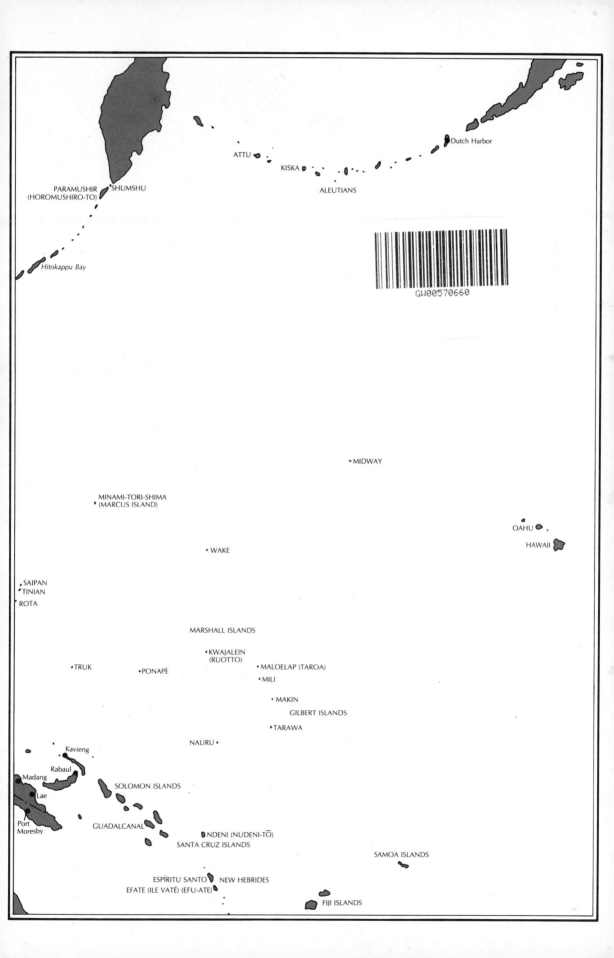

JAPANESE NAVAL ACES
AND
FIGHTER UNITS
IN
WORLD WAR II

JAPANESE NAVAL ACES
AND
FIGHTER UNITS
IN
WORLD WAR II

Ikuhiko Hata and Yasuho Izawa

Translated by Don Cyril Gorham

Airlife
England

English language edition copyright © 1989
by the United States Naval Institute
Annapolis, Maryland

First published in the United States of America in 1989 by United States Naval
Institute Press

This edition first published in the United Kingdom 1990 by Airlife Publishing Ltd.

The original Japanese-language edition published by Kantosha
Publishers, Tokyo, Japan, 1970, under the title Nihn Kaigun
Sentoki-tai. The revised and enlarged edition on which this
edition is based was published in 1975.

Drawings by Noboru Shimonoune

ISBN-1-85310-138-9

British Library Cataloguing in Publication Data available.

Printed in England by Livesey Ltd., Shrewsbury.

Airlife Publishing Ltd.

101 Longden Road,
Shrewsbury, SY3 9EB, England.

CONTENTS

FOREWORD TO THE ENGLISH-LANGUAGE EDITION

At the outbreak of the Pacific War the Allies discovered to their surprise and dismay that the fighter pilots of the Imperial Japanese Navy were relentless, highly skilled foes. In late 1941 and early 1942, Japan's superb Zero fighters, flying from carriers or land bases, wreaked havoc over Pearl Harbor, the Philippines, Singapore, the Dutch East Indies, and New Guinea. To their Allied opponents, understandably, the Japanese pilots were faceless dealers of death. The squadrons in which they fought were only poorly identified. Then the tide of war turned against Japan, and her flyers by the hundreds died bravely in air battles or kamikaze attacks. No one on the Allied side had the chance to learn much about the men they fought in the air. With very few exceptions this cloak of anonymity has continued to hide from the West the identities of Japanese naval fighter pilots and the proud record of their air groups.

Japanese Naval Fighter Units, with Biographies of the Aces (*Nihon Kaigun Sentōki-tai*), the revised and enlarged edition published in Tokyo by Kantōsha Publishers in 1975, has become the classic work in Japan, the most comprehensive source on the pilots and their squadrons. It tells how the air groups were organized, who the aces and leaders were, how they were trained, and how they fared through upwards of eight long years of war. The authors, renowned military historian Dr. Ikuhiko Hata and Dr. Yasuho Izawa, a tireless researcher, have based their study mainly upon interviews and documents, officially and privately held. Complementing the text are numerous rare photographs never before published. The work has here been translated in its entirety into English by Don Cyril Gorham.

With a wealth of information hitherto unavailable outside Japan, the book offers an unparalleled look at just how the Imperial Navy's fighter pilots fought the air war over China and the Pacific. Through their own eyes, with their own perceptions and biases, it chronicles their victories and defeats. I am particularly struck by the constant repetition from one squadron's history to another of the names of a relatively few junior officers and senior NCOs, who as long as they survived bore so much of the burden of leadership.

Some will question the numbers of Allied planes the Japanese claimed they shot down, just as Allied tallies have been doubted. This book presents the Japanese assessment of victories made at the time, without the opportunity to compare them to Allied records. Thus it is the indispensable starting point to begin matching Japanese and Allied accounts of the desperate and decisive naval air battles of the Pacific War. Little excites an aviation enthusiast more than the opportunity to see a campaign from both sides, and this book is a wonderful way to accomplish that goal. It will also serve to spur more vital and detailed research on U.S. naval fighter operations, with the hope that someday there will be as detailed a history of the fighter squadrons and aces of the U.S. Navy and Marine Corps.

JOHN B. LUNDSTROM

AUTHORS' PREFACE

To say that the outcome of the Pacific War was determined by the results of naval air battles is not necessarily an exaggeration. Fighter groups of the Imperial Japanese Navy were constantly in the very center of battle activity; they literally fought to the last man and the last aircraft, until defeated. Although there are no accurate records existing today that give the actual number of casualties, some observations can be made by merely looking at a few of the available casualty figures. Of the twenty-eight fighter pilots belonging to the 36th class of Aviation Students (Hikō Gakusei), graduated in June 1942, twenty-four (86 percent) were casualties; of the twenty-one members of the Kō 4th Class, Flight Reserve Enlisted Trainees (Hikō Yoka Renshū-sei), graduated in September 1941, twenty (95 percent) were casualties.

This book narrates the record of the glories and the difficulties encountered by naval fighter units during the Pacific War (including the China Incident). Part 1 [original book] covers the general history of specific air units, from their initial organization through their disbandment. It is divided into carrier-based and land-based naval air units. Generally, units appear in the order of their initial formation. Where changes in unit designations occurred, however, we have maintained consistency by unit, not necessarily in strict chronological sequence of the dates of their reorganization. Only units that actually participated in combat operations have been included; trainee air units have been omitted. Thus, for example, the Kaikō (Haihow), San-a (Ya Hsien), and Tsukuba air groups, which were training units that did see aerial combat, do not appear in the book. On the other hand, Air Groups 345, 361, and 722 are included because they were active duty units. Among the types of fighter aircraft mentioned in the book, night fighter units have been included, but float fighter units have not.

In Part 2, the Biographies of Aces, we include primarily those pilots who had to their credit a record of personally destroying eleven or more enemy aircraft. Internationally, the term *ace* is applied to those who have shot down five or more aircraft. In Japanese air units, however, there was no tradition of deliberately recording the number of kills by individual pilots. Also, a considerable number of the detailed official battle reports are missing. It was difficult to conduct any overall comparative study. As a result, we restricted ourselves to those aces that had shot down eleven or more aircraft. (For the international comparison of aces, please refer to chapter 12 of the authors' publication *The True Record of World War II, Jitsuroku: Dainiji Sekai Taisen,* published in 1968 by the Tōgensha.) Assessments were made on the basis of air groups' reports on operations, aerial records, newspapers, and magazines, and on the recorded memories of survivors, conversations with survivors, the writings of those who did not survive, and other sources of information.

We have also made distinctions about the reliability of the data and characterized it as official in the case of highly reliable information and unofficial in the case of somewhat less reliable data. In general, we found that the official information tended to be about half of the unofficial data available. A joint or multiple shoot down of an aircraft has been counted as one half of a victory.

We enjoyed the assistance and support of countless numbers of persons in the compilation of the data in this book. We were particularly fortunate in receiving from naval air unit survivors and family survivors extremely valuable support in the form of precious conversations, letters, photographs, and other information.

Dr. Yasuho Izawa did not stint in his vigorous pursuit of data. Without his efforts, this book would probably not have been possible in the form that it has appeared in.

In editing this book, significant contributions were made by the editorial staff of Kantō-sha Publishers, in particular Messrs.

Masanori Fujita and Hiroyoshi Nakamura. We were also extremely fortunate to have had historical research conducted by Messrs. Minoru Akimoto and Noboru Shimo-une. Well beyond our own expectations was the fact that we were able to include aircraft paint designs in the various figures in the book.

We would like to deeply thank all of the foregoing people.

IKUHIKO HATA
December 1970

AUTHORS' PREFACE TO THE REVISED AND ENLARGED EDITION

Over four years have passed since the initial publication of this book. Fortunately, the book has been well received and a number of reprints issued. In 1973, a sister publication of this book, *Japanese Army Fighter Units* (*Rikugun Sentōki-Tai*), was also published. In preparing for the revised and enlarged edition of this book, we made considerable numbers of revisions, taking into account the many comments received from a broad range of readers. In particular, the number of photographs has been significantly increased and a name list of those killed in action has been added, as well as a list of fighter pilots by graduating class.

We would like to express our deep-felt thanks to all of those many persons who have assisted us in this endeavor.

IKUHIKO HATA, YASUHO IZAWA,
AND MASAHARU SUZUKI
July 1975

TRANSLATOR'S NOTE

The group that assembled the data incorporated in the book conducted a very thorough study of available source material, including contacting surviving pilots and members of the families of those pilots no longer with us. It was quite a challenge to translate the book in view of the detailed and technical nature of some of the information. Also a challenge was the attempt to get across to readers the correct feeling of the human aspects expressed in the biographies of individual pilots.

The romanization method used in the translation is the broadly accepted "modified Hepburn system" used in the vast majority of English-language publications dealing with Japan and Japanese subjects. This system can be found in Kenkyusha's *New Japanese-English Dictionary*, 1974. All Japanese names of people are rendered in Western order, given name followed by surname. Whenever possible, place names include both the Western name and the Japanese equivalent. Information appearing in square brackets does not appear in the original book but has been added with the help of authorities in the subject matter to aid the reader. Examples are specific dates, geographical place names where the Japanese original and the usual English equivalent are not the same, historical information, or correction of factual errors. Changes of factual material or wording requested by the authors themselves have been incorporated without acknowledgment. All miles are nautical miles.

In the Japanese book, *Nihon Kaigun Sentōki-tai,* a number of terms concerned with dying are used in relation to the Pacific War. More than half of the eight terms listed below (specifically, gyokusai, jibaku, jiketsu, jisatsu, and tai-atari) indicate that death was caused by an act of will of the person who died. Dr. Izawa, coauthor, commented on one of the terms, jibaku:

"Jibaku ('self-destruction,' 'self-explosion') means that the pilot voluntarily destroys himself with his mount when he realizes that he or his plane has no possibility of returning to the base or to an area held by friendly forces. The Japanese navy forbade a pilot to surrender as a prisoner of war." Such distinctions are important to surviving members of the family and to Japanese culture in general and have been retained in the English translation. The eight Japanese terms meaning death used in the book with an explanation of their circumstances follow:

Bakushi
To be killed by a bomb; used even today in the sense of a death caused by an accidental bomb explosion

Gyokusai
To seek death rather than dishonor, to die with honor; the so-called kamikaze death; can be an individual or a group

Jibaku
To self-explode or self-destruct; usually self-destruction using an airplane or a torpedo

Jiketsu
To kill oneself, to commit suicide; the so-called hara-kiri death

Jisatsu
To kill oneself, to commit suicide; to this day, the most common term for destroying oneself

Senbotsu and *senshi*
To be killed in action, to die in action or in battle; the most generic of the terms dealing with death in action

Tai-atari
Ramming; literally, "body-crashing"; self-destruction by deliberately ramming

an airplane or a manned torpedo or torpedo boat into an enemy surface vessel or otherwise destroying one's own weapon of war

The section Japanese Naval Terminology and Abbreviations, which precedes the text, has been added to the English-language edition to help readers keep in mind the various naval ranks, air organization units, and aircraft terms used throughout the book. The romanized Japanese names are included as a cross-reference.

Each of the Japanese commissioned ranks is preceded by the Japanese word "Kaigun," indicating the navy; the Japanese army used the same ranks, preceded by "Rikugun."

In the outline Japanese Naval Air Organization, several Japanese terms need explanation. The Japanese word "Kōkū-sentai" does not distinguish between carrier- and land-based divisions: the same word is used for both. In the translation if a distinction could be made based on other information, the English terms "Carrier Division" and "Air Flotilla" have been substituted. If not, the Japanese term "Kōkū-sentai" has been retained. The Japanese terms "Kokutai" and "Hikōtai" can both be translated "Air Group" in English. To distinguish between the two land-based units in Japanese air organization, "Air Group" has been used for the larger unit, and the Japanese term "Hikōtai" has been retained for the smaller unit. The only exceptions are those instances where the original Japanese text used the English term "Squadron" or where the context of the term is clear that it was a squadron in our sense of the word.

The numbering of Japanese air groups also needs some explanation. On 1 November 1942, a wholesale renumbering of air groups took place. Under the revised numbering system, the numerical designations have meanings as follows: first digit, type of aircraft; second digit, naval base to which the group was attached; and third digit, number unique to the air group itself. Air groups numbered with four digits were composed of transport aircraft only.

The numbering of air groups in Japan, therefore, was not sequential, and the air group numbers are not read numerically in Japanese. For example, a correct rendering would be "Air Group 131"—"one-three-one"—not "131st Air Group." The first twenty-two air groups were numbered sequentially, however, and are correctly translated using the ordinals: for example, "22nd Air Group."

The third reference list is Principal Japanese Carrier- and Land-based Aircraft. The manufacturer, Japanese name with English translation, designation, date the aircraft entered service, and Allied code name are given for the principal naval aircraft included in the book.

Every attempt has been made to ensure accuracy in the translation. I would like to acknowledge my deep thanks and respect for three individuals in particular. Dr. Ikuhiko Hata, senior author of the book, and Dr. Yasuho Izawa of Tokyo University Hospital, who worked very closely with Dr. Hata in compiling the data, both provided extensive, detailed comments and recommendations. They also provided a brief summary of the contents of the book, which was very helpful.

I must also express my deep thanks to John B. Lundstrom, assistant curator of history at the Milwaukee Public Museum and author of *The First Team: Pacific Naval Air Combat from Pearl Harbor to Midway*. With obvious deep knowledge of the subject matter, his meticulous review and comments were invaluable. He was particularly adept at uncovering factual errors and juxtapositions between the original Japanese and the English translation and providing specific information on Japanese naval terminology.

Finally, I would like to thank members of the Naval Institute Press for bearing with me in many of the nitty gritty problems of putting a translation into shape. Thank you very much. Also, it goes without saying that any omissions or mistakes in the translation as published are the responsibility of the translator and not that of the others who so generously contributed their talents.

JAPANESE NAVAL TERMINOLOGY AND ABBREVIATIONS

RANKS AND ABBREVIATIONS

Commissioned Ranks

Taishō	Admiral	ADM
Chūjō	Vice Admiral	VADM
Shōshō	Rear Admiral	RADM
Taisa	Captain	CAPT
Chūsa	Commander	CDR
Shōsa	Lieutenant Commander	LCDR
Tai-i	Lieutenant	LT
Chū-i	Lieutenant (junior grade)	LTJG
Shō-i	Ensign	ENS

Enlisted Ranks

Before June 1941

Kōkū Heisōchō	Aviation Warrant Officer	WO
Ittō Kōkū Heisō	Aviation Petty Officer, 1st Class	PO1c
Nitō Kōkū Heisō	Aviation Petty Officer, 2nd Class	PO2c
Santō Kōkū Heisō	Aviation Petty Officer, 3rd Class	PO3c
Ittō Kōkūhei	Aviation Seaman, 1st Class	Sea1c

After June 1941

Hikō Heisōchō	Flight Warrant Officer	WO
Jōtō Hikō Heisō★	Flight Chief Petty Officer	CPO
Ittō Hikō Heisō	Flight Petty Officer, 1st Class	PO1c
Nitō Hikō Heisō	Flight Petty Officer, 2nd Class	PO2c
Santō Hikō Heisō⁺	Flight Petty Officer, 3rd Class	PO3c
Hikō Heichō★	Flight Leading Seaman	LdgSea
Jōtō Hikōhei★	Flight Superior Seaman	SupSea
Ittō Hikōhei	Flight Seaman, 1st Class	Sea1c

★ rank established November 1942
⁺ rank abolished November 1942

JAPANESE NAVAL AIR ORGANIZATION

Commands

Administrative Title	Operational Title
Carrier-Based	
Air Fleet	Striking Force
Carrier Division (Kōkū-sentai)	—
Air Group made up of:	
Hikōtai (Hikōtaichō: Group Leader)	—
one for each aircraft type:	
Carrier Fighter (VF)	
Carrier Bomber (VB)	
Carrier Attack (VT)	
organized into:	
Hikōbuntai (Buntaichō: Division Officer)	
divided among each of the carriers	
of the Kōkū-sentai to form a:	
	Carrier Air Group (Hikōkitai)
	with:
	Carrier Fighter Squadron (VF)
	Carrier Bomber Squadron (VB)
	Carrier Attack Squadron (VT)
Land-Based	
Air Fleet	Base Air Force
Air Flotilla (Kōkū-sentai)	Air Attack Force
Air Group (Kōkūtai)	—
Hikōtai (Hikōtaichō: Group Leader)★	—
Hikōbuntai (Buntaichō: Division Officer)	—

Flight formations and numbers of planes

		Before 1944	1944–1945
Daitai	squadron	18–27	16
Chūtai	division	9	8
Shōtai	section	3	4
Buntai	pair	—	2

★ Until early 1944, there was only one hikōtai for each major aircraft type in the group. In early 1944 the air groups were reorganized with two or three numbered hikōtai, which could all operate the same type of aircraft.

PRINCIPAL JAPANESE CARRIER- AND LAND-BASED NAVAL AIRCRAFT

		DESIGNATION	DATE ENTERED SERVICE	ALLIED CODE NAME
Carrier-based Fighters				
Nakajima	Type 3	A1N1 to A1N2	1929	—
Nakajima	Type 90	A2N1 to A2N3	1932	—
Nakajima	Type 95	A4N1	1936	—
Mitsubishi	Type 96	A5M1 to A5M4	1937	Claude
Mitsubishi	Type 0	A6M2 to A6M8	1940	Zeke
		(A6M3	1942	Hamp)
Land-based Interceptor Fighters				
Mitsubishi	Raiden ("Thunderbolt")	J2M1 to J2M6	1943	Jack
Kawanishi	Shiden ("Lightning Flash")	N1K1-J	1943	George
Kawanishi	Shiden-kai (Improved Shiden)	N1K2-J	1944	George
Mitsubishi	Shūsui ("Shining Blade")	J8M1 (experimental rocket fighter)		—
Night Fighters				
Nakajima	Gekkō ("Moonlight")	J1N1 to J1N3	1943	Irving
Yokosuka	Suisei ("Comet")	D4Y2-S	1944	Judy
Yokosuka	Ginga ("Milky Way")	P1Y1-S	1944	Frances
Yokosuka	Ginga ("Milky Way"); also known as Kyokkō ("Aurora")	P1Y2-S	1944	Frances
Nakajima	Saiun ("Iridescent Cloud")	C6N1-S	1945	Myrt
Carrier-based Bombers (Dive Bombers)				
Aichi	Type 94	D1A1	1934	—
Aichi	Type 96	D1A2	1936	—
Aichi	Type 99	D3A1 to D3A2	1940	Val
Yokosuka	Suisei ("Comet")	D4Y2 to D4Y4	1943	Judy
Carrier-based Attack Planes (Torpedo Planes)				
Mitsubishi	Type 13	B1M1 to B1M3	1923	—
Mitsubishi	Type 89	B2M1 to B2M2	1932	—
Yokosuka	Type 92	B3Y1	1933	—
Yokosuka	Type 96	B4Y1	1936	Jean
Nakajima	Type 97	B5N1 to B5N2	1937	Kate
Nakajima	Tenzan ("Heavenly Mountain")	B6N1 to B6N2	1943	Jill
Aichi	Ryūsei ("Shooting Star")	B7A1 to B7A2	1944	Grace

		DESIGNATION	DATE ENTERED SERVICE	ALLIED CODE NAME
Land-based Attack Planes (Medium Bombers)				
Hirosho	Type 95	G2H1	1936	—
Mitsubishi	Type 96	G3M1 to G3M3	1936	Nell
Mitsubishi	Type 1	G4M1 to G4M3	1941	Betty
Land-based Bomber				
Yokosuka	Ginga ("Milky Way")	P1Y1 to P1Y6	1944	Frances
Carrier-based Reconnaissance Planes				
Yokosuka	Type 2	D4Y1-C to D4Y2-C	1942	Judy
Nakajima	Saiun ("Iridescent Cloud")	C6N1 to C6N3	1944	Myrt
Land-based Reconnaissance Planes				
Mitsubishi	Type 98	C5M1 to C5M2	1938	Babs
Nakajima	Type 2	J1N1-C	1942	Irving
Special Attack (Suicide) Plane				
Yokosuka	Ōka ("Cherry Blossom")	MXY7	1944	Baka

PART 1

Japanese Naval Aircraft

JAPANESE NAVAL AIRCRAFT

Nakajima Type 3 Carrier Fighter

The first domestically produced carrier fighter of the Imperial Japanese Navy was the Type 10 Mitsubishi, placed in service in 1921. The Type 3 carrier fighter was officially adopted for service in April of 1929, as a follow-on aircraft to the Type 10. Contracts for the design and manufacture of a prototype Type 3 were awarded to the Gloucester firm in England. After some improvements were added, about fifty aircraft of Type 3 Model 1 (equipped with the Jupiter 6, 420 HP engine) and about one hundred of Type 3 Model 2 (*Kotobuki* Model 2, 450 HP engine) were manufactured. The Model 2 fighter had a maximum speed of 240 KPH and was armed with two 7.7-mm machine guns. Aircraft on board the carriers *Hōshō* and *Kaga* participated in the Shanghai Incident; they recorded the first aerial victory by our nation's forces. Type 3 Model 2 attached to the Kasumigaura Air Group. (Katsuhiro Hashimoto)

Nakajima Type 90 Carrier Fighter

The Type 90 carrier fighter was independently developed by the Nakajima firm and placed in service in April 1932. In spite of the fact that it used the same Kotobuki Model 2 engine used in the Type 3 Model, maximum speed of the Type 90 was increased to 292 KPH and its maneuverability was widely acclaimed. Models 1, 2, and 3 of the fighter, as well as a twin-seat trainer version, were manufactured. Until the early part of the China Incident, these planes were used in the front lines. Type 90 Model 3 carrier fighter with tail legend Ku-259 in the foreground is attached to the Kure Air Group. (Katsuhiro Hashimoto)

Nakajima Type 95 Carrier Fighter

The Nakajima 95 was destined to be the last biplane fighter in the Imperial Japanese Navy. It was developed as a follow-on to the Type 90 carrier fighter and was equipped with the Hikari Model 1 engine (670 HP). The aircraft's structure was redesigned and maximum speed increased to 351 KPH. It was adopted for service in January 1936; a total of 221 units were manufactured. Although some did participate in the China Incident, because of the appearance of the Type 96 carrier fighter soon after, the earlier version was withdrawn from the front lines and used as a trainer. Nakajima Type 95 carrier fighter 3-123 flown by PO1c Yukiharu Ozeki of the 12th Air Group. (Katsuhiro Hashimoto)

Mitsubishi Type 96 Carrier Fighter

The Type 96 carrier fighter was Japan's first cantilevered and all metal monocoque fuselage monoplane, famous in its time as a fuselage design that was well ahead of its contemporaries in other parts of the world. It had a number of ambitious design features, such as flush rivets and washout type wings. When first flown, it also became world famous as an aircraft well ahead of its time. Nine prototype single-place fighters were completed in January 1935; they featured an amazing 450 KPH maximum speed. Early in 1937, manufacture of the Model 1 aircraft equipped with the Kotobuki Improved Model 2 engine (460 HP) was started. Next, the Type 96 Model 2.1 fighter, equipped with the Kotobuki Model 3 engine (600 HP), was produced. Model 2.2 of this fighter, with an enlarged fuselage featuring an enclosed cockpit, was the next to be manufactured. Upon the outbreak of the China Incident in July 1937, the plane was immediately dispatched to the front and achieved brilliant results. Mitsubishi Type 96 carrier fighter belonging to the 12th Air Group, probably the plane of the buntai leader. Wheel spats have been removed. (Yasujirō Abe)

Mitsubishi Type 96 Carrier Fighter

Type 96 Model 2.1 attached to the 13th Air Group, taking off from Kunda airfield, Shanghai. (Family of Isamu Mochizuki)

Mitsubishi Type 96 Model 4 Carrier Fighter

Counting all models of the Type 96 carrier based fighter, almost one thousand units were manufactured. The model that was produced in the greatest quantity was Model 4, equipped with the Kotobuki Model 4 engine (680 HP). Some of those aircraft were still stationed in the front lines in the early part of the Pacific War. Maximum speed was 435 KPH and armament consisted of two 7.7-mm machine guns, used ever since the introduction of Model 1. Type 96 Model 4 carrier fighter piloted by LT Tamotsu Yokoyama, fighter division officer, taking off 12 November 1939 from the carrier *Sōryū,* which was engaged in the battle to seal off the East China Sea. (Yasushi Yokoyama)

Mitsubishi Type 96 Model 4 Carrier Fighter

Type 96 Model 4 fighters participating in a flyby in the year's first formation flight, January 1939. The plane in the center of the formation was flown by LT Hideki Shingō, division officer. (Hideki Shingō)

Mitsubishi Zero Carrier Fighter

The Zero fighter was formally adopted for service in July 1940. Not only did it have speed and heavy armament second to none of the world's leading fighter aircraft at the time, but it also had superior maneuverability and unmatched long-distance cruise capabilities. In the summer of 1940, the Zero went into action on the Chinese mainland with brilliant results. For the rest of the entire period of the Pacific War, it continued to serve as the Japanese navy's primary carrier-based fighter. Two Zero Model 11 aircraft of the 12th Air Group flying over the Chinese mainland. LT Minoru Suzuki flew the fighter marked with a double stripe on its fuselage. (Minoru Suzuki)

Mitsubishi Zero Carrier Fighter

Zero Model 21 fighters on the aircraft carrier *Zuikaku,* operating in the Indian Ocean, April 1942. Model 11 was the first to be placed in production; Model 21 had folding wing tips in order to facilitate storage on board aircraft carriers. (*Air Review*)

Mitsubishi Zero Carrier Fighter

Zero fighter Models 11 and 21 were equipped with the Homare Model 12 engine (950 HP); later production models were equipped with the Homare Model 21 engine (1,100 HP), resulting in increased performance. Zero fighter Model 32, with a wing span one meter shorter than its predecessors, was used in the front lines starting in mid-1942. By the end of 1942, a version with the wing span increased back to its former length and with improved cruising capabilities, the Model 22, also joined the fighting forces. Next, in August 1943, the Model 52 fighter was developed; the Model 52, among all models of the Zero fighter, was the one that was produced in the greatest quantity. Zero Model 22 fighters belonging to Air Group 204 on the eastern airfield on the island of Rabaul, scene of fierce battles. (Torao Saitō)

Mitsubishi Zero Carrier Fighter

Zero Model 22 fighters attached to the aircraft carrier *Zuikaku*, which had brought them to the advance base at Buin in early 1943. (Torao Saitō)

Mitsubishi Zero Carrier Fighter

Zero Model 22 fighters attached to the aircraft carrier *Zuikaku*, at Buin in 1943. (Torao Saitō)

Mitsubishi Zero Carrier Fighter

With the Zero Model 52 Type C, Zero fighters reached a maximum speed of 565 KPH. They were also heavily armed, with two 20-mm machine cannons plus three 12.7-mm machine guns. With the large-scale commitment of new and efficient fighter aircraft by the American forces, these Zeros gradually came to lose their effectiveness. The Zero fighter was manufactured not only by Mitsubishi but also by the Nakajima company. The total number of Zeros manufactured, about 10,430 aircraft, was well ahead of any other type of aircraft built, an unprecedented occurrence in the history of Japanese aviation. Zero Model 32 fighter. (Ryōji ŌHara)

Mitsubishi Zero Carrier Fighter

Zero Model 52 Type C fighters, belonging to the Genzan (Wonsan) Air Group, en route from their Wonsan base in Korea, heading back toward the island of Kyūshū to join in a special attack force operation. (*Air Review*)

Mitsubishi Interceptor Raiden ("Thunderbolt")

Raiden was the Imperial Japanese Navy's first fighter interceptor. Although fourteen prototype interceptors were completed by February 1942, because of malfunctioning of engines and visibility problems, quantity production did not start until September 1943. Toward the end of the war, production was concentrated on the Shiden-Kai ("Lightning Flash, improved"); as a result production of the original Raiden was discontinued after a total of only 470 units had been manufactured. The primary production model of the Raiden, the Type 21, was equipped with the Kasei Model 23 engine (1,575 HP), which gave it a maximum speed of 610 KPH, and armed with four 20-mm machine cannons. This aircraft had other superior characteristics, including the ability to climb to 6,000 meters' altitude in 5 minutes 50 seconds. Armed with four 20-mm machine cannons, the plane was active in the interception of B-29s. Among naval fighters, there was no other that could match the climbing ability as well as the acceleration characteristics of the Raiden. No other Japanese navy fighter could match its superior maneuverability; it was counted among the finest aircraft ever to be produced in Japan. Mitsubishi Raiden during test at test center. (Mitsugu Kofukuda)

Mitsubishi Interceptor Raiden

Model 21 Raiden fighters belonging to Air Group 302 based in Atsugi, flying by Mount Fuji. Air Group 302 played a major role in intercepting B-29s. (Fusai Miyazaki)

Kawanishi Interceptor Shiden ("Lightning Flash")

The Shiden was an ambitious development of an interceptor based on the seaplane fighter Kyōfū ("Mighty Wind"); the first plane was completed in December 1942. Units were supplied with the Shiden starting in early 1944; they saw action in the Taiwan and Philippines areas. Equipped with the small but powerful Homare Model 21 engine (1,825 HP), it had a maximum speed of 574 KPH and was armed with four 20-mm machine cannons. By the time production was switched over to the Shiden-kai, 1,007 of the initial model had been sent into service. Shiden 11 Model Type C fighters, attached to the Genzan Air Group as the interceptors were leaving Wonsan base with extra fuel tanks strapped below their fuselage, April 1945. (*Air Review*)

Kawanishi Interceptor, Shiden-kai

Because the Shiden had a mid-wing body design, it was plagued with poor visibility and undercarriage problems. These defects were removed by changing to a low-wing design, as well as by redesigning the fuselage structure to adapt it better to mass production. This resulted in the Shiden-kai [improved Shiden]; aircraft number one made its maiden flight in December 1943. Naval fighter units anxiously looked forward to using the aircraft because of its superior maneuverability, its heavy armament, and its maximum speed of 595 KPH. The Shiden-kai was even designated as one of the top priority production models in its time. Only some four hundred interceptors of this type were produced by the end of the war; however, the exploits of Air Group 343, which was organized from veteran pilots, are well known. Shiden-kai belonging to Fighter Hikōtai 301, Air Group 343, at snow-covered Matsuyama Air Base. (Minoru Honda)

Nakajima Night Fighter Gekkō ("Moonlight")

The night fighter Gekkō, used for the air defense of the homeland toward the end of the war, was initially developed as an experimental Type 13 twin-engine, long-range fighter to be used for escorting bombers. Because of performance defects, however, it was redesigned and saw service as the Type 2 land-based reconnaissance plane, starting in July 1942. The aircraft was equipped with oblique-firing machine guns developed by LCDR Kozono, then executive officer of Air Group 251. Favorable results were attained in its use as a night interceptor fighter; as a result, it was formally placed in service in August 1943 as a night fighter. Equipped with two Homare Model 21 engines (1,100 HP), its maximum speed was about 500 KPH. A total of 477 were produced. Fighter belonging to Air Group 302.

PART 2

Fighter Unit Histories

鳳 翔 戦 闘 機 隊

HŌSHŌ FIGHTER SQUADRON

The *Hōshō* was Japan's first aircraft carrier; she was built at the Yokosuka Naval Arsenal and completed in 1922. Since she was a small aircraft carrier displacing only ten thousand tons, her capacity to carry aircraft was limited; normally only fifteen aircraft were carried on board. During the early part of the Shōwa period (from 1926 on), the normal complement was a fighter buntai (nine aircraft), a reconnaissance buntai (three aircraft), and an attack buntai (three aircraft).

With the outbreak of the Shanghai Incident on 29 January 1932, the 1st Carrier Division (consisting of the *Hōshō* and the *Kaga*) was posted to the 3rd Fleet. The fleet moved off Shanghai and supported land military operations in the vicinity of the city. The *Hōshō* actually arrived off the mouth of the Yangtze River on 1 February, accompanied by the 3rd Destroyer Division. On the 5th of the month, two carrier attack planes under the command of LT Nagamoto Hirabayashi, escorted by three carrier fighters led by LT Shigehachirō Tokoro, flew over the Shingū area and engaged in aerial battles a number of times with a total of nine Chinese fighter planes.

This was the very first aerial battle recorded in the history of the Japanese air forces. Although the battle results have not been verified, one Chinese fighter landed

because the pilot was seriously injured but took off under the piloting of the deputy commander of the damaged aircraft. During flight, the plane crashed and the pilot was killed in action. Thus, the result was the same as if the aircraft had been shot down by our forces.

Next, upon completion of the airfield being developed at Kunda, a portion of the 1st Carrier Division landed in Shanghai on the 7th of the month and supported ground operations. On the 26th, covered by six carrier fighters (under the command of LT Tokoro) from the carrier *Hōshō*, nine *Kaga* carrier attack planes attacked the Hangchow airfield. On the way back, five enemy fighters were engaged in sporadic battles, with the result that three of them were shot down. The Atsumi Shōtai shot down one plane, and LT Tokoro and PO3c Saitō each shot down one plane as well. A ceasefire order was issued on March 3rd; by the 20th, the 1st Carrier Division returned to the Combined Fleet. It then was engaged in aerial training work.

With the outbreak of the China Incident in July 1937, the *Hōshō*, together with the carrier *Ryūjō*, was posted to the 3rd Fleet, leaving the port of Sasebo on the 12th. Arriving in the Ma-an-shan Islands area, the ship started supporting land operations beginning the 16th of the month. During this

Type 96 Model 4 Carrier Fighter

The lateral paint stripe across the length of the fuselage indicates it is a fighter belonging to the 3rd Carrier Division in accordance with an order issued by the Combined Fleet on 15 November 1940. The body of the aircraft was light gray or silver. The unit designation *GI* was put into use in November 1940.

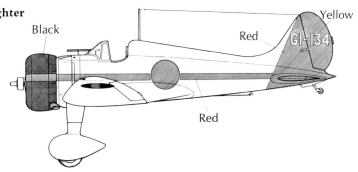

Black

Red

Yellow

GI-134

Red

Aircraft carrier *Hōshō*, which saw action in the China Incident. To the left rear is the carrier *Kaga*. (Hideki Shingō)

period, both *Kaga* and *Ryūjō* groups had opportunity to engage in aerial battles; however, the only results were that on the 25th, three Type 90 carrier fighters led by LTJG Harutoshi Okamoto (from the *Hōshō*) engaged in battle over Shanghai with two Martin heavy bombers, but only one of the latter was shot down.

On 1 September, the *Hōshō* left Shanghai to return to Sasebo for refueling. On the 5th, in the company of the carrier *Ryūjō*, she proceeded south, and starting the 21st of September, conducted several attacks on enemy bases in the vicinity of Canton. During the morning of the 21st despite the bad weather, fifteen carrier fighters (six from the *Hōshō*) of the 1st Carrier Division

escorted twelve carrier bombers and three carrier attack planes in an attack on the Tienho and Paiyun airfields. Some ten or more Curtiss Hawks were engaged in battle, and twelve friendlies (six by the *Hōshō*) were shot down.

Five of the *Hōshō* carrier fighters ran out of fuel and ditched; pilots were rescued by destroyers and other vessels. In the afternoon, nine carrier fighters, six carrier bombers, and three carrier attack planes all from the carrier *Ryūjō* carried out a second attack and engaged in battle with ten Curtiss aircraft [fighters], shooting down five of them. Until the end of the month, attacks were conducted almost daily. During this latter period, however, almost no op-

Type 96 Model 4 Carrier Fighter

The unit marking *CI* was during the period 1941 through March 1942.

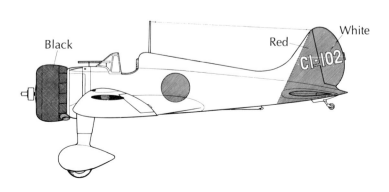

portunities were present to engage in aerial battles. On 3 October, the unit was again off Shanghai, and the aircraft units were dispatched to the Kunda airfield for ground support. The *Hōshō* transferred her aircraft to the *Ryūjō* and returned to the homeland on 17 October.

As of 1 December [1937] the *Hōshō* was placed in reserve. Three years were spent in repairs and conversion work. In November 1940, she returned to the battle front and, together with the *Zuikaku,* formed the 3rd Carrier Division. With the commissioning of new classes of aircraft carriers, the *Hōshō* was retired to the second line. The 3rd Carrier Division was engaged primarily in guard duties for major combatant forces. She greeted the advent of the Pacific War by using her fighters on combat air patrols, as well as engaging in antisubmarine work using her carrier attack planes. With the disbanding of the 3rd Carrier Division in April 1942, the ship continued to perform the same type of duty but was attached to the 1st Fleet. She participated in the Battle of Midway. At that time, her aircraft complement was a mere six carrier attack planes. After June 1942, aircraft were off-loaded and the *Hōshō* became a carrier qualification training vessel for new carrier flight crews. In April 1945, the *Hōshō* was placed in the category Class 3 Reserve Ship; on the first of June she was categorized a Class 4 Reserve Ship. By this time, the majority of her crew had left the ship, and the *Hōshō* greeted the end of hostilities while docked at the Kure Naval Base.

Successive Division Officers:

January 1937–October 1937 LT Kiyoto Hanamoto

November 1940–September 1941 LT Harutoshi Okamoto

September 1941–December 1941 LT Aya-o Shirane

December 1941–April 1942 LTJG Saneyasu Hidaka

赤 城 戦 闘 機 隊

AKAGI FIGHTER SQUADRON

Construction of the *Akagi* was started as a battle cruiser in 1920; as a result of the Washington Naval Treaty, the ship was refitted as an aircraft carrier and was completed by March 1927. In August the same year, she was posted to the Combined Fleet. In November 1931 a major overhaul, which took one year and a half to complete, was begun at the Yokosuka Naval Arsenal; as a result she did not participate in the first phase of the Shanghai Incident [1932]. Even when the China Incident broke out [August 1937], the *Akagi* was in dock for yet another major refitting operation that took almost three years, starting the end of October 1937. The *Akagi* had no opportunity to engage in battle and in comparison with her less efficient sister aircraft carrier *Kaga* was not favored by the gods of war.

In September 1938, the refitted *Akagi* had been converted into a major aircraft carrier with the following specifications: official displacement 41 thousand tons, maximum speed 32.5 knots, with the capability of handling a total complement of ninety-one aircraft consisting of twelve Type 96 carrier fighters (in addition, four spares), nineteen Type 96 carrier bombers (five spares), and thirty-five Type 96 carrier attack planes (sixteen spares). Posted to the 1st Carrier Division in November of the same year, the *Akagi* operated in the southern China and Hainan Island areas from the

end of April 1939 to the middle of February. She then returned to homeland waters and engaged in fleet training activities.

In October 1940, the *Akagi* was placed in reserve; the hull and weapons were reworked. In April 1941, she was next posted to 1st Carrier Division of the 1st Air Fleet and equipped with aircraft. The allowance called for a total of 104 planes: twelve carrier fighters (plus four spares), eighteen carrier bombers (six spares), and forty-eight carrier attack planes (sixteen spares). On 26 November, the *Akagi,* serving as the flagship of the Nagumo Striking Force, departed Hitokappu Bay, steamed into the North Pacific and headed for the U.S. naval base at Pearl Harbor. Early on the morning of December 8th [Tokyo time; 7th], the first attack wave of aircraft left the *Akagi,* led by CDR Fuchida; it consisted of fifteen [Type 97] level bombers, twelve [Type 97] torpedo planes (under the command of LCDR Murata), and nine carrier fighters led by LCDR Shigeru Itaya. At the time, LCDR Itaya also took command of the forty-three [Zero] fighters that constituted the first wave covering force (Seikūtai).

The Itaya unit was over Pearl Harbor by 0750 Honolulu time; since it was a complete surprise attack, the anticipated enemy fighter interceptions did not materialize. After discovering and shooting down one

Model 21 Zero Fighter

The plane that was flown by LCDR Shigeru Itaya, who was group leader of the *Akagi* Fighter Squadron when it attacked the Hawaiian Islands. The two horizontal bands on the vertical tail indicate group leader [hikōtaichō]. The unit designation was used from April 1941 to June 1942.

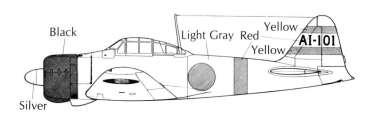

sight-seeing plane and three trainers, the unit strafed the Hickam and Ewa airfields. About twenty-five aircraft were hit and seen burning on the ground; Itaya's number one wingman, PO1c Takashi Hirano, took hits from antiaircraft guns, and he crashed his plane into the ground.

Next, the second wave of attackers, consisting of nine carrier fighters [Zeros] led by LT Saburō Shindō escorting eighteen [Type 99] carrier bombers, arrived over the Pearl Harbor area about one hour later. Since there was no aerial opposition, they strafed Hickam Field but were only successful in setting two enemy aircraft on fire. All our aircraft returned safely.

On the 23rd, the *Akagi* returned safely to the western area of the Inland Sea in the homeland. On 8 January [1942] the *Akagi* sortied south, joining in the attack to capture the Bismarck Archipelago. On the 20th the force attacked Rabaul, on the 21st Kavieng, and on the 23rd, the force attacked Rabaul a second time. There was no opposition. After its mission was accomplished, the force went to Truk Island. When an American task force made an air attack on the Marshall Islands, the *Akagi* force immediately pursued but was not able to engage a single enemy plane. The ship then proceeded to Kendari and on the 19th of February joined the major fighter/bomber force that attacked Port Darwin [Australia]. There was minimal counter attack on the part of the enemy and the carrier fighter unit (nine aircraft led by LCDR Itaya) were able to shoot down four enemy aircraft in coordination with other planes, as well as destroy eight aircraft on the ground.

Next, until 11 March, the *Akagi* Fighter Squadron was engaged in action in the Indian Ocean south of Java. After attacking remaining enemy warships in the area and

Type 96 Model 4 carrier fighter on board the *Akagi*. In the foreground, LTJG Masao Satō (on the right) and LTJG Masao Asai. (Yoshio Shiga)

Aircraft on board the carrier *Akagi* preparing to take off for the attack on Hawaii, 7 December 1941. (Maru)

participating in the Tjilatjap port bombardment, the squadron also took part in the early April attack against Ceylon. During the attack on Colombo on 5 April, nine [Zero] fighters escorted the carrier attack squadron of seventeen aircraft. A furious battle ensued with the British fighters that rose to intercept them; sixteen enemy aircraft (of which seven were probables) were shot down. On our side, all aircraft returned to the carrier safely. During the raid on Trincomalee on the 9th, the carrier fighter squadron shot down six aircraft.

Immediately upon their return to the mainland at the end of April, preparations started for the next phase of operations. On 27 May, the four aircraft carriers *Akagi, Kaga, Sōryū,* and *Hiryū* left the Inland Sea and headed for the attack on Midway Island. During the morning of 5 June [Tokyo time; 4 June] when the first air attack on Midway Island took place, eighteen [Type 99] carrier bombers and nine [Zero]

fighters (led by LT Shirane) were involved. Engaging in aerial battles with the F4Fs and Buffalo that were waiting in ambush immediately in front of the target, the Zero fighters were able to successfully protect the attacking forces as well as shoot down eleven enemy aircraft. They then strafed land targets and destroyed one B-17 on the ground. PO1c Iwama's aircraft, however, was hit by antiaircraft fire and he destroyed his own aircraft. On the other hand, the remaining [Zero] fighters flew combat air patrol in shifts, which they had been doing ever since the first attack unit was launched. Against the repeated attacks by American carrier planes, units of the Shirane group that had returned to their carrier, as well as casuals [transients] (Binjōsha) from the 6th Air Group, also joined in. During the course of twelve interception battles, a total of fifty-one aircraft (of which thirty were in conjunction with other units) were shot down. At 1030, [4

Kaneohe Naval Air Station in Hawaii under attack by Japanese carrier planes. (Yasujirō Abe)

June], the *Akagi* received two hits from enemy carrier bombers and sank later that same night.

The majority of the combat air patrol (CAP) fighters were able to land on the *Hiryū,* which was undamaged; the aircraft were refueled and rearmed and continued to engage in interception battles. Even after the *Hiryū* was fatally damaged, the aircraft remained in the air but eventually ran out of fuel. In the evening hours, they ditched near friendly destroyers and were saved.

Successive Group Leaders:

December 1937–November 1941 LCDR Shigehachirō Tokoro

April 1941–June 1942 LCDR Shigeru Itaya

Successive Division Officers:

December 1938–October 1940 LT Takahide Aioi

December 1938–November 1939 LT Masao Yamashita

April 1940–October 1940 LT Kenjirō Nōtomi

April 1941–December 1941 LT Saburō Shindō

December 1941–June 1942 LT Aya-o Shirane

December 1941–June 1942 LT Masanobu Ibusuki

加 賀 戦 闘 機 隊

KAGA FIGHTER SQUADRON

Construction of the *Kaga* started in 1920 as a battleship for the so-called 8-8 Fleet; however, as a result of the Washington Naval Treaty it was decided to remodel her as an aircraft carrier. The *Kaga* was completed in March 1928. She was posted to the fleet in November of the following year. Together with the *Hōshō,* she constituted the 1st Carrier Division. The complement of aircraft on board ship at the time was twelve operational fighters (plus three spares), six reconnaissance planes (two spares), eighteen attack planes (six spares), for a total of thirty-six aircraft (plus eleven spares). The carrier fighter model being used was the Type 3. Starting at the end of 1930, the carrier underwent one year of repair work; in December 1931, she rejoined the fleet. She became the flag ship for RADM Takayoshi Katō, commander of the 1st Carrier Division.

With the outbreak of the first phase of the Shanghai Incident in January 1932, the 1st Carrier Division was posted to the 3rd Fleet and operated off Shanghai. A Hikōkitai (a detachment of a carrier air group) under the command of division officer LT Yoshitane Yanagimura established its base in Shanghai at Kunda airfield and was used primarily in support of land operations. It was during this period that, on 22 February, three Type 3 carrier fighters under the command of shōtai leader LT Nokiji Ikuta (second aircraft flown by PO3c Toshio Kuroiwa and third aircraft flown by Sea1c Kazuo Takeo) joined three carrier attack planes led by shōtai leader LT Kotani. They then engaged a Boeing 218 (the prototype for the P-12) piloted by American volunteer flier Robert Short. Though LT Kotani was killed in action, Short's aircraft was also shot down. This came to be officially recognized as the first aerial victory by the Japanese navy and is credited to carrier fighters. In actuality, however, it should perhaps be characterized as the result of a joint action conducted by both carrier fighter and carrier attack planes.

A cease-fire order was issued on 3 March, and the 1st Carrier Division returned to the Combined Fleet and engaged in fleet training. Starting in August 1933, the *Kaga* underwent a major remodeling that lasted two years. The flight deck was remodeled from the former three-unit deck to a single-unit, continuous flight deck extending the full length of the ship. Placed back in service in November of 1935, she was posted to the 2nd Carrier Division. A large complement of aircraft was placed on board, consisting of sixteen Type 90 carrier fighter aircraft, sixteen Type 94 carrier

Type 96 Model 4 Carrier Fighter

The unit designation *P* was used starting November 1940. The entire fuselage was either silver or light gray.

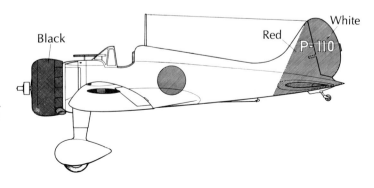

Type 3 carrier fighter pilots who scored the first aerial victory by Japanese forces. From the left: LT Ikuta, PO3c Kuroiwa, and Sea1c Takeo. (*Air Review*)

bombers, and twenty-eight Type 89 carrier attack planes for a total of sixty operational aircraft.

With the outbreak of the Marco Polo Bridge Incident on 7 July 1937, storm clouds gathered menacingly over Japan and China, and the *Kaga* Fighter Squadron underwent base training at Ōmura from July 23rd through August 8th. Between August 10th and 20th, the unit acted in support of the transportation of army units; starting on the 15th, it conducted aerial operations in central China. As of 15 August, aircraft on board the *Kaga* consisted of twenty-two carrier attack planes, fourteen carrier bombers, and sixteen Type 90 carrier fighters.

The first aerial battle in this area occurred on 16 August. Six Type 90 carrier fighters, commanded by LT Chikamasa Igarashi, engaged four enemy aircraft over Kiangwan. Three of the enemy aircraft were shot down, one Corsair and two Douglas.

The next day, on the 17th, four Type 90 carrier fighters under the command of WO Toyoda went into battle and shot down two additional planes over Kiangwan. On the 22nd, two Type 96 carrier fighters were ferried to the front and made their first sortie; however, there were no aerial encounters with the enemy. On 4 September, two Type 96 carrier fighters, under the command of LT Tadashi Nakajima, shot down

Zero Fighter Model 21

Around January 1941. During the same period the Type 96 carrier fighter was also being used.

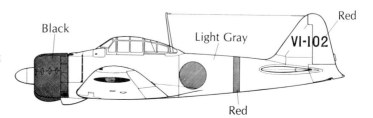

The *Kaga* during China Incident operations with a Type 96 carrier attack plane. (Hideki Shingō)

three Curtiss Hawks. On the 7th, three aircraft led by Igarashi shot down five aircraft, and of the five LT Igarashi single-handedly shot down three enemy aircraft over T'ai Hu. For a period of about ten days starting the 15th of September, the *Kaga* Carrier Air Unit had dispatched to the Kunda airfield six Type 90 fighters, six Type 96 fighters, eighteen carrier bombers, and eighteen carrier attack planes; they served in support of land operations. At the same time, starting on the 19th of the month, Type 96 carrier fighters participated in aerial attacks on Nanking.

The carrier *Kaga* entered Sasebo Naval Base on 26 September. Aircraft on board were replaced by the following: sixteen Type 96 carrier fighters, sixteen Type 96 carrier bombers, and thirty-two Type 96 carrier attack planes. In early October, the carrier moved into operations in the South China area and in November was temporarily sent to the Shanghai area. From that time on, until the end of the battle for Kwangtung in late 1938, the *Kaga* returned only twice to Sasebo Naval Base, both for short periods of time. Using Taiwan as her

base, the carrier periodically went forth in the South China Sea area during a period of about one year. There were a few occasions, however, on which aerial battles occurred. In particular, during the attacks on Tien-ho and Pai-yun, three Type 96 carrier fighters and three Type 95 carrier fighters engaged in battle with British manufactured Gladiators that rather unexpectedly had come up to intercept our aircraft.

Although six enemy aircraft were shot down, one Type 96 carrier fighter as well as two of the less efficient Type 95 carrier fighters were lost. Also, during the attack on Nanyung on 30 August, six carrier fighters and five carrier bombers engaged in a forty-minute aerial battle with a total of twenty-one Gladiators, Deboachins, and Hawks. The carrier fighter unit claimed to shoot down eleven enemy aircraft (including three probables) but lost two, including the commander, LT Teshima. The carrier *Kaga* steamed some 29,048 nautical miles during the one-year period between December 1937 and December the following year. Also, six of the *Kaga* fighters were dispatched to Shanghai and Nanking be-

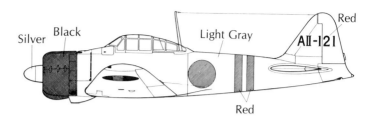

Zero Fighter Model 21

The unit designation *AII* was used from April 1941 to June 1942.

tween 9 December 1937 and 15 January the following year. Also, nine fighters were dispatched to Nanking from 3 March through 4 April 1938.

The *Kaga* had been posted to the 1st Carrier Division since December 1937; in December of the following year, 1938, she was placed in reserve status to undergo remodeling for a period of about two years. Both the flight deck and the hangar areas were enlarged, an island bridge was constructed, and the standard aircraft complement increased as follows: twelve carrier fighters (plus four spares), eighteen carrier

bombers (six spares), forty-eight carrier attack planes (sixteen spares), for a total of seventy-eight aircraft (twenty-six spares). Displacement exceeded 40 thousand tons.

After the above remodeling, the *Kaga* returned to the 1st Carrier Division in October 1940. In April 1941, it was made a part of the newly created 1st Air Fleet. The standard complement of aircraft on board as of October 1941 included eighteen operational carrier fighters, with six held in reserve. The total number of operational aircraft was sixty-three, with twenty-one held in reserve.

Kaga flight crew members huddle before departing on a mission during the China Incident. (Hideki Shingō)

With the outbreak of the Pacific War, the *Kaga* participated in the attack on Pearl Harbor. In the first wave of attacking aircraft, the carrier fighter squadron dispatched nine aircraft under the command of LT Shiga, and on the second wave, nine aircraft under the command of LT Nikaidō. Battle results attained were one enemy aircraft shot down and more than twenty aircraft destroyed on the ground. At the same time, the *Kaga* suffered the worst casualties of the six aircraft carriers, losing WO Gotō and three others in action. After returning to the mainland, the *Kaga* departed for the Southeast area in January 1942. Following the raid on Darwin, the *Kaga* left the other aircraft carriers in the group and returned to Sasebo on 22 March for replenishment of supplies. On 27 May, the *Kaga*, together with three other aircraft carriers of the 1st Air Fleet, left the Inland Sea and participated in the Battle of Midway. During the first wave attack, launched on the morning of 4 June, nine Zero fighters under the command of LT Iizuka shot down twelve aircraft. During air defense battles over the friendly carriers, a cumulative total of thirty-two attacking enemy aircraft were intercepted and shot down. The aircraft carrier *Kaga*, however, was hit by American dive-bombers and sank. Total casualties for the *Kaga* Fighter Squadron numbered six.

Successive Group Leaders:

October 1935–June 1936   LCDR Motoharu Okamura

June 1936–November 1936   LCDR Sadao Koike

Pilots of the *Kaga* Fighter Squadron as of October 1938. Center row: second from left, LCDR Chujirō Nakano, group leader. The faces of the following aces can also be seen here. Extreme left, Jirō Chōno. Center row: right end, Osamu Kudō. Back row: right end, Yoshio Fukui; second from right, Chitoshi Isozaki. (Yasujirō Abe)

November 1936–December 1937 LCDR Takeo Shibata

December 1937–December 1938 LCDR Chujirō Nakano

November 1940–September 1941 LCDR Tadao Funaki

Successive Division Officers:

November 1936–March 1938 LT Chikamasa Igarashi

November 1936–March 1938 LT Tadashi Nakajima

December 1937–September 1938 LT Hideo Teshima

September 1938–December 1938 LT Masao Yamashita

September 1938–December 1938 LTJG Kashira Ikeda

April 1941–April 1942 LT Yoshio Shiga

April 1941–September 1941 LT Kiyokuma Okajima

September 1941–May 1942 LT Yasushi Nikaidō

April 1942–June 1942 LT Masao Iizuka

May 1942–June 1942 LT Masao Satō

竜 驤 戦 闘 機 隊

RYŪJŌ FIGHTER SQUADRON

The *Ryūjō* was a small aircraft carrier completed in June 1933. With a standard displacement of 8 thousand tons and a speed of 29 knots, she was immediately posted to the 2nd Carrier Division, together with the *Akagi*. At the time she was posted to the fleet, her complement of aircraft was: three operational Type 3 carrier fighters with two spares, and nine operational Type 13 carrier attack planes with three spares. In 1934, the carrier was equipped with six each of Type 90 and Type 3 carrier fighters. Starting in 1935, twelve Type 90 carrier fighters were on the ready line; following the outbreak of the China Incident, this was changed to twelve Type 96 carrier fighters on the ready line. As a matter of fact, however, because of a shortage of the new fighters, the *Ryūjō* commenced operations using Type 90 carrier fighters only.

With storm clouds in the Shanghai area blackening in August 1937, the carrier was posted to the 1st Carrier Division (*Hōshō, Ryūjō*) on 6 August. *Ryūjō* left Sasebo on the 12th and arrived off Shanghai on the 16th, then joined the aerial battles. The initial sortie by the fighter squadron on board the *Ryūjō* was during the afternoon of the 22nd, in the aerial battles over Pao-shan. Four aircraft under the command of LT Tadashi Kaneko discovered eighteen Curtiss Hawk fighters that were scouting at a height of three thousand meters and made a surprise attack on them from the rear. Six enemy aircraft were shot down and our side did not even receive a single hit, so complete was the victory. Next, on the 23rd, four aircraft under the command of LTJG Minoru Suzuki discovered a mixed force of twenty-seven enemy aircraft, including P-26s, while they were scouting over Pao-shan. The units engaged in battle and a total of nine enemy aircraft were downed, including those downed by three aircraft of LTJG Suzuki's force. The China Area Fleet commander in chief issued a letter of commendation in connection with this battle.

The *Ryūjō* returned to Sasebo on 2 September and after refueling left port together with the *Hōshō* on the 5th. Between the 20th and the 30th, the two carriers were engaged in South China operations. In particular, during the raid on Kwangtung on the 21st, under the leadership of LCDR Kozono, the first wave of nine carrier fighters served as escort for fifteen carrier attack planes and bombers. The *Ryūjō* by itself accounted for shooting down six enemy aircraft. Similarly, the second wave of nine carrier fighters also covered fifteen carrier attack planes and bombers and shot down six enemy aircraft (one probable). Next, on 3 October, the *Ryūjō* moved off Shanghai; after the 5th, the air group was based at the Kunda airfield, providing aerial protection and support of land operations in the Shanghai and Nanking areas. Reinforced by the *Hōshō*'s air group, the total force came to twenty-one carrier fighters, fifteen carrier bombers, and six carrier attack planes. On 1 December, the *Ryūjō* re-

Zero Fighter Model 21

Fighter flown by PO1c Tadayoshi Koga during the June 1942 Aleutian Islands operation. The unit insignia *DI* was used between April 1941 and July 1942.

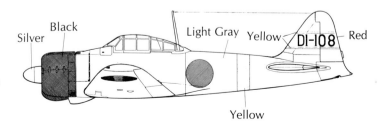

Silver
Black
Light Gray Yellow DI-I08 Red
Yellow

turned to the Japanese mainland and was assigned to training activities. Further, with respect to the 1st Carrier Division attack on Canton, a letter of commendation was issued by the commander in chief of the China Area Fleet.

In 1938, the *Ryūjō* joined with the *Sōryū* to form the 2nd Carrier Division. For about twenty days starting the middle of March, and again in October, the units operated in the South China area in support of the Kwangtung operation. In November 1939, the *Ryūjō* had reached the point where she needed various repairs because of fleet operations extending over a period of six years; she was placed in the reserve fleet. Various parts of the carrier were repaired or modified. During the same period, between February and July 1940, the *Ryūjō* assisted in landing and takeoff training exercises for officer and enlisted pilot trainees of the 12th Combined Air Group.

Following one year's rest and recuperation in this fashion, the *Ryūjō* returned to active service on 15 November 1940. Constituting the 3rd Carrier Division, together with the *Hōshō,* she was posted to the 1st Fleet. The *Ryūjō* carried sixteen Type 96 carrier fighters and eighteen Type 97 carrier attack planes. In April 1941, she alone joined the 4th Carrier Division and was dispatched in June to Micronesia, where she engaged in antisubmarine training exercises. At the outbreak of the Pacific War, the *Ryūjō* and the specially converted (escort) carrier *Kasuga Maru,* which had been commissioned on 11 August, were part of the 4th Carrier Division.

In order to participate in Southern Area operations, the *Ryūjō* departed Saeki Bay on 27 November and entered Palau on 5 December. On the next day *Ryūjō* sortied and by early morning of 8 December, the first day of hostilities, was about one hundred miles east of Davao [Philippines]. Thirteen Type 97 carrier attack planes escorted by nine Type 96 carrier fighters (commanded by LT Takahide Aioi) at-

Type 95 carrier fighter of the *Ryūjō,* flown by LTJG Minoru Suzuki. (Minoru Suzuki)

Fighter squadron pilots on the *Ryūjō* in 1937. LCDR Yasuna Kozono, group leader, is in the center of the middle row (seated). Left of LCDR Kozono is LTJG Minoru Suzuki. (Yoshimichi Saeki)

tacked Davao but met with little resistance. The second wave, consisting of two carrier attack planes and three carrier fighters, made their sortie. PO2c Hiroshi Kawanishi's fighter was hit by antiaircraft guns. He made an emergency landing, burned his aircraft, then committed suicide. On the 12th, the *Ryūjō* then participated in providing support to the Legaspi landing operation; she entered Palau harbor on the 14th. Leaving Palau on the 17th, she next participated in the invasion of Davao, fighting on both the 19th and the 20th. She then participated in supporting the invasion of Jolo Island (until 24 December) and was next posted to the Malayan forces.

On 1 January 1942, the unit moved to Cam Ranh Bay and supported operations in Singapore and in the Dutch East Indies area. In April, the *Ryūjō* moved into the Indian Ocean and engaged in commerce raiding. Once the first phase of operations was ended, the carrier returned to the Inland Sea, arriving on 23 April. Aircraft on board were changed from the Type 96

fighter to Zero models; the complement was then sixteen carrier fighters and twenty carrier attack planes.

In order to participate in the Aleutian Islands campaign, the *Ryūjō*, together with the *Junyō*, left the port of Ōminato and on 3–4 June conducted attacks on Dutch Harbor. During the attack on 4 June a PBY was shot down. The aircraft piloted by PO1c Tadayoshi Koga, however, received antiaircraft fire and made an emergency landing in the tundra on an almost uninhabited island [Akutan]. He was killed in the crash. At a later date, Koga's aircraft was found by an American search party; it was to become the first, almost completely intact Zero fighter (model 21 number 108) that the Americans obtained.

After returning to the homeland, the *Ryūjō* was posted to the 2nd Carrier Division in a July reorganization (*Ryūjō, Junyō,* and the *Hiyō*). At the outbreak of the battle for Guadalcanal, on 16 August, the *Ryūjō* went out on a sortie as an element of the 3rd Fleet. She detached herself from the

The *Ryūjō* Fighter Squadron in 1941, just before the beginning of the war. Front row, from the left: PO1c Ippei Yoshida, WO Mutsuo Sagara, LT (group leader) Takahide Aioi, WO Haruichi Uemura, and (unknown). Rear row, from the left: (unknown), Hiroshi Kurihara, Yukuo Miyauchi, Teruo Sugiyama, Tsugio Shikada, Tomio Yoshizawa, (unknown), Tadayoshi Koga, and Hiromichi Hōjō, all noncommissioned officer pilots. (Tsuguo Shikada)

main unit on the 24th in order to participate in the attacks against the airfield on Guadalcanal. The carrier used fifteen carrier fighters (under the command of LT Nō-tomi) [and six carrier attack planes]. During the fierce battle for the island, a total of fifteen enemy aircraft were downed. During the absence of most of her fighters, however, the *Ryūjō* herself underwent heavy attacks from American carrier aircraft. The carrier attempted to intercept the opposing forces with its remaining ten [seven] carrier fighters and was successful in shooting down eleven of the enemy. In the evening, however, the carrier sank; all combat air patrol fighters ditched and their pilots were rescued by destroyers. The majority of the attack group was able to land in Rabaul.

Successive Group Leaders:

December 1933–October 1935   LCDR
 Ryutarō Yamanaka

October 1935–December 1937   LT Yasuna Kozono

November 1941–February 1942   LT Takahide Aioi

June 1942–August 1942   LT Kenjirō Nōtomi

Successive Division Officers:

November 1936–October 1937   LT Shigeru Itaya

October 1937–   LT Manbei Shimokawa

October 1937–December 1937   LT Kiyoto Hanamoto

December 1937–June 1938   LT Mitsugu
 Kofukuda

November 1940–November 1941   LT
 Masaji Suganami

March 1942–July 1942   LT Minoru Kobayashi

July 1942–August 1942   LT Masao Iizuka

蒼 竜 戦 闘 機 隊

SŌRYŪ FIGHTER SQUADRON

Work on the *Sōryū,* a new and efficient medium-sized aircraft carrier, started in November 1934 at the Kure Naval Arsenal; she was completed in August 1937. Placed in service 1 December, she was posted to the 2nd Carrier Division (of the Second Fleet). Commanded by CAPT Kinpei Teraoka, orders were also issued at this time for the following officers to report for duty: CDR Toshihiko Odawara as Air Officer, LCDR Shigehachirō Tokoro as group leader for the fighter unit, as well as LT Mochifumi Nangō and LT Tamotsu Yokoyama as division officers. Although the aircraft complement on board was to have been twenty-seven Type 96 carrier bombers, twelve Type 96 carrier attack planes, and eighteen Type 96 carrier fighters, because of the shortage of Type 96 fighters at the time, Type 95 fighters were placed into use. Borrowing the *Hōshō* and using the Ōmura Naval Base, carrier takeoff and landing practice was conducted.

On 25 April of the following year, 1938, the decision was made that nine carrier fighters, eighteen carrier bombers, and nine carrier attack planes would be posted under the command of the 2nd Combined Air Group and participate in central China operations, especially in the Yangtze River upriver operation. The aircraft took off from their carrier from off the Ma-an-shan Islands and initially moved to the Nanking airport. The fighter unit engaged for a while in the air defense of Nanking and in support of land operations (carrying two 60-Kg bombs each). With the advances made by the army, in early June the fighter unit moved on to Wuhu, and by mid-June, to the Anking base performing similar duties. Since in all instances these were advances into newly conquered territories, the facilities were inadequate, and at night there were even occasional enemy attacks. In particular, at Anking the quality of water was poor, resulting in a number of personnel becoming sick. During the same period, there were almost daily raids conducted by Soviet-made SB bombers trying to bomb the naval ships in the river. Although *Sōryū* units rose to intercept on each occasion, there were very few encounters with the enemy. WO Sakae Katō, who took off on an intercept mission on 25 June, was able to down one enemy aircraft but his craft lost speed and he destroyed his own aircraft. It is assumed that the cause for this was a temporary loss of consciousness because of physical weakness on the part of the pilot.

Although the unit dispatched from the *Sōryū* was to have been returned to its car-

Type 96 Model 4 Carrier Fighter

This was the plane flown by LT Tamotsu Yokoyama serving as a fighter division officer in the central China area in 1938. The fuselage was silver overall, and the diagonal stripe on the fuselage indicates the pilot is a division officer. The unit insignia *W* was used from the end of 1937 to 1940.

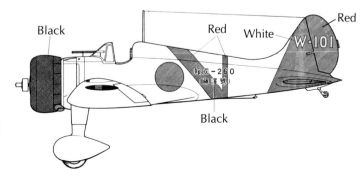

Black

Red   White   Red

報國 - 2 6 0
（藤澤號）

Black

Type 96 Model 4 carrier fighter on the *Sōryū*. (Kiyokuma Okajima)

rier under group leader Nangō, one detachment of fighters remained and was posted to the newly organized 15th Air Group. Later, on 25 September, the *Sōryū* proceeded to South China as the 1st and 2nd carrier divisions were ordered to participate in the battle for Kwangtung. Although they did participate, there were no opportunities to engage the enemy; on 1 December, the carrier returned to the mainland of Japan.

The *Sōryū* was engaged in fleet training exercises during 1940 and 1941; at the same time they loaned aircraft to the forces in China. The carrier's own complement was a mere nine aircraft.

In September 1940, her consort, the *Hiryū*, received orders to move out to assist in the occupation of the northern part of French Indochina. All air units on the *Sōryū* were temporarily transferred on board the *Hiryū*. From 17 September through the early part of October, the unit was active off Hainan Island.

In 1941 also, during early and mid-February, the unit moved into the Taiwan area and supported the blockade of South China.

When the 1st Air Fleet was organized in April 1941, the *Sōryū* was posted thereto. In response to the occupation of the southern part of French Indochina, the air group was dispatched to Ya Hsien (Sanya), Hainan Island, in mid-July.

LT Masaji Suganami, fighter division officer on board the *Sōryū*. (Family of Masaji Suganami)

Model 21 Zero fighters belonging to the *Sōryū* at the Kendari Air Base in February 1942. The Zero fighters to the right and the Type 98 land reconnaissance plane belong to the 3rd Air Group. (Kiyoshi Katō)

With the outbreak of the Pacific War, the *Sōryū* did participate in the December 7th (Hawaiian time) Hawaii strike force and left the bay of Hitokappu, Kurile Islands on 26 November. Eight Zero fighters, led by LT Masaji Suganami, participated in the first wave attack on Pearl Harbor. The unit strafed both Wheeler and Ewa airfields, and set twenty-seven enemy aircraft on fire on the ground; part of the unit also engaged in aerial battles with the enemy. PO3c Shin-ichi Suzuki shot down two aircraft and Sea1c Isao Doikawa shot down three. All our aircraft returned safely. At the same time, losing his bearings at one point, LT Suganami decided to return to Hawaii, taking his five aircraft with him with the intention of destroying himself. With the aid of friendly carrier attack planes, however, he and his unit were able to return safely to the carrier. During the second wave attack on Pearl Harbor, a chūtai of nine aircraft led by LT Fusato Iida strafed the airfield at Kaneohe and destroyed six flying boats. However, LT Iida himself received hits and died heroically by destroying himself. At the time that LTJG Iyozō Fujita had gathered the remnants of the unit together and started on their way back towards the carrier, they were met by enemy fighter aircraft. Although Fujita and PO2c Jirō Tanaka downed one enemy aircraft each, PO1c Takashi Atsumi and PO1c Saburō Ishii were killed. On the way back from Hawaii, the 2nd Carrier Division was ordered to support the Wake Island occupation forces; they attacked the island from 21–23 December. On the 29th, the *Sōryū* dropped anchor at Kure Naval Base.

After rest and recuperation at the Usa Base, the air group returned to its carrier on 11 January 1942. On the next day, the *Sōryū* steamed out of the Inland Sea.

The *Sōryū* participated in the attack on Darwin on 19 February, after having proceeded to the front via Palau. There were, however, no aerial encounters with the enemy. Next, following rest and recuperation at Kendari, the carrier departed on 25 March for Indian Ocean operations. The

Model 21 Zero Fighter

Aircraft flown by LT Masaji Suganami, division officer of the fighter squadron on board the *Sōryū* at the time of the Battle for Midway. The unit designation *B1* was used starting in April 1941.

Sōryū participated in the attack on Colombo on 5 April and the attack on Trincomalee on the 9th. In particular, it is to be noted that during the aerial battle over Colombo, the nine aircraft led by LTJG Fujita shot down fourteen enemy aircraft (three probables) and lost but one plane themselves. On the way back to the mainland, the task force pursued but was not able to catch up with the American task force that had raided Tokyo. On the 22nd, the *Sōryū* anchored at Kure. Shortly thereafter, in order to participate in the Battle of Midway, the carrier left the Inland Sea on 27 May. Nine Zero fighters under the command of LT Suganami participated in the first wave attack on Midway and shot down six American fighters that rose to intercept them.

On the other hand, by the sixth watch, a cumulative eighteen aircraft were able to shoot down thirty-two American attack aircraft that had risen to intercept them. The *Sōryū* did receive hits, however, burned, and sank that evening about two hundred miles north of Midway Island. Most flight crews on board were rescued by screening destroyers and were able to return to the homeland.

Successive Group Leaders:

December 1937–March 1938   LCDR Shigehachirō Tokoro

March 1938–July 1938   LT Mochifumi Nangō

November 1940–August 1941   LCDR Ryōsuke Nomura

Successive Division Officers:

December 1937–July 1938   LT Mochifumi Nangō

December 1937–December 1939   LT Tamotsu Yokoyama

December 1939–October 1940   LT Kiyoto Hanamoto

October 1940–April 1941   LT Kiyokuma Okajima

November 1941–June 1942   LT Masaji Suganami

November 1941–December 1941   LT Fusata Iida

December 1941–June 1942   LTJG Iyozō Fujita

飛 竜 戦 闘 機 隊

HIRYŪ FIGHTER SQUADRON

8 July 1936	Construction started at the Yokosuka Naval Arsenal.
16 November 1937	Launched.
5 July 1939	Completed. (Same type of carrier as the *Sōryū;* 17,300 tons displacement.)
15 November 1939	Posted to the 2nd Carrier Division (2nd Fleet); aircraft complement was nine carrier fighters, commanding officer, CAPT Ichihei Yokogawa, air officer, CDR Masataka Nagaishi.
January 1940	Aircraft loaded and training exercises commenced.
15 September 1940	Carrier air group (includes *Sōryū* aircraft transferred to the *Hiryū*) proceeded to the Hainan Island area.
17 September 1940	Left the port of Kure.
6 October 1940	Entered Yokosuka harbor.
February 1941	Active in South China area.
10 April 1941	2nd Carrier Division was integrated into the 1st Air Fleet.
July–August 1941	Active in the South China Sea; carrier air group proceeded to Ya Hsien (Sanya), Hainan Island.
18 November 1941	2nd Carrier Division left Saeki Bay.
22 November 1941	Arrived at Hitokappu Bay.
26 November 1941	Sortied out of Hitokappu Bay as task force.
7 December 1941	Attacked Pearl Harbor.
21–23 December 1941	Cooperated in the Wake Island invasion campaign.
29 December 1941	Returned to western portion of Inland Sea.
12 January 1942	Sortied out of western portion of Inland Sea.
23–24 January 1942	Ambon invasion campaign.
29 January 1942	Port Darwin air raid.
27 February 1942	Tjilatjap, Java air raid.
5 April 1942	Colombo air raid.
9 April 1942	Trincomalee air raid (attack on the British aircraft carrier *Hermes*).
22 April 1942	Returned to western portion of Inland Sea.
27 May 1942	Sortied out of western portion of Inland Sea.
6 June 1942	Sunk during the Battle of Midway.

Type 96 Model 4 Carrier Fighter

Unit insignia *QII* was used starting November 1940.

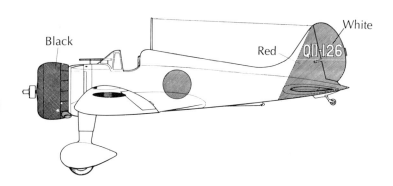

Snapshot of pilots taken between October 1940 and April 1941. Extreme right is LTJG Saneyasu Hidaka. (Family of Hachitarō Hayashi)

The *Hiryū* carrier air group's first taste of battle was the raid on Pearl Harbor. During the attack on Pearl Harbor, six Zero fighters led by LT Okajima participated. They strafed approximately forty aircraft on the ground at Barbers Point [Ewa Field] and were able to set twenty-two of them on fire. At the same time, there were no aerial encounters and all aircraft returned safely to the carrier.

During the second wave attack on Pearl Harbor, nine Zero fighters (of which one aborted to the carrier) led by LT Nōno participated. They strafed Kaneohe and Bellows airfields and were able to set two aircraft on the ground on fire as well as destroy one truck.

The squadron next engaged in an aerial battle during which PO1c Tsugio Matsuyama shot down two enemy fighters. During this same battle, however, the aircraft piloted by PO1c Shigenori Nishikaichi received hits and was lost in action on the way back to the carrier. He was thought to have destroyed himself. After the war, however, it became known that he had made an emergency landing on the island of Niihau, Hawaii, and when surrounded by natives, committed suicide [he was killed by a Hawaiian]. During the raid on Wake Island, the *Hiryū* Air Group received damage. PO3c Isao Tahara, assigned to the *Hiryū* carrier escort, made chase and took revenge in the form of shooting down two

Zero Fighter Model 21

Fighter used by LT Sumio Nōno, *Hiryū* division officer, during Indian Ocean operations. The unit insignia *BII* was used between April 1941 and June 1942.

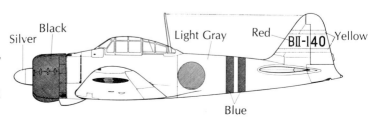

Grumman F4Fs. During the Colombo raid, nine carrier fighters under the command of LT Nōno participated; during a bitter air battle sixteen Hurricanes and eight Swordfish were shot down. LT Nōno himself failed to return to his carrier after an intercept attack on Blenheim bombers.

Special note should be taken of the activities of the *Hiryū* carrier fighter squadron during the Battle of Midway. Nine carrier fighters under the command of LT Shigematsu joined the first wave attack; they shot down a total of eighteen F4Fs and Buffalo that rose to intercept them. The unit itself returned safely to the carrier. The three aircraft carriers *Akagi, Kaga,* and *Sōryū,* however, received hits from attacking American carrier aircraft and were destroyed by fire. The remaining carrier, the *Hiryū,* was able to send out two waves of attack forces by herself; this force severely damaged the American aircraft carrier *Yorktown.* At the same time, casualties on the part of the *Hiryū*'s carrier fighter squadron were not minor, either. Six carrier fighters served as escort for the Kobayashi carrier bombing squadron, with the exception of two aircraft of the Minegishi shōtai that had to return prematurely to the carrier.

Group leader LCDR Shigeru Itaya standing at center (Yoshimichi Saeki)

The remaining four aircraft shot down seven enemy aircraft during an aerial encounter over the American task force. Our side suffered the loss of three aircraft also; LT Shigematsu was the sole survivor who returned to the carrier. Four carrier fighters

TABLE 1. ORGANIZATION OF THE *HIRYŪ* CARRIER FIGHTER SQUADRON DURING THE BATTLE OF MIDWAY

	1ST SHŌTAI	2ND SHŌTAI	3RD SHŌTAI
Attack on Midway	LT Yasuhiro Shige-matsu PO1c Kazuo Muranaka PO2c Haruo Nitta	WO Yoshijirō Mine-gishi PO1c Takaaki Satō PO3c Yutaka Chi-yoshima	PO1c Michisuke To-kuda PO2c Toshiaki Harada Sea1c Shigeru Hayashi
Task Force Attack Unit (1st Phase)	LT Yasuhiro Shige-matsu PO2c Noboru To-daka★ Sea1c Suekichi Yoshi-moto★	WO Yoshijirō Mine-gishi PO1c Hitoshi Sasaki PO3c Yutaka Chi-yoshima★	[No 3rd Shōtai]
Task Force Attack Unit (2nd Phase)	LT Shigeru Mori★ PO2c Tōru Yama-moto★	WO Yoshijirō Mine-gishi PO2c Kenji Kotani	PO1c Akira Yama-moto (*Kaga* plane) PO3c Makoto Bandō (*Kaga* plane)

★ Destroyed himself.

led by LT Mori and reinforced by two carrier fighters from the *Kaga* escorted the Tomonaga torpedo attack squadron and participated in the attack on the American task force. After battling in the air with about thirty American fighters, the unit was able to shoot down eleven of the enemy; however, two aircraft, including the one piloted by LT Mori, were destroyed. On the other hand, to provide combat air patrol directly over the aircraft carrier itself, a total of thirty-three aircraft were used, including planes that had been sent to the *Hiryū* from other carriers. By evening and the tenth watch, a cumulative total of thirty-three enemy aircraft had been shot down. At the same time, five *Hiryū*-based fighters among others were also lost. As a matter of fact, the entire fighter squadron [aircraft] complement was wiped out. Also, the carrier *Hiryū* itself received bomb hits during

the afternoon raids conducted on her, caught on fire, and sank the next morning. The Battle of Midway ended as a crushing defeat for the Japanese.

Successive Group Leaders:

November 1940–April 1941   LCDR Shigeru Itaya

Successive Division Officers:

January 1940–November 1940   LT Shigeru Itaya
November 1940–April 1942   LT Sumio Nōno
November 1940–April 1941   LT Takumi Hoashi
November 1941–January 1942   LT Kiyokuma Okajima
January 1942–June 1942   LTJG [LT?] Yasuhiro Shigematsu
April 1942–June 1942   LT Shigeru Mori

翔 鶴 戦 闘 機 隊

SHŌKAKU FIGHTER SQUADRON

The two aircraft carriers *Shōkaku* and *Zuikaku* were sister ships the construction of both of which started in 1937 as part of the 3rd Armament Strengthening Plan. Both of them were medium-sized carriers, with a standard displacement of 25,675 tons and a speed of 34 knots. Throughout the Pacific War, these two carriers served as the nuclei of task forces.

The first ship to be completed was the *Shōkaku,* completed on 8 August 1941 at the Yokosuka Naval Arsenal. On 1 September the *Shōkaku,* together with the *Kasuga Maru,* constituted the 5th Carrier Division. Immediately upon completion of the *Zuikaku* on the 25th of the same month, she was posted to the 5th, and the *Kasuga Maru* was posted to the 4th Carrier Division. Complements of both carriers were the same: twelve Zero fighters (four spares), eighteen Type 96 carrier bombers (six spares), and eighteen Type 97 carrier attack planes (six spares). Fighter units attached to the 5th Carrier Division were assigned to various bases on the island of Kyūshū, starting 7 October. The fighter squadrons were sent to Ōmura to undergo accelerated training. Aircraft on board each of the carriers were increased to eighteen carrier fighters, twenty-seven carrier bombers, and twenty-seven carrier attack planes. On 18 November, the two ships steamed out of the western end of the Inland Sea and rendezvoused at Hitokappu Bay, Etorofu Island, on the 22nd. On the 26th, they joined the task force that attacked Hawaii. Six carrier fighters from the *Shōkaku* under the command of LT Tadashi Kaneko joined in the first attack wave but did not meet any enemy reaction. The unit then strafed Kaneohe and Bellows airfields and set on fire thirty-three flying boats and other aircraft. The 5th Carrier Division did not participate in the second wave of attack;

twelve aircraft under the command of LT Iizuka served as air cover for the fleet, in shifts.

The 5th Carrier Division, which had been successful in its surprise attack on Hawaii, returned to Kure by 24 December. The aircraft complement was changed so that there were twenty-one each of fighters, bombers, and attack planes. On 8 January 1942 the ships joined in the attack on Rabaul and Lae, returning to Yokosuka on 2 February.

With hardly any time for rest or recuperation, however, the ships sortied on 17 March and participated in Indian Ocean operations, proceeding via Kendari. In particular, during the 9 April raid on Trincomalee ten carrier fighters under the command of LT Kaneko joined in the attack and a major air battle ensued. Twenty-three enemy aircraft were destroyed; on our side, we lost PO1c Hayashi. On both the 7th and the 8th of May, the 5th Carrier Division joined in the Battle of the Coral Sea. During the attack on the 8th on an American task force, nine carrier fighters under the command of LT Hoashi served as escort and shot down thirty aircraft. At the same time, the nine carrier fighter aircraft assigned as air patrol directly over the carriers were able to shoot down twenty-one American dive-bombers, torpedo planes, that attacked the fleet. PO2c Takeo Miyazawa, after shooting down an enemy torpedo plane, piloted his own aircraft into an attacking torpedo plane, moments before it was to release its torpedo and thereby saved the carrier. Although the *Shōkaku* did receive bomb hits on her deck and started burning, emergency measures were successful in extinguishing the flames. Carrier fighters were able to land on the unscathed *Zuikaku.* A Zero fighter, piloted by WO Yukuo Hanzawa, was able to safely land

Shōkaku flight crew, on the eve of the attack on Hawaii, December 1941. (WO and above.) Second row (from the front): fourth person from the right, fighter division officer LT Kaneko. To his left, air officer CDR Wada, CAPT Koji Shiroshima, and LCDR Kaku-ichi Takahashi, air group commander. (Yasujirō Abe)

his aircraft on the *Shōkaku*'s deck, which was bathed in black smoke and had no arresting gear in place. The damaged *Shōkaku* entered the port of Kure on 17 May and repair work commenced. The carrier air group was reorganized and underwent training at Kanoya and at Saeki from the 30th on. It did not participate in the Battle of Midway in June.

With the organization of the new 3rd Fleet on 14 July, the *Shōkaku, Zuikaku,* and the *Zuihō* formed the 1st Carrier Division. The aircraft complement on board the *Shōkaku* was changed to twenty-seven each of carrier fighters and bombers, and eighteen

carrier attack planes. On 16 August, the force sortied out of the Inland Sea in order to join the final battles in the Solomons area.

On the 24th, the *Shōkaku* participated in the Second Battle of the Solomons [Battle of the Eastern Solomons]. As part of the first attack unit, four carrier fighters under the command of LT Shigematsu served as escort for eighteen carrier bombers. The strike group was successful in dropping bombs on the USS *Enterprise,* as well as in shooting down four aircraft. Our side lost one Zero fighter. Next, fifteen Zero fighters under the command of LT Shingō

Zero Fighter Model 21

The plane used by LT Hideki Shingō, group leader of the *Shōkaku* Fighter Squadron during the battles in the South Pacific area. Unit insignia *EI* was used from September 1941 through October 1942.

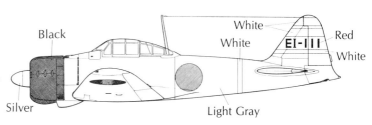

Shōkaku Fighter Squadron flight personnel just before the outbreak of hostilities. Front row, from the left: end, Ichirō Yamamoto; Masao Sasakibara. Second row, from the left: second person, LTJG Masao Iizuka; LT Takumi Hoashi, and WO Yasujirō Abe. Third row, from the right: second person, Sadamu Komachi; third person, Kenji Okabe. Rear row, from left: second person, Yoshimi Minami. (Yasujirō Abe)

were sent to Buka Base from 28 August through 4 September; they were used in the daily attacks on Guadalcanal. At the same time, because of poor weather conditions, on two occasions the aircraft had to return to base. The unit was successful on three occasions, however, the 29th and the 30th, as well as on 2 September when they were able to shoot down a total of fifteen enemy fighter aircraft. At the same time, our side did lose six veteran pilots; sacrifices made

included LT Shingō, who had to make an emergency landing on Guadalcanal, and LT Ibusuki who was hit and also made an emergency landing.

During the Battle of Santa Cruz on 26 October, four carrier fighters under the command of LT Miyajima participated in the first attack, while five carrier fighter aircraft under the command of LT Shingō participated in the second attack, serving as escorts for carrier bomber and attack plane

Zero Fighter Model 22

At the time of the "Ro"-gō operation in November 1943.

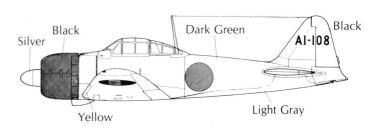

squadrons. They thus joined in the attack on the American task force. Enemy fighter aircraft were few, however, and only five aircraft were shot down. On the other hand, the Zero fighter units that served as CAP for the aircraft carrier numbered, cumulatively, twenty-four and were able to shoot down nine aircraft (three probables). PO1c Ōmori rammed his own aircraft into an enemy bomber that was on the verge of dropping a bomb on the *Shōkaku* and thereby saved the ship. The *Shōkaku* was hit repeatedly, however, and heavily damaged. In a sense, although the damage to the carrier fighter squadron—three aircraft—was minor, there was great attrition in carrier attack planes and bombers. The *Shōkaku* returned to the homeland to undergo reconstruction.

By the end of February 1943 repairs to the *Shōkaku* were complete; the aircraft complement was changed to twenty-seven carrier fighter aircraft, eighteen carrier bombers, and twenty-seven carrier attack planes. On 15 July she proceeded to Truk, where the fighter squadron used the island's airfield for training. Under the command of twenty-four-year-old LT Hōhei Kobayashi, newly assigned as the division officer, the fighter squadron on the *Shōkaku* was reorganized. The air tactical section was changed from the traditional three aircraft formation to a four aircraft formation; efforts were made to improve formation air battle tactics and in-flight navigational techniques. New fighter bomber tactics were also developed. After undergoing such training for one year, the *Shōkaku* Fighter Squadron sortied to Rabaul in order to participate on 1 November in the "Ro"-gō operation.

On the next day, 2 November, all 130 fighter aircraft stationed at Rabaul were used in intercepting a total of about two hundred enemy fighters and bombers. Major results were obtained: 119 aircraft were downed (twenty-two probables). In particular, the twenty-five aircraft of the *Shōkaku* Fighter Squadron took advantage of taking off from the Vunakanau airfield situated on

Zero Model 21 piloted by LT Hideki Shingō, group leader, taking off from the *Shōkaku* in October 1942 during the Battle of Santa Cruz. (Hideki Shingō)

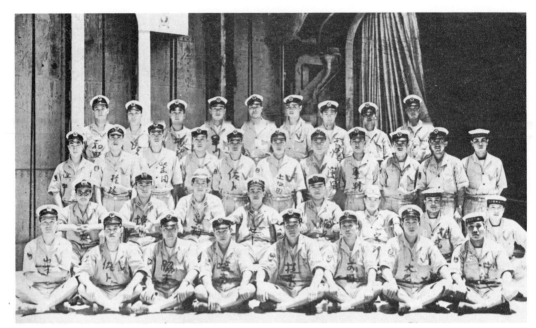

The *Shōkaku* Fighter Squadron in November 1943 on the eve of the "Ro"-gō operation. Second row center is LT Setō, group leader. To his left, LT Kobayashi, division officer. (Takeo Tanimizu)

The *Shōkaku*, repairing damage received from bomb hits. In the distance, the *Zuikaku*. (*The Ships of the World*)

the top of a mountain and shot down forty-seven enemy aircraft (seven were probables). As for individual victories, WO Hitoshi Satō had eight kills, reportedly LTJG Kazunori Miyabe shot down six aircraft, and LT Kobayashi shot down four aircraft. Next, almost daily, the *Shōkaku* Fighter Squadron participated in attacks on the island of Bougainville, as well as actively engaging in Rabaul interception.

By the time the unit made its way to Rabaul on the 13th, the record was 107 aircraft shot down (twenty-three probables). Our side lost eight pilots. Next, responding to the critical situation at the Marshall Islands, the fighter squadrons of the 1st Carrier Division sortied to Roi (Ruotta). Because of crippling damages incurred in the air battles on 5 December, however, the unit returned to Truk on the 8th. In order to refurbish, both the *Shōkaku* and the *Zuikaku* left Truk on the 12th and headed for home. Aircraft were removed from the *Shōkaku;* the group was reborn on 15 February 1944 as part of the newly organized Air Group 601. The *Shōkaku,* which had

sortied off the Marianas, was sunk on 19 June.

Successive Group Leaders:

July 1942–October 1942   LT Hideki Shingō

March 1943–November 1943   LT Masuzō Setō

Successive Division Officers:

September 1941–April 1942   LT Tadashi Kaneko

November 1941–June 1942   LT Takumi Hoashi

April 1942–July 1942   LT Shigehisa Yamamoto

July 1942–November 1942   LT Hisayoshi Miyajima

July 1942–November 1942   LT Masanobu Ibusuki

February 1943–October 1943   LT Hōhei Kobayashi

October 1943–December 1943   LTJG Yasuo Masuyama

October 1943–December 1943   LTJG Ikurō Sakami

瑞 鶴 戦 闘 機 隊

ZUIKAKU FIGHTER SQUADRON

The *Zuikaku* was completed 25 September 1941, one month behind her sister, the *Shōkaku*. She was immediately posted to the 5th Carrier Division and her air group stationed at various air bases on Kyūshū to start training.

The *Zuikaku*'s initial battle was the attack on Pearl Harbor; six Zero fighters under the command of LT Satō joined the first wave attack covering force but did not have any opportunity to engage in aerial battle. In conjunction with the carrier bomber squadron, the fighters strafed Kaneohe Naval Air Station and were able to set on fire more than thirty-two aircraft on the ground. The squadron did not participate in the second wave attack but was assigned to patrol above the carrier, using a cumulative total of twenty-nine aircraft.

On 24 December, the *Zuikaku* returned to the western part of the Inland Sea and, together with the *Shōkaku*, sortied out during the month of January 1942 to assist in the Southern Area operations. In particular, during the air raid on Trincomalee on the 9th, ten carrier fighters under the command of LT Makino covered nineteen carrier bombers; they were able to shoot down twenty enemy aircraft during a battle with British fighters. Two carrier fighters, however, including LT Makino's aircraft, were lost.

On the way back to the homeland, the 5th Carrier Division was assigned to support the MO Operation. The *Zuikaku* sortied to the Solomon Islands area front via Ma-kiang and Truk Island. On both 7 and 8 May, the world's first carrier versus carrier battle (Battle of the Coral Sea) developed. On the 8th, nine [Zero] fighters, six of which were used in support of the torpedo attack squadron of the *Shōkaku* and three in support of the *Zuikaku*'s torpedo attack squadron, all under the command of LT Tsukamoto, joined in the attack on the American task force. They engaged in battle with the enemy fighters that were stationed in defense over their own carriers. "Each unit and each aircraft did valiantly engage in battle," with the result that twenty-nine enemy aircraft (three probables) were shot down. At the same time, the ten fighters [Zeros] that were serving as direct cover for the carriers (commander, LT Okajima) engaged the many incoming American fighter aircraft and shot down thirteen fighters, six torpedo bombers, and five dive-bombers, for a total of twenty-four enemy aircraft downed (two probables). These brilliant results were achieved by our side with only one of our aircraft forced to make emergency landings in each of these two encounters.

At the end of May, both carriers belonging to the 5th Carrier Division returned to the homeland; fighter units resumed training exercises in the southern part of Kyūshū. The *Zuikaku* sortied out of the western end of the Inland Sea on 15 June in order to support the withdrawal of the task force that had been defeated at the Battle of Midway. Following operations in the area

Zero Fighter Model 21

The unit insignia *EII* was used during the period December 1941 through October 1942.

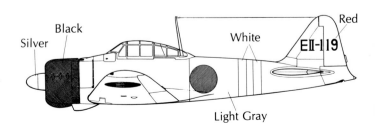

The aircraft carrier *Zuikaku*, built as a sister ship of the *Shōkaku*. (*The Ships of the World*)

south of the Kurile Islands, she entered the port of Ōminato on the 25th. The *Zuikaku* then again returned to the Inland Sea.

As of 14 July, a new task force (the 3rd Fleet) was organized around the disbanded 1st Carrier Division, absorbing the latter's surviving pilots. The *Zuikaku* was posted to the 1st Carrier Division and her air group (twenty-seven each carrier fighters and bombers, and eighteen carrier attack planes) underwent intensive training at Kanoya and Saeki.

With the start of the American offensive to recapture Guadalcanal in August, the *Zuikaku*, together with the *Shōkaku*, sortied out of the Inland Sea and proceeded to the Solomon Sea. On the 24th, during the second phase of the Battle of the Solomons, both sides withdrew from the battle area with inconclusive results. Six carrier fighters, under the command of LT Hidaka, went out to battle in support of the first attack wave. During aerial encounters they were able to shoot down six enemy aircraft. Our side also lost three aircraft, however, including that piloted by PO1c Makino. Next, from 28 August through 4

September, thirty carrier fighters of the 1st Carrier Division proceeded to Buka Island.

The unit participated in a number of attacks on Guadalcanal; fifteen aircraft under the command of LT Hidaka also participated. Details are not available, however. The task force next sortied out of Truk on 9 September and by operating north of the island, cooperated with the offensive being conducted by the army. However, the attack ended in failure; also, the enemy fleet did not show up within the zone of operations of our forces. On the 23rd, our task force returned to the island of Truk.

On 11 October, in support of the second major attack, the task force again sortied out of Truk. On the 26th, our forces engaged the American task force in battle in waters north of Guadalcanal (the Battle of Santa Cruz). Eight *Zuikaku* carrier fighters under the command of LT Shirane joined the first wave attack force. They served in direct support of the carrier bomber squadron and in carrying out attacks on American carriers. Fourteen enemy fighters were shot down. Next, as part of the second wave attack force, four carrier fighters un-

Zero Fighter Model 22
About November 1943

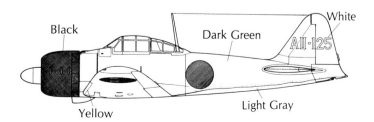

der the command of WO Shigemi Katsuma sortied and were able to shoot down nine aircraft in aerial combat. However, damage to our attacking force was not minor either. A cumulative total of twenty-seven aircraft were used as combat air patrol over the carriers; they were able to shoot down six attacking enemy dive-bombers. During the entire Battle of Santa Cruz, damages to carrier fighter aircraft were five aircraft, including WO Osanai's plane.

Later, the *Zuikaku* returned to anchor at Kure for maintenance and reorganization. On 17 January 1943, she sortied out of the Inland Sea and proceeded to Truk. On the 29th, in order to assist in evacuation operations from Guadalcanal, thirty-six carrier fighters, under the command of LT Nōtomi, advanced to Rabaul.

The squadron next moved to the base at Buin. Assisting in aerial cover operations for evacuating units on three occasions, they were able to shoot down about forty aircraft in air combat operations. Because of the success of this operation, the *Zuikaku* squadron returned to Truk on 17 February.

Next, in order to participate in the "I"-gō operation, carrier air groups of the 3rd Fleet were at Rabaul from 2 April through the 18th. They participated in the attacks on Guadalcanal, Oro Bay, Moresby, and Rabi. Battle results for the *Zuikaku* Fighter Squadron were thirteen aircraft (five probables), but our side did lose three aircraft as well. After the end of this operation, the *Zuikaku* left Truk and arrived back in the Inland Sea on 8 May. Together with the *Shōkaku*, repairs for which were completed by this time, the two carriers engaged in air unit training exercises. On 15 July, the force moved to Truk. With issuance of the command on 28 October to start the "Ro"-gō operation, the 1st Carrier Division's air unit left Truk Island and proceeded to Rabaul. The total number of aircraft, including those of the *Shōkaku*, came to 152. Of this total, [Zero] carrier fighters numbering twenty-four each were from the *Shōkaku* and the *Zuikaku;* together with eighteen from the *Zuihō,* the total was sixty-six fighters.

Starting with the attack on enemy ships

Zuikaku Fighter Squadron personnel, just before taking off from the base at Buin to participate in the battle off Florida Island, 7 April 1943. (Family of Kenjirō Nōtomi)

Fighter squadron flight personnel as they await the attack on Pearl Harbor, to take place the following day, December 1941. Second row (from the front): third person from the right is fighter division officer LT Masao Satō. To his left, LT Masatoshi Makino, LTJG Yūzō Tsukamoto. Last person on right, PO1c Tetsuzō Iwamoto. (Sei-ichi Tsukuda)

Zuikaku Zero fighter Model 22, at the Buin base early in 1943. (Torao Saitō)

off Cape Torokina on the following day, the 2nd, the fighter squadron aboard the *Zuikaku* engaged in daily attack and intercept operations until the carrier's return to port on the 13th. During this period, the squadron realized battle results of forty-seven enemy aircraft shot down (nineteen probables). However, our side also lost eight men, including the brilliant commander LT Nōtomi. The 1st Carrier Division carrier air groups, which had lost 120 aircraft and around half of its flight personnel during a two-week period, withdrew to the island of Truk on 13 November. Some personnel stayed on at Rabaul as a detached unit of the *Zuikaku* (twenty-one of the fighter squadron). Under the command of LT Kenji Nakagawa, the unit stayed in combat until the end of January the following year.

The twenty-six aircraft of the 1st Carrier Division that had returned from Rabaul had no time for rest or recuperation but proceeded to the island of Roi [the Marshalls]. On 5 December, severe damages were suffered as the result of an attack by a large number of American carrier aircraft; ten of our aircraft were lost and the unit was withdrawn to the island of Truk on the 7th.

The two carriers *Shōkaku* and *Zuikaku* left Truk on the 12th and returned to the homeland, in order to reorganize their carrier air units. The following year, on 2 February 1944, the aircraft unit of the *Zuikaku* was removed, reorganized, and absorbed into the newly established Air Group 601.

Next, in June the *Zuikaku* sortied out to engage in the Battle of the Marianas. The *Zuikaku* was that rare aircraft carrier that had not received a single hit despite repeated battle engagements. When she sortied out on 25 October to participate in the *Shōgō* operation, however, the *Zuikaku* received concentrated attacks from American carrier aircraft and sank in waters northeast of the Philippines.

Successive Group Leaders:

June 1942–July 1942   LT Kiyokuma Okajima

November 1942–November 1943   LT Kenjirō Nōtomi

November 1943–December 1943   LT Kenji Nakagawa

Successive Division Officers:

September 1941–January 1942   LT Masao Satō

November 1941–April 1942   LT Masatoshi Makino

January 1942–June 1942   LT Kiyokuma Okajima

April 1942–June 1942   LT Yūzō Tsukamoto

July 1942–November 1942   LT Aya-o Shirane

July 1942–November 1943   LT Shigeru Araki

November 1942–May 1943   LT Hisayoshi Miyajima

October 1943–November 1943   LTJG Takeo Sekiya

瑞 鳳 戦 闘 機 隊

ZUIHŌ FIGHTER SQUADRON

The *Zuihō* was initially designed as a high-speed oiler and was then converted to a small carrier; with a standard displacement of 11,200 tons, she was quite similar to her sister ship, the *Shōhō*. Named the *Zuihō* on 5 December 1940, immediately upon her completion on the 27th she was placed in the Kure Naval Station reserve force. The 12th Combined Air Group used her for training purposes. On 26 March 1941, aircraft were loaded on board the *Zuihō;* as of 10 April, the *Zuihō* and the *Shōhō* constituted the 3rd Carrier Division attached to the 1st Air Fleet. Primary duties of the *Zuihō* were antiair and antisubmarine patrols; she was equipped with sixteen carrier fighters (changed to twelve in December) and twelve carrier attack planes. Her later movements and her war record are noted below.

To mid-February 1942: Stationed in the Inland Sea, used in guarding battleship units.

17 February–2 March 1942: Transported aircraft from Yokosuka to Davao.

2 March–mid-May 1942: Stood by in the western end of the Inland Sea; during this period sortied on 18 April to intercept an enemy task force attack but failed to engage the enemy.

18 May–13 July 1942: Left the Inland Sea and accompanied the battleship force destined for the Battle of Midway; did not engage the enemy, however, and returned to Sasebo.

14 July 1942: As a result of reorganization, was integrated into the 1st Carrier Division (*Zuikaku, Shōkaku,* and the *Zuihō*) and attached to the 3rd Fleet. Aircraft on board increased to twenty-one carrier fighters and six carrier attack planes.

14 July–late August 1942: *Zuihō* outfit-

TABLE 2. ORGANIZATION OF THE *ZUIHŌ* FIGHTER SQUADRON
Battle of Santa Cruz (first wave) 26 October 1942

1ST SHŌTAI	2ND SHŌTAI	3RD SHŌTAI
LT Saneyasu Hidaka	LTJG Shū-ichi Utsumi (KIA)	WO Masa-aki Kawahara
PO1c Jirō Mitsumoto	PO1c Masao Kawasaki (KIA)	PO1c Masaichi Kondō
PO3c Shizuta Takagi (KIA)	PO3c Zenpei Matsumoto (KIA)	PO2c Yasuhiro Nakamura

Type 96 Model 4 Carrier Fighter

The unit insignia *CII* was used from April 1941 through April 1942. Fuselage was silver or light gray.

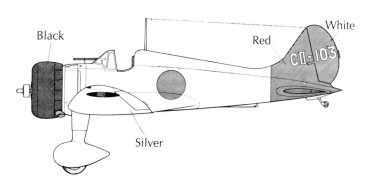

Black

Red

White

Silver

Zuihō Fighter Squadron on the eve of the Battle of Santa Cruz, October 1942. Front row, from the left: WO Masaaki Kawahara, LT Saneyasu Hidaka, LCDR Mikuma Minowa (air officer), LT Masao Satō (group leader), and LT Shū–ichi Utsumi. Rear row: right end, LdgSea Izumi Ishihara; left end, LdgSea Masanao Maki. (Izumi Sanada)

ted in Sasebo; on 24 August, moved to western Inland Sea.

1 September–early October 1942: Left the Inland Sea on 1 September reaching Truk Island on the 6th. Sortied on the 10th to the Solomon Sea area but did not engage the enemy. Ordered to transport aircraft; entered the port of Yokosuka on the 23rd and assisted in the 6th Air Group's advance to Rabaul. On 8 October, transported the group's personnel and aircraft to Rabaul.

1 October 1942–Mid-January 1943: Returned to the 1st Carrier Division on 1 October and joined operations in the Solomon Sea area. On 26 October, joined in the Battle of Santa Cruz. Before dawn, the *Zuihō* received one small bomb hit on her flight

deck and landing operations became impossible.

During the first attack nine carrier fighters under the command of LT Hidaka were dispatched to serve as escort for the *Shōkaku* and *Zuikaku* carrier attack plane and carrier bomber squadrons. Hidaka's unit became engaged in battle with an American attack group that they encountered on the way and were able to shoot down fourteen of the enemy craft. They lost their bearings, however, and four aircraft were missing in action. During the second phase attack, fourteen carrier fighters under the command of LT Satō served as a screen for five carrier attack planes and attacked the U.S. task force.

Zero Fighter Model 21

The unit insignia *EIII* was used from July through October 1942.

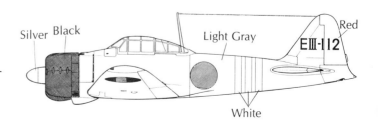

Zuiho Fighter Squadron, on board the *Zuihō*, immediately before the advance to Rabaul, February 1943. Front row, from the left: second person, WO Masaaki Kawahara; LT Saneyasu Hidaka; air officer Matsuda; LT Masao Satō (group leader); WO Akira Yamamoto; and CPO Tsutomu Iwai. Rear row: left end, LdgSea Izumi Ishihara; right end, LdgSea Itaru Shikano. (Izumi Sanada)

Four enemy aircraft were shot down; at the same time, two aircraft of the Satō unit destroyed themselves. On the 28th, the *Zuihō* anchored off Truk Island and following emergency repairs, left on 2 November. On the 7th she dropped anchor at the port of Sasebo; on the 21st, the *Zuihō* moved to the western end of the Inland Sea.

17 January–Early May 1943: Leaving Kure on 17 January, the *Zuihō* ferried aircraft to the island of Truk, arriving on the 23rd. Next, in order to participate in the evacuation operations from Guadalcanal, the carrier was assigned to the 2nd Carrier Division and sortied out of Truk on the 29th. She operated in the seas north of Guadalcanal in indirect guard operations. Completing her duties on 7 February, she returned to Truk on the 9th. Although the *Zuihō* stood by at Truk, from 18 to 28 February her fighter squadron was dispatched to Wewak; from 2 to 13 March the unit went to Kavieng, where it assisted in the reinforcement of army forces in New Guinea. In order to participate in the "I"-gō operation, the *Zuihō* next proceeded to Rabaul. After shooting down a total of eighteen aircraft, the carrier returned to Truk on the 18th.

3 May–early July 1943: The *Zuihō* left Truk on 3 May for rest and recuperation and refitting operations, reaching Sasebo

Zero Fighter Model 22

At the time of the "Ro"-gō operation, November 1943.

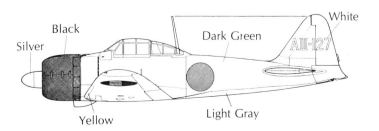

on the 9th. During the middle of the month, the carrier went to Tokyo Bay in preparation for the Attu Island relief operation but the operation was cancelled. The *Zuihō* returned to Sasebo on 2 June and then moved to the western part of the Inland Sea on the 18th.

9 July–early November 1943: On 9 July, the *Zuihō* left Kure loaded with munitions and landing force personnel; she arrived at Truk Island on the 15th. From that date until 5 November, she ferried aircraft between Truk and Yokosuka on three occasions. At the same time, her fighter squadron was dispatched to Kavieng from 29 August through 3 September. On 1 November, ADM Koga issued orders for the "Ro"-gō operation. The air group (eighteen carrier fighters, eight carrier attack planes) was again sent to Rabaul and participated in air battles off Bougainville on the 5th, 8th, and 11th. However, our side also suffered severe damages. In contrast with the battle results for a ten-day period of thirty-five enemy aircraft downed (ten probables), the *Zuihō* Fighter Squadron suffered eight casualties, including the loss of LT Satō. The unit then returned to Truk.

Late November 1943–Mid-February 1944: As of 1 December 1943, aircraft were removed from the *Zuihō,* and she returned to Yokosuka on 10 November. By 16 February 1944, the *Zuihō* had been used on four occasions to ferry aircraft and other war supplies to Truk. On 1 February, the carrier was posted to the 3rd Carrier Division of the 3rd Fleet.

1 February–15 October 1944: The 3rd Carrier Division, composed of the remodeled aircraft carriers *Chitose, Chiyoda,* and *Zuihō,* had planned to have the carriers each equipped with twenty-one carrier fighters and nine carrier attack planes. On 15 February, however, Air Group 653 (sixty-three carrier fighters and twenty-seven carrier attack planes) was organized and all aircraft removed from the three carriers. For about ten days starting the end of March, the *Zuihō* was used to transport supplies to Guam. After training exercises in the Inland Sea, the 3rd Carrier Division departed from the western end of the Inland Sea on 11 May in order to participate in the "A"-gō operation. On the 19th, the *Zuihō* took part in the decisive Battle of the Marianas.

Three aircraft carriers, the *Taihō, Shōkaku,* and *Hiyō,* were sunk; other aircraft carriers were also damaged. The *Zuihō,* however, returned unscathed to the Inland Sea on 24 May. Later, on 10 August the *Zuikaku* was added to the 3rd Carrier Division and reorganization continued. Damages suffered during the "A"-gō Operation were very severe; in addition, during this period American forces invaded the Philippines. Next, the *Zuihō* sortied out of the Inland Sea on 20 October in order to participate in the decisive Shōgō operation. On the 25th, however, the *Zuihō* met an attack from U.S. carrier fighters in the seas northeast of the Philippines and was sunk.

Successive Group Leaders:

June 1942–November 1943 LT Masao Satō

Successive Division Officers:

April 1941–November 1941 LT Takumi Hoashi

February 1942–April 1942 LT Shigeru Mori

April 1942–June 1943 LT Saneyasu Hidaka

June 1943–November 1943 LT Kenji Nakagawa

祥 鳳 戦 闘 機 隊

SHŌHŌ FIGHTER SQUADRON

The *Takasaki* and the *Tsurugizaki* were both initially built to serve as high-speed oilers to accompany the fleet; the two ships were started in 1934 and in 1935, respectively. During construction, they were remodeled to serve as submarine tenders. Once the *Takasaki* had been completed, it was next decided that the *Tsurugizaki* would be converted to an aircraft carrier. In the final analysis, both ships were remodeled to serve as aircraft carriers. The *Takasaki* became what was known later as the *Zuihō,* and the *Tsurugizaki* came to be called the *Shōhō*.

Remodeling of the *Tsurugizaki* was started in November 1940; immediately after the outbreak of the war, she was completed and renamed the *Shōhō*. She was a small aircraft carrier with displacement of 11,200 tons, an overall length of 180 meters, and a maximum speed of 28 knots. Aircraft complement on board consisted of twelve carrier fighters and twelve carrier attack planes.

Immediately upon completion, the *Shōhō* was posted to the 4th Carrier Division. Orders were issued to CAPT Ishinosuke Izawa to serve as captain, to LCDR Toshikazu Sugiyama to serve as her air officer, and to LT Kenjirō Nōtomi to serve as the fighter unit division officer. On 5 January 1942, flight group training began at the Yokosuka Naval Base; however, the *Shōhō* was soon ordered to duty as an aircraft ferry and left Yokosuka on 3 January. At Truk Island, starting on the 10th, she

loaded on board fighters that were destined to be used by the 4th Air Group. The aircraft were delivered to Rabaul on 15 February, immediately after the island had been captured; the *Shōhō* then returned to Truk. During the period from the 20th to the 26th, she sortied out of Truk and sought to engage the enemy task force; however, no enemy forces were sighted. From 7 until 10 March, she returned to the ferrying of aircraft to Rabaul. On 8 April, the *Shōhō* left Truk and entered the port of Yokosuka on the 11th.

On 18 April, *Shōhō* sortied out to engage in fighting off the homeland's first aerial attack, carried out by B-25s of the enemy task force; however, she did not find any enemy and returned to Yokosuka on the 22nd.

In May, Imperial General Headquarters was planning the capture of Port Moresby following the attack on Tulagi. *Shōhō* was placed under the command of the 6th Cruiser Division (four heavy cruisers) of the 4th Fleet and assigned to be used in support of the naval task force accompanying the invasion forces. On 30 April she sortied from the island of Truk.

Aircraft on board the *Shōhō* at the time were the six Zero fighters that had undergone remodelling at Yokosuka just before the departure of the ship from that port; in addition, there were several Type 96 carrier fighters, plus twelve carrier attack planes. Also, the *Shōhō* carried on board unassembled Zero fighters. There was some ar-

Zero Fighter Model 21
Unit insignia *DII* was used during the period December 1941 to May 1942.

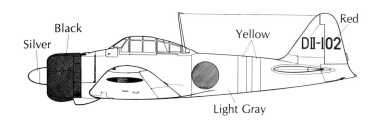

Black
Silver
Yellow
Red
DII-102
Light Gray

Fighter division officer LT Kenjirō Nōtomi at left, 1943 (Kiyokuma Okajima)

gument as to how the *Shōhō* was to be used. Although the 5th Carrier Division proposed that the *Shōhō* aircraft be integrated with the other planes of the carrier division so that their actions could be coordinated, their desires were overridden by the 4th Fleet, which placed higher priority on the escort of convoys.

On 2 May, the *Shōhō* arrived at the Solomon Islands front together with the 6th Cruiser Division. Early the morning of the 3rd, three carrier fighters and three carrier attack planes were dispatched from a point 120 miles west of Tulagi for operations over the Tulagi area in support of land forces. Since the capture of Tulagi was effected during that same day, the *Shōhō* disengaged itself from the operation and steamed north to off the island of Buka. The next day, the 4th, strike groups from the American task force attacked our ships anchored in Tulagi. The *Shōhō* immediately turned back and sped south; however, it was too late and she returned to base. On the 4th, she sortied out of Rabaul and joined the southward advancing Port Moresby invasion force; starting the morning of the 5th, the carrier provided air cover for the invasion force. During the afternoon of the same day, two enemy observation planes were encountered and our units in the air were used to pursue them. No enemy aircraft were shot down, however.

The important base at Truk, Micronesia (Yasujirō Abe)

Starting on the early morning of 7 May, four Zero fighters and two Type 96 carrier fighters (commanded by LT Nōtomi) were used on combat air patrol. Shortly after 0800, a report was received from a reconnaissance plane that aircraft on board the American task force carriers had taken off and preparations were made for all aircraft to take off from the *Shōhō*. However, just after 0900 [1100] and before such preparations were possible, a massive combined force of ninety-three enemy aircraft—fighters, dive-bombers, and torpedo planes—made an attack; seven torpedos and thirteen bombs found their mark on the *Shōhō*. Twenty minutes later the *Shōhō* sank.

The short life span of this aircraft carrier was under six months, following her assignment to operations.

Although the six airborne fighters engaged in patrol operations fought vigorously and shot down five enemy aircraft (one probable; American records indicate three aircraft downed), three of our aircraft were forced to make emergency landings at the Deboyne Base because of the loss of their own carrier. The other three were counted as missing in action.

隼 鷹 戦 闘 機 隊

JUNYŌ FIGHTER SQUADRON

The *Junyō* was launched at the Nagasaki docks of the Mitsubishi Ship Building Company on 26 June 1941. On 3 May 1942, immediately upon her completion, she was posted to the 4th Carrier Division (*Ryūjō, Junyō*) of the 1st Air Fleet. It was decided to equip her with sixteen Zero fighters and twenty-four Type 99 carrier bombers. Starting on 8 May, the air fleet carried out training exercises and had its equipment loaded on board by the Saeki Air Group.

In June, Combined Fleet Headquarters was planning for the Battle of Midway; in conjunction with that battle, a plan for capturing the Aleutian Islands was also under consideration. On 20 April, the 4th Carrier Division was given orders to conduct air attacks in the area of the Aleutians. On 18 May the *Junyō* withdrew from the Saeki base and loaded her own aircraft, plus a portion of the aircraft (twelve planes commanded by LT Miyano) assigned to the 6th Air Group's fighter unit that was scheduled to proceed to Midway upon its capture. The *Junyō* left the western part of the Inland Sea on the 22nd and arrived at Ōminato on the 25th. In this fashion, she came to be assigned to the battle front less than one month after her commissioning. Proceeding eastward through the fog-enshrouded North Sea, she arrived at Dutch Harbor the morning of 3 June and started air operations.

The attack force was commanded by the *Junyō*'s fighter squadron division officer LT Shiga and consisted of the following aircraft: thirteen carrier fighters and twelve carrier bombers of the *Junyō* itself, plus six carrier attack planes and three carrier fighters of the *Ryūjō*, as well as seven fighters under the command of LT Miyano of the 6th Air Group. Since the cloud base was three hundred meters and it was hard for the aircraft to assemble, each unit operated independently. Wherever there was a break in the clouds, units would bomb the enemy; fighters strafed flying boats at anchor and vehicles on land. During the course of such operations, one patrolling PBY was shot down. The second wave attack was then launched; it consisted of six carrier fighters (commanded by LT Shiga) and fifteen carrier bombers. Because of the bad weather, however, the aircraft turned back, although they were able to shoot down two PBYs while aloft. Bad weather was encountered also the next day, the 4th. However, the *Junyō* did send out a force to attack Dutch Harbor; it consisted of five carrier fighters all piloted by experienced personnel (commanded by LT Shiga), eleven carrier bombers, as well as the *Ryūjō*'s six carrier fighters and nine carrier attack planes. After this attack was concluded, the *Junyō* unit met and engaged in air battle with eight P-40s off the northeast point of Umnak Island. Six enemy aircraft were shot down; our side also lost two carrier bombers and two other aircraft that failed to return on their way back to the carrier. The *Junyō* returned to the port of

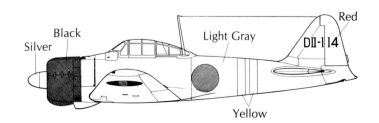

Model 21 Zero Fighter

The unit insignia *DII* was used during the period May to September 1942.

Silver · Black · Light Gray · Red · DII-114 · Yellow

Fighter pilots on the eve of the first attack on Dutch Harbor, June 1942. The following aces can be observed in this photo. Center row: third from the right, LT Shiga, group leader. Rear row: fourth from the left, PO1c Takashi Okamoto. Center row (from the left): PO1c Ichirō Yamamoto, WO Saburō Kitahata; fifth person (from the left): PO1c Kiichi Oda. Front row: third from the left, PO2c Masao Sasakibara. (Masao Sasakibara)

Ōminato on the 24th; she next left Ōminato on the 29th, arriving back in the Inland Sea on 3 July.

The *Junyō* Fighter Squadron started training exercises at two air bases after 1 July; 1 July at the Iwakuni air base, and on the 8th, at the Kagoshima. Because of the loss of four major aircraft carriers during the Battle of Midway, the importance of the *Junyō*'s own group was increased. The fighter squadron absorbed the surviving flight crew personnel of the carriers and re-organized her striking force on 14 July. The 4th Carrier Division was renamed the 2nd Carrier Division: *Junyō*'s on board aircraft allowance was increased to twenty-one carrier fighters, eighteen carrier bombers, and nine carrier attack planes. While the battle in the Solomons was raging, intensive training was in process; on 14 September joint training exercises were carried out at

Saeki. On 4 October, the 2nd Carrier Division, reinforced by the addition of the *Hiyō* and the *Zuihō* of the 1st Carrier Division, reached Truk on the 9th. Those ships were added to the front line forces; they next sortied out of Truk on the 11th.

The *Junyō* next provided aircover for the battleships *Kongō* and *Haruna,* which left on the 13th to bombard Guadalcanal. The 17th was the day scheduled for the attack on the anchorage; nine carrier attack planes and nine carrier fighters each from the *Junyō* and the *Hiyō* (commanded by LT Shiga) sortied. There was a snafu in the assignment of escort duties to the fighter squadrons, however, and all aircraft belonging to the *Hiyō* returned to their carrier. Also, the *Junyō* carrier attack squadron was attacked by enemy fighters; of the total of nine aircraft (one had turned back) six were immediately shot out of the air. The remaining

Fighter squadron pilots on Roi, summer 1943. Second row (from the front): center, LT Miyajima, division officer; right end, LT Sumio Fukuda; left end, WO Masaichi Kondō. Third row (from the left): third person, CPO Shizuo Ishii; sixth person, PO2c Takao Banno. Fourth row (from the left): second person, PO1c Tomita Atake; sixth person, PO2c Wataru Nakamichi. (Akio Masuya)

two aircraft made emergency landings on the north shore of Guadalcanal. Such were the severe damages that our side received.

During the Battle of Santa Cruz, as a follow-on to the attack made by the 1st Carrier Division, eighteen carrier bombers of the 2nd Carrier Division (the *Hiyō* dropped out because of breakdowns and only the *Junyō* was available), escorted by twelve carrier fighters under the command of LT Shiga, left their carriers after 0900 on the 26th in order to carry out an attack on the American task force. The attack force bombed both the aircraft carrier *Enterprise* as well as the battleship *South Dakota;* during air battles, they shot down fourteen enemy aircraft (five probables). During the second phase attack, nine carrier attack planes escorted by five carrier fighters under the command of LT Shirane torpedoed the *Hornet.* Later, during the same afternoon, the *Junyō* sent out a third wave attack

consisting of four carrier bombers and six carrier fighters (LT Shiga) to administer the final blow to the *Hornet.* In all of these attacks, there was no enemy fighter counterattack. At the same time, since these were long distance attacks, two Zero fighters under LT Shirane were unaccounted for and another three aircraft ditched at sea.

On 30 October, the *Junyō* returned to her anchorage at Truk. From 9 through 11 November, she once again operated in the seas north of Guadalcanal. From 18 through 20 December, in order to participate in the "Mu"-gō operation, the carrier assisted in the protection of transport ships to Wewak by the army. Next, the *Junyō* air group was sent to Wewak airfield and engaged in convoy guard duties, starting 17 January of the following year [1943]. The force intercepted incoming B-24s and accomplished its assigned mission; on the 20th, the group returned to Truk Island.

From the end of January to the early part of February, she participated in the evacuation of forces from Guadalcanal; on 21 February, the *Junyō* returned to Saeki. In port, efforts were concentrated on reorganization of her air group and on intensive training exercises.

On 22 March, the *Junyō* left Saeki harbor and arrived at Truk Island on the 27th. In order to participate in the "I"-gō Operation, the air group advanced to Rabaul on 2 April and then engaged in attacks on Guadalcanal, Milne Bay, Oro Bay, and Port Moresby. On the 17th, the carrier was back at Truk. She returned to her home port in Japan on 22 May. The *Junyō* left Yokosuka soon thereafter, on 10 June, and proceeded to Truk Island again. On the 15th, the air group advanced to Roi. Because of the American invasion of Rendova Island in the Solomons starting on 2 July, however, all aircraft assigned to the 2nd Carrier Division (forty-eight carrier fighters, thirty-six carrier bombers, and eighteen carrier attack aircraft) advanced to the base at Buin. Valiantly engaging in daily battles with enemy aircraft, by the end of August the fighter squadrons had shot down more than fifty enemy aircraft (13 probables) but lost nine aircraft on their side. On 1 September, the 2nd Carrier Division was disbanded.

The carrier air group was reorganized as of 1 November [1943] and given a complement of twenty-four carrier fighters, eighteen carrier bombers, and nine carrier attack aircraft. After engaging in exercises in Singapore, the unit next arrived at Truk Island, on 1 December. After being dispatched to Kavieng at the end of December for a period, it then advanced to Rabaul on 25 January 1944. Until the retreat to Truk on 20 February, the unit engaged in fierce air battles with the enemy, day and night; the unit accounted for the downing of about seventy enemy aircraft (thirty probables). Losses on our side, however, were also severe; in fact, the 2nd Carrier Division was wiped out. During the same period, the *Junyō* herself was back in the homeland for repairs and then participated in the Battle of the Marianas in June. After that, the carrier stayed primarily in the western end of the Inland Sea. Toward the end of the war, the *Junyō* was bombed while at anchor in Sasebo Bay; she greeted the end of hostilities in a half-damaged condition.

Successive Group Leaders:

May 1942–December 1942 LT Yoshio Shiga

November 1943–March 1944 LT Saneyasu Hidaka

Successive Division Officers:

June 1942–May 1943 LT Yasuhiro Shigematsu

May 1943–August 1943 LT Hisayoshi Miyajima

July 1943–August 1943 LTJG Keigo Fujiwara

November 1943–January 1944 LTJG Nobu Mae

飛 鷹 戦 闘 機 隊

HIYŌ FIGHTER SQUADRON

During the fall of 1940 it was decided that the new luxury passenger liners being built for the Nippon Yūsen Kabushiki Kaisha (Japan Mail Line), the *Kasuga Maru, Kashiwara Maru,* and *Izumo Maru,* would be commandeered and remodeled as aircraft carriers. The three ships were to become, at a later date, respectively, the *Taiyō,* the *Junyō,* and the *Hiyō.* The *Junyō* and the *Hiyō* were identical vessels, each with a displacement of 24,140 tons, a 210-meter flight deck, and speed of 25.5 knots; they were also each equipped with forty-eight operational aircraft and five spares.

The *Hiyō* was launched in June 1941 at the Kawasaki Kobe Shipbuilding Works and commissioned in July 1942, the following year. On 31 July, she was posted to the 2nd Carrier Division. Although two months later in getting into commission than her sister ship, the *Junyō,* the *Hiyō* came to play a central role as the primary aircraft carrier of the striking force, after flight personnel who had lost their aircraft carriers at the Battle of Midway were transferred to her. There were twenty-one carrier fighters, eighteen carrier bombers, and nine carrier attack planes on the ship. LT Tadashi Kaneko was ordered to the *Hiyō* as her group leader and, together with the *Junyō* Air Group, started training exercises at Iwakuni, Kogoshima, and Kasanbara bases. The *Hiyō* left Kobe on 10 August, entered Kure Naval Base on the 11th, and was posted to the 2nd Carrier Division. At this time, the American forces were

mounting a counteroffensive against Guadalcanal; on 13 August, Imperial General Headquarters ordered the main forces of the Combined Fleet to sortie for the purpose of recapturing the island. The 2nd Fleet sortied out of the Inland Sea on 16 August and proceeded south. The *Ryūjō,* from the 2nd Carrier Division, joined forces with the fleet; however, since their newly formed air groups had as yet not finished training, the *Junyō* and the *Hiyō* remained in the western part of the Inland Sea.

Following the conduct of joint exercises held at Saeki on 14 September, the 2nd Carrier Division left that port on 4 October and reached Truk on the 9th, where she was added to the advance force (under the command of the 2nd Fleet). By 17 October, the 2nd Carrier Division approached north of Guadalcanal; nine carrier fighters each from the *Junyō* and the *Hiyō* bombed the Guadalcanal anchorage. Because of enemy opposition, the carrier attack squadron from the *Junyō* was annihilated but that from the *Hiyō* returned to base safely. On the 20th, the forces moved again to the south and attempted to assist the army's general offensive on Guadalcanal. Engines of the *Hiyō* suddenly developed trouble, however, and she was judged to be out of battle commission. Later in the day on the 22nd, the *Hiyō* returned to Truk, after transferring some of her air group to the *Junyō.* Under the command of group leader Mieno, the remainder of the *Hiyō* Air

Zero Fighter Model 21

The unit designation *DI* was placed in use in July 1942.

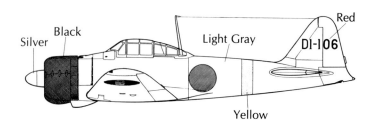

Silver · Black · Light Gray · Red · DI-106 · Yellow

Group (sixteen Zero fighters and seventeen Type 99 carrier bombers) proceeded to Rabaul on the 23rd; the unit then became involved in air operations jointly with forces of the 11th Air Fleet. The following day, on the 24th, the air group dispatched from the *Hiyō* provided air cover for the landing forces attacking Guadalcanal; after that date, the unit made almost daily sorties to fight the enemy.

An element of the force advanced to the base at Buin on 1 November and was engaged in the Battle of the Solomon Sea [Naval Battle of Guadalcanal]. In particular, the unit served as air cover on the 13th and the 14th for eleven ships of the high-speed ship convoy that was sent to Guadalcanal. During the same period, LCDR Kaneko was killed in action and a number of our airplanes had to make emergency landings. The unit dispatched to Rabaul returned to Truk by 11 November. The unit sent to Buin remained in the area until 14 December, however, when it was sent back to the mainland by air transport. After reaching the mainland, the unit rejoined the *Hiyō*, which had returned to the Bay of Saeki on the 18th.

The *Hiyō* left the port of Saeki on 22 March 1943 and proceeded to Truk. Her air group advanced to Rabaul and from 2 to 17 April assisted in the "I"-gō operation. At that time, the complement of aircraft on board the *Hiyō* consisted of twenty-seven Zero fighters and twelve Type 99 carrier bombers. The *Hiyō* Fighter Squadron participated in the attacks off Guadalcanal on the 7th, the attack on Oro Bay on the 11th, the attack on Port Moresby on the 12th, and the attack on Milne Bay on the 14th. Twenty-six enemy aircraft (eleven probables) were shot down; at the same time, the 2nd Carrier Division lost a total of seven carrier fighters and six carrier bombers. On 22 May, the 2nd Carrier Division was back in Tokyo Bay and stood by for the Attu Island rescue operation; that was canceled, however, and the force was again ordered to Truk. After loading the air group at the Kisarazu base, she departed Yokosuka on 7 June.

Fighter group leader of the *Hiyō*, LT Kiyokuma Okajima (*right*) (Kiyokuma Okajima)

The *Hiyō* was attacked by an enemy submarine the same evening in the seas off the eastern coast of Miyake-jima; as a result, the carrier was unable to navigate. She returned to her home port in order to undergo repairs. The *Junyō* thus proceeded by herself to Truk. The small aircraft carrier *Ryūhō* was added to the force in place of the *Hiyō*. However, it was not possible to load on board the *Ryūhō* all of the aircraft that had been on the *Hiyō*; thus, the *Hiyō*'s fighter squadron was air-lifted to Truk, via Iwo Jima and Tinian. In the early part of July, the fighter squadron advanced further to Buin. As of the 15th, all pilots of the *Hiyō* Fighter Squadron had been transferred on board the *Ryūhō*.

During this period and until 15 September, the *Hiyō* was in dock, undergoing repairs and without an aircraft group on board. On 1 November, the group was reestablished with twenty-four Zero fighters, eighteen Type 99 carrier bombers, and nine carrier attack planes. With this complement on board, the *Hiyō* next underwent training exercises in Singapore. In mid-December, the air group received orders to transfer to Truk and left base on the 21st, transported on board the *Hiyō*. From the end of the month through the early part of 1944, the unit was ordered to Kavieng to engage in transport escort work. Under the command of the 2nd Carrier Division commander, CO Shiroshima, the unit proceeded to Rabaul on 25 January. Taking the place of the base air unit, it engaged in air battles night and day.

Under the frontline leadership of LT Hōhei Kobayashi as group leader, the *Hiyō* squadron fought valiantly; by the time the unit drew back to Truk it had accounted for about eighty downed enemy aircraft. We also lost twelve aircraft. During the same period, the *Hiyō* left Truk and arrived back in the Inland Sea 1 January 1944. In March, the carrier was posted to the newly organized 1st Striking Force and assigned to Air Group 652. Although it participated in the Battle of the Marianas, the *Hiyō* was attacked on the 20th by American carrier planes and sank.

Successive Group Leaders:

July 1942–December 1942   LT Tadashi Kaneko

December 1942–January 1943   LT Yoshio Shiga

January 1943–July 1943   LT Kiyokuma Okajima

December 1943–March 1944   LT Hōhei Kobayashi

Successive Division Officers:

July 1942–June 1943   LT Iyozō Fujita

June 1943–July 1943   LTJG Keigo Fujiwara

November 1943–January 1944   LTJG Fujikazu Koizumi

竜 鳳 戦 闘 機 隊

RYŪHŌ FIGHTER SQUADRON

The *Ryūhō* was a small aircraft carrier, which had been converted from a submarine tender, the *Taigei*. Remodeling of the ship commenced in December 1941, right after the outbreak of hostilities; work was completed on 30 Nov 1942 and the ship named the *Ryūhō*. Posted to the 3rd Fleet, she was not initially equipped with any aircraft. On 11 December, the *Ryūhō* left Yokosuka for Truk Island with the mission of ferrying aircraft. The next day, however, she was damaged by torpedoes from an enemy submarine and had to turn back; the *Ryūhō* then underwent repairs until February of the following year.

On 15 January 1943, the 50th Air Flotilla was organized as a training unit and attached to the 3rd Fleet. Together with the *Hōshō*, the *Ryūhō* was posted to the 50th Air Flotilla. From the end of March, the *Ryūhō* served as a training vessel for carrier landing exercises, as well as a target ship for torpedo training.

On 12 June 1943, the *Ryūhō* was posted to the 2nd Carrier Division; the air group on board the *Hiyō* that had been attacked by enemy submarine torpedoes was transferred to the *Ryūhō* (the aircraft were ferried to their destination). On the 16th, the *Ryūhō* left Yokosuka and arrived at Truk on the 21st. When the American forces attacked Rendova Island on 30 June, the Combined Fleet ordered the 2nd Carrier Division Fighter Group to proceed to Buin. After 2 July, the unit then proceeded to Buin, via Rabaul, under the command of ADM Sakamaki. Serving as the advance guard, the *Ryūhō* Fighter Squadron (a complement of twenty-one carrier fighters and nine carrier attack planes) proceeded to Rabaul. The unit then immediately transferred to Buin and participated in the attack off Rendova on the 4th. Later, the 2nd Carrier Division cooperated with the local 26th

Air Flotilla and engaged in fierce air battles over the base for days on end. At the end of fierce battling that lasted slightly over a month, however, half of its flight personnel had been lost in action. As of 1 September all personnel under the command of ADM Sakamaki transferred to the 26th Air Flotilla, and for a while, the 2nd Carrier Division was a unit without any aircraft assigned to it. In as far as battle results of the *Ryūhō* Fighter Squadron are concerned, as of 15 August the unit had shot down approximately thirty enemy aircraft.

Earlier, the *Ryūhō* had left Truk on 19 July and returned to the western end of the Inland Sea. On 1 September, a new 2nd Carrier Division command was organized and work started on resurrecting the unit. There was a shortage of aviation fuel for training purposes on the mainland, however, and it was decided to dispatch her to the south, where fuel was still plentiful and training was carried out. The carrier air group arrived in Singapore on 19 October; the *Ryūhō* itself was used between the mainland and Singapore for the transportation of materials. Next, ADM Koga issued an order on 14 November that the 2nd Carrier Division Air Group, which had not completed even one month's worth of concentrated training, was to proceed to Truk Island by early December. His decision was based on an assessment that an enemy attack in the Gilbert Islands was approaching, which would be in addition to the hard ongoing battles being fought in the Rabaul area.

The 2nd Carrier Division Air Group left Singapore on 10 December and proceeded to Truk, where it stood by for action. In order to help secure the transport of land troops from Truk Island to Kavieng during the early part of January 1944, the unit was next dispatched to Kavieng from 27 December through 9 January, under the command of LCDR Saburō Shindō. On 1 and 4 January, the fighter units blocked attacks from being conducted by enemy carrier aircraft. At the time, aerial battles around Rabaul were gradually turning worse for the Japanese, and at the request of ADM Kusaka, commander of the Southeastern Area Fleet, sixty-nine carrier fighters, thirty-six carrier bombers, and twenty-seven carrier attack planes of the 2nd Carrier Division (the *Junyō*, the *Hiyō*, and the *Ryūhō*) proceeded to Rabaul on 25 January. They relieved the local base air group that had been fighting valiantly day after day. By 20 February, the 2nd Carrier Division had been reduced to thirty-seven fighters, four carrier bombers, and five carrier attack planes. For just under a month before its retreat to Truk, the unit had been engaged in daily, fierce intercept battles. During this period, the *Ryūhō* Fighter Squadron shot down about forty enemy aircraft; however, attrition on our side was not inconsiderable. By mid-February aircraft actually available for use had been reduced to only about four or five.

LCR Saburō Shindō (Kazuo Tsunoda)

Before the activity described above, the *Ryūhō* had left Truk on 22 December and returned to the western part of the Inland Sea by 1 January 1944. As of 4 March, the aircraft belonging to each of the ships of the 2nd Carrier Division had been removed

Air Group Fighter Squadron 652 at the Tawi Tawi anchorage, mid-May 1944. Middle row (from the left): third person, LT Saneyasu Hidaka, air officer Matsuda; LT Dai Nakajima; (unknown); and CPO Tetsuo Kikuchi. Front row (far left): CPO Izumi Ishihara. (Izumi Sanada)

and the air groups replaced by Air Group 652, newly attached to the 2nd Carrier Division. In addition to providing transportation to Saipan for a period of ten days starting the end of March, the ship was used for carrier landing exercises in the western part of the Inland Sea.

The *Ryūhō* left the western end of the Inland Sea on 11 May, when orders were issued to commence the "A"-gō Operation; she then proceeded to Tawi Tawi, where she participated in the Battle of the Marianas on 19 June. As a result of an attack by enemy aircraft on the 20th, the ship received some damage from a near miss; however, there was no effect on her battle worthiness or navigability. On the 24th, the *Ryūhō* returned to the Inland Sea, but the reconstruction of her air group did not progress apace. As a result, the *Ryūhō* did not participate in the Shōgō operation in October. During the same period, the *Ryūhō* was posted to the 1st Carrier Division (Air Group 601) by the reorganization

of 10 July; she was next posted to the 4th Carrier Division (Air Group 634) by the reorganization of 10 August. On 15 November, the *Ryūhō* was then posted to the 1st Carrier Division (the *Amagi, Unryū, Katsuragi, Junyō, Ryūhō,* and Air Group 601). Little progress was made in reconstructing the air group, however; starting the end of October, the *Ryūhō* was assigned to transportation duties to Keelung. Later she was moored at Kure harbor and removed from the Combined Fleet as of 20 April 1945. The *Ryūhō* greeted the end of hostilities tied up to a wharf.

Successive Group Leaders:

July 1943–September 1943   LT Kiyokuma Okajima

Successive Division Officers:

July 1943–September 1943   LTJG Keigo Fujiwara
September 1943–March 1944   LTJG Hiroshi Yoshimura

第601航空隊戦闘機隊（I）

AIR GROUP 601 FIGHTER SQUADRON (I)

At the outbreak of the war, it was the practice for aircraft assigned to aircraft carriers to be posted to their own individual carriers; when getting ready for sorties, they would reassemble and form a combined attack force while in the air. As a result of the reorganization ordered as of 15 February [1944], aircraft and aircraft carriers were separated. Air Group 601 was newly organized around the former 1st Carrier Division Air Group. As of 10 March, the unit was posted to the 1st Carrier Division (*Taihō, Shōkaku, Zuikaku*). The aircraft complement was eighty-one Zero fighters, eighty-one Suisei carrier bombers, fifty-four Tenzan carrier attack planes and nine carrier reconnaissance planes. CDR Toshiiye Irisa was assigned as the commanding officer.

Starting about mid-December 1943, when the 1st Carrier Division air unit was at Rabaul, the nucleus of the flight personnel for the newly formed unit was gathered at Iwakuni base in order to form the main element of the new organization. Included in the nucleus were personnel selected from the various homeland air groups, as well as new personnel who had just completed their flight training, and others. In order to make up the shortage in numbers, some personnel were also transferred from seaplane duty. Later on, survivors from Rabaul and from the Marshall Islands were also added. After completing its organizational stage at Iwakuni, the unit was divided into two parts, one part assigned to the carrier *Shōkaku* or the *Zuikaku* for transport and the second part transported by air, via Taiwan. In mid-February 1944, the unit moved to Singapore for training. The reason that the training locale was in the southern area was because of the shortage of aviation fuel on the mainland for training purposes. The majority of aircraft in Air Group 601 consisted of new Model 52 Zero fighters. The *Taihō* unit (division officer LT Toshitada Kawazoe) was deployed to the Batu Pahat Base; the *Shōkaku* unit (division officer LT Yasuo Masuyama) and the *Zuikaku* units were deployed at Seletar all engaged in intensive training activities. Carrier takeoff and landing exercises commenced in April. Because it was organized earlier, the degree of training of Air Group 601 was at a higher level than that of its sister units, Air Groups 652 and 653. It was anticipated that the 601 would serve as the nucleus of a reactivated striking force (the 3rd Fleet). With the American attack on the Mariana Islands nearing, a striking force (the 1st Striking Force) completed its final training phase at Lingua Base; on 15 May the force assembled and stood by at the Tawi Tawi anchorage south of the Philippines. Because of the appearance of enemy submarines, however, there were few opportunities to practice outside of the bay. Takeoff and landing training were possible only twice a month and there was concern that flying skills would degrade.

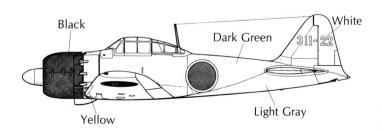

Model 52 Zero Fighter
Taihō unit, around June 1944.

Black

Dark Green

White

311-22

Yellow

Light Gray

Aircraft carrier *Taihō* with Air Group 601 on board (*The Ships of the World*)

By 13 June, the striking force had moved to the central Philippines anchorage at Gimaras. With the beginning of the "A"-Gō operation, the 601 sortied out on the 15th to the seas west of the Marianas; on both the 19th and 20th it engaged in battle with the American task force. In other words, the first wave attack (48 fighters, 53 carrier bombers, 27 carrier attack planes, for a total of 128 aircraft) of Air Group 601 (1st Carrier Division) proceeded to attack a force of American aircraft carriers discovered west of Saipan. However, as the 601 was passing over our own 2nd Fleet, steaming one hundred miles ahead, the fighter unit became disorganized as it met antiaircraft fire from friendly forces. Just about the time that it reorganized and regained battle formation, the 601 was attacked by a large number of American fighters. Seventy-five percent of the unit's strength—thirty-two fighters, forty-one carrier bombers, and twenty-three *Tenzan* carrier attack planes, for a total of ninety-six aircraft—were lost. The only result attained by our side was that one enemy aircraft carrier [battleship] was hit.

A large number of aircraft failed to return, including LT Kawazoe commanding the 1st Daitai (a daitai consisted of two chūtai composed of eight aircraft each), LT Sakami commanding the 2nd Daitai, and LT Fumio Yamagata commanding the 3rd Daitai, among others. The second wave (four carrier fighters, ten carrier bombers, and four carrier attack planes) returned without being able to locate the enemy in the expected area; in addition, eight fighter bombers and one carrier attack plane failed to return.

After the attack force had departed the two carriers, the *Taihō* and *Shōkaku* were torpedoed by American submarines and sank. Aircraft of those two carriers that did

Model 52 Zero Fighter
Zuikaku unit, about June 1944.

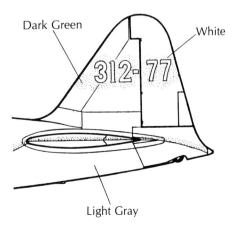

Dark Green

White

313-52

Light Gray

Model 52 Zero Fighter
Shōkaku unit, about June 1944.

make it home landed on the *Zuikaku* and other ships. At dusk the following day, the 20th, American carrier strike planes attacked the Ozawa Striking Force. The eight Zero fighters of Air Group 601 (commanded by ENS Yoshio Fukui) were able, in coordination with the 2nd Carrier Division, to shoot down fifteen enemy aircraft; however, the great majority of our aircraft had to ditch in pitch darkness. The 2nd Carrier Division's own carrier *Hiyō* also sank, and the "A"-Gō operation turned out to be a complete defeat for Japan. In addition, although the remaining elements of the striking force did return to the Inland Sea, surviving operational aircraft of Air Group 601 consisted of only four Zero fighters, two carrier bombers, and one carrier attack plane.

On 10 July, Air Group 601 was posted to the 1st Carrier Division (the *Zuikaku* and the *Ryūhō*); later, 10 August, it was placed under the direct command of the 3rd Fleet. In preparation for scheduled assignment to the *Amagi* and the *Unryū,* the unit was organized into Fighter Hikōtai 161 (forty-eight carrier fighters; commander, LT Hōhei Kobayashi) and Fighter Hikōtai 162 (forty-eight fighter bombers; commander, LT Saneyuki Hida). In addition, Attack Hikōtai 161 (carrier bombers), Attack Hikōtai 262 (carrier attack planes), and Reconnaissance Hikōtai 61 were also added. Training started at the Ōita Base. With the ordering of the Shō-gō [Leyte] Operation in October, the striking force was given the assignment

of serving as a diversionary force and proceeded off the Philippines. The *Amagi* and the *Unryū* stayed back, while the four carriers assigned to the 3rd Carrier Division (the *Zuikaku,* the *Zuihō,* the *Chitose,* and the *Chiyoda*) participated. On the 24th, an attack force of thirty carrier fighters, nineteen fighter bombers, two carrier bombers, and five carrier attack planes, a total of fifty-six aircraft, was sent out against the American task force. Twelve carrier fighters of Air Group 601 (of which six returned) were included in the above total of fifty-six aircraft. After the attack, the planes landed at a land base in the Philippines. The following day, with the exception of fighters used in direct air protection operations that were left behind, the striking force had the surviving five fighter bombers, three carrier attack planes, and one carrier bomber on standby in the Philippines. On the 25th, the striking force met the expected attack by American carrier aircraft; thirteen Zero fighters (eight were from Air Group 601) under the command of LT Kobayashi intercepted and shot down twelve enemy aircraft. At the same time, the four carriers (the *Zuikaku, Zuihō, Chitose,* and *Chiyoda*) were sunk. Flight personnel, led by LT Kobayashi, had ditched their planes and were taken on board a destroyer [the *Hatsuzuki*]; however, that same night the same flight personnel shared the fate of the ship they were riding on when it was shelled by American naval forces and sunk.

第601航空隊戦闘機隊（Ⅱ）

AIR GROUP 601 FIGHTER SQUADRON (II)

It was not as if the former Air Group 601 had been disbanded and reorganized. Though actually the same unit, the character of the unit had been substantially changed from that of a fleet air unit to that of a land-based air unit. As a result, we decided to deal separately with the reorganized 601 unit after it was resurrected following the Battle of the Philippine Sea (October 1944).

As indicated previously, the former Fighter Squadron 601 had been completely wiped out because of the sea battles that occurred on 24–25 October 1944. What remained in the Inland Sea were carriers without any aircraft complements on board. As a result of the revised organization of 15 November, the 3rd Carrier Division was disbanded. The striking force was left with the 1st Carrier Division, under the direct command of the CO of the Combined Fleet and the 4th Carrier Division only (the *Ise* and *Hyuga*). The carriers of the 3rd Carrier Division, the *Junyō, Ryūhō, Amagi, Unryū,* (which had sunk on 29 December), and *Shinano* (which had sunk on 29 November) had been posted thereto. In reality, however, they were reassigned to duty operating between the mainland and the southern areas carrying replenishment supplies instead of airplanes.

The air group had a complement of twenty-four carrier fighters, twelve carrier bombers, and twelve carrier attack planes. LT Hideo Katori was assigned as group

leader of the fighter squadron and LT Hida as group leader for both the carrier bomber and attack plane units. When the air group went to the Matsuyama Base for reorganization and training, there were only two or three persons with actual battle experience. The great majority of flight personnel were graduates fresh from air training units. From December to January 1945, survivors formerly with the fleet air groups who had returned from the Philippines area of battles were integrated into the unit. Fighter Squadron 601 moved its training to the base at Iwakuni.

On 10 February 1945, with few exceptions, Japanese navy vessels were decommissioned. The 1st Carrier Division was among the units also disbanded; Air Group 601 was posted to the 3rd Air Fleet, which was serving as the base air unit. CAPT Toshikazu Sugiyama was assigned the command. At the time of its organization, the unit consisted of the following three elements: Fighter Hikōtai 310 (forty-eight Zero fighters; commander, LT Katori), Attack Hikōtai 1 (forty-eight carrier bombers), and Attack Hikōtai 254 (forty-eight carrier attack planes). In March, unit 254 was reassigned. At the same time, Fighter Hikōtai 308 (forty-eight Zero fighters; commander, LT Kakichi Hirata) and Fighter Hikōtai 402 (forty-eight Shiden fighters; commander, LT Iyozō Fujita) were attached. Later, in early July immediately before deployment for the final battle

Model 52 Zero Fighter, 1945

Black

White

Dark Green 601-121

Light Gray

Yellow

Fighter Hikōtai 310 at Hyakurigahara Base (Air Group 601), 15 March 1945. Front row: fourth from right, LT Hideo Katori; second from left, ENS Tsutomu Iwai. Third row: second from left, WO Kunimori Nakakariya. (Kunimori Nakakariya)

on the homeland, Fighter Hikōtai 402 was assigned to the Tsukuba Air Group. Also, Attack Hikōtai 3 (carrier bombers) was transferred in.

The commander of the 3rd Air Fleet became aware of the American attack on Iwo Jima on 14 February; he ordered the CO of Air Group 601 to dispatch all operational aircraft to the Katori base. Both carrier bomber and carrier attack plane units moved on the same day and started patrolling over the seas off the eastern part of the Kantō region. Twenty aircraft of Fighter Hikōtai 310 previously stationed at Iwakuni had flown to the vicinity of Yokohama by the morning of 16 February. Here they became aware of an American carrier air attack going on in the Kantō region. The 310 landed at Atsugi and then headed for Katori but lost four aircraft as a result of an aerial engagement with a group of F6Fs, over Kasumigaura. During the course of an intercept battle the following day, the 17th, seven Zero fighters were able to make a surprise attack on enemy dive-bombers and shot down six of them. Of the six, LT Katori accounted for four. On the 19th, American forces began their landing operations on Iwo Jima. Air Group 601 had al-

ready started the process of selecting suicide attack force personnel.

In the end, the 2nd Mitate-tai ("Imperial Shield Unit") under the command of LT Hiroshi Murakawa of the carrier bomber force and consisting of twenty suicide attack aircraft, plus twelve escorting fighters (commanded by LTJG Senzō Iwashita) sortied on the 21st via Hachijō-jima. They sank the American carrier *Bismarck Sea* and inflicted major damage on the *Saratoga;* at the same time, the majority of the attacking aircraft shared a similar fate.

By late March, the 3rd Air Fleet had proceeded to Kyūshū in preparation for participating in the Battle of Okinawa. By 1 April, thirty-eight Zero fighters, eight Shiden fighters, and eighteen Suisei carrier bombers of Air Group 601 had been deployed to Kokubu No. 1 Base in southern Kyūshū. In preparation for participating in the Kikusui (Floating Crysanthemum) Operation, CAPT Sugiyama, commanding officer, was placed in command of all the units assembled at the base. These were: Air Group 701 (5th Air Fleet), Air Group 210, Air Group 252, Air Group 601 (3rd Air Fleet), Usa Air Group, Nagoya Air Group, Hyakurigahara Air Group, and the

Fighter Hikōtai 308, Air Group 601, May 1945. Second row (sitting), from the left: CPO Moriji Sako, WO Kenji Okabe, LT Mori, LT Takeo Hirose, LT Kakichi Hirata (group leader), and LTJG Arita. Rear row, from the left: sixth person, WO Ichihei Yoshida. (Ichihei Yoshida)

Genzan (Wonsan) Air Group (10th Air Fleet, main strength in suicide attack force aircraft).

On 1 April, American forces began to land on the main island of Okinawa; the first wave of counterattack units left on 3 April. Carrier Bomber Squadron 601 proceeded south seeking an American carrier force but was unable to meet with the enemy. Thirty-two Zero fighters and eight Shiden fighters under the command of LT Katori engaged in strafing operations in the Okinawa archipelago. In an air battle over Kikaiga-shima with American fighters, sixteen of the enemy (five probables) were shot down and our side lost eight aircraft. On the 6th, Kikusui Operation No. 1 started and the first general air attack, composed primarily of suicide aircraft, was launched. The general offensive continued in the sense that Operation No. 2 was carried out on the 12th, and Operation No. 3 on the 6th. During this period, Fighter Squadron 601 served as an advance strafing unit for the suicide aircraft. It is to be noted that, on the 16th, twenty-six Zero fighters and four Shiden fighters commanded by LT Hirata engaged in air battle with a force of American fighters over Kikaiga-shima

and shot down four of the enemy. Our side also lost four aircraft. Next, four Zero fighters equipped with bombs (under the command of LTJG Makio Aoki) attacked nearby elements of the American task force; none of our aircraft returned. In this fashion, during the two-week period ending on the 17th, Air Group 601 had lost twenty-six fighters and twenty-three carrier bombers. The unit was then relieved by twenty Suisei carrier bombers that had been sent from the Hyakurigahara base; the 601 returned to the Kanto area.

From this time on, Air Group 601 took on a policy of husbanding its strength for later use, stayed at the Hyakurigahara base and concentrated on rebuilding the unit and on training exercises. Because of the shortage of aviation fuel, however, there was no significant increase in skills.

At the same time, the replacement of aircraft from May on went smoothly; by June, operational aircraft were back up to about seventy Suisei carrier bombers and about one hundred Zero fighters. Advantage was taken, on occasion, of participating in the interception of American carrier aircraft and of P-51s based at Iwo Jima. During the same period, in early June, about seventy aircraft on the ground were damaged as a result of low-flying attacks by P-51s carrying aerial rockets. In this instance, in about ten days repairs on all aircraft had been completed. In July, the 3rd Air Fleet assumed new positions in anticipation of the final battle of the homeland. On the 18th, about fifty aircraft of Fighter Hikōtai 308 (unit commander, LT Takeo Hirose) were assigned to the Yamato base in Nara prefecture; also, the approximately eighty aircraft of the Hikōtai 310, under the direct command of the admiral, proceeded to the Suzuka base in Mie prefecture.

With the exception of an intercept battle over Lake Biwa the day before hostilities ended, however, Air Group 601 was to greet the day the war ended as the most powerful fighter squadron left intact in central Japan.

At the end of the war, Attack Hikōtai 1 (about one hundred aircraft) remained at Hyakurigahara and Attack Hikōtai 3 (about fifty aircraft) at Nagoya.

第634航空隊戦闘機隊

AIR GROUP 634 FIGHTER SQUADRON

At the end of June 1942, immediately following the Battle of Midway, the Japanese navy was plagued by a shortage of aircraft carriers and decided to convert two old-style battleships, the *Ise* and *Hyūga,* into carriers. Conversion work was started in March 1943 at the Kure Naval Arsenal; work was completed as of 1 July. The main changes in the remodeling were as follows: the two aft units of the six 36-cm gun turrets were removed. [Each turret held two guns for a total of twelve guns.] In their place [the four guns removed], an aircraft hangar and two catapults were added. The 14-cm secondary batteries were also removed and were replaced by eight, new double-mounted 12-cm high-angle guns (a total of sixteen guns) and nineteen 25-mm triple turret antiaircraft cannons.

The planned allowance of aircraft on board consisted of eleven of the new Suisei carrier bombers (equipped with 500-kg bombs) and eleven Aichi E16A Zuiun reconnaissance float seaplanes [PAUL], for a total of twenty-two aircraft. By the end of April 1944, basic training had about been completed and as of 1 May, the 4th Carrier Division, consisting of the *Ise* and the *Hyūga,* was created. Air Group 634 was attached to the 4th Carrier Division and the group integrated into the 3rd Fleet. CAPT Takahisa Amagai was assigned to command the 634; LT Yoshio Tamura (a graduate of a student reserve unit and a graduate of Waseda University) and LT Tadaharu

Kizuka (graduate of the Naval Academy) were assigned as group leaders. Suisei training was started at the Iwakuni base, while Zuiun training was started at the Kure base. Aircraft allowances would be fourteen Suisei and eight Zuiun aircraft attached to the *Hyūga;* the *Ise* would have the two same types of aircraft but in reverse numerical quantities. On 23 June, the first catapult takeoff exercises were held in Hiroshima Bay. The target was to be able to make it possible for twenty-two aircraft equipped with 500-kg bombs to take off within a period of thirty minutes.

The 4th Carrier Division had been unable to participate in the "A"-gō [Marianas] operation; at the same time, the two aircraft carriers by themselves were insufficient to serve as a tactical battle unit. As a result, it was decided that with the 10 July reorganization, the *Junyō,* and with the 10 August reorganization, the *Ryūhō* (for a total of two additional aircraft carriers) would be added to the 4th. It was further decided to add carrier fighters and attack planes as well. Aircraft allowance was increased to twenty-four carrier bombers and twenty-four float bombers (later twenty-four carrier attack planes were added). Two other units were also added: Fighter Hikōtai 163 (LT Sumio Fukuda, group leader; forty-eight carrier fighter allowance) and Fighter Hikōtai 167 (concurrently commanded by LT Fukuda, group leader; forty-eight carrier fighter allowance).

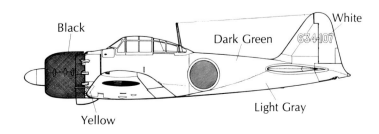

Model 52 Zero Fighter

Unit insignia *634* was used from May 1944 to January 1945.

Black

Dark Green

White

634-107

Light Gray

Yellow

Zero fighter unit attacking in the Leyte Bay area, November 1944. (Kazuo Sugino)

When an American task force attacked on 12 October, the majority of Air Group 653 and the entire Air Group 634 left their assigned ships and participated in battle, operating from bases on land. The approximately sixty Zero fighters of Fighter Hikō-tai 163 and Fighter Hikōtai 167, which were undergoing training at the To-kushima base along with carrier bombers and float bombers, were integrated into the 2nd Air Fleet. Advancing to the Kanoya base in southern Kyūshū, the units partici-pated in the aerial battles off Taiwan.

From the 13th to the 14th, the two air units engaged in attacks on the American task force in conjunction with other squad-rons, using Okinawa as a relay base. Though they next moved to the Taichung base there were no noteworthy battle results. The main strength of these units had arrived by the 23rd, in succession, at Clark Field on Luzon. On the 24th, the fol-lowing day, a major force of the 2nd Air Fleet sortied in search of a group of Ameri-can carriers. On their way they met an in-tercept attack by a powerful group of American fighters. The result was that a large number of our aircraft failed to return to base. Air Group 634 lost LT Fukuda to-gether with seven aircraft under him.

The units next engaged in a number of intercept battles in conjunction with other elements based at Clark Field. A portion of the aircraft advanced to Cebu after attack-ing Tacloban and participated in an attack on Leyte as well as in Cebu intercept bat-tles. Within six months of their arrival in the Philippines, the units had suffered al-most 50 percent attrition. LTJG Otsuji, as commander of the kamikaze special attack force unit, the Baika-tai ("Plum Flower Unit"), was transferred into the area. After the injury of LT Mitsuo Ishizaka at Cebu, on the 4th, during an intercept battle with

B-29s, there were no operationally fit flight personnel left. At the same time, the strength of the carrier bomber squadron deployed to the base at Mabalacat had diminished; also, the float bomber squadron that had transferred from Tungkang to Cavite did not achieve any special battle results. Without achieving any noteworthy results, Air Group 634 itself was reorganized on 8 January 1945 as a float reconnaissance unit and transferred to the 1st Air Fleet. It withdrew to the Taiwan port of Tungkang and was later transferred to the 5th Air Fleet. It greeted the end of hostilities at the Genkai base in northern Kyūshū.

第652航空隊戦闘機隊

AIR GROUP 652 FIGHTER SQUADRON

Air Group 652 succeeded the 2nd Carrier Division and was organized on 10 March 1944. CDR Shōichi Suzuki was the commander in addition to serving as air officer for the flagship *Junyō*. The 652 was attached to the reorganized 2nd Carrier Division (aircraft carriers *Junyō, Hiyō,* and *Ryūhō*). LT Saneyasu Hidaka, group leader, served on board the *Ryūhō;* LT Hōhei Kobayashi on the *Hiyō* and LT Hiroshi Yoshimura on the *Junyō* served as the senior division officers in their respective fighter squadrons.

When we look at the history of this unit before its establishment, as it has already been dealt with in the section concerning the *Junyō* and *Hiyō* fighter squadrons, the 2nd Carrier Division had advanced to Rabaul by the end of January 1944. There it lost more than half of its fighting power in the fierce battles that raged for about three weeks. Commanding officer Shiroshima led a group of fifteen Zero fighters, fourteen carrier bombers, and eight carrier attack planes and retreated to Truk during the period 19–21 February. The unit then pulled back to the homeland on 2 March, leaving its aircraft behind in order to rebuild itself. As a result, the rebuilding of the 652 commenced last among all air units

attached to the 1st, 2nd, and 3rd carrier divisions. There was no time for proceeding to Singapore for training. Starting the end of March, equipment, supplies, and personnel were hurriedly gathered together. Training was scheduled to be completed within two months and was conducted at each of three bases situated at Iwakuni, Saeki, and Ōita.

The aircraft allowance was eighty-one carrier fighters, thirty-six carrier bombers, and twenty-seven carrier attack planes; equipment was slow in arriving. As of 1 April, there were only thirty Model 21 Zero fighters, thirteen Model 52 Zero fighters, and four Type 99 carrier bombers on hand. By the time the unit moved to Tawi Tawi in May, it had been reinforced to a total aircraft complement of 135 planes, including 27 Model 21 Zero fighters and 53 Model 52 Zero fighters. The Model 21 Zero fighter was used as a fighter bomber by equipping it with a 250-kg bomb. The idea was to bomb the flight deck of an enemy carrier at the outset of an attack in order to negate the takeoff and landing capabilities of the enemy. The Zeros would also be used in air combat as fighter aircraft. The majority of pilots had

Model 52 Zero Fighter
1944, on the mainland.

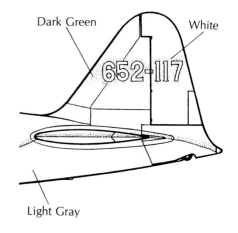

Dark Green   White

652-117

Light Gray

been transferred from carrier attack and bomber duties; almost none had actual battle experience. Although air combat training was conducted, the capabilities of the personnel were considered to be quite modest. Since there were no dive brakes as in the case of carrier bombers, dive-bombing was conducted at a shallow angle of between thirty and forty degrees. Intensity of training, combined with the lack of experience in takeoff and landing on carriers, resulted in a number of accidental crashes during training exercises in Saeki Bay.

With the American offensive on the Marianas nearing, however, the 2nd Carrier Division left Saeki on 11 May carrying on board an incompletely trained hikōtai. The unit arrived at Tawi Tawi southwest of the Philippine Islands on the 16th; here they met the main force of the Ozawa Striking Force. Although the unit stood by for about one month in the area, there were few opportunities to leave the bay for training because of the presence of enemy submarines. There was no opportunity to increase the level of training either.

With the issuance of the command for the "A"-gō operation on 15 June, the Ozawa Striking Force departed the Gimalas anchorage.

After passing through the San Bernadino Strait, the striking force emerged in the seas west of the Marianas and sought battle with the main body of the American task force. On the afternoon of the 18th, search planes sent out discovered several units of the American task force. Although the attack unit was made ready for takeoff, because of the long distances involved no attempt to attack was actually made. After verifying the enemy's position early the next morning, on the 19th, the first attack wave was sent off. Air Group 652 sent out a total of forty-seven aircraft, consisting of fifteen fighters, twenty-five fighter bombers, and seven carrier attack planes. Because of insufficient training and low cloud cover, however, visibility was obstructed and formation assembly was difficult; as a result, the force was split into two units and each proceeded on its own way. There was not only a flight of 350 miles to contend with but the fact that orders were changed, while under way, to a target an additional 50 miles ahead. As a result, while in the process of searching for the anticipated enemy location, the first element was ambushed by enemy fighters and became disorganized. The first unit returned to their carriers with no results attained. At the same time, two fighters, four fighter bombers, and one Tenzan carrier attack plane were lost. The second of the two units returned to their carriers without seeing any trace of the enemy.

The second attack force sent out by Air Group 652 left their three carriers two hours and twenty minutes later. The first unit, consisting of nine Suisei carrier bombers and six Zero fighters, did not sight the enemy for a period of two and a half hours in the anticipated area. Immedi-

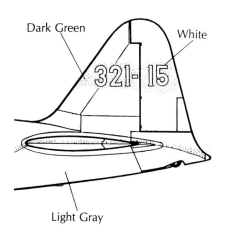

Model 52 Zero Fighter

Junyō Fighter Squadron, about June 1944.
(*Hiyō* units, 322–55. *Ryūhō* units, 323–92.)

Air Group 652 at Tawi Tawi, mid-May 1944. All personnel on board the *Ryūhō* including the carrier bomber and carrier attack squadrons. Last row, eleventh from the left, CPO Tetsuo Kikuchi (a large man). (Izumi Sanada)

ately before they landed back at Rota, however, enemy aircraft carriers were discovered west of the island and an attack was carried out. Five Suisei and one Zero fighter were lost; no battle results were verified. The second unit of the attack force, consisting of twenty-seven Type 99 carrier bombers, twenty Zero fighters, and two Tenzan carrier attack planes, also failed to discover the enemy. After a flight of about three hours, just about when they were ready to land on Guam, the unit was engaged in battle by some thirty Grumman fighters that attacked them. Six enemy aircraft were shot down, but because of the unfavorable situation that they found themselves in, our forces received major damage. Only one Zero fighter, seven carrier bombers, and one Tenzan carrier attack plane landed safely. Despite the unfavorable circumstances, an escorting fighter squadron under the command of LT Kobayashi, resolutely fought back in order to protect the fighter bombers just before they landed. The great majority of the aircraft in the Kobayashi squadron either destroyed themselves or made emergency landings after receiving damage. In this fashion, as of the evening of the same day, forces available to Air Group 652 had shrunk to one third of what they had been; nineteen fighters, nineteen fighter bombers, and eight Tenzan carrier attack planes, for a total of forty-six aircraft.

The following day, the 20th, ADM Ozawa planned another attack using the approximately one hundred remaining aircraft, including the previously described remnants of the 652. During the evening and before a time felt suitable for takeoff had arrived, however, American carrier strike groups made a major attack on them. Air Group 652 had their carrier bombers and attack planes take evasive action in the air; all operable Zero fighters (nineteen fighters and seven fighter bombers) took off to intercept the enemy. Two F6Fs (probable) and nine TBFs (two probables) were shot down. Damages on our side amounted to eleven planes destroyed or failed to return, as well as three planes that ditched. In addition, the *Hiyō* was sunk, and the *Junyō* received hits.

During the same evening, the striking force started its withdrawal; the force had returned to the western part of the Inland Sea by the 23rd, proceeding via Nakagusuku Bay. Operational aircraft available to Air Group 652 were but eleven fighters, five fighter bombers, and one Tenzan carrier attack plane, total, seventeen.

With the reorganization as of 10 July, both the 2nd Carrier Division and Air Group 652 were disbanded. The majority of remaining flight personnel were absorbed into Air Group 653.

第653航空隊戦闘機隊

AIR GROUP 653 FIGHTER SQUADRON

Air Group 653 was organized on 15 February 1944, composed of the air groups that were attached to the 3rd Carrier Division (3rd Fleet), which itself had been newly organized of the three aircraft carriers, the *Chitose, Chiyoda,* and *Zuihō.* Its first base was at Iwakuni. CDR Gunji Kimura was the commanding officer, and LT Kenji Nakagawa served as the group leader and commander of the fighter squadron.

Aircraft allowance was sixty-three carrier fighters, and twenty-seven carrier attack planes; the main strength of the fighter units on board were Model 21 Zero fighter bombers. As a result, on the eve of the "A"-gō operation, forty-five of the sixty-three aircraft were Zero fighter bombers. Of the three carrier divisions that were assigned to the 3rd Fleet, the level of training for Air Group 653 was the lowest. In addition, the majority of pilots were new and officer strength was concentrated in aviation students of the 38th Class (September 1943 graduates) and the 39th Class (January 1944 graduates). In particular, it is to be noted that seven of the ten officers involved were from the latter graduating class.

On 11 May, the three aircraft carriers of the 3rd Carrier Division, with their air units on board, departed the western part of the Inland Sea and proceeded to Tawi Tawi, where they arrived on the 16th and stood by for action. As a result of the American attack on the Marianas, the "A"-gō operation was ordered on 15 June and the Ozawa Striking Force advanced to the waters west of the Mariana Islands. On the afternoon of the 18th, a Tenzan-equipped search unit dispatched by Air Group 653 encountered enemy carrier aircraft in flight. A short while later, search aircraft of Air Group 601 discovered a group of enemy aircraft carriers. At 0730 on the 19th, the following day, the 3rd Carrier Division, which had advanced with the main unit of the 2nd Fleet one hundred miles ahead of other units, took the initiative in launching the first attack wave. This force consisted of eight Tenzan carrier attack planes, forty-five fighter bombers, and fourteen fighters (commanded by LT Nakagawa). The force was blocked, however, by a defensive patrol established twenty miles ahead of the enemy force. At the same time, a portion of the first wave was able to attack the enemy ships and reported that an aircraft carrier and a cruiser had each received one bomb hit. Losses on our side were considerable;

Model 52 Zero Fighter
Chitose unit, about June 1944.

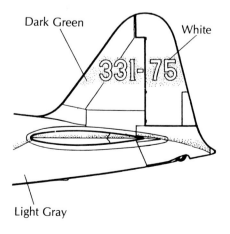

Dark Green

White

331-75

Light Gray

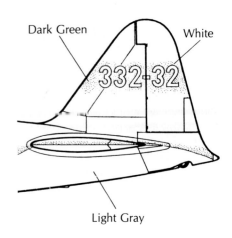

Model 52 Zero Fighter
Chiyoda unit, about June 1944.

two Tenzan aircraft, thirty-two fighter bombers, and eight fighters, for a total of forty-two aircraft, failed to return. The 3rd Carrier Division made preparations for the second wave, led by LT Nakagawa; it consisted of five Zero fighters, nine fighter bombers, and five Tenzan carrier attack planes, for a total of nineteen aircraft. The second wave missed an opportunity for takeoff because of the large number of returning aircraft belonging to various units, damages caused by such planes, and the shortage of fuel. Finally, at 1530, a portion of the attack force did take off. Ultimately, plans for a second wave were abandoned.

Despite the substantial losses sustained, the strike force went ahead and made preparations for a second attack the next day. The 3rd Carrier Division sent off a strike group that afternoon with the intention of tracking and attacking any enemy aircraft that came to attack our forces; this one consisted of two Tenzan carrier attack planes, ten fighter bombers, and four fighters under the command of LT Itō. After a short period of time, American carrier aircraft carried out a major attack on our forces; our own carrier fighters moved into counterattack. In conjunction with Air Group 652, a total of about twenty enemy aircraft were shot down. However, the great majority of our airplanes failed to return or made forced landings; in addition, the *Chiyoda* received one direct and one near miss bomb hit.

In this fashion, operational aircraft of the 3rd Carrier Division had been reduced to two carrier fighters, three fighter bombers,

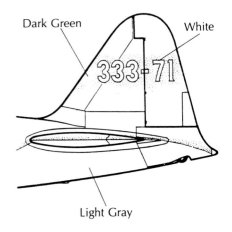

Model 52 Zero Fighter
Zuihō unit, about June 1944.

Model 52 Zero Fighter

Zuihō unit, about October 1944. Number *2* at top of rudder indicates the *Zuihō* unit; two horizontal lines on tail indicate this is the unit leader's aircraft.

and six carrier attack planes, for a total of eleven aircraft. The unit next returned to the homeland.

After the Battle of the Marianas, the navy started rebuilding its strike force capabilities; it was decided to use as its nucleus Air Group 653, which had, comparatively speaking, suffered less damage than the others. Training started at the Ōita base with the aim of being ready for carrier operations by about September. Because of the intensity of training, however, a large number of accidental fatalities occurred. Even so, by September, Air Groups 653 and 634 had reached a level where basic carrier takeoff and landing operations were possible. At the same time, they did not have the confidence to engage in fierce aerial battles. Two covering force units were formed, consisting of the Fighter Hikōtai 164 (headed on a concurrent duty basis by LT Nakagawa, commander; allowance, forty-eight aircraft) and Fighter Hikōtai 165 (LT Nakagawa, commander; allowance, forty-eight Zero fighters). In addi-

tion, Air Group 653 had the following two units: Fighter Hikōtai 166, used solely as a fighter bombing unit and consisting of Model 52 Zero fighters converted to fighter bombers (commander, LT Tetsuo Endō; allowance, forty-eight aircraft) plus Attack Hikōtai 263 (allowance, forty-eight carrier attack planes).

With the attack by an American task force on Taiwan, the main strength of Air Group 653 was integrated into the 2nd Air Fleet, which was serving as the base air unit. Under the direct command of the commanding officer, the 653 engaged in aerial battles offshore of Taiwan and lost almost half of their aircraft. At the same time, the unit did advance via Okinawa to the base at Bamban on Luzon. LTJG Manabu Ishimori led the twenty-four-aircraft unit.

At the same time, some veteran personnel with carrier experience stayed behind; as of the 20th, such personnel were distributed to one or the other of the four carriers of the Ozawa fleet. Leaving the Inland Sea

Model 52 Zero Fighter

1944, in the homeland.

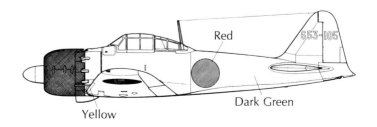

Model 52 Zero Fighter

Zuikaku unit in October 1944. Number *1* at top of tail indicates *Zuikaku* unit. Yellow horizontal lines on vertical tail signify it is the commander's aircraft.

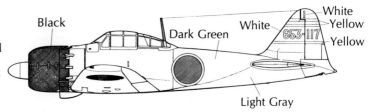

to engage in diversionary operations, 653 headed for the seas northeast of the Philippine Islands. Early on the morning of the 24th, an attack force composed of the 653 joined forces with Air Group 601 for a total of fifty-six aircraft and took off for an attack on American carriers. En route, the attack force was intercepted by a combat air patrol of about twenty Grummans. Units of the *Chitose, Chiyoda,* and *Zuihō* failed to discover the enemy's whereabouts. Only the *Zuikaku* unit (six carrier fighters, eleven fighter bombers, and one carrier attack plane) arrived over the enemy carrier force area; however, the only report received was of white smoke, which was believed to have been caused by a bomb hit. The remaining aircraft, under the command of LT Nakagawa, arrived the following day in Manila, proceeding via Aparri and Tuguegarao in the northern part of Luzon. Immediately upon arrival, half of the

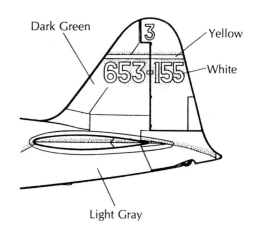

Model 52 Zero Fighter

Chitose unit about October 1944. Number *3* at top of tail indicates the *Chitose* unit. Single horizontal line on tail signifies it is a *shōtai* leader's aircraft.

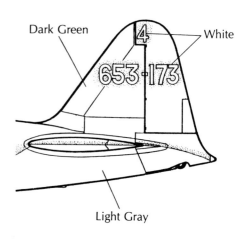

Model 52 Zero Fighter

Chiyoda unit about October 1944. Number *4* at top of tail indicates the *Chiyoda* unit.

Zuihō flight personnel at Tawi Tawi anchorage, May 1944. Center row: eighth person from left, LT Kenji Nakagawa; fourth from right, WO Kunimori Nakakariya. (Kunimori Nakakariya)

aircraft were equipped with bombs and proceeded on a search-and-attack mission against enemy task force elements northeast of Luzon. However, there was no sighting of the enemy. Later, during the same evening, the unit patrolled in the air over the retreating Kurita fleet; 653 did meet and repulse attacking enemy fighters.

Later, Air Group 653 Fighter Squadron was merged with some elements from the mainland that had caught up with them. By the 26th, some twenty-odd personnel, under the command of LT Nakagawa, were assembled at Bamban. In late October, after completing two intercept operations, the unit advanced to the base at Cebu. It participated in the attack on Tacloban,

Leyte, and served as air cover for friendly ship convoys. During the attack on Tacloban conducted in the early morning 3 November, LT Nakagawa and those under him were killed in action. There were no officer pilots whatsoever left in the unit. A few days later, most of the pilots who did survive withdrew to Ōita base. At the same time, the personnel left at Ōita base under division officer LT Yasuo Masuyama had continued to undergo intensive training. In the early part of November, all aircraft were assembled and next proceeded to the Philippines via Taiwan. With the reorganization as of the 15th, Air Group 653 Fighter Squadron was disbanded.

第 12 航 空 隊

12TH AIR GROUP FIGHTER SQUADRON

Following the outbreak of the China Incident on 7 July 1937, the 12th Air Group was formed from the Saeki Air Group as of the 11th. Equipped with twelve Type 95 carrier fighters, twelve Type 94 carrier bombers, and twelve Type 92 carrier attack planes, the group was immediately posted to the 2nd Combined Air Group (Rengō Kōkūtai). On 7 August, the unit advanced to the Chowshihtze (Shūsuishi) airport in Luda (Dairen) where it engaged in convoy escort duties. There were no opportunities for aerial combat, however, and the unit returned to the homeland towards the end of August.

As the war situation in the Shanghai area became more critical, the 12th Air Group was posted to the 3rd Fleet on 5 September and advanced to the Kunda base in Shanghai. The speed and cruising range of the Type 95 carrier fighter, however, was insufficient; in contrast, the 13th Air Group, equipped with Type 96 carrier fighters, played a spectacular role in aerial battles over Nanking. The 12th Air Group was engaged in such unspectacular duties as close ground support and air defense operations. Gradually from October through November, aircraft of the 12th Air Group were changed to Type 96 carrier fighters. With the capture of Nanking in December, the unit advanced to Daikōjō airfield in that city. Joining the 13th Air Group, the 12th participated in the attacks on Nanchang and Hankow.

As of 22 March 1938, the 13th Air Group was reorganized as a land attack plane unit; at the same time, the 12th Air Group was reorganized into a carrier fighter unit. As a result, the combination became a large fighter squadron that was composed of two and one-half units (five divisions) with an allowance of thirty Type 96 carrier fighters, as well as pilots in excess of fifty. In addition, another unit of carrier attack planes (allowance, twelve aircraft) was added. After the newly organized 12th Air Group had consolidated its strength, it used Anking as its base. On 29 April, the emperor's birthday, the unit attacked Hankow with a force of twenty-seven Type 96 carrier fighters serving in support of land attack planes. A fierce aerial battle ensued during which thirty-five enemy aircraft (seven probables) were shot down.

During the course of many repeated attacks on Hankow and Nanchang, and as one part of a major combined force of fighters and bombers, the 12th Air Group continuously showed the world the vigor of Japanese naval fighter groups in overwhelming the Chinese air force units that rose up to intercept them. A general idea can be obtained from taking note of the

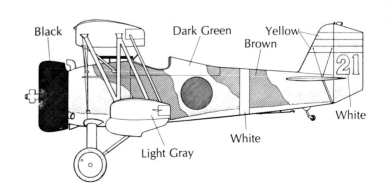

Type 95 Carrier Fighter
On the mainland of China, 1937.

The 12th Air Group Fighter Squadron, summer of 1938. Front row (from the left): third person, LT Yoshitomi; fourth, LCDR Kozono; fifth, LT Nakajima; and sixth, LT Aioi. Second row back (from the left): second person, Toshio Kuroiwa; seventh, Kiyonobu Suzuki; and eighth, Shigetaka Ōmori. Third row back: left end, Tetsuzō Iwamoto. (Shigema Yoshitomi).

Organized on 11 July 1937, immediately after the outbreak of the China Incident, the 12th Air Group was active over the Chinese mainland for a period of four years; it was reorganized on 15 September 1941, just before the outbreak of the Pacific War. During the summer of 1940, the air group was equipped for the first time with the new, advanced Zero fighter. The group is famous for air victories over and around Chungking.

12th Air Group flight personnel, Hankow Air Base, summer 1940. A good number of aces were to develop out of the pilots shown here. Second row, from the right: WO Koshirō Yamashita, division officer LT Fusata Iida, division officer LT Tamotsu Yokoyama, group leader LCDR Mikuma Minowa, commanding officer CAPT Kiichi Hasegawa; skip one; division officer LT Saburō Shindō, LTJG Aya-o Shirane, and WO Ichirō Higashiyama. Third row, from the right: fifth person, PO1c Matsuo Hagiri; skip one; PO2c Yoshio Ōki; PO1c Saburō Kitahata; PO1c Tora-ichi Takatsuka; skip one; PO2c Tsutomu Iwai; skip one; and PO1c Masayuki Nakase. Fourth [back] row, from the right: PO2c Jirō Matsuda; PO1c Kazuo Tsunoda; and, [seventh person], PO2c Keishū Kamihira. (Kazuo Tsunoda)

Type 96 Model 2-1 carrier fighter flown by LT Shigema Yoshitomi (Shigema Yoshitomi)

following figures. During the period from the end of April up to the 19 July attack on Hankow, 112 enemy aircraft were shot down (including twelve probables) with the loss on our side of only five aircraft.

With the fall of Hankow in the autumn of 1938, the 12th Air Group advanced its base to Hankow itself. The majority of ex-

perienced flight personnel were sent back to the homeland; the unit itself stayed engaged in air defense duties in the Wuhan area, though on a reduced scale. The 12th passed almost all of the following two years quietly and without fighting any noteworthy battles. When land attack planes started conducting large-scale strategic bombing

Type 96 Model 2-2 carrier fighter equipped with enclosed cockpit (earlier version). (Yoshimichi Saeki)

Upon returning from an attack on Chengtu, a report is provided VADM Shigetarō Shimada, commander of the China Area Fleet (on the left, in Class 2 uniform), 4 October 1940. Front row (from the left): LT Yokoyama, PO1c Hagiri, WO Higashiyama, LT Shindō, PO1c Kitahata, and LT Shirane. Rear row (left end): PO2 Ōishi. (Kazuo Tsunoda)

attacks on Chungking, the capital of Szechwan Province, and on Chengtu, they began to suffer significant losses from Chinese fighters during each attack because of the limited cruising range of our own supporting fighters. Thus, once again there was eager anticipation for the advent of new and significantly longer range fighters.

What started the response to these pressing demands coming from the front lines was the advent of the Zero-type carrier fighter. On 21 July [1940], an advance unit of six Zeros commanded by LT Yokoyama was transferred from the Yokosuka Air Group, where they were undergoing actual testing, to the city of Wuhan. Soon thereafter nine more of the new fighters were transported locally by air. On 19 August,

twelve Zeros of the Yokoyama unit serving as escort for land attack planes arrived over Chungking but failed to sight the enemy. During a fourth-phase attack carried out on 13 September, however, the thirteen Zero fighters led by LT Saburō Shindō caught over thirty enemy aircraft and shot down twenty-seven of the thirty for a brilliant combat debut.

Later, until the summer of 1941, the 12th Air Group Fighter Squadron, using Zero fighters, not only flew to Chungking and Chengtu but extended their flights to Tienshui in Shansi Province, as well as to Nancheng and Kwangyuang. Once they even flew on a reconnaissance mission over Lanchow. Battle results in such actions, including results attained by the 14th Air Group,

Model 11 Zero Fighter

Flown by PO1c Matsuo Hagiri during the attack on Chengtu, 14 March 1941. Unit designation 3 was used from October 1937 to September 1941.

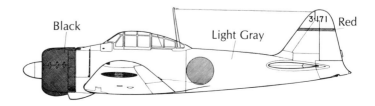

Zero fighter units of the 12th Air Group, which roamed the skies over mainland China. (Minoru Suzuki)

were 103 enemy aircraft shot down and 163 destroyed on the ground. Only three of our own aircraft were lost. Moreover, those three were shot down by ground fire, not in aerial combat.

In such fashion did the 12th Air Group exert control over the Chinese mainland skies for a period of more than four years. On 15 September 1941, just before the outbreak of the Pacific War, the 12th Air Group was disbanded as a result of reorganization. Most pilots were transferred to the Tainan Air Group or to the 3rd Air Group.

Officers of the 12th Air Group and a Zero fighter with twenty-eight kill marks on its fuselage, August 1941. Rear row, from the left: LTJG Yūzō Tsukamoto, group leader Hanamoto, commanding officer Uchida, and air officer Suzuki. Front row, from the extreme left: end, LTJG Jōji Yamashita; third person, LT Ichirō Mukai. The plane was later donated to the Naval Academy. (Yūzō Tsukamoto)

Successive Commanders:

July 1937–November 1937 CAPT Osamu Imamura

November 1937–December 1938 CAPT Morihiko Miki

December 1938–October 1939 CAPT Shun-ichi Kira

October 1939–June 1940 CAPT Takasue Furuse

June 1940–March 1941 CAPT Ki-ichi Hasegawa

March 1941–September 1941 CAPT Ichi-tarō Uchida

Successive Group Leaders:

July 1937–March 1938 LCDR Motoharu Okajima

March 1938–December 1938 LCDR Yasuna Kozono

March 1938–August 1938 LCDR Shige-hachirō Tokoro

December 1938–October 1939 LCDR Takeo Shibata

October 1939–November 1940 LCDR Mikuma Minowa

October 1939–January 1940 LCDR Shigema Yoshitomi

November 1940–September 1941 LCDR Seiichi Maki

TABLE 3. FORMATION OF THE 12TH AIR GROUP
(At the Attack on Chungking, 13 September 1940)

	VICTORIES
1st Chūtai	
1st Shōtai	
Lt Saburō Shindō	1
PO1c Saburō Kitahata	2
PO2c Yoshio Ōki	4
PO2c Kihei Fujiwara	1
2nd Shōtai	
WO Koshirō Yamashita	5
PO2c Toshiyuki Sueda	1
PO3c Hatsumasa Yamaya	2
2nd Chūtai	
1st Shōtai	
LTJG Aya-o Shirane	1
PO1c Masayuki Mitsumasa	2
PO2c Tsutomu Iwai	2
2nd Shōtai	
PO1c Tora-ichi Takatsuka	3
PO3c Kazuki Mikami	2
PO3c Masaharu Hiramoto	1

第 13 航 空 隊

13TH AIR GROUP FIGHTER SQUADRON

The 13th Air Group was organized on the same date as the 12th Air Group, 11 July 1937, by the Ōmura Air Group and was posted to the 12th Combined Air Group. On 7 August, the unit advanced to the Chowshihtze base but returned to its own base by the end of the same month. At the time of its organization, the group consisted of two divisions of Type 96 carrier fighters (twelve aircraft), six Type 96 carrier bombers, and twelve Type 96 carrier attack planes. It was equipped with the newest and most advanced aircraft of all of the navy's air groups. In particular, the Type 96 carrier fighter had just reached a stage of quantity production and was considered to be an epochally advanced fighter aircraft. Just before departure, Type 95 carrier fighters were replaced by the newer aircraft.

On 5 September, orders were received to proceed to Shanghai. On the 9th, the unit deployed via Cheju Island to the Kunda airfield in Shanghai, then under bombardment. For a few days the unit engaged in strafing enemy ground forces in the vicinity of the air base. On 19 September, twelve Type 96 carrier fighters led by LT Shichitarō Yamashita participated in the first phase air attack on Nanking as escort for the seventeen carrier bombers commanded by LCDR Wada. Engaging in air battle with some twenty Curtiss Hawks

and Boeing P-26s that had risen to intercept them, fifteen of the enemy aircraft (three probables) were shot down. All our aircraft returned safely.

The 13th Air Group continued to participate in attacks on Nanking and continued to achieve major battle results. In particular, ever since LT Mochifumi Nangō took over as division officer in place of LT Yamashita, who made an emergency landing in September and was taken prisoner of war, morale had taken a significant upward swing. During an air battle over Nanking on 2 December, six of our aircraft took on a horde of thirty enemy aircraft and after fierce battling shot down thirteen. (Data on the Chinese side admits that twelve interceptors were engaged and that ten of them were lost in action.) Presented with a citation for the unit, Nangō Fighter Squadron became widely known.

With the fall of Nanking, the base of the 13th Air Group was moved to the Daikōjō airfield in the suburbs of the city; the 13th continued to be active and effective in the attacks that were made on Nanchang and Hankow. At the same time, the morale of the enemy was not to be underestimated; the enemy concentrated on attacking the formation leader's aircraft. As a result, combined with the unfamiliarity with formation fighting on the part of the officers who succeeded LT Nangō, casualties did

Type 96 Carrier Fighter Model 1

About September 1937 on the Chinese mainland. The *T* was either black or white; the aircraft number was white.

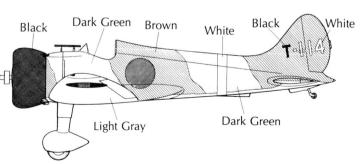

Black — Dark Green — Brown — White — Black — White

Light Gray — Dark Green

13th Air Group Type 96 carrier fighter, Model 1, at Kunda airfield, Shanghai, 1937. (Family of Isamu Mochizuki)

result. For example, LT Norito Ōbayashi and LT Shigeo Takuma were both killed in action within one month of assuming their commands.

As of 22 March 1938, the 13th Air Group was reorganized as a predominantly land attack unit; it was equipped with two units (allowance, fourteen aircraft) of land attack planes and one unit (allowance, twelve aircraft) of carrier fighters. The number of Type 96 carrier fighters being made available, however, was lessening. As a result, in the attacks on Hankow and Nanchang conducted between April and July, the unit's major role was transferred to the 12th Air Group Fighter Squadron. The 13th Air Group itself was withdrawn

to Shanghai. A few of the latter unit's aircraft were assigned to the 12th Air Group and participated jointly with them. No battle results worthy of note came about. As a result of the reorganization of 15 November 1938, the fighter squadron was eliminated and the 13th Air Group became a land attack force only (allowance, eighteen aircraft). In November 1940 the unit was disbanded.

Successive Commanding Officers:

July 1937–March 1938 CAPT Sadatoshi Senda

March 1938–December 1938 CAPT Kanae Kamisaka

Type 96 Carrier Fighter Model 2

The unit designation *4* was used from October 1937 through November 1940. Fuselage was silver or light gray all over. Later, camouflage colors of dark green and liver brown were used on the top and sides.

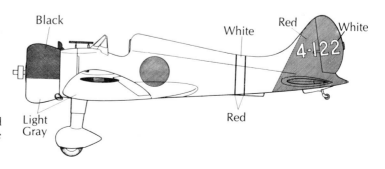

Black

White

Red

White

Light Gray

Red

4·122

December 1938–November 1939   CAPT
  Kikuji Okuda
November 1939–November 1940   CAPT
  Rinosuke Ichimaru

Successive Group Leaders:

July 1937–September 1938   LCDR Tsu-
  guo Ikegami
September 1939–December 1939   LCDR
  Chujirō Nakano
August 1938–November 1938 LCDR
  Shigehachirō Tokoro

TABLE 4. FORMATION OF THE 13TH AIR GROUP
(At the Attack on Nanchang, 25 February 1938)

	VICTORIES
1st Chūtai	
1st Shōtai	
LT Shigeo Taguma	Missing
PO3c Kiyonobu Suzuki	1
PO3c Shigetaka Ōmori	1 (1)★
3rd Shōtai	
PO1c Toshio Kuroiwa	2
PO2c Jirōkichi Kusunoki	3 (1)
Sea1c Tetsuzō Iwamoto	5 (1)
5th Shōtai	
PO1c Sada-aki Akamatsu	4
PO2c Tsuguo Matsuyama	
12th Air Group	
PO2c Fujikazu Koizumi	2
Sea1c Yukiharu Ozeki	3
2nd Chūtai	
2nd Shōtai	
LTJG Yoshio Yotsumoto	1
PO3c Kan-ichi Kashimura	2
Sea1c Kazuo Ochi	Missing
4th Shōtai	
PO1c Tomokichi Arai	2
PO3c Akira Kikuchi	1 (1)
Sea1c Momoto Matsumura	7 (3)
6th Shōtai	
PO1c Masao Naitō	1 (1)
PO3c Kinji Fujiwara	1

★ Parentheses indicate probables.

第 14 航 空 隊

14TH AIR GROUP FIGHTER SQUADRON

The 14th Air Group was organized as of 6 April 1938 and attached to the 5th Fleet. The following May, the unit moved to the just completed base on Santsao (a small island south of Macao) and was assigned operational duties in the South China area. Strength at the time of its organization was 1 unit of carrier fighters (twelve aircraft), 0.5 unit of carrier bombers (six aircraft), and 1.5 units of carrier attack planes (eighteen aircraft). During the fall of the same year, the 14th Air Group was assigned to patrol over anchorage and to direct land support operations in the Kwangtung operation. It did escort land attack forces targeting Kweilin and the bombing attack on Liuchow; however, there were no opportunities for aerial engagement.

With the reorganization of 15 December 1938, strength was increased to one unit of land attack planes (eighteen planes) and one unit of carrier attack planes (eighteen planes). Posted to the 3rd Combined Air Group, it continued to engage in operations in the South China area, using as its base Ishū-tō (near Canton), Santsao Island, and Haihow. As a result of reorganization in November 1939, the group's strength was changed to eighteen carrier fighters and nine carrier bombers. As a reaction to the army's Nanning operation late the same year, the Chinese air force had concentrated their strength in the Liuchow and Kweilin areas. In order to destroy such forces, the 14th Air Group, with the temporary augmentation of units from the *Akagi* and the 12th Air Group Fighter Squadron, conducted two attacks on those two areas.

In other words, at the end of December, thirteen aircraft of the 14th Air Group Fighter Squadron advanced from Haihow to the base at Nanning, which had just been captured. Combining its strength with the 12th Air Group Fighter Squadron under the command of LT Aioi, the forces attacked Liuchow on the 30th. Engaging in battle with the I-15 and I-16 aircraft that rose to intercept them, fourteen of the enemy aircraft were shot down. On 1 January 1940, fourteen aircraft of the 14th Air Group and twelve aircraft of the 12th, under the command of LT Igarashi, attacked Kweilin. Battle results attained were sixteen aircraft shot down and nine aircraft on the ground destroyed by bombing.

In May 1940, the Medium [Land] Attack Plane Unit of the 14th Air Group was temporarily transferred to Hankow for use in the attacks on Szechwan Province. Half a unit of Type 96 carrier fighters, under the command of LT Suhō, accompanied the unit and both served in the defense of the

Type 96 Carrier Fighter Model 4

The aircraft flown by LT Motonari Suhō during the Dai 101-gō operation, September 1940. Unit insignia number *9* was used from April 1938 through September 1941.

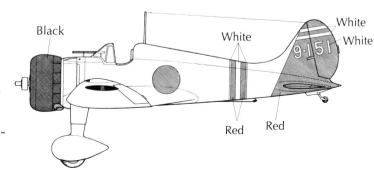

Black White White White Red Red

Type 96 carrier fighter Model 4 of the 14th Air Group. (Kiku-ichi Inano)

base. With the return to South China in September, the unit was supplied with nine of the new advanced Zero fighters.

At this time, because of the occupation of northern French Indochina, it had become possible to use the airfield at Hanoi.

On 14 July, the 14th Air Group Fighter Squadron, in conjunction with the land attack unit of the 15th Air Group, advanced to Hanoi to participate in the operation to cut off the supply line to the Chiang Kaishek forces. The same afternoon it was decided that the southwestern China base of Kunming would be attacked.

Formation consisted of seven Zero fighters, plus twenty-seven land attack planes commanded by LT Mitsugu Kofukuda. After flying above the clouds, the Kofukuda unit arrived two hours later over Kunming and engaged in air combat with a group of I-15, I-16, and Curtiss Hawks. Within a period of fifteen minutes, thirteen enemy aircraft were shot down and four aircraft on the ground destroyed. By evening, all our aircraft had returned safely to base, one plane at a time. They were greeted by a covering force of nine carrier bombers and nine Type 96 carrier fighters. Later, the carrier bombers of the 14th Air Group, the 15th Air Group, and the land attack planes of the Takao Air Group jointly bombed the Tien-Yueh railroad; they also attacked key points in Yunnan Province. In particular, on 12 December,

The 14th Air Group Fighter Squadron, January 1939. Center (seated): left, LT Hideki Shingō; right, LTJG Takumi Hoashi. (Hideki Shingō)

Type 96 Model 4 carrier fighters standing by at Nanning, end of December 1939. (Kiku-ichi Inano)

Type 96 Model 4 carrier fighter that took full advantage of its superior maneuverability. (Kiku-ichi Inano)

Zero fighter unit of the 14th Air Group that returned from an attack on Kunming, 7 October 1940. (Kiku-ichi Inano)

seven Zero fighters led by army reconnaissance aircraft flew the long distance of 340 miles to the Siangyun airfield and set on fire twenty-two aircraft on the ground by strafing.

In July 1941 with the occupation of the southern part of French Indochina, twelve carrier fighters and three land attack planes were sent to Saigon led by the command. At the same time, the main force of the 14th Air Group remained at Hanoi and was disbanded on 15 September 1941.

Successive Commanding Officers:

April 1938–December 1938 CAPT Kōki Abe

December 1938–November 1939 CAPT Hiroshi Higuchi

November 1939–May 1940 CAPT Tameteru Nomoto

May 1940–October 1940 CAPT Shigematsu Ichimura

October 1940–April 1941 CAPT Toshiyuki Yokoi

April 1941–September 1941 CAPT Kin Nakase

Successive Group Leaders:

December 1938–November 1939 LCDR Tadao Funaki

November 1939–May 1940 LCDR Chikamasa Igarashi

May 1940–November 1940 LCDR Asaichi Tamai

14th Air Group Zero fighter unit over South China, autumn 1940. (Motonari Suhō?)

第 15 航 空 隊

15TH AIR GROUP FIGHTER SQUADRON

The 15th Air Group was organized at Ōmura on 25 June 1938; on 10 July, the group advanced to the Anking base. At the time of its organization, the strength of the unit consisted of 1 unit of carrier fighters (twelve aircraft), 1 unit of carrier bombers (twelve aircraft), and 0.5 unit of carrier attack planes (six planes). The actual strength, however, was nine each Type 95 and Type 96 carrier fighters, eighteen carrier bombers, and nine carrier attack planes. Primary duties were to cooperate in the army's Hankow operation and in particular air defense in the areas along the Yangtze River.

Starting in May, two months before the establishment of the unit, carrier fighter and bomber units of the aircraft carrier *Sōryū* had been dispatched to Anking and had participated in operations there. More than half of such aircraft remained in place at Anking and formed the nucleus of the newly formed 15th Air Group. LT Nangō, group leader on the *Sōryū*, was one of the persons left; despite the physically unhealthy local conditions, he engaged in daily intercept work against ground attacks and SB bombers that came to attack vessels navigating the Yangtze River. Upon the establishment of the 15th Air Group, LT Nangō was transferred to the newly created unit as its group leader.

At the time, there were delays in the delivery of Type 96 carrier fighters and the unit was composed of a mixture of both Type 95 and Type 96 fighters. In the fall, finally, all fighter aircraft were replaced with Type 96 carrier fighters.

On 18 July, the newly organized 15th Air Group dispatched fourteen carrier bombers and five carrier attack planes under LCDR Matsumoto, escorted by six carrier fighters led by LT Nangō, to participate in the attack on Nanchang. The carrier fighter squadron, however, was unable to rendezvous with the carrier bomber squadron at the appointed place. Engaging in an air battle over Lake Piyang with an enemy fighter force of eleven aircraft, LT Nangō met a heroic death; he maneuvered his own aircraft into an enemy plane that he was attacking, and both aircraft crashed. At the same time, the carrier bomber unit under LTJG Ogawa pulled off the stunt of landing on the Nanchang airfield, setting enemy aircraft on the ground afire, and then taking off.

Later on, in September, the 15th Air Group was strengthened with an allowance of eighteen carrier fighters, eighteen carrier bombers, and nine carrier attack planes. The unit advanced to Kowkong (Chiuchiang) and participated in the attacks on Hankow. There were no large-scale air en-

Type 96 Model 2 Carrier Fighter

The aircraft used by LT Seiichi Maki during an attack on Nanchang, 17 July 1938. Unit insignia *10* was used from June through November 1938.

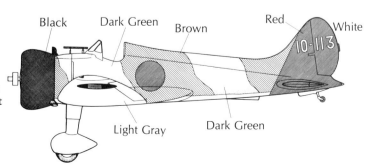

Black · Dark Green · Brown · Red · White · Light Gray · Dark Green

Type 96 Model 4 carrier fighters and Type 95 fighters of the 15th Air Group at Anking base, summer 1938. (Yasujirō Abe)

Type 96 Model 4 carrier fighters at their base. (Yasujirō Abe)

counters, however, and the 15th Air Group was disbanded with the reorganization of 1 December 1938.

Successive Commanding Officers:

June 1938–November 1938 CAPT Kazutari Kabase

Successive Group Leaders:

June 1938–July 1938 LT Mochifumi Nangō

Right, a Type 96 fighter that was shot down. (Yasujirō Abe)

千歳航空隊戦闘機隊

CHITOSE AIR GROUP FIGHTER SQUADRON

Organized initially as a land attack unit at Chitose on Hokkaidō on 1 October 1939, a fighter unit under the command of LCDR Kiyoji Sakakibara was later attached. The unit did not participate in any mainland operations but continued to undergo training. On 15 January 1941, it was posted to the 24th Air Flotilla of the 4th Fleet. From June to August, the unit trained on Saipan; it was next deployed to Micronesia on the eve of the outbreak of war between Japan and the United States. An advance party of the unit led by CDR Ryutarō Yamanaka, executive officer, and one month later the main unit under the commanding officer, CAPT Fujiro Ōhashi, proceeded to Roi. Later, toward the end of November, twelve from the total of thirty-six Type 96 carrier fighters (group leader LCDR Chikamasa Igarashi) were dispatched to the base at Taroa on the eastern edge of the Marshall Islands, along with one chūtai of Type 96 land attack planes. The unit under senior division officer LT Harutoshi Okamoto had been dispatched to Truk Island on board the *Goshū Maru,* but as of the date hostilities opened, not a single aircraft had been assigned to the unit.

On 8 December 1941, the entire land attack unit strength of the Chitose Air Group was assembled at Roi and used to attack Wake Island. Until the capture of the island on the 23rd by landing forces, bombing runs were made daily. Because of insufficient cruising range, however, Type 96 carrier fighters were unable to accompany the bomber force; they were used instead in shifts, for the air defense of Roi and Taroa. At the same time, the Okamoto unit, which had been given the responsibility of providing air defense for Truk, had received Type 96 carrier fighters on 7 December with the entry into port of the *Kamoi.* The aircraft were assembled, test flown, and started operating patrols by the 11th.

On 23 January the next year, 1942, at the time of the capture of Rabaul, executive officer Yamanaka took a flying boat to the island to encourage the army engineer troops on the scene. On the 15th, Yamanaka ordered the unit to advance to Rabaul, using the facilities of an aircraft carrier en route, in order to proceed with preparations for the reception of the fighter squadron. The majority of Chitose pilots, however, had not yet completed carrier landing training. As a result, *Shōkaku* and *Zuikaku* fighter pilots who had flown together with carrier attack plane pilots of the Chitose Air Group took over control of the Type 96 carrier fighters and flew them from Truk out to the carriers. Taking off from the carriers, which were north of Rabaul on the 26th, the next day, they were forced to return because of bad weather conditions. Including those who had no carrier landing experience, all aircraft did return safely to the ships. This was an unprecedented incident for the Japanese navy.

Model 21 Zero Fighter

Unit insignia *S* was used from November 1940 through October 1942.

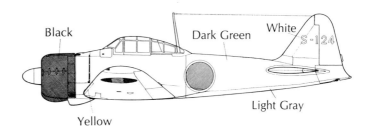

Black Dark Green White S-124

Light Gray

Yellow

Model 21 Zero fighter (S-171) flown by PO3c Hideo Watanabe. (Hideo Watanabe)

A Type 96 Model 4 carrier fighter belonging to the Chitose Air Group has up-ended on Roi Island, end of 1941. (Masami Ōtomo)

The next day, the 27th, the Okamoto unit arrived at Kavieng; the unit then proceeded to the eastern airfield at Rabaul on the 31st. Joining forces with the Kawai unit, which had previously arrived in the area, the two units were posted to the 4th Air Group, which had been newly organized as of 10 February. They were assigned air defense duties at Rabaul.

On the other hand, the main forces of the Chitose Air Group that had been left in the Marshalls (eighteen aircraft at Roi, fifteen aircraft at Taroa) received a baptism of

LCDR Chikamasa Igarashi, group leader, standing, fifth from left. (Akimasa Igarashi)

fire on 1 February from shellings and bombings by American task forces under the command of [Admirals] Halsey and Fletcher. Attack aircraft from the aircraft carrier *Enterprise* attacked Kwajalein, Roi, and Taroa while aircraft from the *Yorktown* attacked Jaluit, Makin, and Mili. Accompanying cruisers bombarded Wotje. In opposition to these attacks, the land attack unit commanded by LT Nakai conducted valiant counterattacks on the Halsey task force. In battles over Roi, a cumulative total of twelve Type 96 carrier fighters were able to shoot down five enemy aircraft; over Taroa, a cumulative total of twenty-two aircraft shot down twelve enemy aircraft. Although no damages whatsoever were suffered by our carrier fighter units, considerable damage was received by land-based installations and ships at anchor.

Later, in March 1942, the main strength of the Chitose Air Group Fighter Squadron in the Marshalls under executive officer Yamanaka advanced to Wake. Progressively replacing its equipment with Zero fighters, the unit concentrated on training activities and air defense. As of 1 April, the strength of the unit, in contrast with its allowance of thirty-six aircraft, consisted of only nine Zero fighters and nineteen Type 96 carrier fighters. These were divided into two elements, fourteen aircraft at Roi and

fourteen at Wake. With the increase in intensity of air battles in the southeastern area, experienced pilots were selected out and assigned to the newly created 1st and 2nd Air Groups. Next, at the end of May, together with fifteen Zeros of the 24th Air Flotilla dispatched to Rabaul, Chitose pilots were also detached to the Tainan Air Group. The Chitose Fighter Squadron served as a training unit for younger pilots.

In early June, on the eve of the Midway operation, the number of carrier fighters on Wake was fifteen; the unit was used to strengthen local air defenses. Under the command of LT Yoshitami Komatsu, who had just arrived in April and who served as the group leader, as well as under the command of Reserve LT Yoshio Murata, who served as the division officer, operations were carried out in shifts. At the end of October of the same year, the entire land attack force of the Chitose Air Group was ordered to proceed to Rabaul. Within the month, the majority of its strength had been wiped out and the unit was returned to the homeland for rebuilding. The fighter squadron itself remained on Wake, however, and was renamed Air Group 201 with the reorganization of 1 December. During this period, the war situation in the area was quite calm; there was not a single air battle.

第 201 航 空 隊（I）

AIR GROUP 201 (I)

Air Group 201 was established on the island of Roi in the Marshalls on 1 December 1942, organized primarily out of the Chitose Air Group and Air Group Fighter Squadron 752. On the same date, the new unit was posted to the 24th Air Flotilla (11th Air Fleet). CDR Ryutarō Yamanaka, former executive officer of the Chitose Air Group, was promoted to commander of the newly established unit. The location of the new unit remained the same: two buntai [divisions] under group leader Komatsu at Wake, a buntai at Roi under LTJG Heitarō Morita, and another buntai also located at Roi but under Reserve LT Yoshio Murata. There were almost no air battles; the unit was engaged in training and in air patrol activities.

In February 1943, Air Group 201 was ordered back to the homeland; leaving their aircraft in the local area, personnel had been transferred to Kisarazu by mid-March. Assigned to the Matsushima base, personnel were regrouped and engaged in training activities. Command passed to CDR Chujirō Nakano at that base, and LCDR Yoshitami Komatsu was promoted to air officer. As the latter's successor, LT Shirō Kawai arrived at the base.

Following the American attack on the island of Attu, the 201 was next scheduled for assignment to the northern area. On 18 May, the posting of the 24th Air Flotilla to the 12th Air Fleet was ordered. On 3 June, twelve Zero fighters advanced to Paramushiro in the northern Kuriles but returned to base in a short time. The unit was next ordered to the southeastern area; its primary strength of forty-five aircraft, together with twenty-seven carrier bombers of Air Group 552, was loaded on board the *Unyō,* a remodeled aircraft carrier. Loading material and supplies as well as ground personnel on the *Aikoku Maru,* the 201 left the port of Yokosuka on 6 July. On the 8th, eighteen Zero fighters under the CO, CDR Chujirō Nakano, himself a former fighter pilot, guided by four land attack planes, left Kisarazu. Proceeding via Iwo Jima, Saipan, and Truk, all aircraft arrived safely at Rabaul on the 12th, after a five thousand–kilometer trek. On the 15th, the aircraft loaded on board the *Unyō* and *Junyō* carrier aircraft arrived from Truk. As of that date, Air Group 201 was posted to the 21st Air Flotilla (11th Air Fleet). According to records held by CDR Nakano, the level of qualifications held by the fifty-two pilots as of the date that action commenced was distributed as follows: eight experienced, twenty medium-level, and twenty-four Class C.

On the 16th, the day after their arrival, preparations to receive the main force of the unit were made by dispatching air officer Komatsu and LTJG Nakajima to the advanced base at Buin, together with two Zero fighters. By the 17th, eight each aircraft were sent to the bases at Buin and Buka; by the 20th, the strength at Buin was

Model 22 Zero Fighter

Unit insignia *WI* was used during the period June 1943 through 1944.

Dark Green · White · W1-1 41 · Yellow · Light Gray

twenty-five aircraft. On the 21st, fifteen Zero fighters under the command of LTJG Tomoyoshi Arai conducted their first offensive, an air raid on Rendova; there were no air battles. On the next day, the 22nd, air combat took place with enemy dive-bombers and enemy fighters that had attacked the 201 unit while they were providing cover for the *Nisshin*. Initial battle results were eight enemy aircraft downed.

Starting at this time and for the next two months or more, desperate battles ensued. In addition to Air Group 201, about fifty fighters belonging to Air Group 204 or to the 2nd Carrier Division were deployed at the two airfields at Buin. Half of Air Group 201 was dispatched to Buin; the other half was held at Rabaul and used for air defense, convoy protection, and other purposes. In July and August, primary activity centered around raids on Rendova and Vella Lavella. By September, enemy pressure began to be felt—the majority of air battles were conducted in the vicinity of the Buin base during the interception of large combined formations of American fighters and bombers numbering over one hundred planes each.

During the intercept battle on 14th September against a cumulative force of more than two hundred American aircraft that came attacking in the morning in five waves, a cumulative total of 117 Zero fighters were used. Twenty-nine fighters, including P-38s, F4Us, and F4Fs, as well as four bombers were shot down; our side lost three aircraft. It is to be noted that CPO Okumura made three sorties during which he shot down nine small aircraft and one larger aircraft (jointly). By doing this, Okumura established the highest single day's kill among all [Imperial] Navy pilots during the entire course of the Pacific War.

Again, on the eve of the American forces landing at Finschhafen (New Guinea) on 22 September, twelve Zero fighters under the command of LT Kawai moved to Rabaul and engaged in battle an enemy ship convoy off Cape Cretin. Suddenly attacked by a large number of enemy fighter aircraft, experienced personnel such as CPO Okumura and WO Hongō as well as four aircraft were lost in action.

Once the month of October was entered, American air attacks on Buin increased even more than before. Fighter units at the Buin base suffered heavy attrition; the number of pilots who fell because of exhaustion and illness because of the poor weather conditions in this equatorial area also increased. In particular, once army units on the island of Kolombangara had withdrawn, advance intelligence was no longer available to our side. The only reliable source of intelligence became the twenty-power telescopes used by watchers in the command post. It became necessary to deploy aircraft aloft to keep watch in order to avoid surprise attacks on the base.

Following the withdrawal of Air Group 204 on 8 October and that of the 26th Air Flotilla command on the 11th to Rabaul, Air Group 201 was left as the only air defense unit in the Buin area. As a result of an enemy air attack on the 22nd, some thirty large holes were created on the runway by bombs. In addition to three fighters that rose to intercept the enemy and did not return, damages consisted of three aircraft that made forced landings and eight aircraft that were set on fire. The nine Zero fighters that remained were transferred to Buka; ground personnel were evacuated both by land and sea. About the same time, both

Model 52 Zero Fighter
Truk, 1944

Black

Dark Green

White

01-114

Yellow

Light Gray

Model 21 fighters in formation, August 1943. (Nearest aircraft is the W-111.) (Masami Ōtomo)

bases located on Ballale Island and at Buka became unusable because of bomb damage.

Under the circumstances, the 201 was withdrawn to Rabaul by the end of October; there they were resupplied with material and personnel from the homeland. Under the underway command of the only division officer left alive, LTJG Yoshio Ōba (who himself died in action later, on 23 December), the 201 continued to engage in attacks on Torokina and Cape Marcus, in intercept operations over Rabaul, and other action until its withdrawal to Saipan in early January of the following year [1944]. During the half year starting July 1943, the number of enemy aircraft shot down by Air Group 201 totaled approximately 450.

On 3 January [1944], Air Group 201 was ordered to withdraw to Saipan. Since their aircraft had been left at Rabaul at one point, the 201 was a unit consisting of thirty pilots only. Commanding officer Nakano returned to the homeland to receive equipment and supplies. On 11 February, he left Yokosuka with twenty-three Zero fighters and advanced to Saipan via Iwo Jima.

A group of eight fighters of the Nakano unit, led by WO Masao Taniguchi, moved to Truk in order to serve as an advance party for Rabaul. All the aircraft were lost, however, as a result of the major air raid on Truk on the 17th. The next morning, the 18th, twenty aircraft under the command of LT Kawai moved to Truk to relieve the local unit, leaving behind four aircraft for rescue purposes. However, this was after the enemy task force had left the scene. All four of the aircraft left behind on Saipan were also destroyed as the result of an air attack conducted by the enemy on the 23rd. The Kawai unit again returned to Saipan on the 28th.

Later, from 14 through 16 March, Air Group 201 (Fighter Hikōtai 305) was transferred to the base on Peleliu, via Guam. On the 30th, a group of American carrier fighters attacked, and twenty aircraft rose to intercept them. Because it was a surprise attack, however, control of the air was in the hands of the enemy. Despite the fact that seventeen enemy aircraft were shot down, our side also suffered damages: nine aircraft failed to return, nine aircraft were

Air Group 201 at Rabaul, November 1943. Front row: fifth from left, Hiroshi Shibagaki. Second row from front (from the left): second person, WO Tetsuzō Iwamoto; fifth, CDR Chujirō Nakano (commanding officer); sixth, group leader LT Shirō Kawai; and end of line (right), WO Teruo Sugiyama. Third row: second person from left, PO2c Hiroshi Okano; and end of line (right), PO1c Masami Shiga. Fourth row: fifth person from the right, CPO Shigeru Takahashi. (Masami Ōtomo)

damaged severely, and two aircraft made crash landings. Commanding officer Nakano, accompanied by a few survivors, withdrew to Davao during April and May; he then busied himself in rebuilding the unit.

Successive Commanding Officers:

November 1939–July 1940   CAPT Kōzō Matsuo

July 1940–September 1941   CAPT Kaoru Umetani

September 1941–December 1942   CAPT Fujiro Ōhashi

December 1942–March 1943   CDR Ryutarō Yamanaka

March 1943–July 1944   CDR Chujiro Nakano

July 1944–November 1944   CAPT Sakae Yamamoto

November 1944–January 1945   CDR Asa-ichi Tamai

January 1945–March 1945   CDR Zen-ichi Nakamura

March 1945–   None

Successive Group Leaders:

November 1939–September 1941   LCDR Kiyoji Sakakibara

September 1941–April 1942   LCDR Chikamasa Igarashi

April 1942–May 1943   LT Yoshitami Komatsu

May 1943–March 1944   LT Shirō Kawai

第 201 航 空 隊（Ⅱ）

AIR GROUP 201 (II)

With the reorganization of 4 March 1944, Air Group 201 was restructured into two units, Fighter Hikōtai 305 (commander, LT Kawai) and Fighter Hikōtai 306 (commander, LT Torajirō Haruta); each unit had an allowance of forty-eight aircraft. An air group at the time under its commanding officer, Nakano, which was active in operations in the Micronesia area, was renamed, as is, Fighter Hikōtai 305 but had been destroyed on the island of Peleliu. As noted previously, remnants had retreated to Davao in the Philippines in April and May and were in the process of reconstructing their unit. On the other hand, ever since its formation, Fighter Hikōtai 306 had been undergoing training at Kisarazu. From mid-April through May the unit advanced successively to bases at Cebu and then Davao. By mid-May the entire strength of thirty-two aircraft was assembled at Cebu and had started training. Toward the end of May, the unit started to operate in direct support of the campaign to eradicate guerillas in the mountains. After the order was issued for the "A"-gō Operation in mid-June, eleven Zero fighters advanced to Yap via Peleliu. A portion of the unit went as far as Guam; after engaging in attacks on vessels off Saipan, it then returned to Cebu in July. By mid-July, one buntai formed out of a mixture of transferees from the 263 and 343 units, which had been disbanded as a result of the reorganization of 10 July, had advanced to Yap under the command of LT Naoshi Kanno. Between the 16th and the 23rd, B-24s made almost daily attacks; valiant intercept battles were conducted including the use of ramming tactics. Results attained were seventeen (nine probables) enemy aircraft shot down and forty-six enemy aircraft destroyed. The unit received a commendation from the commander of the

1st Air Fleet. Our side also suffered casualties, however: five personnel were lost, including the two who rammed enemy planes.

Next, after the failure of the "A"-gō [Marianas] Operation, navy central headquarters estimated that the center of the next phase of the war would move towards the southern part of the Philippines. The 1st Air Fleet, destroyed as a result of banzai ground attacks in the Marianas, was reconstituted and made responsible for air defense in the entire Philippines area. The traditional small air group structure was abandoned in favor of a larger organization. The new organization consisted of fighters that formed Air Group 201, attack aircraft that formed the 761, and reconnaissance and night fighters that formed the 153 (allowance 192 aircraft). As a result, the newly formed Air Group 201 was established from the following four hikōtais: the 305 (commander, LT Masanobu Ibusuki); the 306 (commander, LT Hiroshi Mori-i; in September, LT Kanno); the 301 (commander, LT Usaburō Suzuki); and the 311 Fighter Hikōtai (commander, LT Takeo Yokoyama). Orders were issued to CAPT Sakae Yamamoto as the new commanding officer, CDR Asa-ichi Tamai as the executive officer, and LCDR Tadashi Nakajima as the air officer.

In the early part of August, around the time that ADM Teraoka, the new commanding officer of the 1st Air Fleet, arrived, the 201 assumed duties at Davao. At that time, B-24s were beginning to raid Davao. When September came around, there were repeated raids by combined fighter and bomber units using B-24s and P-38s. It was becoming difficult to maintain an air group in the area. In an attempt to preserve their strength while being rein-

LT Usaburō Suzuki, commander of Fighter Hikōtai 301, Air Group 201 (II). (Ikuhiko Hata)

forced by replacement aircraft from the mainland as well as to conduct training exercises, the main strength of Air Group 201 was dispersed. One part was sent to Legaspi, Mactan Island (opposite Cebu), and another to Nichols. As of 1 September, the number of Zero fighters available reached about 210 aircraft (130 operable). The attack aircraft strength, however, was insufficient. Since there was little hope for success in opposing the attacking American task force, it was decided to employ "skip bombing" (chōhi bakugeki) tactics using bomb-equipped Zero fighters. This tactic called for flying low over the ocean surface, at about ten meters' elevation and at the high rate of speed of 450 kilometers per hour. Approaching to within two hundred to three hundred meters of the target vessel, the plane would drop 250-kg bombs, much like a torpedo attack. The bomb would bounce along on the water's surface and make a direct hit on the side of the

target vessel. Since this was a very dangerous method of attack, little hope was held for the safe return of personnel. Without exception, however, all personnel assigned to Air Group 201 volunteered for such duty. Training started in the latter part of August in the Bohol Strait off Cebu, under the guidance of carrier bomber instructors from the Yokosuka Air Group. At the point that basic training had just been completed, severe damages were received from enemy bombings of Cebu. As a result, there was never a chance to use the new tactic. Following the American carrier air attack on Davao on 9 September, the approximately 150 aircraft on Cebu took refuge at Clark. The next day, on the 10th, word was received that a landing might be made at Davao and the entire unit returned to Cebu. It was later ascertained, however, that the report of a landing was in error. On the 11th, forty aircraft were dispersed to Nichols and twenty aircraft to Mactan.

On the morning of the 12th, approximately one hundred additional aircraft were overcrowding the Cebu area; wave after wave of American carrier aircraft conducted their attacks at that time. Forty-one fighters of Air Group 201 were able to take off despite the disadvantageous circumstances to intercept the enemy; they shot down twenty-three aircraft. Our side also suffered immense damages: twenty-five aircraft, starting with LT Mori-i's plane, either destroyed themselves or failed to return, and fourteen other aircraft made forced landings. In addition, twenty-five aircraft on the ground were set on fire and thirty additional aircraft received either medium or minor damage. Even on the following day, the 13th, about three hundred enemy aircraft raided Cebu and Legaspi; the recently resurrected Air Group 201 suffered heavy damages. Carrying on the momentum, American carrier aircraft raided the Manila area on the 21st and the 22nd. The local Air Group 201 used forty-two aircraft for interception and was able to shoot down twenty-seven of the enemy aircraft. Our side also lost twenty aircraft

Departure of the Kamikaze attack unit Shikishima-tai from the Mabalacat airfield, 25 October 1944. In the foreground with a cane is CAPT Sakae Yamamoto (commanding Air Group 201). (Maru)

in air combat and ten on the ground. The next morning, the 22nd, a volunteer attack force of fifteen Zero fighters outfitted with bombs, accompanied by ten Suisei carrier bombers, attacked an American carrier force east of Lamon Bay. Five bombs found their targets; three strafing runs were made on the enemy carriers, after which the unit returned. Also on the 15th, a Zero fighter unit (twenty-five aircraft) commanded by LT Ibusuki attacked an American task force in the seas east of Luzon and carried out a daring strafing attack.

As can be seen, morale in Air Group 201 was high, but they were unable to stem the overwhelmingly large numbers of American forces. Attrition continued upon attrition; a desperate atmosphere began to prevail because normal attacking techniques were felt to be of no avail. Coincidentally, voices were heard calling for a special attack force. It just so happened that, on 19 October, the admiral in charge of the 1st Air Fleet had been relieved. Also, VADM Takijirō Ōnishi, proponent of special attack forces, had arrived at Clark and ordered executive officer Tamai of Air Group 201 to form a kamikaze special attack force unit. The same evening, twenty-four volunteers under the command of LT Yukio Seki were selected.

Starting the next day, the 20th, the Seki unit was deployed at the two bases located at Mabalacat and Cebu. Each of the units sought out elements of the American task force, but poor weather prevented any encounter with the enemy. The first casualty of a special attack force unit was Reserve LTJG Kōfu Kunō of Fighter Hikōtai 301, the Yamato-tai ("Spirit of Japan") unit, which had departed from Cebu on the 21st and failed to return. The first successful unit was the Shikishima-tai (five aircraft under the command of LT Seki) on the 25th. WO Nishizawa, commanding the direct support unit, verified battle results: the sinking of one aircraft carrier (the *Saint Lo*), a major fire aboard another (the *Kitkun Bay*), and the sinking of one cruiser. Because of their success, the special attack force technique became the rule from then on. Surviving pilots of Air Group 201 were withdrawn to Taiwan by January of the following year. Until they holed up in the mountains west of Clark, all members of Air Group 201 served in special attack operations. More than two hundred were to lose their lives in this heroic fashion.

第252航空隊 (旧元山航空隊戦闘機隊) (Ⅰ)

AIR GROUP 252 (I)
(FORMERLY GENZAN AIR GROUP FIGHTER SQUADRON)

The Genzan Air Group was formed 15 November 1940 at Genzan (Wonsan) on the east coast of Korea; it was a mixed unit consisting of land attack planes and carrier fighters.

Allowance was twenty-seven operational and nine spare land attack planes, plus eighteen operational and six spare carrier fighters (Type 96). The group was attached to the 2nd Combined Air Group; on 15 January 1941, it was transferred to the 22nd Air Flotilla, 11th Air Fleet. Later, on 10 April, the group was transferred to the China Area Fleet; by the end of the month, it and Mihoro Air Group had advanced to the Hankow base (later Siaokan). The land attack squadron was assigned to strategic bombings in Szechwan Province, while the carrier fighter squadron was assigned to air patrol over the base and for direct support of ground forces. LCDR Kiyoto Hanamoto was group leader of the carrier fighter squadron, and LT Takeo Kurosawa served as division officer. Not a single opportunity for air combat presented itself.

In September, the Genzan Air Group was ordered back to its base and continued training activities at Wonsan. The carrier fighter squadron, however, was exempted from this; at one point, the Genzan was composed solely of land attack planes. Next, at the end of October, the Genzan Air Group advanced to Takao; by 1 December it had advanced as far as Saigon. With the outbreak of the Pacific War, the group next participated in the sea battles off the Malay Peninsula, bombings of Singapore, and air battles in the Dutch East Indies. At the end of February the group was moved to Bangkok. During March and April, it participated in patrol operations over the Indian Ocean as well as in the Akyab (Sittwe) [Burma] operation. On 1 May, the unit advanced to Rabaul, via Taiwan. During the same period, in April the Genzan Air Group again had a carrier fighter unit attached (allowance of thirty-six aircraft, unit head LT Tadashi Kaneko, and in May, LT Hideki Shingō). Pilots were recruited from experienced personnel who had fought with the Tainan Air Group and the 3rd Air Group in southern area operations and had returned from the front; training exercises started at the Kisarazu Base in May. On the other hand, the land attack plane unit of the Genzan, after having advanced to Rabaul and participated in the Battle of the Coral Sea and other opera-

Model 21 Zero Fighter
During the Genzan Air Group days. Unit insignia G was used during November 1940 through October 1942.

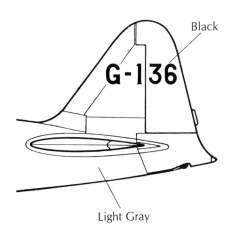

Black

G-136

Light Gray

Air Group 252, Roi Island, July 1943. Second row, from the left: WO Toshiyuki Sueda, LTJG Masao Kuramoto, LTJG Tsutomu Kawai, LT Yūzō Tsukamoto, CAPT Yoshitane Yanagimura (commanding officer), LCDR Tadao Funaki, skip one, and WO Shizuo Kojima. Third row, from the right: sixth person, CPO Isamu Miyazaki. Last row, from the left: sixth person, CPO Bunkichi Nakajima. (Yūzō Tsukamoto)

tions, was transferred to the homeland. Training exercises started at Misawa base on 1 July.

On 20 September at the Tateyama base, the Genzan Air Group Fighter Squadron became an independent unit and was renamed the Air Group 252. At the same time it was posted to the 22nd Air Flotilla.

CAPT Yoshitane Yanagisawa was ordered to be the commander; LCDR Tadao Funaki, the air officer; and LT Masaji Suganami, the group leader. It became a major fighter unit with an allowance of sixty carrier fighters. On 30 October, the main force of Air Group 252 was placed on board the aircraft carrier *Taiyō* and departed Kisarazu; by 9 November, they had advanced to Rabaul. Over the period of almost five months until February or March of the following year, when the unit transferred to Micronesia, it participated in the fierce aerial battles going on in the southeast area at the time. The baptism of fire was during an attack on Guadalcanal on the 11th; eleven Zero fighters under the command of LT Shigehisa Yamamoto carried out the attack in coordination with Air Group 253 and Air Group 582. With only

Model 21 Zero Fighter

Unit insignia *Y2* was used from June 1943 through February 1944.

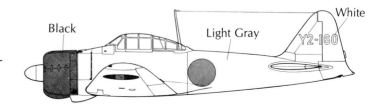

Black · Light Gray · White · Y2-160

one kill to their credit, all aircraft returned safely. Next, twelve aircraft led by LT Suganami operated in support of daylight torpedo attacks being carried out by the land attack plane unit. Battle results attained by participating in the attacks on vessels off Guadalcanal were eight enemy aircraft shot down. On the following day, the 13th, the battleship *Hiei,* damaged by the previous day's sea battle, was protected by a unit of six Zero fighters. Unfortunately, on the way back inclement weather forced all aircraft to ditch in Rekata Bay, LT Yamamoto suffered severe injuries and had to be sent home.

At one of the crucial moments in the battle for Guadalcanal, November 12 through 14, the navy mustered its entire air and surface strength in support of the transport of the 38th Division to Guadalcanal. Zero fighter units participated daily, in shifts, in air cover operations over the convoy. At the same time, we also made considerable sacrifices. LT Suganami, group leader of Air Group 252, was among those so sacrificed. While the unit shot down fourteen enemy aircraft over the convoy during the 14th, LT Suganami was seen to depart on his own way back from the rendezvous point but was never seen again.

Later, Air Group 252 fought from bases at Rabaul, Ballale, Lae, and Munda. The unit also participated in the air defense of various bases in the Solomon Islands and in New Guinea. Battle results were 145 enemy aircraft (thirty-six probables) shot down for a loss on our side of sixteen pilots.

On 1 February 1943, Air Group 252 was ordered to proceed to the air defense of the Micronesia area, relieving Air Group 201. Over a period of three months, successive moves were made as follows. Headquarters were established at Roi and two buntai stationed at Wake (commanding, LT Yūzō Tsukamoto, later replaced by LT Suhō); one buntai each was established at Taroa (Maloelap Atoll, commanding, LT Suhō, later LT Tsukamoto) and Nauru (commanding, Reserve LT Kōichi Yoshida). In addition to patrol duties, training exercises were also conducted. Until around fall of the same year, there were very few enemy attacks—no more than two or three intercepts of B-24s.

In September, however, there were signs that a central Pacific advance by the American forces would commence. On the 19th, an American Task Force attacked the Gilbert Islands. As a result, twelve Zero fighters under the command of LT Tsukamoto advanced to Tarawa on the same day to intercept incoming B-24 aircraft. On the 24th, the unit returned to Taroa. On 6 October, Wake Island was attacked by about one hundred American carrier fighters. The local Zero fighter unit was able to muster a total of twenty-six aircraft for intercept work and shot down fourteen aircraft. Our side also suffered the loss of sixteen experienced pilots serving on board sixteen aircraft, starting with the loss of WO Sueda. After LT Tsukamoto received news of the attack on Wake he headed there, braving a six-hundred-mile flight over water leading six Zero fighters, reinforced by seven land attack planes. Just thirty miles short of the target, however, a surprise attack of F6Fs coming through the clouds overhead forcibly dispersed the unit. Only three aircraft reached their destination, a severely potholed Wake Island. Almost all aircraft on the ground had been severely damaged or destroyed by fire. A few days later, surviving pilots retreated to Roi, by airlift.

Anticipating that the next target for the enemy would be the Gilberts, Air Group 252 planned to advance to Tarawa. Before that happened, however, American forces landed on the island on 21 November. Following four days of fierce battles, our outnumbered Tarawa and Makin garrison units all suffered tragic, heroic deaths. At the time, Air Group 252 had dispersed sixteen aircraft to Roi, eighteen to Taroa, and twelve to Nauru. On the 24th, LT Suhō led nineteen Zeros, each equipped with two 60-kg bombs and left Taroa with the intention of engaging in low-level strafing and bombing attacks on the island of Makin. They were met by a force of thirty F6Fs, however, and engaged in fierce air combat with them, shooting down ten (five probables) enemy aircraft. Our side also lost nine aircraft. The next day, the 25th, twenty-four aircraft under the command of LTJG Sumio Fukuda sortied for an attack on Makin. Later, this unit was again intercepted by a group of F6Fs and lost six aircraft.

Later, Air Group 252 marshaled its entire strength of about thirty aircraft on Taroa. For about one month starting in late December, it conducted intercept operations under the command of LTJG Fukuda against the frequent raids conducted by B-24s. Although able to shoot down about fifty enemy aircraft using the technique of continuous direct overhead formation air attacks [head-on attacks] (Renzoku chokujō kōgeki-hō), our side continued to suffer air and ground losses. In particular, damage to air base facilities was extensive. With the intercept battle of 30 January 1944 as the last engagement, preparations for fighting ground battles were begun in anticipation of enemy landing operations. The 120 personnel that had been isolated on Wotje, Taroa, and Braun [Eniwetok] were evacuated to Truk on the night of 5 February, using a total of eight flying boats and land attack planes. Survivors of Air Group 252 returned to the homeland.

第252航空隊 (Ⅱ)

AIR GROUP 252 (II)

As has been noted, Air Group 252 was destroyed during air battles over the Marshall Islands. Immediate measures were taken, however, to reconstitute the group; training began at the Tateyama base 20 February 1944. Also at that time, the unit was integrated into the 27th Air Flotilla (12th Air Fleet). Former air officer CDR Funaki was promoted to commanding officer; aircraft allowance was forty-eight. Starting the 1st of April, with air and ground units separated, Fighter Hikōtai 302 (commanding, LT Nobuo Awa) was attached to the 252. At the end of March, the Air Group 252 training base was moved from Tateyama to Misawa. Operational aircraft in use as of early May numbered fifty-five Zero fighters. With the issuance of orders for the "A"-gō [Marianas] operation in June, the Hachiman Unit was organized on the 15th, constituted primarily from the Yokosuka Air Group. Air Group 252 was posted therein. On the 21st, twenty-three Zero fighters, and on the 25th, another sixteen aircraft advanced to Iwo Jima.

On the 24th, American carrier fighters attacked Iwo Jima in great force; the locally stationed Air Group 252 used its entire resources in intercept work. Nineteen enemy aircraft were downed; our side also lost ten aircraft, including that flown by group leader Awa. Enemy attacks occurred on the 3rd and 4th of July; though thirteen enemy aircraft were shot down, our side also lost

fourteen aircraft. In such fashion the air battles over Iwo Jima resulted in a one-sided defeat for Japan. Later, the main strength of Air Group 252 withdrew to the Tateyama base; at the same time, a number of aircraft, in relays, remained on Iwo Jima until November. They were involved in intercepting attacking B-24s. LT Hidehiro Nakama (Fighter Hikōtai 317 division officer) participated in nineteen interception battles from the time of his arrival at the end of September, shot down two aircraft, and damaged three others. On the 21st, LT Nakama rammed into an enemy aircraft and was killed. He was honored with a special two-rank promotion as well as mention in an All Units Bulletin.

With the B-29s based in the Marianas beginning to make raids on the homeland, a one-way attack operation, using Iwo Jima as a staging point, was planned on the Saipan airfield. On 27 November, eleven bomb-equipped Zero fighters under the command of LTJG Kenji Ōmura of Fighter Hikōtai 317, called the Mitate-tai ("Imperial Shield Unit"), raided Saipan; none of the aircraft returned. As a result of the reorganization on 10 July, Air Group 252 was reconstituted into four hikōtais as follows: 302 (commander, LT Masao Iizuka), 315 (commander, LT Masumi Setō), 316 (commander, LT Torajirō Haruta), and 317 (commander, LT Kazumasa Mitsumori). Each unit had an allowance of forty-eight

Model 52 Zero Fighter

This aircraft belonged to Fighter Hikōtai 316 and was flown by CPO Nario Taguchi on 3 May 1945 when B-29s were intercepted over Kokubu base. Unit insignia used during 1944–45. Fuselage numbers of the 316 were *01–99*.

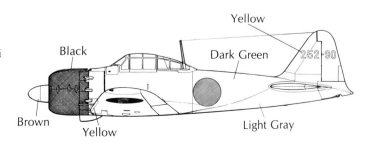

Yellow

Black

Dark Green

252-90

Brown

Yellow

Light Gray

Fighter Hikōtai 316, Air Group 252, right before sortie for Okinawa, Spring 1945. Front row center (seated) from the left: LTJG Yatarō Hayashi, LT Yasujirō Abe (group leader), and LTJG Susumu Kawasaki. Third row, from the right: third person, CPO Shigeru Takahashi. (Family of Hachitarō Hayashi)

aircraft. At the same time, the 252 was placed under the direct command of the 3rd Air Fleet. Training bases were moved to Mobara (Fighter Hikōtai 316) and to Tateyama (Fighter Hikōtai 315 and 317), and training continued. With the activation of the Shō-gō [Leyte] operation in October, however, the main force of Air Group 252, led by senior group leader LCDR Minoru Kobayashi of Fighter Hikōtai 317, ad-

vanced to Clark Field in the Philippines on the 22nd, proceeding via Okinawa and Taiwan. During the general offensive conducted on 24 October, 126 carrier fighters and 63 carrier attack planes, including 26 aircraft of Air Group 252, participated there, all under the command of LCDR Kobayashi. Before reaching the enemy task force, however, a group of F6Fs under the command of CDR [David] McCampbell

Model 52 Zero Fighter

Belonging to Fighter Hikōtai 311. Fuselage numbers used were *101–99*.

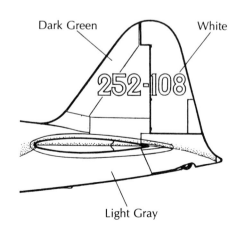

Model 52 Type C Zero fighter taking off. (Masami Ōtomo)

made a surprise attack on them and inflicted severe damage. A total of sixty-seven aircraft failed to return; there were no noteworthy battle results. Air Group 252 lost eleven aircraft, including the aircraft flown by the formation leader, Kobayashi.

Later, 252 participated in the Leyte operation and was active in searching and attacking enemy task forces as well as in intercept work over bases. By mid-November, three unit heads (Kobayashi, Iizuka, and Haruta) had been killed in action. Those pilots who did survive either joined suicide units, transferred to other units, or returned home to help in the reconstitution of units.

Around February 1945, Air Group 252 established its headquarters at Mobara. The various air groups, each with an allowance of forty-eight Zero fighters, were dispersed to the two bases at Mobara and Tateyama to undergo further training: Fighter Hikōtai 304 (commander, LCDR Hachirō Yanagisawa), 308 (commander, LT Kakichi Hirata; in March transferred to Air Group 601), 311 (commander, LT Kōsuke Tabuchi), 313 (commander, LT Yasuo Masuyama), and 316 (commander, LT Yasujirō Abe).

On 16 February, the occasion of the first

American carrier air attack [against Japan], both Fighter Hikōtai 308 and 311 rose up to intercept them over the Bōsō Peninsula. With a cumulative total of forty-five aircraft, the two units battled with thirty F6Fs and achieved battle results of twenty-four aircraft (ten probables). At the same time, our side lost nine aircraft. Although raids on the next day, the 17th, and again on the 25th were intercepted, considerable damage was also inflicted on our side. In this fashion, the aircraft still available to Air Group 252 had diminished to thirty-nine aircraft (twenty-three operable) as of the 25th.

At the end of March, as American attacks on Okinawa threatened, Air Group 252 dispatched a total of 144 Zero fighters to the Kokubu base in southern Kyūshū. These were planes of Fighter Hikōtai 304, 313, and 316, as well as the 3rd Attack Hikōtai (*Suisei* carrier bombers). In addition, about one-half of the forty-eight carrier bombers were also dispatched. The units were placed under the command of Air Group 601.

On 3 April, two aircraft constituting the first wave of special attack forces (bomb-equipped Zero fighters) of the 252 unit (which included the Fighter Hikōtai 304

Air Group 252 Zero fighters at Misawa Base, May 1944. Left, Model 52s; right, Model 21s. (Kazuo Tsunoda)

and 313) and referred to as Kamikaze Special Attack Unit No. 3, the Mitate-tai, commanded by LT Minoru Honda, himself 3rd attack unit division officer, vigorously attacked American vessels off Okinawa. This was the first of thirty-nine persons who would die the death of heroes by the 23rd.

During the Kikusui No. 3 operation conducted on 16 April, LCDR Yanagisawa, newly arrived in the area, led a group of twelve Zero fighters of Air Group 252 and sortied forth in an attempt to sweep the skies in the southwestern islands front area. Engaging in battle with F6Fs over Amami Ōshima, our side shot down thirteen enemy aircraft also lost five aircraft. On the next day, the 17th, ten aircraft in coordination with Air Group 601 formed an air control unit and left on a second attack to clear the skies. This time, three aircraft, including that flown by LCDR Yanagisawa, failed to return. In such fashion, during the period between 1 and 17 April, Air Group 252 lost fifteen Zero fighters and five Suisei carrier bombers. The unit was then withdrawn to the Kantō Plains area. Later, the Air Group 252 did assign Fighter Hikōtai 304 (commander, LCDR Saneyasu Hidaka) to Wonsan and Fighter Hikōtai 316 to Mobara in an attempt to intercept B-29s and

P-51s. In general, however, aircraft were husbanded, waiting for the final battle on the homeland, and greeted the end of hostilities in that condition.

Successive Commanding Officers:

November 1940–October 1941 CAPT Ishinosuke Izawa
October 1941–September 1942 CAPT Takanari Maeda
September 1942–February 1944 CAPT Yoshitane Yanagimura
February 1944–July 1944 CDR Tadao Funaki
July 1944–November 1944 CAPT Tatsuji Fujimatsu
November 1944–June 1945 CAPT Masahisa Saitō
June 1945– CDR Kiyoji Sakakibara

Successive Group Leaders:

November 1940–August 1941 LCDR Kiyoto Hanamoto
April 1942–May 1942 LT Tadashi Kaneko
May 1942–July 1942 LT Hideki Shingō
July 1942–December 1942 LT Masaji Suganami
December 1942–March 1944 LT Motonari Suhō

第 1 航空隊戦闘機隊

1ST AIR GROUP FIGHTER SQUADRON

The 1st Air Group was organized at Kanoya on 10 April 1941 and then immediately posted to the 21st Air Flotilla, 11th Air Fleet. CAPT Keikichi Araki was the commanding officer and LCDR Takeo Shibata served as air officer. Allowance was thirty-six land attack planes and twenty-four carrier fighters. Type 96 fighters were assigned to the group; LT Tamotsu Yokoyama was ordered in to serve as group leader.

Immediately after the establishment of the 1st Air Group, the land attack unit was moved to the South Sea Islands area and started torpedo attack exercises in May. In July, the unit advanced to Hankow and repeatedly attacked Szechwan Province. In September, the unit returned to its base. The carrier fighter squadron was also used in air patrols over hot and humid Hankow, between 29 July and 31 August. In a reorganization that anticipated the outbreak of the Pacific War in September, the 1st Air Group Fighter Squadron was abolished. The majority of its pilots were absorbed into the newly created 3rd Air Group, or into the Tainan Air Group. The land attack unit moved to Taiwan and participated in Philippines and Dutch East Indies operations.

Following the finish of the attack on Kupang, the unit assembled at Ambon in February. On the 20th, the 4th Air Group land attack unit suffered heavy losses attacking an enemy carrier task force off Rabaul. It was decided that the unit would be relieved and transferred to the southeast area of operations. The 1st Air Group then moved to Rabaul and, starting the end of February, engaged in local patrol activities as well as in attacks on Port Moresby. Next, the 1st Air Group's land attack unit advanced to the Marshalls as of the end of March. On 10 April, the majority of its forces were transferred to Taroa and engaged in patrol activities. With the reorganization of 1 April, the 1st Air Group was transferred to the 24th Air Flotilla; at the same time it was decided that the attached carrier fighter squadron would be reactivated. Allowance was twenty-seven operational and nine reserve aircraft; however, actual operable aircraft strength as of that date consisted of thirteen Type 96 carrier fighters. One buntai of pilots in the unit was composed of transferees from the Chitose Air Group Fighter Squadron. Since the local area was quiet, with no combat going on other than air patrol activities using Type 96 carrier fighters, activities were centered around training exercises. On the other hand, experienced personnel were selected out and dispatched to the southeast area, where fierce battles were ongoing. For example,

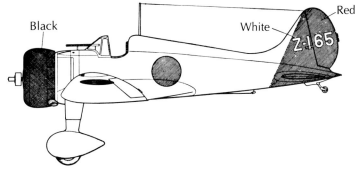

Type 96 Model 4 Carrier Fighter

Aircraft flown by PO1c Kuniyoshi Tanaka, around July 1941. The entire fuselage was either silver or light gray. Unit insignia Z was used April 1941 through July 1942.

Black

White

Red

Z-165

towards the end of May, fifteen Zero fighters (mixed with aircraft from the Chitose Air Group), under the command of LT Jōji Yamashita, advanced to Rabaul and participated in air battles over eastern New Guinea and the Solomon Islands. Following the arrival of this initial increment, pilots who had finished their training at Taroa were successively dispatched to Rabaul. During this same period in mid-August, an American raiding force transported by submarines made a surprise landing on the island of Makin and, after some combat, left the island. The 1st Air Group Fighter Squadron, led by LTJG Heitarō Morita, together with nine carrier fighters of the Chitose Air Group (commander, LT Yoshitami Komatsu) sortied on a mission to search and attack the enemy fleet. They were unable to locate the enemy, however, and returned to base empty-handed. Again, on 29 August, one each land attack and carrier fighter buntai advanced to Mili Island and assisted in the Nauru and Ocean (Banaba) invasions. On 11 September, the carrier fighter unit returned to Taroa.

With the reorganization of 1 November 1942, the 1st Air Group was renamed Air Group 752. In December it was decided that the land attack unit would be returning to the homeland. The carrier fighter element was integrated into the Chitose Air Group and stayed on in the Micronesia area.

第 3 航 空 隊

3RD AIR GROUP

Along with the Tainan Air Group, the 3rd Air Group was among the most distinguished naval fighter units of the entire Pacific War. The group survived the war as perhaps the sole fighter unit that was always victorious, from the beginning of the war in the Philippines, through the air battles over the Dutch East Indies, and on into the attack on Darwin [Australia].

The 3rd Air Group was organized on 10 April 1941 as a unit designed for land attack [bomber] operations; it was attached to the 11th Air Fleet. In July, the unit advanced to Hanoi in northern French Indochina; in September, it was reorganized into a fighter unit. With hostilities between Japan and the United States imminent, the 3rd Air Group was expected to play a key role as a fighter unit in the battle for air control, together with the Tainan Air Group, in the southern area of operations.

In contrast to the fact that air groups were traditionally composed of a number of different types of aircraft, the 3rd was constituted only of fighters; this was a first, historically speaking. Its allowance was also increased to fifty-four operational carrier fighters (eighteen aircraft in reserve, separately) and nine land reconnaissance planes. Actual strength on the eve of the outbreak of hostilities was forty-five Zero Model 21 fighters and twelve Type 96 carrier fighters. In addition, there were thirteen Zero fighters (commanding officer, LT Tadatsune Tokaji) and three land recon-

naissance planes that were detached to the 22nd Air Flotilla Headquarters Fighter Squadron in southern French Indochina. The unit was to participate in the Malay area operation. Many pilots had been transferred in from the 12th Air Group; when compared to Tainan Air Group personnel, the ratio of senior, experienced personnel was higher. Even newer personnel had around one thousand hours' flight time to their credit.

Veteran fighter squadron CO CAPT Yoshio Kamei was assigned as the unit's commanding officer; CDR Takeo Shibata, as executive officer and, concurrently, air officer. Equipment and personnel were assembled at Kanoya; the main force of the unit moved to Takao [in Taiwan] in mid-October. Under the direction of group leader Yokoyama, furious training commenced in preparation for the assault on the Philippines. In particular, in order to make it possible to fly the long, one-way distance of five hundred miles to Manila, tests were conducted on a continuing basis to lessen fuel consumption. Since confidence was gained that it was possible to fly 1,200 miles and conduct a twenty-minute air battle, in late October commander Kamei ordered that the intermediate stop technique of landing and refueling on aircraft carriers be abandoned. He also submitted a report to his superiors recommending that Zero fighter units be directly dispatched for action.

Model 21 Zero Fighter

The (vertical) band on the fuselage and the band on the tail indicate the aircraft is used by a division officer. Unit insignia X was used during the period April 1941 through October 1942.

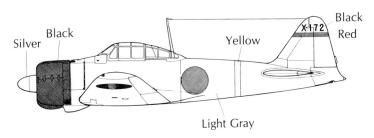

Silver — Black — Yellow — X-172 — Black — Red — Light Gray

3rd Air Group just before departure from Kao-hsiung (Japanese name, Takao) base, 8 December 1941.
(Katsutarō Kobayashi)

On the first day that hostilities commenced, 8 December, fifty-three Zero fighters (of which two turned back) under the command of LT Yokoyama left Takao and attacked the airfields at both Iba and Clark, while escorting land attack planes. After wiping out more than ten enemy fighters that rose to intercept them, the unit strafed aircraft on the ground. By gunfire, more than twenty aircraft on the ground were destroyed or set on fire. During the course of this one day, our air supremacy in battles over the Philippines was assured. Losses inflicted on the 3rd Air Group were a mere two aircraft. On the 10th, thirty-four aircraft attacked in the vicinity of Manila and engaged in a major air battle. Substantial battle results were attained; forty-four enemy aircraft were shot down and forty-two aircraft set on fire. Attacks were repeated later, on the 12th and the 13th, but the American air force in the Philippines had been decimated, and no sign of the enemy was to be seen.

As a result, the 3rd Air Group started its move on the 23rd, directly from Takao to the next scheduled area, the Davao base [Mindanao]; most of its strength was in place by the 29th. On the 28th, seven Zero fighters and one land reconnaissance

plane attacked the island of Tarakan [off Borneo] and engaged in air combat with nine Buffalo fighters. Almost all enemy aircraft were demolished. Next, on 11 January 1942 Japanese forces captured Manado [Celebes]; from the 12th through the 19th the group's base was moved forward.

On the 15th and 16th, the next scheduled target of Ambon was attacked. Starting the 25th, the entire strength of the group was assembled at the recently captured Kendari base [on Celebes]. Part of the unit was used in attacking Kupang on the island of Timor, starting the 26th. The main force moved to Balikpapan [Borneo] on 2 February in preparation for engaging in aerial battles over eastern Java. At one point, the 3rd Air Group was placed under the command of the Tainan Air Group.

On 3 February, twenty-seven Zero fighters under the command of LT Yokoyama and guided by land reconnaissance planes, in cooperation with twenty-seven Zeros of the Tainan Air Group, entered the clear skies over Surabaya. There they engaged in a major air battle with Dutch and American fighter units that had been standing by for their arrival. During the battle, thirty-nine enemy aircraft were shot down

3rd Air Group command as of the end of August 1942. Front row (from the left): third person, LT Takahide Aioi (group leader); LCR Kiyoji Sakakibara (air officer); CDR Takeo Fukuda (executive officer); and center, CAPT Yoshio Kamei (commanding officer). (Takahide Aioi)

A major formation of 3rd Air Group Zero fighters prepare to sortie over the Celebes plain, 1942. In the lead is the aircraft flown by the commander, LCDR Aioi. (Takeshi Sakamoto)

Model 21 Zero fighters and Type 98 land reconnaissance planes at Kendari base. (Katsutarō Kobayashi)

and twenty-one aircraft on the ground severely damaged or set on fire, all in one fell swoop. Together with the Tainan Air Group, approximately ninety enemy aircraft were destroyed; almost complete air superiority over Java was achieved in the course of this one day.

Later, until mid-February, the 3rd Air Group was dispersed at bases in Balikpapan, Makassar (Ujung Pandang), and Ambon. The group was engaged in attacking eastern Java, the Timors, and in flying air cover for the Bali Island invasion convoy. With the capture of Kupang, the main force of the 3rd Air Group moved into the suburban Buton airfield between 23 February and 8 March. A portion of the group was moved, together with elements of the Tainan Air Group, to the island of Bali after its capture and engaged in enemy troop mop-up operations. The group also participated in an attack on the American [seaplane tender] *Langley*. With the termination of the Java campaign at the end of March, the various elements were reunited with the main force located at Kupang.

Battle results for the 3rd Air Group for the period 12 January through 3 March are calculated to be (based on letters of appreciation) eighty-six enemy aircraft shot down and ninety severely damaged or set on fire. If these figures are added to the battle results achieved since the outbreak of hostilities, they amount to about 150 enemy aircraft downed and about 170 aircraft severely damaged or set on fire. On our side, only eleven Zero pilots were killed in action.

On 3 March, the 3rd Air Group, which had advanced to Kupang, sent out seventeen Zero fighters under the command of LT Miyano on a long range mission of attacking the key northwestern Australian towns of Broome and Wyndham. The Zero fighters forced about twenty enemy flying boats to stay on the water and set the entire group of enemy aircraft on fire by strafing. On 10 March, a part of the 3rd Air Group was integrated into northern units and ordered to return to the homeland. In April and later, the main force of the 3rd Air Group used Kendari and Kupang as primary bases. A part of the unit was dispatched to Ambon and used in air defense over the Arafura Sea, in addition to repeatedly providing escorts for land attack planes bombing Darwin. At the time, enemy forces assigned the duty of protecting the Darwin area were P-40s of the U.S. Army Air Forces. Zero fighters were able to take advantage of their overwhelming superiority. Although major air results were attained, our side was concerned over the P-40's tactic of making single hit-and-run attacks and then withdrawing. Starting with LT Tokaji, some casualties did result from this. During the same period, from 3 to 19 March, one buntai was dispatched to Sabang (off Sumatra).

In September 1942, in order to partici-

Model 22 Zero fighter (X-151), the favorite mount of PO2c Kiyoshi Itō. (Kiyoshi Katō)

pate in the Guadalcanal operation, twenty-one Zero fighters, twenty-seven pilots, and four land reconnaissance planes under air officer Sakakibara were transported to Rabaul by means of the aircraft carrier *Taiyō*. They were placed under the command of the Tainan Air Group. Until their return in the early part of November to the south-west area, the unit was engaged in almost daily attacks on Guadalcanal, air cover for convoys, and air defense of key areas. Although battle results were sixty-eight enemy aircraft (twenty probables) shot down, our side lost eight pilots. With the reorganization of 1 November 1942, the 3rd Air Group was renamed Air Group 202.

Model 21 Zero fighter of the 3rd Air Group at Rabaul base. (Torao Saitō)

第 202 航 空 隊

AIR GROUP 202

With the reorganization of 1 November 1942, the 3rd Air Group was renamed Air Group 202. At the time, the major strength of the 3rd Air Group was in the process of being transferred from Rabaul after engaging in the furious air battles going on around Rabaul, in the southeast area. Escorting a convoy to Lae on 1 November as its last operation in the area, the unit was returned to its original southwest area base. Joining the caretaker unit at Kendari, the unit continued training exercises. During the same period, the group was dispatched for the defense of Ambon, Babo [West New Guinea], Tual [Aru Islands], Kupang [Timor Island], Makassar, and other strategic areas. On occasion, training and recreational activities were provided on the island of Bali. Up till the spring of 1943, small numbers of B-24s, Beaufighters, and other enemy aircraft made occasional attacks on the previously mentioned strategic areas and the 202 intercepted them. On 3 and 5 March, the group provided escorts for land attack planes and flew south from the Kupang base against Darwin. On the 15th, four Spitfire fighters, considered by the Royal Air Force to be among their best planes, were shot down.

During the previous year, air defense in this area had been the responsibility of P-40s of the U.S. Army Air Forces. In the fall of 1942, however, a group of about one hundred Spitfires, including veterans of the fighting in Europe (commanding, [Wing Commander Clive] Caldwell) arrived from Britain. By the early part of 1943 this British unit had been deployed in bases around the Darwin area. Based on such enemy moves, Imperial General Headquarters arrived at the judgment that the primary offensive on the part of enemy forces during the second half of 1943 would be in the southwest area, centered around Darwin. In addition to strengthening the forces allotted to the 23rd Air Flotilla, the army sent in Type 100 heavy bomber regiments and engaged in aggressive aerial operations in the area in an attempt to crush the enemy's intent to retaliate before such could occur. Under the leadership of newly assigned group leader Suzuki, Air Group 202 engaged in intensive training activities at the Kendari base in anticipation of the new operations. Particular attention was paid to over-ocean navigational techniques, permitting a flight of 450 miles and the improvement of formation fighting tactics.

Model 52 Zero Fighter

Fighter Hikōtai 603. Unit insignia *02* was used during March–July 1944. Plane numbers used were in the *1100* grouping.

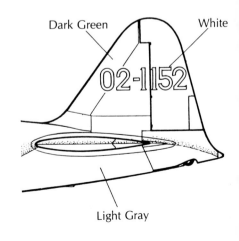

Dark Green   White

02-1152

Light Gray

Air Group 202 officers at Kendari: Center, (white uniform), CDR Motoharu Okamura (commanding officer). Second person to the right, LCDR Suzuki (group leader). (Minoru Suzuki)

On 2 May, twenty-seven Zero fighters that had been stationed in Kupang (commander, LCDR Suzuki), together with twenty-five Type 1 land attack planes of Air Group 753, which had staged in from Kendari, engaged in a furious battle with thirty-three Spitfires [over Darwin]. During a fifteen-minute period, twenty-one enemy aircraft were shot down; all of our aircraft, including land attack planes and Zero fighters, returned safely. According to records of the Royal Australian Air Force, actual losses were thirteen aircraft (two pilots); in any event there is no doubt that it represented an overwhelming victory on the part of the Zero fighters. Later

on, through the early part of September, Air Group 202 conducted six attacks on Darwin, Brocks Creek, and other areas.

Total battle results attained since March were 101 aircraft (including twenty-two probables), counting only those enemy aircraft that were shot down in aerial combat; in contrast, Australian records indicate thirty-eight shot down. Our side suffered the loss of only three Zero fighters and two land attack planes.

This was at a time when the myth of "The Invincible Zero Fighter" (Fuhai no Zero-sen), which had pervaded the southeast area, was beginning to crumble. The one-sided victory on the part of Zero

Model 22 Zero Fighter

Unit insignia *X2* used between June 1943 and 1944. After the name was changed from "3rd Air Group" to "Air Group 202," the *X* insignia continued in use from November 1942 through June 1943.

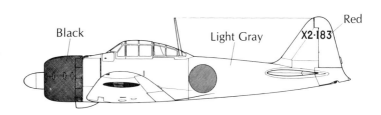

Zero fighter of Air Group 202 (Kiyoshi Katō)

fighters, escorting land attack planes, made a long-range attack on Merauke. After the bombing attack was ended, seven Zero fighters that were serving as a commando unit (Yūgeki-tai) were trapped [by P-40s], and three of our aircraft, including the plane flown by ENS Morio Miyaguchi, were lost. For a while thereafter, the 202 did not engage in aggressive operations. In December, approximately twenty pilots led by WO Tadao Yamanaka were transferred to Air Group 204 at Rabaul because of the need to assist in air battles in the southeast area, which appeared to be in peril.

On 4 March 1944, Air Group 202 was posted to the 22nd Kōkū-Sentai (14th Air Fleet) (on 5 May, it was next posted to the 1st Air Fleet) and was scheduled to proceed to the central Pacific area. At this time, the unit was also divided into Fighter Hikōtai 301 (commander, LCDR Minoru Suzuki) and Fighter Hikōtai 603 (commander, LCDR Hideki Shingō). Each group had a complement of forty-eight aircraft. Toward the end of February, forty-three aircraft of Fighter Hikōtai 301 advanced to Harushima airfield on Truk, via the island of Tinian. Although at one time it had been temporarily transferred to Ponape, the unit engaged in air defense operations over Truk until the end of May. The occasional raids by B-24s were intercepted. Also during this period, one buntai was detached and sent for a short time to provide air defense over Mortlock Islands and the island of Ponape. When an American task force made an attack on 30 April, seven Zero fighters led by LTJG Kawakubo escorting a carrier bomber unit broke off and shot down sixteen aircraft in aerial combat. Our side lost four aircraft.

fighters over Darwin is considered to be of particular note. There are a number of reasons that accounted for these victories. Among them are that Air Group 202 already had experience of over a year in the local area; that sufficient training, rest, and recuperation were available; and that a high ratio of veteran pilots was involved. In contrast, perhaps it should be mentioned that Spitfires tended to prefer dogfights, at a time when the very same tactic was most favored by [the more experienced] Zero fighter pilots.

Once Air Group 202 had concluded its part in the drive on Australia with the 7 September attack on Brocks Creek, the unit moved to Tual in the Aru Islands in order to strike at American army air force units that had reportedly advanced into Merauke, located in southwestern New Guinea. On the 9th, twenty-seven Zero

Model 52 Zero Fighter

A plane of Fighter Hikōtai 301. Unit insignia *301* was used March–July 1944. Plane numbers used were in the *100* group.

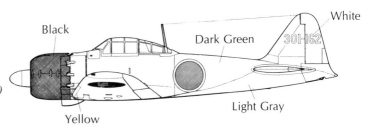

During the period 23–24 May, the main force of twenty-eight fighters led by LCDR Suzuki left Truk Island; proceeding via Guam, Yap, Peleliu, and Wasile, they arrived at Sorong [West New Guinea] on 1 June. Joining forces with Fighter Hikōtai 603, it participated in the Biak operation from the 2nd to the 12th. The unit moved to Peleliu on the 13th, proceeding via Yap. On the 19th, about twenty aircraft participated in attacks on ships off Saipan. On the other hand, Fighter Hikōtai 603, which had been transferred in from Air Group 331 left Sumatra with thirty-three aircraft. Proceeding via Surabaya, Kendari, Davao, and Palau, the unit advanced to the island of Mariaon [Wolei Atoll]. By early March, the unit was engaged in intercepting B-24s. At the end of March, however, the unit moved to Truk and was absorbed into the main force. During the 30 April American task force attack, fifteen Zero fighters led by LTJG Hiroshi Suzuki sortied, providing screen for the carrier bomber strike force. During air battles, eleven enemy aircraft were shot down, but our side also lost four aircraft. At the end of April, one buntai of eighteen Zeros (accompanying the Air Group 503 carrier bomber squadron), was dispatched to Biak Island and then to Halmahera. The buntai protected convoys and intercepted B-24s. On 23 May, the main strength of fourteen aircraft, under the command of unit commander Shingō, left Truk and proceeded to Sorong (part of the unit moved to Wasile) via Guam and Yap, arriving on 1 June. After joining Fighter Hikōtai 301, unit strength rose to about fifty aircraft. Until

the 12th, the unit was engaged in the Biak operation. As of the 10th, twenty-one of our aircraft, including those that destroyed themselves, had been lost. The remaining sixteen aircraft transferred to Peleliu, via Wasile, on the 17th. On the next day, the 18th, the group combined forces with other units and participated in attacks on shipping off Saipan. One part of the unit advanced to Guam and participated in attacks on Saipan and in air cover operations. Following such action toward the end of the same month, the unit engaged in the interception of B-24s at Yap and Peleliu. After retreating to Davao, Air Group 202 was disbanded in the reorganization of 10 July.

Successive Commanding Officers:

April 1941–August 1942   CAPT Yoshio Kamei

August 1942–October 1942   CAPT Kaoru Umetani

October 1942–August 1943   CAPT Motoharu Okamura

August 1943–March 1944   CDR Sadagorō Uchida

March 1944–July 1944   CDR Shigeki Negoro

Successive Group Leaders:

September 1941–March 1942   LT Tamotsu Yokoyama

March 1942–March 1943   LT Takahide Aioi

March 1943–April 1943   LT Minoru Kobayashi

April 1943–March 1944   LCDR Minoru Suzuki

台 南 航 空 隊

TAINAN AIR GROUP

Among all naval air groups the Tainan Air Group was the best known and the unit with the largest number of aces. [Saburō] Sakai's well-known book (the English version was published under the title *Samurai*) vividly describes the competition between such aces as Hiroyoshi Nishizawa, Saburō Sakai himself, Jun-ichi Sasai, Toshio Ōta, and others to see which of them could shoot down the largest number of enemy aircraft.

The Tainan Air Group was established on 1 October 1941 at Tainan [Taiwan] as a unit of fighters only. It was then immediately incorporated into the 23rd Air Flotilla. CAPT Masahisa Saitō was named as the CO, CDR Yasuna Kozono as executive and air officer. Vigorous training activities commenced under the direction of group leader LT Hideki Shingō.

In anticipation of participating in operations in the southern area, the unit was strengthened in that its aircraft allowance was increased to fifty-four carrier fighters (an additional eighteen spares) and six land reconnaissance planes. Just before the outbreak of hostilities, actual strength consisted of forty-five Model 21 Zeros, twelve Type 96 carrier fighters, and six land reconnaissance planes. In addition, fourteen Zero fighters and a few Type 96 carrier fighters under the command of LT Kiku-ichi Inano were transferred to the fighter squadron attached to the 22nd Air Flotilla for the purpose of engaging in Malayan operations.

On 8 December 1941, the first day of battle, forty-four Zero fighters of the Tainan Air Group under the command of group leader LT Shingō escorted land attack forces that attacked Iba and Clark Field on Luzon in the Philippines. Enemy aircraft that came to intercept were few in number; nine of them were shot down. After the land attack planes finished their bombing runs, the fighter group strafed aircraft on the ground, despite the AA barrage. About sixty aircraft on the ground were destroyed, including B-17s. In that single day, the trend of the air battle for the Philippines was set. Our side's losses consisted of only one aircraft that destroyed itself and four that failed to return to base.

Following this, on the 10th, 11th, and the 13th, remaining enemy forces were routed by attacks on enemy airfields in the vicinity of Manila. After the third phase attack, there was almost no enemy aircraft opposition. During the same period and in coordination with the army landings at Legaspi, one chūtai under the command of LT Masuzō Setō moved into the captured Legaspi airfield. By the 14th, the airfield

Model 21 Zero Fighter

Aircraft used by PO1c Saburō Sakai. Slanted band on fuselage, blue. Band on vertical tail indicates aircraft flown by a shōtai leader. On aircraft flown by a chūtai leader, there are two bands on the vertical tail and the fuselage stripe is vertical. Unit insignia *V* used during October 1941 through October 1942.

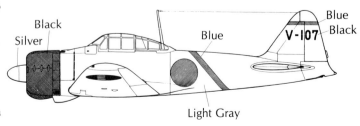

The flight crew at Jolo Island, January 1942. Middle of center row, [CAPT Masahisa] Saitō, commanding officer; to his left, [CDR Yasuna] Kozono, XO; right end, group leader [LT Hideki] Shingō. Back row, fifth from the left, LTJG Sasai. Front row, second from the left, WO Miyazaki. (Hideki Shingō)

had been secured. The main unit also patrolled over Vigan anchorage, on a rotation basis.

The battle for the Philippines reached the end of its first phase towards the end of December. The Tainan Air Group, which had been split up between Tainan and Legaspi, was ordered to go a considerable distance over the ocean to an airfield recently captured on the remote island of Horo. Starting the 26th, forty-one Zero fighters were moved successively to the island by 7 January of the following year. As early as 30 December, in anticipation of the move into the Dutch East Indies, the Zero fighter unit had attacked the island of Tarakan for the first time. By 11 January 1942 the island had been captured. Starting on the 16th, the unit successively moved its base forward. The speed of its advance was amazing: the attacks on Balikpapan started by the 18th and those on Bandjermasin by the 20th.

On the occasion of the army landing on Balikpapan on 24 January 1942 the group provided aerial cover, in relay, from its base located on Tarakan. On several occasions, allied bombers, including massed B-17s, were repulsed. Because of the hindrance of the B-17's heavy firepower, however, it was not easy to shoot down these enemy bombers.

It was a tough battle. During air combat over the Java Sea on the 8th, however, confidence was gained by the pilots when two enemy aircraft of the B-17 type were shot down successfully by the use of head-on attacks.

On 30 January, the entire Tainan Air Group was moved, together with the 23rd Air Flotilla headquarters to the Balikpapan base. Starting 3 February, and in conjunc-

Model 21 Zero fighter (V-117) flying in the clouds. Believed to have been piloted by a chūtai leader or a group leader. (Family of Susumu Ishihara)

Tainan Air Group

First organized on 1 October 1941, the Tainan Air Group was reorganized on 1 November 1942 and renamed Air Group 251. Active in the South Pacific, it produced more aces than any other unit of all the Imperial Japanese Navy air groups.

Tainan Air Group flight personnel, Rabaul Air Base, 4 August 1942. Front row, from the right: fourth person, PO3c Utō Kazushi; and, skipping five [ninth person], PO3c Take-ichi Kuniwake. Second row, from the right: second person, LTJG Takeyoshi Ōno; skip one; division officer LT Jōji Yamashita; division officer LT Kiku-ichi Inano; group leader LCDR Tadashi Nakajima; commanding officer CAPT Masahisa Saitō; executive officer and air officer CDR Yasuna Kozono; division officer LT Shirō Kawai; division officer LTJG Jun-ichi Sasai; skip one; PO1c Tora-ichi Takatsuka; and WO Sahei Yamashita. Third row, from the right: fifth person in, PO3c Masuaki Endō; PO1c Toshio Ōta; skip two; PO1c Yoshio Ōki; skip one; PO1c Hiroyoshi Nishizawa; PO1c Saburō Sakai; and PO1c Mototsuna Yoshida. Fourth row, from the right: seventh person, PO2c Ichirōbei Yamazaki; skip four persons, Sea1c Keisaku Yoshimura. (Kiku-ichi Inano)

tion with the 3rd Air Group, the Tainan Air Group engaged in aerial combat over eastern Java. During air annihilation battles over Malang and Surabaya, major damage was inflicted on the main Allied air forces. During this same period, one chūtai was detached on 8 February and moved to Makassar in support of the Bali landing forces. On the 20th, concurrent with the capture of the island, the Tainan group moved into the Denpasar airfield. The group then successively gathered together its entire force and engaged in operations until 9 March, when the Dutch East Indies foray was completed. The unit spent about one month at Denpasar replenishing its forces and recu-

perating. At the same time, nine of their aircraft were transferred to the Philippines after 22 March and provided air cover for the Corregidor bombings.

With the reorganization as of 1 April, the Tainan Air Group was integrated into the 25th Air Flotilla (allowance, forty-five aircraft) and received orders to proceed to Rabaul. A portion of veteran flight personnel returned to the homeland, under the command of LT Shingō. About two weeks later, flight personnel arrived at Rabaul on board the transport ship *Komaki Maru*. By the 16th, the entire force, including CO Saitō and the new group leader, Nakajima, had also arrived. As of the first of the

Tainan Air Group, Rabaul east airfield, November 1942. (Compare with the photo on p. 134.) Front row, from the left: second person, CPO Takeo Okumura; CPO Yoshio Ōki, ENS Noboru Yamakawa, special service; LTJG Takeyoshi Ōno; LCDR Tadashi Nakajima; CAPT Masahisa Saitō; CDR Yasuna Kozono; LT Shirō Kawai; WO Sahei Yamashita; and CPO Hiroyoshi Nishizawa: Center row, from the left: PO2c Hiroshi Okano, skip one, PO2c Yoshi-ichi Nakaya, skip one, PO2c Daizō Fukumori. Center row, from the right: seventh person, PO1c Kōzaburō Yasui; fifth person, PO2c Mitsuo Hori. Rear row, from the left: PO1c Shigeru Takahashi, skip one, PO1c Sadao Uehara, skip one, and PO1c Masuaki Endō. (Shin-ichi Hirabayashi)

month, equipment and pilots that had previously been transferred to the Tainan Air Group from the local 4th Air Group Fighter Squadron had also been integrated into the organization.

Aircraft in commission as of 25 April were as follows: at Rabaul, two Zero fighters, six Type 96 carrier fighters, and, at Lae, about twenty-four Zero fighters. The replacement of expendable materials however, was very sluggish; as a result, up until about August actual operational aircraft were limited to around twenty.

Following its move to Rabaul, the Tainan Air Group was, in the main, dispatched to the forward base at Lae. Starting 17 April and using a system whereby pilots were rotated in turn back to Rabaul for rest and recuperation, as well as by speeding up

the training of new arrivals, the group started air battles over eastern New Guinea. Even if we restrict our attention to attacks on Port Moresby alone, during the four-month period from April through July, a cumulative total of fifty-one missions were carried out; the total number of aircraft sorties was 602. Battle results, counting only aircraft shot down, were 246 (including forty-five probables). In addition, if battle results of the attack on Horn Island, Lae intercept battles, Buna airfield patrols, and other engagements are added, the total comes to about three hundred enemy aircraft downed. In contrast, on our side damages were limited to twenty aircraft that either destroyed themselves or failed to return to base. The majority of downed enemy aircraft were American and

Australian fighters, primarily P-39s. In many instances they were lured into spiral battles (senkai sentō) [dogfights], a strong specialty of the Zero's; the result was that our side in many instances won lopsided victories.

On the morning of 7 August, the U.S. First Marine Division, supported by a carrier task force, made an unexpected landing on Guadalcanal, Solomon Islands. The construction of an airfield was still under way at the time. Eighteen Zero fighters of the Tainan Air Group, which had been standing by for an attack on Rabi (Rambi), changed their objective; under the leadership of LCDR Nakajima, they escorted our own land attack planes. After flying the then unheard of long distance for single seater fighter craft of 560 miles each way, the unit was still able to engage in air combat with intercepting U.S. Navy F4F fighters. Our losses were two aircraft, with forty-three enemy aircraft shot down (including seven probables).

TABLE 5. FORMATION OF TAINAN AIR GROUP
(At the Attack on Guadalcanal, 7 August 1942)

	VICTORIES
1st Chūtai	
1st Shōtai	
LCDR Tadashi Nakajima	
PO1c Hiroyoshi Nishizawa	6 fighters
PO1c Keisaku Yoshimura	5 (2)★ fighters
2nd Shōtai	
WO Tora-ichi Takatsuka	4 (1) fighters; major damage caused by mid-air fire
PO1c Sadao Yamashita	2 (2) fighters; received four hits
PO2c Susumu Matsuki	4 (2) fighters
2nd Chūtai	
1st Shōtai	
LT Shirō Kawai	1 fighter
PO1c Mototsuna Yoshida	Missing in action
PO3c Ichirōbei Yamazaki	2 (1) fighters
2nd Shōtai	
PO1c Yoshio Ōki	Returned to base because landing gear malfunctioned
PO2c Nobuo Tokushige	4 (1) fighters; 1 dive-bomber
PO2c Kunimatsu Nishiura	Missing in action
3rd Chūtai	
1st Shōtai	
LTJG Jun-ichi Sasai	4 (1) fighters; 1 dive-bomber
PO1c Toshio Ōta	4 (2) fighters
PO2c Masuaki Endō	1 fighter; 2 dive-bombers
2nd Shōtai	
WO Saburō Sakai	1 fighter; 2 dive-bombers; received three hits
PO2c Enji Kakimoto	1 fighter; 1 dive-bomber
PO3c Kazushi Utō	4 (2) fighters

★ Parentheses indicate probables or number of aircraft jointly destroyed.

Flight personnel just before departure, August 1942. Front row (from left): end, group leader Tadashi Nakajima; WO Takatsuka; PO1c Ōki; LT Kawai; LTJG Ōno; WO Yamashita; and last (right end), PO3c Okano. (Kiku-ichi Inano)

Model 21 Zero fighter used by PO2c Yoshisuke Arita. At Denpasar base, February 1942. (Family of Susumu Ishihara)

Later, until the order to return to the mainland of Japan was received in November, furious air battles continued to be fought. However, Zero fighters, which of necessity had to fly very long distances, were intercepted by F4Fs of the U.S. Marines, which had the advantage of using bases closer at hand. As a result, veteran pilots were successively lost. During the three-month period of August through October and including the battle for eastern New Guinea, compared to the destruction of 201 enemy aircraft (thirty-seven probables) by the Tainan Air Group, the number of Zero fighter pilots killed in action mounted to thirty-two. The weakened Tainan Air Group (renamed Air Group 251 as of the reorganization of 1 November) was ordered back to the mainland of Japan in November. Leaving their equipment behind, the fewer than twenty surviving ground crew and pilots boarded a transport ship and left for the homeland. At Toyohashi base the unit would start being brought back up to strength.

第 251 航空隊

AIR GROUP 251

With the reorganization of 1 November 1942, all air groups at the front lines were scheduled to be changed to a numerical designation system. The Tainan Air Group, then located at Rabaul, was renamed Air Group 251. In mid-November, Air Group 251 was ordered to return to the homeland to regroup. At the end of the year, the group started to rebuild itself at the Toyohashi base. Aircraft allowance was sixty carrier fighters, eight land reconnaissance planes, and four transport planes. The executive officer, CDR Kozono was promoted to CO, LCDR Tadashi Nakajima ordered to be air officer, and LT Ichirō Mukai, group leader. Using a core consisting of the ten or more pilots who had returned safe and sound from Rabaul as its nucleus, training at Toyohashi base emphasized formation fighting. By April 1943 the required level of skills had been attained and orders were issued on 1 May to proceed to Rabaul. Ground personnel, supplies, and equipment were loaded on board the transport *Mogami-gawa Maru* and arrived at Rabaul on 7 May. The air unit, after island-hopping to Truk and assembling, then waited for the weather to clear. On the 10th, fifty-eight Zero fighters and seven land reconnaissance planes led by LT Mukai advanced to the east airfield at Rabaul.

Including members of the advanced party, total Zero fighter pilot strength was as follows: four division officers, six buntai [junior officers] members, sixty-three petty of-

LTJG Takeyoshi Ōno, Air Group 251 (Ikuhiko Hata)

Model 22 Zero Fighter

Aircraft flown by CPO Hiroyoshi Nishizawa. Unit insignia *U1* was used during 1942 and 1943. If the fuselage was painted light gray, the *U1* was in black (only the plane number was in white). There were times when the *U1* was erased by being painted over in black or dark green.

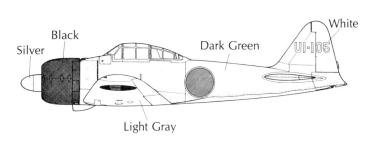

Silver
Black
Dark Green
White
UI-105
Light Gray

East airfield, Rabaul (Kiku-ichi Inano)

ficers and seamen, total seventy-three. Of this number, however, only ten had actual combat experience.

On the 14th, the fourth day after its advance to the field, thirty-two Zero fighters escorted eighteen land attack planes of Air Group 751 and started out on an attack on Oro Bay. Combating intercepting P-38s and P-40s, thirteen enemy aircraft (five probables) were shot down; all of our aircraft returned safely. In June, an American advance into the central Solomons was considered imminent, and reports were received of the concentration of enemy aircraft at bases on Guadalcanal and in the Russells. A second-phase attack, to be carried out by fighter units only, was next planned. On 7 June, thirty-six aircraft of

Gekkō night fighter of Air Group 251 at Rabaul, 1943. (Maru)

group 251 and, similarly on the 12th, thirty-two aircraft of the 251 sortied together with Air Groups 204 and 582, proceeding via Buka Island. In both cases, major battles were fought with enemy fighters that rose up to intercept our planes over the Russell Islands. Battle results attained by Air Group 251 were the highest of all units involved. Each sortie accounted for twenty-three aircraft (five probables) and eleven aircraft shot down; our side also lost eight aircraft. Next, on the 16th, thirty aircraft from Air Group 251 participated in the attack on vessels off Lunga (Guadalcanal), flying in support of carrier bombers; ten enemy aircraft were shot down. Our side also suffered major losses; seven of our aircraft were shot down.

On the 30th, American forces landed on Rendova in the central Solomons; Air Group 251 immediately sortied in order to counterattack. As a result of strenuous fighting, the unit lost eight of the twenty-four aircraft participating, including planes flown by LT Mukai and LTJG Ono. Battle strength of group 251 was drastically reduced. Despite such conditions, however, the unit continued intercept operations, almost daily, under the leadership of the remaining senior division officer, LTJG Takashi Oshibuchi. Attacks were in the Rendova area, using Rabaul and Buin as bases. As of 1 September, Air Group 251 was scheduled to be reorganized as a night fighter unit; pilots were transferred to the 201, the 253, and other air groups.

Between May, when the unit advanced to Rabaul, and the end of August, approximately 230 enemy aircraft were shot down by Zero fighter units. In contrast, our side lost thirty-four pilots.

In connection with the battle record of

Group leader, LCDR Tadashi Nakajima (Yoshio Shiga)

Air Group 251 particular mention should probably be made of the role played by the Gekkō ["Moonlight"; a twin-engined] night fighter. This aircraft was initially designed to serve as a long-range escort fighter for bomber units. Because of faulty performance capabilities, however, the aircraft were provided to Air Group 251 in the summer of 1942 for use as land reconnaissance planes. Executive officer Kozono was acutely aware of the lack of any intercept method for combating night raids on Rabaul. It was he who thought up the idea of having these aircraft equipped both above and below the fuselage with obliquely angled cannons, thus turning them into night fighters. After his return to the homeland, Kozono overcame strong opposition on the

Gekkō, 1944

Located in the southern area. Upper portion of fuselage and sides, dark green. Lower side, light gray, or, otherwise, black all over.

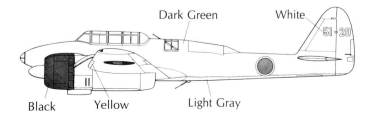

part of air headquarters as well the Yoko-suka Air Group and actually implemented his idea. Using two aircraft that had been remodeled immediately before the May 1943 advance into the southeast area of operations, air tests were conducted at Toyohashi to increase confidence in the newly equipped aircraft. It was only after this testing that the aircraft were sent to Rabaul.

The baptism of fire came about the night of 21 May. CPO Kudō, piloting his Gekkō, was able to identify in the light of the thirteen-day-old moon B-17s that had taken off after midnight. He successfully shot down two of them. Following this, during the night of 10 June, WO Ono used his Gekkō to shoot down two (one proba-ble) enemy aircraft. During the night of the 11th, again Kudō shot down one enemy aircraft; on the night of the 13th, he simi-larly shot down another aircraft. Once again, on the night of the 15th, Kudō's air-craft shot down two enemy aircraft; he then shot down another aircraft on the night of the 30th. As a result, enemy air attacks ceased for the time being. At the same time, since attacks in the Buin area had begun, Gekkō night fighters, rein-forced by additional aircraft sent out from the homeland, advanced in early July to the island of Ballale.

By the end of July, not only had six B-17s, B-24s, and Hudson bombers been shot down during night operations but the night fighters were also being used in operations against enemy ships in the Rendova area. As of 1 September, Air Group 251 was converted into an exclusively night fighting unit, with an allowance of twenty-four such aircraft. In addition to night intercep-tion duties, the 251 was used in daytime reconnaissance, as well as night attacks on land units and vessels. Because of the inten-sification of enemy daytime raids in the Buin area, during the day the Gekkō unit stood by at Rabaul; after dark it would ad-vance to Buin. On flights to and from the Buin area, the unit would also be assigned patrol duties. After October, the 251 moved back to Rabaul and continued to

engage in night operations; part of its force was next detached to Kavieng. Together with the fact that enemy bomber counter-measures were being developed against night-fighting tactics and the fact that pri-mary emphasis shifted to daytime raids, the battle results were almost nil.

In early 1944, the main strength of Air Group 251 advanced to Kaedeshima base (Moen Island), Truk Atoll. As a result of attacks made on the 17th and the 19th by American carrier fighters, the nine Gekkō fighters based locally were destroyed. Later, on 1 April, the unit was reinforced and reorganized as Fighter Hikōtai 901 (commander, LT Yutaka Sugawara; allow-ance twenty-four aircraft). Actual aircraft on hand, however, numbered only about six planes. The two to three aircraft that had remained at Rabaul (remodeled by re-moving the downward-angled guns and re-placing them with three turret-type, up-ward-angled guns) continued to engage in night operations until May; they then with-drew to Truk to join the main unit. Al-though participating until the end of June in intercepting nighttime B-24 attacks, there were almost no battle results. With the re-organization of 10 July, Fighter Hikōtai 901 was integrated into Air Group 153 and scheduled to go to the Philippines. At the same time, Air Group 251 was disbanded.

Successive Commanding Officers:

October 1942–December 1942 CAPT Masahisa Saitō
December 1942–September 1943 CDR Yasuna Kozono
September 1943–March 1944 CDR Ikuto Kusumoto
March 1944–July 1944 CDR Takeo Shi-bata

Successive Group Leaders:

October 1941–April 1942 LT Hideki Shingō
April 1942–February 1943 LCDR Ta-dashi Nakajima
February 1943–June 1943 LT Ichirō Mu-kai
June 1943–July 1943 LT Dai Sonokawa

22航戦司令部付戦闘機隊

FIGHTER SQUADRON ATTACHED TO 22ND AIR FLOTILLA HEADQUARTERS

This fighter unit was not originally a part of the regular table of organization. It was a unit that was temporarily established and attached to the headquarters of the 22nd Air Flotilla in order to participate in the Malayan and Dutch East Indies operations during the initial phases of the outbreak of hostilities. The 22nd Air Flotilla initially comprised the land attack planes of three air groups: the Genzan, Kanoya, and Mihoro. In anticipation of bombing Singapore as well as of attacks by the British Far Eastern Fleet, army fighter regiments were made responsible for air superiority in those areas. On 22 November 1941, however, immediately before the outbreak of the war, it was decided that a unit of navy fighters would be detached and added to the local forces.

Fourteen Zero fighters and three land reconnaissance planes of the Tainan Air Group under the command of division officer LT Kiku-ichi Inano, plus thirteen Zero fighters and three land reconnaissance planes from the 3rd Air Group under the command of division officer LT Tadatsune Tokaji, were selected. In addition, nine Type 96 carrier fighters from the same two air groups (four Tainan Air Group planes and five 3rd Air Group planes) were added. CDR Yutaka Yamada (executive officer of the Takao Air Group) was ordered to command the unit being dispatched, while LCDR Shigehachirō Tokoro was ordered to fill the capacity of air officer.

The Yamada unit left the two bases at Tainan and Takao on the 26th and 27th and completed their advance to the Saigon base by 1 December, proceeding via Hainan Island. En route to their destination, however, two Zero fighters had to make emergency landings on Luichow Peninsula because of foul weather, and two pilots were missing in action. On the 4th, the main force of the Yamada unit moved to the base at Soc Trang, south of Saigon, and stood by for action. A twelve-aircraft type 96 carrier fighter unit (to which were added three aircraft that had been attached to the fleet sent to the southern area of operations; commander, LTJG Masayoshi Baba) was also used for patrolling over Saigon. With hostilities imminent, starting on the 6th, Yamada unit Zero fighters were assigned to provide air cover in shifts for Malayan invasion force vessels. Land reconnaissance planes were active in surreptitious reconnaissance activities over Singapore.

Starting early in the morning of the 8th, the day hostilities commenced, nine fighters flew air cover over Singora, the landing point. Around 0930 hours, the Tokaji Shōtai, which was on the second watch, shot down an attacking Blenheim bomber. The Tokaji aircraft itself, however, received hits and had to make an emergency landing. In addition, three other aircraft ditched but all pilots were rescued. For a while after this, the Yamada unit was responsible for supporting subsequent ship

Model 21 Zero Fighter
At Kota Bharu, December 1941.

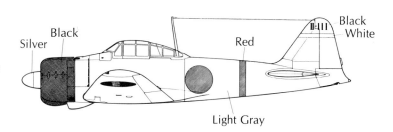

Silver · Black · Red · Black White · Light Gray

convoys between French Indochina and Malaya. On the 22nd, nine aircraft of the Ineno unit were sent to Miri in North Borneo [Sarawak] and, in place of the float-plane unit, assigned air defense duties at the Kuching anchorage. During the same period, attacks were made on the Ledo airfield [West Borneo] on the 25th and on the island of Tarakan on the 28th. In addition, on the 28th, three Blenheim bombers that came to attack Miri were intercepted and all three shot down.

During this period, nineteen Zero fighters and five land reconnaissance planes of the main body awaited repairs to the airfield at Kota Bharu. On the 26th, the unit advanced from Soc Trang to Kota Bharu on the Malay Peninsula. Joining the Inano Buntai, which had returned to base, the squadron participated in the battle for air superiority over Singapore (the S operation) starting 12 January 1942. The first day the entire force of twenty-one Zero fighters was used as escorts for eighty-one land attack planes; however, bad weather prevented access overhead in the target area. On the 13th, similarly, the aircraft returned to base. On the 15th, for the first time, an attack was carried out successfully but there were no air encounters. At the same time, on the 16th, twelve Zero fighters that protected land attack planes of the Genzan Air Group engaged in air combat with the twenty Buffalo that intercepted them. They were able to shoot down ten (one probable) of the enemy. Battle results: only one land reconnaissance plane failed to return on our side.

Later, until the 29th the two units worked in shifts and attacked Singapore, almost daily, as well as escorting land attack planes. The cumulative number of aircraft sorties during this period was 150 (of which 60 aircraft turned back); 40 enemy aircraft were shot down, and 30 aircraft on the ground destroyed by bombing (this includes battle results of the land attack planes as well). Losses on our side are recorded as two land attack planes, two Zero fighters, and one land reconnaissance plane, all of which destroyed themselves. On 5

February, the main force of the Yamada unit (twenty-one Zero fighters and four land reconnaissance planes) advanced to the base at Kuching; here they were integrated into a unit in the southern area of operations preparatory to participating in air operations over the Dutch East Indies. At the same time, the Type 96 carrier fighter unit (nine aircraft) was integrated into the Mihoro Air Group; the unit next moved out from the base at Kuantan and on to Kahang [Kelang, Malaya]. On 9 February, fifteen Zero fighters and one land reconnaissance plane of the main unit started out to provide the first attack on Batavia, capital of Java. They engaged in fierce air combat with the intercepting enemy aircraft. Twelve enemy aircraft were shot down and eight were destroyed on the ground; all our aircraft returned safely.

On the 13th and the 14th, the unit provided air cover, in shifts with other units, for convoys that were on their way to invade Palembang [Sumatra] (the L operation). Ten attacking Hudson bombers were shot down on the 14th. On the 23rd, the unit proceeded to the recently captured airfield at Muntok (Bangka Island). On the 25th, thirteen Zero fighters and one land reconnaissance plane escorting twenty-seven Genzan Air Group land attack planes set forth on an attack against Batavia for the second time. Although four enemy aircraft were shot down as a result of aerial encounters, our side also lost one Zero fighter and one land reconnaissance plane in combat. The main force of the Yamada unit completed its Dutch East Indies operations and departed from Muntok on the two days of 15 and 16 March; the unit transferred to Bangkok.

During the same period, the main force of the Type 96 carrier fighter unit, which had been assigned to the Mihoro Air Group, departed from Kuantan; some aircraft were left behind. Coordinating its movements with movements of the land attack plane units, the main force moved from Kuantan to Kelang, to Gelumbang (South Sumatra), and then on to Karijachi (Java). Duties were to patrol around bases

Zero fighter assigned to the 22nd Air Flotilla command, camouflaged by palm tree leaves. (Kiku-ichi Inano)

and to provide air cover for ship convoys. There were no opportunities for air battle however; by 9 March, all elements of the unit had assembled at the island of Penang. As of the 15th, the unit rejoined the 22nd Air Flotilla. Navy headquarters had planned to integrate the Yamada unit into the Kanoya Air Group as of 1 April and to use them in the northern area of operations. The 11th Air Fleet requested, however, that two chūtai, about twenty aircraft, remain in the area as fighter units in order to have them available for use in operations in the Indian Ocean area; this was allowed. As a result, CDR Yamada received orders to serve as Mihoro Air Group commander. As of 20 March, his unit was to be dis-

banded and absorbed into the Kanoya Air Group. Twenty aircraft of the fighter squadron however, advanced to Tavoy in southern Burma; from 29 March to 3 April, they conducted air patrols over the Andaman Islands. There were no enemy air raids and the unit returned to Bangkok. On the 4th, in order to participate in the Akyab (Sittwe) operation [West Burma], together with land attack planes of the Genzan Air Group, the unit moved to Rangoon. After the attack of the 6th was over, the unit returned to Bangkok on the 7th. For information on the later activities of this unit as the Kanoya Air Group Fighter Squadron, refer to the history of Air Group 253.

第４航空隊戦闘機隊

4TH AIR GROUP FIGHTER SQUADRON

The 4th Air Group Fighter Squadron was organized at Truk on 10 February 1942 and immediately integrated into the 24th Air Flotilla of the 4th Fleet. Allowance was twenty-seven land attack planes and twenty-seven carrier fighters. CAPT Gashi Moritama was ordered in as the commanding officer, and CDR Takashi Miyazaki as the air officer.

The land attack unit was organized from one chūtai each from the 1st Air Group, Chitose Air Group, and Takao Air Group. On the 14th, commanding officer Moritama led the first contingent of three aircraft from Truk, advancing to the Vunakanau airfield at Rabaul. The air flotilla had the services of LT Harutoshi Okamoto as group leader; he had come from Truk to Rabaul at the end of January at the head of one chūtai of the Chitose Air Group Fighter Squadron. One chūtai equivalent of pilots, including LT Shirō Kawai and others, were also added to the unit at that time. In order that the unit could be assigned responsibilities for air defense over Palau just before the outbreak of hostilities, the Kawai unit had been organized around thirteen Type 96 carrier fighters, selected from the Tainan Air Group in Taiwan and from the 3rd Air Group. Loaded on board the specially converted escort carrier *Kasuga Maru,* the Kawai unit was transported to Peleliu and was standing by ready for action by 5 December.

At this time, Rabaul was being subjected every few days to night raids conducted by small groups of multi-engined aircraft. Type 96 carrier fighters of the 4th Air Group (separately, on 25 January an additional three Zero fighters had arrived and had assembled as of the 28th), aided by the use of search lights, attempted night intercept operations with no effect.

On 9 February, Surumi and Gasmata in the western portion of New Britain Island were captured; they were under development as staging bases for launching air attacks over the eastern part of New Guinea. Some of the Type 96 carrier fighters immediately advanced to the area; on the 11th, they engaged in air combat with three Hudson bombers that had come in to attack. All three were shot down.

On the 17th, the *Shōhō* ferried in six Zero fighters, the first such to arrive in Rabaul; it was then decided to start attacks on Port Moresby. The first attack was carried out on the 24th with fighters escorting nine land attack planes; no shadow of the enemy was seen, however. On the 28th, six Zero fighters under the command of LT Okamoto escorted seventeen land attack planes in an attack on Port Moresby. No air opposition was encountered, but a group of flying boats anchored in the port were discovered. Four Catalina aircraft were set on fire by low-level strafing. At the same time, one Zero fell victim to ground fire.

On 8 March, our army landed and captured Lae and Salamaua in northeastern New Guinea. The airfield at Lae was secured. On the 11th, seven Zero fighters

Model 21 Zero Fighter

Plane flown by PO1c Hiroyoshi Nishizawa. Unit insignia *F* was used during February through October 1942.

started using the airfield for intercept operations as well as for attacks on Port
Moresby. On 14 March, eight land attack
planes and twelve Zero fighters (commander, LT Kawai) engaged in air combat
with P-40s that had risen to intercept them
at far off Horn Island off the northeastern
tip of Australia. Eight enemy aircraft (including two probables) were shot down
but our side lost two aircraft, including the
one flown by LTJG Iwasaki.

With the reorganization as of 1 April, the
4th Air Group became a unit of land attack
planes only, and the former 4th Air Group
Fighter Squadron was posted to the Tainan
Air Group. As of the same date, the
strength of the Tainan Air Group located at
Rabaul and at Lae was ten Zero fighters and
eleven Type 96 carrier fighters. The group
continued to engage in air defense and attack operations. By mid-month, the main
force of the unit had advanced and joined
them at Rabaul.

第 6 航 空 隊

6TH AIR GROUP

The 6th Air Group was established at Kisarazu Base on 1 April 1942 and on the same day posted to the 26th Air Flotilla. CAPT Chisato Morita was CO, LCDR Asa-ichi Tamai the air officer, and LT Hideki Shingō, group leader.

Aircraft allowance was sixty carrier fighters and eight land reconnaissance planes; however, at the time of the unit's organization, actual strength consisted of only six aircraft. The unit started gradually to receive shipments of Zero fighters, of which there was a production shortage. By the end of the month, the number of aircraft available for use had risen to about twenty-nine Zero fighters and fourteen Type 96 carrier fighters. The core of pilots was composed of veterans of the Tainan Air Group and the 3rd Air Group who had finished their tours in the southern area of operations and had returned to the homeland. At the same time, the majority of personnel consisted of inexperienced men around the age of twenty who had finished the flight training course at the end of the previous year or in March of the current year; their skill level was low.

The first taste of combat came sooner than anticipated. In mid-April, the 11th Air Fleet had received communications intelligence indicating that an American task force would be approaching the homeland. As a result, ninety carrier fighters (including fifteen aircraft from the 6th Air Group) and eighty land attack planes were mobilized and stood by in the Kantō region, ready for action. The presence of the American carrier task force was detected by a patrol vessel six hundred miles east of the homeland. After sending off sixteen B-25 bombers under the command of LTCOL [James H.] Doolittle, the American task force turned back towards the east. Planning on a daylight torpedo attack, at 1245 the CO of the 26th Air Flotilla ordered the departure from Kisarazu base of twenty-nine land attack planes, escorted by twelve Zero fighters of the 6th Air Group (commander, LT Shingō) plus twelve Zero fighters from the *Kaga*. However, no trace of the enemy could be found. After traveling more than six hundred miles over the ocean, the planes reversed course; they were back at base by nightfall. During the same period of time, the B-25s carried out a surprise attack on the mainland, catching us off guard. After bombing Tokyo and various other places, the planes flew off towards the Chinese mainland. The opportunity to intercept them had been lost.

Stimulated by the Doolittle raid, plans for the Midway operation, which had been under consideration for some time, started materializing rapidly. The 6th Air Group received secret orders to land and occupy Midway after its capture; the group continued to conduct exercises. It is recorded that, as of 20 May, available aircraft numbered thirty-three Zero fighters; pilot strength consisted of twenty-five A class,

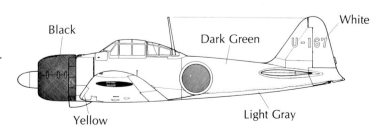

Model 22 Zero Fighter
Plane flown by PO1c Masayoshi Okazaki, 8 October 1942. Unit insignia *U* was used April–October 1942.

Black

Dark Green

White

U-167

Yellow

Light Gray

zero B class, and thirty-one C class personnel. Among the pilots scheduled to participate in the occupation, there were only a few of them who had even completed their carrier landing training. As a result, personnel and aircraft were split up into groups and placed on board each of the aircraft carriers involved in the operation. The allocation was as follows. To the *Akagi*: CO Morita, the new group leader, LT Tadashi Kaneko, and others, plus six zeros; to the *Kaga*: Air Officer Tamai and nine aircraft; and finally, three aircraft each to the *Sōryū* and *Hiryū*. During 24 and 25 May, personnel and aircraft were transferred on board the carriers located off Iwakuni. On the 19th, twelve zeros under the command of senior division officer LT Miyano were placed on board the *Junyō*. The plan was that after participating in the Aleutian operation, the unit would be moved south and proceed to Midway.

On 3 June, seven aircraft, including that flown by LT Miyano, together with six Zero fighters from the *Junyō* (commander, LT Shiga) escorted the carrier bomber force that attacked Dutch Harbor. In the second phase attack during the PM, three aircraft including LT Miyano's participated. On the following day, the 4th, LT Miyano and one other aircraft participated in another attack during which they engaged P-40s and shot down three of them. Also, two aircraft on combat air patrol over the aircraft carriers shot down two attacking PBY flying boats.

On the other hand, the Nagumo Striking Force was moving towards the island of Midway; on the morning of 4 June, its carriers launched the first attack. Immediately thereafter American land- and carrier-based aircraft conducted wave after wave of attacks; in the end, all four aircraft carriers were sunk. During the same period, LT Kaneko, accompanied by two other aircraft from the *Akagi*, left his carrier for combat air patrol; they shot down five enemy aircraft.

In the final analysis, the 6th Air Group lost all of its aircraft and was forced to return to the homeland. Gathering at Kisarazu base, the unit resumed training exercises. At this time, because of the American forces' attack on the Solomons on 7 Au-

Advance party of the 6th Air Group, en route from Kisarazu to Rabaul in August 1942. Left end, detachment leader, LT Mitsugu Kofukuda; fourth person from left, CPO Momoto Matsumura. Plane in the background is a Junkers Ju 88, purchased from Germany. (Ryōji Ōhara)

gust, ferocious air battles were developing in the southeast area. Our local forces requested the immediate dispatch of the entire 6th Air Group. Since it was not reasonable to commit green pilots to the front lines, however, it was decided that initially only experienced personnel would be sent out in an advance detachment. The new group leader, LT Kofukuda, led eighteen aircraft, guided by two land attack planes, and advanced by air to Rabaul on 21 August; all of his aircraft arrived safely, after having proceeded via Iwo Jima, Saipan, and Truk. For single seater fighters to conduct such a long-distance transfer was without precedent and was thought to be of considerable significance.

In early September, the advance detachment of the 6th Air Group sortied in attacks against Rabi, Port Moresby, and Gua-dalcanal. With the completion of the airfield at Buin on 8 October, the detachment moved in and provided direct cover for 6th Cruiser Division warships that had started out to bombard Guadalcanal. Because of bad weather conditions, however, five people were lost, starting with LTJG Kazuto Kuba and WO Sagane.

The main force of the 6th Air Group, consisting of twenty-seven aircraft (commander, LT Miyano), CO Morita, materials, equipment, and ground personnel, arrived at Rabaul on 7 October on board the carrier *Zuihō*. Here they met the advance detachment and soon thereafter the entire air group advanced to the base at Buin. With the reorganization of 1 November, the 6th Air Group was renamed Air Group 204 and continued to engage in air operations in the southeast area.

第 204 航空隊

AIR GROUP 204

Air Group 204 is the successor organization to the 6th Air Group and was established as a result of the reorganization of 1 November 1942, at which time it was renamed Air Group 204. Although the allowance called for sixty carrier fighters and eight land reconnaissance planes, actual strength numbered about half of those figures. The unit was composed of a mixture of the first model (Model 21) of the Zero fighter and the second model (Model 32).

From October on, Air Group 204 continued to use Buin as its base; duties were attacking Guadalcanal, providing air cover for Guadalcanal reinforcement convoys, air defense in the Buin area, and other assignments. Fighter units that were active at the time in the southeast area of operations, in addition to the 204, were air groups 252, 253, and 582. At one point, even the fighter squadron on board the *Hiyō* participated in the Guadalcanal operation. In carrying out large scale air operations, in many cases these various fighter units would act in unison. In air combat with enemy fighters, Zero fighter units maintained a superiority in performance and in skills. The gap with enemy forces gradually began to lessen, however; once 1943 came, both sides were about equal.

LT Kofukuda, group leader of Air Group 204 is quoted as having made the following observation: "We had absolute confidence of overcoming the enemy if forces on each side are roughly equal. . . .

If the strength on our side was half of that of the enemy, there would be a draw following a fierce battle. If our side were one-third as strong, we would have a rather tough fight on our hands. If our side had only one-fifth of the enemy strength, we would not have a chance of winning." What caused the unexpectedly large attrition of pilots was not necessarily aerial combat but the conduct of combat air patrols over warships and convoys destined for Guadalcanal. In particular, in the case of important convoys, escort operations would continue until sundown. Pilots in the final shift were forced to ditch, abandoning their aircraft and then being rescued by friendly destroyers. Such a procedure resulted in the loss of a number of veterans. The same fact is also apparent when we consider that for the period through the end of 1942, ten pilots were lost in air combat operations, whereas sixteen were lost as a result of other causes.

ADM Yamamoto of the Combined Fleet moved his flag to Rabaul in April 1943 and issued orders for the start of the "I"-gō operation.

Air Group 204 withdrew its main force to Rabaul and in coordination with [carrier] fighter squadrons of the 3rd Fleet, the air groups 253 and 582 participated in the attacks off Guadalcanal (the 7th), on Port Moresby (the 12th), and on Milne bay (the 14th). Victories totaled twenty enemy aircraft shot down. It was decided that ADM

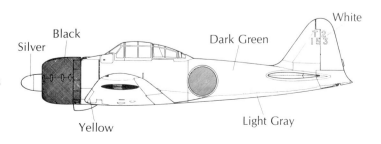

Model 22 Zero Fighter

Unit insignia *T2* was used during the period June 1943 through 1944. Plane numbers in the *190s* indicate the aircraft is a Model 32.

Yamamoto and his staff on 18 April would conduct a tour of inspection of the Buin base. The admiral and his staff would be traveling on board two land attack planes. Six Zero fighters of Air Group 204 (commander, Reserve LTJG Takeshi Morisaki) escorted the admiral and his staff. Based on information from decoded radio messages, however, the American air forces were aware of the plan and sent a unit of P-38s from Guadalcanal to intercept our aircraft over Cape Moira [southern Bougainville]. Despite vigorous battle by escorting fighters, both land attack aircraft were shot down; ADM Yamamoto died in action. One reason for this outcome is that the command at Rabaul, believing that control of the air was completely on the Japanese

TABLE 6. FORMATION OF AIR GROUP 204
(At the Attack on Guadalcanal, 16 June 1943)

	VICTORIES
1st Chūtai	
1st Shōtai	
LT Zenjirō Miyano	Failed to return
PO2c Hisahide Hashimoto	
PO1c Toyomitsu Tsujinoue	3; severe injuries
PO2c Yoshio Nakamura	Severe injuries
2nd Shōtai	
PO1c Masaichi Oshōdani	1
PO2c Kazu Tamura	Failed to return
PO1c Hachirō Tsuboya	
PO2c Katsuyoshi Tanaka	
2nd Chūtai	
1st Shōtai	
LTJG Takeshi Morisaki	Failed to return
PO2c Shigemasa Asami	1
PO2c Tomoji Nakano	2 (1)*
PO2c Takao Banno	Light injuries
2nd Shōtai	
CPO Hideo Watanabe	
PO2c Kijū Hitomi	3
PO2c Shō-ichi Sugita	
PO2c Masakazu Kobayashi	
3rd Chūtai	
1st Shōtai	
WO Hatsuo Hidaka	
PO2c Sei-ichi Kurosawa	1
PO2c Saji Kanda	Failed to return
PO2c Sei-ichi Nakasawa	
2nd Shōtai	
CPO Hiroshi Suzuki	
PO2c Tetsuo Hidaka	2
PO2 Kiyosaburō Watanabe	
PO2c Ryūji Yagi	

* Parentheses indicate probables

Model 32 Zero fighter that aimed at increasing speed by use of a shortened wing span. (Torao Saitō)

side, had inadvertently reduced the number of escort aircraft. Also, the pilots of the six aircraft were not necessarily the best that might have been selected. All of the escorts returned safely and claimed to have shot down six enemy aircraft (two probables). Actual loss on the side of the American air forces was only one plane.

The death of ADM Yamamoto marked a significant turning point in southeastern area operations, which were just beginning to show signs of becoming a hard struggle. There was also fatigue resulting from continuing combat operations; morale gradually started to decline. In particular, losses of Type 1 land attack planes, which were deficient in defense capabilities, increased. CO Sugimoto of Air Group 204 thought up the idea of equipping Zero fighters with 30-kg bombs and using them as fighter bombers. In order to supplement the shortage of attack forces, training exercises were carried out despite severe ongoing battles.

About this time, LT Kofukuda returned to the homeland and LT Miyano was promoted to group leader. The LT vigorously led his forces and continued resolutely attacking the enemy. The fighter bombing method of fighting was attempted during the 7 June attack on the Russell Islands; eight of the total of twenty-four aircraft carrying out the attack were equipped with bombs. Heavy ground fire resulted in major damage to our side. This method of attack was abandoned after this one attempt. On 16 June, LT Miyano joined a dive bomber escort unit equipped the way that he himself had propounded; however, he was killed in action during air combat off Lunga. At one point, Air Group 204 had reached a condition where there was not a single officer pilot left in the unit.

On 30 June American forces started to move north from the central Solomons to attack Rendova Island; on 14 July they landed on Munda [New Georgia].

Zero fighters on the flight line. Model 22 in foreground; to the left, Model 32. (Torao Saitō)

In mid-August, Air Group 204 again moved up to Buin and established headquarters there. During the same period, the 204 absorbed the fighter squadron of the now-disbanded Air Group 582 and the carrier fighter squadrons of the 2nd Carrier Division. Engaging in daily attacks and intercept operations, Air Group 204 suffered mounting losses; in early October, the unit retreated to Rabaul. After October, the preponderance of air combat moved to the Rabaul area; Air Group 204, together with air groups 201 and 253, formed the nucleus of the air units at this base. In addition to participating in spectacular intercept operations, they were also involved in attacks on Torokina and Cape Marcus. On 26 January 1944, leaving behind some pilots who were

Air Group 204 at Buin, September 1943. Second row (from the left): fifth person, LT Okajima; seventh, LCDR Chikamasa Igarashi; ninth, LTJG Fukuda, tenth, CPO Hagiri; right end, CPO Ishihara. Third row: left end, Kiyoshi Sekiya. Fourth row (from the left): fifth person, Takao Banno; ninth, Tomita Atake, and tenth, Wataru Nakamichi. Fifth row (from the right): third person, Toshihisa Shirakawa. (Akimasa Igarashi)

Model 32 Zero fighter (T2-135) taxiing (Torao Saitō)

transferred to Air Group 253, the remaining twelve aircraft of Air Group 204, together with the 26th Air Flotilla command, withdrew to Truk for recuperation and the rebuilding of their units.

At Truk, Air Group 204 was reinforced with fresh pilots who had arrived from the homeland and were waiting for them. Intending to advance again to Rabaul, training exercises were started. What happened, however, was that the air raid conducted by an American carrier task force on 17 February decimated the 204 organization. The 26th Air Flotilla command had become aware through radio intelligence that enemy forces were approaching; local units were on alert all during the 16th. Since nothing unusual was observed, however,

Zero fighters fly in formation over the airfield. (Torao Saitō)

the alert condition was returned to a peacetime basis, and personnel were granted leave. At the same time, on the morning of the 17th, radar provided warning of the approach of strong enemy forces; orders were immediately issued for interception. Because of the wave after wave of attacks that followed, all of Truk Atoll was dealt a devastating blow, in effect enacting a "Second Pearl Harbor Attack."

The thirty-one Zero fighters belonging to Air Group 204, together with eight Zero fighters of Air Group 201 and about ten aircraft of Air Group 501 (a bomb-equipped Zero fighter unit) engaged in several daring air battles and shot down about thirty enemy aircraft. By nightfall [17 February], however, there was only one operable Zero fighter left. Air Group 204 alone suffered the loss of eighteen pilots killed in action. Survivors were transported to the homeland by medium land attack planes; the unit itself was disbanded 4 March. It is to be noted that overall battle results achieved by the 6th Air Group, since the date of its establishment, amounted to about one thousand enemy aircraft shot down, counting only the results of air combat.

Successive Commanding Officers:

April 1942–March 1943 CAPT Chisato Morita

March 1943–September 1943 CAPT Ushie Sugimoto

September 1943–March 1944 CDR Takeo Kurita

Successive Group Leaders:

April 1942–May 1942 LT Hideki Shingō

May 1942–July 1942 LT Tadashi Kaneko

July 1942–March 1943 LT Mitsugu Kofukuda

March 1943–July 1943 LT Zenjirō Miyano

July 1943–September 1943 LCDR Saburō Shindō

September 1943–December 1943 LT Kiyokuma Okajima

September 1943–January 1944 LT Yoshio Kurakane

January 1944–March 1944 LTJG Torajirō Haruta

第 2 航空隊 (第 582) 戦闘機隊

2ND AIR GROUP (582) FIGHTER SQUADRON

Organized on 31 May 1942 at Yokosuka as a mixed carrier fighter and carrier bomber air group, the 2nd Air Group was posted to the Combined Fleet on the same day. CDR Sakae Yamamoto was ordered in as the CO, and LCDR Katsutoshi Yagi as the air officer. Allowance at the time of its organization was sixteen carrier fighters and sixteen carrier bombers; however, with the reorganization of November, this was increased to thirty-six carrier fighters and twenty-four carrier bombers.

Initially, the 2nd Air Group Fighter squadron was scheduled to participate in future operations against the New Hebrides and New Caledonia, together with the 6th Air Group. On 29 July, equipment, materials, and personnel were loaded on board the specially converted escort carrier, *Yawata Maru* and she left Yokosuka. On 6 August, fifteen Zero fighters and sixteen Type 99 carrier bombers, under the direct command of CDR Yamamoto, took off from the carrier and advanced to the east airfield at Rabaul. On the 15th, the unit was integrated into the Eighth Fleet.

The seventh of August happened to be the day that the American forces started their counteroffensive against Guadalcanal. From the very first, the 2nd Air Group unit was involved in fierce air combat. On the morning of the 7th, nine carrier bombers (commanded by LT Fumito Inoue) left to attack enemy ships off Guadalcanal, fully aware that it was to be a one-way trip; in this attack alone, [all nine] aircraft were lost. Again, the fighter squadron was as-

signed combat air patrol over Rabaul and together with fighters of the Tainan Air Group was able to shoot down a B-17 that had come on a reconnaissance mission.

Zero fighters assigned to the 2nd Air Group were the second model (models 22 and 32), which were improvements over the initial model (Model 21). Horsepower had been increased by changing to an engine equipped with a two-stage supercharger; this had increased the speed somewhat. At the same time, because of the increase in weight, cruising range was reduced. As a result, the aircraft was viewed as being rather unsuitable for the long-range attack operations then being conducted in the Solomons area. They were used primarily in operations in the eastern part of New Guinea.

On the 22nd, the 2nd Air Group Carrier Fighter Squadron (commander, LT Yoshio Kurakane), together with a part of the Tainan Air Group, advanced to Buna airfield [New Guinea]. On the 24th, an attack was made on Rabi and the first real air combat with P-39s occurred. Nine of the enemy aircraft (two probables) were shot down; all of our planes returned safely. On the 26th and 27th, attacks were repeated, this time with carrier bombers participating. However, our side lost two carrier bombers and two zero fighters (separately, four of the Tainan Air Group as well). In particular, two carrier fighters, including one piloted by PO1c Iwase, were caught in a surprise attack by P-39s just as they were

Model 32 Zero Fighter

Unit insignia Q was used during July through October 1942.

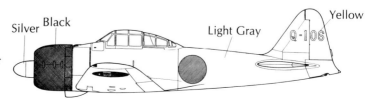

Silver Black Light Gray Yellow

Q-106

Air Group 582 at Buin, June 1943. Front row, from the left: LTJG Usaburō Suzuki, CDR Sakae Yamamoto (commanding officer), LCDR Saburō Shindō, LTJG Gi-ichi Noguchi, WO Kazuo Tsunoda, and WO Yoshihiko Takenaka. Second row (seated), from the left: third person, Daizō Fukumori; Ki-ichi Nagano; skip one; Nobutaka Yanami; skip one; Tomezō Yamamoto. Rear row: left end Shin-ichi Hirabayashi; from the right, fifth person, Kiyoshi Sekiya; fourth person, Bangorō Myōkei; right end, Shigehiko Itō—all noncommissioned officer pilots. (Family of Ki-ichi Nagano)

taking off from Buna airfield; both planes were destroyed.

In the above fashion, the 2nd Air Group made repeated attacks on Port Moresby and on Rabi until 8 September, using Buna as its base. From the early part of September, the 2nd Air Group participated in the drive on Guadalcanal. The first attack by the unit was made by three aircraft on the 4th, but the enemy was not to be seen. On the 12th, fifteen Zero fighters, and on the 14th, eleven Zero fighters were used in other attacks. Battle results in the two cases came to eleven and ten enemy aircraft shot down. During the same period, an additional ten fighters and three carrier bombers were provided to the air group. As soon as the Buka base was ready on 28 September, CO Yamamoto advanced with

twenty-one Zero fighters. This unit conducted a number of attacks on Guadalcanal in support of the 25 October general offensive conducted by the army.

Next, from 11 November through 14 November, the 2nd Air Group (renamed Air Group 582 as of 1 November) assisted in supply operations to Guadalcanal, as well as participating in the difficult task of providing air cover. Starting the middle of the month, the main body of the air group again headed for eastern New Guinea. Using Lae as a staging base, the unit made frequent sorties escorting ship convoys headed for Buna, in addition to conducting air control operations in the Buna area.

On 7 and 8 January 1943, Air Group 582, acting in coordination with army fighter units, participated in protecting

Model 22 Zero Fighter

Unit insignia *T3* was used during June 1943 through March 1944. (The fighter squadron was dissolved 1 August 1943.) Right after the formation of the 2nd Air Group, *Q* was used.

convoys en route to Lae. Between the end of January and the early part of February, the 582 advanced to bases at Buin and Munda [New Georgia]. The group's entire strength was used in supporting the evacuation from Guadalcanal referred to as the "Ke"-gō operation. In particular, during the sea battle off Isabel Island on 1 February, twenty-one Zero fighters (commander, LT Saburō Shindō) provided direct support to fifteen carrier bombers and performed in a daring fashion; however, five carrier bombers and two fighters were lost. As an example of a special type of operation, the following is of interest. On 10 February, in the attempt to ensure that secret documents that may have been left on the submarine *I-1,* stranded and abandoned on the north shore of Guadalcanal, would be destroyed, eight carrier bombers accompanied by forty-two Zero fighters (of which fourteen aircraft were from Air Group 582) were used to bomb the beached sub. One bomb did hit near the conning tower.

With issuance of orders for the "I"-gō operation in April 1943, Air Group 582 participated therein using its entire strength. Starting off with the attack off Guadalcanal on the 7th, during attacks on Port Moresby (12th of the month), as well as during the attack on Milne Bay (14th), a cumulative total of eighteen carrier bombers and fifty-eight fighters sortied.

Next, for the purpose of conducting an inspection of the Buin base, ADM Yamamoto of the Combined Fleet and his staff boarded two Type 1 land attack planes and left Rabaul on the 18th. However, the two aircraft were shot down by P-38s that lay in ambush over the dense forest in the Cape Moira area, based on radio intelligence received about the moves of the admiral. The group died with tragic bravery. Immediately upon receipt of a report on this matter, the 582 sent out six carrier bombers to search for the downed planes. As a matter of fact, during the early morning of this same day, a cumulative total of sixteen fighters of Air Group 582, under the command of WO Tsunoda, had flown off in

pursuit of P-38s that had reportedly arrived in the area. The P-38s were not found. The tragic event of the deaths of the admiral and his staff occurred after those planes had returned to base. Intent upon taking revenge against P-38s, Air Group 582 made reprisal on the 22nd over Rabaul, led by WO Tsunoda, and on the 29th over Buin, led by PO2c Sekiya, by shooting down one P-38 each.

Later, using Buin and Munda as bases, Air Group 582 directly confronted the American air forces on Guadalcanal and continued to engage in fierce battles. In particular, on 13 May, and again on 7 and 12 June, the fighter squadron alone advanced into the area over Russell Island and engaged in large-scale aerial combat operations; a total of twenty-eight enemy aircraft were destroyed. During intercept battles over Buin on 5 June, seventeen enemy aircraft were destroyed. On 16 June, in coordination with other units, Air Group 582 sent out twenty-four carrier bombers and sixteen carrier fighters (commander, LCDR Shindō) in an attack on enemy vessels off Lunga [Guadalcanal]. The fierce battle resulted in four enemy aircraft being shot down, but our side also lost eight carrier bombers and four carrier fighters. Despite such meritorious battling on our part, American forces that had counterattacked in the central Solomons area drove on to Rendova Island on 30 June. Air Group 582 engaged in counterattacks almost daily. With 12 July as the final day of operations, the fighter squadron was disbanded; the air group itself became solely a carrier bomber unit. This was formally ordered on 1 August. (Later on there was a transition to a carrier attack plane unit.) A portion of surviving [fighter] pilots were sent back to the homeland but the majority were assigned to the 201, 204, and other air groups. In a little under one year, the curtain was rung down on Air Group 582 Fighter Squadron, a unit that had built up such a brilliant tradition. It is to be noted that battle results during this period reached about 220 aircraft destroyed, counting only those shot down in air combat.

第253航空隊 (旧鹿屋航空隊戦闘機隊)

AIR GROUP 253
(FORMERLY KANOYA AIR GROUP FIGHTER SQUADRON)

Air Group 253 was established on 1 April 1936 at Kanoya, Kagoshima Prefecture, as a land attack plane unit. One and a half units (eighteen aircraft) of Type 95 land attack planes and one unit of Type 95 carrier fighters (twelve aircraft, group leader LCDR Asa-ichi Tamai) were attached thereto. With the outbreak of the China Incident in August 1937, the Kanoya Air Group was integrated into the 1st Combined Air Group and advanced to the base at Taipei [Taihoku]. Starting with the first overseas bombing attack on the 15th, the unit was active in bombing attacks on key areas in central and southern China all the way through November. The carrier fighter squadron was given duties of providing air defense in and around Taipei. In December, the 253 moved to Shanghai; the land attack squadron was active in bombing key areas in central China such as Hankow and Nanchang. Because of insufficient cruising range, Type 95 fighters were unable to accompany the other planes and there were no opportunities for air combat. At the end of March 1938, the 1st Combined Air Group was ordered back to the homeland; at the same time, the carrier fighter squadron was eliminated. From this time on, the Kanoya group operated only land attack planes. At the time the Pacific War started, it was posted to the 21st Air Flotilla and participated in the Malayan and Dutch East Indies area operations. Among other feats, the unit was responsible for sinking the [British battleship] *Prince of Wales*.

After completion of its southern area tour, the Kanoya Air Group returned to Kisarazu base, around 10 March 1942. Soon after that it again became involved in southwest area operations; it was engaged in searches over the Indian Ocean area, based at Sabang [off Sumatra] and at Rangoon. At the same time, as of 1 April, the decision was made to attach to the Kanoya group a carrier fighter squadron (group leader, LT Toshitaka Itō; allowance thirty-six aircraft). The majority of the personnel involved in this new unit were transferees from the fighter squadron that was attached to the former 22nd Air Flotilla headquarters, which had assembled at Bangkok following completion of their Dutch East Indies operations. For the next six months or so, until September, the unit was engaged in air defense operations as well as in training exercises, based at Sabang and at Andaman. With the growing importance of the southeast area of operations, the unit was ordered to proceed to Rabaul. About 19 September, twenty-three land attack planes and one buntai (nine aircraft, commander, LT Itō) of Zero fighters advanced to Kavieng [New Ireland]. In early October, the unit was reinforced to a total of about twenty-four Zero fighters. Next, starting with the 21 September attack on Port Moresby, the Kanoya group became involved in air battles surrounding Guadalcanal. During the attack on Guadalcanal carried out on the 29th, the Kanoya group engaged in its first air combat operation, shooting down four enemy aircraft.

Model 21 Zero Fighter

During the Kanoya Air Group period. Unit insignia K was used between November 1940 and September 1942.

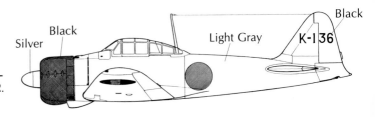

Silver · Black · Light Gray · Black · K-136

Model 21 Zero fighters training at Penang base, summer of 1942. (On the left is the K-125.) (Kiku-ichi Inano)

Next, as of 1 October, the Kanoya Air Group was renamed the Air Group 751. As a result of the reorganization of 1 November the land attack plane squadron and the carrier fighter squadron were separated. The carrier fighter squadron was renamed at this point Air Group 253. CDR Yoshito Kobayashi was ordered in as the CO and LCDR Sei-ichi Maki as the air officer; aircraft allowance was forty-eight carrier fighters and eight land reconnaissance planes. Next it was attached to the 21st Air Flotilla and maintained its main strength at Kavieng. Some elements were sent to Rabaul, Buka, Surumi, and elsewhere. During the approximately eight-month period before mid-May 1943, when it withdrew to Saipan, the 253 carried out vigorous attacks on Guadalcanal and on Oro Bay, and was active in screening convoys and in air defense and intercept operations. Through air combat alone, battle results amounted to approximately 110 enemy aircraft; our side also lost thirty or more pilots killed in action.

At the end of June [1943], the war situation in the southeast area of operations had become more serious because of the American forces' attacks on Rendova. In early July, one chūtai of the 253 was dispatched to Buin. Following a number of air engagements, LTJG Saitō was lost. Attendant upon the disbanding of the 21st Air Flotilla on 1 September of the same year, Air Group 253, which had been taking rest and recuperation as well as undergoing refitting at Saipan, was next integrated into the 25th Air Flotilla (allowance, ninety-six aircraft),

Model 52 Zero Fighter

Unit insignia *U3* was used during the period September 1943 through 1944. At the time of initial reorganization, *K* (for the Kanoya Air Group days) was used.

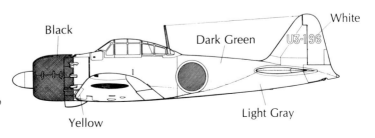

Black

Dark Green

White

U3-196

Yellow

Light Gray

Model 21 Zero fighter at Bangkok. (Ken-ichi Abe)

based at Rabaul. Between early and mid-September, the unit moved to Tobera airfield at Rabaul. Replacing the exhausted air groups 201 and 204, the 253 fought as the nucleus in the daily air battles over eastern New Guinea and northern Solomons. In particular, after mid-October allied air attacks on Rabaul became very frequent and the 253 had to send out thirty to forty aircraft on each occasion to engage in daring intercept operations. By the end of January 1944, fighter units operating in air defense over Rabaul had dwindled to only Air Group 253 and units dispatched from the

2nd Carrier Division. Many experienced personnel were lost in battle; by mid-February operable aircraft of the 253 had been reduced to about twenty or more aircraft only. At the same time, intercept operation results were substantial; results were in excess of five hundred enemy aircraft downed during the period September 1943 through February 1944. Battle result reports towards the end of this same period were of low reliability; when compared with announcements made on the American side, ours are believed to have been inflated by a factor of five to ten times.

On 17 and 18 February 1944, our important Micronesia area base at Truk was demolished as a result of attacks by American carrier task forces. Air units at Rabaul were ordered withdrawn to Truk. On the 20th, the main force of Air Group 253 left Truk and moved to Rabaul; only nine Zero aircraft, under the command of WO Shigeo Fukumoto, were left in Rabaul.

Air Group 253, fatigued by the continuing combat, started rest, recuperation, and refitting at the Takeshima base on Truk Island. On April 30th, however, the unit suffered yet another air raid by American carrier fighters; twenty of our aircraft failed to return to base. In addition, there was damage to aircraft on the ground; total operable aircraft were reduced to merely five. Moreover, starting in mid-March, B-24 raids became frequent. The 253 tried to intercept them using No. 3 [aerial] bombs and other weapons and did attain some kills. However, losses on our side were also not inconsiderable. Next, with the reorganization of 1 April, Air Group 253 was divided into two hikōtai, Fighter Hikōtai 309 (commander, LT Tatsu-o Hirano) and Fighter Hikōtai 310 (commander, LCDR Haru-

Model 52 Zero Fighter
At Truk, 1944.

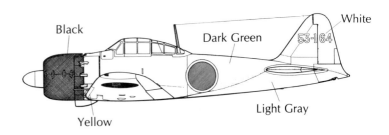

Black

White

Dark Green 53-164

Yellow

Light Gray

Air Group 253 at Kavieng on New Years Day, 1943. Second row (from left): second person, CPO Takio Yoshida; LTJG Yōichi Kenmochi; LT Masao Iizuka; LT Toshitaka Itō (group leader); LTJG Saburō Saitō; WO Tadashi Torakuma; and CPO Shizuo Ishii. Third row (from left): sixth person, Shigeru Shibukawa. Fourth row (from left): fifth person, Minoru Honda. (Shigeru Shibukawa)

Air Group 253 at Tobera, February 1944. Front row (from left): fifth person, Masajirō Kawato. Second row (from left): second person, CPO Tetsutarō Kumagaya; fourth, LCDR Okamoto (group leader); fifth, CDR Fukuda (commanding officer); sixth, LTJG Haruta; seventh, CPO Tetsuzō Iwamoto; eighth, Shigeo Fukumoto; ninth, Sadamu Komachi; and tenth, Kaoru Takaiwa. Third row, left end, Sekizen Shibayama. Fourth row (from left): seventh person, Ken-ichi Takahashi. (Kenji Takahashi)

toshi Okamoto; each unit with an allow-ance of forty-eight aircraft).

As of 16 June immediately before the is-suance of the order for the "A"-gō opera-tion [Marianas], however, the total number of operable aircraft did not exceed thirteen Zero fighters. On the 19th, the entire force of Air Group 253 was ordered to advance to Guam in coordination with movements of the First Striking Force. Under the com-mand of LCDR Okamoto, thirteen fighters left Truk as escorts for the attack plane unit. Just before landing at Guam, how-ever, several score of F6Fs made a surprise attack on the Okamoto unit. After fighting against heavy odds, the second formation lost five aircraft, including that flown by LT Hirano, formation commander. Even the aircraft that did manage to land on the ground were all heavily damaged by fire. Before any final suicide attack might have been made, the survivors escaped by trans-port vessels, submarines, and in other ways to the homeland.

On 10 July, Air Group 253 was dis-banded. Seven Zero fighters that had re-mained at Truk were transferred to the Eastern Caroline Air Group; until about October, a small number of fighters con-tinued to intercept B-24s. Units left at Ra-baul repaired their damaged Zero fighters and attempted guerilla intercept action. They did make a contribution to the overall war effort by strafing and bombing Green Islands (Nissan), conducting reconnais-sance under fire, and other actions. Imme-diately upon the disbanding of Air Group 253, surviving pilots were transferred to the Southeast Area Fleet Command; until the end of the war, they continued to be active, based at Rabaul.

Successive Commanding Officers:

November 1942–July 1943   CDR Yoshito Kobayashi

July 1943–June 1944   CDR Tarō Fukuda

June 1944–July 1944   CDR Shō-ichi Oga-sawara

Successive Group Leaders:

November 1942–August 1943   LT Toshi-taka Itō

August 1943–January 1944   LCDR Haru-toshi Okamoto

January 1944–March 1944   LT Tatsu-o Hirano

第 281 航空隊

AIR GROUP 281

Air Group 281 was newly established at Maizuru Air Base on 20 February 1943. On 1 March it was attached to the Yokosuka Naval Station and started operations at Tateyama base. CDR Shigehachirō Tokoro was assigned as the CO; LT Taka-ichi Hasu-o as the group leader; and LTJGs Torajirō Haruta, Ichirō Imamura, and Isamu Mochizuki as division officers. The allowance was forty-eight Zero fighters, and if officers of division rank are excluded, newly graduated pilots with no battlefield experience were in the majority.

Most of the training was completed around May 1943. It was decided that, as of the 18th, the unit would be posted to the 27th Air Flotilla of the 12th Air Fleet and sent to the northeast area. Transiting via Misawa and Mihoro, the unit arrived at the Paramushir base in the northern Kuriles on the 23rd. At the time, the American forces had landed on the island of Attu and fierce fighting was continuing. Although there were occasions on which the land attack unit based at Paramushir would travel long distances over northern seas and attack American ships off Attu, it was difficult for the fighter unit to accompany the group because of cruising range factors.

In May, the garrison on Attu Island met with a glorious end; in addition, for a while tension in the northern area lessened. After August, B-24s started sporadic air raids on the Kurile Islands; it was the army's 54th Fighter Regiment that participated in the

majority of air battles that ensued. Group 281 went on antisubmarine missions on a few occasions, but there were no opportunities to engage in air combat operations. As of the end of August, operable aircraft consisted of twenty Model 21 Zero fighters; however, on the 25th, twenty-five additional aircraft were flown in from Ta-

Genji Aoki and Zeros of Air Group 281 at Tateyama, April 1943. (Genji Aoki)

Model 22 Zero Fighter
About 1944.

CDR Shigehachirō Tokoro (*front right*), CO of Air Group 281 (Kiku-ichi Inano)

teyama. As a result, the total number of operable aircraft was increased to forty-two; the aircraft were dispersed to three separate airfields on the island.

With the increasing intensity of air battles in the southeast area in November, sixteen Zero fighters from Air Group 281 led by LTJG Haruta (as well as WO Tetsuzō Iwamoto, SupSea Nobu-o Ogiya, and others) were detached. Traveling from island to island, the aircraft arrived at Rabaul on the 14th and were transferred to Air Group 204.

Next, in response to the emergency in the Gilbert Islands area, it was decided that the 24th Air Flotilla would proceed to the Marshall Islands to take the place of the emaciated 22nd Air Flotilla. On 24 November, Air Group 281 was integrated into the 24th Air Flotilla and ordered to proceed to the Marshalls.

The first unit to move, twenty-one aircraft under the command of CO Tokoro, left Kisarazu on the 27th and advanced to the base at Roi on 3 December, proceeding via Tinian, Truk, and Brown [Island, Eniwetok Atoll]. The second contingent of eighteen aircraft left Tateyama on 1–2 December; following the same course, they arrived at Roi on the 6th. As of the 8th, all aircraft had completed the transit. Base personnel, equipment, and materials next arrived on Roi on the 10th, having been transported on the destroyer *Kasumi*.

On 5 December, however, Roi was attacked by a large group of fighters from an American carrier task force; Air Group 281, which had just arrived, sustained losses. Although land-based radar had detected the approach of enemy forces at the 80-km point on this date, the intercept battle situation had become unfavorable for our side because of delayed communications. Air Group 281 also participated in intercept operations, using twenty-seven of its planes, but ten aircraft were lost in action.

Carrier fighter squadrons of the 1st Carrier Division suffered heavy losses during the course of the day's air battles and had to withdraw to Truk. As a result, the responsibility for air defense in the Roi area became that of Air Group 281.

On 14 December, thirteen Zero fighters led by LT Hasuo were dispatched to the island of Mili at the southeastern end of the Marshall Islands. After participating in intercept operations against multi-engine aircraft on a number of occasions, the unit returned to Roi after attacking Makin Atoll as its final operation. Starting the latter part of December, multi-engine aircraft began to attack Roi and Kwajalein. On 30 January 1944, American task forces launched major attacks against various targets in the Marshall Islands. In retaliatory attacks launched by our forces through the 31st, the majority of aircraft stationed locally (twenty-five carrier fighters), with the exception of one part of the land attack plane unit that had taken refuge at Truk, was demolished on the ground.

On 1 February, which was the following day, American amphibious forces began landing on the two islands of Kwajalein and Roi following massive ship bombardments. By the 6th, the island garrisons had met an honorable death. It is understood that after the 30th all members of Air Group 281, starting with the CO, transformed themselves into a naval infantry unit and all died a glorious death. Since there are no survivors, however, details are not clear as to exactly what happened from the advance of the unit to Roi Island until the unit's decimation.

第 261 航 空 隊 （虎）

AIR GROUP 261 (TORA)

Air Group 261 was established on 1 June 1943 at Kagoshima base and was referred to as the Tora ("Tiger") unit. On 1 July, it was posted to the newly created 1st Air Fleet; CDR Taketora Ueda came on board as the CO and LT Masanobu Ibusuki as group leader. Although the allowance called for thirty-six Zero fighters, it was later increased to seventy-two fighters; intense training activities started at the Kagoshima base.

In February 1944 the 1st Air Fleet command was ordered to advance to the Marianas; Air Group 261 also started its move from Kagoshima to Katori base on the 19th. Because of poor weather, however, over one half of the aircraft made emergency landings in the Kinki area of the homeland and aircraft rendezvous was delayed. On the 22nd, sixty-eight aircraft did leave Katori and advanced to Iwo Jima. At this time, the first American air attack on the Marianas occurred; advance units of the 1st Air Fleet were heavily damaged. Waiting until after the American task force had withdrawn, on the 24th and 26th, Air Group 261 split itself into two units and then advanced to Saipan. Also, approximately six hundred base personnel plus equipment and supplies were transported on board the *Chitose* and entered Saipan harbor on 26 February.

On 30 March, in response to the American task force attack on Palau, thirty-two fighters of Air Group 261 under the command of LT Ibusuki, escorted the Suisei carrier bomber squadron of Air Group 523 and left Saipan. Proceeding via Guam, a search for the enemy in the vicinity of Palau was conducted but met with negative

CDR Taketora Ueda, CO of Air Group 261. (Ikuhiko Hata)

Model 52 Zero Fighter
About 1944.

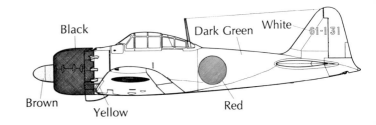

Model 21 Zero fighter of Air Group 261 (National Archives)

results. During the evening, the group of aircraft landed on Peleliu Island. Early the next morning a large group of American carrier fighters attacked; the 261, together with air groups 263 and 201, rose to intercept them. Although eighteen enemy aircraft (three probables) were shot down, our units came under heavy attack while flying at a low altitude preparatory to assembling. Our side suffered major losses; indeed, twenty of the twenty-three aircraft involved failed to return. In addition, four persons received light or serious injuries, and eight aircraft were heavily damaged or set on fire while on the ground. Surviving pilots were evacuated to Saipan and the remaining personnel, augmented by additional aircraft, started to rebuild their units.

When April came, raids by PBY flying boats and B-24s on Saipan and Mariaon [Woleai Atoll] became frequent; Air Group 261 took its turn in air defense operations over Mariaon [Woleai]. On 23 April, twenty-seven aircraft led by LT Ibusuki advanced to Mariaon [Woleai] and shot down four B-24s (two by ramming tactics); our side also lost four aircraft. This battle was

commended by the commander of the Combined Fleet and a citation promulgated throughout the fleet.

Later, efforts were made to regain strength, using Airfield No. 2 on Saipan as a base. By mid-May, the number of aircraft available had been built back up to forty-two, the number of operable aircraft to thirty-four. By the end of May in the Biak Island area, the time appeared ripe. Under orders of the Combined Fleet, twenty-seven fighters of Air Group 261 led by LT Ibusuki departed from Saipan on 2 June. Proceeding via Yap and Peleliu islands, on the 6th the unit arrived at Wasile on Halmahera Island. But on 12 June all twelve aircraft that were sent to Biak failed to return. Hearing of the American attacks in the Mariana area, the unit again returned to Guam and Yap.

One buntai, led by LT Ken-ichi Ban, stayed on in Saipan and Yap during this same period and came under attack by American forces. Also during this period the unit faced the day of the final battle of the "A"-gō operation. In addition to attrition to aircraft caused by the various moves made by the unit, pilots increasingly became ill with tropical diseases. As a result, no effective opposition was possible except for small numbers of aircraft that were used in attacking enemy ships off Saipan or in air defense operations over Guam. By the 21st, there were only two aircraft left on Guam; the majority of pilots, starting with LT Ibusuki, escaped in groups by using land attack planes. A few also escaped by submarine but died in action as a result of the submarines themselves being sunk. Until 15 July, several persons, including CPO Minpo Tanaka, remained on the island and repeatedly carried out attacks on Saipan. It is recorded that during the period of the "A"-gō operation (27 May–15 July), Air Group 261's victories were in excess of seventy-six enemy aircraft shot down. At the same time, the number of our aircraft that destroyed themselves and of pilots who failed to return to base totaled twenty-eight.

On 10 July, Air Group 261 was disbanded and the majority of surviving personnel transferred to Air Group 201.

第 331 航 空 隊

AIR GROUP 331

Air Group 331 was organized at Saeki on 1 July 1943 and attached to the Southwest Area Fleet. It was a mixed unit consisting of twenty-four Zero fighters (group leader, LCDR Hideki Shingō) and twenty-four Type 97 carrier attack planes (division officer, LT Saneyuki Hida). CDR Hisao Shimoda was ordered in as the CO. In order to advance to the Sabang base at the northern edge of Sumatra during the month of August, thirty-six carrier fighters and eighteen carrier attack planes were loaded on board the aircraft carrier *Junyō,* which departed Saeki on the 15th. Next, on the 27th, all aircraft took off from the carrier while she was still off Singapore and flew to Sabang. Among the more green pilots were a large number of men who had not received any training in carrier takeoffs or landings. A few days later, the light cruiser *Kashi-i* arrived, transporting base equipment and goods and ground personnel. At this time there were no enemy air raids in the Sumatra area; however, submarine operations were brisk. In the Andaman and Nicobar islands, there were some enemy bomber attacks. As of 1 September, the carrier attack plane squadron was removed and reorganized as Air Group 551. It was next moved to the Kotawaringin base. Together with Air Group 331, the group was integrated into the 28th Air Flotilla; the two groups joined forces in antisubmarine patrols, protection of ship convoys, etc. Also, a portion of Air Group 331 was dispatched to Car Nicobar, Port Blair, Mergui [South

Burma], and Waingapu where they engaged in intercepting the occasional raids conducted by B-24s. On a number of occasions, there were some battle results; in early December the unit moved to Burma. Jointly with the navy's [land] attack plane units and the army's air regiments, attacks were made on the key city of Calcutta in eastern India. For example, twenty-seven Zero fighters led by LCDR Shingō, advanced from Sabang to Tavoy on the first day, to Magwe in central Burma on the second day; on the 3rd day, 5 December, they succeeded in bombing Calcutta, escorting the land attack planes of the 705th Air Group. Six (of which two probables) of the intercepting Hurricane fighters were shot down; all of our aircraft returned safely. In mid February 1944, in an attempt to reinforce the Micronesia area defenses that had become somewhat thinned out because of air raids on Truk conducted by American carrier task forces, Air Group 331 received orders to move. As of 4 March, the entire force of thirty-three fighters was reorganized into Fighter Hikōtai 603 and posted to Air Group 202. Proceeding via Singapore, Surabaya, Kendari, and Davao, the unit advanced to the island of Mariaon [Woleai Atoll] on 24 March.

At the same time, a new fighter unit (allowance of twenty-four aircraft) had been organized at Iwakuni base; in mid-May, one buntai thereof led by Reserve LT Akira Tanaka advanced to Sabang. Next, the unit

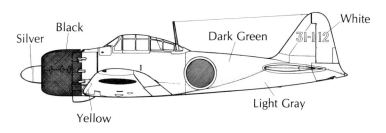

Model 52 Zero Fighter
About 1944.

Silver · Black · Dark Green · White · 31-112 · Light Gray · Yellow

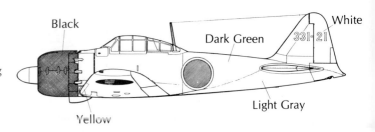

Model 52 Zero Fighter
Unit insignia *331* used during fall 1944 through 1945.

moved to Penang and continued to engage in training activities, in particular, fighter bombing tactics. Because of the advance of American forces into the Marianas, however, on 15 June twelve fighters were ordered to proceed to the island of Peleliu, arriving on the 17th. Next, one portion of the unit moved to Yap Island and engaged in patrol operations until the end of the month. There were no opportunities to engage in combat, however; on 4 July, the unit moved to Davao and then returned to Penang.

As of 1 September, the number of aircraft available (those operable are shown in parentheses) was eighteen (sixteen) Model 21 Zero fighters, seven (five) Model 52 Zero fighters, and seven (two) carrier bombers. Later, during October, Air Group 331 was reorganized into a mixed group consisting of Fighter Hikōtai 309 (commander, LT Kisuke Hasegawa; allowance, forty-eight aircraft) and Attack Hikōtai 253 (allowance, forty-eight carrier attack planes). The main strength of the first named unit left Penang on 18 September and moved to Balikpapan [Borneo]. From the end of the same month, American air forces attacked Balikpapan. By mid-October a number of intercept operations were conducted jointly with Air Group 381 and considerable battle results achieved. On the 19th, eight Zero fighters led by LT Hasegawa, together with fifteen aircraft of Air Group 381 led by LT Keijirō Hayashi, moved to the base at Mabalacat [Luzon]. As of 1 October, the number of aircraft available (number operable) were as follows: thirty (twenty) Zero fighters of Fighter Air Group 309 at Balikpapan, and five (four) Zero fighters that were dispersed to Sandakan [Borneo], Kuching, and Penang. Fighter Hikōtai 309 then withdrew in February 1945 to Seletar in Singapore, next to the base at Johore. In May, all aircraft were ordered back to the homeland; thirteen Zero fighters returned to the Ōmura base on the 15th. The very same day the unit was disbanded and the remaining carrier attack squadron absorbed by Air Group 381.

Group leader, Hideki Shingō at Sabang, early 1944 (Hideki Shingō)

第501航空隊戦闘機隊

AIR GROUP 501 FIGHTER SQUADRON

Air Group Fighter Squadron 501 was initially organized in July 1943 as a carrier bomber unit. After advancing to Rabaul in October, attrition forced the unit to transfer to Truk by the end of January of the following year. In February, it was decided to add Zero fighters equipped with bombs to the group. Taking advantage of Zero fighters locally available that were themselves en route to other destinations, training in fighter bombing tactics was started at the Takeshima airfield. Early on during this training period, however, specifically on the two days of 17 and 18 February, Truk was attacked by a large number of carrier planes from an American task force. Although Air Group 501 did intercept them with a cumulative total of twenty-five aircraft, on the very first day our side lost

eleven aircraft. For all intents and purposes, unit 501 was decimated.

With the reorganization of 4 March, it was decided that Air Group 501 would be rebuilt back in the homeland. The allowance was revised to forty-eight carrier fighters and twenty-eight carrier bombers; it was also integrated into the 26th Air Flotilla. The carrier fighter unit became Fighter Hikōtai 351 (commander, LT Takeo Yokoyama). Organization of the new unit started at Kisarazu the early part of March. On 20 March, the first group of ten Zero fighters advanced to the Peleliu base, having traveled via Kaohsiung, Nichols, and Davao.

As early as the 30th, a large group of carrier planes from an American task force had conducted air raids; the 501, jointly

Takeshima airfield at Truk (Yasujirō Abe)

with Air Group 201, rose to intercept them with a force of twelve Zero fighters. Partly because of the lack of training, our forces were miserably defeated. In return for shooting down four enemy aircraft, five of our aircraft, including that flown by the commander, LT Tomojirō Yamaguchi, failed to return. The remaining seven aircraft received bomb hits on the ground; in addition, nine Type 99 carrier bombers were destroyed by fire. Next, the Zero fighters that had been repaired were transferred to Davao in early April; they were then flown back to Kisarazu.

In their place, a second group of seventeen aircraft of the Fighter Hikōtai 351 advanced to Davao by air in the latter part of April. These aircraft were used in the training of pilots, who were beginning to gather at the local base. For the "A"-gō operation, Lasam was scheduled to be the main base, with Babo [New Guinea] and Peleliu serving as deployment areas. In late May, the unit was combined with the fighter bomber unit of Air Group 201. Without participating in the "A"-gō operation, Air Group 501 was disbanded as of 10 July. Fighter Hikōtai 351 was also abolished and pilots integrated into Air Group 201.

第 254 航 空 隊

AIR GROUP 254

Air Group 254 was newly organized on 1 October 1943 and immediately posted to the Hainan Guard Command (Kainan Keibi-fu). Advancing to Ya Xian (Sanya) on Hainan Island, the unit was assigned duties in air defense in the Hainan Island and Hong Kong areas, as well as protection of the sea lines of communication in the South China area. Aircraft allowance was twenty-four carrier fighters, four carrier attack planes, and one transport. Officer assignments were as follows: CAPT Kurō Hori as the CO; LT Isamu Matsubara, a student reserve (graduate of Waseda University) who had completed seaplane training, as group leader; and as the senior division officer, LTJG Hiroshi Maeda of the 69th class, Naval Academy. The unit had been well trained. There were few experienced personnel, however; the majority of pilots were youths who had just finished their flight training courses. From the date of its establishment, a detachment under the command of LTJG Gi-ichi Minami was dispatched to Hai-k'ou (Hoihow). In addition, a few aircraft were also dispatched to Hong Kong.

An increasing number of B-24 and B-25 raids by American airforce units stationed in China started about the time the unit arrived at their base. The Zero fighter squadron of Air Group 254 was active in interception operations over Hainan Island and Hong Kong. Starting in 1944, the raiding forces came with escorts of P-40s, and later, escorts of P-38s. As a result, on a number of occasions our forces attacked Nanning, the source base for the American raids. Our raid on 5 April was conducted by twenty-three Zero fighters equipped with bombs. The aircraft were flown primarily by instructors from the training units known as the Sanya [Ya Hsien, also Ya Xian on Hainan Island] Air Group and the Haikow Air Group; in addition, there were nine aircraft of Air Group 254 serving as escorts (overall commander, LT Maeda) all of which provided air support for advancing ground forces. The fighter bombers, however, met a surprise attack by P-40s diving out of dense clouds; there were many casualties, including LTJG Nakahara. Later on, this particular type of [ground] support operation was abandoned.

For about one year following its establishment, Air Group 254 was engaged primarily in intercepting sporadic raids con-

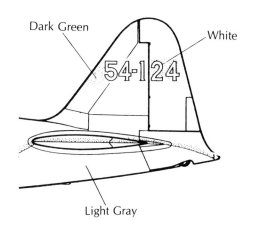

Model 52 Zero Fighter
Unit insignia *54* used from 1943 through summer 1944.

Seated on chairs are LT Akira Sugiura (left) and LTJG Takeshi Inoue (right), Air Group 254. Both were killed in action 5 January 1945. (Kaoru Inoue)

ducted by American air forces stationed in China. Because of the attacks on Taiwan by American carrier task forces in October 1944, however, a unit consisting of sixteen Zero fighters (commander, LT Akira Sugiura) left Hai-k'ou the evening of the 13th and moved to Tainan. Placed under the control of the Taiwan Air Command, the unit was assigned air defense duties. On the 14th, forty enemy aircraft were engaged in

air combat and the unit shot down three F6Fs. On the 16th, six aircraft under the command of LTJG Minami, as an escort, participated in an attack on an enemy task force. In the resulting air combat, two F6Fs were shot down. The unit stayed on in Taiwan for a while afterward; then nine Zero fighters advanced to the base at Nichols, near Manila, on the 27th. The next day, the unit moved to the base at Mabalacat. Until

Dark Green   White

Light Gray

Model 52 Zero Fighter
Unit insignia *254* used from autumn 1944 through January 1945.

LTJG Takeshi Inoue's Zero when Air Group 254 moved to Tainan base, Taiwan, for the Philippines campaign. (Takeshi Inoue)

the middle of November, the unit was fully involved in the advance on Leyte, providing air cover for ship convoys as well as in participating base intercept operations almost daily. Losses were considerable; by 12 November, operable aircraft were reduced to one or two planes. The unit was next ordered back to its parent organization. As of 1 January 1945, Air Group 254 was disbanded and absorbed into Air Group 901. It participated in air defense operations and was dispatched to Ya Hsien [Ya Xian] as a part of the 901. As a result of intercept operations conducted on 5 and 16 January, however, six aircraft including that flown by LT Sugiura were lost; in April, the unit retreated to Shanghai.

第 263 航空隊 (豹)

AIR GROUP 263 (HYŌ)

Air Group 263 was organized on 1 October 1943 at Genzan [Korea]. Aircraft allowance was thirty-six Zero fighters, later increased to seventy-two planes. The group was immediately posted to the 1st Air Fleet and commenced training at Matsuyama Air Base. Normally referred to as the Hyō, ("Panther") unit, the commanding officer was CDR Asa-ichi Tamai and the group leader, LT Yasuhiro Shigematsu. There were few experienced pilots; the majority of personnel in the unit were seventeen- to eighteen-year-old youths who had completed their Kō 10th Flight Reserve Enlisted Trainee Class in November. Intense training was conducted, however, and even though the unit lacked full training, orders were issued to the 1st Air Fleet to advance to the Marianas.

Eighteen aircraft of the advance party, including the commander, left Katori base on 20 February [1944] and advanced to Tinian Island via Iwo Jima, arriving on the 21st. Facilities and defenses at the Tinian airfield at this time, however, were not completed; insufficient preparations had been made for taking care of the aircraft that were arriving. In addition, as early as the 23rd, American carrier task forces conducted a major raid using both fighters and bombers. Air Group 263, initially scheduled to provide escorts for carrier bomber units, immediately plunged into intercept operations. Eleven aircraft under LTJG Wajima either destroyed themselves or

failed to return; six additional planes were destroyed on the ground. Thus the unit received a blow tantamount to annihilation.

As a result, group leader Shigematsu and other survivors returned to Matsuyama by air transport in order to receive replacement aircraft. Replacement pilots were added to the unit. At the end of February and again in mid-March, carrier fighters totaling forty-nine aircraft once again advanced to the Marianas (Airfield No. 1 on Guam). Separately, approximately five hundred ground personnel, equipment, and supplies were loaded on board the *Chiyoda,* arriving at Saipan on 5 March.

On 30 March, jointly with Air Group 261, the 263 moved twenty-five aircraft to Peleliu. The next day, on the 31st, eighteen aircraft led by LT Shigematsu left for intercept work. In contrast to the victory tally of five enemy aircraft shot down, however, our losses were fifteen aircraft that either destroyed themselves or failed to return. This was in addition to three aircraft on the ground that were either burned or sustained severe damage. The survivors returned to Saipan by air transport; in the homeland, they were provided with replacement aircraft and then returned to Guam.

In order to participate in the Biak operation, the main force of Air Group 263, consisting of twenty-eight aircraft led by the CO, Tamai, transferred to Peleliu on 25 May. Next, the unit advanced to Wasile

Model 52 Zero Fighter
About 1944.

Silver Black Dark Green White 63-172 Yellow Light Gray

Air Group 263, Matsuyama base, March 1944. Second row, from the left: sixth person (right of the propeller) LT Yasuhiro Shigematsu (group leader); seventh person, LTJG Nobuhiko Mutō. (Hiroharu Kaihō)

[Halmahera Island]. Because of the American forces advancing on the Marianas, however, thirty aircraft returned to Guam on the 30th. Of the eight aircraft belonging to the unit that remained behind, four were destroyed in air combat over Guam on the 11th. From the 15th to the 18th, the entire force available to Air Group 263 in Guam was used for air combat and in attacks on ships off Saipan. Losses amounted to more than twenty aircraft; by the final decisive day for the "A"-gō operation, the 19th, the 263 had lost almost all of its combat capability.

Later, replacement aircraft were received from the homeland and the number of operable aircraft reached the level of more than ten. Some of the planes returned to Guam. The remaining six aircraft under LT Shigematsu were on their way to transfer to Peleliu on 8 July when they met a surprise attack conducted by Grumman fighters. Our unit lost five aircraft; one plane just barely made its escape and arrived at Peleliu. Pilots remaining at Guam continued to react with the few available aircraft against sporadic attacks by the enemy. About 18 July, the number of operable aircraft was down to zero. Personnel escaped using land attack planes or other means.

As of 10 July, Air Group 263 was disbanded. The eight Zero fighters that had remained at Peleliu were transferred the next day to Davao. The majority of pilots were absorbed into Air Group 201.

第 321 航空隊 (鵄)

AIR GROUP 321 (TOBI)

Air Group 321 (Tobi, "Hawk") was organized at the Mobara Air Base on 1 October 1943 as the first night-fighter unit of the navy. It was posted to the 1st Air Fleet; training exercises started at Tateyama base. The CO was CDR Tokutarō Kubo, a graduate of flying-boat operations; its group leader was LT Ichirō Shimoda, a carrier (dive-) bomber pilot by experience. Initially, the allowance was eighteen aircraft (with six aircraft separately as spares); in February 1944, however, this was increased to fifty-four aircraft (sixteen held separately as spares). The type of aircraft supplied the unit was the night fighter Gekkō, first used during the summer of 1943 in the Solomons battle front.

This particular type of aircraft was produced as a result of experience gained during the fall of 1938 in the China Incident. It was a land-based three-seat fighter equipped with two Experimental Type 13 engines, intended to serve as a long-distance escort aircraft for bomber units. First flown in May 1941, the aircraft did not attain its expected performance. As a result, during the summer of 1942, it was converted to a two-seat land reconnaissance aircraft (Type 2 land reconnaissance aircraft) and production in quantity ordered. The unit was assigned to the Tainan Air Group at Rabaul. It was CO Kozono's idea to replace the traditional rear, upward-swivel machine gun with 20-mm cannons fixed at an angle, facing upward in the rear and downward in front. In this fashion, the aircraft was to be turned into a night fighter. From May 1943 on this aircraft was effectively employed in battle in the Rabaul and Buin areas; it was named the Gekkō at this time. It was next decided that Air Group 321 would be incorporated into the 1st Air Fleet, newly established by the Imperial General Headquarters as the "Greater East Asia Final Showdown Unit" (Dai Tō-a Kessen Butai). The 321 was to serve exclusively as a night-fighting unit.

On 1 February 1944, Air Group 321 was posted to the 61st Air Flotilla; on the 17th, it was ordered by the Combined Fleet to dispatch one half of its force to Saipan and the other half to Tinian. In several flights, twelve Gekkō aircraft under the command of LT Shimoda had advanced to Tinian by the 21st; they were immediately ordered into antisubmarine patrol work. On the 23rd, however, an American carrier task force attacked the Marianas and most of the recently arrived advance unit of the 321 was destroyed in a single day. At dawn, Air Group 321 itself sent out five Gekkō aircraft under the command of LT Shimoda to search for the enemy. They were unable to locate the enemy fleet, however. After engaging in battle with five Grummans, two of our aircraft failed to return. LT Shimoda's own aircraft had to make an emergency landing and was heavily damaged. Aircraft in the Tinian area were also destroyed as a result of enemy air raids; six of our aircraft were set on fire and two aircraft heavily damaged. No aircraft survived. By the end of February, however, replacement aircraft did arrive regularly from the homeland. As of 1 March, eleven aircraft were based at the 3rd airfield on Tinian. It is un-

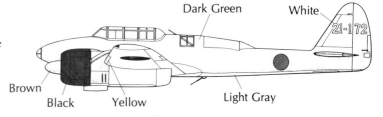

Gekkō, about 1944.

Upper part and sides of the fuselage were dark green; lower part light gray, or black all over.

Dark Green · White · Brown · Black · Yellow · Light Gray · 21-172

derstood that additional aircraft were next distributed to various bases in the Micronesia area; however, details are not available.

It has also been reported that around April, five aircraft were assigned to Guam and seven to Tinian. Also about the same time, it was reported that four out of the ten flight crews were qualified for night fighting; it was also reported that equipment and material, plus six aircraft (three were completely equipped) were available for use.

Movements of Air Group 321 during the "A"-gō operation period are not clear because the CO, the group leader, and the majority of headquarters personnel met with honorable deaths when Tinian was lost on 2 August. Some fragmentary information is available, however, as can be seen in the data reported below. About 15 May, six aircraft were deployed to Guam, two to Tinian, and fifteen to Katori. The four aircraft that were dispatched to Yap in early June engaged in daily early morning patrol operations. Separately, the six aircraft that had been dispatched to Peleliu were bombed and four of them burned as a result of B-24 air raids. On the 17th, the unit dispatched to Yap joined forces with the unit dispatched to Peleliu and participated in night intercept operations against B-24s. Towards the end of the month, the four

Group leader LT Ichirō Shimoda (Minoru Suzuki)

aircraft, still operable, had retreated to Davao. WO Ishii on Truk had shot down a B-24.

The Gekkō aircraft assigned to Air Group 321 were for the most part not used for the initially intended purpose of service as night fighters. They were used primarily in antisubmarine patrol, protection of convoys, or in early morning patrols and other ways. On 10 July 1944 Air Group 321 was disbanded.

Airfield on Tinian (Yasujirō Abe?)

第 381 航 空 隊

AIR GROUP 381

On 1 October 1943, the same day that Air Group 381 was established with an allowance of thirty-six fighter bombers and posted to the 23rd Air Flotilla (13th Air Fleet), the unit was also dispatched to Kendari on the island of Celebes. The first CO was CAPT Katsuji Kondō; in October 1944, CAPT Daizō Nakajima took over. LT Takeo Kurosawa was the group leader. As a result of the reorganization of 1 April 1944, however, the 381 became a major air group in the sense that carrier fighters and night fighters were added to its allowance. It was divided into Fighter Hikōtai 602 (allowance of forty-eight fighter bombers; commander, LT Kurosawa) and Fighter Hikōtai 902 (allowance of twenty-four night fighters; commander, LT Hideo Matsumura). In addition, Fighter Hikōtai 311 (allowance of forty-eight [Model 52-]A [Zero] fighters, commanded by LT Kunio Kanzaki) was created at Kendari; this unit included transferees from Air Group 202. From the end of 1943, a few of the new Raiden ("Thunderbolt") fighter interceptors were assigned to Fighter Hikōtai 602 in order to provide air defense over the Balikpapan oil fields. The plan was to gradually replace all aircraft with the Raiden. The unit itself continued to train at the Toyohashi base, using Zero fighters.

As of February, ten Raiden and thirty-five Zero fighters were available; however, there appeared to be little hope of receiving additional Raiden interceptors. On 7 March as a follow-up move to the dispatch of an advance team in February, LT Kurosawa led the main force of the unit, consisting of Zero fighters, and advanced to Balikpapan, via Davao. (In September six Raiden arrived.) By mid-March, the main force of the 381 was using the base at Raikan, near Makassar, Celebes Island. In part, the unit engaged in air defense operations over Balikpapan. In response to the advance of American forces into western New Guinea, and acting jointly with Fighter Hikōtai 311, elements of unit 381 were dispatched to Surabaya, Tarakan, Ambon, Waingapu, Sorong, Babo, and other places. Fighter Hikōtai 311, led by the newly assigned group leader LT Shin Yamanouchi, was detached from Air Group 381 as of 5 May and transferred to Air Group 153, an air reconnaissance group. Advancing to the Sorong area, it participated in the Battle of Biak. During the course of continued combat from 5 through 16 June, the units achieved battle results of thirty-two enemy aircraft shot down. Our side also suffered, however; fifteen aircraft either destroyed themselves or failed to return, and combat effectiveness was lost as a result. On the other hand, Fighter Hikōtai 902 had been reinforced with float fighter pilots formerly assigned to Air Group 934, which had retreated from Ambon to Surabaya. Equipment available at Balikpapan were two Gekkō aircraft as of mid-April. Later on the unit was gradually reinforced and by Octo-

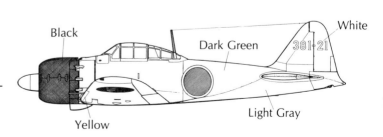

Model 52 Zero Fighter

Unit insignia *381* used between autumn 1944 and August 1945.

Black

Dark Green

White

381-21

Yellow

Light Gray

Group leader LT Takeo Kurosawa (*seated, third from right*). Later, CO of Fighter Hikōtai 602. (Yasunobu Nabara)

ber had gone up to about ten aircraft. As of 1 September, the number of aircraft available (number operable) was as follows: at Balikpapan, forty (thirty-one) Zero fighters of Fighter Hikōtai 602 and eight (five) Gekkō aircraft of Fighter Hikōtai 902; at Kendari, thirty-two (fifteen) Zero fighters; nine (seven) Raiden; and two (two) Gekkō of Fighter Hikōtai 602 plus two (two) Gekkō aircraft of Fighter Hikōtai 902 at Surabaya.

Starting in September, American heavy bombers began to bomb Menado (Celebes). WO Kamihira and others of Fighter Hikōtai 602, which had been dispatched to Menado, were able to inflict telling blows on the enemy by using no. 3 [aerial] bombs. Starting the end of September, the American air forces attacked Balikpapan using large formations of aircraft consisting of one hundred to two hundred aircraft each. Our side responded using the entire strength available to air groups 331 and 381

and engaged in a number of fierce intercept battles with the incoming forces.

Because of the abundance of fuel for training purposes, among other reasons, the skill level of the fighter hikōtais was high, and considerable battle results were achieved. (During 30 September, and 3, 10, and 14 October, the two groups together accounted for shooting down more than eighty aircraft. Even the American side has admitted to the loss of nineteen B-24s and six P-47s and P-38s.) Initially, only bombers were used. With the attack of 10 October, however, escort fighters started accompanying the [enemy] bombers and losses on the part of fighters on our side also mounted. In particular, it became difficult for Fighter Hikōtai 902's Gekkō units to engage in daytime intercept operations. As a result, the aircraft were shifted to night bombings of the island of Morotai and other areas. In mid-March 1945, the main strength of the fighter units was

Field command tent at Kupang (during Air Group 202 period). (Minoru Suzuki)

moved to Singapore to participate in ship convoy protection and other operations in the French Indochina area. Ten Zero fighters and two or three Gekkō aircraft were left behind at Balikpapan.

In early April, orders were received to move fighter units back to the homeland. On or about the 10th, all aircraft were transferred to Batavia; there were no aircraft whatsoever left at Balikpapan. During this same period, Fighter Hikōtai 902 advanced to the base at Denpasar on the island of Bali. It then moved forward to Kupang to assist in the evacuation of army troops from Timor Island. The unit was primarily employed in the protection of ship con-

voys. In early April, the main forces of fighter hikōtais 602 and 901 returned to the homeland. Air Group 381 was reorganized to include aircraft that had belonged to the 11th Air Group (fighter training unit, Johore), the 12th Air Group (carrier bombers), and the 13th Air Group (land attack planes) before they were disbanded. The allowance at this point in time was twenty-four fighters, twelve land attack planes, twelve carrier attack planes, and twenty-four medium trainer planes. Next, the 381 was transferred to Sumatra to participate in special attack force operations; it greeted the end of hostilities while still undergoing training.

第 265 航空隊 (狼, 雷)

AIR GROUP 265 (ŌKAMI, KAMINARI)

Air Group 265 (Ōkami, "Wolf"; Kaminari, "Thunder") was established at Kagoshima base on 15 November 1943. Aircraft allowance was thirty-six Zero fighters, later increased to seventy-two. Immediately upon its organization it was posted to the 1st Air Fleet and started training activities at Kasanbara base. In January of the following year, however, the air group was moved to the Hsinchu (Shinchiku) base on Taiwan. CO was CDR Terujirō Urata and group leader, LT Usaburō Suzuki. Youthful pilots were in the majority, and the lack of skills was keenly felt. Even at the end of May, the situation was such that the skill levels of pilots stood at two class A, eight class B, and twenty-six class C.

Though initially scheduled to be sent to the Philippines, it was decided that the 265 would take the place of Air Group 341 and proceed to the Marianas. Based on an order received on 8 April 1944, the initial group of thirty-two aircraft moved on the 1st and the 2nd of May from Hsinchu to airfield no. 1 at Saipan, proceeding via Kasanbara, Katori, and Iwo Jima. The second group of sixteen aircraft moved out immediately before the "A"-gō operation, while the remainder moved on to Iwo Jima during the operation itself. Base personnel and materials were transported from Yokohama on the *Shōun Maru*, which arrived on 11 June at the scheduled primary deployment area on Rota Island.

Starting from the early part of May, Air Group 265 at Saipan intercepted attacks made by enemy heavy bombers. In order to participate in the Biak operation, thirty-two Zero fighters left Saipan on 1 June and advanced to the Kau base on Halmahera Island; proceeding via Yap, they arrived at

(*Seated, front*) LT Usaburō Suzuki (while a LTJG) (Family of Ki-ichi Nangō)

Model 21 Zero Fighter
Around 1944

Black

Dark Green

White

65-120

Yellow

Light Gray

their destination on the 5th. During the same period, on 11 June, American carrier task forces staged a major attack on the Marianas. The remaining twelve aircraft under the command of LT Ikura did intercept the enemy but almost all of our aircraft were lost. On the other hand, during the period of the 14th through 17th, the main force of Air Group 265 moved to the island of Peleliu. Also, six aircraft led by LT Yasuhiko Ukimura arrived at Yap on the 14th. The next day the unit participated in an attack on enemy vessels off Saipan as escort for a carrier bomber unit; the unit shot down one F6F. However, our side also lost two aircraft; the rest landed at Guam.

During the "A"-gō operation, the main force of Air Group 265 moved to Guado (Guadobusu), Yap; a part of the unit was also deployed to Guam. Activities of the unit at Guam are not clearly known. The former unit, the main force of the 265 under LT Suzuki, intercepted a number of B-24 attacks. It appears, however, that with the exception of a single enemy aircraft shot down, no victories were attained. On the other hand, the unit that had advanced to Iwo Jima was active in intercepting attacks by American carrier aircraft that took place on the 15th. It is understood that our unit received devastating damages; however, the details are not clear.

By early July, surviving aircraft of Air Group 265 had been withdrawn to Davao; as of the 10th, the unit was disbanded. Most pilots, including LT Suzuki, group leader, were absorbed into Air Group 201. Those personnel who had advanced as far as Rota remained there until the end of the war.

第 301 航 空 隊

AIR GROUP 301

Air Group 301 was established by the Yokosuka Air Group on 5 November 1943 and was a part of the Yokosuka Naval Station. CDR Katsutoshi Yagi was ordered in as the CO and LT Iyozō Fujita as group leader. The air group was scheduled to receive a new type fighter interceptor that had just recently been placed in quantity production; it was named the Raiden. Training was initiated on the assumption that the unit would be proceeding to Rabaul; on 1 February 1944, the unit was posted to the 26th Air Flotilla. On 20 February, however, Air Group 301 was transferred to the 22nd Air Flotilla (the 4th Fleet; assigned to the 14th Air Fleet after 4 March). On 5 May, as a result of its being posted to the 1st Air Fleet, it was decided that the unit would be sent to Truk Island's Kaedeshima base, a very tense area in Micronesia. However, because of the activation of the Kon ("Tidal Wave") operation, the unit was ordered on the 27th to advance to the [New Guinea] area. On the 29th, twenty Zero fighters and forty-nine Raiden interceptors moved to Tateyama.

As of 4 March, Air Group 301 was reorganized into two hikōtais: Fighter Hikōtai 316 (allowance, forty-eight carrier fighters; group leader, LT Tadashi Minobe) and Fighter Hikōtai 601 (allowance, forty-eight interceptors; group leader, LT Fujita). Based on a recommendation submitted by LT Minobe, a seaplane pilot who had gotten the idea when he was engaged in air combat over Rabaul, Fighter Hikōtai 316 was made into a night fighter unit composed of Zero fighters. The majority of pilots had been two-seater floatplane pilots and had finished night flying exercises at the Atsugi base around May. As a result, the unit had to sortie as a daylight fighter unit manned by personnel who had hardly perfected their aerial combat techniques in daylight because of the original conception in using such units.

On 2 June, eighteen aircraft (commander, LT Jūji Torimoto) belonging to Fighter Hikōtai 316 advanced to the base on Tinian, proceeding via Iwo Jima. Ten in-

Air Group 301 CO, CDR Katsutoshi Yagi (Takahide Aioi?)

Model 52 Zero Fighter
About 1944

Black

Dark Green

White

01-147

Yellow

Light Gray

terceptors rose to fight a group of American carrier fighters that conducted an air raid on the 11th. The unit received devastating damages when their combat operations were just beginning.

The main force of Fighter Hikōtai 316 had been held up in their advance by poor weather; on the 11th, nineteen aircraft under the direct command of CO Yagi moved to Iwo Jima. On the afternoon of the 15th, eighteen aircraft under the command of LT Shigeo Jūni rose up and intercepted approximately sixty American carrier planes. Because of inadequate training in air combat techniques, however, a miserable defeat ensued. Sixteen aircraft failed to return, and one aircraft made a forced landing; the sole surviving aircraft was that of PO1c Mitsugu Yamazaki. Such were the harrowing results of the day.

On the same date, the American forces launched a massive invasion of Saipan. When the order for the "A"-gō operation was issued, all operable forces available to both sea- and land-based air groups were to be assembled with the 19th as the target date. Base air units in the eastern part of the homeland were ordered to assemble at Iwo Jima. Fighter Hikōtai 601 had gathered at the Tateyama base and was planning to advance to Iwo Jima but was prevented from so doing by continuing bad weather conditions. In addition, certain concerns about the performance of the aircraft supplied to the unit, the Raiden, arose. In the final analysis, the unit replaced its aircraft with Zero fighters. On the 21st, nine aircraft, and then on the 25th, thirty-one aircraft proceeded to Iwo Jima. On two occasions, the first contingent of nine aircraft rose to intercept incoming American carrier fighters, numbering approximately 180 F6Fs; five of the enemy were shot down. Four aircraft were lost on our side, however, including that flown by the commander, LT Katsumi Kōda. Next, during the afternoon of 3 July, thirty-one aircraft (commanded by LT Fujita) rose to intercept some one hundred attacking F6Fs. While flying in a single

TABLE 7. FORMATION OF AIR GROUP 301
(At Intercept Battles over Iwo Jima, 15 June 1944)

	FATE
1st Chūtai	
1st Shōtai	
LT Shigeo Jūni	Killed in action
CPO Kazuo Ōishi	Killed in action
PO1c Sotojirō Demura	Killed in action
LdgSea Shūzō Nakagawa	Killed in action
2nd Shōtai	
CPO Suminori Kawabata	Killed in action
PO1c Akio Nagashima	Killed in action
PO2c Takeo Yoshitake	Killed in action
LdgSea Kaihaku Kumagaya	Killed in action
3rd Shōtai	
PO1c Isamu Hirano	Killed in action
PO1c Mitsugu Yamazaki	
2nd Chūtai	
1st Shōtai	
LTJG Chōbei Morita	Killed in action
PO1c Hiroshi Shigemitsu	Killed in action
LdgSea Kesaji Sugihara	Killed in action
LdgSea Kazuwa Honda	Killed in action
2nd Shōtai	
WO Fukuju Kawakami	Force-landed
PO1c Yukio Kubota	Killed in action
PO2c Kaname Shibata	Killed in action
LdgSea Mitsuo Shiraishi	Killed in action

LT Ryō-ichi Koga on his Raiden in his Air Group 301 days, March 1944. (Ryō-ichi Koga)

column at low altitude headed for the northern part of Iwo Jima, the unit attempted to gain altitude and was attacked from the flank. As a result, the various units became separated and a confusing battle developed. Ten enemy aircraft (three probables) were shot down; our side lost seventeen aircraft. On the next day, the 4th, approximately 160 enemy aircraft made an attack. Fighter Hikōtai 601 sent out its entire operable aircraft strength, cumulatively totaling fourteen aircraft. Six enemy aircraft were downed; however, three aircraft on our side were lost and the remaining aircraft were damaged by AA (antiaircraft) fire from warships. Surviving pilots went back to the homeland by boarding transport planes that had been flown out. As of 10 July, Air Group 301 was disbanded.

Looking at Mount Suribachi from the Genzan airfield on Iwo Jima. Aircraft are Zero fighters of Air Group 252. (Katsuki Kobayashi)

第 341 航空隊 (獅子)

AIR GROUP 341 (SHISHI)

Air Group 341 (Shishi, "Lion") was organized on 15 November 1943 at the Matsuyama base, scheduled to be equipped with the new efficient Shiden fighter. The group was posted to the 1st Air Fleet on the same date. LCDR Shō-ichi Ogasawara (replaced by CAPT Motoharu Okamura in May 1944, in turn replaced by CDR Tadao Funaki in October) was ordered in as the air group CO and LT Aya-o Shirane, division officer in the Yokosuka Air Group, as group leader. It is to be noted that many of the pilots serving under division officers Motoi Kaneko and Masa-aki Asakawa, both LTJGs, were inexperienced personnel who had just completed their flight training. The allowance at the time the unit was organized was thirty-six interceptors (Type C fighter aircraft); this was increased to seventy-two aircraft the following February. Production of the Shiden was delayed, however, and the unit had to be supplied initially with Zero fighters. In mid-February, the first Shiden aircraft arrived; takeoff and landing training exercises started.

Defects appeared in the undercarriage and elsewhere; the schedule for placing the new aircraft in operation was considerably delayed. It was only in June that the air group was able to start formation air combat exercises. Approximately 250 advance party personnel moved to the island of Rota on 2 April, in anticipation of the air group's March deployment to that air base located in the Marianas. (The personnel remained on the island until the end of the war.) Despite these preparations, deployment of the air group itself was canceled.

The training base for Air Group 341 was changed from Matsuyama to Kasanbara on 5 December 1943 and then to Tateyama on 14 January. Thirteen aircraft of Fighter Hikōtai 401, commanded by LT Kaneko, departed from Tateyama on the 12th and advanced to Iwo Jima in order to assist in air transport operations. During an intercept battle against American carrier fighters on the 15th, however, ten Zero fighters, including the commander's aircraft, were lost, and the unit was withdrawn to the homeland. On 10 July, with the increase in Shiden aircraft, Air Group 341 was reorganized into two elements; Fighter Hikōtai 401 (group leader, LT Shirane; allowance forty-eight aircraft) and Fighter Hikōtai 402 (division officer, LT Iyozō Fujita; allowance forty-eight aircraft). Since the Tateyama base was restricted in size and not suitable for training exercises using such high speed aircraft as the Shiden, those activities were transferred to the Meiji base in Aichi Prefecture. In addition, Fighter Hikōtai 701 (commander, LCDR Hideki Shingō; replaced in August by LT Kunio Iwashita) was established as an air control organization with relatively experienced personnel on board. This fighter hikōtai was actually an air control unit of the T Attack Force, which was a specially organized body composed of various types of

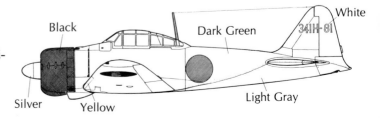

Model 21 Zero Fighter
Aircraft of Fighter Hikōtai 401, about 1944. The *H* indicates Fighter Hikōtai 401. Fighter Hikōtai 402 used an *S*.

Black

White

Dark Green

341H-81

Silver

Yellow

Light Gray

Fighter Hikōtai 401, Air Group 341, March 1944. Second row, from the left: third person, CPO Takashi Okamoto; LTJG Asakawa; LT Shirane (group leader); LTJG Kaneko; and Reserve LTJG Hikomori Kimiyama. Third row, from the left: fifth person, CPO Hiroshi Ōhara; twelfth person, CPO Yoshio Torishima. (Hiroharu Kaiho)

aircraft assigned to it. The organization continued to train with the Yokosuka Air Group.

On 31 August, the first group of seventeen Shiden aircraft and in mid-September, the second group of twenty-five aircraft of Fighter Hikōtai 401 advanced to Kao-hsiung. Assigned to intercept work against American air force planes that flew in from the Chinese mainland, the ratio of operationally available Shiden was very low; in addition, difficulties were encountered in conducting training exercises. The main force of Fighter Hikōtai 402 was transferred in the latter part of September to the base at Miyazaki. The number of aircraft available

(operable) as of 1 October was as follows: Fighter Hikōtai 401 had thirty-two Shiden (twenty) at Kao-hsiung; eleven Zero fighters (six) at Miyazaki; Fighter Hikōtai 402 had thirty Shiden (twenty-five) at Miyazaki with another twenty-two (eighteen) Zero fighters at the same base.

Because of American task force attacks on Formosa, the main strength of the 2nd Air Fleet was deployed to the southern part of Kyūshū in October. Starting on the 12th, air battles developed off Taiwan.

The Shiden unit at Kao-hsiung (commander, LT Masa-aki Asakawa) became active in intercept operations; although ten enemy aircraft were shot down, our side

Shiden
Fighter Hikōtai 701

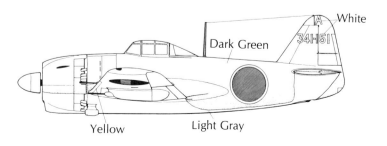

also lost fourteen aircraft. Thus, unit strength was reduced to one-half in very short order. Under the leadership of LT Shirane, who had replaced LT Iwashita, who had fallen ill, Fighter Hikōtai 701 escorted the T Attack Force and advanced to Okinawa via Taiwan. About the same time, Fighter Hikōtai 402 also arrived on Taiwan. In this fashion, the main strength of Air Group 341, consisting of thirty-six aircraft (twenty-one operable) had gathered at the Mabalacat base on Luzon by the 23rd. On the following day, the 24th, the 341 sortied as covering force in the general offensive but lost a high number of aircraft. By nighttime of the same day, the 341 had been reduced to a total of only four operable aircraft. In November, Fighter Hikōtai 701 was removed from the T Attack Force and posted to Air Group 341. LCDR Shirane was in overall command of the three hikōtai. Using the highly experienced Fighter Hikōtai 701 as its core element, the unit participated in the attack on Leyte, engaging in base air defense, protecting ship convoys, attacking torpedo boats, and other actions. The Shiden aircraft could not be utilized to their full capabilities, however, because of the low level of skill of the pilots; breakdowns were frequent and the rate of operation was quite low. Even in air combat, the Shidens were overwhelmed by P-38s and P-47s, contrary to expectations.

LCDR Shirane was killed in action during the 24 November attack on Leyte. As his replacement, LT Iwashita, who had recovered from his illness, assumed command. Fighter Hikōtai 402 group leader Fujita was placed in overall command of Shiden units; by the end of December, operable aircraft in the combined three hikōtai reached about eight in number. Following a heavy attack made in mid-December on a ship convoy off Mindoro (twelve Shiden participated under the command of LT Iwashita), Shiden aircraft were primarily employed in daytime attacks, taking advantage of their superior speed in the conduct of opposed reconnaissance against enemy carrier task forces. In particular, LT Takuo Mitsumoto of Fighter Hikōtai 402

was successful in regularly discovering enemy aircraft carriers. By the end of the year, some pilots of Air Group 341 were even selected to serve in special attack force units.

The morning of 4 January 1945, thirteen Shiden aircraft that had just arrived from the homeland the previous day were lined up on the flight line being readied for providing air cover for a convoy. Two P-47s came in very low and swept the field with murderous fire. In a single moment, eight aircraft were set on fire; four pilots as well as five maintenance crewmen were killed. The Shiden units of Air Group 341 were almost annihilated.

On 7 January, the American forces sent a huge invasion convoy into Lingayen Gulf; accompanied by heavy naval gunfire support, amphibious operations started on the 9th. All of our operable aircraft available in the Clark Field area were used as special attack force units. LT Iwashita of Air Group 341 led four Shiden aircraft that had been repaired overnight and transferred to Tuguegarao in northern Luzon. The unit participated in attacks on Lingayen Gulf but within a few days had lost all of its aircraft. Commanding officer Funaki, group leader Sonoda, and ground personnel under the two officers transformed themselves into naval infantry and holed up in the mountains west of Clark. They were responsible for the 17th Battle Sector and fought valiantly. The majority of personnel had been killed in action, however, by the time the war ended. Pilots under the command of LT Fujita fought their way to Tuguegarao by land, fending off attacks by guerilla forces. Those personnel were able to escape by means of transport aircraft sent from Taiwan to the area from time to time and did return to the homeland.

Successive Commanding Officers:

November 1943–May 1944 CDR Shōichi Ogasawara

May 1944–October 1944 CAPT Motoharu Okamura

October 1944– CDR Tadao Funaki

第 153 航 空 隊

AIR GROUP 153

Newly organized on 1 January 1944 as a reconnaissance unit (allowance, twelve aircraft; later increased to twenty-four), Air Group 153 was immediately posted to the 23rd Air Flotilla (13th Air Fleet) and deployed to Kendari base. With American forces attacking western New Guinea in April, the main strength of the 153 advanced for about a month to Wakde Island. Starting on the 2nd, the unit engaged in scouting operations.

As of 5 May, the 23rd Air Flotilla was posted to the 1st Air Fleet and readied itself for action in New Guinea operations. At the same time, Fighter Hikōtai 311 (commander, LT Kunio Kanzaki, followed by LT Shin Yamauchi; allowance, forty-eight Type A [Zero] fighters, though actual numbers were about one-half of those figures) was transferred into Air Group 153. Part of the latter force was detached to Sorong. At the time, the next target that the American forces would attack was thought to be the Marianas, Palau, or the Biak Island area. On 22 April, however, American forces landed on Hollandia and in the Aitape area. As a result, it became quite clear that there would be further advances westward following the northwestern New Guinea area (Kame Chiku) [Vogelkopf sector] operations.

Starting in early May, allied forces bombers made increasingly frequent attacks in the Sorong and Manokwari areas. Using Sorong as their primary base, Zero fighters of Fighter Hikōtai 311 would intercept each attack using ten aircraft or fewer. Although by the 26th they were able to shoot down twenty-one B-24s and other aircraft, our side also suffered six aircraft lost. As of the 26th, the numbers of aircraft available to Fighter Hikōtai 311 were as follows: five at Sorong, fifteen at Kendari, and separately a few training aircraft. On the 27th, the American forces that had landed on Wakde Island commenced landing on Biak Island.

The Combined Fleet had been waiting for an opportune moment to launch the final battle of the "A"-gō operation; they decided to conduct the final decisive engagement around the island of Biak. Under cover of surface fleet units, a [counter] landing force was activated. Also, a powerful segment of the 1st Air Fleet, which had been stationed in the Micronesia area, was moved to the island of Halmahera. Air Group 202 stationed at Sorong was advanced to the Babo area; in cooperation with Fighter Hikōtai 311, it participated in the attack on Biak, as well as in air defense operations.

At the same time, attrition because of the continuing battles fought each day was considerable. Between 27 May and 5 June, Fighter Hikōtai 311 alone lost nine aircraft; there was only one aircraft left to the unit. In particular, in the 29 May strafing and bombing of the airfield at Biak, all four aircraft led by WO Shinji Ishida were lost.

Gekkō

Aircraft belonging to Fighter Hikōtai 901. In August 1944, this aircraft rammed a B-24 during intercept operations and was destroyed.

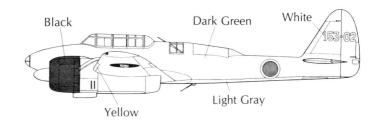

Black Dark Green White

153-02

Yellow

Light Gray

Air Group 153, Fighter Hikōtai 901, at Nichols Field, Manila, toward the end of October 1944. As a result of battles on 20 October, three Gekkō aircraft and four Zero fighters failed to return. Shown with the remaining group personnel, consisting of reserve students of the 13th and 14th classes, is LCDR Minobe, holding his walking stick. (Tadashi Minobe)

Also, in a similar attack made on 2 June, three out of the six participating aircraft under the command of LT Kikumasa Fujita failed to return; another aircraft made a forced landing. Although during this period a few replacement aircraft did arrive, the unit itself was withdrawn to Kendari for regrouping. With the American landings on Saipan, ten Zero aircraft and one Suisei carrier bomber advanced to Peleliu Island via Wasile on the 18th, with the intention of eventually proceeding to the Marianas.

On the 20th, the unit advanced farther to the island of Yap. On 11 July, six aircraft advanced to Truk via Mariaon [Woleai]; however, there were no opportunities for engaging in air combat.

With the reorganization as of 10 July, Air Group 153 was turned into a reconnaissance and night fighter unit; it was used for screening operations under the direct command of the 1st Air Fleet. The unit began rebuilding itself at Davao in the Philippines. Fighter Hikōtai 311 was transferred into Air Group 201. The unit was scheduled to be constituted of two Hikōtai. One, Reconnaissance Hikōtai 102, a reconnaissance unit attached to the 201 from its initial organization; and the second, Fighter Hikōtai 901 (commander, LT Tadashi Minobe; allowance twenty-four night fighters), which had been transferred in from Air Group 251. In his capacity as group leader of Fighter Hikōtai 316 (Air Group 301), LT Minobe had personal experience in the training of a night fighter unit composed of Zero fighter aircraft, starting in early 1944. During intercept operations over Iwo Jima in June, however, most of the unit's aircraft were lost. By early August, the unit had advanced to Air Base No. 2 on Davao, with fresh equipment, supplies, and personnel.

Immediately after their arrival on station, B-24s started nighttime air raids on Davao. The Gekkō aircraft unit was active in interception at night, but because of insufficient speed and radar problems, very few combat results were attained. Only one operation is important. On the night of 2 September the aircraft captained by PO1c Yoshimasa Nakagawa rammed and shot down an enemy aircraft; Nakagawa himself was able to return alive. Early in September, the intention of the American carrier task forces to attack the southern Philippines became apparent. As a result, all operable aircraft of Fighter Hikōtai 901, which consisted of nine Gekkō aircraft (three at Davao, one at Tacloban, three at Zamboanga, and two at Nichols) and two Zero night fighters (one each at Davao and Tacloban), were gathered together at Tacloban [Leyte]. On the 9th, three Gekkō aircraft left on a search and attack mission in the seas east of the Philippines but were intercepted by Grumman F6Fs. Two aircraft failed to return, including the one flown by the commander, LT Kunio Mori. Even the remaining one aircraft lost its observer; the pilot, CPO Saburō Sue, was able to make an emergency landing. He was the only one to return alive.

In mid-September, the main force of Fighter Hikōtai 901 moved to Nichols Field on Luzon. In the American attack on Manila by carrier planes on the 21st and the 22nd, two Gekkō aircraft were able to hold the enemy task force on target. One of the aircraft (CPO Sue, WO Take-aki Shimizu) hit an aircraft carrier by a bomb. With the landing of American forces on Leyte in mid-October, Fighter Hikōtai 901 was ordered to support army units that were going to conduct a counterlanding operation on the same island. Ordered to suppress enemy torpedo boats in the Ormoc Bay area, group leader Minobe led four each Gekkō aircraft and Zero night fighters and advanced to Cebu. Almost every night for a period of four weeks his unit would attack; they were able to consign six enemy torpedo boats to their watery graves. At one point, enemy torpedo boat activities were completely halted. At the same time, casualties on the part of the night fighter unit were considerable. During a two-month period, three division officers were lost, as well as fourteen aircraft that failed to return. At the end of November, LCDR Minobe was ordered back to the homeland in order to rebuild the night fighter unit.

During the period from the end of 1944 until the early part of 1945, Fighter Hikōtai 804 (commander, LT Ei-ichi Kawabata), Fighter Hikōtai 812 (commander, LT Masashi Tokukura), and Fighter Hikōtai 851 (commander, LT Yutaka Sugawara) were all integrated into Air Group 153. In a short period of time, however, the unit was transferred to Taiwan and then to the homeland. After American forces landed on Luzon, headquarters of Air Group 153 and its ground personnel fled into the mountains west of Clark Field and engaged in guerilla activities. By the time the war ended, the majority of personnel, from CO Wada on down, had been killed in action.

Successive Commanding Officers:

January 1944–February 1944   CDR Moriyoshi Yamaguchi

February 1944–July 1944   CDR Rikihei Inokuchi

July 1944–November 1944   CAPT Nobukichi Takahashi

November 1944–   CAPT Tetsujirō Wada

第343航空隊 (初代, 隼)

AIR GROUP 343 (I)
(1ST FORMATION, HAYABUSA)

Air Group 343, the home unit of which was Matsuyama Air Base, was organized at Kagoshima base on 1 January 1944 and immediately posted to the 1st Air Fleet. Normally referred to as the Hayabusa ("Peregrine Falcon"), command was in the hands of CDR Masao Takenaka, a former flying boat pilot; the unit's group leader was LT Shinya Ozaki, a former float fighter pilot.

Assigned primarily to air defense operations, Air Group 343 was scheduled to use the new Shiden fighter, which was at the operational testing stage. Production of the aircraft was delayed, however, and there was little possibility of their becoming available. Thus, with only a single Shiden aircraft actually received, by the end of February the unit abandoned any idea of using the new fighter and switched to Zero fighters instead. At the time of the unit's organization, pilots numbered around sixty; however, only six of them were experienced. The majority were youthful personnel of the Kō class of enlisted trainees who had graduated from the 10th class, Flight Reserve Enlisted Trainee course the previous November.

In February 1944 fighter units attached to the 1st Air Fleet, which had been sent in advance of the 343 unit, suffered major losses as a result of enemy air raids on the Marianas. Consequently, the schedule of Air Group 343 was speeded up and the first unit of twelve aircraft, led by group leader Ozaki, advanced to airfield no. 1 on the island of Tinian on 24 March, proceeding via Katori and Iwo Jima. As of 1 May, headquarters of the unit and the third segment sent out had both arrived and the entire air group was deployed. Ground personnel were transported by the carrier *Ryūhō* in early April.

Even after deployment to the front, training was continued. As of 15 May, the total of aircraft on hand was fifty-three, of which forty-two were operational. From the number of aircraft available for use, Air Group 343 was the strongest unit of all in the 1st Air Fleet's fighter force. With the start of the Biak operation on 25 May, the main body of Air Group 343 was ordered to deploy to Palau. Leaving behind one chūtai commanded by LT Kakurō Kawamura, key personnel of the headquarters element including CO Takenaka, with thirty-seven Zero fighters led by LT Ozaki, advanced to Peleliu Island. Further, on 9 June, upon completion of the Airai base on the main Palau island, the unit advanced to

Model 52 Zero Fighter
Unit insignia *43* was used from January through July 1944.

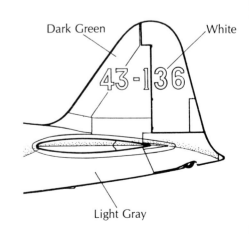

Dark Green · White · 43-136 · Light Gray

Air Group 343 (1st Formation), at the Kagoshima base, early 1944. Second row: center (in uniform), CDR Masao Takenaka, commanding officer; right of Takenaka, LT Shinya Ozaki, group leader; sixth person in from the left, CPO Isamu Doigawa. (Hiroharu Kaihō)

the base and was made responsible for the air defense of all of the Palau Islands.

On 11 June, American forces raided the Marianas and on the 15th invaded Saipan. The unit left behind on Tinian used eight aircraft for interception during the attack of the 11th and then moved on to Guam. Details are not known.

On the other hand, headquarters of the 1st Air Fleet directed headquarters of Air Group 343 to participate in the final battle of the "A"-gō operation, using Yap Island as its base and shuttling in and out of Guam. On the 17th, LT Ozaki led a group of twelve aircraft and advanced to Yap Island. The same evening his unit attacked vessels off Tinian; two aircraft landed on Rota Island and remained there until the end of the war.

On the 19th, the day of the final battle, LT Ozaki was killed in action during combat operations over Guam. While LT Ozaki and one other aircraft were flying patrol they engaged in battle with two enemy fighters. One of the enemy aircraft was shot down. Ozaki, who had been tailed by the other enemy aircraft, made a sudden dive almost to the surface of the ocean and then just as rapidly zoomed up; the result was that the enemy aircraft following LT Ozaki flew into the water. LT Ozaki himself was hit and badly injured. After making an emergency landing on the airfield, he died while being transported to the hos-

pital. Further, it is believed that the sole existing Zero fighter (43-188), which was discovered on Guam and returned to Japan in 1963, was that of LT Ozaki.

Later, the 343 continued to engage in attacking enemy vessels off Saipan or in intercept battles, based on Yap and on the Guam islands, until the end of June. However, LT Kawamura and other key officers were lost; remnants were able to reach Airai on the 28th. On 10 July, Air Group 343 was disbanded.

LT Shinya Ozaki, hikōtai leader, Air Group 343. (Ikuhiko Hata)

第343航空隊（2代，剣）

AIR GROUP 343 (II)
(2ND FORMATION, TSURUGI)

Air Group 343 (2nd Formation, Tsurugi "Lance") was organized at the Matsuyama base on 25 December 1944 and immediately posted to the 25th Air Flotilla (3rd Air Fleet). This unit was created based on an inspiration held by CAPT Minoru Genda, a former fighter pilot and at the time the senior officer in charge of aviation at the operations division at the Naval General Staff. CAPT Genda's concept was to regain control of the air through the use of Shiden-kai ("improved Shiden") aircraft, at the time the most advanced fighter available. He himself transferred out of the Naval General Staff and assumed the role of commanding officer of the new unit. As executive officer, CDR Tadashi Nakajima (later CDR Takahide Aioi), and as air officer, LCDR Yoshio Shiga, were ordered in. As can be seen, the senior officers were highly qualified, all having a background in fighters. Pilots, from the group leader on down, were outstanding, experienced personnel selected out of various units. At the time, this fighter unit had the highest degree of skills of all the fighter units in our navy.

The nucleus of the newly organized Air Group 343 consisted of the following three elements: Fighter Hikōtai 301 (group leader, LT Naoshi Kanno), Fighter Hikōtai 701 (group leader, LT Takashi Oshibuchi), and Fighter Hikōtai 407 (group leader, LT Yoshishige Hayashi). Allowance for each element was forty-eight aircraft; immediately upon organization, the three elements started training exercises at Matsuyama, Ōita, and Izumi bases, respectively. By the end of January 1945, all three hikōtai were assembled at Matsuyama. Also in January, Fighter Hikōtai 401 (group leader, LT Masa-aki Asakawa), which was then undergoing regrouping using as its nucleus a few survivors who had returned from the Philippines, and Fighter Hikōtai 402 (group leader, LT Iyozō Fujita) were posted to the 343. The latter unit, Fighter Hikōtai 402, was transferred to Air Group 601 in March. The former unit, Fighter Hikōtai 401, was dispatched to Tokushima base to serve as a training unit for younger pilots.

A characteristic of Air Group 343 was that it placed an emphasis on the acquisition of advance intelligence so that the effectiveness of interceptor operations would be heightened. As a result, the 4th Reconnaissance Hikōtai (group leader, LT Toshio Hashimoto; allowance twenty-four aircraft) was attached to the 343. The 4th was equipped with the high-speed carrier reconnaissance plane Saiun ("Iridescent Cloud"). Among other points that were emphasized by CAPT Genda, the commanding officer, were: stress on formation combat, the improvement of air-to-air radio communications, and assuring victory in the case of fighter battles. In order to enhance morale, each hikōtai was also given a popular name: the Shinsen-gumi ("Elite Guard"), 301; the Ishin-tai ("Imperial Restoration Unit"),

Shiden-Kai

Aircraft belonging to Fighter Hikōtai 301, 16 April 1945; used by CPO Mitsuo Hori. Unit insignia *343* was used during December 1944 through August 1945. Letter *A* indicates aircraft belonged to Fighter Hikōtai 301.

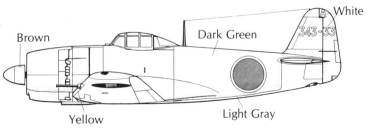

White

Brown

Dark Green

343-33

Yellow

Light Gray

Fighter Hikōtai 701, Air Group 343, July 1945. Front row, from the left: second person, LT Ryō-ichi Yamada; CAPT Minoru Genda; and LCDR Yoshio Shiga; right end, ENS Kazuo Muranaka. Second row, from the left: third person, Ryūji Yagi; fifth person, Masao Sasakibara; sixth person, Yasuo Matsumoto; and seventh person, Hiroshi Okano—all noncommissioned officer pilots. [Banner at left reads: "Ready area for Restoration Fighter Unit flight personnel."] (Masao Sasakibara)

701; the Tenchūgumi ("Heavenly Punishment Unit"), 407; and the Kiheitai ("Commando Unit"), 4th Reconnaissance. Banners were placed in front of barracks and other means taken to stimulate spiritual determination. At the same time, the captain's operating philosophy was, in general, scientific, logical, and to a large extent had taken into consideration American concepts. Equipment, materials, personnel, and other facilities were provided top priority. Perhaps it could be said that the unit was the last trump card played by the Japanese navy. At the time of its organization, supplies of the Shiden-kai were late in forthcoming and the unit was composed of

Shiden-Kai

Interceptor belonging to Fighter Hikōtai 407, 21 April 1945, Flown by PO1c Shōjirō Ishii. Letter *B* indicates Fighter Hikōtai 407.

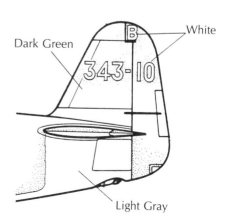

Shiden-kai flown by PO1c Tomokazu Kasai of Fighter Hikōtai 301. The rail below the wing gun is used for holding rockets. (Tomoichi Kasai)

Shiden aircraft. Commencing mid-February, aircraft were regularly replaced with the Shiden-kai, starting with Fighter Hikōtai 301. By mid-March, the majority of aircraft had been replaced with the newer model. It became possible to engage in formation combat using sixteen aircraft per formation. The navy had completed all preparations for an opportune moment for action; the time arrived when American carrier task force attacks on western Japan started on 18 March. At the time, there were 170 pilots in the 343 unit; of this number 35 possessed class A qualifications. Early the morning of the 19th, the 343, which had been made aware of an approaching major air raid in the Kure area, dispatched Saiun reconnaissance planes to form a patrol line over the southern coast of the island of Shikoku. In addition, three hikōtai totaling fifty-four Shiden-kai aircraft were placed on the ready line. At 0650, a report was received from a Saiun commanded by ENS Mitsuru Takada (killed in action, All Units Bulletin issued) that an enemy carrier strike force was proceeding north. All aircraft took off under the leadership of senior commander LT Oshibuchi; by 0930 they were able to zero in repeatedly on F6F, F4U, and SB2C formations. As a result of fighting very effectively in the air, forty-eight enemy fighters and four dive-bombers were shot down. For our air forces, which were then at a low ebb, this was indeed an epochal victory. In addition to sixteen aircraft on our side that either rammed enemy aircraft or failed to return, losses amounted to only five aircraft that were burned while on the ground, as well as a few aircraft that made forced landings. As a result of the air battles fought on this date, nineteen American pilots were captured. It is said that these pilots evaluated highly the skills of Air Group 343.

With the outbreak of the Battle of Okinawa in April, CO Genda led his Air Group 343 to the Kanoya base on the 8th. Coming under the command of the 5th Air Fleet (formally posted as of 5 May), the 343 participated in the Kikusui ("Floating

Shiden-Kai

Aircraft belonging to Fighter Hikōtai 701, 12 April 1945. Flown by PO1c Takumi Sugitaki.

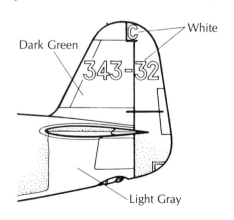

Fighter Hikōtai 301 pilots. Front row (from left): unknown, LT Kanno, unknown, CAPT Genda, LCDR Shiga, unknown, unknown. 2nd row: 2nd from left, WO Mitsuo Hori; 3rd from right, CPO Shōichi Sugita. [Placard on right reads: Kaigun Shinsen-gumi Shikisho ("Naval Elite Guard Unit Command Post")]. (Tomoichi Kasai)

Chrysanthemum") Operation No. 2 starting on the 12th. It was hard to attack the main island of Okinawa because of the *Shiden-kai*'s limited cruising range. Using Kanoya, Kokubu, and Ōmura as bases, however, during the period ending 22 June six sorties were made in the Amami Ōshima and Kikaigashima areas in an attempt to clear the way for action by special attack force units. In each sortie, enemy fighters were encountered, but our side attained effective battle results. In contrast with the 165 aircraft that went out on these sorties and the 106 enemy aircraft that were shot down, records indicate that our side suffered only twenty-nine aircraft that either destroyed themselves or failed to return to base. In addition, a considerable number of aircraft suffered engine failures or received hits; these were forced to make emergency landings. Next, during the period 18 April through 11 May, the 343 was based at Kokubu Air Base No. 1; it concentrated on the

interception of B-29s that had started to attack southern Kyūshū.

A cumulative total of 120 aircraft were sent off and twelve enemy aircraft shot down. It was not easy to shoot down B-29s while in a formation attack pattern, even using the four 20-mm cannons with which the Shiden-kai was equipped. Losses on our side amounted to three aircraft that destroyed themselves, including that of LT Hayashi, plus seven aircraft that made emergency landings. Fifteen aircraft incurred major damage while still on the ground. On 3 May, Air Group 343 withdrew to Omura and was used against enemy flying boat attacks in the Gotō Islands area. During the month of April, five enemy aircraft were destroyed. During June and July, the number of experienced flight personnel lessened, and the replenishment of materials and supplies was insufficient. In particular, once B-24s started their bombing runs based on Okinawa, ground damage increased. The number of operable aircraft of Air Group 343 had dropped to around twenty aircraft. Based on a policy promulgated by the 5th Air Fleet, measures were taken to husband pilot strength. At the same time, there were instances where the circumstances were favorable and the entire force of available aircraft was sent out. In particular, during the 2 June air battles over Kagoshima Bay, twenty-one aircraft led by LT Keijirō Hayashi, newly assigned as group leader in Fighter Hikōtai 407, were able to make a surprise attack from a superior position on a formation of twenty-three F4Us. The result was a one-sided battle that ended with eighteen enemy aircraft being shot down.

Again, during the 24 July air battles over the Bungo Strait, battle results were sixteen enemy aircraft shot down. Imperial words of approval were received. At the same time, our side lost four aircraft, including that flown by LT Oshibuchi.

Subsequent to this time, there were no large scale air battles. Both LT Hayashi (22 June) and LT Kanno (1 August) were killed in action; a decimated senior staff greeted the end of hostilities.

According to CAPT Genda's records, the approximate half a year total of battle results of Air Group 343 amounted to about 170 enemy aircraft shot down. Seventy-four pilots were lost on our side.

第 345 航 空 隊 (光)

AIR GROUP 345 (HIKARI)

Air Group 345 (Hikari, "Light") was organized on 1 January 1944 at the Naruo base and immediately posted to the 62nd Air Flotilla (1st Air Fleet). Allowance was seventy-two interceptors (eighteen spares); the unit was scheduled to be equipped with Shiden-Kai. In the final outcome, however, such aircraft never became available. CDR Kōrokurō Tatemi was ordered in as the CO, and LCDR Miyoshi Sonoda as group leader. Training started using Zero fighters but progress was exceedingly slow. While equipment, supplies, and personnel were still being assembled, the final Battle of the Marianas began. With the disbanding of the 62nd Air Flotilla on 15 June, Air Group 345 was transferred to the 2nd Air Fleet. On 10 July, however, Air Group 345 itself was also disbanded.

第 221 航空隊 (嵐)

AIR GROUP 221 (ARASHI)

Air Group 221 (Arashi, "Storm") was organized at the Kasanbara base in Kagoshima Prefecture on 15 January 1944 and immediately posted to the 62nd Air Flotilla (1st Air Fleet). LCDR Ichirō Himeno (later, CDR), a former sea plane pilot, was ordered in as the commanding officer, while LT Toshio Shiozuru came in as group leader. Allowance was fifty-four carrier fighters, with eighteen others in reserve. Training started around the middle of February but the equipment (Zero fighters) was late in arriving; at the end of the month, a mere ten aircraft were operable. Later, the number of aircraft increased gradually; by the end of June there were fourteen Model 21 Zero fighters and twenty-four Model 52s. During this period the order to commence the Tōgō operation was issued. Elements of Air Group 221 were temporarily deployed in the following manner in order to prepare for attacks by American carrier task force elements: eight aircraft to Kasumigaura starting 25 February and sixteen aircraft to Kisarazu, starting 19 June. However, no action was seen. With the reorganization of 10 July, the 221 was transformed into a major air group consisting of four hikōtai. It was then posted to the 2nd Air Fleet. CAPT Masahisa Saitō was ordered in as the commander, CDR Kiyoji Sakakibara as the executive officer, and LCDR Harutoshi Okamoto as the air officer. Units that were integrated into the newly organized Air Group 221 consisted of the following: Fighter Hikōtai 308 (commander, LT Hisaya Hirusawa), the 312 (commander, LT Shiozuru), the 313 (commander, LT Shirō Kawai), and the 407 (commander, LT Yoshishige Hayashi). The allowance for each unit was forty-eight aircraft. Fighter Hikōtais 308, 312, and 313 trained at Kasanbara base, while Fighter Hikōtai 407 trained at the Kagoshima base. On three occasions in mid-August, the fifty-one Zero fighters of Fighter Hikōtai 312 advanced to the Shinchiku (Hsinchu) base in Taiwan and engaged in air defense as well as ship convoy protection operations.

On 12 October, a large force of carrier aircraft from an American task force raided Taiwan. Fighter Hikōtai 312, under the command of LT Keiji Katagi, used a cumulative total of forty-three aircraft to intercept the incoming raiders. In contrast with the battle results of twenty-three enemy aircraft (seven probables) shot down, fif-

Zero Fighter Model 52

Aircraft belonging to Fighter Hikōtai 313, around August 1944. Unit symbol of the 313 was *21*.

Dark Green — White

21-57

Light Gray

Zero Fighter Model 52

In the homeland, around January 1944.

Black — Dark Green — White — Yellow — Light Gray

Zero Fighter Model 52

Aircraft of Fighter Hikōtai 312, around August 1944. Unit symbol of the 312 was *221*.

Black — Dark Green — White — Yellow — Light Gray

Zero Fighter Model 52

Fighter Hikōtai 308 aircraft, around August 1944. *A* was inserted for Fighter Hikōtai 308.

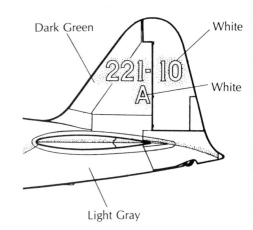

Dark Green — White — White — Light Gray

Zero Fighter Model 52

Aircraft of Fighter Hikōtai 407, around August 1944. *D* was inserted for unit 407.

Dark Green — White — Light Gray

Fighter Hikōtai 407 flight personnel belonging to Air Group 221, shown while undergoing training in April 1944 in the homeland. Extreme right is LT Hayashi, group leader. In the center, with his back to us is CPO Minoru Honda. (Minoru Honda)

teen of our aircraft either destroyed themselves or failed to return. Next, on the 15th, sixteen Zero fighters (eleven from Fighter Hikōtai 312) escorted four land attack planes in an attack on enemy task forces off Taiwan. The majority of the aircraft, including that flown by LT Katagi the leader, turned back while still en route to the objective area; also, in air combat with Grummans conducted over enemy forces, two Zero fighters were lost. Also on the 16th, fourteen Zero fighters under the command of LT Shiozuru sortied as escort for one carrier bomber and three land attack planes. However, because of fog the aircraft turned back while flying over Takao (Kao-hsuing).

On 14 October Air group 221 situated on the island of Kyūshū staged to Taichung and Shinchiku (Hsinchu) to participate in battles off Taiwan. The strength of the unit as of the 18th was thirty aircraft at Taichū (Taichung) and forty aircraft at Hsinchu.

On the 23rd, four hikōtai, consisting of sixty aircraft of Air Group 221, advanced to the Angeles base on Luzon. The next day, the 24th, the unit participated in the general offensive that was carried out against enemy carrier task forces operating east of Luzon. Later on, the air group participated in a number of operations including attacks on Leyte and base air defense. During the same period, one element advanced to Jolo Island; seven of the aircraft, basing themselves at Menado [Celebes], engaged in the 21 October nighttime surprise strafing attack on the island of Morotai. With the reorganization of December, the following additional units were attached to Air Group 221: Fighter Hikōtai 303 (commander, LCDR Kiyokuma Okajima), the 304 (commander, LT Takashi Oshibuchi), the 315 (commander, LCDR Masuzō Setō), and the 317 (commander, LT Minoru Kawazoe). It was thus enlarged to a six-hikōtai organization and became the main air control unit towards the end of the air battles over the Philippines. On 20 December, the last of the remaining crack aircraft, numbering twenty (belonging to

Fighter Hikōtai 308), advanced to the Angeles base under the command of LCDR Kawai. On the 24th, however, unit commander Kawai received hits on his aircraft during air combat over Clark and had to parachute into the mountains to the west; he was lost in action. A considerable number of aircraft were lost in the air as well as on the ground. As a result of the action on the two days of the 25th and the 26th, further attrition came about; Air Group 221 received a death blow. On 8 January of the following year, commanding officer CDR Katsutoshi Yagi, accompanied by surviving pilots of his unit, went to Taiwan.

Ground crews were reorganized as naval infantry under the command of LCDR Tadao Saeki; by the end of the war, a large number of them had been killed in guerilla battles in the mountains.

Successive Commanding Officers:

January 1944–July 1944   LCDR Ichirō Himeno

July 1944–November 1944   CAPT Masahisa Saitō

November 1944–February 1945   CDR Katsutoshi Yagi

February 1945– LCDR Tadao Saeki

第 256 航空隊

AIR GROUP 256

Air Group 256 was established at the Ryūka (Lunghwa) airfield in Shanghai on 1 February 1944 and attached to the China Area Fleet. Allowance was twenty-four carrier fighters and eight carrier attack planes. The unit was given duties of air defense over Shanghai, antisubmarine patrol in adjacent waters, and the protection of ship convoys. At the same time, the carrier fighter squadron was also made responsible for advanced training provided youthful pilots. In that sense, it was more of a training unit than it was an actual fighting unit. The commanding officer was CAPT Ichitarō Uchida and group leader, LCDR Yoshirō Kaneko; LTJG Hiroshi Mori-i (replaced by group leader, LT Keizō Yamazaki in April) was group leader for the carrier fighter squadron. At the time of its organization, the number of operable aircraft was fifteen Zero fighters and five Type 97 carrier attack planes. In addition, a few fighter trainers were also attached to group 256.

At the time of the American carrier task force raids against Taiwan in October 1944 Air Group 256 was strengthened by the ordering to the unit of selected veteran pilots. On the 13th, ten Zero fighters led by LT Yamazaki departed Lunghwa on a sortie but were forced back because of inclement weather. Only two aircraft, including that flown by WO Kazuyoshi Toyoda, were able to reach Taiwan. Avoiding contact with attacking enemy fighters over Hsinchu, the aircraft were able to land at Taichung. On the 14th and the 15th, they joined forces with Air Group 254 and sortied on air defense operations. On the 15th, nine Zero fighters led by LT Yamazaki again advanced to Tainan. On the 16th, five aircraft sortied together with Air Group 254 aircraft providing screen in an attack on enemy task forces. During air battles two F6Fs were shot down; two of our own aircraft returned after making forced landings at Laoag in the northern Philippines.

On the 27th, six Zero fighters of Air Group 256 (commander, WO Toyoda) were integrated into Air Group 254 and given orders to advance to the Philippine Islands. Arriving at Nichols on the same day, they then transferred to Malbalacat. They were assigned to participate in the attacks on Leyte, as well as engage in base air defense operations. By early November, the number of operational aircraft had been reduced to zero. Two pilots were reassigned to Air Group 201 for special attacks. On the 7th, unit commander Yamazaki caught up with them after leaving Taiwan; by the 15th, only three pilots remained alive. They withdrew to Tainan. On the 17th, orders were received returning them to their original unit; the group returned to Shanghai together with whatever personnel had survived in Taiwan. During the one month or more that air groups 254 and 256 were dispatched to Taiwan and the Philippines, they lost twenty-four pilots; battle

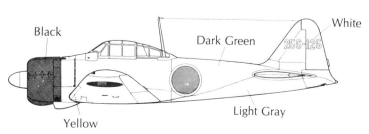

Zero Fighter Model 21

In China, 1944. Planes numbered in the *150* series were Model 52s; planes numbered *1–149* were Model 21s.

Black

Yellow

Dark Green

White

256-125

Light Gray

results were eighteen enemy aircraft (four probables) shot down.

During the same time at the Lunghwa airfield, LT Chiyoyuki Shibata was serving as commander of the caretaker unit; training activities were continued. As of 1 November, the number of aircraft on hand was eleven Model 21 Zero fighters (three were dispatched to Hong Kong, and five to Taiwan), thirteen Model 52 Zero fighters (eight were in Taiwan), three Raiden interceptors, six Type 97 carrier attack planes, and six observation floatplanes.

Starting in November, B-29s on the way to and from bombing the homeland were engaged by the 256 in intercept operations but with almost no results. On 15 December, Air Group 256 was disbanded and integrated into Air Group 951.

第 203 航 空 隊

AIR GROUP 203

The Atsugi Air Group was established in April 1943 as a training unit for pilots assigned to the fleet; it was renamed Air Group 203 effective 20 February 1944. Immediately upon the renaming, it was posted to the 51st Air Flotilla (12th Air Fleet) and was scheduled to engage in air defense operations in the area of Hokkaidō and the Kurile Islands.

The commanding officer was CAPT Ryutarō Yamanaka, continuing on as the commander from the days when the unit was the Atsugi Air Group. Although the aircraft allowance was ninety-six carrier fighters, there were only fifty-nine Zero fighters and twelve Gekkō night fighters at the time of its activation. Headquarters was at Atsugi and a unit dispatched to Kisarazu. The latter unit was posted to Air Group 302 as of 14 March. After the reorganization on 15 April, Air Group 203 assumed the following structure: two hikōtai consisting of Fighter Hikōtai 303 (commander, LCDR Kiyokuma Okajima) and Fighter Hikōtai 304 (commander, LT Takashi Oshibuchi). Each unit had an allowance of forty-eight aircraft. On 30 March, forty-six aircraft of the main unit left Atsugi for the Chitose base in Hokkaidō; they were assigned to air defense activities in the northern Kuriles, replacing Air Group 281, which had proceeded to the Marshall Islands the previous year end and had met with an honorable demise.

Toward the end of April, as soon as the snows melted, one unit consisting of one buntai of Zero fighters and three Gekkō aircraft was sent to the Kataoka base on Shumshu Island and another unit of similar configuration to the Musashi base on the island of Paramushir. From mid-May to the end of the month, the main force of the air group under the command of Yamanaka advanced to the Kataoka base. On 13 May, Air Group 203 scored its first victory when it shot down a U.S. Navy Ventura patrol bomber that came in on an attack from the Aleutians. On 15 June, a cumulative total of sixty aircraft were used in intercepting incoming American bombers; two PVs were destroyed and one B-24 heavy bomber also shot down. One of the damaged enemy aircraft was forced into making an emergency landing in the Soviet territory of Kamchatka.

By the time heavy snows began in the fall, the unit had participated in three to four intercept operations; there was trouble with radar equipment, however, and few kills were obtained. During this same period, the Musashi base underwent a night bombardment on 26 June conducted by American cruisers and destroyers. As a result, major damage was inflicted upon us in that eight Zero fighters were destroyed by fire and seven aircraft received heavy damage; in addition sixteen aircraft received hits. As of the end of June, the number of operable aircraft was as follows: thirty-two Zero fighters with the main unit

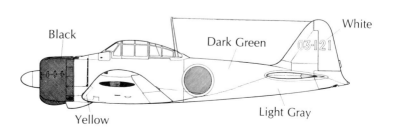

Zero Fighter Model 21

Unit insignia *03* was used during February through summer 1944.

Black · Dark Green · White · 03-121 · Yellow · Light Gray

CPO Tanimizu of Fighter Hikōtai 303 with his favorite aircraft (Model 52 Zero fighter); the side is inscribed with marks indicating the number of aircraft he shot down. (Takeo Tanimizu)

at Kataoka, one Gekkō aircraft, and the nineteen Zero fighters dispatched to Musashi. In addition, there were a few aircraft that remained at Mihoro.

As the summer drew to a close, it was decided that the main force of Air Group 203 would be moved to Hokkaidō. On 11 August, the main unit moved to the Mihoro base; only the nineteen Zero fighters of the Shumshu Detachment (commander, LT Mutsuo Urushiyama) were left in the northern Kurile Islands. On 2 September,

Zero Fighter Model 52

Unit insignia *203* was used during autumn 1944 through August 1945.

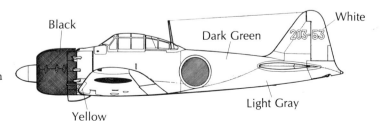

Black

White

Dark Green

203-53

Yellow

Light Gray

Fighter Hikōtai 303 (Air Group 201) at Kasanbara in early 1945. Second row (from the front): fourth person from the right is LCDR Kiyokuma Okajima (group leader). (Kiyokuma Okajima)

in preparation for American task force landings on the homeland and in order to participate in the Tō-gō operation, fifty of the sixty-three aircraft at Mihoro were dispatched to the Hyakurigahara base under the command of LCDR Okajima. However, the unit returned to Mihoro on the 14th. During the same period of time, on the 18th, orders were received to integrate Fighter Hikōtai 303 (twenty-seven aircraft) into the T Attack Force. The unit moved first to Mobara and then to Kagoshima on the 25th, standing by for action. On 12 October, with the start of air battles off the coast of Okinawa, Fighter Hikōtai 303 joined the T Attack Force and participated in attacks on American carrier task forces. The unit next advanced to the Philippines via Okinawa and Taiwan. At the same time, the Air Group 203 main unit also received its orders to participate in the Shō-gō operation.

During 11–12 October, the unit deployed to Izumi via Katori, reaching their destination on the 13th. On the 14th, twenty-nine Zero fighters of Fighter Hikō-tai 304 led by LT Oshibuchi left Izumi and advanced to the Okinawa north airfield. During the same afternoon, twenty-three aircraft left as an air control unit to attack American task forces. No sign was seen of the enemy, however, and the majority of aircraft returned to Okinawa; some of them returned to Taiwan. On the next day, the 15th, the unit sortied off the coast of Taiwan in support of the Ginga-tai ("Galaxy" Unit). On the 16th, fourteen aircraft commanded by LT Oshibuchi joined Air Groups 221, 252, and 634 on a sortie; they were successful in shooting down six enemy aircraft (jointly) after engaging in battle with Grummans.

On the 22nd, the unit joined the main unit, which had managed to catch up with them, as well as with reinforcements that had arrived at Taichung. On the 22nd, twenty-nine aircraft advanced to Bamban on Luzon. Commanding officer Yamanaka accompanied them with the two MC transports being used to transport maintenance personnel. During the general offensive on the 24th, sixteen aircraft from Fighter Hikōtai 304 (commander, LT Oshibuchi) joined in the attacks on American carrier task forces east of Luzon. Later and until the end of the month, Fighter Hikōtai 304 joined forces with Fighter Hikōtai 303 and other air groups that had assembled at Clark Field in conducting search and destroy missions against American carrier forces, as well as participating in the Leyte attack.

Once November came, however, the forces stationed at Clark Field endured almost daily raids conducted by American carrier aircraft. Losses continued to mount from intercept operations; strategic emphasis was placed on operations by the special attack force units. A large number of special attack force pilots were selected from Air Group 203 as well; sixteen persons, including LTJG Ichirō Watanabe, died a hero's death. With the reorganization of 15 November, the emaciated unit 203 had its Fighter Hikōtai 303 transferred to Air Group 201, and Fighter Hikōtai 304 to Air Group 221. The 203 itself was integrated into the 25th Air Flotilla (3rd Air Fleet); on the 20th, the main body of the 203 withdrew to Kasanbara in southern Kyūshū in order to regroup. In addition, Fighter Hikōtai 812 (twenty-four Gekkō aircraft), which had been integrated into Air Group 203 during the latter part of October, moved forward to the Philippines for action.

By the end of December, however, after action in the bombings of Leyte and engaging in night intercept operations, unit 812 was decimated. The new Air Group 203 was constituted of Fighter Hikōtai 303,

which had retreated from the Philippines, and Fighter Hikōtai 312 (commander, LT Yoshihiro Hayashi; later succeeded by LT Kunio Kanzaki). Both units had an allowance of forty-eight aircraft. At the same time there were delays in equipment and supplies. As of 18 March 1945, available strength was as follows: Fighter Hikōtai 303, with thirty-two aircraft (fifty-seven pilots) located at Kagoshima and Izumi, and the 312, with thirty-one aircraft (fifty-one pilots) located at Kasanbara.

On 18 and 19 March, American carrier aircraft raided the southern part of the island of Kyūshū for the first time. Although Air Group 203 did intercept and shoot down twelve enemy aircraft, our side also lost eleven aircraft. On the 21st, eleven aircraft under the command of LCDR Okajima serving as an air control unit participated in the first sortie by the Jinrai Special Attack Force (see Air Group Fighter Squadron 721 (Jinrai), p. 226). The attackers themselves, however, were wiped out and the venture was unsuccessful. With the outbreak of the Okinawa operations on 1 April, Air Group 203 was posted to the 5th Air Fleet and participated in direct support of special attack force operations. Losses were not inconsiderable. In May 1945, Air Group 203 was integrated into the 72nd Air Flotilla and withdrew to the Tsuiki base. Here the strength was increased to that of a major fighter organization consisting of the following five Hikōtai (total complement of 240 aircraft): Fighter Hikōtai 303 (commander, LT Osamu Kurata), the 309 (LT Hideo Matsumura), the 311 (LT Kisuke Hasegawa), the 312 (LT Kōsuke Tabuchi), and the 313 (LT Yasuo Masuyama). In preparation for the final battle in the homeland, Air Group 203 followed a policy of conserving its manpower; in this way, it greeted the end of the war.

第 302 航 空 隊

AIR GROUP 302

Air Group 302 was established 1 March 1944 at Kisarazu as an air defense fighter unit assigned to the Yokosuka Naval Base for protecting the nation's capital. CAPT Yasuna Kozono, a veteran campaigner well known among naval fighter pilots, was named as the commanding officer. At the time of its organization, the allowance was forty-eight interceptors and twenty-four night fighters. There were few true veterans of fighter aircraft; the majority of pilots had been transferred from other branches of the service, such as seaplanes, flying boats, carrier bombers, and others. Both the air officer, LCDR Ki-ichirō Nishihata, and the group leader, LT Kushi-chirō Yamada (who later himself became the air officer), were former seaplane pilots. At the time of its establishment, training was started with one unit of Raiden aircraft at Yokosuka and one unit of Gekkō aircraft at Kisarazu. The command used one corner of the headquarters of the Yokosuka Air Group. A large number of reserve student pilots who were graduates of universities and technical colleges was assigned to the unit. During the latter part of March, leaving about one hundred headquarters personnel behind at Yokosuka, the main force of Air Group 302 transferred to the Atsugi base, where it took over duties of Air Group 203, which itself had been transferred elsewhere.

Atsugi was in an ideal geographical location for the interception of enemy aircraft coming in over the Kantō coastal area because it was located only five minutes away from Eno-shima and fifteen minutes away from Tokyo. At the same time, the airfield was not completely set up and there was too much red earth dust. In order to permit fighter aircraft on the ready line to take off immediately, CO Kozono mobilized construction workers and hurriedly built several runways on each side of the main runway. On 5 May, headquarters of the 302 was moved to Atsugi. At the time it was thought that air raids on the Kantō area by the superbomber B-29 were inevitable.

Great expectations were placed on Air Group 302 as the sole air defense fighter unit available in the area. Intensive training in CO Kozono's own unique method of intercepting B-29s was carried out. In particular, emphasis was placed on the technique of using obliquely angled cannon. This technique had been found to be successful by Kozono during his days with Air Group 251 when the unit was engaged in nighttime interception of heavy bombers in the southeast area. Not only were angled guns mounted on the Gekkō, they were also placed in the after fuselage of Zero fighters, the Raiden, and other single-seat fighters.

In the case of the Zero fighter, in addition to the forward firing fixed guns, a 20-mm gun was placed at a thirty-degree angle from the plane's center line on the upper portion of the rear of the canopy. This was

Raiden
Aircraft flown by CPO Take-hiko Baba. Unit insignia *YoD* was used from March 1944 through August 1945.

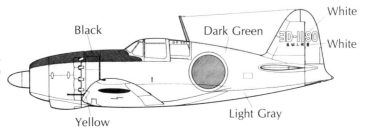

Black — Dark Green — White — White — Light Gray — Yellow

an attempt to permit, even during daytime intercept actions, the upward firing of guns while the interceptor itself would dive under and off to the side of the target plane, flying a parallel course. The innovation was carried out despite the opposition of pilots who disliked any increase in aircraft weight. Also, from the point of view of the actual results attained, it was not considered to have been very effective.

In such fashion Air Group 302 was built up almost to its full battle strength. On 1 November 1944, the 302 encountered the first raid by B-29s from bases in the Marianas. At the time, Air Group 302 was constituted of the following: two buntai of Raiden aircraft; the 1st Hikōtai, made up of one buntai of Zero fighters (commander, LT Yamada, followed by LT Hiroshi Morioka); the 2nd Hikōtai, made up of two Gekkō buntai, plus one Ginga buntai (commander and senior division officer, LT Makoto Kudō; LT Tomiya Miyazaki, LT Seikan Hayashi, and others); and the 3rd Hikōtai, made up of two Buntai of Suisei night fighters (commander, LT Hidetada Fujita). The number of operable aircraft were ten Raiden, twenty-seven Zero fighters, fifteen Gekkō night fighters, two Ginga night fighters, and six Suisei night fighters. By 1945, the main strength of the unit was in the thirty or so Raiden aircraft (see Table 8).

From August to October of 1944, one Gekkō buntai under the command of LTJG Endō was dispatched to northern Kyūshū to engage in intercept operations against B-29s. Considerable numbers of kills were attained and confidence in the unit's abilities was increased as a result. Next, in No-

vember, LT Endō was sent to Hachijō-jima with three aircraft. The intention was to use Chichi-shima [Bonin Islands] radar in intercept operations; this was found to be difficult, however, and the unit was soon withdrawn from Hachijō-jima.

Because B-29s flew at an altitude above ten thousand meters, unexpectedly higher than that initially imagined, almost all early period intercept operations of Air Group 302 were unsuccessful. During a reconnaissance raid conducted by enemy aircraft on 1 November, it became quite clear that it would take an intercept fighter almost thirty minutes to reach that altitude. It was decided that, starting the following day, three Zero fighters would be used in rotation for patrol, both before and after the noon hour. During the raids on the 5th, LT Morioka was able to score the first success in this area. Full-scale formation raids by B-29s commenced on 24 November. Air Group 302 had itself become experienced in conducting intercept battles. On 3 December, using a variety of aircraft cumulatively totaling seventy-four (including twenty-four Raiden interceptors) the 302 was able to shoot down nine enemy aircraft (three probables) with eight destroyed. From this time on, some kills were always obtained in each intercept operation conducted. In particular, it was noted that intercept operations using the Raiden fighter units were the most effective. Because of the lack of aircraft and limited crusing range, however, repeated or continuous attacks were not possible. Thus, it was not possible to deal the enemy forces decisive blows; in addition, our own damages resulting from the air raids continued to mount. With the

TABLE 8. OPERABLE AIRCRAFT, BY TYPE

	RAIDEN	ZERO FIGHTER	GEKKŌ	GINGA	SUISEI	TYPE 99 CARRIER BOMBER	OTHER
End Sept. 1944	14	28	17	0	6	4	
1 Jan. 1945	26	22	16	8	9		7
1 Feb. 1945	31	18	14	6	7		8
1 Mar. 1945	24	20	13	12	7		5

Raiden interceptors of Air Group 302 taking off. (*Air Review*)

start of raids by carrier aircraft in February 1945 and assaults by P-51s based at Iwo Jima, which commenced in April, it became increasingly difficult for the sluggish night fighters to sortie. In addition, damages suffered on the part of Raiden and Zero fighter units that were believed deficient in antifighter tactical experience also increased.

During the same period, the Battle of Okinawa started. Starting in the early part of April and lasting for a period of about one month, Air Group 302 dispatched around half of its force of Zero fighter and Raiden fighter units to southern Kyūshū, where they participated in the attacks on Okinawa and in intercepting B-29s. Again, for a period of about ten days starting on 12 May, eight Suisei night fighters were dispatched to the Itami base and were used in assisting in the air defense of the Osaka Kobe area.

After May, the number of actually operable aircraft of Air Group 302 was down to around ten or so. In August, in anticipation of the final battle for the homeland, aircraft were dispersed to Komatsu and Maebashi, leaving only a few planes in undergound hangars at Atsugi. The morning of August 15th, the day the war ended, also became the last opportunity for air combat for Air Group 302. Four Raiden and eight Zero fighters led by LT Morioka engaged in battle with six Grummans over Atsugi. They were able to shoot down one enemy aircraft; however, our side also suffered losses. Four aircraft, including the one flown by LT Taguchi, were lost. Immediately after the end of this air battle the imperial rescript ordering the end of the war was issued. Commanding officer Kozono, however, proclaimed his intention to fight to the very end; he refused to obey the cease-fire order. Kozono dispatched personnel of his unit to various areas to issue a declaration of his intention; he also gathered together aircraft that had become available as a result of the disbanding of other air groups. With the persuasion of Prince Takamatsu and others, however, and the hospitalization of Kozono on the 20th on mental grounds, circumstances within Air Group 302 gradually returned to normal. With the arrival of a new commanding officer and the disarming of all aircraft, it was possible for the 302 a week later to receive the first contingent of American occupation forces arriving at Atsugi without incident.

It has been reported that battle results attained by Air Group 302 came to about three hundred enemy aircraft downed. (Records of Air Officer Nishihata.)

第 361 航 空 隊 (晃)

AIR GROUP 361 (AKIRA)

Air Group 361 (Akira, "Radiant") was established at the Kagoshima base on 15 March 1944 and immediately posted to the 62nd Air Flotilla (1st Air Fleet). LCDR Kiyoji Sakakibara was ordered in to hold the posts of both commanding officer and executive officer. Fighter Hikōtai 407 (allowance of forty-eight interceptors; group leader, LT Yoshishige Hayashi) was attached to the 361. Although the group was scheduled to be equipped with Shiden interceptors, training started immediately using Zero fighters. Equipment and materials as well as pilots gradually arrived; from around April, flight training began in earnest at the Kagoshima base. This was after Air Groups 261 and 343 had been transferred to the Marianas and the base itself had become vacant. Equipment and supplies did not become available on schedule, however; even as of 1 May, the number of operable aircraft stood at eleven, with ten planes still undergoing maintenance. In addition, a considerable number of aircraft had been manufactured in a slipshod manner. There was also an insufficient number of pilots and not even a division officer ordered in to the unit. In the final analysis, Air Group 361 was disbanded as of the reorganization of 10 July; Fighter Hikōtai 407 was integrated into Air Group 221. Without any record of battles fought, Air Group 361 was to end its short history of four months' duration.

第 131 航 空 隊

AIR GROUP 131

Air Group 131 was organized on 10 July 1944 at Yokosuka as a combined day land reconnaissance and night fighter unit. It was attached to the 3rd Air Fleet and soon started training at the Katori base. Air Group 131 was composed of two units, the 11th Reconnaissance Hikōtai (twenty-four land reconnaissance planes) and Fighter Hikōtai 851 (commander, LT Yutaka Sugawara; allowance of twenty-four night fighters). The former unit was equipped with the new and powerful Saiun, the latter unit with the Gekkō. As of 1 August, the actual number of operable aircraft available

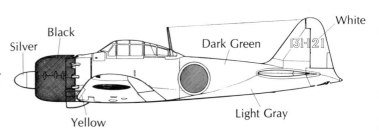

Zero Fighter Model 52
Aircraft flown by PO1c Kō-tarō Nagahama during interception of carrier aircraft, 16 February 1945.

Black
Silver
White
Dark Green
131-121
Yellow
Light Gray

Most of the officer cadre of the Fuyō Butai and personnel of Fighter Hikōtai 901, just before Kikusui Operation No. 1, early April 1945. Second row: wearing a tunic, LCDR Tadashi Minobe, air officer of Air Group 131. (Tadashi Minobe)

to Fighter Hikōtai 851 was eight planes. Starting about the end of July, two to three aircraft and some ground personnel were dispatched to Iwo Jima and participated in air defense and patrol operations, on a rotation basis. Although the unit did engage in a number of intercept operations against B-24s, with the reorganization as of 15 November, Air Group 131 was reconstituted as a carrier bomber and carrier attack plane unit. Fighter Hikōtai 851 was transferred to the northeast area.

With American attacks impending on Okinawa in March 1945, Air Group 131 was reorganized as follows; using Fighter Hikōtai 901, which had returned from the Philippines, as its core, Fighter Hikōtai 804 and 812 were added. In this fashion, the 131 was reconstituted as a night fighter unit and transferred to Kanoya base in southern Kyūshū, using the name Fuyō Butai ("Lotus Unit"). It was placed under the operational control of the Kantō area air com-

mand. The majority of experienced pilots were attached to the 901 and 804 fighter units (each with twenty-four Type C [night] fighter aircraft). The approximately forty aircraft, composed of Zero night fighters and Suisei aircraft, were commanded by Air Group 131's air officer, LCDR Tadashi Minobe. Based in Kanoya by the end of March, the unit engaged in the ferocious air battles over Okinawa. Fighter Hikōtai 812 (twenty-four Type C fighters) and personnel under training were led by LT Masashi Tokukura and became absorbed in training activities at the Fujieda base, Shizuoka Prefecture.

Fuyō Butai did not use any special attack force methodology; the unit used a small number of aircraft, flown by experienced personnel, in early dawn strafing and bombing raids on enemy airfields in Okinawa. In other cases, they would conduct surprise attacks on enemy task forces; in this fashion, they served to clear the way for our own special attack force units to operate. Till the end period of the Battle of Okinawa, Fuyō Butai repeatedly and stubbornly continued to engage in night attacks and was able to achieve effective battle results. The unit was able to develop their own special techniques for night fighting. The initial sortie conducted was on the night of 4 April; eight Suisei and four Zero night fighters were used. During April, a total of ninety-three sorties by Suisei and sixty sorties by Zero night fighters were made. Our side lost ten aircraft.

Later, the Kanoya base became subject to enemy air raids; the Fuyō Butai moved to Iwakawa base on 20 May. Iwakawa base was located in a mountainous and wooded area, given over primarily to agriculture. About one-tenth of the acreage was used for the airfield; the runways were grass. When the runways were exposed from use, branches and leaves were used to camouflage the area. In addition, other camouflage measures in the general area were using portable houses, putting cattle out to pasture, and other means. Iwakawa airfield was not discovered by American military aircraft until after the war had ended. To the very end, it was possible to fully exploit the advantages of this hidden airfield.

As indicated above, even when the war ended substantial military strength was still available in the forty-five Suisei night fighters and twenty-five Zero night fighters at Iwakawa. Moreover, there were forty Suisei and ten Zero night fighters, as well as twenty trainer planes available at Fuji-eda, located inland. These aircraft were standing by awaiting the final battle for the homeland. The means of using Fuyō Butai assets was affected quite a bit by the intricate, logical, yet zealous guidance provided by Minobe, air officer. The use of special attack force battle techniques was avoided until the very last. By the same token, by the time the Ketsu-gō operation started, preparations had been made for a technique that would have night fighters loaded with bombs slide onto the decks of enemy aircraft carriers in order to sweep all aircraft on board into the sea. Such techniques, however, were never implemented.

During the Okinawa operation, Fuyō Butai flew a cumulative number of about six hundred aircraft on sorties; their losses were sixty or more aircraft that destroyed themselves or failed to return and seventy-seven personnel killed in action.

第 332 航 空 隊

AIR GROUP 332

Air Group 332 was organized at the Iwakuni base on 1 August 1944 as a Kure area air defense fighter group; it was assigned to the Kure Naval Station. Allowance was forty-eight interceptors and sixteen two-seat, reconnaissance floatplanes. CDR Takeo Shibata was ordered in as the commanding officer, LCDR Masao Yamashita as air officer, and LCDR Yoshio Kurakane as group leader, respectively. The predecessor organization was the Kure Air Group Fighter Squadron, also stationed at Iwakuni. At the time that Air Group 332 was organized it had forty-five (twenty-eight operable) Zero fighters, twelve (two operable) Gekkō night fighters, and two Raiden (neither operational) interceptors. Later on, the number of Gekkō and Raiden aircraft on hand was increased; as of 1 November, actual operational aircraft numbered twenty-seven Zero fighters, fifteen Raiden, and six Gekkō aircraft.

On 6 November, the main Zero fighter force of Air Group 332 was given orders to proceed to the Philippines. The following day, twenty aircraft, led by LTJG Susumu Takeda, moved to Clark Field in the Philippines, proceeding via Kanoya and Takao (Kao-hsiung). They were next integrated into Air Group 201. As a result of the ferocious fighting that ensued on the battle front, however, the unit was soon decimated. Also as of 6 November, eight Zero fighters (equipped with obliquely angled guns) and six Gekkō aircraft were dis-

patched to the Atsugi base. Assigned to air defense operations in the Kantō area, the unit was next ordered back to its home base on 15 December. At the same time, the main force of Air Group 332 received its own transfer orders in order to assist in the air defense of the Kobe-Osaka area. As a result, Zero fighter and Raiden interceptor units (nine Zero fighters, eleven Raiden) under the command of air officer Yamashita deployed to the airfield at Naruo. Under the command of LT Seikan Hayashi (division officer), the Gekkō unit also deployed to Itami airfield; for air defense duties, it was placed under the command of the commanding general, 11th Army Air Division. The first sortie made by Air Group 332 was an interception operation against B-29s that came raiding the Kyūshū area on 25 October. Sixteen Zero fighters took off from Iwakuni and headed for northern Kyūshū; however, they failed to encounter the enemy, and there were consequently no battle results. Next, on 22 December, a cumulative total of sixteen Raiden and seven Zero fighters intercepted incoming B-29s over Naruo. CPO Ochi, flying his Zero fighter, recorded the first victory for the unit when he shot down one B-29.

On 3 January 1945, six Zero fighters and two Raiden aircraft were used to intercept B-29s over Osaka; LTJG Jūsaburō Mukai shot down one enemy aircraft. During an intercept operation on the 14th, LTJG Mu-

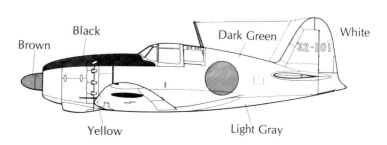

Raiden

Aircraft flown by CPO Akeshi Ochi, April 1945. Unit insignia *32* was used from August 1944 through 1945.

Brown · Black · Dark Green · White · 32-101 · Yellow · Light Gray

CPO Ochi piloted his Raiden to a belly landing. (Family of Susumu Ishihara)

Air Group 332 flight crews at a ready position enjoy a few moments of respite between battles. (Family of Susumu Ishihara)

kai was again able to shoot down one aircraft (a probable), but his own aircraft received hits and crashed; he himself was injured. Although Air Group 332 continued to intercept successive raids conducted by B-29s, no noteworthy additional battle results were attained. After the battle for Okinawa began in April, the Raiden units of Air Groups 302, 332, and 352 were deployed in a coordinated operational intercept effort against raiding B-29s, which were determined to suppress our special attack force bases located in southern Kyūshū. During the 23rd through the 25th, seventeen Raiden of Air Group 332 proceeded to the Kanoya base; by 12 May they had participated in a number of intercept operations. The aircraft then returned to their home base.

As of 25 May, Air Group 332 was integrated into the 72nd Air Flotilla (5th Air Fleet); allowance was forty-eight interceptors and twenty-four night fighters. On 3 August, the unit was transferred to the 53rd Air Flotilla (3rd Air Fleet) standing by for the battle for the homeland; the unit greeted the end of hostilities at Naruo base.

Successive Commanding Officers:

August 1944–February 1945   CDR Takeo Shibata

February 1945–August 1945   CDR Katsutoshi Yagi

第 352 航空隊 (草薙)

AIR GROUP 352 (KUSANAGI)

Air Group 352 (Kusanagi, "Heavenly Grass-Mowing Sword") was newly organized as of 10 August 1944 for air defense of the Sasebo, Nagasaki, and Ōmura areas. Command was located at Ōmura; at the outset, CAPT Ryūji Terasaki, commanding the Ōmura Air Group, a training group, assumed the concurrent command of the 352. LT Kunio Kanzaki was ordered in as group leader.

Allowance at the time it was organized was forty-eight interceptors and twelve night fighters; the air group itself was actually composed of three elements—the Zero fighter unit, the Raiden interceptor unit, and the Gekkō night fighter unit. In August, the number of operable aircraft was twenty-eight to thirty Zeros, no Raiden, and three to four Gekkōs. By June 1944, B-29s based in remote parts of China had started to raid northern Kyūshū. Though attached to the Sasebo Naval Base as a B-29 intercept unit, the 352 was placed under the control of the army's supreme defense commander (Western Army Command) for purposes of air defense. Eight night fighter teams under the command of LTJG Sachio Endō from Air Group 302 had been previously dispatched to the Gekkō unit of

Air Group 352. Of those teams, three were ready for night fighting action.

The first battle took place during 20 August 1944 (P.M.). Thirty-three Zero fighters and four Gekkō aircraft sortied; army and navy aircraft jointly shot down a total of twenty-eight enemy planes. Air Group 352 shot down one aircraft and destroyed one other. LTJG Endō, flying his Gekkō aircraft, was forced to make an emergency landing on Chejudo Island (Quelpart); he reported his own tally as three enemy aircraft (one probable) shot down, as well as minor damage inflicted on two other planes. Next, during the daytime intercept battles on 25 October, a cumulative number of fifty Zero fighters, thirteen Raiden, and six Gekkō aircraft took off; each attacking once or twice, the group shot down one enemy aircraft and shot up sixteen others.

During daytime intercept battles fought on 21 November, a cumulative sixty-nine Zero fighters, Raiden, and Gekkō aircraft took off to intercept the enemy. Jointly with the Ōmura Air Group, Air Group 352 was able to achieve the following significant battle results: twelve enemy aircraft shot down (nine by the 352), ten planes set on fire, seven aircraft left smoking, and

Raiden
Flown by ENS Nobuo Kikuchi, March 1945. Unit insignia *352* was used from August 1944 through August 1945. Plane numbers used: Raiden, *01–99;* Zero fighters, *101–99;* Gekkō, *201–99.*

White

Dark Green

352-17

Light Gray

fourteen other aircraft hit. The reasons for this success lay in the fact that an effective intercept structure had been set up; this consisted of a Gekkō patrol line placed one hundred miles west of Ōmura, which was used in coordination with radar operations. It was during the battles of this day that the aircraft flown by LTJG Mikihiko Sakamoto rammed an enemy plane; he himself died in action. Later on, attacks from the mainland of China ceased; after November, B-29s based in the Marianas started to raid the Kantō, Kinki, and Chūkyō [Nagoya] areas of the homeland. The Gekkō unit led by LT Endō reverted to Air Group 352.

Air Group 352 continued to engage in training in anti-B-29 battle tactics, in particular the technique of using San-gō (No. 3) aerial bombs. During the spring of 1945, the group was faced with an American invasion of Okinawa. As of 1 March, strength was as follows: thirty-nine Zero fighters (twenty-one operable), thirty-nine Raiden (eighteen operable), eight Gekkō (four operable), and six Suisei night fighters (three operable). In order to participate in the Kikusui operation (special attack force), which started on 6 April, the Zero fighter unit commanded by LT Shinei Uematsu advanced to the Kokubu base; there it was integrated into the air control

unit and participated in a number of air battles. The Raiden unit led by Reserve LTJG Yoshihiro Aoki was posted for about three weeks to the composite Raiden unit located at the Kanoya base. Although participating in intercepting B-29s, there were no victories; as a matter of fact, the unit merely compounded losses to their own aircraft as a result of damage from being bombed.

With the 25 May reorganization, Fighter Hikōtai 902 (Gekkō planes; commander, LT Fujito Hoshiko) of Air Group 381, which had been active in the southwest area, was added to the 352. At the time, the available equipment was: twenty-eight Zero fighters of various models (eighteen operable), twenty-five Raiden (five operable), twelve Gekkō (seven operable), and seven Suisei (none operable).

After the dropping of the atomic bomb on Nagasaki on 9 August [1945], the first aerial reconnaissance flights made were conducted by Zero fighters of Air Group 352.

Successive Commanding Officers:

August 1944–December 1944 CAPT Ryūji Terasaki

December 1944–July 1945 CAPT Bunzō Shibata

July 1945– CAPT Tatsuto Yamada

第 210 航空隊

AIR GROUP 210

Air Group 210 was organized at Meiji base in Aichi Prefecture on 15 September 1944 as a training unit; it contained a number of different types of aircraft. It was posted to the 3rd Air Fleet.

At the time of its establishment, the 210 was a very large unit having an allowance of forty-eight carrier fighters, forty-eight interceptors, twelve night fighters, twenty-four land reconnaissance planes, twenty-four carrier bombers, and twenty-four carrier attack planes. Planes on hand as of 31 December consisted of various types of aircraft: twenty-nine Zero fighters, thirty-one Shiden interceptors, twelve Gekkō night fighters, eight fighter trainers, forty-seven Suisei carrier bombers, eleven Type 99 carrier bombers, eighteen Tenzan carrier attack planes, and three Type 97 carrier attack planes. The number of base personnel was also large, reaching 3,300. Hikōtai organization was: two Type A fighter units; two Type B fighter units; half of a Type C unit; plus one each land reconnaissance, carrier bomber, and carrier attack plane units. Senior division leaders (and later, group leaders) of the fighter units were LT Kazumasa Mitsumori (Shiden aircraft) and LT Toshio Shiozuru (Zero fighter).

Starting the end of 1944, B-29s based in the Marianas began to raid the homeland. At the same time that Air Group 210 engaged in training activities, its instructors and teachers were also assigned to air defense operations. The first intercept action was against B-29s that raided the Nagoya area in daylight on 13 December. Fourteen Zero fighters, four Shiden, and three Gekkō aircraft sortied; results were limited to two enemy aircraft destroyed. During intercept battles on the 18th, however, three enemy aircraft (one probable) were shot down. In January 1945, a unit was created for dispatch to Tokushima, primarily around the Shiden; the unit was assigned air defense responsibilities in the Osaka and Kobe areas. The main force of the unit was responsible for the Nagoya area; each time there were raids, some victories were attained. On 16 and 17 February, American carrier aircraft raided the Tōkai area.

During the morning of the 16th, fourteen Zero fighters of Air Group 210 tangled with approximately fifty enemy aircraft in the skies over Hamamatsu. Sixteen (four probable) enemy aircraft were shot down; the following morning, another two enemy aircraft were shot down, also over Hamamatsu. Our side lost one aircraft; such were the results of the battles.

In March, in anticipation of the American invasion of Okinawa, Air Group 210 was reorganized into a primary tactical unit. Under the command of air officer Maki, the unit was deployed to southern Kyūshū in late March. The fighter unit, consisting of thirty-two Zero fighters and fourteen Shiden interceptors, advanced to Kokubu Base No. 1 and was placed under the command of Air Group 601. The unit participated in Okinawa special attack force operations as an air control unit. Until their

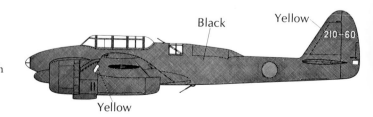

Gekkō

Unit insignia *210* was used from September 1944 through August 1945.

Black

Yellow

210-60

Yellow

Gekkō night fighters of Air Group 210 (*Air Review*)

return in mid-April to their former base, the unit was under the leadership of the two group leaders, Shiozuru and Mitsumori; it participated in a number of battles for air superiority over the Okinawa Islands, starting off with the first Kikusui special attack conducted on 6 April. Relative to the meager results attained (six aircraft shot down), losses were high (ten aircraft).

On 5 May, Air Group 201 was reorganized into a pure fighter unit (allowance, ninety-six carrier fighters) and posted to the 53rd Air Flotilla. The unit continued to carry out air defense duties. As a result of the policy of preserving forces for the final battle of the homeland, the end of the war was greeted with few battle results worthy of mention.

Flight personnel standing by to participate in air defense battles, Tokushima base. Second from right, ENS Shigeo Sugio. (Shigeo Sugio)

第721航空隊（神雷）戦闘機隊

AIR GROUP 721 FIGHTER SQUADRON (JINRAI)

In June 1944, when VADM Fukudome, commander of the 2nd Air Fleet, was inspecting Air Group 341 he received a report from CAPT Motoharu Okamura, a former fighter pilot, proposing the formation of a unit that would specialize in suicide attack operations only. Following consideration of this proposal at headquarters, it was adopted. It was in this fashion that Air Group Fighter Squadron 721 (Jinrai, "Heavenly Thunder") was born at Kōnoike base on 1 October 1944. CAPT Okamura, who had originally suggested the idea, was ordered in as the CO, and CDR Kunihiro Iwaki, a veteran of seaplanes, as the air officer (later executive officer). The unit was attached to Yokosuka Naval Base. The aircraft selected to be used as the ramming device was called the Ōka [literally "Cherry Blossom"; colloquially, by the United States, the Baka ("Idiot") bomb]. This craft was designed by special service ENS Shōichi Ōta, a transport pilot who had been active in air transport operations in the Rabaul area. The first model was built at the Tokyo Imperial University Air Research Laboratories and at the Naval Air Technology Arsenal (Kaigun Kōkū Gijutsu-chō). In order to maintain the secrecy of the project, the temporary name "Marudai" was assigned to the aircraft, based on ENS Ōta's name. The Ōka (Model 11) was a small, single-seat wooden glider carrying a 1.2-ton explosive charge in its nose. The bomb was to be hung underneath the fuselage of its mother aircraft, a Type 1 land attack plane; it would then be carried to within about twenty kilometers of its target. The aircraft would next release the Ōka to perform as a high speed special attack force aircraft. Although capable of gliding through the air for about thirty kilometers when dropped from an altitude of six thousand meters, the Ōka bomb itself was equipped with five rockets in its tail. The firing of those rockets enabled it to extend its cruising range somewhat. The greatest concern at the time of its trial manufacture was the fact that the mother craft was a slow and sluggish Type 1 land attack plane. There would thus be a good possibility that both the mother ship and the bomb itself would be shot down before their arrival in the battle zone. Wada, commander of the Naval Air Technology Arsenal, pressed the operational headquarters, stressing that unless fighter support was sufficient, the chances for success would be slim. As a result, a reinforced fighter unit was attached to Air Group Fighter Squadron 721.

The Fighter Hikōtai 306 (commander, LCDR Hachirō Yanagisawa, later LT Kunio Kanzaki and LT Daihachi Nakajima; allowance of forty-eight aircraft) was attached to the 721. For a period of time during the Battle of Okinawa, Fighter Hikōtais 305 and 307 were also added.

Successful drop tests of the Ōka bomb were carried out on 23 October 1944. A

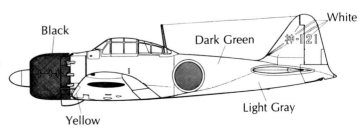

Zero Fighter Model 52

Unit insignia *Jin* ("God") was used from October 1944 to August 1945.

Black

Dark Green

White

神-121

Yellow

Light Gray

Air Group 721 personnel exchange the [traditional] final drink of water in a sake cup before takeoff. (Wataru Nakamichi)

trainer aircraft (Model K-1) was successfully flown on the 31st, with WO Nagano serving as the test pilot. Mass production was started immediately. By spring of the following year [1945], 750 of the gliders had been produced.

Starting in mid-November, Air Group 721 Fighter Squadron began training at Kōnoike base. By the end of the same month, fifty Ōka bombs had been loaded on board the aircraft carrier *Shinano* at Yokosuka, for use in Philippine operations. As the aircraft carrier was passing through Kumano-nada, however, she was torpedoed by an American submarine; the Ōka bombs sank with the carrier.

When the land attack squadron of Air Group 721 finished its short period of training in February 1945, it was posted to the 5th Air Fleet and moved to the Kanoya base in southern Kyūshū. The fighter squadron itself was located at Miyazaki base. On 19 March, when American carrier planes first raided western Japan, the land attack squadron was at the Kanoya and Usa bases. In addition, Fighter Hikōtai 305 (twenty-seven Zero fighters) was deployed to Ka-

noya, while Fighter Hikōtais 306 and 307 (totaling sixty-four Zero fighters) were deployed to the Tomitaka base. On the same date, the main thrust of the attack by the enemy was directed towards the Kyūshū area; fighters on the ready line at Usa belonging to Attack Hikōtai 728 were hit and burned.

On the other hand, Zero fighters of Fighter Hikōtais 306 and 307 had departed to intercept enemy aircraft; reported battle results totaled twenty-two enemy aircraft downed. At the same time, their own losses were great: twenty-three aircraft either destroyed themselves or failed to return to base. On the 21st, reconnaissance aircraft reported the presence of an American carrier task force operating in the seas south of Shikoku Island. ADM Ugaki of the 5th Air Fleet ordered Attack Hikōtai 711 at Kanoya to engage in a large-scale, daytime Ōka bomb attack. Supporting fighter aircraft strength for the eighteen land attack planes carrying the bombs (commander, LCDR Gorō Nonaka), however, was a mere fifty-five planes because of losses that had occurred on the 18th.

Moreover, because of poor maintenance and other factors, the actual number of aircraft that took part in the raid was restricted to the nineteen aircraft from Air Group 721 (direct escort) and the eleven aircraft (commander, LCDR Kiyokuma Okajima) from Air Group 203 (air control unit). Commanding officer Okamura, concerned over the insufficient number of support fighters available, recommended to his superiors that the attack be canceled. In the final case though, the aircraft sortied under a decision made by ADM Ugaki himself. The Jinrai unit was intercepted by some fifty enemy fighters en route to the target; as a result, and despite the defense put up by escorting fighters, all aircraft of the land attack force were shot down and destroyed before any Ōka bombs were released. Although the fighter unit did shoot down ten enemy aircraft, ten fighters led by 307 division officer LT Mutsuo Urushiyama failed to return. The very first Jinrai attack thus resulted in failure.

In late March, with the outbreak of Okinawa operations, it was decided that Air Group 721 Fighter Squadron would be used primarily as a fighter bomber unit that could be used to breach enemy patrol zones. CDR Nakamura was assigned duties of commanding and training the new unit. In using the Ōka bomb, the former policy of sending out a large formation was abandoned and changed to one of a constant dribble kind of attack (tenteki kō-geki). With this new tactic, a few Ōka bomb–carrying aircraft, without direct support as such, would be intermingled with special attack force planes to carry out their own attacks. The number of fighter bomber special attack force pilots who died in action during the entire Battle of Okinawa reached forty-eight (mentioned in All Units Bulletin).

On the other hand, the first success achieved by any Ōka bomb special attack forces was on 12 April, during Kikusui Operation No. 2. Eight Type 1 land attack planes carrying the bombs took off on this date. Before they were shot down by the enemy, six of those aircraft had reported that they had been able to release their Ōka bombs. Following his safe return to base, the pilot of the mother aircraft that carried the Ōka bomb piloted by Reserve LTJG Saburō Doi reported that Doi's Ōka was the only bomb that made a direct hit on an enemy warship; the hit resulted in a plume of smoke five hundred meters high. Forty Ōka bombs were released during the entire Battle of Okinawa; the only war vessel sinking verified by the American side was the sinking of the destroyer *M. A. Able* by LTJG Doi. At the same time, hits on five other enemy warships, including destroyers are on record. The last attack conducted by Air Group 721 Fighter Squadron was on 22 June, when six Oka bomb–carrying aircraft and six fighter bombers sortied; however, battle results are not clear. In any event, battle results attained through the use of this bomb were vastly less than initially anticipated. The reason for this was the sluggishness of the Type 1 land attack plane that was being used to carry the bombs. The navy decided to end the use of Ōka bomb Model 11. In its place, the navy started developing bomb Model 22 (the explosive charge was reduced to six hundred Kilo), which used as its mother ship the highly advanced Ginga. It was next decided that Air Group 722 (belonging to the 3rd Air Fleet; commander, CAPT Isao Watanabe), which was established at the Kō-noike base on 15 February 1945 and had been scheduled to receive the Model 11, would reoutfit their aircraft to operate with the Model 22 bomb. Training started but there was an accident during air release tests of the Model 22 conducted on 12 August; as a result, ENS Nagano died in the line of duty. The end of the war arrived before preparations were completed for large-scale production of the Ōka bomb.

第 205 航 空 隊

AIR GROUP 205

Air Group 205 was organized on 5 February 1945 at Taichu (Taichung) on Formosa and immediately posted to the 1st Air Fleet. In June it was transferred to the 29th Air Flotilla (Takao Guard Command). The unit had three elements: Fighter Hikōtai 302 (commander, LT Takeshi Murakami), 315, and 317, each with an allowance of forty-eight carrier fighters. The 205's total aircraft allowance came to 144 planes. CDR Asa-ichi Tamai was ordered in as the commanding officer, LCDR Minoru Suzuki as air officer.

Key personnel of Air Group 205 had come from among survivors of the 1st Air Fleet, which had retreated from the Philippines to Formosa. Following the American landings on Luzon in January 1945 the majority of personnel had lost their aircraft; they were gathering in Tuguegarao and in Echague in northern Luzon, looking for a land escape route. In accordance with orders from Imperial General Headquarters, air groups on Taiwan had mobilized land attack, heavy bombers, transports, and other types of aircraft for rescue operations. Between 9 and 29 January, some 1,060 personnel had been rescued from the Philippines, using night flights primarily.

At the time Air Group 205 was organized, the confusion accompanying the evacuation of troops was subsiding. At the same time, in contrast with the twenty-three Zero fighters on hand, there were only two pilots available. That situation

was gradually rectified. By 10 March, there was a total of 112 pilots (eight of Class A technical proficiency) distributed among Fighter Hikōtai 302 (Taichū/Taichung), 315 (Tainan/T'ai-nan), and 317 (Shinchiku/Hsinchu). At the same time, actually operable aircraft numbered only around twenty. With the American invasion of Okinawa in late March, the decision was made that the entire 1st Air Fleet in Taiwan would be turned into a special attack force. Commanding officer Tamai moved to the advance airfield on Ishigaki-jima, while LCDR Okamoto similarly advanced to Miyako-jima, both in order to direct special attack force operations. Starting on 1 April and almost daily, Zero fighters armed with bombs and provided a few escort fighters took off on missions. Mostly using Ishigaki-jima as a transit point, they were dispatched to seek out and attack enemy task forces in the seas south of Okinawa. However, due to inadequate supplies of materials and equipment, it was difficult to launch large-scale sorties as was the case with the 5th Air Fleet in Kyūshū. Most of the sorties were small in scale, using ten or fewer aircraft. At its height, the number of aircraft did not exceed the forty planes (of which twenty-eight were equipped with bombs) on hand as of 13 April. Special attack force planes of the 205 were identified as the Taigi-tai ("Noble Cause Unit"). When the war ended, the total number of pilots who sortied and died in the line of

Zero Fighter Model 52

Unit insignia *205* was used from February through August 1945.

Black

Dark Green

White

205-141

Yellow

Light Gray

action was thirty-two (All Units Bulletin). It is difficult to verify the battle results in view of the difficulties of separating battle results of the 205 from those of the 5th Air Fleet stationed in Kyūshū. It would appear that British task forces, which were responsible for air control over Taiwan and were operating in the Sakishiwa Guntō (Okinawa) area, were the main objective of operational action. According to Royal Navy records, bomb hits on 4 May on the aircraft carriers *Formidable* and *Indomitable,* as well as the bomb hits of the 9th on the *Victorious,* and the *Formidable* (for the second time) have all been credited as battle results of the Taigi-tai.

Special attacks by Air Group 205 subsided by the end of May; from June on, only dribble attacks were carried out once or twice a month until the war's end.

第 312 航 空 隊

AIR GROUP 312

Air Group 312 was organized on 5 February 1945 as a fighter unit that was equipped, for the first and only time in the history of Japanese aviation, with an interceptor propelled by a rocket engine. The interceptor was called the Shūsui ("Shining Blade").

The Shūsui was a copy of the Messerschmitt Me 163 rocket-powered fighter the German Air Force [Luftwaffe] had managed to make operable just before that nation's defeat in war. Based on blueprints brought back to Japan by technical CDR Iwaya, who traveled by submarine back to the homeland in July 1944, the design of the aircraft was started by the end of the same month. As a result of extraordinary efforts on the part of the army, navy, and civilian personnel and agencies involved, the design was completed within one month. The fuselage was manufactured in several parts by Mitsubishi and other aircraft manufacturers, the engine by the Naval Air Technology Arsenal and Mitsubishi Engine Company.

The planned Shūsui was a tailless aircraft with a wingspan of nine and a half meters, an empty weight of 1.4 tons, and a total equipped weight of about three tons. It could climb to ten thousand meters in three and a half minutes, had a maximum speed of about 770 kilometers per hour, and a cruising range, after reaching an altitude of ten thousand meters, of about five and a half minutes at full speed. The rocket engine used hydrogen peroxide as fuel; thrust at takeoff was 1,500 kilograms.

Air Group 312 was established in order to provide priority training for pilots planning to use the Shūsui. CAPT Takeo Shibata, a veteran navy fighter pilot, was selected as the commanding officer. LCDR Masao Yamashita was ordered in as air officer, and LCDR Yorio Yamagata, a veteran of seaplanes, as group leader. Headquarters was located in a corner of the Yokosuka Naval Arsenal. Air officer Yamashita was responsible for the training unit that was attached to the Kasumigaura Air Group. The latter was equipped with two buntai of Zero fighters (twenty-four aircraft standard), as well as gliders to permit glider landing practice. The majority of pilots, however, were young with little actual battle experience; the few veterans in the unit were men who had just recovered from illnesses. Concern was expressed over such persons piloting a rocket-propelled aircraft that required a high degree of technical proficiency. However, starting with CAPT Shibata, expectations and hopes for the Shūsui were high. As a result, not only was intensive training carried out but a method was studied whereby on-the-ground guidance could be effected in order to compensate for inadequate air time. The method of attack devised by commanding officer Shibata was as follows.

Using suitable guidance from the ground, the Shūsui would climb at a steep angle and position itself behind a B-29 formation; it would then accelerate to reach an altitude of ten thousand meters in three minutes plus. Then the aircraft would attack using the 30-mm cannons, one of which was placed in each wing; finally, circumstances permitting, the pilot would chase and finish off the enemy plane. Following this scenario, the Shusui, which had by this time exhausted its fuel supply and would be half the weight it was, would glide in for a landing. Although some quarters proposed the use of the ramming tactic, commanding officer Shibata took an absolute stand in opposition to it.

In December 1944, the Mitsubishi plant at Oh-e completed the first fuselage unit, overcoming such harsh circumstances as being the target of bombing attacks from time to time. The fuselage was immediately transferred to Yokosuka where it awaited the completion of its engine. On 7 July 1945, Air Group 312 division officer LT Toyohiko Inuzuka flew the aircraft in its first test flight at Yokosuka.

The Shūsui took off after a ground run of ten seconds and then started a very rapid climb; sixteen seconds later, at an altitude of about 250 meters, smoke started coming out. The glider lost speed and crashed in a corner of the airfield, suffering major damage. LT Inuzuka himself was severely injured and died the following day. The reason for the malfunction was immediately ascertained; the valve at the mouth of the fuel tank was defective. The result was that there was a sudden cutoff of the fuel supply while climbing. Immediate repairs were made; manufacture of the second model was planned with a due date of 6 August. The war ended, however, while the project was still incomplete. The Shūsui production plans on the part of both the army and the navy were very ambitious. Initial planning called for 155 aircraft by March 1945, followed by 1,200 aircraft by September, in turn followed by 3,600 aircraft by March 1946. Because of air raids and other factors, however, major setbacks were encountered in the schedule; only five aircraft were actually completed by the time the war ended. Air Group 312 was disbanded without ever having engaged in combat.

横須賀航空隊戦闘機隊

YOKOSUKA AIR GROUP FIGHTER SQUADRON

Historically speaking, the Yokosuka Air Group is the oldest air group in the navy. It was first organized on 1 April 1916 and continued in existence until the war ended. Initially, emphasis was placed on training and education. With the establishment of air groups in various parts of the nation, the Yokosuka Air Group started to collect all the different types of aircraft in use. It came to have as its main responsibilities research into air combat tactics and operational testing of new model aircraft. In addition, it was responsible for advanced navigational training, centered around the advanced course (Kōtō-ka) and the special course (Tokushū-ka). From 1930 until 1939, responsibility for the training of flight reserve enlisted personnel was also assigned to the unit.

Starting around 1929 or 30, naval air groups were first organized by type of aircraft used. Under group leader Kamei at Yokosuka, battle tactics studies started. Selecting the better pilots from the entire armed forces, these men came to be used in the development of aerial battle tactics unique to the Japanese navy, centered around single aircraft combat. Also, starting around 1932, special flight teams (tokushu hikō chiimu) were established under the direction of LT Kobayashi, division officer. Techniques used by such special flight teams were displayed to the public during aircraft donation commemoration ceremonies and other occasions. What later came

to be known as the "Genda Circus" is a reference to the acrobatic performances of a three-aircraft formation; the planes were usually flown by petty officers Hei-ichirō Mase and Atae Aoki, under the guidance of LTs Okamura and Genda.

Test pilots of the flight testing department (hikō jikken bu), Naval Air Technology Arsenal, situated at the Yokosuka base, were responsible for basic flight testing of new model fighters. When the aircraft were to undergo actual flight tests, they were handed over to the Yokosuka Air Group Fighter Squadron. In both instances, the cream of the naval fighter pilots were selected for duty in the two organizations. With the reorganization of 10 July 1944, the flight testing department was abolished and its functions transferred to and carried on by the newly established evaluation department (shinsa bu) of the Yokosuka Air Group.

It was February 1944 when the Yokosuka Air Group first took up battle stations; during the latter part of February, two land attack chūtai were sent to the Marianas at the time that the 1st Air Fleet conducted its phase-one advance on the islands. Towards the end of March, the units sortied off Palau, but the fighter squadron itself was not moved. About this time it was decided that the Tō-gō operation would be implemented if enemy task forces were thought ready to attack the homeland. Only the land attack unit of the Yokosuka Air Group

Shiden-Kai

Unit insignia *Yo* was used from January 1922 through August 1945.

Yellow

Dark Green White

Yellow

Light Gray

Yokosuka Air Group Petty Officer pilots, 1944. Front row (left): Ryōji Ōhara. Back row (from left): second person, Masami Shiga; third, Tomita Atake; fourth, Kiyoshi Sekiya, all aces. (Masami Ōtomo)

was to be used in this phase. It was decided, however, that the total strength of all naval aviation forces would be used in the June "A"-gō operation. The "A"-gō operation was ordered implemented simultaneously with the American forces landing on Saipan, which took place on the 15th. The Hachiman Butai ("God of War Unit") was temporarily created out of the majority of Yokosuka Air Group forces and the 27th Air Flotilla. Under the leadership of RADM [Tei-ichi] Matsunaga, CO of the 27th Air Flotilla, the unit was placed under the direct command of the Combined Fleet and moved forward to Iwo Jima. It positioned itself so the unit could participate in the Battle of the Marianas, from the north side.

Allowance of the Yokosuka Air Group Fighter Squadron consisted of forty-eight carrier fighters, forty-eight interceptors, and twelve night fighters; LCDR Tadashi Nakajima served as group leader. A total of 112 aircraft were ordered to advance: fifty-two Zero fighters, seventeen Type 1 land attack planes, fifteen Suisei carrier bombers, twenty Tenzan carrier attack planes, and eight land reconnaissance planes. The poor weather that continued during the rainy season at this time, however, prevented the movement of planes to Iwo Jima. Although attack aircraft successively advanced to the front, Zero fighter units started withdrawing while still only part way to their target.

The idea of continuing on to Guam after attacking enemy task forces by participating in the First Striking Force general offensive of the 20th became impossible to realize.

Commanders in the Yokosuka Air Group, 1945. From the left, LT Kunio Iwashita, LCDR Masanobu Ibusuki, and LT Yūzō Tsukamoto. A Shiden-kai can be seen in the right rear. (Mitsugu Kofukuda)

In the final analysis, the main strength, twenty-seven aircraft, of the Zero fighter unit led by LCDR Nakajima was able to finally advance to Iwo Jima on the 22nd. On the 25th, the second group of twenty-four Zero fighters and five Gekkō aircraft also arrived. On the 24th, American carrier forces made a major attack on Iwo Jima. Together with air groups 301 and 252, the twenty-seven aircraft of the Yokosuka Air Group Fighter Squadron (commander, LT Sadao Yamaguchi) rose to intercept enemy forces. Although seventeen (6 probables) enemy aircraft were shot down, our side also lost nine planes. Later, during the afternoon of the same day, nine carrier attack planes, three carrier bombers, and twenty-three Zero fighters (of which nine were from the Yokosuka Air Group) sortied on a search and destroy mission looking for enemy task forces. Just about dusk the planes were intercepted by enemy fighters in the vicinity of Uracus Island; as a result, seven carrier attack planes and ten Zero fighters (four belonging to the Yokosuka Air Group) failed to return. In the evening, sixteen Ginga [bombers] sortied un-

Shiden undergoing flight tests conducted by the evaluation department. CPO Ōhara, pilot. (Ryōji Ōhara)

der the leadership of LT Ōbuchi; only one aircraft was successful in attacking the enemy while the other aircraft failed to locate the enemy. Seven of our aircraft were missing as well.

On 3 and 4 July, Iwo Jima was again subjected to large-scale attacks by American carrier aircraft. On the 4th, the island was also bombarded by warships. Coincidental with the accidental explosion of an ammunition depot, which took place on the 3rd, the great majority of planes on the ground were destroyed. Flight crews who had lost their aircraft but were still alive as of the 6th were returned to the homeland by air transport.

During the course of those three battles, the Yokosuka Air Group was able to shoot down fifty-two enemy aircraft; in return, however, twenty-two highly qualified personnel including LT Yamaguchi were lost on our side. When this assessment is compared with the losses announced by the American side, it could be said that the air battle for Iwo Jima turned out to be complete failure on the part of the vaunted Yokosuka Air Group Fighter Squadron, which was so proud of its traditions and which considered itself to be the elite of all air groups.

In February 1945, during the course of intercept operations against American carrier aircraft that took place over the Kantō area, the Yokosuka Air Group managed to clear itself completely of this stain on its honor. On 16 February, a mixed group of some ten aircraft consisting of Zero fighters from the Yokosuka Air Group Fighter Squadron and the evaluation department under the command of LT Yūzō Tsukamoto, plus Shiden-kai and Raiden aircraft, fought valiantly under the leadership of LCDR Masanobu Ibusuki and LTs Yūzō Tsukamoto and Shigehisa Yamamoto.

In particular, during the P.M. of the 17th and despite the falling snow, a successful surprise attack was made from a height of 2,500 meters on nineteen F6Fs and F4Us that had almost reached their rendezvous point in the skies over the Atsugi area. Chasing the enemy aircraft back to the sea, the ten planes shot down the entire enemy force of nineteen aircraft (six probables), a brilliant achievement. During the course of those events, CPO Takashi Yamazaki was hit and parachuted to the ground. Mistaken for an enemy pilot by local civilian people he was clubbed to death. From that time on, fighter unit personnel wore the emblem of the rising sun on their flight suits.

Later on, in addition to intercepting attacking B-29 bombers, the Yokosuka Air Group Fighter Squadron sent one buntai, under the command of LT Kunio Iwashita, to southern Kyūshū in April when the Battle of Okinawa broke out. Assigned to the support of special attack force aircraft as well as to air defense operations following the end of Kikusui Operation No. 3 in midmonth, the unit returned to its original base. After April, the Yokosuka Air Group Fighter Squadron followed a policy of husbanding its forces; the unit greeted the end of the war following that policy.

PART
3

Biographies
of
Aces

LTJG Hiroyoshi Nishizawa (Fumiko Satō)

LTJG Hiroyoshi Nishizawa

LTJG Nishizawa was known during the Pacific War period by the military on both sides of the war as Japan's top ace.

Nishizawa was born in 1920 in a mountain village in Nagano Prefecture, the fifth son of Shuzōji, his father, and Miyoshi, his mother. Following graduation from higher elementary school, he worked for a time in a textile factory and then responded to a poster recruiting volunteers to join the Flight Reserve Enlistee Training Program (Yokaren). He was accepted by the program and in June 1936 qualified as a student in the Otsu 7th Class. In March 1939, he completed the flight training course and scored sixteenth out of a class of seventy-one.

Following service with the Ōita, Ōmura, and Suzuka air groups in October 1941, immediately before the outbreak of the war, Nishizawa was assigned to the Chitose Air Group, which was responsible for the Inner South Sea area air defense. In February 1942, he was transferred to the 4th Air Group and moved to Rabaul. On 3 February, Nishizawa scored his first aerial victory when he shot down an enemy aircraft in the skies over Rabaul. In April, he was transferred to the Tainan Air Group

and went to eastern New Guinea. After American forces attacked Guadalcanal on 7 August, Nishizawa also participated in the Battle of the Solomons. Before his withdrawal to Toyohashi in November, Nishizawa had recorded thirty (officially recognized) aircraft he had personally shot down.

During the air battle fought on 7 August, he not only shot down six Grumman F4Fs, but when he realized his plane had been hit, he turned his aircraft around and decided to make a suicide attack. He failed to find any enemy aircraft and just barely made it back to base. With the advance of Air Group 251 in May 1943 to Rabaul for the second time, Nishizawa next participated in air battles in the southeast area of operations. In September he was transferred to Air Group 253 and in October, returned to the homeland.

Nishizawa's aerial battle skills continued to increase in masterly technique; he was honored with a gift from ADM Kusaka of the Southeast Area Fleet of a military sword enscribed, Bukō Batsugun ("For Conspicuous Military Valor"). He was held in complete trust by both superiors and subordinates. It is even said that during the course of one air battle when Nishizawa's return to base was delayed, ADM Kusaka himself stood by for many hours at the airfield awaiting his return, showing his deep personal concern over the fate of a mere noncommissioned officer. As far as the official record is concerned, Nishizawa scored six aircraft shot down by mid-June. The air groups then discontinued the practice of recording kills by individuals as such and Nishizawa's own record is not clear in this area.

In November, Nishizawa was promoted to WO and assigned to Air Group 203, transferring from Atsugi to duty in northern Kurile air defense operations. With the activation in October 1944 of the Shō-gō operation, he proceeded on the 24th to Mabalacat, Luzon, as a member of the northern unit. On the following day, the 25th, Nishizawa took off leading a flight of three aircraft that were serving in direct support of the first kamikaze suicide attack launched. Brushing aside interference from F6Fs, he shot down two enemy aircraft, completed his mission, and landed on the island of Cebu. The next day, however, the 26th, while he was returning to base on a transport after leaving his own aircraft behind, the transport was attacked by two F6Fs in the skies over Calapan, Mindoro Island; Nishizawa died in action. This ace was always convinced that he led a charmed life and would never be shot down in aerial combat; however, there was nothing he could do to save himself when he was on board an air transport. Following Nishizawa's death, the commander of the Combined Fleet honored him with mention in an All Units Bulletin and gave him a special double promotion. Because of the confusion toward the end of the war, however, the publication of the bulletin was delayed. Funeral services were held on 2 December 1947. He was given the posthumous name Bukai-in Kōhan Gikō Kyoshi.★ The following figures have been reported as the total number of aircraft shot down by Nishizawa: 147 aircraft (reported to his family), more than 150 aircraft (newspaper articles at the time of his death in action), as well as 102 aircraft, and other figures. It is believed, however, that the figure of eighty-six aircraft mentioned to group leader Okamoto of Air Group 253 at the time of the evacuation from Rabaul is the most trustworthy count. If we add the final air battle results, the figure would then

be eighty-seven aircraft shot down. Officially, the estimate would be around sixty to seventy aircraft. In any event, it is the highest score ever recorded in the history of both army and navy fighter units.

As in the case of other geniuses, a number of legends have arisen surrounding Nishizawa; he also left a variety of quite different impressions on different people. Said to have been lively and social, he was also said to have been taciturn, aloof, stubborn, and obstinate. Although accomplished in the arts of jūdō and sumō, he had a pale face and complained about having problems with his internal organs. He was a man of complex traits [personality].

Nishizawa at Rabaul (Maru)

★ The Buddhist phrase contains several elements: reference to the deceased person in a form reserved for members of the nobility or other high personages, "Bukai-in"; the posthumous name "Kōhan Gikō"; and a term including information that the person is deceased and a member of the Zen sect of Buddhism. The phrase could be translated:

> In the Ocean of the Military,
> Reflective of all distinguished pilots,
> An honored Buddhist person.

LTJG Tetsuzō Iwamoto (Kenji Takahashi)

LTJG Tetsuzō Iwamoto

Born in a farmhouse in Shimane Prefecture in 1916, after graduating from the Masuda Agricultural and Forestry School, Iwamoto entered Kure Naval Barracks as a seaman in June 1934. The next year he transferred to maintenance duty. In December 1936 he graduated from the 34th Pilot Training Course and became a fighter pilot.

In February 1938, Iwamoto took part as the youngest pilot ever to fight in central China operations. Assigned to the 12th Air Group, he first saw combat on 25 February during the attack on Nanchang; he shot down five enemy aircraft. With that as a start until September, when he returned to the homeland, he flew eighty-two sorties and shot down fourteen aircraft. He became the top ace of naval fighter units during the China Incident. In the Pacific War, he served on board the carrier *Zuikaku* and participated in the battles of Hawaii, the Indian Ocean, and the Coral Sea. In August 1942 he was transferred to become an instructor in a training unit.

He was next transferred to Air Group 281, newly organized in March 1943 and spent about half a year at Paramushir Island engaged in northern area air defense operations. In November he was part of a unit of

fifteen aircraft dispatched to Rabaul; his unit affiliation was then changed to Air Group 204 and later to the 253. For more than three months, Iwamoto was engaged in almost daily interception operations. Toward the end of February 1944, he withdrew to Truk Island and participated in intercept attacks on B-24s. In June, Iwamoto returned to the homeland. In September, he was attached to Fighter Hikōtai 316, Air Group 252, and promoted to ensign. In October, he participated in air battles off Taiwan and then advanced to the Philippines. By the end of October he had returned to the homeland. In the spring of 1945, he was transferred to Air Group 203 and advanced to Kyūshū. After participating in air battles over Okinawa, he greeted the end of the war.

Iwamoto's battle record as a front-line fighter pilot lasted close to eight years; there are no other aces that compare with him when it comes to the length or the variety of air battle experience. With the exception of his time with Air Group 204 (a total of twenty enemy aircraft shot down, with five probables during a one-month period), the air groups that he was assigned

LTJG Iwamoto (Family of Tetsuzō Iwamoto)

to during the Pacific War did not maintain records on individual kills. It is therefore difficult to calculate the total number of aircraft he did shoot down. Iwamoto died from illness after the war. In detailed reminiscences that he compiled and which have not yet been published, he claims an astounding 202 enemy aircraft downed (142 were the result of battles in the Rabaul area). From a conservative point of view, it may perhaps be more appropriate to estimate the number of aircraft downed to be around eighty. He referred to himself as Kotetsu (a well-known swordsmith of the late sixteenth century). He was of a chivalrous bent; his favorite aerial technique was a vertical-dive, single pass kill. It could be that Iwamoto's score even exceeds that of Nishizawa, which would make him the top ace of Japan.

ENS Shō-ichi Sugita with Fighter Hikōtai 301, Air Group 343, 1945. (Tomoichi Kasai)

ENS Shō-ichi Sugita

Born in 1924 in a mountain village in the prefecture of Niigata, Sugita withdrew from agricultural school and volunteered for service with the navy in 1940, at the age of fifteen. In March 1942, he graduated from the Hei 3rd Flight Reserve Enlisted Trainee Class and was assigned to the 6th Fighter Hikōtai (Air Group 204). He was literally a wartime pilot.

Although Sugita did participate in the Battle of Midway, there was no opportunity for air combat. In the fall of 1942, he participated in the Solomons battle front as one of the youngest pilots. Based in Buin,

he engaged in aerial combat operations for almost one year until his return to the homeland as a result of his aircraft receiving hits on 26 August [1943]. Sugita himself parachuted to safety, though he suffered burns all over his body.

Sugita's first victory was on 1 December 1942, when he single-handedly, physically barreled in on a B-17 during intercept operations over Buin. He sheared off the right wing of the B-17, and then shot down the enemy aircraft. This was an example of the uniquely combative spirit that Sugita exhibited. On 18 April 1943 he was among the six Zero fighters that escorted the Type 1 land attack plane used by ADM Isoroku Yamamoto, who was heading for an inspection trip around Buin. Although Sugita was able to shoot down two of the enemy aircraft that attacked the group, his efforts were of little avail because the admiral's plane itself was shot down. In March 1944, Sugita was posted to Air Group 263 and participated in operations in the Marianas and Caroline islands. Transferring to Air Group 201 in July, he was next active on the Philippine front. In January 1945, Sugita was posted to the newly organized Fighter Hikōtai 301, Air Group 343. Serving under LT Kanno, he flew the Shiden-kai in homeland defense as well as Okinawa aerial operations. On 15 April, because of a delayed warning report, he was attacked by enemy fighter aircraft while taking off from Kanoya airfield. Sugita and his aircraft both burned; he died in action.

Earlier during the spring of 1945, Su-

BIOGRAPHIES OF ACES • 243

gita, together with ENS Sakai, were deco-
rated for having shot down a large number
of enemy aircraft. Immediately upon Sugita's death in action, he was posthumously
honored by the publication of his name in
an All Units Bulletin, and he was given a
special double promotion. His personal destruction of seventy enemy aircraft and
joint destruction with others of another
forty aircraft have been officially recognized in his personal commendation. There
are some questions with respect to the particular findings, however; it may be more
appropriate perhaps to view the total number of aircraft shot down as being in the
thirties. Sugita was a rambunctious person
of manly disposition; in a sense, he was a
fighter pilot who was an incarnation of the
fighting spirit.

Sugita at Rabaul, 1943 (Ryōji Ōhara)

LTJG Saburō Sakai at Lae, 9 June 1942 (Maru)

LTJG Saburō Sakai

The top ace among pilots alive today,
LTJG Sakai wrote *Samurai in the Big Sky:
The Record of the Air Combat of Saburō Sa-
kai,* a best-seller that was translated into a
number of foreign languages [in English as
Samurai].

Born in a farmhouse in Saga Prefecture
in 1916, Sakai enlisted as a seaman at Sasebo Naval Barracks in May 1933. After
graduating at the top of the 38th Pilot
Training Class in November 1937, he was
posted in September 1938 to the 12th Air
Group and participated in central China operations. Aerial combat operations, however, were almost over at that time; Sakai's
only achievement was that during the 5
October attack on Hankow, he recorded
his first aerial victory.

In April 1941 he was posted for the second time to the 12th Air Group and advanced to Hankow. He participated in the
air attacks on Chengtu and Lanchow. In
June he was promoted to the rank of PO1c
and was transferred to the Tainan Air
Group in the month of October. Immediately upon the outbreak of war, he participated in aerial battles in the Philippines and
Dutch East Indies as a shōtai leader. In
April [1942], he advanced into Rabaul and
Lae and was active as the senior pilot in the
Sasai Chūtai. On the first day of the air
battle for Guadalcanal, 7 June [August], Sakai was hit by [.30-caliber] bullets fired by
an SBD's rear gunner, and received severe

head wounds. Despite his injuries, however, he managed to return to Rabaul and was transported back to the homeland. Official records show that during this period the number of aircraft shot down by Sakai had reached twenty-eight. Later, he was transferred first to the Ōmura Air Group and then to the Yokosuka Air Group; in June 1944 he participated in intercept action at Iwo Jima. From that time on, Sakai gave up aerial combat because of failing eyesight. At the end of the hostilities, he was an instructor at both the Yokosuka Air Group and Air Group 343.

It is said that the total number of enemy aircraft shot down by Sakai numbered sixty-four; the majority of those kills were during the early stages of the war and in the New Guinea battle area. Sakai was a typically hard-working ace; his aerial combat techniques were finely crafted and logical in nature. It is notable that he never lost a single wingman, in some two hundred or so sorties. He is also credited with being the pilot who, on 10 December 1941, shot down over Luzon the B-17 bomber flown by Colin Kelly, the American air hero. On 9 June 1942 over Lae, he turned the tables on an attacking B-26 and inflicted severe damage on the enemy aircraft in which Senator Lyndon B. Johnson, later to become the president, was riding. [Recent research has shown Johnson's plane never reached the target area.] Also, around the same time, Sakai, together with his colleagues Nishizawa and Ōta, engaged in an ostentatious display of a formation loop over the Port Moresby airfield. Sakai was indeed a man with many colorful episodes in his life.

Sakai at Hankow, 1938 (Yoshimichi Saeki)

WO Takeo Okumura

WO Takeo Okumura during his Tainan Air Group days, 1942. (Shin-ichi Hirabayashi)

Okumura was born in 1920 in Fukui Prefecture; in 1935 he entered the Kure Naval Barracks. In September 1938 he graduated from the 42nd Pilot Training Class and was next assigned to the 14th Air Group in March 1940 and went to the South China battlefront. On 7 October, as a member of the force that attacked Kunming led by LT Mitsugu Kofukuda, Okumura had his first taste of battle and shot down four enemy fighter aircraft.

In July 1942, Okumura was assigned on board the aircraft carrier *Ryūjō* and advanced into the Solomons battle area. He participated in the 24 August attack on Guadalcanal; although reported lost at one point, he managed to return alive. Since the

Okumura (*far left*) at Atami, 1943 (Fumiko Satō)

Ryūjō had been sunk in the meantime, Okumura was next transferred to the Tainan Air Group at Rabaul. From the early part of September through late October, he participated in the attacks on Guadalcanal and shot down fourteen enemy aircraft (officially recognized).

In December, Okumura returned to the homeland; by May of the following year he was transferred to Air Group 201. In July [1943], he advanced to Buin in the Solomon Islands group and participated in furious, almost daily attack and intercept operations in the area. In particular, during intercept operations over Buin conducted the morning of 14 September involving five sequential air battles, he shot down a total of ten enemy aircraft. The aircraft shot down included eight fighters, one dive-bomber, and one larger aircraft (B-24), which was shot down jointly. Although this score is unofficial, it is said to be the highest number of enemy aircraft shot down during a single day for the entire Pacific War. In recognition of this feat, ADM Kusaka, commanding the Southeast Area Fleet, presented Okumura with a white sheathed military sword inscribed with the words Bukō Batsugun ("For Conspicuous Military Valor"). A week after attending the ceremonies in which he received the sword, WO Okumura participated in another attack operation, on the 22nd. The attack was on an enemy convoy off Cape Cretin [New Guinea]; the attacking unit was led by LT Shirō Kawai. During the combat with fifty enemy fighter aircraft under poor weather conditions, Okumura's whereabouts became unknown, and he is presumed to have died in action. Okumura's commanding officer recommended a two-rank promotion, but that did not materialize. Okumura's disposition was bright and cheerful; glimpses of genius could be seen in his air battle techniques.

It is said that the total number of aircraft downed by Okumura was four during the China Incident and fifty during the Battle of the Solomons. The latter figure is believed to be somewhat exaggerated; perhaps a figure around thirty would be more appropriate.

WO Toshio Ōta during his Tainan Air Group days. At Rabaul, August 1942. (Kiku-ichi Inano)

WO Toshio Ōta

Born in a farm house in Nagasaki Prefecture in 1919, following graduation from higher elementary school Ōta enlisted at the Sasebo Naval Barracks in 1935. In September 1939, he graduated from the 46th Pilot Training Class and became a fighter pilot. After serving with the Ōmura and Yatabe air groups, he was posted to the 12th Air Group in June 1941. Although Ōta advanced as far as Hankow, there were no opportunities for aerial combat.

In October of the same year, Ōta was transferred to the Tainan Air Group and saw action in the Philippines and Dutch East Indies areas. During the attack on Luzon carried out on the first day of the war, 8 December, Ōta recorded his first battle kill. On 29 January of the following year, he received bullet wounds in a battle with B-17s over Balikpapan [Borneo]; for a while after that he did not participate in any air battles.

Ōta's brilliant battle record started in April 1942 when as a member of the Sasai Chūtai he advanced to Rabaul and engaged in a spectacular race with his own colleagues Sakai, Nishizawa, and others to see who could account for the most enemy aircraft shot down. After August, Ōta participated in the continuing attacks on Guadalcanal; he was lost in action during an air battle on 21 October [1942] after shooting down one enemy aircraft. Ōta is presumed to have died in action.

Ōta was a gentle person, with a smile always on his face; he was liked by both superiors and subordinates and was friendly with all. At the same time, the sense of combat deep down in his heart was extremely strong; in one incident over Lae Ōta persisted over one hour in pursuing a B-17 before finally shooting it down.

Ōta is officially credited with a total of thirty-four aircraft shot down. Although he died rather early in the war, in the Sasai Chūtai, Ōta had the highest pace of victories in the competition for the highest number of enemy aircraft shot down. It is believed that if he had lived longer, his score would have been no less than that of Nishizawa or Sakai.

Ōta with Tainan Air Group (Family of Toshio Ōta)

WO Kazuo Sugino during his *Kasuga Maru* fighter unit days, 1942. (Akimasa Igarashi)

WO Kazuo Sugino

Born in Yamaguchi Prefecture in 1921, Sugino was working in a cement factory when he volunteered for the navy; he enlisted in June 1939. In February 1941, Sugino entered training with the Hei 3rd Flight Reserve Enlisted Training class; he completed the 17th Flight Training Course in March 1942. In April of the same year, he was posted to the 6th Air Group.

During the Battle for Midway, Sugino served on board the aircraft carrier *Akagi* with the intention of being stationed on the island after its capture. There was no opportunity for aerial engagement however; following the sinking of the carrier he was on, he was rescued out of the sea and returned safely to the homeland. Next, he was transferred to the converted carrier *Kasuga Maru* and assigned duties in ship convoy and air transport operations. In October, he became an instructor at the Ōmura

Air Group; he was next ordered, in February 1943, to serve on board the aircraft carrier *Zuikaku*. He advanced to Truk Island. Under division officer LT Hōhei Kobayashi, Sugino was intensively trained in air combat and dive-bombing techniques. In November, Sugino accompanied the carrier air group advance into Rabaul. Even after the main unit had withdrawn, Sugino stayed behind with Air Group 253. Until the time of his return to the homeland in March 1944, he was engaged in almost daily intercept operations. Sugino's first combat was on 2 November 1943, when he shot down three enemy aircraft.

Following his return to the homeland, he served as an instructor with the Tsukuba Air Group and other units; following that, in August 1944, he was transferred to Air Group 634. After participating in air battles off Taiwan and over the Philippines, Sugino withdrew to Taiwan in February 1945. He was next assigned as an instructor of special attack force pilots at the Hakata Air Group until the war ended.

Since Sugino's air combat experience started after the end of 1943, he is not too well known. According to flight records still available, the following facts are known. Sugino's total flight time was 1,994 hours, he engaged in 495 combat missions (about one hundred included air combat), and he shot down thirty-two aircraft. After the war, he served in the Maritime Self Defense Forces.

Sugino during his Tsukuba Air Group days, 1944. (Kiyoshi Katō)

WO Shizuo Ishi-i (Family of Shizuo Ishi-i)

WO Shizuo Ishi-i

Born as the eighth of nine children of a farm family in Fukushima Prefecture in 1920, Ishi-i enlisted in the navy in 1937. Transferring from maintenance duties to pilot training, he graduated from the 50th Pilot Training Class in June 1940. The following April he was posted to the 12th Air Group and participated in the fighting in central China. Although there were few air battles of note during the period, PO3c Ishi-i was favored by the gods of war. He racked up his first battle results on 22 May, during an attack on Chengtu when he shot down one SB bomber. By the time of his transfer to the Tainan Air Group in October, he had achieved a score of three enemy aircraft shot down.

During the Pacific War, he was active in Philippines and Dutch East Indies air operations. Transferred to the Ōmura Air Group in April 1942, he was assigned on board the *Junyō* in September and moved into the southeast area of operations. After participating in the Solomons and New Guinea battlefronts, he was transferred to Air Group 204 in September 1943. Following distinguished service in both offensive and defensive air operations in Buin and Rabaul, Ishi-i was killed in action over Rabaul on 24 October during the course of an intercept battle.

Rather unusual for a person from the northeastern hinterlands, Ishi-i was quick to learn and a bright pilot. He was particularly adept at attacking and shooting down larger aircraft. In January 1943, during support operations in connection with convoy shipments to Wewak [New Guinea], Ishi-i managed to demolish two attacking B-24s all by himself. His activities during the one and a half months immediately before he was killed in action were particularly outstanding; he had been operating at the high pace of seventeen aircraft shot down (four jointly). The date 23 September is of particular interest. Twenty-seven Zero fighters of Air Group 204, led by LTJG Sumio Fukuda, carried out an attack on Viroa. During this attack, thirteen of the intercepting American fighters were shot down; of this number, Ishi-i himself accounted for five (one jointly). The total number of aircraft shot down by Ishi-i during the entire period reached twenty-nine aircraft (officially recognized).

LTJG Kaneyoshi Mutō during his Yokosuka Air Group days, before an attack on Iwo Jima. (Masami Ōtomo)

LTJG Kaneyoshi Mutō

Mutō was born in Aichi Prefecture in 1916; he enlisted in 1935 as a fireman at the Kure Naval Barracks. Half a year later, however, he successfully entered and passed the 32nd Pilot Training Class and was posted to the Ōmura Air Group upon graduation. With the outbreak of the China Incident, he was posted to the 13th Air Group as a Sealc. Mutō participated in central China battle operations. During his first taste of battle, on 4 December in an attack on Nanking, he engaged in combat with an I-16 fighter and shot it down. In December, he was transferred to the 12th Air Group and participated in the battles over Nanking, Nanchang, Hankow, and other areas.

In September 1941, after serving with the Ōita, Suzuka, and Genzan Air Groups, Mutō was posted to the 3rd Air Group. With the outbreak of war, he engaged in air combat operations over the Philippines and Dutch East Indies, serving as number two for group leader Yokoyama. The following April, Mutō was transferred to the Genzan Fighter Squadron (Air Group 252) and advanced to Rabaul in November [1942]. Until March of the following year, he was

WO Ishi-i (Family of Shizuo Ishi-i)

active in air operations in the Solomons and eastern New Guinea. Promoted to WO in November 1943, he was next transferred to the Yokosuka Air Group. During June and July 1944 he advanced to Iwo Jima and was assigned duties in air defense operations and in attacks on enemy task forces. When the year 1945 came, he engaged in air defense operations in the Kantō area. During the latter part of June, at the earnest request of CAPT Genda, Mutō was transferred to Air Group 343, for escort duties with LT Kanno, replacing ENS Sugita, who had been killed in action. On 24 July, in an air battle fought over the Bungo Strait, Mutō was killed in action.

Mutō was well known as a person whose personality as well as skills had fully matured. In particular, it is interesting to recall that he single-handedly challenged (flying a Shiden-kai) twelve F6Fs over Atsugi in February 1945. Mutō shot down four of the enemy aircraft, each with a single burst of gunfire. This episode has been transmitted even in our own time as reminiscent of the actions of Musashi Miyamoto (a famed swordsman of the early seventeenth century) at the battle of Ichijōji Kudari-matsu. Although the total number of aircraft shot down by Mutō is not clear, it is estimated to be around twenty-eight planes. Short in stature, Mutō was a man whose entire body exuded vitality; he was a friendly and cheerful ace who was liked by everybody who came in contact with him.

Mutō, age twenty-nine, during his Yokosuka Air Group days. (Family of Kaneyoshi Mutō)

LCDR Jun-ichi Sasai (Maru)

LCDR Jun-ichi Sasai

Called the "Richthofen of Rabaul," Sasai was the top ace among graduates of the Naval Academy. The exploits of the Sasai Chūtai, in which he led such experts as Sakai, Nishizawa, Ōta, and others, are vividly described in Saburō Sakai's popular book, [Samurai].

Born in 1918 in Tokyo as the eldest son of naval engineering CAPT Kenji Sasai, during his early years Sasai was not in good health. From about the time he entered Tokyo Municipal High School No. 1, he regained his health and came to hold a grade in the art of jūdō. In 1939 he graduated with the 67th class of the Naval Academy; shortly before the outbreak of war, in November 1941, he completed the 35th Aviation Student Course (Hikō Gakusei Kyōtei) and was immediately assigned to the Tainan Air Group. As early as 10 December he participated in the attack on Luzon but was forced to withdraw because of engine trouble.

Sasai's initial victory was recorded on 3 February 1942 during an air battle over Java. After April, when he moved out to Rabaul, Sasai's air combat skill improved rapidly and his score of kills increased dramatically. But he lost his most valuable subordinate, Saburō Sakai, on 8 [12] August, soon after the first day of the battle for Guadalcanal. Shortly afterward, on 26 August, Sasai led eight others to Guadalcanal, fought against fifteen F4Fs, and failed to return. Although Sasai's fate has not been verified, it is assumed that he was shot down by the American Marine Corps fighter ace CAPT Marion Carl.

In a letter sent out immediately before his death, Sasai reported that he had shot down fifty-four aircraft and implied that he would soon exceed the record established by Richthofen (eighty aircraft); however, the official figure remains at twenty-seven aircraft downed. Following his death, the exploits of Sasai were announced to all the units and he was given the honor of being promoted two ranks, to LCDR.

Since his days at the academy when his classmates referred to him as Shamo ("Gamecock"), he disliked losing and was a vigorously combative person. He was a typical fighter pilot, with a direct yet very sincere character.

LCDR Sasai (Maru)

LTJG Sada-aki Akamatsu during his 3rd Air Group days. (Yasunobu Nabara)

LTJG Sada-aki Akamatsu

Akamatsu was born in 1910 in Kōchi Prefecture, the son of the head of a weather observatory station. Following graduation from Kainan High School, he volunteered for the navy and entered Sasebo Naval Barracks in 1928. He is among the veteran fighter pilots who graduated in March 1932 from the 17th Pilot Training Class.

After serving on the *Akagi,* the *Ryūjō,* and the *Kaga,* as well as in the Yokosuka and Ōmura air groups, Akamatsu was assigned to the 13th Air Group in December 1937 following the outbreak of the China Incident. At the time he engaged in central China battle operations, he was twenty-seven years of age and a senior PO1c aviator. He was renowned for his bravery in action, such as when he shot down four enemy aircraft at one crack during the attack on Nanchang on 25 February 1938. By the time of his transfer to serve on board the carrier *Sōryū,* he had a record of having shot down eleven aircraft.

Promoted to WO in April 1941, Akamatsu was assigned to the 3rd Air Group

during World War II and served in the Philippines and the Dutch East Indies. In May 1942, Akamatsu returned to the homeland. Later, in July 1943, he was transferred to Air Group 331 and participated in the December attack on Calcutta. He returned soon after to the homeland. Until the war ended, Akamatsu served with Air Group 302 at Atsugi, piloting his Raiden fighter and participating in the air defense of the nation's capital.

With a background of fourteen years in fighters and flight time exceeding six thousand hours, Akamatsu was well known among his colleagues for his heroic acts as well as his eccentricities. Although he himself claimed a score of 350 enemy aircraft shot down, it is judged that the actual number was around twenty-seven.

Akamatsu during his Air Group 302 days (Family of Sada-aki Akamatsu)

CDR Naoshi Kanno during his Air Group 343 (Shinsen-gumi) days. (Tomoichi Kasai)

CDR Naoshi Kanno

Born in 1921 in Miyagi Prefecture, Kanno graduated from the Naval Academy in December 1941 with the 70th class. He finished the 38th Aviation Student Course in September 1943 and is counted among the wartime aces.

In April 1944, Kanno advanced to the Micronesia area as division officer in Air Group 343 (1st formation). By July he had been transferred to the position of division officer with Fighter Hikōtai 306, Air Group 201, and next became group leader. He experienced ferocious air battles in the Yap Island and the Philippines areas. In particular, during a series of intercept operations over Yap against incoming B-24s in July, Kanno's unit was responsible for destroying more than sixty enemy aircraft. Kanno himself rammed and damaged an enemy aircraft, and for this valor his unit was given a unit citation by the admiral commanding the 1st Air Fleet. In October when the first Kamikaze Suicide Attack Unit was organized, it was thought that he would be assigned to be its leader. At the

time concerned, however, Kanno was back in the homeland to procure additional aircraft; in his place, LT Seki was nominated to be the commanding officer of the special unit.

Even during air battles over the Philippines, a time when there were successive defeats for our forces, Kanno showed an indomitable will and led his forces brilliantly. In particular, during an aerial encounter on 27 October over the island of Marinduque, he led a group of seventeen aircraft of various types and engaged in combat with sixteen Grumman F6Fs. Battle results were twelve enemy aircraft downed. During this period, Kanno requested special attack force [Kamikaze] duty any number of times; he was never accepted, however, because of his superior skills in air combat operations. With the organization of Air Group 343 (2nd formation) in December 1944, he was ordered in as group leader for Fighter Hikōtai 301 (Shinsen-gumi, "Elite Guard"). In this post he was active in air defense operations over the homeland as well as in air battles over Okinawa. While engaged in air combat over Yakushima, however, an explosion took place within the barrel of his 20-mm gun and maneuvering difficulties ensued.

Kanno during his aviation student days (Minoru Suzuki)

Kanno turned down an offer of help from one of his wingmen, WO Mitsu-o Hori. After the battle was over, WO Hori did his best to locate Kanno but with no results. In a status of lost in action, Kanno was deemed to have been killed in action.

After his death, Kanno was given the honor of mention in an All Units Bulletin and a posthumous promotion of two ranks. Kanno was short in stature, had the fighting spirit of a bull dog, and was rather wild in temperament. The total number of aircraft downed by Kanno was twenty-five (officially recognized).

ENS Nobu-o Ogiya (Family of Nobu-o Ogiya)

ENS Nobu-o Ogiya

The name of Ogiya is not well known even among his own colleagues because of the fact that his air combat activities covered only a short period of three months, from the end of 1943 until his death in action in February 1944, a period during which the tide was turning against our forces. The pace of the record he compiled in shooting down eighteen aircraft over a period of thirteen days over Rabaul, however, is the highest figure for such concentrated shoot-downs on record in Japan. Ogiya's record exceeded even that compiled by WO Shinohara, the Japanese army's top ace, during the Nomonhan air battle [against the Soviet Union, in August and September 1939].

Ogiya was born in 1918 in Ibaragi prefecture, into a family descended from a line of swordsmen. After graduating from Minato Commercial School, Ogiya himself for a time desired to become a swordsman and did attain the third rank in [Kendō] fencing. He ultimately chose the path of being a warrior in the skies, however, and enlisted in the navy in 1938. After graduating with the 48th Pilot Training Class in January 1940, he was posted to the fighter

Ogiya during his pilot trainee days (Family of Nobu-o Ogiya)

squadron of the Chitose Air Group. At the time the war broke out, he was assigned to air defense operations in the Micronesia area but saw no air combat action. He was next transferred to Air Group 281 and advanced to the northern Kuriles.

Transferring to Air Group 204 in November 1943, Ogiya next got involved in the furious air battles over Rabaul. At the time he was almost twenty-six years old. His first shoot-down of an enemy aircraft was during the 16 December attack on Cape Marcus. By the end of January of the following year, when he was transferred to Air Group 253, Ogiya had shot down a total of twenty-four aircraft (officially recognized) during day in and day out air combat. In particular, during an intercept battle over Rabaul on 20 January [1944], he was actually able single-handedly to flame five enemy aircraft (two F4Us, two SBDs, and one P-38).

Following an intercept battle on 13 February [1944], however, Ogiya's aircraft, with thirty-two cherry blossoms painted on its fuselage, failed to return to base.

LTJG Shigeo Sugi-o at Tokushima base, 1945. (Shigeo Sugi-o)

LTJG Shigeo Sugi-o

Born in Miyazaki Prefecture, Sugi-o was inspired by the activities of civilian aviator Yūkichi Gotō, also a native of his hometown of Nobeoka. From his youth, Sugi-o wanted to be a pilot; in 1934 he passed the exams for the Otsu 5th Flight Reserve Enlisted Trainee Class. In March 1938 he finished his flight training course. In September of the following year, he was posted to the 12th Air Group and saw action in central China. This was at a time, however, when air battles had settled down somewhat. He did participate in the support of the attack on Hengyan and other areas by a land attack plane unit but had no opportunity for air combat. One year later he returned to the homeland.

In April 1941, Sugi-o was posted to the 12th Air Group for the second time and advanced to the base at Hankow. The gods of war did not favor him, however, and his only accomplishment was the shoot-down of one transport during an attack on Kwangyuan. In October he was transferred to the newly established 3rd Air Group and as a shōtai leader, participated in air battles in the Philippines and the Dutch East Indies. During a strafing attack on Iba airfield, Luzon, on 8 December, Sugi-o's aircraft was hit by ground fire. Although his fuel gauge indicated zero, Sugi-o managed to return to Kao-hsiung [Takao]. On another occasion, during an air battle over Batangas, Sugi-o and his colleagues were able to surround a six-aircraft formation of old-style P-26s operated by Filipino pilots; jointly with his wingmen, Sugi-o shot down four enemy aircraft (in actuality two aircraft). Again, on 3 February 1942 in an aerial encounter over Surabaya, he was able to shoot down, at one time, nine enemy aircraft with his own shōtai formation of three aircraft, by using a surprise attack. In April, Sugi-o advanced to Timor and participated in a series of attacks on Darwin until August and was able to overwhelm P-40s flown by U.S. Army air units. From September through November he was dispatched to Rabaul and engaged in the furious air battles over Guadalcanal. In this latter instance, he was acting in the place of his chūtai leader. Following his return to the southwestern area, Sugi-o was promoted to WO and participated in the attacks on Darwin. In April 1943, he was able to trod the earth of his homeland for the first time in two years.

Half a year later, however, he was transferred to the Haihow Air Group and engaged in the flight training of Otsu class pilots. He also participated in the 1944 spring offensive on Nanning. In this engagement he battled with U.S. Army Air Forces P-40s stationed in China. In May of the following year, he returned to the homeland, transferring to the Kōnoike Air Group. In September, he was transferred to Air Group 201; in May 1945, to the Tsukuba Air Group. Sugi-o greeted the end of the war while serving as an instructor in Shiden fighters. Although conservative in nature, he was proud of his skills; it is estimated that the number of aircraft he shot down was more than twenty.

Sugi-o at Haihow base (Shigeo Sugi-o)

WO Ki-ichi Nagano during his Atsugi Air Group days (Family of Ki-ichi Nagano)

WO Ki-ichi Nagano

Born in Shizuoka Prefecture in 1922, Nagano entered the navy in June 1939; in July 1941, at the age of eighteen, Nagano graduated with the 56th Pilot Training Class. He was posted to the Chitose Air Group in October; at the time the war broke out he was assigned to air defense duties on Taroa Island in the Micronesia area. In June 1942, he was transferred to the 2nd Air Group (Air Group 582) and returned to the homeland. In August, however, he advanced to Rabaul; for about one year, until July of the following year, Nagano fought valiantly in the hard air battles in the southeast area. The official record alone records the shootdown of nineteen aircraft (three probables); he was destined to be the top ace in Air Group 582.

Starting from March 1943, Air Group 582 no longer maintained records on individuals; thus the victories attained by Nagano during the latter part of his time in combat are not clear. If we sum up the available figures, however, it would appear that the number would reach twenty or more. In particular, during the air battle over Guadalcanal on 25 October 1942, Nagano flew one of eight Zero fighters led by

LTJG Futagami. After circling and observing the airfield at a height of two hundred meters, just when the unit was to start strafing aircraft on the ground, it found itself suddenly surrounded by a formation of attacking Grumman F4Fs coming in from overhead. Following a deadly struggle, four of our aircraft, including that flown by the leader, were lost. PO1c Nagano single-handedly fought back, and despite the fact that his aircraft had received ten or more hits, he was able to shoot down four of the enemy (one probable) and return to base alive. In writings found after his death, the twenty-year-old Nagano had observed, "It would not be an exaggeration to say that this was the day in which I was reborn. It is one day that I will never forget."

In July 1943, he was transferred to the Atsugi Air Group and then to Fighter Hikōtai 304, Air Group 203. In April of the following year, he advanced to the Kurile Islands and was assigned air defense duties. Half a year later, he was transferred to southern Kyūshū and, following activation of the Shōgō [Leyte] operation in October [1944], participated in the air battles off Taiwan. On the 22nd, he advanced to the Bamban base in the Philippines and engaged in interception battles and in supporting attacks on ship convoys, participated in the attack on Leyte and also in almost daily base intercept operations. On

6 November, in an intercept battle with American carrier aircraft over Bamban, Nagano was killed in action.

Total number of aircraft downed, nineteen (officially recognized).

Nagano during his Air Group 582 days, at Buin. (Family of Ki-ichi Nagano)

PO2c Kazushi Utō during his Tainan Air Group days, August 1942. (Kiku-ichi Inano)

WO Hiroshi Okano (Masami Ōtomo)

PO2c Kazushi Utō

Utō was a gentle, white-faced, young-looking pilot known affectionately to his colleagues in the Tainan Air Group as "Poppo." (Utō's name can also be read "Hatō," so his nickname can be taken to mean "the sound made by doves.") Despite this name, however, he served as a wing-man for Saburō Sakai and unpretentiously kept on racking up his score of kills.

Born in Ehime Prefecture in 1922, Utō graduated with the Otsu 9th Flight Training Class in October 1941. The following February he was assigned to the Tainan Air Group; in April he moved out to Rabaul and then on to Lae. After achieving his first victory in the Port Moresby attack of the 10th, he was next transferred to the New Guinea and Solomon battlefronts. During a period of less than six months, until he was lost in action during an attack on Guadalcanal on 13 September, Utō shot down nineteen aircraft (officially recognized).

WO Hiroshi Okano

Born in Ibaragi Prefecture in 1921, Okano enlisted at the Yokosuka Naval Barracks in June 1938. In May 1941, he graduated with the 54th Pilot Training Class and was assigned to the Yokosuka Air Group; in September, to the Chitose Air Group. When the war broke out he was assigned to air defense operations in the Marshall Islands, flying a Type 96 carrier fighter. In April 1942, Okano was transferred to the 1st Air Group. In late May, he was assigned as a member of the reinforcement group led by LT Jōji Yamashita, which was dispatched to bolster the Tainan Air Group in Rabaul. For a period of about half a year until he returned to his original unit in November, Okano participated in furious air battles in the southeast area of operations. During the same period, PO3c Okano achieved his first victory over Moresby on 25 June; he then went on to down a total of six enemy aircraft (including one probable). In December 1942, Okano was transferred to Air Group 201 and participated in air defense operations in the Marshall Islands area. In March of the following year, he withdrew to the homeland. Following additional training at Matsushima base, in July [1943], with the advance of Air Group 201 to the southeast area of operations, Okano took passage on board the aircraft carrier *Unyō* and advanced to Buin base [on Bougainville]. At the time that he was promoted to CPO in November, he was also transferred to Air Group 331. During daily air combat operations over a period of about four months until his transfer to the southwest area of operations, Okano kept racking up his score of kills.

In March 1944, he was transferred from Air Group 331 to Fighter Hikōtai 603, Air Group 202. After participating in the Biak operation, in September he returned to the Ōmura Air Group. Okano greeted the end of the war while serving with Fighter Hikōtai 701, Air Group 343. Total number of aircraft downed, nineteen. Even after the end of the war, Okano continues to be active as a pilot in Japan today.

PO1c Masajirō Kawato (Masajirō Kawato)

PO1c Masajirō Kawato

Kawato is well known for the rather unique set of records he established; he engaged in three ramming attacks, was hit and shot down twice, and had to parachute to safety on four other occasions.

Born in 1925 to a farming family in Kyoto Municipality, in May 1942 Kawato entered the Maizuru Naval Barracks. Passing through the Hei 12th Flight Reserve Enlisted Trainee Class and then the 28th Flight Training Course, he graduated in July 1943. In late September, he was air-transported to Truk as one member of a reinforcement team of more than forty.

Kawato was provided with a Zero fighter and on 10 October posted to Air Group 253, which at the time was heavily engaged in combat operations.

He was only eighteen years old when he became a Sea1c flyer; his flight time was just barely over the three-hundred-hour mark. His superiors laughed at him saying, "I wonder if a young boy like you can actually fight in a war." Kawato, on his part, immediately displayed a reckless but resolute fighting spirit and proved his mettle with the Rabaul fighter unit.

Kawato's first ramming attack was made during an intercept battle over Rabaul on 2 November when he engaged in a frontal attack on a formation of B-25s. After the shoot-out, Kawato attempted to evade enemy aircraft by flying under a flaming enemy plane but rammed into it and had to parachute. He was rescued from the ocean and did not even receive a single scratch. The second ramming attack occurred during an intercept battle on the 11th. Immediately after he had shot down an enemy carrier bomber that had been attacking friendly ships in the bay, Kawato suddenly found himself attacked from the rear by an enemy fighter. Kawato's aircraft was hit and started burning; he had to parachute to the surface of the ocean from a height of 150 meters and was rescued. Because of burns and a wound in his left leg, he was forced to forgo air combat for about one month.

Next, on 17 December, he made a head-on attack on a P-39 to shoot it out with the enemy aircraft. He was unable to avoid the enemy aircraft, however, and the two planes collided in midair. Both pilots parachuted to the ocean surface; Kawato was rescued by a high-speed vessel. Paying no attention to his injuries, Kawato participated in air combat on the following day. Later on, he was waiting for a chance to ram the tail of a B-24 and was able to do so on 6 February 1944 in the skies over Rabaul. He made a successful parachute landing and, despite receiving six injuries, was safely rescued from the water.

On 20 February, almost all fighter units stationed in Rabaul were withdrawn to Truk. SupSea Kawato and a few of his fellow pilots and aircraft, however, remained on the island. Gathering together discarded materials from which Zero fighters were assembled, the group engaged in guerilla intercept operations, conducted reconnaissance flights and attacks on the Green Islands (Nissan), the Admiralities, and other areas. During this period, with the disbandment of Air Group 253, Kawato's unit became the 105th Air Base Support Squadron from July on. In the evening of 9 March 1945, PO2c Kawato, piloting a two-seat Zero fighter (PO2c Shimizu was on board with him), set out to intercept B-25s. The aircraft was later reported to be missing in action. Kawato was deemed to have been killed in action. The facts were later found to be as follows: Kawato discovered an enemy destroyer and while attacking, received antiaircraft gun hits and plunged into the ocean. Despite the serious wounds he had received, Kawato was able to reach the shore. While living by himself in the jungle he was taken prisoner by Australian forces; in December, he returned home to Japan from the Leyte prison camp. Total number of aircraft shot down, eighteen.

PO1c Kawato (Ikuhiko Hata)

PO1c Kawato (Masajirō Kawato)

ENS Saburō Saitō (Saburō Saitō)

ENS Saburō Saitō

Born in Yamagata Prefecture in 1917, Saitō enlisted in the navy in 1934 and was assigned to sea duty. In January 1939 he graduated with the 44th Pilot Training Class and then further trained at both the Ōita and the Ōmura air groups. That October he was posted to the 12th Air Group and advanced to Hankow; however, soon after he was transferred to the Ishū-tō base in southern China. Saitō was assigned to LT Aioi's buntai and saw his first air combat on 30 December and 10 January of the following year when he participated in the attacks on Kweilin. In January 1940, he was transferred to serve on board the *Akagi* and then was posted to the Ōita, Tokushima, and Tsuiki air groups. Upon being promoted to CPO in November 1942, he was transferred to serve on board the *Zuikaku*. In January 1943 he advanced to Rabaul to assist in the withdrawal from Guadalcanal. On 1 February, the *Zuikaku* Fighter Squadron, in coordination with the base fighter unit, escorted a carrier bomber unit that was attacking enemy vessels off Tulagi. During this air combat, Saitō scored his first victory when he, jointly with others, shot down an F4F.

On 4 and 7 February, Saitō served as

part of the air patrol for an evacuation ship convoy and shot down two enemy aircraft on each of the two days. He next participated in the "I"-gō operation in April and joined in the attacks conducted off Guadalcanal, in Oro Bay, on Moresby, and in Milne Bay. Although the *Zuikaku* later returned to the homeland for a while, the ship again advanced to Truk in July. On 1 November, the carrier's air group was sent to Rabaul in order to participate in the Ro-gō operation. On 2, 5, 8, and 11 November, WO Saitō served as the shōtai leader in intercept operations. He also participated in attacks carried out off Cape Torokina on the 2nd and the 3rd. During these operations, Saitō shot down a total of eight air-

Saitō during student trainee days (Saburō Saitō)

craft (including one jointly) consisting of P-38s, F4Us, B-25s, and other planes. During these operations and the course of this one week of ferocious battles, over 70 percent of the pilots of the *Zuikaku* Fighter Squadron were lost in action.

Returning to Truk on the 13th, Saitō later moved with seven aircraft to Roi Island on the 26th. He then moved to Taroa Island on 3 December and engaged in air defense operations. On the 5th, as he returned to land at Roi Island, he engaged in a battle with raiding American carrier fighters and shot down four aircraft. At the same time four aircraft, including that of the leader ENS Ōyama, were lost. The following day, Saitō withdrew to Truk using a land attack plane and was then transferred to the Tokushima Air Group. In July, he was transferred to Fighter Hikōtai 317 and

posted to Air Group 252 at Mobara. In order to participate in the Shō-gō [Leyte] operation, he proceeded on 13 October to the Philippines via Kasanbara, Okinawa, and Taiwan.

Saitō next participated in the general offensive carried out on the 24th; he engaged in air combat with American fighters over the waters east of Luzon. After he shot down one enemy aircraft, Saitō received hits on his aircraft. He had to make an emergency landing on the shore of Lamon Bay and was injured. Rescued by an army guard unit, he was returned to the homeland. He was unable to get up out of bed, however, till after the war came to an end. Total flight time 2,118 hours; the number of enemy aircraft shot down by Saitō listed in air records indicate eighteen for sure and another six, either jointly or as probables.

ENS Masayuki Nakase (Kunimori Nakakariya)

ENS Masayuki Nakase

Born in 1918 in Tokushima prefecture, Nakase enlisted and joined the Yokosuka Air Group in 1934 because he wanted to volunteer for the Otsu 5th Flight Reserve Enlisted Trainee Class. In March 1938 he finished the Flight Training Course and was promoted to PO3c. After serving with the Ōmura Air Group, he was next attached to the 14th Air Group during the latter part of 1938. He spent half a year on the China front but had no opportunity to engage in combat. While serving with the Yokosuka Air Group, he was assigned to the 12th Air Group at Hankow as part of the first Zero fighter unit that went into combat in July 1940. During the 4 October attack on Chengtu, Nakase, together with WO Ichirō Higashiyama, PO1c Hagiri, and PO2c Hideo Ō-ishi, engaged in the daring operation of landing on Taipingsze airfield and setting the field command post on fire. Although the 14 March 1941 attack on Chengtu was his first air battle, Nakase was able to shoot down six Soviet-made improved I-15 [fighters] (including one probable) all by himself. During the 26 May attack on Nancheng, Nakase shot down three more planes. In September he was transferred to the 3rd Air Group. Starting with the first attack on the Philippines on the day the war broke out, 8 December, Nakase became one of the core NCO pilots who fought valiantly in Philippines and Dutch East Indies area air battles. On 9 February, near Makassar on the island of Celebes, Nakase was hit while strafing enemy armored cars and died heroically by killing himself. Soon after, his name was published in an All Units Bulletin and he was also given the honor of a two-step promotion to the rank of Special Service Flight Ensign.

Nakase had a gentle character and was known as an all-around athlete. He was always the first to take action; it is said that there was a touch of genius in his air combat technique. Total number of enemy aircraft shot down, eighteen.

LTJG Akio Matsuba during Atsugi Air Group days, 1943. (Family of Ki-ichi Nagano)

LTJG Akio Matsuba

Born in Mie Prefecture in 1914, Matsuba graduated with the 26th Pilot Training Class in March 1935; he had spent a total of ten years in flight operations by the time the war ended. He was a true veteran, well honed in both spirit and techniques.

In November 1936, Matsuba was assigned aboard the *Kaga* for service. The China Incident broke out the following year, 1937. During the course of an air battle that occurred over Shanghai on 16 August [1937], Matsuba engaged in combat for the first time; jointly with another pilot he shot down a Douglas 0-38 reconnaissance bomber. The end of that same year, he returned to the Kasumigaura Air Group and then was successively transferred to the *Ryūjō* aircraft carrier, and then to the Iwakuni, Genzan, and Ōita air groups. In November 1943, Matsuba was transferred to Fighter Hikōtai 601, Air Group 301; at the end of the following June, [1944], he advanced to Iwo Jima. During intercept operations on 3 and 4 July, he shot down six F6Fs. In July he was transferred to the Fighter Hikōtai 701, which consisted of Shiden fighters. As a member of the T Force, he participated in air combat operations off Taiwan and in the air battle for Leyte. He was next transferred to Air Group 343 and was twice wounded during air defense operations over the homeland. He continued to fight valiantly until the war ended. Total number of enemy aircraft shot down, eighteen.

WO Takeo Tanimizu during his 6th Air Group days, on board the *Junyō,* June 1942. (Takeo Tanimizu)

WO Takeo Tanimizu

Graduating from the 17th Flight Training Course in March 1942, Tanimizu was posted to the 6th Air Group in April; he was among those pilots who were trained during the war. In June he was assigned on board the aircraft carrier *Kasuga Maru,* transferred to the *Shōkaku* in February 1943, and advanced to Rabaul in November. Tanimizu's first combat experience was on 2 November, when he shot down two P-38s during an intercept battle. He stayed on in Rabaul and, until his transfer to the Tainan Air Group in March of the following year, participated in daily intercept battles over a four-month period. At the Tainan Air Group, he not only served as an instructor in training but also participated in intercept operations as well as in air defense combat operations off Taiwan. In November while Tanimizu was escorting a ship convoy off Amoy, a P-51 attacked him by surprise; his aircraft was hit and burned. Tanimizu himself parachuted into the ocean and was hospitalized for burns. Toward the end of 1944, he returned to the homeland and was assigned to Air Group 203 until the end of the war. He participated in Kyūshū area air defense operations as well as in the Okinawa operation; he greeted the end of the war at Usa base.

Flight time, 1,425 hours; total number of aircraft shot down, eighteen.

WO Sadamu Komachi

WO Sadamu Komachi during his *Shōkaku* days, 1941. (Yasujirō Abe)

Born in Ishikawa Prefecture in 1920, Komachi graduated with the 49th Pilot Training Class in June 1940 and was assigned on board the *Shōkaku* the following year. He participated in each of the following sea battles: Hawaii, Indian Ocean, the Coral Sea, the Second Solomons Battle [Eastern Solomons], as well as the South Pacific [Santa Cruz].

Returning to the Ōmura Air Group at the end of 1942, in December 1943, Komachi was next transferred to Air Group 204 and then to Air Group 253. He was active in intercept operations over Rabaul and Truk and received honors from his commanding officer for his interception of B-24s using the Type 3 [aerial] bomb (sangō bakudan). On 19 June [1944], in order to participate in the final battle for the Marianas, he left Truk headed for Guam, under the command of LCDR Harutoshi Okamoto. Minutes before landing at his destination, however, Komachi's aircraft was damaged by Grumman F6Fs. Though badly burned, Komachi himself was able to make an emergency landing on the coast and was rescued. A few days later he escaped from the front in a land attack plane and returned to the homeland. He greeted the end of the war with the Yokosuka Air Group. Komachi was a wild character, known as a daredevil pilot. Total number of aircraft shot down, eighteen.

ENS Kuniyoshi Tanaka during his 13th Air Group days (Mitsunori Nakajima)

ENS Kuniyoshi Tanaka

Tanaka was known as one of the leading aces during the China Incident. Born in Saga Prefecture in 1917, he enlisted in the navy in 1934. In March 1936 he graduated with the 31st Pilot Training Class and was posted to the Ōmura Air Group. After the outbreak of the China Incident, however, in October 1937 he was transferred to the 13th Air Group and advanced to Shanghai. Tanaka's first air combat experience was on 9 December, the day of the attack on Nanchang and the day that Kashimura returned alive with his [badly damaged] aircraft. Tanaka used up his entire ammunition supply in shooting down a Curtiss, a Hawk, and a Corsair.

At the time, the number of pilots in fighter units far exceeded the number of available aircraft and it was quite hard to gain battle experience. The youngest pilot, Sea1c Tanaka, however, was favored by the gods of war and participated in six air battles, the highest number for anybody at the time. He shot down a total of twelve enemy aircraft. In July, he returned to the Ōmura Air Group. Later, he served on board the Ryūjō as well as with the Suzuka and the Kanoya air groups. In October

1941 Tanaka was promoted to PO1c, transferred to the Tainan Air Group and thus entered the Pacific War. During the first attack on Luzon on 8 December, Tanaka served as wingman (number two) to group leader Shingō and the two shared the destruction of one P-40. He next served in the Dutch East Indies and showed particular adeptness in the special technique of attacking B-17s. In other words, while conducting air patrols over a ship convoy in the Balikpapan area on the morning of 24 January 1942, Tanaka attacked an incoming formation of seven B-17s. Although receiving hits and wounded himself, he made several passes and shot down a B-17. Then the B-17 collided with another B-17; Tanaka lingered long enough to verify that both bombers fell and crashed.

On 8 February, Tanaka joined the nine Zero fighters led by LT Shingō in a battle over the Sea of Java. Discovering a nine-aircraft formation of B-17s flying eastward (commanded by LCDR [CAPT J. L.] Dufrane, [Jr.]), the Zero fighters split to left and right and attacked the American planes in a pincer movement. Each of three enemy aircraft were successively attacked from the

Tanaka at the Daikōjō airfield in Nanking, January 1938. (Kuniyoshi Tanaka)

front with the result that two aircraft, including that of the leader of the enemy formation, were shot down. In April 1942, Tanaka was transferred to the Ōita Air Group as an instructor and returned to the homeland. He was unable to return to

combat, however, because of a valvular disease of the heart. He greeted the end of the war after serving as an instructor with the Tsukuba and the Kasumigaura air groups. Total number of aircraft shot down, seventeen (officially recognized).

ENS Yoshio Ōki during his 12th Air Group days (Kazuo Tsunoda)

ENS Yoshio Ōki

Born in Ibaragi Prefecture in 1916, Ōki entered the navy as a fireman in 1933; he later changed to maintenance man. In July 1937 he graduated with the 37th Pilot Training Course and became a fighter pilot.

In July 1940, Ōki transferred from the Yokosuka Air Group to the 12th Air Group. During an air raid on Chungking on 13 September by a Zero fighter unit, Ōki experienced his first combat; he shot down four enemy aircraft. In July 1942, he was attached to the Tainan Air Group and participated in the New Guinea and Solomons air operations until November. In the same month, he withdrew to the homeland; the following May, Ōki returned to the Solomons battle front, advancing to Rabaul as a member of Air Group 251. On 16 June, in an air battle over the Russell Islands, Ōki was killed in action. Total number of aircraft shot down, seventeen (officially recognized).

WO Masao Masuyama during his 3rd Air Group days (Kiyoshi Katō)

LTJG Keishū Kamihira (Family of Keishū Kamihira)

WO Masao Masuyama

Born in Nagasaki Prefecture in 1921, Masuyama graduated with the 49th Pilot Training Class in June 1940; after being assigned to the Sasebo and 14th air groups, he was next assigned to the 3rd Air Group when the war began. Starting with the attack on Luzon on 8 December, Masuyama participated in combat in the Philippines and Dutch East Indies; he then advanced to the island of Timor. Until his return to the homeland in April 1943 to serve in the Naval Air Technology Arsenal Test Department as a test pilot, he was engaged in Darwin attack operations.

During the above period, from September until November 1942, Masuyama was dispatched to Rabaul under the command of LCDR Kiyoji Sakakibara and LT Takahide Aioi. In this fashion, Masuyama also joined a number of air battles over Guadalcanal as well. Total flight time, 1,540 hours; total number of aircraft shot down, seventeen.

LTJG Keishū Kamihira

Born in Yokohama City in 1920, Kamihira graduated from the Second High School of Yokohama, responded to recruitment for the Kō 1st Flight Reserve Enlisted Trainee Class, newly established in September 1937, and passed the exams. He graduated in June 1939 and was successively assigned to the Ōita, Ōmura, and Yokosuka air groups. Following these assignments, in August 1940 Kamihira was posted to the 12th Air Group and advanced to the base at Hankow. On 14 March 1941, Kamihira valiantly sortied as number two wingman for PO1c Hagiri on the attack on Chengtu; Kamihira managed to shoot down four enemy aircraft (one probable) at one time. In October 1941, he was next transferred to the Tainan Air Group. Starting off with the shoot-down of one enemy aircraft during the attack on Luzon the day the war started, Kamihira saw combat in Philippines and Dutch East Indies air operations. In April 1942, he was transferred to the newly organized 6th Air Group and participated in the Aleutian operation, traveling on board the aircraft carrier *Junyō* joining members of the unit scheduled to occupy Midway. Kamihira was transferred to the Ōita Air

Group in July; the following April he was promoted to the rank of WO. In October [1943], he was transferred to Air Group 381 and engaged in air defense operations in the Borneo and Celebes areas. In intercepting B-24s, Kamihira used the Type 3 aerial bomb and achieved substantial battle results. In particular, in the Menado intercept operation of 5 September 1944, Kamihira achieved great success; he single-handedly shot down two P-38s and five B-24s (two probables). He was later wounded and returned to the homeland. He greeted the end of the war as a special attack force instructor. Kamihira was a large man, almost five feet six inches tall, and weighed about 149 pounds; he was a pilot representative of the best of the Kō class of pilots. In 1970, while piloting a Maritime Safety Agency helicopter, Kamihira died in a crash near Hakodate City.

ENS Minoru Honda

Born in Kumamoto Prefecture in 1923, Honda graduated from the Kō 5th Pilot Training Course in January 1942 after the war had begun. Although he was assigned to a fighter squadron attached to 22nd Air Flotilla Headquarters, the southern area operations had already ended and he had no opportunity to engage in air combat.

In April, Honda was transferred to the fighter squadron attached to the Kanoya Air Group (later renamed Air Group 253) and moved around various bases in the southwest area. In September [1942] he advanced to Rabaul (later to Kavieng) and participated until May of the following year in air battles in the New Guinea and Solomons areas. In April 1944, he was transferred to Fighter Hikōtai 407; in October Honda next advanced to the Philippines. Following his return to the homeland, Honda was assigned to Fighter Hikōtai 407, Air Group 343, and was active in the air defense of the homeland, where he greeted the end of the war. At the present time, he is a test pilot of the MU-2 aircraft. Total number of aircraft shot down, seventeen.

ENS Minoru Honda during his Fighter Hikōtai 407, Air Group 343, days. (Minoru Honda)

WO Kiyoshi Itō during his Tsukuba Air Group days (Kiyoshi Katō)

WO Kiyoshi Itō

Born in Niigata Prefecture in 1921, Itō graduated from the 12th Flight Training Course in November 1941, immediately before the outbreak of the war. He was immediately posted to the 3rd Air Group and thus greeted the Pacific War. The majority of pilots in the 3rd Air Group at the time were all veterans, however, each with one thousand or more flight hours to their credit; as a result, Itō had no opportunity to participate in air combat during the earlier stages of the war. On 4 April 1942, Itō saw combat for the first time when he participated in the attack on Darwin and shot down one enemy aircraft. Since that time and until August he participated in a number of attacks on Darwin and showed amazing growth in skills. In September, with the temporary diversion of the main force of the 3rd Air Group to the southeast area under the leadership of LT Aioi, Itō advanced to Rabaul. By the time he returned to the southwest area in late November, Itō had participated in the fierce air battles that were going on over Guadalcanal and New Guinea.

Following his return to the southwest area, Itō was engaged in air defense operations over the Arafura Sea, as well as participating in attacks on Darwin from early spring 1943 until November. As a result of a full two years of continuous combat experience, Itō had participated in thirty air battles, shot down or destroyed thirty aircraft (seventeen shot down, thirteen destroyed), and was given a special commendation. After his return to the homeland, he served as an instructor in the Ōita and Tsukuba air groups and thus greeted the end of the war. After the war, Itō changed his name to Katō.

(Left) ENS Tora-ichi Takatsuka during his Tainan Air Group days, Rabaul, 4 August 1942. (Kiku-ichi Inano)

ENS Susumu Ishihara during his Tokushima Air Group days (Family of Susumu Ishihara)

ENS Tora-ichi Takatsuka

Born in Shizuoka Prefecture in 1914, Takatsuka was a veteran pilot who graduated with the 22nd Pilot Training Class in November, 1933. During the China Incident, he participated in the 13 September 1940 attack on Chungking by the Zero fighter squadron attached to the 12th Air Group; he shot down three aircraft.

In October 1941, Takatsuka was promoted to WO and released to inactive duty; however, he was immediately mobilized and assigned to the Tainan Air Group. In June 1942 he advanced to Rabaul and, using his unspectacular but crafty air battle techniques, kept on piling up victories. Takatsuka was missing in action over Guadalcanal on 13 September during air combat; he is deemed to have died in action. Total number of aircraft shot down, sixteen (officially recognized).

ENS Susumu Ishihara

Born in 1921 in Aichi Prefecture, Ishihara entered the navy in October 1938 as a student of the Kō 3rd Flight Reserve Enlisted Trainee Class and graduated in April 1941 from the Flight Training Course. He was ordered to the newly organized 1st Air Group and took his station at Kanoya. He advanced to Hankow in July but was engaged only in air patrol operations and had no opportunity for combat; he returned to Kanoya in September. In October, Ishihara was transferred to the Tainan Air Group; with the outbreak of the war, he next participated in air operations in the Philippines and Dutch East Indies. On the first day of war, 8 December, PO2c Ishihara, serving as number two for the 3rd Shōtai of the Wakao Chūtai, strafed Clark Field. On the 10th, Ishihara scored his first victory in a battle over Del Carmen. In April 1942, he returned to the homeland to serve as an instructor at the Tokushima Air Group. In June 1943 he advanced to the southeast area of operations. He was soon transferred to

Air Group 204; while based primarily at Buin and Rabaul, Ishihara engaged in ferocious air attacks and intercept operations. Ishihara was particularly good at shooting down larger aircraft. On 18 October, he shot down three B-26 medium bombers over Rabaul; on 2 November, he similarly shot down three other aircraft. In December, he was transferred to Air Group 202 and moved to the southwest area of operations. In March of the following year [1944], he moved to Truk; after participating in the Biak operation, in late May Ishihara advanced to Yap because of the American attack on the Marianas. On 18 and 19 June [1944] Ishihara sortied with his colleagues in an attack on enemy vessels off Saipan. On the 18th in particular, he engaged in combat with enemy fighters; Ishihara shot down four aircraft jointly with other pilots. In July he returned to the mainland and was transferred to the Kure Air Group. From August until the end of the war, he flew Zero fighters and Raiden interceptors in the Kure and Osaka area as a member of Air Group 322, which was responsible for local air defense. Ishihara was engaged in intercepting B-29s. Total number of aircraft shot down, sixteen (officially recognized). After the war, Ishihara became a jet pilot with the Air Self-Defense Force but died in the line of duty as the result of an accident (ASDF Major).

Ishihara with his favorite aircraft, at Surabaja, Java, February 1942. (Family of Susumu Ishihara)

CDR Zenjirō Miyano (Maru)

CDR Zenjirō Miyano

Born in 1917 in Osaka Municipality, Miyano graduated from the Naval Academy in 1938 with the 65th class. In April 1940, he completed the 32nd Aviation Student Course and was attached to the 12th Air Group the following year. Although participating in the China Incident, he had no opportunity for air combat. In October 1941, Miyano was promoted to LT and became a division officer in the 3rd Air Group. On 8 December, the day the war broke out, he recorded his first victory during an attack on Luzon. He was next transferred to the Philippines and Dutch East Indies. In April 1942, Miyano was ordered in as division officer with the 6th Air Group, which was scheduled to occupy Midway. He took passage on the carrier *Junyō* in June and participated in the attack on Dutch Harbor. Soon after his return to the homeland he advanced to Rabaul and served first as division officer in Air Group 204, later as its group leader. He was always in the forefront of things and spent almost one year on the battle front.

Miyano was both respected and popular with his superiors as well as his subordinates as a truly superior fighter unit leader. At the same time, he was the first in the

Japanese navy to use the four-aircraft formation, the first to develop new fighter bombing techniques, and to otherwise break new ground in battle tactics. Miyano proposed the dangerous task of escorting a slow moving dive-bomber after it had completed a low-level bombing attack. He volunteered for this duty in an attack on a ship convoy on 16 June 1943 off Lunga on Guadalcanal. While engaged in a dog fight with enemy fighters, Miyano failed to return. Following his death, he was given the honor of mention in an All Units Bulletin and a posthumous two-rank promotion, to the rank of naval CDR. It is said that Miyano by himself shot down sixteen aircraft; his unit's score stood at 228 aircraft.

WO Ryōji Ōhara during his Yokosuka Air Group days (Ryōji Ōhara)

WO Ryōji Ōhara

Born in Miyagi Prefecture in 1921, he was a wartime pilot who was graduated with the Hei 4th Flight Training Course in July 1942.

Immediately upon graduation, Ōhara was assigned to the 6th Air Group; in October of the same year he advanced to Buin as a replacement. After achieving his first victory during the attack on Guadalcanal on 23 October [1942], and until October of the following year, when he returned to the Yokosuka Air Group, Ōhara participated in ferocious air battles in the Solomons, Rabaul, and New Guinea and managed to stay alive. In particular, on 13 May 1943 he sortied as number two (wingman) for LT Miyano during air combat over the Russell Islands and shot down one Corsair fighter. Immediately after, his own aircraft received thirty-eight hits and its horizontal stabilizer was damaged. He managed to extricate himself; on the way back, he valiantly counterattacked two Corsairs that were following him and shot down one of them. He then made an emergency landing on the island of Kolombangara. With respect to this particular air battle, Ōhara was later given a good conduct commendation by the commander of Air Group 204. Following his return to the homeland, he continued to be assigned to the Yokosuka Air Group. After participating in the Kantō air defense battles in spring 1945, he greeted the end of the war. After the war, he joined the Maritime Self-Defense Force. Number of aircraft shot down, sixteen.

WO Bunkichi Nakajima (Family of Bunkichi Nakajima)

WO Bunkichi Nakajima

Born in 1918 in Toyama Prefecture, Nakajima entered the navy after having worked as a janitor in a police station. He graduated in September 1936 from the 33rd Pilot Training Class and at the age of seventeen, became the youngest PO3c ever to serve as a fighter pilot. He was immediately assigned to the Kanoya Air Group; with the outbreak of the China Incident, Nakajima advanced to Taiwan and participated in air defense operations. In March 1938, he was transferred to the 13th Air Group and in July, to the 15th Air Group. However, he was not favored by any opportunity for air combat. In September 1941, Nakajima was assigned to the 3rd Air Group. With the outbreak of the war, he participated in air combat in the Philippines and the Dutch East Indies. In November 1942, he was transferred to Air Group 252 and advanced to Rabaul. For a period of three months before he was transferred to the Marshall Islands in February of the following year [1943], Nakajima participated in air operations in eastern New Guinea and over Guadalcanal.

On 6 October 1943, because of the huge American carrier task forces that attacked Wake Island, Nakajima took off from Maloelap with a group of seven land attack planes that were intended as reinforcements; the group was provided an escort of an equal number of Zero fighters (commander, LT Yūzō Tsukamoto). As they neared Wake Island the group was attacked by enemy fighters. After the dogfights were over, five aircraft were able to land; two other aircraft, including that flown by CPO Nakajima, were lost in action. He is believed to have died in action. Number of aircraft destroyed, sixteen.

and graduated with the Hei 2nd Flight Training Class in November 1941 and was immediately assigned to the Chitose Air Group. When the war broke out he was assigned to air defense duties in the Micronesia area. On 1 February 1942 when an American task force attacked, Nakaya took off from Roi Island and shot down one dive-bomber; this was his first combat. In August, he was dispatched to Rabaul as part of a reinforcement group for the Tainan Air Group. Until the end of October, he participated in air combat operations in the Solomons area.

Nakaya returned to Air Group 201 in December and was assigned to air defense duties in the Marshall Islands. In the spring of the following year, he withdrew to the homeland; in July [1943], he again advanced to Buin. He participated in daily combat but managed to stay alive. During this time one of the episodes he participated in was the following. Nakaya tried to force a P-38 to land on a friendly airfield so that it could be captured. Before he was able to do that, however, his own colleagues, unaware of what Nakaya was trying to accomplish, shot down the P-38. On another occasion, Nakaya moved up on a two-plane formation of P-38s and forced them to crash into each other in midair. In December, he was transferred to Air Group 331 and went to Sabang [Sumatra]. In March 1944, he was transferred to Air Group 202, then to Air Group 221, and finally back to the homeland. He greeted the end of the war as an instructor with the Tsukuba and Yatabe air groups. Although not spectacular in any sense, Nakaya had a steady and thoroughgoing nature. Number of aircraft shot down, sixteen.

WO Yoshi-ichi Nakaya during his Tainan Air Group days (Shin-ichi Hirabayashi)

WO Yoshi-ichi Nakaya

Born in 1921 in Nagano Prefecture to a farm family, Nakaya first worked in a bicycle store and then enlisted in the Navy. He transferred out of maintenance work

CPO Kunimichi Katō during his Air Group 210
days, 1945. (Kunimichi Katō)

CPO Kunimichi Katō

Next to Masajirō Kawato, Katō was the
youngest of all the naval fighter aces. Born
in 1923 in Aichi Prefecture, he graduated
from the Hei 10th Flight Training Course
in January 1943. After being posted to the
Ōmura Air Group, Katō was attached to
Air Group 254 on Hainan Island. Although
inexperienced, he was a qualified sharp-
shooter; at this sport he had won a cup
while stationed at the Sasebo Naval Station. His first combat was during the summer of the same year, 1943; without taking
time to put on flight gear, Katō took off
and shot down a raiding P-38. Starting the
end of 1943, mixed formations of B-24,
B-25, P-38, and P-40 aircraft of the U.S.
Army Air Forces based in southwestern
China began to raid Kwangtung, Hong
Kong, and Hainan regularly. Through daring intercept operations, LdgSea Katō
came to assume the position of top ace of
Air Group 254. Before his transfer to Air
Group 210 in the fall of 1944 when he returned to the mainland, Katō had shot
down a total of nine aircraft. Later on, he
participated in homeland air defense operations from Meiji base. In particular, during
the first raid on the homeland by an American carrier task force, which took place on
16 February 1945, Katō single-handedly
tackled an enemy carrier fighter formation
of ten planes in the air over Hamamatsu.
He shot down three of the enemy aircraft.
Next, he advanced to the Kokubu base and
participated in a number of support activities for Okinawa-based special attack force
operations. Flight time, 882 hours; number
of aircraft shot down, sixteen.

ENS Masami Shiga before taking off for an air battle over Okinawa, April 1945. (Masami Ōtomo)

ENS Masami Shiga

Born to a farm family in Ibaragi Prefecture in 1919, Shiga enlisted in the navy in 1937 and was assigned to maintenance duties. In June 1940, he graduated with the 50th Pilot Training Class and was transferred to piloting fighters. In September 1941, he was assigned to the Chitose Air Group. At the outbreak of war, Shiga was engaged in air defense operations based at Taroa Island, in the Micronesia area. On 1 February of the following year, Shiga scored his first victory while intercepting attacking American carrier aircraft. He was next stationed in the Marshall Islands but spent his time without any opportunity for combat. In July 1943, Shiga was assigned to Air Group 201 and advanced to the Buin base, Solomon Islands. For about half a year, until his transfer to the Yokosuka Air Group in February 1944, Shiga experienced fierce fighting on the Solomons, Rabaul, and New Guinea battlefronts.

In June 1944, he was dispatched to Iwo Jima and participated in a number of air battles as wingman for Saburō Sakai. During the 24 June attack on an enemy task force, Shiga was able to fly safely through the night and return to base alive. In February 1945, he was transferred to Air Group 203 and greeted the end of the war while engaged in air battles over Okinawa. After the war, he joined the Air Self-Defense Force but returned to inactive duty at retirement age. Number of aircraft shot down, sixteen. After the war, Shiga changed his name to Ōtomo.

ENS Kunimori Nakakariya at the Matsuyama base before taking off for the Marianas, May 1944. (Kunimori Nakakariya)

ENS Kunimori Nakakariya

Born in 1920 in Kagoshima Prefecture, Nakakariya entered Yokosuka Air Group in June 1937 as a student of the Otsu 8th Flight Reserve Enlisted Trainee Class. In March 1940 he graduated from the Flight Training Course and then served with the Ōita, Ōmura, and Kanoya air groups. In April 1941, he was ordered into the 12th Air Group; Nakakariya then proceeded to the Hankow base. On 26 May, a flight of eleven Zero fighters under the command of LT Minoru Suzuki left Ichang base and sortied on a long-range attack on Tienshui and Nancheng. PO3c Nakakariya engaged in a battle with incoming enemy fighters; in this first combat, he shot down two enemy aircraft. In September, he was transferred to the 3rd Air Group. Following the outbreak of the war, Nakakariya participated in air battles over the Philippines and the Dutch East Indies.

Next, he advanced to Kupang on Timor Island and participated in air defense operations over the Arafura Sea, as well as in attacks on Darwin. During the fall of 1942, the main force of the 3rd Air Group advanced to Rabaul, but Nakakariya remained behind at Kupang, continuing on his air defense duties.

In May 1943, for the first time in two and a half years, Nakakariya returned to the homeland and was assigned as an instructor at the Ōmura Air Group. Upon promotion to WO in May of the following year, he was transferred to Air Group 653 and participated in the June [1944] sea battle off the Marianas. Next, with issuance of the order for the Shō-gō operation in October 1944, Nakakariya was ordered to the Philippines.

Nakakariya in celebration of an air battle in which two aircraft were pitched against eighteen aircraft, 26 May 1941. (Aircraft shown belonged to Masayuki Nakase.) (Kunimori Nakakariya)

He parted with the main force that was to sortie with an aircraft carrier and proceeded by air to the Bamban base, Luzon, via Okinawa and Taiwan. He then rejoined the main force and advanced to Cebu. Nakakariya was next involved in the attack on Leyte, as well as in intercept operations over the base. In mid-November, however, for the purpose of replenishing their war strength, WO Nakakariya and other surviving pilots were transferred back to the homeland and posted to Air Group 601. Nakakariya greeted the end of the war while participating in air defense operations over the homeland and in the air battles over Okinawa.

Total number of aircraft shot down, sixteen.

WO Hideo Watanabe during his student trainee days (Hideo Watanabe)

WO Hideo Watanabe

Born in 1920 in a farm family in Fukushima Prefecture, Watanabe enlisted in the navy in 1937 and was graduated from the Hei 2nd Flight Training Course in November, 1941, immediately before the outbreak of the war. In March of the following year, he was posted to the Chitose Air Group and assigned air defense duties in the Micronesia area. In March 1943, he was transferred to Air Group 204 and advanced to Rabaul as well as to Buin. He participated in the ferocious air battles over the Solomons.

After the death on 16 June [1943] of group leader Miyano, the situation was such that there were almost no officer or WO pilots left. As a result, the youthful twenty-three-year-old CPO Watanabe served in place of the chūtai leader; on occasion, Watanabe served in place of the daitai leader and acted as formation officer of the Air Group 204 Fighter Squadron. Watanabe shot down one B-24 on the evening of 26 August when he single-handedly tackled a combined enemy fighter-bomber force attacking Buin; he then shot down one Grumman F4F fighter. Just as he shot down the latter, however, he himself received a bullet through the right eye, from behind; he was severely wounded with a fracture of the forehead. Despite these injuries, however, Watanabe regained control of his aircraft just above the surface of the ocean and managed to land safely on land. He then lost consciousness and was hospitalized. For this gallantry, Watanabe, while still confined to the naval hospital at Rabaul, was awarded a military sword by ADM Kusaka, commander of the Southeast Area Fleet. The sword was inscribed with the words, Bukō Batsugun ("For Conspicuous Military Valor"). Watanabe was then returned to the homeland but was not able to go back on duty before the war ended. Number of aircraft shot down, sixteen.

WO Wataru Nakamichi during his Air Group 721 days (Wataru Nakamichi)

WO Wataru Nakamichi

Born in Osaka City in 1922, Nakamichi had been working in a tin can factory before he enlisted at the Kure Naval Barracks in 1940. In May of the following year, desiring to become a pilot, Nakamichi entered the Tsuchiura Air Group. In July, he was graduated with the Hei 4th Flight Reserve Enlisted Trainee Class and received pilot training with the Kasumigaura and Ōita air groups. On 21 July, he was graduated from the 21st Pilot Training Course. Ordered on board the *Junyō* in December 1942, he was next transferred, in the summer of 1943, to Air Group 204. He advanced to the Buin base and for the approximately nine months until the following March when he returned to the homeland was heavily engaged in furious air battles in the southeast area of operations. During this period, his personal victories amounted to nineteen aircraft (nine, joint, or probable).

Later and until the war ended, Nakamichi was assigned duties in the homeland. In particular, after November 1944, Nakamichi was assigned to the Air Group 721 Fighter Squadron (Jinrai, "Heavenly Lightning"); here he served in direct support of the Jinrai [Ōka] Special Attack Force units.

Number of aircraft shot down, fifteen (officially recognized).

LT Yoshimi Minami (Ikuhiko Hata)

LT Yoshimi Minami

Minami was known as Kashimura, the 2nd; Minami died as a member of a Special Attack Force Unit [Kamikaze] in the Philippines. Born in Kagawa Prefecture in 1915, Minami entered the navy in 1933, volunteering for flying duty. In November 1935, he graduated from the 30th Pilot Training Class. In July 1937, he was posted to the 13th Air Group (and next, the 12th Air Group), via the Omura Air Group. He participated in the Shanghai battlefront. Starting with the third air attack on Nanking on 20 September, Minami participated in air battles over Nanchang and Hankow. He shot down nine aircraft and, for a while, occupied the position of top ace in the 12th Air Group.

In particular, during the 31 May 1938 attack on Hankow, nine aircraft of the Yoshitomi Chūtai tangled with about fifty enemy fighters; during the ensuing dogfights, PO3c Minami shot down one enemy aircraft. He then received a hit in his plane's fuel tank; moreover, he found himself surrounded by twelve enemy aircraft. Since he had run out of ammunition, Minami employed a ramming tactic. Then, despite the fact that the left wing of his aircraft had been sheared off from the red ball

of the rising sun outward, Minami started on his way back to base. He made an emergency landing on the banks of the Yangtze River and set his aircraft on fire. Fortunately for Minami, friendly search aircraft were able to spot him; he was rescued by a patrol boat and returned safely to base.

In September 1938, Minami returned to the homeland; he was then assigned to the Saeki and Ōita air groups, then to duty on board the *Hiryū* and the *Zuihō*. In October 1941, he was transferred to the *Shōkaku* and participated in sea battles in the Hawaiian Islands, Indian Ocean, and Coral Sea areas. Transferred to the Ōmura Air Group in June 1942, he was next promoted to WO and transferred to Air Group 601 in February 1944. He was assigned to serve on board the newly built aircraft carrier *Taihō*. On 19 June, he participated in an attack on an American task force as a member of a fighter escort during the battle off the Marianas. After several dogfights he returned to his carrier, the *Taihō,* but was wounded at the time that it was sunk.

Following his return to the homeland, Minami was attached to Air Group 653; on

Minami during his *Shōkaku* days, 1941. (Yasujirō Abe)

24–25 October, he participated in the battles off the Philippines. Next he sortied out during the Leyte operation; as a member of the Kasagi Unit of the Kamikaze Special Attack Force units he plunged into an American task force and was killed in action. After his death, he was given a special two-grade promotion to navy LT. He was one of the few aces who were killed while serving in a special attack force unit. Number of aircraft shot down, fifteen (officially recognized).

ENS Satoshi Yoshino (Saburō Saitō)

ENS Satoshi Yoshino

Born in Chiba Prefecture in 1918, Yoshino was accepted at the age of sixteen, in June 1934, as a student of the Otsu Fifth Flight Reserve Enlisted Trainee Class. Graduating in August 1937, he then took the Flight Training Course and completed it in March 1938. Proceeding via the Ōmura Air Group and duty on board the *Sōryū*, Yoshino was next attached to the Chitose Air Group Fighter Squadron, newly established in October 1940.

Immediately before the outbreak of the war, Yoshino had advanced to the Marshall Islands in October 1941 and was engaged in air defense operations in the Micronesia area. In February of the following year, he was transferred to the 4th Air Group and advanced to the base at Rabaul. On the 11th, while four Type 96 carrier fighters led by PO1c Yoshino were on patrol over Gasmata (Surumi) [New Britain], they met three Hudson bombers of the Royal Australian Air Force. Immediately, two of the enemy aircraft were destroyed. Two days later, on the 13th, Yoshino added another plane to his score, also over Gasmata. The unit was then re-equipped with Zero fighters; on 11 March, the first day of the advance to Lae, Yoshino led seven aircraft, which then shot down one enemy aircraft. Until April, when the Tainan Air Group transferred into the area, Yoshino was the core of the 4th Air Group Fighter Squadron. During attacks on Port Moresby, Horn Island, and intercept operations, Yoshino racked up total victories of four enemy aircraft shot down.

Even after his promotion to warrant officer and his transfer to the Tainan Air Group, Yoshino continued to participate in the attacks on Moresby and in intercept operations over Lae. On 9 June Yoshino intercepted a flight of B-26s over Lae, and pursued them to Cape Ward Hunt, where he was pounced upon by an eleven-plane formation of P-39s. Yoshino failed to return and is presumed to have died in action. Number of aircraft shot down, fifteen (officially recognized).

WO Shigeru Shibukawa during his Tsukuba Air Group days (Shigeru Shibukawa)

LCDR Motonari Suhō during his 12th Air Group days, spring 1938. (Yoshio Shiga)

WO Shigeru Shibukawa

Born in Osaka Municipality in 1923, Shibukawa enlisted in the navy in 1940. After graduating from the 23rd Flight Training Course in September 1942, he was assigned to Air Group 253 in December of the same year. Early in 1943, Shibukawa advanced to Kavieng and participated in air battles in the Solomons and New Guinea. Shibukawa withdrew to Saipan in May 1943 for rest and recuperation, but again advanced to Rabaul in early September.

Shibukawa participated in attack and intercept operations until the end of October [1943]. On 1 November, he escorted units attacking ships off Cape Torokina [Bougainville] and shot down one Grumman F6F. Later, however, he was hit from behind and his left hand wounded, and he returned to the homeland in a hospital ship. After recovering from his wounds, Shibukawa was assigned to the Tsukuba Air Group, where he greeted the end of the war while engaged in training activities.

Flight time, 767 hours; number of aircraft shot down, fifteen (from his flight log).

LCDR Motonari Suhō

Born in Tottori Prefecture in 1912, Suhō graduated with the 62nd Naval Academy Class in 1934. After serving in the fleet, he next completed the 28th Aviation Student Course in September 1937. Following advanced training at the Saeki and Yokosuka air groups, in February 1938, Suhō was assigned to the 12th Air Group as a brand new ensign; he advanced into the central China battlefront area. Soon injured as a result of an air accident, he was able to leave the hospital after a period of two weeks. On 29 April, Suhō saw his first action when he managed to shoot down one enemy aircraft during an attack on Hankow. His own aircraft received hits, however; on the way back to base Suhō had to make an emergency landing at Anking because he ran out of fuel. Next, on 4 July, he flamed an additional two aircraft during an air battle over Nanchang. He was then transferred to the 15th Air Group and returned to the homeland within a matter of ten days.

After serving as a training instructor at the Kasumigaura and Ōita air groups, he was promoted to LT in October 1939. He was next ordered to serve as group leader,

14th Air Group. He thus again headed for the China front. On 30 December of the same year, as well as on 10 January [1940], Suhō participated in the attacks on Liuchow and on Kweilin, flying his aircraft via Nanning. As a result of daring air combat, Suhō shot down two aircraft during each of the two engagements. In the fall of 1940 at Hankow, he was given sophisticated training in the use of Zero fighters. On 7 October, Suhō advanced to Hanoi and as the shōtai leader of the second unit of six Zero fighters led by LT Kofukuda, advanced with the unit to Kunming. By himself he shot down four aircraft; Suhō chased one of the planes down into a valley and forced it to crash without Suhō himself firing a single shot.

In November, Suhō was transferred to the Genzan Air Group; the following April [1941] he was transferred to the Naval Air Technology Arsenal as a test pilot. For about a year and a half, he was engaged in the operational testing of Zero fighters and Raiden interceptors. In December [1942], Suhō was ordered to serve as group leader, Air Group 252, succeeding LT Suganami, who had been killed in action. Suhō advanced to the base at Munda [New Georgia] in the Solomons. For a period of about two months, until his transfer in February of the following year to the Micronesia area, Suhō participated in various operations such as defense action over Munda and Ballale Island, attacks on Buna, protecting the retreat from Guadalcanal, assisting in transport convoys proceeding to Lae, and other activities. Later he was assigned as the commanding officer of the unit dispatched to Wake. The unit was destroyed completely, however, as a result of a major enemy air attack on 6 October. Surviving pilots were quartered on Roi Island after being transported there by land attack planes sent out to rescue them.

On 24 November, LT Suhō led a group

Suhō's favorite aircraft during his 14th Air Group days (Kiku-ichi Inano)

of nineteen Zero fighters and sortied on a strafing and bombing attack against Makin [Gilbert Islands], immediately following its capture by enemy forces. En route to the destination, the unit was suddenly attacked by a force of F6Fs over the ocean. The aircraft flown by Suhō received the first hit of the engagement, a hit in its fuel tank; he was forced to break off and land on Mili Island. The attack itself ended without success.

In March 1944, Suhō returned to the homeland. In May he was promoted to LCDR and assigned to the Genzan Air Group and later as air officer of the Tsuiki Air Group. Suhō greeted the end of the war while engaged in ground duties. LCDR Suhō was quiet and self-posessed, a pure expert soldier type; he is said to have been the greatest officer pilot as far as flying skill was concerned. Suhō's score of eleven enemy aircraft shot down by him alone was the highest among all officers participating in the China Incident. After the war, he served as a jet pilot for the Air Self-Defense Force and rose to the rank of general, ASDF, before his retirement. Total number of aircraft shot down, fifteen.

WO Minpo Tanaka immediately before the end of the war, at Iwakuni base. (Kenji Takahashi)

WO Minpo Tanaka

Born in Nagasaki Prefecture in 1923, Tanaka was one of the youngest aces who entered the Otsu 11th Flight Reserve Enlisted Trainee Class in June 1939. Graduating from the 23rd Flight Training Course in September 1942, he was posted to Air Group 261, 1st Air Fleet, in June the following year.

When storm clouds over the Marianas became ominous toward the end of February 1944, Tanaka advanced to Saipan as part of the buntai commanded by ENS Ichirō Higashiyama. During the evening of 30 March, Tanaka moved to Peleliu under the command of LT Ibusuki. When he joined in intercepting an attack by a force of American carrier aircraft on the following day, the 31st, it turned out to be Tanaka's first taste of battle. During the course of the same air battle, however, Air Group 261 lost twenty of its twenty-eight aircraft.

Tanaka later moved to Mariaon Island (Woleai Atoll) and began intercepting PBYs; using a frontal, downward dead-angle attack (shikaku no zen-kahō kōgeki) [in U.S. Navy parlance, a high-opposite or head-on attack], he shot down two enemy aircraft. In the early part of June, Tanaka moved to Halmahera Island; he then joined other pilots at Yap in preparation for the Battle of the Marianas. On the 18th, Tanaka helped in escorting the Ginga-tai ("Milky Way Unit") and participated in an attack on an American ship convoy off Saipan. After a fierce battle, he shot down two F6Fs; Tanaka then went on to land on Guam. Tanaka himself kept on participating in ongoing daily intercept battles, but the number of operable aircraft shrank, and persons from the commanding officer and below escaped from the island. Only what came to be referred to as "that wild Tanaka and his gang of four" remained behind;

they kept on fighting almost daily, attacking ship convoys off Saipan, strafing airfields, and participating in air defense operations until mid-July. On the day that American forces landed on the island, Tanaka took off carrying a 60-kg bomb and bombed the invasion beach being used by the American forces. He then escaped to Mariaon [Woleai], proceeding via Palau, and eventually arrived at Cebu.

Tanaka was next transferred to Air Group 201 and engaged in direct support of the kamikaze special attack force units. In January 1945, Tanaka returned to the homeland and was assigned to Air Group 252 and then 203. He greeted the end of the war engaged in air defense operations in the Kantō and the Kyūshū areas, providing screen support to Okinawa special attack force units.

Tanaka held a record for having had his aircraft shot down three times but still escaping by parachuting; the number of aircraft shot down by him was fifteen. After the war ended, he became a pilot for All Nippon Airways, where he continues to serve today.

ENS Kenji Okabe (Yasujirō Abe)

ENS Kenji Okabe

Okabe is the ace that holds the official record for shooting down eight enemy aircraft (three probables) in a single air encounter. Born in Fukuoka City in 1915, Okabe enlisted in the navy after graduation from Shūyūkan High School. In November 1937, he graduated from the 38th Pilot Training Class and was then posted to the Saeki and Ōmura air groups. In July 1937, he was posted to the 12th Air Group and proceeded to the battlefront in China; however, he had no opportunity to engage in combat. Just before the outbreak of the Pacific War, Okabe was ordered on board the *Shōkaku;* during the attack on Hawaii, he served as part of the combat air patrol for the carriers. An air battle over Trincomalee on 9 April 1942 was Okabe's first taste of battle; he shot down two [RAF] Hurricane fighters. During the Battle of the Coral Sea on 8 May, Okabe was assigned combat air patrol duties. He would wait at a high altitude diving point until a U.S. dive-bomber formation came into view; he would then swoop down on his prey. In this fashion he was able to shoot down eight aircraft in succession. Because his own carrier had received hits, however, Okabe was unable to land on her; he ditched and was rescued.

Tanaka, February 1945 (Minpo Tanaka)

In July 1943, he was again assigned to the *Shōkaku,* and on 1 November he advanced to Rabaul. Including the major air raid of the 2nd, Okabe participated in a number of intercept operations. He was later transferred to the Ōmura Air Group. Then in July 1944, he was assigned to the newly established Air Group 634. This was at a time when there were no longer any aircraft carriers remaining that he could serve on. With issuance of orders in October to start the Shō-gō operation, Okabe proceeded via Okinawa and Taiwan, eventually arriving in the Philippines. After participating in the Leyte operation, Okabe returned to the homeland toward the end of the year. He greeted the end of the war while posted to Air Group 601.

Okabe tended to be a theoretician. At the same time, he was an ace with strong character; he openly expressed opposition to the concept of the special attack forces. Number of aircraft shot down, fifteen.

PO1c Masu-aki Endō, Tainan Air Group at Rabaul, August 1942. (Kiku-ichi Inano)

PO1c Masu-aki Endō

Graduating with the Otsu 9th Flight Reserve Enlisted Trainee Class in October 1941, just before the outbreak of hostilities, Endō was posted to the Tainan Air Group in February of the following year. In April, he advanced to Rabaul and to Lae, where he participated in the air battles over eastern New Guinea and the Solomons. He managed to live through all of these fierce operations.

In November, Endō returned to the homeland for reorganization purposes. In May 1943, he joined in the advance of Air Group 251 into the southeast area of operations; using Rabaul as a base, he fought for a string of air operations. On 7 June, during an air battle in which thirty-six carrier fighters under the command of LT Ichirō Mukai sortied on a mission to attack the Russell Islands, Endō shot down a P-38. He was then shot at by P-39s that had come to the rescue of their colleague. Realizing the hopelessness of his situation, Endō rammed the P-39 and died in action. Total number of aircraft shot down, fourteen (officially recognized).

PO1c Ichirōbei Yamazaki (Family of Ichirōbei Yamazaki)

PO1c Ichirōbei Yamazaki

Yamazaki was born in 1920 in the mountains near the village of Hinohara, Nishi Tama County, Tokyo Municipality. After entering the Yokosuka Naval Barracks in 1937, he graduated from the 54th Pilot Training Class in May 1941. In February 1942, Yamazaki was posted to the 4th Air Group and advanced to Rabaul after having served with the Ōita Air Group. In April, he was transferred to the Tainan Air Group. Until August, Yamazaki used Rabaul and Lae as bases and was active in the eastern New Guinea and Solomons battlefronts.

During the same period, the following incident occurred. After Yamazaki had pursued a Lockheed [Hudson] bomber by himself, his aircraft received hits and he had to make an emergency landing deep in the mountains [of New Guinea]. He was helped by the local natives, built a log raft, floated downstream and returned to base safely. In May, Yamazaki was wounded during air combat over Moresby. During the attack on Buna on 16 August, he was again hit and had to make an emergency landing. He was injured and returned to the homeland. In May of the following year, he was posted to Air Group 251 and again advanced to Rabaul. During an attack on Rendova Island on 4 July [1943], Yamazaki was killed in action. Total number of aircraft shot down, fourteen (officially recognized).

WO Mototsuna Yoshida

Born in Okayama Prefecture in 1918, Yoshida enlisted at the Kure Naval Barracks in June 1935. He served as a fireman on board the *Chōgei;* the following year he was transferred to maintenance work. In January 1939, Yoshida graduated from the 44th Pilot Training Class and became a fighter pilot. After being posted to the Ōita Air Group and then to the Ōmura Air Group, he was next posted to the 12th Air Group in September 1939 and served on the China battlefront. During the enemy bombing of Hankow on 14 October, Yoshida was wounded. Following his recovery, Yoshida moved to the South China area and participated in the attacks on Liuchow and Kweilin. In July 1940 Yoshida became an instructor with the Yokosuka Air Group. In February 1942, Yoshida was posted to the 4th Air Group Fighter Squadron stationed at Rabaul. On the 23rd, he single-handedly intercepted a B-17 over Rabaul and shot it down.

After Yoshida was wounded in March, he was away from air combat for a period of time. He was promoted to the rank of PO1c in April and posted to the Tainan Air Group. From May on, Yoshida served as number two (wingman) for LT Shirō Kawai and participated in a series of attacks on Moresby, achieving kills in almost every instance. During the attack on Tulagi on 7 August, Yoshida was lost in action during combat with American carrier fighters. He is believed to have died in action. It is recorded that during his Rabaul days, Yoshida's personal shoot-downs were twelve definite, one probable, and three joint.

Top, WO Mototsuna Yoshida (Saburō Saitō)

ENS Yukiharu Ozeki during his 12th Air Group days, at Anking. (Yasujirō Abe)

ENS Yukiharu Ozeki

Born in Aichi Prefecture in 1918, Ozeki enlisted at the Kure Naval Barracks in 1935. In January of the following year, he was selected for the 32nd Pilot Training Class and graduated in July; he was then posted to the Ōmura Air Group. In December 1937, he was attached to the 12th Air Group and set out for the central China battlefront. For a period of close to one year, until October of the following year, he was active as one of the youngest fighter pilots. He had his first taste of battle during the 25 March 1938 attack on Nanchang; PO3c Ozeki, at the tender age of twenty, engaged in a valiant air battle with a group of I-15s and I-16s, shooting down three enemy fighters.

Later he was successively posted to the Saeki, Ōmura, and the Genzan air groups; then, in September 1941 immediately before the Pacific War began, he was ordered attached to the 3rd Air Group. He participated in air combat in the Philippines and the Dutch East Indies. In particular, during the attack on Luzon on 10 December, Ozeki participated in the ferocious battles as one of the wingmen for LT Ichiro Mukai; jointly with Mukai, Ozeki shot down five aircraft.

In April 1942, he was promoted to PO1c and transferred to the newly organized 6th Air Group. In June, Ozeki was on board the aircraft carrier *Junyō* as a member of the Midway Island occupation forces and participated on the raids on Dutch Harbor. Upon cancellation of the operation, Ozeki returned to the homeland.

Toward the end of the same year, Ozeki advanced to the base at Buin, Solomons Islands, as a member of Air Group 204. He participated in the day in and day out air battles until May of the following year. Following his return to the homeland, Ozeki served with the Atsugi Air Group. In February 1944, he was transferred to Fighter Hikōtai 304, Air Group 203. After being assigned to air defense duties in the Kurile Islands and following activation of the Shō-gō operation, Ozeki was next transferred to southern Kyūshū in October. On the 21st, he was placed in command of the rear guard and moved on to Taiwan. Joining the main force, Ozeki moved to the base at Bamban [Luzon] in the Philippines. During the general offensive on the 24th, Ozeki headed out for an attack on an American task force but was intercepted by enemy fighter forces. As a result of the ensuing dogfights, Ozeki failed to return to base.

Total number of aircraft shot down, according to official figures, was over fourteen.

ENS Ozeki (Family of Ki-ichi Nagano)

ENS Masao Taniguchi (Masao Taniguchi)

ENS Masao Taniguchi

Born in Fukuoka Prefecture in 1919, Taniguchi enlisted in the navy in 1936 and graduated from the 51st Pilot Training Class in July 1940. In April of the following year, he was transferred aboard the *Akagi* where he greeted the beginning of hostilities. Taniguchi participated as a member of the fighter escort in the attacks on Hawaii, Darwin, and Colombo. During the attack on Trincomalee on 9 April 1942, Taniguchi recorded his first victory. He next participated in the Midway operation and was assigned to the combat air patrol over the aircraft carriers. Taniguchi was able to shoot down three incoming enemy torpedo planes, but the *Akagi* had been sunk in the meantime. Taniguchi ditched and was rescued by a destroyer. Following his return to the homeland, he was transferred on board the *Shōkaku* and participated in both the Second Battle of the Solomons [Battle of the Eastern Solomons, 24 August 1942] as well as the Battle of the South Pacific [Battle of Santa Cruz, 26 October 1942].

After his transfer to the Ōmura Air Group in November, he was moved to the newly organized Air Group 331 in July 1943. Advancing to Sabang [Sumatra], Taniguchi participated in the 5 December attack on Calcutta. During the same month, Taniguchi was ordered attached to Air Group 201 and moved to the heavy fighting area of Rabaul. During the course of approximately one month, until the end of the following January when the unit retreated from Truk, Taniguchi shot down eight aircraft (three probables) in air combat. Taniguchi also sortied and participated in intercepting the American carrier fighters that attacked Truk on 17 February [1944], as well as in intercept operations over Peleliu on 30 March. After retreating to the Philippines and while attempting to regroup on 23 October, Taniguchi was hit and severely wounded during air combat over Manila. He was forced to make an emergency landing and was sent back to the homeland with severe injuries. Taniguchi greeted the end of the war without ever being able to get up out of his sickbed. Total aircraft shot down, fourteen (officially recognized).

WO Ken-ichi Takahashi (Kenji Takahashi)

WO Ken-ichi Takahashi

Born in Nagano City in 1924, Takahashi entered the Otsu 13th Flight Reserve Enlisted Trainee Class in 1940; he completed the 26th Flight Training Course in March 1943. He was then successively posted to the Nagoya and Atsugi air groups, after which he was attached to Air Group 204 toward the end of September 1943. Takahashi was thus thrust into the furious battles going on in the Rabaul area. His first kill came during air combat over Rabaul on 24 October; he later participated in the continuing intercept and attack operations in the area. Upon the withdrawal of Air Group 204 to Truk at the end of January of the following year, Takahashi was transferred to Air Group 253. Following participation in intercept battles over Rabaul, Takahashi withdrew to Truk together with Air Group 253 directly after the heavy mid-February attack on that island had taken place.

During the "A"-gō operation on 19 June 1944, Takahashi started out from Truk under the command of LCDR Okamoto, heading for Guam. Minutes before landing, however, Takahashi was attacked by enemy fighters and just barely managed to land his plane. A few days later, Takahashi escaped to Truk using a land attack plane. He then traveled on board a submarine and finally reached the homeland.

In July he was transferred to Fighter Hikōtai 308 and posted to Air Group 221. In mid-October, in order to participate in the Shō-gō operation, he advanced to Clark Field in the Philippines, traveling via Taiwan. He participated in the attacks on Leyte as well as in intercept operations. During the same period, on occasion, Takahashi advanced to Jolo Island and engaged in the dawn attacks against Morotai Island.

Takahashi returned to the homeland in January 1945. He greeted the end of the war while performing education and training duties at the Tsukuba Air Group. Number of aircraft shot down, fourteen.

ENS Kiyoto Koga (Ikuhiko Hata)

ENS Kiyoto Koga

Koga is known throughout the Japanese navy as its first ace. Born in 1910 in Fukuoka Prefecture, he was first a newspaper delivery boy and then volunteered for the navy, enlisting at the Sasebo Naval Barracks in 1927. In May 1931, he graduated from the 16th Pilot Training Class and became a fighter pilot. After being assigned to the Ōmura and Yokosuka air groups, Koga was ordered attached to the 13th Air Group with the outbreak of the China Incident. In August 1937, he advanced to the base at Shanghai.

Koga's first combat encounter was during the first attack on Nanking carried out on 19 September; he shot down two Curtiss Hawks. During several raids on Nanking and Nanchang, Koga fought valiantly as a shōtai leader under LT Nangō. With the shoot-down of three aircraft over Nanking on 6 October, Koga's victories mounted to seven aircraft. During the course of around six air battles fought before 9 December, he shot down a total of thirteen aircraft. Upon the occasion of his return to the homeland, Koga was given a personal citation by the admiral commanding the China Area Fleet and was given a special promotion to flight warrant officer. During night air defense maneuvers carried out by the Yokosuka Air Group on 15 September of the following year, Koga was confused by the searchlights and crashed. He was severely wounded and died the next day, in the line of duty.

Koga was a hardworking person but did not project himself very much under normal circumstances. At the same time, he possessed a vigorous spirit for combat and considerable courage. Koga was indeed an Isamu Kondo ("the swordsman") kind of ace who had matured by actual combat experience.

LTJG Watari Handa during his *Kaga* days, 1937.
(Family of Kiyonobu Suzuki)

LTJG Watari Handa

Handa, together with Toshio Kuroiwa, was an ace representing the era of single-aircraft combat battles [dogfights]. Born in Fukuoka Prefecture in 1911, Handa entered the navy in 1928 and served on ships for a period of five years. In March 1933, he graduated from the 19th Pilot Training Class and was assigned to the aircraft carrier *Ryūjō,* then to the Ōmura and Yokosuka air groups. After that, with the outbreak of the China Incident, Handa was ordered on board the aircraft carrier *Kaga* in August 1937. He advanced to the warfront at Shanghai. At the time he was a twenty-six-year-old PO1c. Koga's first victory was achieved on 7 September when he flew as number two (wingman) for LT Chikamasa Igarashi in a three-aircraft formation that was supporting a carrier attack unit. Over Tahu there was a battle with seven Curtiss Hawks; Handa shot down one of them.

During the 20 September air raid on Nanking, Handa shot down another three aircraft. In June 1938 he was transferred to the 15th Air Group and participated in air battles over Nanchang. Before his return to the homeland in November, he had shot down six aircraft. In November 1940, he was promoted to warrant officer and released to inactive duty. However, he was remobilized on the same day. In February 1942, after the war had broken out, he was transferred to the Tainan Air Group. Handa took full advantage of his experience and expertise and showed proof in air operations in the Dutch East Indies, Rabaul, and New Guinea. A case of consumption [tuberculosis] worsened, however, and he was returned to the homeland at the end of the same year. After struggling with this disease for six years, in 1948 Handa died of illness acquired in the line of duty.

Total number of aircraft shot down, thirteen (officially recognized).

LTJG Akira Yamamoto (Masami Ōtomo)

LTJG Akira Yamamoto

Born in 1913 in Shizuoka Prefecture, Yamamoto graduated from the 24th Pilot Training Class in July 1934 and became a fighter pilot.

After serving with the Tateyama and Ominato air groups, he was ordered to serve on board the *Hōshō*. Upon the outbreak of the China Incident he was sent to central and southern China. On 27 September 1937, while serving as number two for LT Hanamoto on an air raid on Canton, Yamamoto discovered two Curtiss Hawks. He challenged them single-handedly and shot down the enemy number two wingman's plane. This was Yamamoto's first victory. In December he returned to the mainland and was transferred to the Kasumigaura Air Group. In October 1939 he was ordered attached to the 12th Air Group and participated in the China battlefront until July of the following year.

Next, he served as an instructor at the Ōita Air Group. Immediately before the start of hostilities, Yamamoto was ordered on board the *Kaga*. During the attack on Pearl Harbor, Yamamoto served as leader of the 4th Shōtai in the first wave fighter escort. Immediately before arriving in the target area, PO1c Yamamoto discovered a civilian sightseeing plane enjoying a leisurely Sunday morning cruise. With one burst of gunfire, Yamamoto shot down the aircraft; this was the very first aerial victory of the Pacific War.

He next moved in to strafe Hickam Field; Yamamoto by himself burned six aircraft on the ground. During the Battle of Midway, Yamamoto was assigned to combat air patrol over his carrier. Intercepting an attacking force of enemy dive-bombers and torpedo planes, Yamamoto and his shōtai jointly accounted for five aircraft. However, since the *Kaga* had received bomb hits, Yamamoto landed on the carrier *Hiryū*. He next supported the Tomonoga carrier attack squadron, which took off to torpedo the American aircraft carrier *Yorktown*. After a furious engagement with enemy fighters, Yamamoto was able to shoot down four of them.

In July, Yamamoto was transferred on board the *Zuihō* and participated in the Battle of Santa Cruz on 26 October. Promoted to warrant officer, he was next dispatched to the base at Rabaul in March and April 1943. While providing air cover for ship

Yamamoto during his Yokosuka Air Group days, 1944. (Ryōji Ōhara)

convoys as well as participating in attacks on Port Moresby, Buna, Oro Bay, and Guadalcanal, Yamamoto shot down a total of four additional aircraft. In May, he was transferred to the Yokosuka Air Group. In June 1944, he participated in the air battles over Iwo Jima; he was wounded by gunfire from a ship but recovered a short while later. When the first homeland bombing attack by B-29s was carried out on 24 November, Yamamoto was among those who intercepted the incoming force over Yachimata. Though his aircraft was hit he managed to extricate himself; however, his parachute failed to open and Yamamoto plunged to his death.

Warm and sincere, Yamamoto was a veteran pilot who was modest enough to always volunteer to be the rear guard in any major air battle. Total number of aircraft shot down, counting only the available official records, thirteen.

ENS Momoto Matsumura during his 12th Air Group days (Mitsunori Nakajima)

ENS Momoto Matsumura

Born in Yamaguchi Prefecture in 1915, Matsumura enlisted in the navy in 1934 as a maintenance man. He graduated from the 29th Pilot Training Class in November 1935 and became a fighter pilot. When the China Incident broke out, Matsumura was ordered to the 12th Air Group and advanced to Shanghai. In December, he was transferred to the 13th Air Group; however, by March of the following year he had been transferred back to the 12th Air Group for the second time. Matsumura sortied on a number of air battles over the mainland of China.

During his first taste of battle on 25 February in the attack on Nanchang, Matsumura was serving as number three wingman in PO1c Tomokichi Arai's unit. During a heavy dogfight, Matsumura had the distinction of single-handedly shooting down seven aircraft (three probable). Again, on 31 May during an air battle over Hankow while attached to the Yoshitomi Chūtai, Matsumura engaged in a wild dogfight with a large force of enemy fighters and shot down three of the enemy.

In January 1939, Matsumura was transferred on board the *Akagi;* he later served as

Matsumura (*center*) during his 12th Air Group days, with his buddies (Mitsunori Nakajima)

an instructor with the Iwakuni and Ōita air groups. In July 1942, he was attached to the 6th Air Group and, starting the latter part of August, advanced by air to Rabaul, staging from island to island. In April of the following year, he was promoted to WO and returned to the homeland. During the same period, Matsumura participated in attacks on Guadalcanal, as well as in intercept operations over Buin and Munda. He then served as an instructor with the Iwakuni, Suzuka, and Kōnoike air groups. In August 1944, Matsumura was transferred to the Fighter Hikōtai 161, Air Group 601. In October, in order to participate in the Shō-gō operation, the unit sortied from the western end of the Inland Sea. On the two days of the 24th and the 25th of the battle off the Philippines, Matsumura flew combat air patrol over his aircraft carrier. Since the aircraft carrier *Zuikaku* had been sunk, he had to ditch; he was picked up by the destroyer *Hatsuzuki*. During the night of the 25th, the *Hatsuzuki* was surrounded by American ships and sank. LT Hōhei Kobayashi, the group leader, WO Matsumura, and others were lost in action and are deemed to have died in the line of duty.

Total number of aircraft shot down, thirteen (officially recognized).

LTJG Gitarō Miyazaki during his Tainan Air Group days, February 1942. (Hideki Shingō)

LTJG Gitarō Miyazaki

Born in 1917 in Kōchi Prefecture, Miyazaki entered the Otsu 4th Flight Reserve Enlisted Trainee Class in 1933; he completed a flight training course in May 1937. He was next assigned to the Saeki Air Group after which he went on to the Takao Air Group. In September 1938, Miyazaki was transferred to the 12th Air Group and participated in the central China battlefront.

However, at the time almost no trace of any enemy activity could be observed. Miyazaki's first victory was achieved on 5 October during the attack on Hankow, when he was able to corner and shoot down one of the few remaining I-16s.

In June 1939, Miyazaki was transferred to the Yokosuka Air Group; after serving

Miyazaki during his 12th Air Group days (*left*), with Mitsugu Mori (*right*). (Katsuhiro Hashimoto)

with the Takao Air Group, he was reassigned to the 12th Air Group for the second time in April 1941. He advanced to the base at Hankow but there were no notable air battles to speak of. During an attack on Chengtu on 11 August, Miyazaki did shoot down one aircraft.

Promoted to WO in October 1941, Miyazaki was next attached to the Tainan Air Group. On the first day of the war, Miyazaki shot down one aircraft during the attack on Luzon. He was then promoted to shōtai leader and participated in air combat in the Philippines and Dutch East Indies. In April 1942, he advanced to Rabaul and Lae and fought valiantly. On 1 June, despite his own illness, Miyazaki participated in the attack on Port Moresby. Miyazaki's aircraft was set on fire by one of the enemy fighters that made a surprise attack on the attacking planes. A midair explosion ensued, and Miyazaki was killed in action.

From his earlier assignment to the 12th Air Group, Miyazaki was always close to Saburō Sakai, almost as if he were Sakai's shadow. Their first victories were recorded at the same time and Miyazaki was to die in direct view of Sakai. Although slim in stature, Miyazaki held the second rank in jūdō and was the strongest arm wrestler (Indian style) in the entire Tainan Air Group. After his death in action, Miyazaki was honored by mention in an All Units Bulletin; he was further honored with a posthumous two-grade promotion and advanced to Special Service Flight LTJG. Number of air battles participated in, thirty-seven. Miyazaki's shōtai is officially recognized as having shot down forty-four aircraft, set six planes on fire, and destroyed thirty other aircraft.

ENS Sahei Yamashita during his Tainan Air Group days, 1942. (Shin-ichi Hirabayashi)

ENS Sahei Yamashita

Born in Shizuoka Prefecture in 1918, Yamashita entered the navy in 1934 as a member of the Otsu 5th Flight Reserve Enlisted Training Class; he also completed a flight training course. Along with PO1c Yoshino, a classmate, Yamashita was next attached to the Chitose Air Group in October 1940. When the war broke out, Yamashita was in the Marshall Islands, assigned to air defense operations in the Micronesia area.

Promoted to warrant officer in April 1942, Yamashita was then dispatched to Rabaul. Towards the end of May, he was formally transferred to the Tainan Air Group and advanced to the base at Lae. His first experience of battle was during the 27 May raid on Moresby; jointly with the shōtai he was assigned to, Yamashita shot down a P-39. Later, WO Yamashita continued to increase his score of kills while in the eastern New Guinea battleground. In August after the American forces had landed on Guadalcanal, he participated in the raids on the island and continued to build up his score of kills. When the Tainan Air Group was withdrawn to the homeland in the early part of November, Yamashita was transferred back to Air Group 201 (the former Chitose Air Group Fighter Squadron) and assigned to the Micronesia area air defense operations. On 9 February 1943, Yamashita and four of his colleagues intercepted a B-17 that had come to reconnoiter over Nauru Island and shot it down. After the kill, however, Yamashita lost his way about 150 miles north of the island; he is deemed to have been killed in action. A personal tally of thirteen enemy aircraft is officially recognized.

WO Toshio Kuro-iwa during his 12th Air Group days, 1938. (Yoshio Shiga)

WO Toshio Kuro-iwa

Together with LT Nokiji Ikuta, Kuro-iwa is famous as one part of the duo that shot down the American volunteer flyer Short. Born in Fukuoka Prefecture in 1908, Kuro-iwa enlisted in the navy in 1926. He is one of the earliest fighter pilots who graduated in December 1928 with the 13th Pilot Training Class. At the outbreak of the first Shanghai Incident in January 1932, Kuro-iwa boarded the aircraft carrier *Kaga*, advanced to Shanghai and served as number two wingman for LT Ikuta. On 22 February, Kuro-iwa flew in support of three carrier attack planes under the command of LT Kotani. Taking off on his own, Kuro-iwa engaged in battle with the Boeing P-12 piloted by Short, which had attacked the Kotani unit. Short's aircraft was attacked from the rear by a fighter piloted by Ikuta; at the same time, the aircraft flown by PO3c Kuro-iwa came in close under the rear of the enemy plane. Both planes fired their guns and the P-12 was shot down. ADM Nomura of the Third Fleet issued commendations on the occasion. This battle result is officially recognized as the first aerial victory by the Japanese air forces.

In the spring of 1938 during the China Incident, Kuro-iwa was attached to the 12th Air Group. He exhibited his daredevil skill during a three-month period of action in the central China battlefront when he shot down thirteen aircraft. He left the service the following year and entered the reserves. Entering the Dai Nippon Kōkū ("Greater Japan Airlines") firm, Kuro-iwa was engaged in air transport operations. On 26 August 1944, however, he was lost off the Malay Peninsula and is deemed to have died in the line of duty. Kuro-iwa was known as an expert in single air combat and had the reputation of being a rather eccentric fighter pilot, both daring and uninhibited.

LTJG Hideo Maeda during his 12th Air Group days (Akimasa Igarashi)

LTJG Hideo Maeda

Born in Mie Prefecture in 1920, Maeda responded to a call for students for the Kō 1st Flight Reserve Enlisted Trainee Class in September 1937 and was accepted. After being trained at the Yokosuka and Kasumigaura air groups, he completed a flight training course in June 1939 and was promoted to PO3c. After being assigned to the Ōita and Ōmura air groups, Maeda was next posted to the 12th Air Group in January 1940. Although he did participate in the war on the central China battlefront, his duties were primarily restricted to air defense of key areas and cooperative efforts in support of naval ground forces.

In November, he returned to the Yatabe Air Group as an instructor; after the war broke out, he was posted on board the *Kasuga Maru*. After being assigned to the Ōmura Air Group, Maeda was promoted to warrant officer in April 1943. In October, he was transferred to Air Group 204 and advanced to Rabaul.

Toward the end of January 1944, for a period of three months until his unit was withdrawn to Truk Island for replenishment, Maeda was engaged in the almost daily intercept operations. He also participated in the drives on Cape Marcus and Cape Torokina. When American carrier aircraft raided Truk on 17 February, Air Group 204 mobilized thirty-one aircraft to intercept them. They were crushed by the superior, wave-type attacks employed by the American forces, however, and lost eighteen aircraft. WO Maeda himself, after shooting down two enemy planes, was among those pilots who failed to return to base. Although his battle experience was a short period that did not even reach six months in duration, Maeda was a pilot with a mature personality; both his combat spirit and technical skills were well honed. His death was felt as a loss. Maeda was mentioned in an All Units Bulletin and also given a special two-grade promotion by the admiral of the Combined Fleet. Officially recognized number of personal shootdowns, thirteen aircraft.

PO3c Hiroshi Shibagaki during his trainee days (Family of Ki-ichi Nagano)

ENS Masa-ichi Kondō during his *Junyō* days, January 1943. (Wataru Nakamichi)

PO3c Hiroshi Shibagaki

Born in Niigata Prefecture in 1924, Shibagaki enlisted in the navy in May 1942 at the age of eighteen. As a member of the Hei 12th Flight Reserve Enlisted Trainee Class, he entered the Iwakuni Air Group in August. After finishing the 28th Flight Training Course, he graduated in July 1943. In the fall of the same year, Shibagaki was assigned to Air Group 201 and advanced to Rabaul.

Shibagaki's first shoot-down was during an intercept operation on 7 November. The following January he was transferred to Air Group 204 and participated in the daily intercept operations around Rabaul. During a period of more than two months, until 22 January [1944] when he was killed in action, Shibagaki exhibited outstanding battle results; he shot down thirteen aircraft (officially recognized).

ENS Masa-ichi Kondō

Born in 1917 in Ehime Prefecture, Kondō graduated from the 27th Pilot Training Class in July 1935 and was posted to the Ōmura Air Group. In November 1936, while on board the aircraft carrier *Ryūjō*, he greeted the outbreak of the China Incident. On 23 August, the *Ryūjō* was off Shanghai; PO1c Kondō was serving as number two wingman for LTJG Minoru Suzuki. While on patrol over Paoshan, nine enemy fighters were encountered and a bitter air battle ensued. Without any loss on our side, ten aircraft were downed. Kondō celebrated his first experience of combat by shooting down two of the ten planes. Kondō continued to be favored by the gods of war. He participated in the attack on Canton on 21 September; after his transfer to the *Kaga* the following year he continued to participate in attacks on Canton. In June he was transferred to the 15th Air Group and in November returned to the homeland. In October 1939, he was transferred to the 12th Air Group; he next participated in the 30 December attack on Liuchow as well as the attack on Kweilin on 10 January of the following year. In all of these operations Kondō showed battle successes.

Once the Pacific War started, in July 1942 he was ordered on board the *Zuihō;* on 26 October he participated in the Battle of Santa Cruz. Nine aircraft from the *Zuihō* carrier fighter squadron (commanding, LT Saneyasu Hidaka) were used for escorting the first attack wave on its way to attack American carriers. In the sky our planes passed American torpedo planes and their fighter escorts that had come from the *Enterprise* and were on their way to attack Japanese aircraft carriers. LT Hidaka decided independently to leave the attack group and challenge the American aircraft to a fight. In a matter of minutes, six enemy fighters and eight torpedo planes were shot down and demolished. PO1 Kondō himself flamed three of the enemy aircraft. At the same time, however, during this air battle, the Hidaka unit lost its bearings and each shōtai was left to find its own way back. Four aircraft, including that flown by LTJG Utsumi, failed to return.

In November, Kondō was transfered to the *Junyō* and participated in the third Battle of the Solomons [the Naval Battle of Guadalcanal]; he was engaged in supporting transports destined for Wewak, in the Guadalcanal evacuation operation, and in the "I"-gō operation. In May 1943, Kondō returned to the homeland to participate in the effort to relieve Attu Island. On 2 July, the *Junyō* fighter squadron was ordered to proceed to Buin and was thrust into the offensive and defensive operations around Rendova [central Solomons]. On 15 August, Kondō sortied in support of carrier bombers en route to attack Vella Lavella. After he had shot down one aircraft, Kondō was severely wounded in his left leg; he had to maneuver his plane using his right leg only. He managed to return to Buin and was hospitalized. Kondō was sent back to the homeland and entered a hospital for treatment for a period of one year and three months. He then returned to Air Group 203. Kondō greeted the end of the war without any further combat action. Kondō was not a showy fighter pilot but a tenacious person possessing excellent skills. Total number of aircraft shot down, thirteen.

ENS Kondō (Masa-ichi Kondō)

ENS Shigetaka Ōmori (Family of Shigetaka Ōmori)

ENS Shigetaka Ōmori

Born in 1916 in Yamanashi Prefecture, Ōmori enlisted in the navy in May 1933; he was graduated from the 33rd Pilot Training Class in September 1936 and became a fighter pilot. In February 1938, he was posted to the 13th Air Group and participated in the central China battlefront. After scoring his first victory on 25 February during the attack on Nanchang, he was transferred in March to the 12th Air Group and was active in central China air battles until December.

Ōmori was later successively posted to the *Akagi,* then to the Tsukuba, and Ōminato air groups. He greeted the outbreak of the Pacific War on board the *Hōshō.* In May 1942, Ōmori was transferred on board the *Akagi.* In June, during the Battle of Midway, Ōmori served as shōtai leader in the *Akagi* fighter chūtai led by LT Shirane. While escorting the first attack wave headed for Mi (Midway) Island, Ōmori battled with intercepting American fighters and shot down two F4Fs. Following his return to the aircraft carrier, and without any time to rest, Ōmori again took off for combat air patrol over the carrier. Intercepting enemy torpedo planes that came attacking the carrier, Ōmori and his colleagues jointly shot down six aircraft in daring fashion. However, Ōmori's aircraft received fourteen hits; in addition, the *Akagi* had started burning, so Ōmori landed on the *Hiryū.* During the afternoon of the same day, PO1c Ōmori took off from the *Hiryū* and helped protect the carrier. Even the aircraft carrier *Hiryū,* the last carrier available, received hits and started burning. At seven o'clock in the evening, flying until his fuel was exhausted, Ōmori and LT Shirane ditched near the light cruiser *Nagara.* Both pilots were rescued.

After return to the homeland, Ōmori was transferred to the *Shōkaku.* On 26 October, he was assigned to combat air patrol during the Battle of Santa Cruz. As shōtai leader, PO1c Ōmori intercepted oncoming enemy dive-bombers and shot down five. After this, Ōmori discovered that one enemy aircraft was on the verge of dropping a bomb on the *Shōkaku.* Sensing that there was not a moment to spare, Ōmori rammed his aircraft into the enemy aircraft, thus protecting the aircraft carrier from its danger. Ōmori died with tragic bravery. Because of his sacrificial effort, he was

Ōmori during his 12th Air Group days (Family of Shigetaka Ōmori)

mentioned in an All Units Bulletin and given the honor of being promoted two grades to the rank of Special Service Flight Ensign. ENS Ōmori seldom spoke, was of small stature, and had a kind and conservative character. At the same time, he was filled with a fierce spirit for combat; he was a youthful pilot, well liked by both his superiors and his subordinates.

LTJG Matsuo Hagiri (Matsuo Hagiri)

LTJG Matsuo Hagiri

Known as "Mustachio Hagiri," Hagiri had a head for details and spent a long time with the Yokosuka Air Group in the testing of new aircraft and weapons. Hagiri's actual combat time was comparatively brief. Possessor of a strong physical body, at one time he underwent a special examination of his heart after recording 9.5 Gs in a diving experiment, which broke all previous records.

Born in Shizuoka Prefecture in 1913, Hagiri started out as a fireman but then transferred to aviation. After graduating from the 28th Pilot Trainee Class in August 1935, he was posted to the Yokosuka Air Group. In August 1940, he was ordered attached to the 12th Air Group. Transporting a new Zero fighter by air to Hankow, Hagiri participated in the first sortie by a Zero fighter unit, which took place on 19 August. Chungking was the target of the raid, but no enemy were sighted. During the 4 October attack on Chengtu, after the shoot-down of one aircraft, the following stunt was pulled by some fighter pilots, including Hagiri. Higashiyama, Ōishi, Nakase, and Hagiri landed their planes on the Taipingsze airfield and set the airfield on

Hagiri during his *Sōryū* days, with his favorite aircraft. (Matsuo Hagiri)

fire. The four then took off from the field. Later, Hagiri single-handedly made a surprise attack on three enemy fighters in formation and shot down two of them.

During the attack on Chengtu the following March, Hagiri shot down three Improved I-15 fighters. Returning to the homeland the next summer, he was promoted to warrant officer and ordered to the Yokosuka Air Group. In July 1943, however, Hagiri was transferred to Air Group 204 and participated in the Solomons battlefront.

tlefront. Two months later, on 24 September, Hagiri shot down two aircraft in an encounter over Buin but was then severely wounded; he was returned to the homeland. Until the end of the war, Hagiri was assigned to the operational testing of equipment and to air defense duties at the Yokosuka Air Group. During an intercept operation against B-29s in April 1945, Hagiri was again wounded. Total number of aircraft shot down, thirteen.

LT Fujikazu Koizumi (Katsutarō Kobayashi)

LT Fujikazu Koizumi

Born in Fukui Prefecture in 1916, Koizumi entered the Yokosuka Air Group in June 1931 as a member of the Otsu 2nd Flight Reserve Enlisted Trainee Class; he also graduated from a Flight Training Course in April 1935. He was then successively posted to the Saeki and Kasumigaura air groups and then wound up back with the Saeki Air Group. While at the last named post, Koizumi greeted the outbreak of the China Incident.

The same month, Koizumi was assigned to the 12th Air Group and participated in the central China battlefront. At first, air defense and air support for naval ground forces were the primary areas of operations in the Shanghai area. There were few opportunities for aerial engagement. During the attack on Nanchang on 25 February 1938, PO2c Koizumi sortied in the capacity of a shōtai leader. In his first air combat, he battled with some forty Soviet-built I-15s and I-16s and shot down two of them. In April, he was sent back to the Ōmura Air Group; then, in December, transferred to serve on board the *Ryūjō*. He was next assigned to the Ōita Air Group and then to the Hyakurigahara Air Group. In September 1941, Koizumi was attached to the newly organized 3rd Air Group and greeted the opening of hostilities between Japan and the United States in that post.

On 8 December, WO Koizumi participated as leader of a shōtai in the first air attack on Luzon. During the second attack carried out on the 10th, Koizumi and his colleagues fought a pitched battle with the enemy over Clark [Field]. They shot down seven aircraft (one probable) of the opposition. Later on, Koizumi participated in air battles over the Dutch East Indies, in the attacks on Darwin and Wyndham [Australia], as well as in other operations. During the month of September, the main force of the unit was temporarily dispatched to the southeast area, but ENS Koizumi remained behind with the caretaker unit. He was assigned air defense duties in northern Australia. In the spring of 1943, Air Group 202 resumed its attacks on Darwin; on a number of occasions, the unit was able to overwhelm the Spitfire aircraft that rose to intercept them.

In May, ENS Koizumi returned to the homeland for the first time in a year and a half and was posted to the Tokushima Air Group. Immediately upon promotion to LTJG in November, Koizumi was ordered to serve as division officer on the *Hiyō*. On 25 January 1944, in response to the threatening situation in the southeast area, Koizumi joined the 2nd Carrier Division and advanced to Rabaul.

When LTJG Koizumi sortied to engage in air combat over Rabaul on the 27th, it was the first air battle he had fought in the area; in the ensuing confusion Koizumi lost his way. He is deemed to have been killed in action.

Total number of aircraft shot down, thirteen.

ENS Isamu Miyazaki (Ryōji Ōhara)

ENS Isamu Miyazaki

Born in Kagawa Prefecture in 1919, Miyazaki enlisted in the navy in 1936. After serving for four and a half years with the fleet, he volunteered to become a pilot and was graduated from the Hei 2nd Flight Training Course in November 1941. He was then assigned to the Yokosuka Air Group; in October of the following year, Miyazaki was transferred to Air Group 252 and on 9 November advanced to Rabaul. Flying one of the Zeros that accompanied group leader LT Suganami on the 12th, Miyazaki escorted a land attack plane unit that made a daytime torpedo attack against an enemy convoy riding at anchor off Guadalcanal. Miyazaki gained his first taste of battle when he used up all of his ammunition in the destruction of one F4F aircraft. For a period of about four months until February 1943, when Air Group 252 moved to the Marshall Islands for air defense operations, Miyazaki participated in the fierce air battles that occurred over the Solomons and New Guinea.

When Wake Island was attacked by American carrier aircraft on 6 October 1943, Miyazaki escorted Type 1 land attack planes that were destined to replenish forces on the island. Miyazaki took off from Maloelap Atoll but en route to his destination became involved in battle with a force of F6Fs. After the dogfights ended, Miyazaki landed his aircraft on Wake Island, alone; he returned to base the following day, hitching a ride on a land attack plane. From the end of November through the end of the following January, Miyazaki engaged in intercept operations against B-24s that raided Maloelap Atoll. In February, he returned to the homeland. In January 1945, Miyazaki was transferred to the newly formed Fighter Hikōtai 301, Air Group 343; he greeted the end of hostilities while engaged in air defense operations over western Japan. Total number of aircraft shot down, thirteen.

PO3c Keisaku Yoshimura (Kiku-ichi Inano)

PO3c Keisaku Yoshimura

Born in Niigata Prefecture in 1922, Yoshimura enlisted in the navy in 1939 at the age of seventeen. In July 1941, he graduated from the 56th Pilot Training Class and was attached to the 1st Air Group. In October, he was transferred to the Tainan Air Group to undergo further training on Taiwan. As of 1 December, Yoshimura was dispatched to southern French Indochina as part of the fighter squadron attached to the 22nd Air Flotilla Headquarters. He then participated in Malayan and Dutch East Indies area operations; at the end of May, Yoshimura returned to his main unit at Rabaul.

Sea1c Yoshimura next advanced to Lae and was assigned as number three wingman in the 3rd Shōtai, Kawai Chūtai. On 16 June, he participated in a raid on Moresby; in the aerial combat against more than twenty P-39s, he shot down two enemy aircraft. Following his return to base, Yoshimura next chased after a P-39 that had come raiding over Lae and shot it down.

During the attack on Tulagi on 7 August, Yoshimura acted as a wingman for the group leader, LCDR Nakajima, and engaged in a pitched battle with F4Fs. By himself, Yoshimura flamed five enemy aircraft (including two probables). When PO3c Yoshimura joined in the attack on Guadalcanal on 25 October, however, he was involved in battle with more than ten F4Fs. Yoshimura received hits and his aircraft caught on fire; he heroically crashed his own airplane. At the time he was only twenty years of age and in his prime. During the period of less than half a year that he spent at Rabaul, Yoshimura's personal score totaled nine aircraft destroyed, four probables, and one shared kill. All of the downed aircraft were fighters.

ENS Kan-ichi Kashimura during his Yokosuka Air Group days, November 1938. (Shigema Yoshitomi)

ENS Kan-ichi Kashimura

Well known as the ace "Kashimura, who returned on one wing," Kashimura was born in 1913 in Kagawa Prefecture and entered the navy following his graduation from Marugame High School. In July 1934 he graduated from the 24th Pilot Training Class and was successively posted to the Ōmura, Yokosuka, and Kanoya air groups. In October 1937 he was transferred to the 13th Air Group and participated in the central China battlefront. His first combat experience occurred when he was attached to the Nangō unit on a raid on Nanking on 22 November; he shot down two aircraft. During the attack on Nanchang on 9 December, he battled with a large number of Curtiss Hawks. After shooting down one enemy aircraft, Kashimura's aircraft collided with another aircraft that had come in during a head-on attack, and his own aircraft started falling. However, Kashimura was able to right his plane just before it touched ground. He then proceeded to pilot his aircraft in a calm but adroit fashion, taking corrective balancing action to compensate for the almost two-thirds of his plane's left wing that had been

sheared off. He was able to return to base. Even landing at his base was difficult; he tried four different times before finally making it. Immediately upon touching ground, Kashimura's aircraft somersaulted and the tail of the plane was sheared off. Kashimura himself did not receive even a scratch during the entire ordeal. This miraculous return of the pilot alive was widely written up in newspapers. Navy minister Yonai sent to Kashimura the following words inscribed with a brush on a photo of the Kashimura aircraft as it was being flown with only one wing: "Shidai Shigen, Shigen Shimyo" ("Enormous responsibilities, enormous strength; enormous masterly techniques, masterful adroitness").

After this and with a score of eight aircraft to his credit, Kashimura was transferred back to the Yokosuka Air Group in

Kashimura's "Renowned One-Wing" aircraft, just before it touched ground upon returning to base. (Family of Isamu Mochizuki)

March 1938. From the end of 1939, for a period of three months, he was posted to the 12th Air Group and paticipated in the attacks on Liuchow and Kweilin. He then returned to the Yokosuka Air Group again. In December 1942, he was posted to Air Group 582 and participated in the Battle of the Solomons. On 6 March 1943, Kashi-

mura failed to return following an air battle over the Russell Islands. He is deemed to have been killed in action.

Kashimura was an expert in dogfights, brimming with combative spirit. On the other hand, he was also a theoretician concerning air combat education and had a major impact on the pilots who followed him.

ENS Takeo Kanamaru during his Tsukuba Air Group days (Takeo Kanamaru)

ENS Takeo Kanamaru

Born in Yamanashi Prefecture in 1920, Kanamaru enlisted in the navy and was graduated from the 44th Pilot Training Class in January 1939. In August, he was posted to the 12th Air Group and proceeded to central China but had no opportunity for air combat. Later he was transferred on board the *Akagi,* then to the Ominato and Ōita air groups. In June 1943,

he was posted to Air Group 202 and went to the northern Australia battlefront. Kanamaru experienced his first combat on 30 June, when as number two wingman for LCDR Suzuki, he escorted a land attack plane unit that raided Brocks Creek. Fighting with the Spitfires that rose to intercept them, Kanamaru achieved his first aerial victory. Next he participated in the repeat raids carried out on 6 and 7 September, as well as in the long-distance attack on Merauke [New Guinea] carried out on 9 September. In December, together with about twenty other pilots, Kanamaru was transferred to Air Group 204 at Rabaul and participated in the ongoing daily intercept operations that were being conducted. On 7 January [1944], Kanamaru was severely wounded after he had shot down three enemy aircraft and was forced to make an emergency landing. During the one-month period preceding this emergency landing, Kanamaru shot down twelve aircraft (two probables). He returned to the homeland in a hospital ship and was hospitalized for half a year. After recovering from his wounds, Kanamaru was posted to the Tsukuba Air Group; he greeted the end of the war at Naruo airfield. Number of aircraft personally shot down, twelve (officially recognized).

PO1c Kiyoshi Shimizu during his trainee days (Family of Susumu Ishihara)

WO Tetsuo Kikuchi during his *Shōkaku* days, 1942. (Izumi Sanada)

PO1c Kiyoshi Shimizu

Born in Kyoto City in 1919, Shimizu enlisted in the navy in 1940 and served as a maintenance man in the China battlefront. He then switched to aviation and was graduated from the 24th Flight Training Course. Posted to Air Group 253, Shimizu was next active in the southeast area of operations. In November [1943], he was transferred to Air Group 204. With the withdrawal from Truk of Air Group 204 on 25 January [1944], Shimizu was posted once again to Air Group 253. He was killed in action the following day, during an intercept operation.

Shimizu's air combat life was a matter of a few months spent at Rabaul. He appeared to project irresistable force, however; in a mere twenty some days following his first shoot-down of an enemy plane on 4 January 1944, he flamed twelve enemy aircraft (officially recognized). Shimizu was to fall as the cherry blossoms fall.

WO Tetsuo Kikuchi

Born in Iwate Prefecture in 1916, Kikuchi enlisted in the navy in 1934 and initially served as a maintenance man. In January 1938 he graduated from the 39th Pilot Training Class and became a fighter pilot. In May of the following year, he was posted to the 14th Air Group and participated in the southern China battlefront; there was no opportunity for air combat. In April 1939, he returned to the Kasumigaura Air Group as an instructor and was next posted to the Yatabe Air Group. In September 1941, he was promoted to PO1c and ordered to the *Akagi*. Although he participated in the attack on Hawaii, his duties were confined to patrol operations over the carrier. Next, in April 1942, Kikuchi participated in Indian Ocean operations; during the attack on Colombo on the 5th, Kikuchi served as number two wingman for the group leader, LCDR Itaya. Kikuchi engaged in fierce battle with Royal Air Force fighters and although this was his first taste of air combat as such, he personally shot down five aircraft (two probables).

Kikuchi next participated in the Midway operation in June, flying as number two wingman for LT Shirane, and was part of the first wave fighter escort that was sent out. During air combat over Midway Island, he shot down four aircraft (two probables). After returning to his carrier, Kikuchi engaged in air patrol duties directly over the carrier. Battling with raiding American forces, Kikuchi flamed three aircraft, jointly with others. Since the aircraft carrier *Akagi* had been sunk, Kikuchi was accommodated in the *Hiryū*. During the afternoon, however, the *Hiryū* was also set on fire; Kikuchi was trapped inside the ship. He was able to make his escape and was rescued. Following his return to the homeland, he was transferred to the *Shōkaku*. With the commencement of offensive/defensive operations around Guadalcanal in August, Kikuchi moved out to the southeast area of operations and participated in the Second Battle of the Solomons [Battle of the Eastern Solomons]. For about one week starting the end of August, Kikuchi was dispatched to Buka Island and sortied on a number of attacks on Guadalcanal.

Promoted to CPO in November, Kikuchi was next transferred to serve as an instructor with the Tsuiki Air Group. In September 1943, he was reassigned to carrier duty and served on board the *Ryūhō, Hiyō,* and *Junyō.* From the end of December for one week, Kikuchi was dispatched to the Kavieng Base [New Ireland]. On 25 January 1944, he advanced to Rabaul and until his withdrawal from the island on 19 February, participated in the daily intercept battles. In March, he was posted to Air Group 652 (*Ryūhō*) and sortied during the "A"-gō operation in June. On the 19th, Kikuchi took off on an attack on enemy carrier forces as a shōtai leader in the second wave fighter escort. The enemy carrier force could not be sighted; immediately before their landing on Guam, Kikuchi's unit was attacked by a force of enemy fighters. The Zero fighter unit that had done its utmost in protecting the carrier bomber unit was now caught operating from a disadvantageous position. While reacting to the enemy fighter force, one plane after another of the unit was shot down; the unit met a tragic end.

Although CPO Kikuchi managed to shoot down two enemy planes, he became utterly exhausted and committed suicide by diving his plane into the sea. Kikuchi was robust, weighing more than 165 pounds, and required the assistance of ground crewmen in climbing into his fighter. At the same time, his maneuvering in the air was quite nimble and he established a reputation for clever air combat techniques. Kikuchi was the heroic and self-appointed "boss" of all the petty officers on board his carrier. He conscientiously involved himself in the training of others. As a matter of fact, he was of such a unique character that on several occasions he declined unofficial notifications of being promoted to warrant officer (WO) because of his affection for the petty officers around him. Although the only remaining official records of his record in shooting down aircraft indicate twelve (seven joint and probables), it is estimated that the total number would reach twenty.

LCDR Sada-o Yamaguchi during his Yokosuka Air Group days, 1944. (Masami Ōtomo)

LCDR Sada-o Yamaguchi

Born in Hiroshima Prefecture in 1919, Yamaguchi graduated with the 67th Naval Academy class in July 1939. In November 1941, he finished the 35th Aviation Student Course and was immediately posted to the 3rd Air Group in Taiwan. It was here that he greeted the commencement of hostilities between Japan and the United States on 8 December. The 3rd Air Group had a large number of veteran pilots, and Yamaguchi was hardly ever given an opportunity to sortie. After additional training and duty in flying patrols over the base, Yamaguchi experienced his first combat when he flew as leader of the 2nd Shōtai within the lead chūtai during an attack on Surabaya on 3 February 1942. The shōtai jointly shot down two aircraft.

Yamaguchi was soon promoted to leader of the chūtai; during the spring and on into the summer, he participated in a number of raids on Darwin while based on the island of Timor. From September to the end of October, he advanced to Rabaul and participated in a number of raids on Guadalcanal. In particular, during an air battle on 3 October after his shōtai had jointly shot down three aircraft, LTJG

Yamaguchi's aircraft received hits. He had to make an emergency landing on the northern coast of Guadalcanal but was rescued by friendly forces on the ground and made it back to base.

In mid-November, Yamaguchi and his unit went back to his original post at Kendari; in May of the following year [1943], he was promoted to LT. During the spring and the summer, he participated in a number of raids on Darwin and kept on piling up kills in combat with Spitfires of the Royal Air Force. In July, Yamaguchi was ordered to the Yokosuka Air Group as a senior student (kōtōka-gakusei) and returned to the homeland. Upon graduating from this course in October, he was next assigned as division officer in Air Group 204 and sent out to the heavy fighting on Rabaul battlefront. By the time he withdrew to Truk toward the end of January 1944, Yamaguchi had shot down five air-

Yamaguchi during his Air Group 202 days (Minoru Suzuki)

craft. In May, he again returned to the homeland and served as division officer in the Yokosuka Air Group Fighter Squadron. In June, he was posted to the Hachiman unit and advanced to Iwo Jima in order to participate in the "A"-gō operation. On three occasions he intercepted American carrier fighter forces that came raiding. During the afternoon of 24 June he sortied on an attack on enemy task forces and fought valiantly. On 4 July, however, during the course of an intercept battle, Yamaguchi was killed in action. Total number of aircraft shot down, twelve.

LT Chitoshi Isozaki during his Air Group 210 days. (Kiyoharu Ishikawa)

LT Chitoshi Isozaki

Isozaki was a veteran pilot who held a record of flying more than four thousand hours over a thirteen-year period, counting only fighter flight time. He showed exemplary traits not only in air combat techniques but also as a leader. Isozaki started out as an ordinary seaman, fourth class, and rose to the rank of lieutenant.

Born in Matsuyama City in 1913, immediately after graduating from Matsuyama High School, Isozaki enlisted in the navy. In March 1933 he completed the 19th Pilot Training Class and became a fighter pilot. Following postings to the *Ryūjō* and the Kasumigaura Air Group, he greeted the outbreak of the China Incident. In October 1937, he was transferred to serve on board the *Kaga* and spent about one and a half years at the battlefront. At the end of 1939, Isozaki was transferred to the 12th Air Group and participated in attacks on Kweilin. He was not favored by the gods of war, however, and had no opportunity for air combat.

In November 1940, Isozaki was promoted to warrant officer; in October 1941, he was posted to the Tainan Air Group and served in southern area operations. One half year later, he returned to the Ōmura Air Group as an instructor. In April 1943 he was promoted to ensign and advanced to Rabaul, attached to Air Group 251. When he scored his first kill in an air battle over the Russell Islands on 16 June, Isozaki was already over thirty years old. He later served as division officer in Air Groups 204 and 201 and managed to survive for a period of half a year in the harsh air combat situation centering around Buin and Rabaul. In March 1944, Isozaki was posted to Air Group 302 at Atsugi, and later to the 210. In May of the following year, he was transferred to the Fighter Hikōtai 301 as division officer; while engaged in air defense operations in the southern Kyūshū area, Isozaki greeted the end of the war. Total number of aircraft shot down, twelve.

ENS Masao Sasakibara (Masao Sasakibara)

ENS Masao Sasakibara

Born in Aomori Prefecture in 1921, Sasakibara graduated from the Kō 4th Flight Training Course in September 1941 and was posted on board the aircraft carrier *Shōkaku*. After participating in Hawaiian and Indian Ocean operations, he joined the fighter escort that attacked an American carrier task force on 8 May 1942 during the Battle of the Coral Sea. He shot down four aircraft. Next, during the Aleutian operation in June, he was temporarily transferred to the *Junyō* but was returned to the *Shōkaku* after the end of the operation. In August, he sortied in the south Pacific area. During the Second Battle of the Solomons [the Battle of the Eastern Solomons] on 24 August, he flew on combat air patrol. On the 28th, Sasakibara was dispatched to the base on Buka Island as a member of a fifteen-aircraft unit commanded by LT Shingō. On both the 29th and the 30th, Sasakibara participated in attacks on Guadalcanal, shooting down one enemy aircraft during each raid. Next, on 26 October, he participated in an attack on an enemy task force during the Battle of Santa Cruz, again as one of the wingmen for LT Shingō.

In February, CPO Sasakibara was dispatched to the Rabaul base in order to assist in the withdrawal from Guadalcanal. On 4 February, Sasakibara joined the attack on Guadalcanal as a member of a fifteen-carrier fighter unit commanded by LT Kenjirō Nōtomi. After shooting down two carrier bombers and two fighters, Sasakibara next exchanged shots with another enemy aircraft in a head–on pass. It was a draw; Sasakibara received hits and was forced to ditch in the water. He was rescued but was hospitalized because of a severe wound to his forehead. Sasakibara returned to the homeland; in June 1945, he was transferred to Air Group 343, where he greeted the end of the war. Total number of aircraft shot down, twelve.

LTJG Kushirō Yamashita during his 12th Air Group days (Kazuo Tsunoda)

LTJG Koshirō Yamashita

Born in 1910 in a farmhouse in Kōchi Prefecture, Yamashita enlisted at the Yokosuka Naval Barracks in 1927 as a fireman. In May 1931, he was transferred to the Kasumigaura Air Group as a member of the 17th Pilot Training Class. He completed the course in March of the following year and became a fighter pilot. He was then successively posted to the Ōmura Air Group, on board the *Akagi,* and finally to the Yokosuka and Kanoya air groups. Yamashita greeted the start of the China Incident while assigned on board the *Ryūjō.* From August on into November, the *Ryūjō* was operating off central and south China. PO1c Yamashita participated in the 21 September attack on Canton as a shōtai leader. On this day, Yamashita single-handedly shot down one aircraft and jointly shot down another aircraft, his first victories. After participating in a number of attack operations and operations in direct support of naval ground forces, Yamashita returned to the homeland.

Later in May 1940, after serving as an instructor at the Suzuka Air Group, WO Yamashita was ordered posted to the 12th Air Group. Although he had reached the age of thirty, he valiantly advanced to Hankow and for a period of about one year exhibited amazing adroitness in air battles over the mainland of China.

For example, during an attack on Chungking by Zero fighters on 13 September of the same year, Yamashita sortied as the leader of the 2nd Shōtai, 1st Chūtai. The unit engaged in heavy fighting with the close to thirty enemy fighters that rose to intercept them. A total of twenty-seven enemy aircraft were shot down. WO Yamashita himself shot down the spectacular total of five enemy aircraft. In particular, it is interesting to note that the final aircraft shot down by Yamashita had been pursued to within fifty meters of the ground and then forced to crash into a rice paddy. After this, Yamashita and PO Kitahata flew a spectacular loop-the-loop fifty meters over the Paishih Railroad Station. Again, on March 14th the following year during an attack on Chengtu, during the course of dogfights conducted at a low altitude in dense mist, Yamashita shot down three aircraft (one probable). Putting together the number of aircraft downed during other air battles, Yamashita had shot

Yamashita during his Ōmura Air Group days (Kiyokuma Okajima)

down more than ten enemy aircraft during the course of one year. Yamashita assumed the position of leading ace in the 12th Air Group.

Later on, while posted to the Kasumigaura, Tainan, and Tsuiki air groups, Yamashita was assigned duties in instructing the younger pilots coming up. In January 1944, he was transferred to Fighter Hi-

kōtai 304, Air Group 201, and advanced to Palau in the Micronesia area. During an intercept battle against a large-scale attack by American carrier aircraft on 30 March, however, Yamashita was killed in action. At the time he was thirty-four years of age, and this was his first combat action in the Pacific War theater.

ENS Kōzaburō Yasui (Minoru Honda)

ENS Kōzaburō Yasui

Born in 1916 in Kyoto Municipality, Yasui enlisted in the navy and graduated from the 40th Pilot Training Class in February 1938. At the end of the following year, 1939, Yasui was posted to the 14th Air Group and saw action in the southern China front.

In November 1940, he returned to the homeland to serve as an instructor at the Hyakurigahara Air Group. In November 1941, immediately before the outbreak of the war, Yasui was posted to the fighter squadron attached to the 22nd Air Flotilla Headquarters and advanced to French Indochina. From January to February of the following year, 1942, Yasui participated in

the bombings of Singapore, in patrolling for ship convoys in the northern Borneo area, and other duties. Yasui did make some kills, but the details are not known. In May 1942, Yasui was promoted to PO1c and transferred to the Kanoya Air Group Fighter Squadron. In August, he was transferred to the battle-hardened Tainan Air Group and advanced to Rabaul. On the 24th, PO1c Yasui experienced his first battle action when he attacked Rabi (Rambi) [New Guinea] in the southeast area and engaged in a pitched battle with P-39s. Yasui shot down three of the opposing aircraft (one probable). With this as a starter, during the course of more than two and a half months of air combat until his return to the homeland in early November, Yasui would shoot down about ten aircraft.

In March 1943, he was transferred to the Ōita Air Group as an instructor. In March 1944, he was ordered to Air Group 652. In June, he participated in the sea battles off the Marianas. During the morning of the 19th, Yasui escorted a carrier bomber unit of the 2nd Carrier Division during an attack on an American task force in the seas west of the Marianas. The unit was unable to find the enemy. Just before he landed on Guam, Yasui was attacked by a group of American fighters and both he and his colleagues were lost in action. Yasui is deemed to have died in action. Total number of aircraft shot down, eleven (officially recognized).

ENS Ichirō Yamamoto (Yasujirō Abe)

ENS Ichirō Yamamoto

Born in a fishing village in Ehime Prefecture in 1918, Yamamoto enlisted in the navy following graduation from higher elementary school. He was selected for the 50th Pilot Training Class in December 1939 and graduated in June of the following year. After being posted to the Ōita and Sasebo air groups and service on board the Zuihō, Yamamoto was next transferred to the Shōkaku, just before the outbreak of the war. Yamamoto participated in the raid on Pearl Harbor, being assigned screening duties over his carrier. He next participated in battles in the Indian Ocean as well as in the Coral Sea. In particular, on 8 May 1942, Yamamoto joined the fighter escort commanded by LT Takumi Hoashi and protected the unit that was to attack the American aircraft carrier. In air combat conducted over enemy vessels, Yamamoto shot down an impressive total of four aircraft, by himself. Further, during the Battle of Santa Cruz on 26 October, he was assigned to the combat air patrol over his carrier and intercepted raiding American torpedo planes as well as dive-bombers. Jointly with two of his colleagues, Yamamoto racked up a total of nine enemy aircraft shot down.

In November, Yamamoto was promoted to CPO and transferred to the Ōita Air Group as an instructor. At the end of the following year he was again assigned on board a carrier. In May 1944, he was promoted to warrant officer. Upon issuance of orders to activate the "A"-gō operation, Yamamoto flew sorties from on board the aircraft carrier Zuikaku (Air Group 601). On 19 June, Yamamoto served as a shōtai leader in the Zuikaku fighter squadron and led a flight of three as part of the first wave that took off to attack an American task force. En route to their target, however, the unit met a powerful force of F6Fs. Counterattacking from an inferior position and after a hard struggle, he shot down two enemy aircraft; this was at the same time Yamamoto's unit continued to provide an escort. His own aircraft received hits, however, and Yamamoto decided to destroy himself together with his aircraft. Total number of aircraft shot down, eleven.

LT Yoshio Wajima (Shin-ichi Hirabayashi)

LT Yoshio Wajima

Born in Hokkaidō in 1911, Wajima graduated from the 18th Pilot Training Class in November 1932; he was a true veteran, an old-timer among fighter pilots. After the outbreak of the China Incident he was attached to the 12th Air Group and participated in the central China battlefront. In April 1938 he was transferred to the 14th Air Group and then took part in the fighting in south China. His duties, however, were confined to patrol and direct support of land operations; there was no opportunity to engage in air combat. In April 1939, Wajima was transferred to the Kasumigaura Air Group as an instructor; in May of the following year, he was promoted to warrant officer. In September [1940], he was next attached to the Chitose Air Group. When the war broke out, Wajima was assigned air defense duties at Taroa Island, in the Micronesia area, using a Type 96 carrier fighter.

On 1 February 1942, American carrier aircraft made a surprise attack on the Marshall Islands. The carrier fighter unit on Taroa Island carried out a number of intercept operations. WO Wajima shot down three aircraft by himself; he was thirty years old at the time and this was his first kill. In May, Wajima was transferred to the newly organized 2nd Air Group (later called Air Group 582) and returned to the homeland. In August, Wajima advanced to Rabaul. For a period of about four months, until his return to the Yokosuka Air Group in December upon his promotion to ensign, Wajima participated in the heavy air battles involved in defensive and offensive operations around Guadalcanal. He took full advantage of his well-honed skills and shot down ten aircraft (three probables).

With the establishment of Air Group 263 in October 1943, he was assigned to the unit as a division officer. On 21 February 1944, LTJG Wajima advanced to the base at Tinian in the Marshall Islands, as part of the advance unit. During the course of air combat with a force of American carrier aircraft that raided the island on the 23rd, Wajima was killed in action. Total number of aircraft shot down, eleven (officially recognized).

WO Kiyoshi Sekiya

WO Kiyoshi Sekiya during his Yokosuka Air Group days, 1944. (Masami Ōtomo)

Born in Tochigi Prefecture in 1921, Sekiya enlisted in the navy in 1939; in November of the following year, he was selected for the Hei 2nd Flight Reserve Enlisted Trainee Class. Sekiya was graduated from the 12th Flight Training Course in November 1941, immediately before the outbreak of the war. In the spring of 1942, he was posted to the 3rd Air Group but did not initially have any chance to sortie for combat. On 16 June 1942, during a raid on Darwin, Sekiya experienced his first battle.

In the fall of the same year, he was attached to Air Group 582 and advanced to Rabaul. He participated in air battles over the Solomons, as well as those over eastern New Guinea and kept on steadily piling up his battle scores. In July 1943, Sekiya was transferred to Air Group 204. In November, he was transferred back to the homeland and posted to the Yokosuka Air Group.

In order to participate in the June 1944 "A"-gō operation, CPO Sekiya advanced to Iwo Jima. He failed to return after participating in the first intercept operation over Iwo Jima, on the 24th of the month. He is deemed to have died in action. Total aircraft shot down, eleven (officially recognized).

WO Tomezō Yamamoto during his Air Group 582 days, 1942. (Shin-ichi Hirabayashi)

WO Tomezō Yamamoto

Born in Kitami, Hokkaidō, in 1922, Yamamoto enlisted in the navy in 1939 and then was selected, in November 1940, for the Hei 2nd Flight Reserve Enlisted Trainee Class. He was posted to the Tsuchiura Air Group; in November 1941, he completed the 12th Flight Training Course while part of the Ōita Air Group. He was then immediately transferred to the Chitose Air Group and assigned air defense duties in the Micronesia area. In June of the following year, Yamamoto was transferred to the 2nd Air Group (Air Group 582) and returned to the homeland. In August, however, he advanced to Rabaul. Yamamoto achieved his first victory on 12 September during an attack on Guadalcanal when he shot down two aircraft. From then until July of the following year, Yamamoto was active in air combat in the Solomons and eastern New Guinea. Despite his youth, his score was in excess of fourteen aircraft shot down (six probables or joints).

In particular, during an intercept battle over Shortland on 5 June 1943, Yamamoto produced an amazing combat record when he, jointly with others, shot down five dive-bombers; in addition, he shot down one F4U aircraft by himself.

In August he was transferred to the Atsugi Air Group and returned to the homeland. In November, Yamamoto was promoted to PO1c. In February of the following year, he was next posted to Air Group 203; with the melting of the snows, the unit moved to Shumshu Island in the northern Kuriles. He was assigned duties in intercepting larger American aircraft that came raiding locally from bases in the Aleutians. On 24 June, CPO Yamamoto took off from the airfield to engage in patrol action; immediately after takeoff, however, at an altitude of fifty meters he lost speed and crashed. Yamamoto died in action.

PO1c Matao Ichioka during his flight trainee days (Family of Ki-ichi Nagano)

PO2c Take-ichi Kokubun during his Tainan Air Group days, at Rabaul, August 1942. (Kiku-ichi Inano)

PO1c Matao Ichioka

Born in Gifu Prefecture in 1925, Ichioka was a member of the Hei 12th Flight Reserve Enlisted Trainee Class and in July 1943, graduated from the 28th Flight Training Course. At the end of September, he was posted to Air Group 204 and advanced to Rabaul.

After Ichioka scored his first kill on 25 December when he shot down one aircraft during an intercept battle, he continued to participate in the daily air battles despite his youth. During the one-month period of January 1944, Ichioka shot down thirteen aircraft (five probables or joints). After transfer of the main unit of Air Group 204 to Truk Island at the end of January, Ichioka was himself transferred to Air Group 253, at Tobera base (in Rabaul). Ichioka kept on fighting energetically; however, on 19 April [1944], he was killed in action.

PO2c Take-ichi Kokubun

Born in Fukushima Prefecture in 1921, Kokubun enlisted in the navy in 1938 and was graduated from the 49th Pilot Training Class in June 1940. After being successively posted to the Ōita, Sasebo, and Mihoro air groups, Kokubun was next posted to the Chitose Air Group in September 1941, where he was assigned air defense duties in the Micronesia area. In February 1942, he was transferred to the 4th Air Group and advanced to Rabaul. On 1 April, Kokubun was next transferred to the Tainan Air Group and plunged into the furious air battles going on in the southeast area of operations. Starting with his first shoot-down of a P-39 in an air battle over Moresby on 18 May, and through the end of July, and despite his youth, Kokubun kept on piling up scores in patrol and other action during attacks on Moresby, intercept operations over Lae, patrolling in the Buna anchorage area, and other actions. With the advance of American forces to Guadalcanal in August, he also participated in air combat in the Solomon Island area as well. On 2 September, nine Zero fighters led by LT Kawai escorted land attack planes that raided

Guadalcanal. On this occasion, PO3c Kokubun was lost in action after engaging in
combat with about ten F4Fs. He is deemed
to have been killed in action. Although his
experience in air battles was not even six

months in duration, it is recorded that Kokubun achieved eight confirmed shoot-
downs, two probables, and three joint
shoot-downs.

LTJG Hatsu-o Hidaka at Kasumigaura (Hatsu-o
Hidaka)

LTJG Hatsu-o Hidaka

Born in Kagoshima Prefecture in 1915, Hidaka enlisted in the navy and graduated
from the 24th Pilot Trainee Class in July

1934 to become a fighter pilot. In November 1935, he was assigned on board the
Kaga; upon the outbreak of the China Incident [1937], the unit advanced off Shanghai. Hidaka's first kill was recorded on 11
November 1937, when he pursued three attacking Northrop bombers and shot down
one of them. Next, during the raid on Canton on 13 April of the following year, Hidaka added two more aircraft shot down to
his tally. In June [1938] he was transferred
to the 15th Air Group; he participated in
the 18 July raid on Nanchang during which
LT Nangō was killed in action. Hidaka
shot down two aircraft on this raid; the following December, he returned to the
homeland. Hidaka then went on to serve
successively as an instructor with the Kasumigaura, Kure, and Ōmura air groups.
In October 1942, Hidaka was promoted to
warrant officer and attached to Air Group
204. Toward the end of December, he advanced to the base at Buin, in the Solomon
Islands. Hidaka fought valiantly in support
of LT Miyano but had to be hospitalized
with malignant malaria. He was transferred
back to the homeland; Hidaka greeted the
end of hostilities as an instructor at the
Yatabe Air Group.

Total number of aircraft shot down,
eleven (officially recognized).

LTJG Yoshio Ōishi (Family of Yoshio Ōishi)

LTJG Yoshio Ōishi

Born in 1923 in Shizuoka Prefecture, Ōishi qualified for the Otsu 9th Flight Reserve Enlisted Trainee Class in June 1938 and enlisted at the Yokosuka Air Group. In October 1941, he graduated from the Flight Training Course and was posted to the Ōmura Air Group. At the end of July 1942, Ōishi was ordered to serve on board the *Zuikaku* and immediately advanced to the Solomons area. His first air combat was during the Battle of Santa Cruz on 26 October. On this occasion, four Zero fighters of the *Zuikaku* air control unit (commander, WO Katsuma Shigemi) composed the second wave and escorted carrier attack planes heading for an American carrier task force. A fierce air battle ensued with enemy fighters that came to intercept the unit; Ōishi, jointly with others, shot down nine aircraft (two probables). Toward the end of January 1943, the *Zuikaku* Fighter Squadron was dispatched for two weeks to Rabaul to assist in the evacuation from Guadalcanal. On 1, 4, and 7 February, Guadalcanal was attacked and heavy air battles took place; in each case, victories continued to mount. Next, in order to participate in the "I"-gō operation in April, Ōishi advanced to Rabaul for the second time. He then participated in the attacks on Guadalcanal, Oro Bay, Moresby, and Milne Bay. Ōishi shot down two aircraft.

Afterward, the *Zuikaku* squadron underwent further training in the homeland and on Truk Island. On 1 November, the unit advanced to Rabaul and participated in repeated attacks on Torokina [Bougainville] and in intercept operations until the 11th. The unit then withdrew to Truk. War clouds over the Marshall Islands were getting more ominous, however, and without any pause for rest the unit was moved to Roi. During air combat on 5 December, the unit was demolished; CPO Ōishi, however, did survive and returned to the homeland. He was then assigned as an instructor at the Ōita and Tsukuba air groups. In June

LTJG Ōishi (*top*) (Family of Yoshio Ōishi)

1944, Ōishi was transferred to the Fighter Hikōtai 302, Air Group 252.

With the activation of the Shō-gō operation in October, Ōishi advanced to the Philippines via Okinawa and Taiwan. On the day of the general offensive, the 24th, Ōishi took off for an attack on an American task force off the eastern coast of Luzon. He shot down one aircraft in combat. He then continued to participate in a number of air battles in the Philippines until the end of the year. In January 1945 he withdrew to Taiwan and was transferred to Air Group 205. With the coming of the final battle for Okinawa, Ōishi was posted to a special attack force unit.

On 4 May, twenty-one Zero fighters of the 17th Taigi-tai ("Noble Cause Unit"), equipped with bombs and escorted by seven Zero fighters, attacked enemy vessels off Okinawa. That same evening, WO Ōishi took off by himself from Ilan (Giran) base on a battle result verification flight; he was lost in action. Ōishi is deemed to have been killed in action and was given a special two-grade promotion, to naval LTJG.

Because of inadequate records, the number of his victories that can be verified is only about eleven. However, Ōishi was the top ace of the *Zuikaku* Fighter Squadron; the actual number shot down is estimated to be at least fifteen.

LTJG Tsutomu Iwai during his 12th Air Group days (Kazuo Tsunoda)

LTJG Tsutomu Iwai

Born in Kyoto Municipality in 1919, Iwai graduated from the Flight Training Course for the Otsu 6th Flight Reserve Enlisted Trainee Class in August 1938. In January 1940 he was posted to the 12th Air Group and advanced to the base at Hankow. On 13 September, thirteen Zero fighters led by LT Saburō Shindō battled enemy fighters over Chungking and shot down an outstanding total of twenty-seven enemy aircraft. In this air battle, Iwai flew as number three in LT Shirane's shōtai and shot down two enemy aircraft. Next, during the attack on Chengtu on 26 October, Iwai, together with Sea2c Koshirō Yamashita, strafed the airfield. Following the strafing, an unarmed trainer aircraft was attacked and shot down while flying over the field.

In November 1940, Iwai returned to the homeland. After being successively posted to the Tsukuba, Saeki, and Ōmura air groups, in November 1942 he was transferred on board the carrier *Zuihō*. In January 1943, Iwai advanced to Rabaul and participated in support of the evacuation from Guadalcanal, in Lae convoy operations, as well as in the attack on Buna. Further, during the "I"-gō operation in April, he participated in the attacks on Guadalcanal, Oro Bay, Port Moresby, and Milne Bay.

In August 1944, Iwai was ordered back [home] to the 601st Air Group and underwent additional training at Matsuyama Base. With the activation of the Shō-gō operation in October, Iwai next boarded the *Zuikaku* and advanced to the seas east of the Philippines. Fifty-six carrier bombers were sent out 24 October, after noon, to attack an enemy task force. WO Iwai was a part of the fighter escort commanded by LT Hōhei Kobayashi. Before they arrived at their target, the unit was intercepted by enemy fighters. After the end of the air combat, Iwai separated himself from the main force and landed at Aparri, Luzon. Together with pilots from other carriers, Iwai was placed under the command of LT Nakagawa and next advanced to Manila. On the following day, Iwai flew air cover for VADM Kurita's ships retreating from the area; two enemy torpedo planes that attacked were shot down. Iwai then landed at Batangas. For the next few days, he participated in the attacks on Leyte, flying from Clark [Field]. He then hitchhiked on an army heavy bomber and returned to the base at Matsuyama.

In November, Iwai was promoted to ensign. During the spring of 1945, Iwai next advanced to southern Kyūshū and participated in the air battles over Okinawa. At the end of April, he moved to Hyakurigahara; he greeted the end of the war at the Suzuka base.

Iwai during his 12th Air Group days (Tsutomu Iwai)

LCDR Iyozō Fujita, spring 1941 (Minoru Suzuki)

LCDR Iyozō Fujita

Born in Shantung Province, China in 1917, Fujita attended Kitsuki High School in Ōita Prefecture and then graduated with the 66th Naval Academy class in September 1938. In June 1940, he completed the 33rd Flight Training Course; in September of the following year he was ordered to serve on board the *Sōryū*. Fujita's first taste of battle was on 7 December in the attack on Pearl Harbor, when he served as a shōtai leader in the second wave fighter escort. Division officer LT Fusata Iida died a tragic death from antiaircraft fire during his strafing of the Kaneohe base. LTJG Fujita gathered together the remaining fighters and headed for Point Kaena, the rendezvous point for return to the carriers. On the way, however, Fujita's group met a P-36 formation that included 2nd LT [Gordon H.] Sterling, [Jr.], and others and a dogfight ensued. After one enemy aircraft had been shot down, Fujita's plane was hit; Fujita just barely managed to make it back to the carrier. Immediately upon landing on the deck of the carrier, one of the cylinders of the engine fractured and fell off.

After his return to the homeland, Fujita was promoted to LT and then participated in attacks on Darwin and in Indian Ocean operations. In June 1942, Fujita flew in the Battle of Midway as one of the combat air patrols. During the first intercept battle, Fujita plunged into a formation of B-26s and shot down three planes (two jointly). After returning to the carrier and refueling, he again took off and next attacked a formation of enemy torpedo planes. Fujita's success was amazing; in a matter of a few moments, four torpedo planes (three jointly) and three fighters (two jointly) were shot down. His aircraft received hits in its fuselage fuel tank from friendly antiaircraft fire, however, and the plane caught on fire. Fujita parachuted into the ocean from a height of two hundred meters. After four hours drifting in the sea, he was picked up by the destroyer *Nowaki* and was able to return to the homeland.

After his return, Fujita was ordered to serve as division officer on board the *Hiyō;* in October, he made sorties in the Solomons battlefront. Because of mechanical problems on board the carrier, the majority of the air group was moved to Rabaul on the 20th, and then to Buin. Until mid-December, the aircraft were engaged in air battles around Guadalcanal.

Staying in Rabaul for less than one month, Fujita was next transferred to the Tsuiki Air Group in June in order to participate in the April 1943 "I"-gō operation. In November, Fujita was ordered in as group leader for the newly organized Air Group 301; in June and July [1944] he participated in the air defense battles in the Iwo Jima area. In July, he was transferred to serve as group leader for Fighter Hikōtai 402, which had been equipped with Shiden fighters. Consolidated into Air Group 341, the unit next made sorties during October in air battles off Taiwan. After hard fighting in the Philippines, the unit lost much of its strength and was withdrawn to the homeland in January 1945. Fujita greeted the end of the war at the Fukuchiyama base.

Shooting down ten aircraft (seven jointly) during the Battle of Midway is on the record; along with the scores made by Okumura and Okabe, this figure is among the highest number of aircraft kills recorded in one day. After the war, Fujita returned to the skies and is today active as a pilot for Japan Air Lines.

WO Yoshijirō Shirahama during his Fighter Hikōtai 310 days (Kunimori Nakakariya)

WO Yoshijirō Shirahama

Born in Tokyo in 1921, Shirahama voluntarily enlisted at the Yokosuka Naval Barracks in 1938. In 1941, he finished the 56th Pilot Training Class as a seaplane pilot. After being successively posted to the Kashima, Hakata, and Kure air groups, he was next transferred to the 16th Air Group. Immediately upon the outbreak of the war, he participated in the Mindanao Island invasion operation. Shirahama then was posted to the 32nd Air Group and, later, to the Ōtsu Air Group. Later, at the Tsuiki Air Group he was transferred to carrier fighter pilot duties. In December 1943, he was ordered attached to the 1st Air Flotilla command. As a member of the reorganized task force air control unit, Shirahama advanced to Singapore. Soon after he served on board the aircraft carrier Shōkaku at the Linga anchorage and continued to undergo

intensive training. During the sea battle off the Marianas on 19 June, Shirahama served as number two wingman for LT Fumio Yamagata, commander of the 3rd Daitai, the first wave sent out by Air Group 601. On the way, the unit was cut off by American fighters and a wild melee ensued. After shooting down one enemy aircraft, Shirahama returned alone to the Zuikaku. During the evening of the next day, the 20th, Shirahama engaged in heavy combat with American carrier planes and shot down three. He then ditched in pitch darkness. He was rescued by a destroyer and was able to return to the homeland.

CPO Shirahama, who had returned alive, became a key figure in the reconstruction of the striking force. As senior pilot of Fighter Hikotai 166, Air Group 653, he concentrated his energies on training at the Ōita base. With the activation of the Shō-gō operation in October 1944, the main force of the unit advanced with the striking force, off the Philippines. However, CPO Shirahama remained behind. During the latter part of October, he was ordered into air transportation duties and advanced to Bamban base on Luzon, via Taiwan. He then went on to the Cebu base. There he met up with the main force of his unit and participated in intercept operations, as well as in the attack on Leyte. Shirahama lost his aircraft, however, and two weeks later returned to Ōita.

When the 601 was reorganized in December, Shirahama was transferred to Fighter Hikotai 310 and instructed at the Matsuyama and Iwakuni bases. In February 1945, he moved to the Kantō area where, on the 16th and the 17th, he participated in intercept operations against American carrier aircraft. Toward the end of March, in order to participate in the final battle for Okinawa, Shirahama proceeded to the Kokubu base in southern Kyūshū. In particular, during the air battle over Kikai-shima, (or Kikai-ga-shima), Shirahama shot down three aircraft by himself. In May, he returned to the Kantō area and greeted the end of the war while stationed at the Suzuka base. Number of aircraft personally shot down, eleven.

LCDR Sumio Fukuda during his Air Group 252 days, on Maloelap Atoll. (Family of Sumio Fukuda)

LCDR Sumio Fukuda

Born in Tokushima Prefecture in 1919, Fukuda graduated with the 69th class of the Naval Academy in March 1941. In February 1943, he completed the 37th Aviation Student Course and was immediately ordered on board the carrier *Junyō*. As early as April, Fukuda had advanced to Rabaul in order to participate in the "I"-gō operation. The attack on Guadalcanal on the 7th was his first battle experience; however, he did not have an opportunity to engage in air combat.

Fukuda next took part in the attack on Oro Bay on the 11th and the attack on Port Moresby on the 12th, after which he returned to the homeland. During mid-July, the *Junyō* Fighter Squadron advanced to the base at Buin and participated in the ferocious, almost daily air battles. On 1 September, all pilots assigned to the *Junyō* Fighter Squadron were transferred, in place, to the local base air unit. LTJG Fu-

kuda was posted to Air Group 204. At the time, almost all officer pilots of Air Group 204 had been killed in action because of the continuing fierce air battles. As a result, LTJG Fukuda served as commander of the unit for about two months, until his transfer to Air Group 252 on 4 November. During the same period, Fukuda commanded intercept operations over Rabaul and Buin; personally, he also shot down six enemy aircraft (two probables).

Following his transfer to Air Group 252, Fukuda was involved in air defense operations at the Taroa base in the Marshall Islands. On 25 November, Fukuda led a force of twenty-four Zero fighters on a strafing and bombing run against Makin Island. En route, however, his unit was intercepted by a force of about fifty F6Fs; eleven enemy aircraft were shot down (four probables). WO Kojima and six aircraft were lost, however, and the attack was abandoned; the unit returned to base. Beginning the latter part of December, B-24s started wave-formation bombing attacks on Taroa. Under the immediate and valiant command of LTJG Fukuda, the locally stationed Air Group 252 fought ferociously

Fukuda during his *Junyō* days, January 1943. (Wataru Nakamichi)

and repeatedly engaged in close attacks. By using repeated head-on attacks (renzoku chokujō kōgeki-hō) they were able to shoot down about fifty enemy aircraft in a period of one month. The majority of their equipment and supplies, however, was lost by the end of January 1944. Remaining pilots escaped to Truk by transport aircraft, eventually reaching the homeland.

In March, LTJG Fukuda was promoted to LT and assigned as an instructor to the Kōnoike Air Group. In July following the end of the "A"-gō operation, however, he was transferred to serve as the commander of the newly organized Fighter Hikōtai

163, Air Group 634. He conducted training activities at the Tokushima base. Because of the activation of the Shō-gō operation in October [1944], however, the unit advanced to Clark Field in the Philippines, via Okinawa and Taiwan. On the 24th, the day of the general offensive, LT Fukuda led all operational aircraft of Air Group 634 aloft for an attack on an American carrier task force located east of Luzon. They were met en route by a strong group of American fighters, however, and LT Fukuda was lost in action. He is deemed to have been killed in action. Total number of aircraft shot down, eleven.

ENS Yoshina-o Kodaira during his *Shōkaku* days, 1942. (Yoshina-o Kodaira)

ENS Yoshina-o Kodaira

Born in Nagano Prefecture in 1918, Kodaira enlisted in the paymaster corps of the navy in 1935. In November 1938, however, he graduated from the 43rd Pilot Training Class and was assigned, successively, to the Saeki and Ōita air groups. In September 1939, he was transferred to the 14th Air Group and participated in the southern China battlefront. Kodaira's first

air engagement was on 30 December, during a raid on Liuchow. On 10 January of the following year, he shot down two aircraft during an attack on Kweilin.

Later, after engaging in air support operations for naval ground forces and being stationed in French Indochina, he returned to the Ōmura Air Group in October 1940 [1941?]. In April 1942, he was ordered to serve on board the *Shōkaku*; during the Battle of the Coral Sea he flew air patrol over the carrier. In August, he made sorties in the southeast area of operations and then participated in the Second Battle of the Solomons [Battle of the Eastern Solomons]. Near the latter part of the month, Kodaira was dispatched for a period of one week to Buka Island; there he participated in a series of attacks on Guadalcanal. Next, Kodaira served on combat air patrol in the South Pacific area of operations. He shot down a dive-bomber on one occasion but then his aircraft received hits, forcing Kodaira to return to his carrier. In February 1944, Kodaira transferred from being an instructor at the Tsuiki Air Group to Air Group 601 (on board the *Shōkaku*). During the Battle of the Marianas on 19 June, Kodaira was a member of the escort for the first wave attack of the 1st Carrier Division. Before the strike was able to reach its target, however, they had to battle a large force of enemy fighters. As a result, two enemy aircraft were shot down; after that Kodaira's own aircraft received hits and he had to return alone. Kodaira made an emergency water landing but was picked up by the destroyer *Fujinami*.

After his return to the homeland, Kodaira was transferred to a reorganized striking force. He was ordered to serve on board the converted aircraft carrier *Chiyoda* as a member of Fighter Hikōtai 164. On 24 October, the ship participated in a battle off the Philippines. The attack group itself was decimated before reaching the target. After shooting down one F6F, Kodaira managed to reach Aparri in the northern part of Luzon, together with some other surviving aircraft. The following day, the unit advanced to Manila and flew air cover for Kurita's forces, which were on the run. Next, Kodaira participated in the Leyte operation, based at Clark Field. On 8 November, he had an accident as he was taking off and sustained injuries. Kodaira was then returned to the homeland. Later he moved from Izumi to Huangchuan, to Mobara, to Kōriyama and then greeted the end of the war as a member of Fighter Hikōtai 304. After the end of the war, Kodaira joined the Air Self-Defense Force but retired under the age limit. Total number of aircraft shot down, eleven.

Kodaira at Tomioka base, 1943. (Yoshina-o Kodaira)

WO Mitsu-o Hori during his Fighter Hikōtai 301, Air Group 343 days. (Mitsuo Mikami)

WO Mitsu-o Hori

Born in Gifu Prefecture in 1921, Hori finished the Flight Training Course for the Otsu 10th Flight Reserve Enlisted Trainee Class in March 1942, after the war started. In May he was ordered to the Tainan Air Group and assumed duties at Rabaul. At the time the Tainan Air Group had a large number of veterans and there were few opportunities for Hori to participate in any offensive operations. He did participate in a few intercept operations, however. In November, Hori was transferred to Air Group 582 and participated in southeast area air operations.

On 7 January 1943, while protecting a convoy bound for Lae, Hori fought with some P-38s, received hits, and had to bail out. He was injured but was rescued and returned to the homeland. Later on Hori became an instructor at the Sanya [Ya Hsien, Hainan Island] Air Group, after serving with the Ōmura Air Group. On 15 April 1944, a Zero fighter unit organized of instructors from the Ya Hsien and Kaikō [Haihow] air groups raided Nanning. The attacking unit was caught by surprise by P-40s and received major damage. After he shot down one aircraft, CPO Hori's own aircraft was hit and he made an emergency landing on Hainan Island. In June, Hori was transferred to the Takao Air Group. While training reserve students, he also participated in air defense battles off the coast of Taiwan. In January 1945, Hori was transferred to the newly organized Fighter Hikōtai 301, 343rd Air Group. As one of the senior pilots, Hori engaged vigorously in air defense operations in western Japan as well as in air battles in the Okinawa area until the war ended. After the war, Hori joined All Nippon Airways and is active to this day as a plane captain (Hori changed his name to Mikami). Total number of aircraft shot down, eleven.

CPO Ken-ichi Abe during his Kanoya Air Group days (Ken-ichi Abe)

CPO Ken-ichi Abe

Born in 1923 in a fishing village in Ōita Prefecture, Abe graduated in October 1941, just before the outbreak of the war, from the Otsu 9th Flight Reserve Enlisted Trainee Class. Initially he was trained at Usa Air Group as a carrier bomber pilot; he was then transferred to fighter operations. After completing advanced training in February 1942 at the Ōita Air Group, he was assigned to the fighter squadron attached to the 22nd Air Flotilla Headquarters. He participated in the southern battlefront but found no opportunity to engage in air combat. In April, Abe was transferred to the Kanoya Air Group Fighter Squadron (later, Air Group 253); in September, he advanced to Rabaul. Abe's first combat experience was during the attack on Guadalcanal, which was carried out on 29 September. PO3c Abe, jointly with PO1c Tsumoru Ōkura, shot down four aircraft (one probable). Abe continued to engage in air combat from then on, in the Solomons and in eastern New Guinea; he also kept adding to his score of kills. The 1 April 1943 air battle over the Russell Islands, during which he shot down two F6Fs, was a turning point. On 6 May, Abe suffered injuries, including broken bones, and was returned to the homeland. Abe greeted the end of the war before he was even able to get out of his sickbed. Total number of aircraft shot down are five for sure, two probables, and five jointly.

ENS Saburō Kitahata during his 12th Air Group days (Kazuo Tsunoda)

ENS Saburō Kitahata

Born into a farm family in Hyogo Prefecture in 1915, Kitahata enlisted in the navy in June 1932. In February 1933, he was selected for the 21st Pilot Training Class and graduated in September. When he entered the Ōmura Air Group for further training following graduation, he was a youthful, eighteen-year-old PO3c. Later on he served on board the *Ryūjō,* then with the Kasumigaura Air Group, and for a second time on board the *Ryūjō,* followed in turn by assignment to the Saeki Air Group. In July 1937 with the outbreak of the China Incident, Kitahata was ordered attached to the 12th Air Group and in September advanced to Shanghai. Initially assigned to air defense and support of naval ground forces, he had no good opportunity to engage in air combat operations. Once 1938 arrived, Kitahata did participate in the attacks on Nanchang, Hankow, and elsewhere. To what extent he achieved any victories, however, is not clear.

In September he was transferred on board the *Sōryū,* and in the fall, he participated in the Kwangtung operation. In December 1939, Kitahata was transferred to the Yokosuka Air Group. In July 1940, he

was again transferred to the 12th Air Group and advanced to the base at Hankow, transporting the new advanced Zero fighter. During the first attack on Chungking on 19 August, PO1c Kitahata flew as number two wingman for LT Saburō Shindō; however, the enemy was not sighted. On 13 September, an air battle took place with about thirty enemy fighter aircraft that rose to intercept their unit on the way to attack Chungking. An overwhelming victory was achieved by our side. After PO1c Kitahata shot down two aircraft, he strafed the Paishih Railroad Station airfield before returning to base. Next, during the 26 October attack on Chengtu, Kitahata made a sortie as 3rd Shōtai leader of the Zero fighter unit (eight aircraft) led by LT Iida. Jointly, the unit flamed ten enemy aircraft, fighters, and trainers.

In April 1942, he was promoted to warrant officer and in May was ordered on board the *Junyō.* Kitahata participated in both the 3 and 4 June raids on Dutch Harbor. There was no air combat during the raid of the 3rd. During the raid of the 4th, however, a ten-odd plane formation of

Kitahata during his *Junyō* days (Masao Sasakibara)

P-40s attacked the carrier bombers as they were gathering at the return rendezvous point. A hard battle ensued; however, during the battle, two Zero fighters, one piloted by Kitahata and the other by Ozeki came to the rescue. In a matter of moments, the two pilots saved the situation; one shot down three and the other shot down two enemy aircraft. WO Kitahata, who was pressing hard behind enemy aircraft at the time, happened by chance to discover, despite the mist, the location of the Otter Point airfield, the sole base available to American air units in the area.

Following its return to the homeland,

the *Junyō* next proceeded to the southeast area in October. WO Kitahata participated in the attack on Guadalcanal on the 17th and in the Battle of Santa Cruz on the 26th. He then returned to his base on Truk Island. On 17 January of the following year, a portion of the aircraft unit was dispatched to Wewak and assigned duties to intercept raiding B-24s. During an intercept battle on the 23rd, while Kitahata was battling a three-plane formation of B-24s, his aircraft was hit. Kitahata deliberately crashed his plane with tragic bravery. Total number of aircraft shot down, in excess of ten planes (officially recognized).

ENS Teruo Sugiyama, Air Group 201, at Rabaul, November 1943. (Masami Ōtomo)

ENS Teruo Sugiyama

Born in Yamaguchi Prefecture in 1920, Sugiyama was selected for the Otsu 7th Flight Reserve Enlisted Trainee Class in

June 1936 and graduated from the Flight Training Course in March 1939. After being successively assigned to the Suzuka, Ōmura, and Genzan air groups, Sugiyama was next ordered on board the *Ryūjō* after hostilities had commenced. He participated in the June 1942 Aleutian operation.

Next, Sugiyama took part in the Solomons battlefront. During the attack on Guadalcanal conducted on 24 August, PO1c Sugiyama was assigned to the combat air patrol over the carrier. He shot down two enemy dive-bombers; however, because of the sinking of the *Ryūjō*, he had to ditch and was rescued by a destroyer. Following his return to the homeland in the fall of 1943, he was promoted to warrant officer. Sugiyama was next ordered to Air Group 201 and advanced to Rabaul. The following January [1944], he was first assigned to Air Group 201 and then transferred to Air Group 253. He continued to fight vigorously in the daily intercept operations at Rabaul. In a period of a little under four months, Sugiyama shot down more than ten aircraft (three probables). During an intercept operation on 4 February [1944], Sugiyama was killed in action.

Total number of aircraft shot down, ten (officially recognized).

LCDR Hōhei Kobayashi (Yoshina-o Kodaira)

LCDR Hōhei Kobayashi

Kobayashi graduated from the Naval Academy with the 67th class in 1939; he then completed the 36th Aviation Student Course in June 1942 and was ordered to the *Shōkaku* Fighter Squadron. Kobayashi's first taste of combat was on 26 October, during the Battle of Santa Cruz while he was flying combat air patrol. In November, he was transferred to the position of Tsuiki Air Group division officer. In February 1943, however, he transferred back to his post of *Shōkaku* division officer. At the Truk base, he conducted training in formation air fighting and in dive-bombing tactics. In November, Kobayashi was transferred to the *Hiyō* as group leader. Toward the end of January 1944 he advanced to Rabaul. Until the time he withdrew to Truk in mid-February, Kobayashi kept fighting right up on the front lines during the daily air battles. In March, he was transferred to Air Group 652 as division officer.

During the final battle for the Marianas on 19 June, Kobayashi served as commander of the fighter escort belonging to the 2nd Carrier Division, which was on its way to attack the American fleet. Kobayashi was unable to sight the enemy however; in addition, just before landing on Guam, his unit was surprised by a large force of Grummans. Though operating from a disadvantageous position, the Kobayashi unit valiantly turned and counterattacked the enemy. Shielding the attack force with their very bodies, one by one the pilots destroyed themselves. LT Kobayashi also received hits on his aircraft and had to make an emergency landing in the water; he was later rescued. Kobayashi then participated in battles off the Philippines as the commander of the resurrected *Zuikaku* Fighter Squadron. On 25 October, after he had completed his duties on combat air patrol, Kobayashi was rescued by the destroyer *Hatsuzuki*. During a sea battle later on that same night, however, Kobayashi shared the same fate as the destroyer he was on board. Kobayashi was renowned as a military leader, with superior technical skills, a large sense of responsibility, and brimming with the spirit of combat. Total number of aircraft shot down, in excess of ten (officially recognized).

WO Yoshirō Hashiguchi during his 3rd Air Group days (Katsutarō Kobayashi)

WO Yoshirō Hashiguchi

Born in Fukuoka City in 1918, Hashiguchi enlisted in the navy in 1937 and was graduated from the 42nd Pilot Training Class in September 1938. After being successively posted to the Saeki, Ōita, and Ōmura air groups, he was assigned to the 12th Air Group and went to central China in June 1939. During the course of a bombing raid conducted by the enemy in October, Hashiguchi was wounded and required more than two months hospitalization and treatment before regaining his health. In January 1940, Hashiguchi returned to the Suzuka Air Group to serve as an instructor and then, in November 1941, was ordered posted to the 3rd Air Group (Air Group 202). Following the outbreak of the war, Hashiguchi saw action in air combat over the Philippines and Dutch East Indies. In particular, on 9 February 1942 he and one of his colleagues strafed the radio station on Ile Yande (Yande-tō) and set it on fire. Hashiguchi received a bullet wound through the right thigh from defensive fire. Hashiguchi calmly stanched the bleeding himself and continued his assigned mission of reconnaissance. He flew another two hours and forty minutes before returning to base.

From April through the summer, Hashiguchi participated in the attacks on Darwin; PO2c Hashiguchi next advanced to Rabaul in September. For about two months, he participated in a series of raids on Guadalcanal. In particular, he led two of his colleagues in an attack on 18 October when a fierce air battle ensued. The shōtai jointly shot down a total of seven aircraft (two probables). In November, Hashiguchi returned to the southwest area of operations and participated in a number of attacks on Darwin as number two wingman for succeeding group leaders. In June 1943, Hashiguchi was transferred to the Ōita Air Group.

In December, he was transferred to a carrier squadron and conducted training as the senior [enlisted] pilot attached to the *Shōkaku* Fighter Squadron, Air Group 601. He next participated in the June 1944 "A"-go operation and managed to return alive. In July, he was transferred to Fighter Hikō-tai 164, Air Group 653. In October, in order to take part in the Shō-gō operation, he started out via land bases on his way to Okinawa. His aircraft malfunctioned, however, and he was transferred on board the aircraft carrier *Chiyoda*. Hashiguchi made a number of sorties in the Battle of [Cape Engano]. At the time his carrier was sunk, the 25th, Hashiguchi was lost in action. He is deemed to have been killed in action. Number of aircraft shot down, in excess of ten (officially recognized).

Hashiguchi's favorite plane, during his 3rd Air Group days. His kills are marked on the tail. (Katsutarō Kobayashi)

CDR Yasuhiro Shigematsu during his student trainee days (Kiyokuma Okajima)

CDR Yasuhiro Shigematsu

Born in Tokyo in 1916, Shigematsu attended Tokyo Municipal High School No. 8 and graduated from the Naval Academy in September 1938 as a member of the 66th class. In April 1941 he completed the 34th Aviation Student Course; in September he was ordered to serve on board the *Hiryū*. Shigematsu was the youngest officer pilot who participated in the attack on Pearl Harbor.

In January 1942, Shigematsu was promoted to division officer and served in the Dutch East Indies and Indian Ocean areas. During the Battle of Midway in June, he was initially assigned as escort for the first attack wave. Then, after returning to his carrier, he played a spectacular role in support of the Kobayashi carrier bomber squadron that sought American carrier task forces. Shigematsu was rescued after the sinking of the *Hiryū* and was next transferred to the *Junyō*, also as a division officer. During the Battle of Santa Cruz on 26 October, he served in the fighter escort for the first attack wave and participated in the attack on the American carrier task force. On this date, Shigematsu's aircraft developed malfunctions after take off from the

carrier and he immediately returned to the carrier. Shigematsu then took a replacement fighter and chased after the main body to catch up with them.

In the spring of 1943, in order to participate in the "I"-gō operation, Shigematsu was transferred to the Yokosuka Air Group. In October he was named group leader in the newly organized Air Group 263. The following February, Shigematsu led an advance party to the Marianas; however, in an exchange with a force of American carrier aircraft that took place on the 22nd, the unit suffered severe losses. After receiving reinforcements, the unit participated in battles in the Marianas and at Palau. On 8 July, Shigematsu led the group of five remaining aircraft, flown by CPO Shō-ichi Sugita and others, en route to Pa-

Shigematsu during his aviation student days (Family of Yasuhiro Shigematsu)

lau. During the course of air combat in the Yap area, however, Shigematsu was killed in action.

Following his death, Shigematsu was given the honor of being mentioned in an All Units Bulletin, as well as given a special posthumous promotion of two ranks. Although small of stature, he was an all-around athlete; he was called "Undōshin no katamari" (a bundle of athletic vigor). Total number of aircraft shot down is estimated to exceed ten.

CPO Tomokazu Kasai during his Air Group 343 days (Tomokazu Kasai)

CPO Tomokazu Kasai

Born in Hyōgo Prefecture in 1926, Kasai joined the Tsuchiura Air Group in 1942 as a student of the Kō 10th Flight Reserve En-listed Trainee Class. In November 1943 he finished the 32nd Flight Training Course, was promoted to PO2c, and ordered to Air Group 263. Halfway through his training, in March 1944 he was ordered to advance to the Marianas; however, en route he had to make an emergency landing on Pagan Island because of poor weather. Arriving late in Saipan, he joined CPO Shō-ichi Sugita as one of his wingmen. In May, he advanced to Kau base on Halmahera Island. With the landing of American forces in the Marianas, Kasai returned to Palau and participated in attacks on enemy vessels off Saipan, using Yap and Guam as advanced bases. Kasai lost his own aircraft but escaped from Guam in a land attack plane and went to Palau, and then on to Davao.

With the disbanding of Air Group 263 on 10 July, Kasai was next transferred to Fighter Hikōtai 306, Air Group 201. Under the leadership of LT Kanno, the unit advanced to Yap. For one week starting on the 16th, the unit was engaged in intercepting incoming B-24s. PO1c Kasai's aircraft received hits and he had to ditch but was rescued. Next, Kasai withdrew to Cebu and concentrated on training activities in ship-bombing tactics. After the American invasion of Leyte in October, Kasai served as wingman for Kanno and for Sugita; he participated in attacks and intercept operations and provided direct support to special attack force units. After that, in December, Kasai returned to the homeland and was transferred to Fighter Hikōtai 301, Air Group 343. He was with the latter unit until the war ended. Number of aircraft personally shot down, ten.

WO Tomita Atake (Tomita Atake)

WO Tomita Atake

Completing the 47th Pilot Training Class in October 1939, Atake was posted to the Chitose Air Group the following year. Immediately before the outbreak of the war, he was assigned to air defense duties in the Marshall Islands. In the early dawn of 1 February 1942, PO3c Atake (former name, Hara) intercepted a force of raiding American carrier aircraft. Of the two [Type 96 carrier fighters] that were the first to take off for the interception, LT Kurakane's aircraft was hit and he had to ditch. Atake flew at low altitude; even then, he challenged the enemy aircraft to air combat despite his own disadvantageous position. An aileron on Atake's wing was damaged because it had brushed against the wing of an F4F; Atake was forced to land.

After serving as an instructor at the Ōita Air Group, Atake was ordered on board the *Junyō* in late 1942. In April 1943 he advanced to Rabaul; during an attack on a large formation of enemy aircraft off Guadalcanal on the 7th, Atake shot down two Grummans (one probable). In mid-July, he advanced to the base at Buin; however, just before landing, Atake met a surprise attack by enemy fighters and was shot down. He ditched and was rescued by a friendly destroyer. From that point until the end of August, he was active in the daily air battles fought over the Solomons. He was transferred to Air Group 204 in September. Before his return to the homeland at the end of the year, Atake shot down five enemy aircraft while attached to Air Group 204. In February 1944 he was transferred to the Yokosuka Air Group; in June he advanced to Iwo Jima. During the large scale air battle of the 24th, however, Atake was shot down and made another emergency landing. Wounded, he was transported back to the homeland. After recovering from his wounds, Atake was attached to Air Group 1001, a transport unit. He greeted the end of the war while attached to Fighter Hikōtai 313 at Kōnoike. Total number of aircraft shot down, approximately ten.

CDR Takahide Aioi at the Ōita Air Group, 1943. (Takahide Aioi)

CDR Takahide Aioi

Born in Hiroshima Prefecture in 1912, Aioi graduated from the Naval Academy as a member of the 59th class in 1931. In July 1934 he completed the 25th Aviation Student Course and became a fighter pilot. After being posted to the Tateyama Air Group, on board the *Ryūjō*, and then to the Saeki Air Group, he was posted to the 12th Air Group in December 1937 [1936?] and advanced to Chowshitze. However, he soon returned to Ōmura. In August, as a result of the outbreak of the Shanghai Incident, Aioi advanced to Kunda airfield. Using a Type 95 fighter, Aioi was engaged primarily in overhead patrols and in support of naval ground forces. In December [1937], he was promoted to LT and returned to the homeland as division officer in the Kasumigaura Air Group. However, the following March he was transferred as division officer to the 12th Air Group and participated in combat in the central China battlefront.

Aioi's first battle experience was during the attack on Hankow, on 29 April; during the confused fighting that ensued, he shot down two I-15 fighters.

Next, during the attack on Nanchang on

26 June [1938] Aioi took three aircraft of the shōtai with him and detached his group from the main force. They found themselves surrounded by about twenty enemy fighters, and after a hard struggle each of the aircraft shot down two of the enemy planes. LT Aioi himself barely managed to elude his pursuers but did get back and land at Anking. After participating in a number of air battles over Nanchang and over Hankow, in December, Aioi was ordered on board the *Akagi* as a division officer. For a time in October 1939 he was transferred to the 12th Air Group and advanced into South China. In January 1940, however, he returned to the *Akagi*. After next being posted to the Ōita and Yokosuka air groups, Aioi greeted the day war began between Japan and the United States as group leader on board the *Ryūjō*. On the morning of 8 December, he led a group of nine carrier fighters from off Mindanao and participated in the attack on Davao escorting the carrier attack planes. There was no enemy opposition, however. In February 1942, he was transferred to the 3rd Air Group as group leader; in November he was promoted to LCDR. Until April 1943, Aioi continued to serve as Air Group 202 group leader and fought vigorously at the front in

Aioi during his 12th Air Group days, at Hankow. (Takahide Aioi)

the attacks on Darwin and the counteroffensive against Guadalcanal. In August 1944, he was transferred to Air Group 601 as group leader and commanded the unit from the ground. In October, during the battle off the Philippines, the *Zuikaku* was sunk (he happened to be on board); Aioi had to be rescued by a destroyer. After landing in the Philippines, Aioi returned to the homeland in the spring of 1945. When the war ended, he was executive officer of Air Group 343.

Renowned as a representative commanding officer of naval fighter units, after the war Aioi entered the Maritime Self-Defense Force and rose to the rank of admiral. After serving as commander in chief of the Self-Defense Fleet as his final post, Aioi retired. He has been credited with shooting down scores of enemy aircraft.

LTJG Kagemitsu Matsu-o (Reserves) (Family of Kagemitsu Matsu-o)

LTJG Kagemitsu Matsu-o (Reserves)

Born in Fukuoka Prefecture in 1920, Matsu-o graduated from the Miyazaki Agriculture and Forestries College in December 1941; he was selected as a reserve student in the navy in February 1942. After receiving flight training at the Kasumigaura, Iwakuni, and Ōita air groups, he was commissioned as a naval reserve ensign in February 1943.

In August, Matsu-o was posted to Air Group 253 and immediately advanced to Rabaul. Starting the latter part of September, Matsu-o was engaged in combat almost regularly in the drives on Ant Atoll, Cape Marcus, Torokina, and Buna, in addition to participating in intercept operations over Rabaul. On 23 December, during the course of intercepting a combined force of American aircraft numbering about eighty fighters and bombers over Rabaul, Matsu-o was killed in action.

Although his time in combat was but a brief three months, Matsu-o had a personal kill record of over ten aircraft. He is thought to be the only ace among all the reserve fighter pilots of the Pacific War. Further, his younger brother by blood was also a pilot, a graduate of the Military Academy; this brother was killed in action one year later in the southern part of Taiwan.

CDR Aya-o Shirane (Family of Aya-o Shirane)

CDR Aya-o Shirane

Born in 1916 as the fourth son of Takesuke Shirane, later to assume the post of cabinet secretary, the younger Shirane attended Tokyo Municipal High School No. 4 and then was graduated from the Naval Academy. In March 1939 he completed the 31st Aviation Student Course and became a fighter pilot. In September of the same year, he was posted to the 12th Air Group and advanced to Hankow. On 19 August 1940, he participated in the first attack on Chungking that used the new and advanced Zero fighter. During a subsequent attack on Chungking carried out on 13 September, Shirane was a member of the thirteen aircraft unit commanded by LT Saburō Shindō. The unit shot down twenty-seven enemy fighters. Even LTJG Shirane, for whom this was his first combat experience, shot down one aircraft.

In May 1941, Shirane was promoted to lieutenant. During the Pacific War, he participated in the attacks on Darwin, operations over the Indian Ocean, and in the Midway operation as a division officer on board the *Akagi*. In July 1942, he was transferred to the *Zuikaku* as division officer and fought vigorously in the Second Battle of the Solomon Sea [Battle of the Eastern Solomons] and in the Battle of Santa Cruz. In November [1942] he was ordered back to the Yokosuka Air Group. In November 1943, he was selected group leader in Air Group 341; this unit was equipped with the new and powerful Shiden fighter. Toward the end of October 1944, Shirane led the Shiden unit that he had personally trained (Fighter Hikōtai 701) and advanced to the base at Mabalacat on Luzon. The unit participated in the air battles over Leyte. On 24 November, while battling P-38s from the U.S. Army Air Forces' 433rd Squadron, Shirane decided to end it all by crashing his aircraft. Shirane was a fighter unit commander who was at once composed, taciturn, and yet finely honed in spirit and skills; he was well liked and trusted by both superiors and subordinates. Total number of aircraft shot down, nine (officially recognized).

LT Isamu Mochizuki during his LTJG days
(Family of Isamu Mochizuki)

LT Isamu Mochizuki

Born in Saga Prefecture in 1906, Mochizuki enlisted in the navy in 1925; he was a real old-timer, in the sense that he completed the 9th Pilot Training Class in November 1926. After serving on board the *Hōshō* and the *Kaga,* he was posted to the Ōmura Air Group. Starting in November 1932 for a period of four years, Mochizuki came to be renowned as the very epitome of pilots posted to the fighter units' Mecca, the Yokosuka Air Group. In November 1936, he was promoted to warrant officer and transferred to the Ōmura Air Group. Upon the outbreak of the China Incident, he was posted to the 13th Air Group and advanced to the Kunda base in Shanghai. He had already reached the age of thirty-one; however, for the half-year period until he returned to the homeland in January of the following year, Mochizuki was very active and shot down a total of seven enemy fighters with his outstanding air combat

techniques and his indomitable fighting spirit.

Later, he served as an instructor in a number of homeland-based air groups; in October 1941, Mochizuki was promoted to Special Service Flight Ensign. In March 1943 he was ordered to serve as division officer in the newly organized Air Group 281 and was stationed in the northern Kuriles. When the war situation in the Marshall Islands became critical, however, he advanced to the Roi base. American carrier raids had already destroyed the majority of aircraft on the ground; it was no longer possible for rescue operations by submarine or aircraft to be successful. When American forces landed on the island on 6 February 1944, Mochizuki is presumed to have met his death by participating in a banzai attack [gyokusai].

LT Mochizuki's flying experiences extended over a period of eighteen years. He was the man who during his Yokosuka Air Group days first established the so-called half loop and roll technique (hineri-komi gihō) used in dogfighting. This technique later spread throughout all services. Mochizuki was known not to have any peers in expertise in single-plane dogfighting.

Mochizuki during his 13th Air Group days
(Family of Isamu Mochizuki)

LTJG Kaname Harada (Hideki Shingō)

LTJG Kaname Harada

Born in Nagano Prefecture in 1916, Harada graduated from the 35th Pilot Training Class in February 1937. After being posted to the Saeki Air Group, he was next attached to the 12th Air Group in October and advanced to the central China battlefront. There was no opportunity for air combat, however, and he was returned to the homeland in January 1938. Harada then served as an instructor in the Saeki, Tsukuba, Hyakurigahara, and Ōita air groups; in September 1941 he was transferred to serve on board the *Sōryū*. During the attack on Pearl Harbor, Harada was assigned patrol duties over the carriers. During the attack on Colombo on 5 April 1942, Harada engaged in air combat with British fighters and, to his credit, shot down five (two probables) single-handedly. During an intercept of Hudson [Blenheim] bombers that attacked the striking force on the 9th, Harada and others jointly shot down two aircraft. Next, Harada participated in the Battle of Midway and served on combat air patrol. During the course of three intercept operations, he shot down five enemy torpedo bombers (three jointly). Since the *Sōryū* had been sunk, however, Harada had to ditch and was picked up by a destroyer. In July, Harada was transferred to serve on board the *Hiyō*. In early October he left the homeland to participate in the Guadalcanal operation. During the attack on Guadalcanal on 17 October, while Harada escorted the carrier attack plane squadron, he engaged in combat with a force of enemy fighters that had made a surprise attack on him by taking advantage of their superior altitude. After Harada had shot down one aircraft (a probable), he was hit and suffered severe injuries. He was forced to make an emergency landing close to the Rekata base. Harada was taken back to the homeland in a hospital ship and treated for wounds to his left shoulder and arms. Harada greeted the end of the war without having been able to regain his health. Number of aircraft shot down, nine (officially recognized).

ENS Toshiyuki Sueda (Kazuo Tsunoda)

ENS Toshiyuki Sueda

Born in Fukuoka Prefecture in 1913, Sueda enlisted in the navy in 1933 and graduated from the 32nd Pilot Training Class in July 1936. He was then posted to the Ōmura Air Group. Immediately upon the outbreak of the China Incident, Sueda was posted to the 13th Air Group and advanced to Kunda base, Shanghai. He participated in the first air raid on Nanking carried out on 19 September 1937; during this attack, which was Sueda's first combat experience, he shot down two aircraft. During the 6 October attack on Nanking, and despite the fact that his machine guns were not operating properly, Sueda kept pursuing an enemy aircraft until it crashed to the ground. This made him well known as the proponent of the "knock'em down without shooting 'em" (Mutekatsu-ryū gekitsui) method. At the same time, Sueda's aircraft was hit; because of damage to its compass, he was unable to find his bearings to return to base. Sueda then followed the banks of the Yangtze River and was able to return to base by evening. In November, after his return to the homeland, he was assigned to the 12th Air Group; in May 1940 he advanced to Hankow. He participated in the attack on Chungking that was carried out on 13 September. Next, he was posted to the 14th Air Group in South China. On 7 October, he participated in the attack on Kunming; then, in November, he reverted to the Ōita Air Group. In October 1942, Sueda was promoted to warrant officer and transferred to Air Group 252. Toward the end of December, Sueda advanced into the southeast area of operations. On 27 December in air combat over Munda, he shot down two aircraft but also received hits himself and made an emergency landing. From this date until March 1943, he continued to be active in the area. He was then assigned air defense duties at Wake Island. On 6 October 1943, after he took off to intercept a large group of enemy carrier aircraft that came raiding, Sueda failed to return. He is deemed to have been killed in action. Number of aircraft shot down: during the China Incident, six; during the Pacific War, three (officially recognized).

WO Kiyonobu Suzuki during his 12th Air Group days (Family of Kiyonobu Suzuki)

WO Kiyonobu Suzuki

Born in Fukuoka Prefecture in 1914, Suzuki enlisted in the navy in May 1933 as a fireman; in August 1935, he graduated from the 28th Pilot Training Class and changed his speciality to that of fighter pilot. After serving with the Ōmura Air Wing, he was posted to the Suzuka Air Group, where he was at the outbreak of the China Incident. He advanced to Taihoku (Taipei), where he was engaged in air defense duties. Toward the end of October 1937, he was transferred to the 13th Air Group and moved to the base at Shanghai.

Suzuki's first battle encounter was on 2 December [1937] during the air raid on Nanking. PO3c Suzuki flew as number three wingman for the 2nd Shōtai, which consisted of six Type 96 carrier fighters commanded by LT Nangō. After a fierce engagement with a force of I-16 fighters, Suzuki shot down two aircraft (one probable) and was given a unit commendation. Next, during the 25 February [1938] attack on Nanchang, he sortied as number two wingman for LT Takuma and shot down another enemy aircraft. Suzuki's aircraft was hit, however, and he was wounded; the commander's aircraft was missing in

action as well. In March, Suzuki was transferred to the 12th Air Group; before his return to the homeland in September, he participated in a number of central China air battles. With respect to combat services performed by Suzuki during this period, he was rewarded by a rare award of the Order of the Golden Kite, 5th Class. At the same time, Suzuki's personal victory tally during his time with the 12th Air Group is not clear.

After serving as an instructor with the Saeki and Ōita air groups, Suzuki was ordered on board the *Kaga* in October 1941. During the attack on Pearl Harbor, he participated in the action as a shōtai leader, attached to the second wave fighter escort. There was no sight of the enemy, however; even the results of the previous strafing of airfields could not be verified because of the smoke generated by the bombings. After participating in attacks on Darwin, Suzuki next took part in the Midway operation in June 1942. During the morning of the 4th, Suzuki participated in the fighter escort that attacked Midway Island; jointly with his chūtai, he shot down twelve aircraft. Following his return to the carrier, Suzuki

Suzuki during his 13th Air Group days (Family of Kiyonobu Suzuki)

took off on two occasions for combat air patrol over the carriers. Using daring combat tactics, Suzuki and his shōtai were able to shoot down a total of fourteen enemy torpedo planes and bombers. During the same evening, he ditched and was rescued by the destroyer *Hagikaze*.

Following his return to the homeland, PO1c Suzuki was transferred to serve on board the *Junyō*. During the Battle of Santa Cruz on 26 October, he joined the escort that accompanied the second attack wave and headed for an attack on American carrier forces. Together with the other fighter that was flying with him, Suzuki failed to return and is deemed to have been killed in action. Total number of aircraft shot down, in excess of the (officially recognized) nine.

ENS Ki-ichi Oda during his *Junyō* days, June 1942. (Masao Sasakibara)

ENS Ki-ichi Oda

Born in Niigata Prefecture in 1913, Oda enlisted in the navy in 1931 and served in the paymaster corps. In November of the following year, however, he graduated from the 18th Pilot Training Class and changed his speciality to that of fighter pilot. After being posted to the Ōmura and Yokosuka air groups, he served on board the *Hōshō* and then returned to the Yokosuka Air Group. In August 1937, immediately following the outbreak of the China Incident, he was transferred on board the *Kaga* and advanced to Shanghai. During the historic first attack on Nanking on 19 September, the main force of the attack unit consisted of twelve Type 96 carrier fighters belonging to the 13th Air Group. Three fighters from the *Kaga* under the command of LT Igarashi were also added to the main force. Both the commander's and the number two wingman's aircraft developed malfunctions and returned to their carriers. Only the number three wingman, PO2c Oda, was able to advance to the target area. In air combat over the capital, Oda shot down three Curtiss Hawks (one probable). Next, on 7 October during the attack on Shaoguan, Oda added one other aircraft to his score. In December he returned to the Kasumigaura Air Group. In March of the following year, he was transferred to the 13th Air Group; in June, to the 15th Air Group. And he was again active in the central China battlefront. In November, Oda returned to the homeland.

Later, at the time the 1st Air Fleet was being organized, Oda was ordered on board the aircraft carrier *Sōryū*. During the attack on Pearl Harbor, Oda sortied as the leader of the 3rd Shōtai, second wave fighter escort, and strafed Kaneohe Naval Air Station. In April 1942 he participated in the Indian Ocean operation; after fierce air combat over Colombo, he shot down three aircraft. On the 9th, while he flew combat air patrol over the carriers, a formation of Hudson aircraft [Blenheim bombers] that came raiding was intercepted; Oda's shōtai downed four of the enemy aircraft. During the Battle of Midway in June, Oda participated in combat air patrol actions over his carrier. He was rescued after the *Sōryū* was sunk and returned to the homeland.

In May of the following year, Oda was promoted to warrant officer and placed in the reserves. He was mobilized on the same day, however, and next served as an instructor at the Iwakuni and Kure air groups. In April 1944, Oda was ordered to Air Group 261 and advanced to a base in the Marianas, from where he participated in a number of battles in the Micronesia area. In July, he was transferred to Fighter Hikōtai 306 and stayed on at Truk. Oda then hitched a ride on the submarine I-365 in order to return to the homeland. On 10 December, however, during the trip back to the homeland, the submarine was sunk in the Ogasawara area and Oda shared its fate. Deemed to have been killed in action as of that date, Oda was also promoted to naval ensign. Total number of aircraft shot down, nine (officially recognized).

LTJG Mitsugu Mori during his 12th Air Group days (Family of Shigetaka Ōmori)

LTJG Mitsugu Mori

Born in Shizuoka Prefecture in 1908, Mori enlisted in the navy in 1927; he graduated from the 14th Pilot Training Class in May 1929. Mori was among the old-timers of the fighter pilot corps. During the First Shanghai Incident, which took place in 1932, Mori was on board the *Kaga* and advanced to the Shanghai airfield. He participated in direct support of ground action as well as in patrol duties, but a truce soon developed and he was withdrawn from the area. Mori was next posted to the Ōmura Air Group, served on board the *Akagi,* and was then posted to the Yokosuka and the Tateyama air groups. In January 1938, he was ordered attached to the 13th Air Group; with the reorganization of March, he was transferred to the 12th Air Group.

One week after he arrived at his post, on 18 February, PO1c Mori participated in the first air raid on Hankow as a shōtai leader. In this capacity, Mori joined the 12th Air Group (commander, LT Kaneko) in supporting the land attack plane unit and participated in the air attack on Hankow. Engaging in combat with the more than thirty enemy fighters that rose up to intercept them, Mori took full advantage of his skills

Oda (*right*) during his *Kaga* days (Hideki Shingō)

in dogfights. Though this was his first battle experience, Mori shot down four aircraft on this one occasion; of the four, two of the enemy aircraft collided with each other when Mori dodged his plane suddenly, using the frontal dodging (katasukashi) technique.

From this date until his return to the homeland about one and a half years later, Mori participated in a number of attacks on Hankow, Nanchang, and other areas. In each instance, he scored victories. As a result, he was given the rare honor of being presented with the Order of the Golden Kite, 5th Class. Unfortunately, however, the number of aircraft that were shot down by Mori during this period is not clear. Starting January 1939, he served as an instructor with the Suzuka Air Group; the following May, Mori was promoted to warrant officer and placed in the reserves. However, he was mobilized on the same day. In July 1942, Mori was ordered on board the *Hiyō* and again returned to the air combat front. At the time he was thirty-four years old but his finely honed air combat skills had not dulled. In October, Mori advanced to Rabaul and the base at Buin; for about one month he participated in a series of attacks on Guadalcanal. On the 11th, Mori shot down one F4F and, on the 14th, a dive-bomber. He himself was hit, however, ditched in the water, and was rescued. The following April in order to participate in the "I"-gō operation, he was again dispatched to Rabaul. He flew sorties in the attacks on Guadalcanal, Oro Bay, Moresby, and Milne Bay; he added two to the list of aircraft he had shot down. In May, he was promoted to ensign and returned to the homeland, where he became a test pilot with the [Naval] Air Technology Arsenal. In August of 1944, Mori was promoted to lieutenant junior grade and immediately retired. In 1960, Mori died of illness while in his birthplace. Number of aircraft shot down: during the China Incident, more than four; and during the Pacific War, five. These figures have been officially recognized.

Mori during his 12th Air Group days (Shigema Yoshitomi)

LTJG Kazu-o Tsunoda (Kazu-o Tsunoda)

LTJG Kazu-o Tsunoda

Born in Chiba Prefecture in 1918, Tsunoda qualified for the Otsu Flight Reserve Enlisted Trainee Class as a trainee and entered the Yokosuka Air Group. In March 1938, he completed the 5th Flight Training Course and was promoted to PO3c. After being posted to the Saeki and Ōmura air groups, he served on board the *Sōryū;* in February 1940 he was ordered to the 12th Air Group and advanced to the Hankow base. On 26 October, eight Zero fighters under the command of LT Fusata Iida carried out the third attack on Chengtu; Tsunoda had his first air combat experience at this time while flying as number two wingman for WO Yamashita. Tsunoda shot down one unarmed trainer.

In November, Tsunoda was transferred to the Tsukuba Air Group and returned to the homeland; in April 1942, he was promoted to warrant officer. At the end of May, he was next attached to the newly organized 2nd Air Group (later, Air Group 582). In August, Tsunoda advanced to the base at Rabaul and began participating in air combat in the southeast area. For a period of about ten months until his return to

the homeland in May of the following year, Tsunoda fought vigorously in attacks on Guadalcanal and Buna, as well as in intercept operations in the Rabaul and Buin areas. In particular, on 14 November 1942, WO Tsunoda commanded a group of eight aircraft that provided air cover for a transport convoy headed for Guadalcanal. After engaging in air combat with attacking enemy dive-bombers, he shot down one aircraft but was then hit and had to ditch near the Russell Islands. Tsunoda was rescued by the destroyer *Amagiri.*

Starting May 1943, Tsunoda served as an instructor at the Atsugi Air Group; in March [1944] he was transferred to Fighter Hikōtai 302, Air Group 252. For a period of one week starting on 30 June, Tsunoda advanced to Iwo Jima. During the same period, on both 3 and 4 July, large forces of American carrier fighters were intercepted and one F6F shot down. Next, on 14 July, Tsunoda again advanced to Iwo Jima and spent more than one month in intercept operations against B-24s.

In October, in order to participate in the ongoing air battles off Taiwan, Tsunoda left Kyūshū and advanced to Clark Field on the 22nd, proceeding via Okinawa and Taiwan. Here he was engaged in support of special attack force units; in November,

Tsunoda during his Air Group 582 days, 1942. (Shin-ichi Hirabayashi)

ENS Tsunoda himself was posted to a special attack force unit, the Baika-tai ("Japanese Apricot Flower Unit"). In the early part of December, Tsunoda advanced to the base at Cebu together with three of his colleagues seeking an opportune moment to attack enemy ship convoys. However, there was no such opportunity; toward the end of the same month, Tsunoda withdrew to Clark. In February [1945] he walked on foot to Tuguegarao in the northern Philippines and then escaped to Taiwan.

In Taiwan, Tsunoda was posted to Fighter Hikōtai 317, Air Group 205, and joined the special attack force unit Taigi-tai ("Noble Cause Unit"). After the Okinawa operation started, Tsunoda flew a number of sorties with the objective of attacking British task forces. There were no good opportunities for attack, however, and he greeted the end of hostilities at the Ilan (Giran) base. Number of aircraft shot down personally, nine. (Figure is officially recognized shoot-downs only.)

WO Jūzō Okamoto (Katsutarō Kobayashi)

WO Jūzō Okamoto

Born in Tokushima Prefecture in 1916, Okamoto enlisted in the navy in 1933; he graduated with the 31st Pilot Training Class in March 1936 and became a fighter pilot. In July 1937, he was posted to the 13th Air Group and participated in the central China battlefront. On the evening of 19 September, Okamoto achieved his first victory when he flew as the number three wingman for LT Shichirō Yamashita, in the second wave attack on Nanking. During the sixth wave attack on the 22nd, Okamoto added one other aircraft to his list.

Again, during the 22 December attack on Nanchang, PO3c Okamoto shot down two aircraft (one probable); he then returned to the homeland. Later, after serving as an instructor at the Saeki, Ōita, and Suzuka air groups, Okamoto participated in the southern China battlefront as a member of the 14th Air Group. In September of the following year [1941], he was transferred to the 3rd Air Group, in which post he greeted the beginning of hostilities between Japan and the United States. In the attacks on Luzon on 8 and 10 December, Okamoto participated as a shōtai leader. In the course of these two attacks and as the result of vigorous air combat, Okamoto and others jointly shot down six aircraft. The following April, Okamoto returned to the homeland and was transferred to the newly organized 6th Air Group. In June he boarded the *Junyō* and joined the attacks on Dutch Harbor carried out on the 3rd and 4th. After his return to the homeland in the fall of the same year, Okamoto was involved in the Solomons battlefront. On 11 October, he left Buka base to engage in patrol operations off the Guadalcanal anchorage. On the way back, five aircraft under the command of LTJG Kuba were missing because of inclement weather; all pilots are deemed to have been killed in action. The veteran pilot PO1c Okamoto was among those lost. Number of aircraft shot down personally, nine (officially recognized).

WO Yoshi-o Nakamura

Born to a farm family in Hokkaidō in 1923, Nakamura enlisted in the navy in 1940 as a fireman. In February 1941, however, he was posted to the Tsuchiura Air Group as a pilot trainee member of the Hei 3rd class. In January 1942, Nakamura entered the 18th Flight Training Course and then received additional training with the Ōmura Air Group. In July, he was posted to the 6th Air Group as a PO1c; in October, he advanced to Rabaul.

For a period of about one year thereafter, Nakamura survived furious air battles in the area, using Rabaul and Buin as his bases. In particular, on 7 June 1943 during an air battle over the Russell Islands, Nakamura shot down three aircraft (one probable). On the 16th, Nakamura flew as number four wingman for LT Miyano's shotai but was hit and wounded and had to make an emergency landing on Kolombangara Island. In January 1944, he was transferred to Air Group 302 and returned to the homeland. After serving in the Yokosuka Air Group, he was next transferred to the Fighter Hikōtai 701, Air Group 343, in January 1944. It was at this post that Nakamura greeted the end of the hostilities. Total flight time, 1,830 hours; total number of aircraft shot down, nine (officially recognized).

WO Yoshi-o Nakamura during his Air Group 302 days (Yoshi-o Nakamura)

LT Ichirō Higashiyama during his 12th Air Group days (Kazu-o Tsunoda)

LT Ichirō Higashiyama

Born in Nagano Prefecture in 1915, Higashiyama entered the Yokosuka Air Group as a student of the Otsu 2nd Flight Reserve Enlisted Trainee Class. He graduated from a Flight Training Course in April 1935 at the top of his class, received an Imperial Award from the Japan Academy, and became a fighter pilot. After serving in the Tateyama Air Group, Higashiyama was posted to the Yokosuka Air Group for two years. Then, in December 1937, he was ordered to serve on board the *Sōryū*. The following May, he joined the unit dispatched to Nanking and participated in the central China battlefront. In July, Higashiyama was transferred to the 15th Air Group under the command of LT Nangō; using Anking as his base, Higashiyama participated in support of naval ground forces, in the attack on Nanchang, in the interception of SBs [bombers], and in other action.

Higashiyama's first taste of battle came on 28 June when his own shōtai intercepted three SBs and shot down two of them. On 14 July, in the course of intercepting nine SB bombers, PO1c Higashiyama and PO3c Yoshiharu Matsumoto shot down three of the invaders. Next, during the attack on

Nanchang on the 18th, Higashiyama sortied as number two wingman for the commander, LT Nangō. After a pitched battle, Higashiyama himself shot down two enemy aircraft. Nangō's aircraft collided with a falling enemy aircraft, and Higashiyama was a witness to the fall of the commander's aircraft into the lake.

In November 1938, Higashiyama returned to the Yokosuka Air Group for the second time and was involved in the operational testing of newly developed, more powerful aircraft. During this same period, in August 1939, Higashiyama suffered serious injuries from a skull fracture that occurred as the result of an accident in the air; he did recover, however. After being promoted to warrant officer in May 1940, he was transferred to the 12th Air Group. He then air transported a Zero fighter, the first of its type to be used in combat, to Hankow. On 19 August, Higashiyama joined in the first attack on Chungking but returned to base without sighting the enemy.

During the third attack on Chengtu on 4 October, Higashiyama flew as 3rd Shōtai leader. During the previous evening, Higashiyama, Hagiri, Nakase, and (Hideo) Ōishi had put their heads together and connived a plan for landing on the enemy airfield and setting it on fire. On the day concerned, aircraft on the ground at the Taipingsze airfield had already been set on fire by strafing. The group landed on the field as planned; Higashiyama and Nakase then set the command post on fire. Following this act, Higashiyama and his colleague PO3c Iki Arita next attacked a formation of SBs and jointly shot down three of the enemy bombers. All pilots then returned safely to base. In March 1941, Higashiyama returned to the Yokosuka Air Group and continued with the practical testing of aircraft. Called the "Boss of the Yokosuka Air Group" (Yokosuka-kū no nushi), Higashiyama was next ordered to serve as division officer in the newly organized Air Group 261. The following February [1944], Higashiyama advanced to Saipan. On 30 March, in response to a raid on Palau by an

American task force, thirty-two aircraft of Air Group 261 commanded by group leader LT Ibusuki escorted a carrier bomber group and moved to the base on Peleliu Island. The following day, however, a major force of American carrier fighters attacked for the second time. The Zero fighter unit that rose to intercept them was still en route to their rendezvous point when they were attacked from above by a group of American fighters. Casualties suffered almost amounted to annihilation. LTJG Higashiyama himself fought vigorously and shot down three enemy aircraft; however, his own aircraft received hits and caught on fire. Higashiyama parachuted but received major burns and was transported to Saipan. He faced the landing of American troops while still hospitalized and is deemed to have met with an honorable death as of 8 July.

LT Higashiyama was trusted by both superiors and subordinates; he possessed both an outstanding character and outstanding skills. He was a superior pilot, considered to be a good representative of graduates of the Flight Reserve Enlisted Trainee Class system. Total number of aircraft shot down, nine (officially recognized).

LT Yoshi-o Fukui (Yoshi-o Fukui)

LT Yoshi-o Fukui

Born in Kagawa Prefecture in 1913, Fukui enlisted at the Sasebo Barracks in 1931, initially serving as a maintenance man. He graduated from the 26th Pilot Training Class in March 1935, however, and changed his speciality to that of fighter pilot. After serving in both the Ōmura and Kanoya air groups, Fukui was posted on board the Ryūjō when the China Incident broke out. In August [1937], the carrier moved off Shanghai but was primarily engaged in support of naval ground action. On the 22nd, while Fukui was flying as number two wingman in LTJG Kaneko's four-aircraft formation on a patrol mission over Paoshan, the formation happened on eighteen Curtiss Hawks. A fight immediately ensued, and eight enemy aircraft were shot down; of this number, three were credited as personal victories of PO2c Fukui.

The carrier next moved off southern China. During the first air attack on Canton on 21 September, Fukui's unit escorted the attacking force. When the unit neared the target area, it was PO2c Fukui with his superior vision who first discovered a group of enemy fighters. Fukui plunged into the group and shot down two. In December he was transferred to the Yokosuka Air Group; the following April he was returned to carrier duty and ordered to serve on board the Kaga. Until late in the fall, Fukui was engaged primarily in action in the southern China area. During the same period, Fukui surprised and shot down one Curtiss Hark aircraft during the 13 September [1938] attack on Liuchow; he also made repeated strafing attacks on ground targets.

In December, Fukui was transferred on board the Akagi. Later on he served as an instructor at the Yatabe, Kanoya, Hyakurigahara, and Ōita air groups. During the same period, in April 1941 Fukui was promoted to warrant officer. In June 1943, for the first time in some time, Fukui was ordered to serve on board a carrier, the *Zuihō*. He thus returned to front-line duty and by 1 November had advanced to Rabaul. On the following day, the 2nd, Rabaul was hit by a major combined air raid by fighters and bombers. Our own side sent out more than one hundred fighters to intercept them and did achieve major battle results. After ENS Fukui had shot down a B-25 at a low altitude just barely over the top of a palm grove, he was surrounded by a formation of P-38s; his aircraft received hits and caught on fire. Fukui parachuted but received burns on his right foot. Three days later he was back in action and continued to participate in a number of intercept and attack operations. Fukui then returned to Truk.

In February 1944 he was transferred to Air Group 601, boarded the *Zuikaku,* and participated in the "A"-gō operation. On 19 June, Fukui served as a shōtai leader of the first wave fighter escort in an attack on an American task force. During air combat he shot down one aircraft (probable). The next day, the 20th, Fukui was flying on patrol in the evening when he intercepted an incoming American torpedo plane. Fukui then made a night landing on his carrier. In July, Fukui was transferred to Fighter Hikōtai 165, Air Group 653. On 24 October, Fukui participated in the sea battle off the Philippines and sortied from the *Zuikaku* en route to attacking an American task force. After the attack, Fukui returned to his aircraft carrier; following the sinking of the carrier itself, he was rescued by an escorting destroyer. Next, in November, Fukui was transferred to Fighter Hikōtai 304 and advanced, by land bases, to the base at Bamban, Philippines. In January 1945, Fukui withdrew to the homeland and greeted the end of the war while attached to Air Group 352. Fukui's career in flying lasted more than ten years; he was a skilled master, possessor of a composed and fine character, in addition to being a well-seasoned fighter. Total number of aircraft shot down, eleven (four probables).

LT Fukui (Yoshi-o Fukui)

CDR Tadashi Kaneko during his *Ryūjō* days (Minoru Suzuki)

CDR Tadashi Kaneko

Born in Tokyo as the son of a lawyer, Kaneko attended Tokyo Municipal High School No. 1 and entered the Naval Academy; he then graduated with the 60th class in 1932. In July 1935, he completed the 26th Aviation Student Course and became a fighter pilot.

LTJG Kaneko greeted the outbreak of the China Incident as a shōtai leader of the fighter squadron on board the aircraft carrier *Ryūjō*. On 22 August 1937, Kaneko led three pilots on a patrol in nearby Shanghai and happened to meet a formation of eighteen Curtiss Hawk fighters. During the ensuing fierce air combat, Kaneko showed conspicuous gallantry; six of the enemy aircraft were shot down. The lieutenant junior grade himself accounted for destroying two of these, and he became instantly famous, nationwide. Later, after participating in the attack on Canton in September, Kaneko returned to the homeland. In August 1938 he returned to the central China battlefront as division officer in the 15th Air Group. Un-

til the end of that year, Kaneko was involved primarily in base air defense and in direct support of ground forces.

Following his return to the homeland, Kaneko was next posted to the 12th Air Group in April 1939 as division officer and advanced to Hankow; however, there were no opportunities for air combat. In May 1940, Kaneko served as division officer in the Ōmura Air Group, and in October, in the same capacity in the Mihoro Air Group. In September 1941, Kaneko was transferred to the newly commissioned aircraft carrier *Shōkaku,* again as division officer. He participated in the attack on Pearl Harbor, the attack on Salamaua, and in Indian Ocean operations. In May 1942, Kaneko was transferred to the 6th Air Group as group leader, and in order to participate in the occupation of Midway, the group advanced towards the battlefront by taking passage on the aircraft carriers. LT Kaneko happened to be on board the *Akagi*. On 4 June, he observed the wave formation attacks on his aircraft carrier by American carrier aircraft and could no longer contain himself. Taking off from the carrier with four of his pilots, Kaneko intercepted and shot down two large torpedo planes.

After his rescue following the sinking of the *Akagi* and return to the homeland, Kaneko was transferred to the *Hiyō* as group leader; in October, the unit advanced into the Solomons area. Because of an engine malfunction of the aircraft carrier, however, the air group was diverted to the base at Rabaul. Starting the latter part of October, Kaneko participated in the almost daily forays conducted during the Guadalcanal attack operation. LCDR Kaneko, who had been advanced to that rank on 1 November, was always at the forefront of any battle action. In particular, during the 11 November attack on Guadalcanal Kaneko shot down three F4Fs. On the 14th, LCDR Kaneko took off from Buin leading eleven of his colleagues to provide escort to the ship convoy that was transporting the 38th Division. About 1430 the same day, while in combat with enemy car-

Kaneko (*second from left*) during his 12th Air Group days (Mitsugu Kofukuda)

rier fighters and bombers, Kaneko was hit and ended it all by crashing his aircraft.

Kaneko was known as an excellent leader, equipped with highly developed senses and the will to fight. His death was mourned by many. Total number of aircraft shot down, in excess of eight (officially recognized).

CDR Sachi-o Endō during his *Sōryū* days (Yasujirō Abe)

CDR Sachi-o Endō

Endō is the hero who became famous as the "King of B-29 Killers" (B-29 Gekitsui-ō) during intercept operations against B-29s that raided the homeland. Born in a remote mountain village in Yamagata Prefecture in 1915, Endō enlisted at the Yokosuka Air Group as a member of the 1st Flight Reserve Enlisted Trainee Class in June 1930. After completing the Flight Training Course at Kasumigaura, he graduated in August 1933. Trained as a pilot of carrier attack planes at the Tateyama Air Group, Endō served on board the *Akagi* and with the Kasumigaura and Ōmura air groups. In December 1937, he was transferred on board the *Sōryū*. During the spring of 1938, Endō advanced to the central China area and joined a unit dispatched to Nanking.

For about two months, he cooperated with the land operations being conducted along the banks of the Yangtze River. In December 1939, he was assigned to the Hyakurigahara Air Group as an instructor and later served in the same capacity with the Tateyama and Ōmura air groups. During this same period, Endō was promoted to warrant officer in May 1940, to ensign in November 1942, and in November of the following year, to lieutenant junior grade.

From May 1942, Endō was assigned to Kasumigaura to teach in the Flight Reserve Enlisted Trainee program. In January 1943, he was ordered posted to Air Group 251 and changed to piloting Type 2 land reconnaissance planes. Endō was made responsible for testing the first model of an aircraft equipped with the obliquely angled cannon, a system devised by commanding officer Kozono for use with the night fighter Gekkō. Confident of its success, Endō advanced to Rabaul in May and sortied on a number of night intercept operations. In these engagements, the glory went to PO1c Kudō and WO Satoru Ono. ENS Endō was not favored by the gods of war, was wounded in action, and returned to the homeland.

Simultaneously with the establishment of Air Group 302 in March 1944, Endo was ordered to serve as division officer of a Gekkō night fighter unit. Training was conducted at Atsugi base. In June, when B-29 attacks came to be directed to the northern Kyūshū area, LTJG Endō was dispatched to Air Group 352 at Ōmura base. At that time, Endō was placed in charge of six aircraft and eight Gekkō flight crews. During the 20 August raid by B-29s, LTJG Endō single-handedly pursued a B-29 that was dropping away from its formation. Endō, however, had to make an emergency

landing on Cheju Island. At the same time, Endō's own victories were two enemy aircraft shot down, one probable, and two damaged. Next, during the 25 October air combat with B-29s raiding Ōmura base, Endō pursued a damaged B-29 for quite a period of time and finally brought it down. In November he was withdrawn to Atsugi. For a period of time, Endō advanced with three of his fellow pilots to Hachijō Jima but soon returned to the base at Atsugi.

From mid-December on, Endō was active in the night interception of B-29s that attacked the Kantō and Tōkai regions. He almost always racked up kills. On the afternoon of 14 January 1945, Endō shot down one aircraft and destroyed a second during daylight interception of enemy aircraft over Enshū Nada. However, his own aircraft was hit and caught on fire. Endō first ordered his observer, CPO Ozaki, to escape by parachute (he was killed in action); he then piloted the burning aircraft over Atsumi Peninsula. Finally, at an altitude of about three hundred meters, Endō attempted to parachute but died in action as a result of severe burns. Adding the last score to the rest, records show that Endō shot down eight and heavily damaged another eight aircraft, counting B-29s only. In October of the previous year, Endō had received words of praise from the commanding general of the western area, as well as a commendation from the admiral commanding the Sasebo Naval Station for his exploits in shooting down B-29s over Kyūshū. After his death, Endō received a further commendation from the admiral commanding the Yokosuka Naval Station, also a promulgation issued by the supreme defense commander. Endō was also given a two-rank promotion to naval commander.

LT Takeyoshi Ōno

LT Takeyoshi Ōno during his Tainan Air Group days, 1942. (Shin-ichi Hirabayashi)

Born in Ishikawa Prefecture in 1921, Ōno graduated with the 68th class of the Naval Academy in 1940. In June 1942 he finished the 36th Aviation Student Course and was immediately ordered to the Tainan Air Group, situated at Rabaul. His initial combat experience was on 27 August over Buna. While on patrol leading two of his colleagues, Ōno single-handedly tackled a P-39 and shot it down. By shooting down five aircraft before returning to the homeland in early November, Ōno showed remarkable progress in combat effectiveness. Hopes were even held that Ōno would be the reincarnation of LTJG Sasai, who had been killed in action. In May 1943, Ōno took part as a division officer of Air Group 251 in the second advance to Rabaul. Starting with the attack on Oro Bay on 14 May, Ōno flew sorties as the mainstay commander of the battles over the Russell Islands on the 7th and 12th June, and the attacks on ships off Lunga Point on the 16th. In particular, during the attacks of the 12th and the 16th, despite his youthfulness, Ōno served as the overall commander of Air Group 251 Fighter Squadron. He single-handedly shot down two aircraft, and jointly, an additional two aircraft. Ōno flew as division officer in the attack on Rendova on the 30th; however, in the ensuing combat melee, Ōno died in action by destroying his own aircraft. Total number of aircraft shot down, eight (officially recognized).

CPO Kaoru Takaiwa during his Air Group 253 days, at Tobera airfield, 1944. (Kenji Takahashi)

CPO Kaoru Takaiwa

Born in Nagano Prefecture in 1923, Takaiwa entered the Otsu 13th Flight Reserve Enlisted Trainee Class at the age of seventeen. He completed his flight reserve training course at Tsuchiura and the Flight Training Course (26th) at the Nagoya and Ōita air groups. Takaiwa then underwent advanced training with the Suzuka and Atsugi air groups. He was next ordered posted to Air Group 201 in December 1943 and advanced to the heavy fighting in the Rabaul battlefront area. Starting with his first victory on the 17th, immediately after his arrival at Rabaul, Takaiwa showed his prowess by personally shooting down ten aircraft (three probables) in the succeeding two weeks.

With the move of Air Group 201 to Truk on 3 January 1944, Takaiwa himself was transferred to Air Group 253; he then fought vigorously in the daily intercept operations being conducted in the area. Although his personal victories for this period are not clear, as a minimum, they are believed to exceed the number achieved during the time Takaiwa was attached to Air Group 201. During an intercept operation on 10 February, youthful, twenty-year-old PO1c Takaiwa was missing in action and is deemed to have been killed in action.

ENS Shigetoshi Kudō

Born to a farm family in Ōita Prefecture in 1920, Kudō enlisted in the navy in 1937 and was initially assigned as a maintenance man. In August 1940, however, he graduated from the 53rd Pilot Training Class and changed his speciality to that of pilot of land reconnaissance planes. After serving with the Saeki Air Group, he was assigned to the Tainan Air Group in October 1941. Kudō participated in the Philippines and Dutch East Indies operations by providing pathfinder service to fighter units and also as a reconnaissance pilot. In the spring of 1942, he advanced to Rabaul.

On the morning of 29 August 1942, he intercepted eight B-17s over Rabaul in a Type 98 land reconnaissance plane, shot down a B-17, and probably shot down an-

ENS Shigetoshi Kudō during his Tainan Air Group days (Family of Shigetoshi Kudō)

other by aerial bombs. At the time, Rabaul was under constant night attack by enemy medium and heavy bombers using Moresby and other air bases. Not much in the way of damage occurred, however. At the same time, certain psychological effects of such raids could not be ignored; our forces were eagerly awaiting the arrival of a new, more powerful night fighter. What was devised as the result of such demand was the Gekkō, equipped with obliquely angled cannons that commanding officer Kozono of Air Group 251 propounded.

Between the time that Kudō returned to the homeland in the fall of 1942 and May of the following year, when he again advanced to Rabaul, CPO Kudō had been training with the new night fighter. On 21 May, the first of the long-awaited night fighter aircraft became available. At 0200 the following day, Kudō took off in a night fighter with LTJG Yutaka Sugawara as observer. Taking advantage of the available moonlight and with the help of friendly searchlights, about 0240 a B-17 was held on target and shot down, using the obliquely angled cannons. Around 0330 the same day, another aircraft was shot down. At 0430, Kudō landed back at the Rabaul base, amid rousing cheers of the personnel who witnessed his return. Starting with this particular victory, a few of the Gekkō aircraft enabled us to regain night air control over Rabaul. In July, Kudō further advanced to the Ballale base [Bougainville], where he engaged in night intercept operations.

The victories achieved by Kudō and his aircraft continued to mount; on 11 and 13 June, one B-17 each day; on the 26th, two aircraft; and on the 30th, one aircraft. Next, during the evening of 7 July, one Hudson bomber was shot down over Buin by use of the downward-looking, obliquely angled cannon. Eventually, a grand total of eight aircraft were shot down during a two-month period. Famed as the "King of the Night" (Yoru no ōja) from Rabaul, Kudō was given a military sword with the inscription, "For Conspicuous Military Valor."

Starting the fall of 1943, the emphasis in bombing raids changed to the conduct of daytime raids. In addition, countermeasures on the part of the enemy also advanced, and it became more difficult to shoot down aircraft at night. In February of the following year, Kudō returned to the homeland and was reassigned to the Yokosuka Air Group, where he was given duties in the air defense of the homeland. During an emergency landing in May 1945 caused by an air accident, Kudō was injured; as a result, he greeted the end of the war while still convalescing. In 1960, Kudō died as a result of the same injury.

Kudō during his Yokosuka Air Group days. (Tadashi Nakajima)

LTJG Satoru Ono (*top*) during his *Kaga* days
(Satoru Ono)

LTJG Satoru Ono

Born in Ōita Prefecture in 1915, Ono enlisted in the navy in 1932. While serving as
a fireman at the Ōmura Air Group, he volunteered to become a pilot and joined the
23rd Pilot Training Class in September

1933. Graduating in April 1934, he was
posted to the Ōmura Air Group as a Sea2c,
as a pilot of carrier bombers. At the time he
was nineteen years old.

After serving on board the *Ryūjō* and the
Kaga, he was posted to the Kasumigaura
Air Group; immediately upon the outbreak
of the China Incident, Ono returned to
serve on board the *Kaga* again. He was active in bombing attacks in various parts of
central and southern China. In particular,
during the attack on Canton on 13 April
1938, despite the fact that he was flying a
carrier bomber, Ono engaged in air combat
with enemy aircraft and shot one of them
down. During the offensive against Nanchang on 18 July, Ono was posted to the
15th Air Group and flew as number two
wingman for the commanding officer,
LCDR Matsumoto. Together with LTJG
Ogawa, Ono landed on an enemy airfield
and set the aircraft on the ground afire. In
addition, he performed the feat of shooting
down an additional two aircraft in air combat. As a result, Ono became well known
almost overnight.

In November of the same year, Ono returned to the homeland. After serving as an
instructor with the Ōmura and Usa air
groups, he was promoted to PO1c. In February 1942 he was transferred to the Yokosuka Air Group and conducted operational
tests of the Gekkō aircraft. In April he was
transferred to the Tainan Air Group and
advanced to Rabaul, from which he conducted reconnaissance missions over a wide
area. With the landing of American forces
on Guadalcanal on 7 August, he next conducted frequent reconnaissance forays in
the Solomons area, with good results. Although he returned to the homeland in November, Ono again advanced to Rabaul in
May of the following year. Using the night
fighter Gekkō, remodeled and equipped
with the obliquely angled cannons, Ono
served with LTJG Kisaku Hamano (observer) as a team; the two of them fre-
quently took off for night interceptions of
enemy bombers. The results were such that
Ono came to be referred to as "King of the
Night," along with CPO Kudō.

Ono's first combat experience was during the night of 5 June 1943, when he shot down two bombers (B-24s); on the night of 10 June, he shot down two more aircraft (B-17s, one probable). In July, Ono advanced to the Ballale base and fought vigorously in both night intercept and night bombing operations. He returned to the Atsugi Air Group in January 1944.

In April, Ono was transferred to Fighter Hikōtai 804, Air Group 322, and then promoted to ensign in May. In October 1944, Ono was posted to Air Group 141 and advanced to the Philippines. Using Nichol's airfield as his base, Ono sortied on night bombing attacks on Leyte using a Gekkō aircraft. During the same period, his own aircraft was attacked by enemy fighters and at one time was riddled with 147 bullet holes.

At the end of the same year, Ono pulled back to the homeland and was transferred to Air Group 352. Until the end of the war, he was engaged in intercepting B-29s; however, he only managed to shoot one down before the war actually came to an end. Total number of aircraft shot down, eight (officially recognized).

Ono was known throughout the navy as a manly and masterful pilot.

ENS Kazu-o Muranaka with Fighter Hikōtai 701, Air Group 343, at Ōmura base, end of July 1945. (Masao Sasakibara)

ENS Kazu-o Muranaka

Born in Fukuoka Prefecture in 1919, Muranaka enlisted in the Otsu 6th Flight Reserve Enlisted Trainee Class in June 1935 and graduated from the Flight Training Course in August 1938. He was successively posted to the Saeki, Ōita, and Ōmura air groups. On 14 August 1939, he was posted to the 14th Air Group and dispatched to participate in the southern China battlefront. In December, a Type 96 carrier fighter unit of the 14th Air Group advanced from Haihow to Nanning, which had been encircled by the enemy. PO3c Muranaka caught up with the fighter unit a bit later on the 27th. During the afternoon of the very same day, Muranaka and Sea1c Nojima, who was flying along with him, immediately took off on combat air patrol. The two of them discovered an enemy formation of single-engine aircraft and engaged them in battle; after pursuing the enemy, they jointly shot down two enemy aircraft (one probable). This not only was Muranaka's first combat experience, it also marked the first victories achieved by the 14th Air

Group. Next, after participating in the 10 January attack on Kweilin, Muranaka returned to the Suzuka Air Group in August 1940.

In November 1941, immediately before the outbreak of the war, he was transferred to serve on board the *Hiryū*. During the attack on Pearl Harbor, Muranaka joined the first attack wave's fighter escort; since he was unable to observe any trace of the enemy, he strafed Ewa Field. Later on, Muranaka participated in attacks on Darwin, in the Indian Ocean operation, and the Midway operation. In particular, on 4 June 1942, during the Midway operation, Muranaka took off as a member of the first wave fighter escort and engaged in battle with enemy fighter aircraft that rose to intercept them. Muranaka's was the sole aircraft providing air protection for the *Hiryū* carrier attack squadron, from the beginning to the end.

After his return to the carrier, Muranaka again took off for combat air patrol and intercepted incoming enemy attack forces. After shooting down three aircraft (one probable), Muranaka's own aircraft was hit and he had to ditch. He was rescued by the destroyer, *Nowaki*. After recovering from his injuries, Muranaka was first assigned to the aircraft carrier *Shōkaku* and then to the *Junyō*. He participated in both the Second Battle of the Solomons [Battle of the Eastern Solomons] in August, and in the Battle of Santa Cruz in October. In November, Muranaka advanced to the base at Rabaul and flew sorties during the Guadalcanal operation. In April of the following year, he returned to the homeland to serve as an instructor with the Tokushima Air Group.

In May 1944, Muranaka was transferred as an instructor to the 11th Air Group (Singapore); this was a unit for advanced training in the use of fighter aircraft. In May 1945, Muranaka was promoted to ensign and transferred to Fighter Hikōtai 701, Air Group 343, returning to Ōmura. On 24 July, Muranaka shot down one aircraft in air combat over the Bungo Suidō. After taking part in a number of other air battles, Muranaka greeted the end of the war. After the war, he served as a member of the Air Self-Defense Force and retired with the rank of major. Total number of aircraft shot down, six for sure, three probables.

Muranaka (*front row, second from left*) during his Saeki Air Group days (Mitsunori Nakajima)

LCDR Mochifumi Nangō during his *Sōryū* days, 1938. (Mitsugu Kofukuda)

LCDR Mochifumi Nangō

Nangō made his name during the early part of the China Incident as a top commander of fighter units. After his death, he became known as Gunshin Nangō Shōsa ("LCDR Nango, War God").

Nangō's grandfather was a high official in the Navy Ministry during its early days, as well as being one of the elder statesmen who were members of the National Diet; Nangō's father was a rear admiral and had served as head of the Kōdō-kan [a martial arts emporium in Tokyo]. Born into such a navy-oriented family, after Nangō attended the high school section of the Peers School (Gakushū-in), he entered the Naval Academy. Graduating in 1927 with an excellent scholastic record, he was ordered to sea duty. In November 1932, Nangō finished the 22nd Aviation Student Course and became a fighter pilot.

After serving on board the *Akagi* and with the Yokosuka Air Group, Nangō was next ordered to England to serve as an assistant naval attache in the Japanese embassy. After two years of residence in London, he returned to Japan. Following the outbreak of the China Incident, he was transferred in October 1937 to the 13th Air Group and participated in the central China battlefront as a division officer.

On 2 December [1937] six Type 96 fighters led by LT Nangō advanced over Nanking and engaged in fierce combat with thirty enemy fighters that had come up to intercept them. Counting the two that the lieutenant himself shot down, a total of thirteen enemy aircraft were shot down. For achieving such victories, the admiral of the China Area Fleet immediately sent to Nangō a letter of commendation.

In December, Nangō was transferred to serve as group leader on board the *Sōryū*. During the summer of 1938, Nangō was transferred to the newly established 15th Air Group as group leader and was sent again to China; this time he went to Anking in order to assist in the Wuhan operation. During the course of an air battle over Nanchang on 18 July, Nangō shot down one Gladiator fighter, despite the fact that his own aircraft was burdened with an extra fuel tank. Unfortunately, however, Nangō's aircraft was struck by an enemy aircraft that was falling out of control; Nangō himself crashed into the lake and died in action. At the time he was thirty-three years old, unmarried, and his death

Nangō at Nanking airfield (Family of Mochifumi Nangō)

was mourned by people very widely in Japan. It is said that vice minister of the navy, Isoroku Yamamoto, when he attended the wake held by Nangō's family, wept in front of the altar. Nangō was a gentle, well-trained, model youthful officer who enjoyed the trust and love of those both above him and below him. Inside Nangō burned a strong sense of combat. The following episode characterizes Nangō. On the way back from an attack on Anking,

during which his aircraft had been hit by enemy fire, Nangō held on to a piece of ruptured oil piping for a period of two and half hours, until he managed to return to base.

Total number of aircraft shot down, eight. In addition, it is interesting to note that Nangō's younger brother by blood, LTCOL Shigeo Nangō (killed in action), became one of the army's top fighter unit aces also.

ENS Tadashi Torakuma during his 13th Air Group days (Katsuhiro Hashimoto)

ENS Tadashi Torakuma

During the early part of the China Incident, Torakuma was known among all fighter pilots for his daring. Born in Ōita Prefecture in 1911, he enlisted in the navy in 1929. Changing from maintenance man to piloting, Torakuma graduated from the 20th Pilot Training Class in July 1933 and was posted to the Ōmura Air Group. He later served on board the *Ryūjō* and was again posted to the Ōmura Air Group. With the outbreak of the China Incident, Torakuma was transferred to the 13th Air Group and

on 17 September [1937], advanced to the Kunda base in Shanghai. Two days later, on the 19th, PO1c Torakuma sortied as a shōtai leader in the first attack on Nanking. This was also his first combat flight and he shot down two aircraft.

During the sixth attack on Nanking on the 22nd, Torakuma was on his way back to base, alone, when he was jumped by an enemy Curtiss Hawk fighter near Changchow. Torakuma's aircraft was peppered from behind with a total of twenty-one 13-mm and 7.7-mm bullet hits, but they were all deflected and did not penetrate the fuselage. Torakuma then turned the tables on the attacking aircraft and shot it down. This incident not only proved the superiority of the all-metal, monocoque fuselage design of the Type 96 carrier fighter but also served as an important lesson learned in battle that helped lead to the recognition of the need to develop guns of larger caliber.

Next, during the course of an attack on Nanking on 12 October, one segment of the eleven carrier fighters led by LCDR Nakano found themselves surrounded and under attack from a force of Breda fighters; three of our aircraft were lost. The Torakuma Shōtai itself lost Sea1c Ino but did shoot down five enemy aircraft. Torakuma's own aircraft received hits, but he made an emergency landing and was rescued. This was the first time that a Type 96 fighter had been lost as a result of air combat.

With a score of seven aircraft downed to his credit, Torakuma returned to the homeland in November. In December of the following year, he was transferred to the 12th Air Group and again advanced to Hankow. However, there were no opportunities for air combat. In October 1939, Torakuma received severe injuries during an enemy bomber raid and was returned to the homeland. In April 1941, Torakuma was promoted to warrant officer and retired to inactive duty; on the same date, he was mobilized and assigned to the Ōita Air Group as a training instructor. In June [1942], he was transferred to the Kanoya Air Group and advanced into the southwest area, to Kavieng. In December, Torakuma was transferred to the Ōmura Air Group and returned to the homeland. On 16 April 1943, while engaged in flight training, Torakuma met with an accident and died in the line of duty. Torakuma referred to himself as Torakuma Hyōzō ("Torakuma Panther"). He was a pilot well known for his extraordinary skills and his intrepid spirit.

ENS Jirō Chōno (Yoshimichi Saeki)

ENS Jirō Chōno

Born in Ehime Prefecture in 1907, Chōno enlisted in the navy in 1927 and then completed the 15th Pilot Training Class in April 1930 and became a fighter pilot. When the China Incident broke out, Chōno was serving as shōtai leader of the fighter squadron on board the aircraft carrier *Kaga*. Chōno's first combat occurred on 11 November 1937, when he and PO3c Hidaka pursued three Northrop bombers that had come raiding off the Maanshan Islands. Each pilot shot down one enemy aircraft. During the attack on Canton on 13 April 1938, Chōno served as escort for eighteen carrier bombers. The shōtai led by the commander of the raid turned back midway, however, and PO1c Chōno found himself the leader of a total of five aircraft, consisting of two Type 96 carrier fighters and three Type 95 carrier fighters. After air combat with more than twenty enemy fighters over the target area, a total of six aircraft were shot down, including the two that were shot down by Chōno.

Chōno continued to participate in air combat operations in southern China. In particular, during the attack on Nan-yung on 30 August, Chōno served as the leader of the 2nd Shōtai of the six Type 96 carrier

Torakuma (*left*) during his 12th Air Group days (Mitsunori Nakajima)

fighters that were being led by LT Teshima. Chōno flew in support of the six carrier bombers on the mission. After a pitched battle with about twenty enemy fighters, despite the fact that his aircraft had received fifteen hits, Chōno single-handedly shot down four aircraft (one probable). Toward the end of the same year, Chōno returned to the homeland and was promoted to warrant officer. In 1940, he was transferred to the 14th Air Group and was again active in the southern China battlefront. During the attack on Kunming on 21 February 1941, Chōno's aircraft took hits from antiaircraft guns, and he decided to destroy his own aircraft and thus died in action. Number of aircraft shot down personally, seven (officially recognized).

CPO Masao Sugawara (Masao Sugawara)

CPO Masao Sugawara

Born in Akita Prefecture in 1924, Sugawara enlisted with the Tsuchiura Air Group in December 1940 as a member of the Otsu 15th Flight Reserve Enlisted Trainee Class. In September 1943, he completed the 29th Flight Training Course and in January of the following year was posted to Air Group 252. He was attached to Fighter Hikōtai 302 and underwent training at Misawa base. In order to participate in the June 1944 "A"-gō operation, however, Sugawara advanced to Iwo Jima on the 21st, proceeding via Tateyama, flying as number two wingman for group leader Awa.

During the morning of the 24th, while the unit was standing by in the process of being loaded with 250-kg bombs for use in an attack on the enemy fleet, it met with an attack by a force of American carrier aircraft. The Awa unit took off immediately, but flying at low speed, all aircraft including that flown by the group leader crashed. PO1c Sugawara escaped to the south and then reversed course, coming back to make a surprise attack on a formation of Grummans, shooting down three of them. Following this action, Sugawara's own aircraft was hit and he parachuted into the ocean. After swimming for ten hours, Sugawara was rescued. In an intercept battle on 3 July, Sugawara shot down one F6F aircraft, during which his own aircraft received thirty-four hits. Landing back at base on one wheel only, Sugawara did not suffer even a scratch.

The following day, the 4th, Sugawara again fought valiantly and shot down two more enemy aircraft. One of the aircraft shot down during this particular action was a gunnery observation plane. This plane had taken off by itself under cover of American fleet gunfire support but was then shot down with one burst of fire. At one point, orders were issued to prepare to combat an invasion by the enemy. On the 6th, however, Sugawara withdrew to the homeland, taking passage aboard a transport aircraft. He was later transferred to Air Group 601 and participated in air battles over Okinawa. Sugawara greeted the end of the war at the Yamato base in Nara Prefecture. Total number of aircraft shot down, seven (officially recognized).

LTJG Osamu Kudō during his days on board the *Kaga* (Minoru Suzuki)

LTJG Osamu Kudō

Born in Ōita Prefecture in 1915, Kudō entered the Otsu Flight Reserve Enlisted Trainee Class in 1931 at the age of sixteen. In April 1935, he completed the 2nd Flight Training Class and was posted to the Ōmura Air Group. In July 1937, he was posted to the 13th Air Group and then advanced to Shanghai. On 19 September, Kudō participated in the first phase attack on Nanking as one of the colleagues of LTJG Kanno. Kudō shot down one aircraft in combat over the capital but then his own aircraft received hits; he had to ditch in the Yangtze River. Kudō was rescued.

In November, Kudō returned to the homeland. The following January, he was ordered on board the aircraft carrier *Kaga* and for the rest of the year participated in a number of attacks in the southern China area. In particular, on 30 August during the attack on Nan-yung, Kudō shot down two of the British Gladiators that came to intercept their flight.

Kudō later served on the *Akagi,* was posted to the Hyakurigahara Air Group, and was promoted to warrant officer. In September 1941, immediately before the outbreak of the war between Japan and the United States, he was transferred to the 3rd Air Group. During the 10 December attack on Luzon, Kudō, jointly with others, shot down nine aircraft. On 3 March 1942, during the attack on the key city of Broome in northwestern Australia, WO Kudō was strafing the ground at a low altitude when his aircraft received hits. Kudō is deemed to have died in action by destroying his own aircraft. Following his death, Kudō was mentioned in an All Units Bulletin issued by the admiral of the Combined Fleet and, in addition, was given the honor of a two-rank promotion to Special Service Flight Lieutenant Junior Grade. Number of aircraft personally shot down, seven (officially recognized).

WO Tokushige Yoshizawa (Maru)

WO Tokushige Yoshizawa

Born in Akita Prefecture in 1923, Yoshizawa enlisted at the Yokosuka Naval Barracks as a seaman in June 1940. In October of the following year, desiring to be a flyer, he was posted to the Tsuchiura Air Group as a student in the Hei 7th Flight Reserve Enlisted Trainee Class. In March 1943, he completed the Flight Training Course; in the fall of the same year, he assumed duties with Air Group 201 at Buin, in the Solomon Islands.

At the end of the year, Yoshizawa moved to Rabaul and participated in the almost daily intercept battles that were going on. During the same period, he personally shot down more than nine aircraft.

Following his transfer to Air Group 204 Yoshizawa remained in Rabaul attached to the Air Base 105 unit, even after Air Group 204 itself had withdrawn to Truk. On 9 January 1945, CPO Yoshizawa took off on a mission to reconnoiter the Admiralty Islands, flying a two-seat Zero fighter assembled at Rabaul [from parts of other Zeros]. He never came back to base and is deemed to have been killed in action. Twenty-seven years after Yoshizawa took off on his final sortie, in August 1972, a Zero fighter and a human skeleton were dragged up from the waters at a depth of eight meters by Australians, just off the mouth of the river at Cape Lambert. These relics were returned to Japan in February 1975; it is believed that they are the remains of Yoshizawa's aircraft.

APPENDIX A

NAVAL FIGHTER UNIT ACES (by Name and Record)

1. The term "Ace" is applicable to any person who has shot down five or more aircraft; however, in the following table the listing is restricted to those responsible for the downing of eight or more aircraft.
2. In the "Class" column, Western numerals indicate Naval Acadamy class number. "Pilot" indicates Pilot Training Class. "Kō," "Otsu," and "Hei" indicate the respective classes within the Flight Reserve Enlisted Trainee system. "Res." indicates classes held for reserve flight officers.
3. In the "Status" column, the date shown is that of the person's death. If blank, the person survived the war.
4. In the "Records" column, "(Off.)" means that the figure has been officially recognized (i.e., a detailed battle report (sentō shōhō), a letter of appreciation (kanjō), a letter of commendation (hyōshō), and/or air flight logs (kōkū kiroku).
5. An asterisk by the name indicates mention in an All Units Bulletin (Zengun Fukoku), and the person was given a double-rank promotion (exclusive of special attack force personnel).
6. Most birth dates are during the reign of Emperor Taisho (1912–1926).

Name	Final Rank	Class	Native Prefecture	Birth Date	Status	Records Total	China Incident
*Hiroyoshi Nishizawa	WO	Otsu 7	Nagano	27 Jan 1920	16 Oct 1944	87	
Tetsuzō Iwamoto	LTJG	Pilot 34	Shimane	14 Jun 1916		c. 80	14
*Shō-ichi Sugita	CPO	Hei 3	Niigata	1 Jul 1924	4 Apr 1945	c. 70	
Saburō Sakai	LTJG	Pilot 38	Saga	26 Aug 1916		64	2
Takeo Okumura	CPO	Pilot 42	Fukui	27 Jan 1920	22 Sep 1943	54	4 (Off.)
Toshio Ōta	PO1c	Pilot 46	Nagasaki	20 Mar 1919	21 Oct 1942	34 (Off.)	
Kazuo Sugino	WO	Hei 3	Yamaguchi	5 Aug 1921		32	
Shizuo Ishii	CPO	Pilot 50	Fukushima	18 Nov 1920	24 Oct 1943	29 (Off.)	3 (Off.)
Kaneyoshi Mutō	ENS	Pilot 32	Aichi	18 Jun 1916	24 Jul 1945	28	5
*Jun-ichi Sasai	LTJG	67	Tokyo	13 Feb 1918	26 Aug 1942	27 (Off.)	
Sada-aki Akamatsu	LTJG	Pilot 17	Kochi	30 Jul 1910		27	11
*Naoshi Kanno	LT	70	Miyagi	13 Oct 1921	1 Aug 1945	25	
Nobuo Ogiya	WO	Pilot 48	Ibaragi	20 Feb 1918	13 Feb 1944	24 (Off.)	
Shigeo Sugio	LTJG	Otsu 5	Miyazaki			20+	
Kazushi Utō	PO3c	Otsu 9	Ehime	18 Aug 1922	13 Sep 1942	19 (Off.)	
Ki-ichi Nagano	CPO	Pilot 56	Shizuoka	26 Oct 1922	6 Nov 1944	19 (Off.)	
Hiroshi Okano	WO	Pilot 54	Ibaragi	27 May 1921		19	
*Masayuki Nakase	PO1c	Otsu 5	Tokushima	1 Jul 1918	9 Feb 1942	18	9
Akio Matsuba	LTJG	Pilot 26	Mie	25 Oct 1914		18	2
Sadamu Komachi	WO	Pilot 49	Ishikawa	18 Apr 1920		18	
Takeo Tanimizu	WO	Hei 3	Mie	14 Apr 1919		18	
Masajirō Kawato	CPO	Hei 12	Kyōto	19 Sep 1925		18	
Saburō Saitō	ENS	Pilot 44	Yamagata	1 Oct 1917		18	
Yoshio Ōki	CPO	Pilot 37	Ibaragi	1 Feb 1916	16 Jun 1943	17 (Off.)	4 (Off.)
Kuniyoshi Tanaka	ENS	Pilot 31	Saga	2 Mar 1917		17 (Off.)	12
Masao Masuyama	CPO	Pilot 49	Nagasaki	2 Mar 1921		17	
Keishū Kamihira	LTJG	Kō 1	Kanagawa	3 Dec 1920		17	4
Minoru Honda	ENS	Kō 5	Kumamoto	5 Jan 1923		17	
Kiyoshi Itō	WO	Hei 2	Niigata	13 Nov 1921		17	
Susumu Ishihara	ENS	Kō 3	Aichi	9 Jan 1921		16 (Off.)	
Tora-ichi Takatsuka	WO	Pilot 22	Shizuoka	22 Feb 1914	13 Sep 1942	16 (Off.)	3 (Off.)
*Zenjirō Miyano	LT	63	Osaka	2 Mar 1917	16 Jun 1943	16	
Ryōji Ōhara	WO	Hei 4	Miyagi	25 Feb 1921		16	
Bunkichi Nakajima	CPO	Pilot 33	Toyama	20 Oct 1918	6 Oct 1943	16	
Yoshi-ichi Nakaya	WO	Hei 2	Nagano	15 Sep 1921		16	
Kunimichi Katō	CPO	Hei 10	Aichi	Jun 1923		16	
Masami Shiga	ENS	Pilot 50	Ibaragi	15 Feb 1919		16	

(continued)

NAVAL FIGHTER UNIT ACES (by Name and Record) (*continued*)

Name	Final Rank	Class	Native Prefecture	Birth Date	Status	Records Total	China Incident
Hideo Watanabe	WO	Hei 2	Fukushima	22 Jun 1920		16	
Kunimori Nakakariya	ENS	Otsu 8	Kagoshima	13 Mar 1920		16	
Yoshimi Minami	ENS	Pilot 30	Kagawa	15 Dec 1915	25 Nov 1944	15 (Off.)	9
Satoshi Yoshino	WO	Otsu 5	Chiba	21 Feb 1918	9 Jun 1942	15 (Off.)	
Wataru Nakamichi	WO	Hei 4	Osaka	22 Aug 1922		15 (Off.)	
Shigeru Shibukawa	WO	Hei 6	Osaka	12 Aug 1923		15 (Off.)	
Motonari Suhō	LCDR	62	Tottori	14 Dec 1912		15	11
Minpo Tanaka	WO	Otsu 11	Nagasaki	3 Oct 1923		15	
Kenji Okabe	ENS	Pilot 38	Fukuoka	7 May 1915		15	
Masuaki Endō	PO1c	Otsu 9	Fukushima	20 Dec 1920	7 Jun 1943	14 (Off.)	
Ichirōbei Yamazaki	PO1c	Pilot 54	Tokyo	5 May 1920	4 Jul 1943	14 (Off.)	
Mototsuna Yoshida	PO2c	Pilot 44	Okayama	1 Jan 1918	7 Aug 1942	14 (Off.)	
Masao Taniguchi	ENS	Pilot 51	Fukuoka	7 Jan 1919		14 (Off.)	
Yukiharu Ozeki	WO	Pilot 32	Aichi	2 Feb 1918	24 Oct 1944	14+ (Off.)	3 (Off.)
Ken-ichi Takahashi	WO	Otsu 13	Nagano	5 May 1924		14	
Kiyoto Koga	WO	Pilot 16	Fukuoka	30 Jun 1910	16 Sep 1938	13 (Off.)	13 (Off.)
Watari Handa	LTJG	Pilot 19	Fukuoka	22 Aug 1911		13 (Off.)	6 (Off.)
Akira Yamamoto	ENS	Pilot 24	Shizuoka	13 Jun 1913	24 Nov 1944	13 (Off.)	1 (Off.)
Sahei Yamashita	WO	Otsu 5	Shizuoka	22 May 1918	9 Feb 1943	13 (Off.)	
Momoto Matsumura	WO	Pilot 29	Yamaguchi	21 Sep 1915	25 Oct 1944	13 (Off.)	10 (Off.)
Toshio Kuroiwa	WO	Pilot 13	Fukuoka	25 Dec 1908	25 Aug 1944	13 (Off.)	13 (Off.)
*Hideo Maeda	WO	Kō 1	Mie	11 Jul 1920	17 Feb 1944	13 (Off.)	
*Gitarō Miyazaki	WO	Otsu 4	Kōchi	19 Jun 1917	1 Jun 1942	13 (Off.)	2
Hiroshi Shibagaki	SupSea	Hei 12	Niigata	9 Dec 1924	22 Jan 1944	13 (Off.)	
Masa-ichi Kondō	ENS	Pilot 27	Ehime	5 Nov 1917		13	6 (Off.)
*Shigetaka Ōmori	PO1c	Pilot 33	Yamanashi	15 Jan 1916	26 Oct 1942	13	
Matsuo Hagiri	LTJG	Pilot 28	Shizuoka	10 Nov 1913		13	7
Isamu Miyazaki	ENS	Hei 2	Kagawa	5 Oct 1919		13	
Fujikazu Koizumi	LTJG	Otsu 2	Fukui	1 Mar 1916	27 Jan 1944	13	2
Kan-ichi Kashimura	WO	Pilot 24	Kagawa	5 Jul 1913	6 Mar 1943	12 (Off.)	10 (Off.)
Keisaku Yoshimura	PO1c	Pilot 56	Niigata	16 Feb 1922	25 Oct 1942	12 (Off.)	
Takeo Kanamaru	WO	Pilot 44	Yamanashi	30 Nov 1920		12	
Tetsuo Kikuchi	CPO	Pilot 39	Iwate	13 Aug 1916	19 Jun 1944	12	
Kiyoshi Shimizu	PO1c	Hei 7	Kyōto	3 Feb 1919	26 Jan 1944	12 (Off.)	
Chitoshi Isozaki	LT	Pilot 19	Ehime	12 Jan 1913		12	
Sada-o Yamaguchi	LT	67	Hiroshima	13 Jan 1919	4 July 1944	12	
Masao Sasakibara	ENS	Kō 4	Aomori	17 Nov 1921		12	
Koshirō Yamashita	ENS	Pilot 17	Kōchi	8 Apr 1910	30 Mar 1944	11 (Off.)	11 (Off.)
Kiyoshi Sekiya	CPO	Hei 2	Tochigi	5 Feb 1921	24 Jun 1944	11 (Off.)	
Kōzaburō Yasui	WO	Pilot 40	Kyōto	11 Aug 1916	19 Jun 1944	11 (Off.)	
Tomezō Yamamoto	CPO	Hei 2	Hokkaidō	30 Sep 1922	24 Jun 1944	11 (Off.)	
Yoshio Wajima	LTJG	Pilot 18	Hokkaidō	7 May 1911	23 Feb 1944	11 (Off.)	
Matao Ichioka	PO2c	Hei 12	Gifu	31 Mar 1925	19 Apr 1944	11 (Off.)	
Takeichi Kokubun	PO3c	Pilot 49	Fukushima	1 May 1921	2 Sep 1942	11 (Off.)	
Hatsuo Hidaka	LTJG	Pilot 24	Kagoshima	7 May 1915		11 (Off.)	5
Yoshio Ōishi	WO	Otsu 9	Shizuoka	25 May 1923	4 May 1945	11	
Tsutomu Iwai	LTJG	Otsu 6	Kyōto	20 Jul 1919		11	3
Iyozō Fujita	LCDR	66	Ōita	2 Nov 1917		11	
Yoshijirō Shirahama	CPO	Pilot 56	Tokyo	15 May 1921		11	
Mitsuo Hori	WO	Otsu 10	Gifu	4 Mar 1921		11	
Sumio Fukuda	LT	69	Tokushima	20 Nov 1919	24 Oct 1944	11	
Yoshina-o Kodaira	ENS	Pilot 43	Nagano	18 Apr 1918		11	2
Ichirō Yamamoto	WO	Pilot 50	Ehime	19 Jun 1918	19 Jun 1944	11	
Saburō Kitahata	WO	Pilot 21	Hyōgo	12 Jan 1915	23 Jan 1943	10+ (Off.)	4 (Off.)
Teruo Sugiyama	WO	Otsu 7	Yamaguchi	4 Jan 1920	4 Feb 1944	10 (Off.)	
Jirō Tanaka	CPO	Pilot 39	Saitama	8 Sep 1919	10 Dec 1942	10 (Off.)	
Shinsaku Tanaka	CPO	Otsu 12	Kumamoto	17 Apr 1924	12 Sep 1944	10 (Off.)	
Takao Banno	PO2c	Pilot 53	Aichi	2 Dec 1921	7 Oct 1943	10 (Off.)	

NAVAL FIGHTER UNIT ACES (by Name and Record) (*continued*)

NAME	FINAL RANK	CLASS	NATIVE PREFECTURE	BIRTH DATE	STATUS	RECORDS Total	RECORDS China Incident
Isamu Ishii	CPO	Hei 10	Osaka	15 Jan 1924	11 May 1945	10 (Off.)	
Kazuo Hattori	LdgSea	Hei 10	Aichi	4 Dec 1921	30 Mar 1944	10+ (Off.)	
Yoshikazu Nagahama	CPO	Kō 2	Fukuoka	26 Aug 1921	6 Sep 1943	10+ (Off.)	
Sei-ichi Kurosawa	PO2c	Hei 4	Saitama	20 Dec 1922	6 Aug 1943	10 (Off.)	
Yoshirō Hashiguchi	CPO	Pilot 42	Fukuoka	10 Sep 1918	25 Oct 1944	10+	
*Yasuhiro Shigematsu	LT	66	Tokyo	23 Jun 1916	8 Jul 1944	10+	
Hōhei Kobayashi	LT	67	Gumma	1 Mar 1918	25 Oct 1944	10+	
Kagemitsu Matsuo	Res. ENS	Res. 10	Fukuoka	27 Aug 1920	23 Dec 1943	10+	
Shigeru Takahashi	ENS	Kō 5	Miyagi	5 Oct 1922		c. 10	
Tomokazu Sasai	CPO	Kō 10	Hyōgo	8 Mar 1926		10	
Tomita Atake	WO	Pilot 47	Chiba			c. 10	
Katsuyoshi Yoshida	WO	Kō 6	Hyōgo	2 Jul 1923		10	
Takahide Aioi	CDR	59	Hiroshima	4 Jan 1912		10	5
Ken-ichi Abe	CPO	Otsu 9	Ōita	1 Mar 1923		10	
Sekizen Shibayama	WO	Otsu 13	Saitama	15 Dec 1922		c. 10	
Isamu Mochizuki	LTJG	Pilot 9	Saga	15 Sep 1906	6 Feb 1944	9 (Off.)	9 (Off.)
Aya-o Shirane	LCDR	64	Tokyo	7 Aug 1916	24 Nov 1944	9 (Off.)	1 (Off.)
Toshiyuki Sueda	WO	Pilot 32	Fukuoka	27 Jan 1914	6 Oct 1943	9 (Off.)	1 (Off.)
Kiyonobu Suzuki	PO1c	Pilot 28	Fukuoka	5 Feb 1914	26 Oct 1942	9 (Off.)	3 (Off.)
Jūzō Okamoto	PO1c	Pilot 31	Tokushima	18 Sep 1916	11 Oct 1942	9 (Off.)	4 (Off.)
Ki-ichi Oda	WO	Pilot 18	Niigata	5 Apr 1913	10 Dec 1944	9 (Off.)	4 (Off.)
Mitsugu Mori	LTJG	Pilot 14	Shizuoka	5 May 1908		9+ (Off.)	4+ (Off.)
Kazuo Tsunoda	LTJG	Otsu 5	Chiba	11 Oct 1918		9 (Off.)	1 (Off.)
Hideo Morinio	LTJG	Pilot 41	Hiroshima	3 Oct 1917		9 (Off.)	1
Jirō Matsuda	LTJG	Kō 1	Nagasaki	26 Apr 1918		9 (Off.)	2 (Off.)
Kaname Harada	LTJG	Pilot 35	Nagano	11 Aug 1916		9 (Off.)	
Hideo Izumi	PO2c	Kō 3	Toyama	19 Jun 1921	30 Apr 1942	9 (Off.)	
Susumu Matsuki	PO3c	Kō 4	Niigata	15 Feb 1922	13 Sep 1942	9 (Off.)	
Yoshio Nakamura	WO	Hei 3	Hokkaidō	20 Jan 1923		9 (Off.)	
Saji Kanda	PO2c	Hei 2	Ōita	22 Sep 1921	19 Jun 1943	9 (Off.)	
Tadao Yamanaka	ENS	Pilot 44	Kōchi	23 Jan 1918		9 (Off.)	
Toshihisa Shirakawa	PO1c	Kō 6	Kagawa	23 Jul 1924	22 Sep 1943	9 (Off.)	
Tokushige Yoshizawa	CPO	Hei 7	Akita	18 Jun 1923	6 Jan 1945	9 (Off.)	
Teigo Ishida	CPO	Hei 6		28 Jun 1920	16 Apr 1945	9 (Off.)	
Ichirō Higashiyama	LTJG	Otsu 2	Nagano	25 Aug 1915	8 Jul 1944	9	6 (Off.)
Yoshio Fukui	LT	Pilot 26	Kagawa	10 Apr 1913		9	6 (Off.)
Shigetoshi Kudō	ENS	Pilot 53	Ōita	14 Feb 1920		9 (Off.)	
Tadashi Kaneko	LCDR	60	Yamagata		14 Nov 1942	8 (Off.)	3 (Off.)
Masao Iizuka	LT	66	Tochigi	6 Jul 1916	15 Oct 1944	8 (Off.)	
Takeyoshi Ōno	LTJG	68	Ishikawa	18 Jan 1921	30 Jun 1943	8 (Off.)	
*Yukio Endō	LT	Otsu 1	Yamagata	9 Sep 1915	14 Jan 1945	8 (Off.)	
Toyoo Moriura	PO3c	Otsu 9	Kumamoto	20 Nov 1922	25 Oct 1942	8 (Off.)	
Hiroshi Suzuki	CPO	Kō 5	Chiba	30 Nov 1922	13 Oct 1944	8 (Off.)	
Kaoru Takaiwa	PO1c	Otsu 13	Nagasaki	27 May 1923	10 Feb 1944	8 (Off.)	
Yoshio Iwaki	PO1c	Kō 2	Karafuto	Feb 1923	24 Aug 1942	8 (Off.)	
Yū-ichi Ema	WO	Pilot 22	Nara	18 Nov 1912	29 Oct 1944	8 (Off.)	2 (Off.)
Kō-ichi Magara	PO1c	Pilot 28	Mie	8 Jun 1914	14 Sep 1942	8 (Off.)	
Katsuma Shigemi	WO	Pilot 20	Shimane	27 Jan 1914	4 Feb 1943	8 (Off.)	3 (Off.)
Kurakazu Gotō	PO1c	Kō 6	Fukuoka	19 Nov 1921	9 Sep 1943	8 (Off.)	
Shigeru Yano	PO1c	Pilot 44	Tochigi	20 Feb 1917	17 Apr 1942	8 (Off.)	
Yoshihisa Tokuji	WO	Otsu 6	Miyazaki	29 Sep 1919	19 Jun 1944	8 (Off.)	
Satoru Ono	LTJG	Pilot 23	Ōita	15 Mar 1915		8 (Off.)	3
Kazuo Muranaka	ENS	Otsu 6	Fukuoka	27 Feb 1919		8	1
Shigefumi Nangō	LT	55	Tokyo		18 Jul 1938	8	8

APPENDIX B

KEY FIGHTER PILOTS KILLED IN ACTION (by Date)

1. Rank indicated is at the time of death in action.
2. In the "Class" column, Western numerals indicate Naval Academy class number (for example, 57 means 57th class). "Pilot" (Sō) indicates Pilot Training (Sōjū renshūsei) class number. "Kō," "Otsu," and "Hei" represent the respective Aviation Student (Hikō yoka renshūsei) Course number, and "Res." (Yo) indicates Reserve Flight Officer (Yobi hikō shikan) class number.
3. Deaths by accident are included.
4. An asterisk means that an All Units Bulletin was issued and a double rank promotion given out.

Name	Rank	Class	Unit	Date of Death	Place	Major Unit History and Other Data
Shichirō Yamashita	LT	57	13th Air Group division officer	26 Sep 1937	Central China	Prisoner of war; then died
Nagaharu Umeda	PO3c	Pilot 32	13th Air Group	12 Oct 1937	Nanking	Also PO3c Torata Takiguchi (Pilot 25) and PO1c Masazumi Ino (Pilot 30)
Hei-ichirō Mase	WO	Pilot 8	12th Air Group	8 Nov 1937	Shōkō [near Shanghai]	AA fire
Rizō Harada	PO1c	Pilot 29	12th Air Group	15 Nov 1937	Shanghai	AA fire
Kōji Miyazaki	PO3c	Pilot 29	13th Air Group	22 Nov 1937	Nanking	
Norito Ōbayashi	LT	55	13th Air Group division officer	22 Dec 1937	Nanchang	
Naoshi Teramatsu	PO3c	Pilot 31	13th Air Group	9 Dec 1937	Nanking	
Ryōhei Ushioda	LT	57	12th Air Group division officer	7 Jan 1938	Nanchang	
Takashi Kaneko	LT	59	12th Air Group division officer	18 Feb 1938	Hankow	Also PO1c Shigeo Miyamoto (Otsu 1) and Sea1c Hiroji Hayakawa (Pilot 29)
Inao Hamada	PO1c	Pilot 34	13th Air Group	18 Feb 1938	Hankow	
Shigeo Takuma	LT	58	13th Air Group division officer	25 Feb 1938	Nanchang	Also PO1c Hisao Ochi (Pilot 31)
Naoshi Eitoku	PO1c	Pilot 14	*Kaga*	13 Apr 1938	Canton	Also PO3c Yukio Miyasato and PO3c Yūji Mōri, (both Otsu 3)
Ken-ichi Takahashi	PO2c	Pilot 19	12th Air Group	29 Apr 1938	Hankow	Also PO3c Kinji Fujiwara (Pilot 29)
Hiromitsu Takahara	Sea1c	Pilot 36	12th Air Group	31 May 1938	Hankow	
Sakae Katō	WO	Pilot 11	15th Air Group	28 Jun 1938	Anking	
Kyūshichi Kobayashi	PO1c	Pilot 18	12th Air Group	4 Jul 1938	Nanchang	Also PO2c Toku Murata (Pilot 32)
Mochifumi Nangō	LT	55	15th Air Group group leader	18 Jul 1938	Nanchang	
Naohisa Shinjō	LTJG	62	15th Air Group	3 Aug 1938	Hankow	Also PO2c Hitoshi Fukasawa (Pilot 27)
Namitarō Matsushima	PO3c	Pilot 30	15th Air Group	3 Aug 1938	Hankow	Prisoner, returned

KEY FIGHTER PILOTS KILLED IN ACTION (by Date) (*continued*)

NAME	RANK	CLASS	UNIT	DATE OF DEATH	PLACE	MAJOR UNIT HISTORY AND OTHER DATA
Masumi Tsutsumi	PO1c	Pilot 24	*Kaga*	16 Aug 1938	Canton	
Hideo Teshima	LT	58	*Kaga* division officer	30 Aug 1938	Nan-yung	Also PO2c Seizaburō Sugino (Otsu 3)
Kiyoto Koga	WO	Pilot 16	Yokosuka Air Group	16 Sep 1938	Yokosuka	Accident
Hironori Shimomura	PO2c	Pilot 33	13th Air Group	23 Oct 1938	Central China	AA fire
Sukesada Senda	PO1c	Otsu 2	*Ryujō*	16 Mar 1939	Homeland	Accident
Shirō Ayukawa	PO1c	Pilot 28	*Akagi*	9 May 1939	Homeland	Accident
Genkichi Ogawa	PO3c	Pilot 40	14th Air Group	5 Jun 1939	South China	
Mitsuo Kaneko	PO1c	Pilot 22	Tsukuba Air Group	9 Aug 1939	Homeland	Accident
Kanetake Okazaki	LTJG	62	12th Air Group	3 Oct 1939	China	
Isamu Ochi	PO3c	Pilot 41	12th Air Group	14 Oct 1939	Hankow	Killed by bombing
Hiroshi Fujita	PO2c	Pilot 42	14th Air Group	30 Dec 1939	Liuchow	
Hiroo Natori	PO1c	Otsu 2	12th Air Group	8 Mar 1940	Hankow	Accident
Jirō Chonō	WO	Pilot 15	14th Air Group	21 Feb 1941	Kunming	AA fire
Manbei Shimokawa	LT	58	Yokosuka Air Group division officer	17 Apr 1941	Yokosuka	Accident
Ei-ichi Kimura	PO1c	Otsu 5	12th Air Group	20 May 1941	Central China	AA fire
Kishirō Kobayashi	PO1c	Pilot 48	12th Air Group	23 Jun 1941	Lanchow	AA fire
Masayuki Mitsumasu	PO1c	Otsu 5	3rd Air Group	8 Nov 1941	China	Accident; also PO1c Ei-ichi Nakasawa (Pilot 48)
Osamu Hatanaka	Sea1c	Pilot 54	Tainan Air Group	24 Nov 1941	Taiwan	Accident
Shime Inoue	PO1c	Pilot 35	22nd Air Flotilla Command	26 Nov 1941	South China Sea	Accident; also PO2c Ryūgen Shimotaba (Kō 3)
*Fusata Iida	LT	62	*Sōryū* division officer	7 Dec 1941	Hawaii	AA fire, 12th Air Group
*Saburō Ishii	PO2c	Pilot 41	*Sōryū*	7 Dec 1941	Hawaii	Lost on return to base; 14th Air Group; also PO1c Shun-ichi Atsumi (Kō 2)
*Ippei Gotō	WO	Pilot 19	*Kaga*	7 Dec 1941	Hawaii	13th Air Group
*Tomio Inenaga	PO1c	Otsu 7	*Kaga*	7 Dec 1941	Hawaii	13th Air Group Re the two pilots above: also PO2c Seinoshin Sano (Pilot 41) and PO2 Tōru Haneda (Pilot 35)
*Takashi Hirano	PO1c	Kō 1	*Akagi*	7 Dec 1941	Hawaii	12th Air Group
*Shigenori Nishikaichi	PO1c	Kō 2	*Hiryū*	7 Dec 1941	Hawaii	Emergency landing, suicide [actually killed]
Ryōichi Nakamizo	WO	Otsu 3	Tainan Air Group	8 Dec 1941	Luzon	*Kaga*
Yoshio Hirose	PO3c	Pilot 40	Tainan Air Group	8 Dec 1941	Luzon	12th Air Group In both cases: also PO1c Yasuhisa Satō (Otsu 6), PO1c Yasujirō Kawano (Otsu 7), and PO3c Yoshio Aoki (Pilot 56)
Saburō Yoshii	PO3c	Pilot 45	3rd Air Group	8 Dec 1941	Luzon	Also PO3c Fumio Itō (Pilot 45)
Hiroshi Kawanishi	PO2c	Pilot 38	*Ryūjō*	8 Dec 1941	Davao	Emergency landing, suicide
Masaharu Higa	Sea1c	Pilot 40	Tainan Air Group	10 Dec 1941	Luzon	12th Air Group
Tamotsu Kojima	PO2c	Pilot 41	3rd Air Group	10 Dec 1941	Luzon	12th Air Group; also PO1c Kiyoharu Tezuka (Otsu 7)

(*continued*)

KEY FIGHTER PILOTS KILLED IN ACTION (by Date) (*continued*)

Name	Rank	Class	Unit	Date of Death	Place	Major Unit History and Other Data
Hiroshi Kuratomi	PO3c	Pilot 44	Tainan Air Group	13 Dec 1941	Luzon	12th Air Group
Kaneo Suzuki	PO2c	Pilot 46	3rd Air Group	13 Dec 1941	Luzon	
Toshio Kikuchi	PO1c	Otsu 7	Tainan Air Group	24 Dec 1941	Legaspi	14th Air Group
Hiroshi Suyama	PO1c	Pilot 54	22nd Air Flotilla Command	15 Jan 1942	Singapore	
Yoshihiro Sakuraba	PO2c	Pilot 44	22nd Air Flotilla Command	18 Jan 1942	Malaya	12th Air Group
Isao Hiraishi	PO2c	Pilot 27	*Kaga*	23 Jan 1942	Rabaul	
Yoshimitsu Harada	WO	Otsu 1	Tainan Air Group	24 Jan 1942	Merauke	AA fire
Akira Wakao	LT	65	Tainan Air Group division officer	25 Jan 1942	Balikpapan	Also PO3c Akimizu Seki (Otsu 9)
Yoshikane Sasaki	PO1c	Kō 1	3rd Air Group	26 Jan 1942	Ambon	
★Toshiyuki Sakai	PO1c	Pilot 25	Tainan Air Group	29 Jan 1942	Balikpapan	12th Air Group
Hatsumasa Yamaya	PO2c	Pilot 40	3rd Air Group	3 Feb 1942	Surabaya	Also PO3c Shō-ichi Shōji (Pilot 48)
Masaru Morita	PO3c	Otsu 9	3rd Air Group	3 Feb 1942	Surabaya	
Kyōji Kobayashi	Sea1c	Pilot 55	Tainan Air Group	3 Feb 1942	Marang	
★Masayuki Nakase	PO1c	Otsu 5	3rd Air Group	9 Feb 1942	Celebes	12th Air Group; AA fire
★Masao Asai	LT	63	Tainan Air Group division officer	19 Feb 1942	Surabaya	12th Air Group
Hajime Toyoshima	Sea1c	Pilot 56	*Hiryū*	19 Feb 1942	Darwin	
Tomekichi Ōtsuki	Sea1c	Pilot 56	3rd Air Group	20 Feb 1942	Bali	
Isaburō Yawata	PO3c	Pilot 44	3rd Air Group	22 Feb 1942	Bali	Killed by bombing
Makoto Ueda	PO3c	Otsu 9	Tainan Air Group	24 Feb 1942	Borneo	
Sueharu Ide	PO1c	Otsu 6	22nd Air Flotilla Command	25 Feb 1942	Batavia	AA fire, 12th Air Group
★Toyoo Sakai	PO1c	Otsu 6	Tainan Air Group	27 Feb 1942	Indian Ocean	Attack on the *Langley*
Katsuaki Nagatomo	PO1c	Pilot 49	4th Air Group	28 Feb 1942	Moresby	
★Osamu Kudō	WO	Otsu 2	3rd Air Group	3 Mar 1942	Broome	AA fire, 13th Air group, *Kaga*
Tsutomu Kobayashi	PO1c	Otsu 5	Ōita Air Group	11 Mar 1942	Homeland	Accident, 12th Air Group
Nobuhiro Iwasaki	LTJG	67	4th Air Group	14 Mar 1942	Horn Island	Also PO1c Genkichi Ōishi (Pilot 54)
Keiji Kikuchi	PO3c	Pilot 47	4th Air Group	22 Mar 1942	Lae	
Kyōichi Yoshii	PO2c	Pilot 34	4th Air Group	23 Mar 1942	Port Moresby	
Sachio Higashi	Sea1c	Pilot 56	*Sōryū*	5 Apr 1942	Colombo	
Yukihisa Tan	PO2c	Kō 4	Tainan Air Group	7 Apr 1942	Lae	
Sumio Nōno	LT	61	*Hiryū* division officer	9 Apr 1942	Off Ceylon	Intercepting Blenheims.
Masatoshi Makino	LT	65	*Zuikaku* division officer	9 Apr 1942	Trincomalee	Also Sea1c Tatsu Matsumoto (Pilot 50)

KEY FIGHTER PILOTS KILLED IN ACTION (by Date) (*continued*)

NAME	RANK	CLASS	UNIT	DATE OF DEATH	PLACE	MAJOR UNIT HISTORY AND OTHER DATA
Fujio Hayashi	PO1c	Otsu 7	*Shōkaku*	9 Apr 1942	Trincomalee	
Toshio Makinoda	PO1c	Kō 1	*Hiryū*	9 Apr 1942	Trincomalee	
Masayoshi Sonoyama	PO3c	Pilot 47	3rd Air Group	13 Apr 1942	Kupang	
Yoshimi Sakai	PO2c	Kō 4	Tainan Air Group	17 Apr 1942	Port Moresby	
Shigeru Yano	PO1c	Pilot 44	3rd Air Group	17 Apr 1942	Kendari	12th Air Group, accident
Shirō Murakami	PO1c	Pilot 54	3rd Air Group	25 Apr 1942	Darwin	
Yoshimitsu Maeda	PO3c	Hei 3	Tainan Air Group	28 Apr 1942	Lae	
Hideo Izumi	PO2c	Kō 3	Tainan Air Group	30 Apr 1942	Lae	
★Yoshisuke Arita	PO1c	Kō 3	Tainan Air Group	1 May 1942	Port Moresby	12th Air Group
★Haruo Kawanishi	Sea1c	Pilot 56	Tainan Air Group	2 May 1942	Port Moresby	
Toshikazu Tamura	PO2c	Kō 4	*Shōhō*	3 May 1942	Tulagi	Accident
Shigeshi Imamura	WO	Pilot 29	*Shōhō*	7 May 1942	Coral Sea	12th Air Group
Tadao Aoki	PO2c	Kō 4	*Shōhō*	7 May 1942	Coral Sea	12th Air Group In both cases: also PO2c Takeo Inoue (Kō 4), PO2c Yukio Hayakawa, and PO2c Hachirō Kuwabara, (both Kō 2)
Takeo Miyazawa	PO1c	Kō 3	*Shōkaku*	8 May 1942	Coral Sea	Ramming
Hisashi Ichinose	PO2c	Kō 4	*Zuikaku*	8 May 1942	Coral Sea	
Yasushi Nikaidō	LT	64	*Kaga* division officer	8 May 1942	Off Izu	Accident
★Toshiaki Honda	PO3c	Pilot 49	Tainan Air Group	13 May 1942	Port Moresby	12th Air Group
Tōru Ōshima	PO1c	Kō 1	Tainan Air Group	14 May 1942	Port Moresby	12th Air Group, 4th Air Group
Tadao Fujiwara	PO2c	Kō 5	Tainan Air Group	16 May 1942	Lae	
Kaoru Yamaguchi	LTJG	67	Tainan Air Group	17 May 1942	Port Moresby	Also PO2c Tsutomu Itō (Kō 4)
Masao Watanabe	Sea1c	Hei 2	Tainan Air Group	25 May 1942	Lae	
Hisao Komori	PO2c	Pilot 45	Tainan Air Group	29 May 1942	Port Moresby	
★Gitarō Miyazaki	WO	Otsu 4	Tainan Air Group	1 Jun 1942	Port Moresby	
Yoshihiro Kobayashi	WO	Otsu 5	Kanoya Air Command	2 Jun 1942	Port Blair (Nicobar Islands)	Emergency landing
Shigeru Mori	LT	64	*Hiryū* division officer	4 Jun 1942	Midway	12th Air Group
Yoshimi Kodama	WO	Otsu 2	*Hiryū*	4 Jun 1942	Midway	12th Air Group, *Zuikaku*
Masato Hino	PO1c	Pilot 27	*Hiryū*	4 Jun 1942	Midway	13th Air Group, 15th Air Group, *Kaga*
Noboru Todaka	PO2c	Otsu 8	*Hiryū*	4 Jun 1942	Midway	
Tōru Yamamoto	PO2c	Pilot 41	*Hiryū*	4 Jun 1942	Midway	
Michisuke Tokuda	PO1c	Pilot 40	*Hiryū*	4 Jun 1942	Midway	In three cases above: also PO3c Yutaka Chiyoshima (Pilot 50), PO2c Haruo Nitta (Pilot 48), PO2c Ichirō Sakai (Otsu 8), and Sea1c Suekichi Yoshimoto (Pilot 54)

(*continued*)

KEY FIGHTER PILOTS KILLED IN ACTION (by Date) (*continued*)

Name	Rank	Class	Unit	Date of Death	Place	Major Unit History and Other Data
Hiroyuku Yamaguchi	Special Service ENS	Otsu 1	*Kaga*	4 Jun 1942	Midway	
Iwao Hirayama	PO1c	Pilot 38	*Kaga*	4 Jun 1942	Midway	
Yukuo Tanaka	PO1c	Otsu 6	*Kaga*	4 Jun 1942	Midway	Re the three pilots above. also PO1c Hiromi Itō (Pilot 47), PO2c Shigeto Sawano (Pilot 46), and PO1c Ei-ichi Takahashi (Pilot 53)
Shinaji Iwama	PO1c	Kō 2	*Akagi*	4 Jun 1942	Midway	
Tōichirō Hanyu	PO3c	Pilot 43	*Akagi*	4 Jun 1942	Midway	Re the two pilots above: also PO2c Yōzō Kawada (Kō 4), and Sea1c Shinpei Sano (Pilot 49)
Takeo Takashima	PO2c	Pilot 44	*Sōryū*	4 Jun 1942	Midway	Also PO3c Teruo Kawamata (Pilot 54) and Sea1c Genzō Nagasawa (Pilot 50)
Tadayoshi Koga	PO1c	Kō 3	*Ryūjō*	4 Jun 1942	Aleutians	12th Air Group, emergency landing, killed in action
Satoshi Yoshino	WO	Otsu 5	Tainan Air Group	9 Jun 1942	Lae	4th Air Group; also PO1c Sakyō Kikuchi (Kō 3)
Katsuji Matsushima	WO	Pilot 15	3rd Air Group	13 Jun 1942	Darwin	15th Air Group; also Sea1c Mikio Tanikawa (Pilot 56)
Takeichirō Hidaka	Sea1c	Hei 2	Tainan Air Group	16 Jun 1942	Lae	
Mitsuo Suizu	Sea1c	Pilot 54	Tainan Air Group	4 Jul 1942	Lae	Rammed into B-25
Katsumi Kurihara	LTJG	67	Chitose Air Group	20 Jul 1942	Port Moresby	Also PO1c Katsumi Kobayashi (Kō 3) and PO3c Yoshimi Ōnishi (Otsu 9)
Tadashi Satō	LTJG	68	Kanoya Air Group	30 Jul 1942	Andaman	
Yoshio Motoyoshi	Sea1c	Pilot 53	Tainan Air Group	2 Aug 1942	Buna	
Mototsuna Yoshida	PO2c	Pilot 44	Tainan Air Group	7 Aug 1942	Guadalcanal	14th Air Group; also PO2c Kunimatsu Nishiura (Kō 4)
Tadashi Hayashitani	LTJG	67	Tainan Air Group	8 Aug 1942	Guadalcanal	Also PO3c Yutaka Kimura (Otsu 9)
Shunkichi Tashiro	LTJG	68	3rd Air Group	8 Aug 1942	Kendari	Accident
Takumi Murata	LTJG	68	Tainan Air Group	13 Aug 1942	Lae	
Masami Arai	PO3c	Otsu 9	Tainan Air Group	14 Aug 1942	Lae	
Norio Tokushige	PO2c	Pilot 42	Tainan Air Group	17 Aug 1942	Port Moresby	12th Air Group
Tadatsune Tokaji	LT	64	3rd Air Group division officer	23 Aug 1942	Darwin	
Nobutoshi Furukawa	PO2c	Pilot 45	3rd Air Group	23 Aug 1942	Darwin	In both cases above: also PO2c Itsuzō Shimizu (Kō 5) and PO3c Yoshiyuki Hirata (Otsu 10)
Yoshio Iwaki	PO1c	Kō 2	*Shōkaku*	24 Aug 1942	Solomons	*Akagi*
Shigeru Makino	PO1c	Pilot 27	*Zuikaku*	24 Aug 1942	Solomons	Also PO2c Gorō Sakaida (Pilot 43) and PO2c Toshiharu Ōkubo (Kō 5)
Matsutarō Takaoka	Sea1c	Pilot 54	*Zuikaku*	24 Aug 1942	Solomons	*Kaga*, sank with aircraft carrier

KEY FIGHTER PILOTS KILLED IN ACTION (by Date) (*continued*)

NAME	RANK	CLASS	UNIT	DATE OF DEATH	PLACE	MAJOR UNIT HISTORY AND OTHER DATA
Jinsaku Nojima	PO2c	Pilot 42	*Ryūjō*	24 Aug 1942	Guadalcanal	Also Sea1c Shōji Ishihara (Pilot 55)
*Jun-ichi Sasai	LTJG	67	Tainan Air Group	26 Aug 1942	Guadalcanal	
Kunisuke Yūki	LTJG	68	Tainan Air Group	26 Aug 1942	Guadalcanal	Also PO3c Ken-ichi Kumagaya (Otsu 9)
Ki-ichi Iwase	PO1c	Pilot 34	2nd Air Group	26 Aug 1942	Buna	12th Air Group, also PO3c Daizō Ihara and PO3c Kiyoshi Nakano (both Otsu 9)
Jōji Yamashita	LT	66	Tainan Air Group division officer	27 Aug 1942	Rabi	
Sadao Yamashita	PO1c	Pilot 34	Tainan Air Group	27 Aug 1942	Rabi	Re two pilots above: also PO2c Enji Kakimoto (Pilot 47), PO3c Takeo Matsuda (Pilot 56), and Sea1c Kihachi Ninomiya (Pilot 56)
Mitsuyoshi Takasuga	PO3c	Pilot 51	*Shōkaku*	28 Aug 1942	Buka	Accident, *Akagi*
Seiji Iishi	PO2c	Pilot 50	*Shōkaku*	29 Aug 1942	Guadalcanal	
Tsuguo Ogihara	PO1c	Pilot 30	*Shōkaku*	30 Aug 1942	Guadalcanal	13th Air Group
Kō Nakamoto	PO1c	Pilot 31	*Shōkaku*	30 Aug 1942	Guadalcanal	12th Air Group Re two pilots above: also PO1c Jin-ichirō Kawanishi (Kō 3) and PO3c Yoshizō Tanaka (Pilot 46)
Tsuyoshi Sumita	WO	Pilot 26	*Zuikaku*	30 Aug 1942	Guadalcanal	*Shōkaku*
Terusada Chūman	PO1c	Kō 1	*Zuikaku*	30 Aug 1942	Guadalcanal	Also PO3c Minoru Awao (Otsu 10)
Takeichi Kokubun	PO3c	Pilot 49	Tainan Air Group	2 Sep 1942	Guadalcanal	4th Air Group, also Sea1c Kenichirō Yamamoto (Pilot 54)
Shigejirō Murakami	Sea1c	Hei 2	6th Air Group	11 Sep 1942	Guadalcanal	
Torakichi Okazaki	PO2c	Pilot 44	2nd Air Group	12 Sep 1942	Guadalcanal	12th Air Group, *Shōhō*
Tora-ichi Takatsuka	WO	Pilot 22	Tainan Air Group	13 Sep 1942	Guadalcanal	12th Air Group
Kazushi Utō	PO3c	Otsu 9	Tainan Air Group	13 Sep 1942	Guadalcanal	4th Air Group Re the two pilots above: also PO2c Susumu Matsuki (Kō 4) and PO3c Noboru Satō (Otsu 9)
Kō-ichi Magara	PO1c	Pilot 28	2nd Air Group	13 Sep 1942	Guadalcanal	Chitose Air Group
Gi-ichi Yamanouchi	WO	Otsu 2	3rd Air Group	27 Sep 1942	Guadalcanal	13th Air Group, 14th Air Group
Yū-ichi Kobayashi	Sea1c	Hei 2	6th Air Group	2 Oct 1942	Guadalcanal	
Takeru Imahashi	PO1c	Kō 1	Kanoya Air Group	3 Oct 1942	Guadalcanal	Attached to 22nd Air Flotilla Command
Toshikazu Iwata	PO2c	Pilot 40	Kanoya Air Group	3 Oct 1942	Guadalcanal	Also Sea1c Tsu Suematsu (Pilot 56)
Jōji Taniguchi	PO2c	Kō 5	3rd Air Group	3 Oct 1942	Guadalcanal	Also PO2c Masashi Tomita (Kō 5)
Shigeo Morimoto	Reserve ENS	Res 7	3rd Air Group	5 Oct 1942	Celebes	Accident
Masaharu Hosono	PO3c	Hei 3	6th Air Group	7 Oct 1942	New Ireland	Accident while moving; also LdgSea Yoshirō Shōji and Sea1c Sōroku Kawakami
Kazuto Kuba	LTJG	68	6th Air Group	11 Oct 1942	Solomons	Ditched
Yū-ichi Sagane	WO	Otsu 5	6th Air Group	11 Oct 1942	Solomons	Ditched

(*continued*)

KEY FIGHTER PILOTS KILLED IN ACTION (by Date) (*continued*)

Name	Rank	Class		Unit	Date of Death	Place	Major Unit History and Other Data
Jūzo Okamoto	PO1c	Pilot	31	6th Air Group	11 Oct 1942	Solomons	13th Air Group and 3rd Air Group Re the three pilots above: also Sea1c Shigeto Kawakami (Hei 3) and Sea2c Shigeo Hirano (Hei 3)
Mitsu-uma Hirai	WO	Otsu	2	6th Air Group	13 Oct 1942	Buka	Killed by bombing, *Kaga*, *Ryūjō*, 12th Air Group
Banri Itō	Sea1c	Hei	2	3rd Air Group	13 Oct 1942	Guadalcanal	
Chūji Sakurai	PO2c	Kō	5	Tainan Air Group	15 Oct 1942	Guadalcanal	Also Sea1c Yoshifusa Iwasaka (Hei 3)
Tomoji Sawada	PO2c	Kō	4	Kanoya Air Group	18 Oct 1942	Guadalcanal	Also Sea2c Mitsuo Gotō (Hei 3)
Tamotsu Fujita	PO3c	Otsu	10	Kanoya Air Group	18 Oct 1942	Guadalcanal	POW, returned
Takeo Inaba	WO	Pilot	19	*Hiyō*	19 Oct 1942	Solomons	*Kaga*
Sadamu Tamai	Sea1c	Hei	2	6th Air Group	20 Oct 1942	Guadalcanal	
Toshio Ōta	PO1c	Pilot	46	Tainan Air Group	21 Oct 1942	Guadalcanal	12th Air Group
Masayoshi Baba	LTJG		67	Kanoya Air Group	23 Oct 1942	Guadalcanal	Attached to 22nd Air Flotilla Command; also Sea2c Hachirō Mitsunaga (Hei 3)
Mukumi Kanemitsu	LTJG		68	6th Air Group	23 Oct 1942	Guadalcanal	
Gunji Suzuki	PO1c	Otsu	7	6th Air Group	23 Oct 1942	Guadalcanal	Re the two pilots above: also PO3c Shimpei Takagaki and PO3c Hiroshi Fukuda, (both Kō 6)
Kōji Ikeda	PO3c	Otsu	10	3rd Air Group	24 Oct 1942	Goodenough Bay	Bad weather
Rokuzō Iwamoto	PO1c	Pilot	42	3rd Air Group	25 Oct 1942	Guadalcanal	AA fire; also PO2c Naoichi Maeda (Kō 5)
Keisaku Yoshimura	Sea1c	Pilot	56	Tainan Air Group	25 Oct 1942	Guadalcanal	Also PO3c Ryusuke Gotō and PO3c Toyoo Moriura, (both Otsu 9)
Tokitane Futagami	LTJG		68	2nd Air Group	25 Oct 1942	Guadalcanal	Also PO3c Toyoo Morita (Otsu 9) and Sea1c Naoichi Ubukata (Hei 2)
Shirō Ishikawa	PO2c	Kō	5	2nd Air Group	25 Oct 1942	Guadalcanal	POW, returned
Kyōichirō Ogino	PO2c	Pilot	44	*Hiyō*	25 Oct 1942	Guadalcanal	12th Air Group
Yukuo Hanzawa	WO	Otsu	5	*Shōkaku*	26 Oct 1942	Battle of Santa Cruz	12th Air Group; also PO2c Katsuo Kanno (Hei 3)
Suekichi Osanai	WO	Otsu	2	*Zuikaku*	26 Oct 1942	Battle of Santa Cruz	13th Air Group, *Akagi*
Tomio Kamei	PO1c	Kō	2	*Zuikaku*	26 Oct 1942	Battle of Santa Cruz	
Kasuke Hoshiya	PO2c	Pilot	39	*Zuikaku*	26 Oct 1942	Battle of Santa Cruz	Re above two pilots: also Sea1c Takashi Nakagami (Pilot 53) and PO3c Kōzō Takayama (Hei 3)
*Shigetaka Ōmori	PO1c	Pilot	33	*Shōkaku*	26 Oct 1942	Battle of Santa Cruz	Ramming, 12th Air Group, *Akagi*
Kiyonobu Suzuki	PO1c	Pilot	26	*Junyō*	26 Oct 1942	Battle of Santa Cruz	13th Air Group, 12th Air Group, *Kaga*; also Sea2c Kiyoshi Nakamoto (Hei 3)
Shigeru Okamoto	WO	Otsu	5	*Zuihō*	26 Oct 1942	Battle of Santa Cruz	
Zenpei Matsumoto	PO3c	Pilot	48	*Zuihō*	26 Oct 1942	Battle of Santa Cruz	

KEY FIGHTER PILOTS KILLED IN ACTION (by Date) (*continued*)

Name	Rank	Class	Unit	Date of Death	Place	Major Unit History and Other Data
Akira Takita	Sea1c	Otsu 11	6th Air Group	30 Oct 1942	Buka	In the four cases above: also LTJG Shū-ichi Utsumi (68), PO1c Kazuo Seki (Otsu 7), PO1c Masao Kawasaki (Otsu 6), and PO3c Shizuta Takagi (Hei 2)
Toshio Kaneko	PO1c	Pilot 29	Air Group 251	1 Nov 1942	Lae	12th Air Group
Katsutoshi Kawamada	LTJG	67	Air Group 202	3 Nov 1942	Guadalcanal	Tainan Air Group; also LdgSea Wataru Takeda (Hei 2)
Isamu Yoshiwara	PO2c	Otsu 10	*Hiyō*	11 Nov 1942	Guadalcanal	Also PO2c Toshio Morita (Otsu 10)
Isao Itō	PO2c	Otsu 10	Air Group 582	12 Nov 1942	Guadalcanal	
Zenji Ono	WO	Otsu 2	*Junyō*	13 Nov 1942	Guadalcanal	*Kaga;* also CPO Tatsuzō Hasegawa (Otsu 8) and CPO Tasuke Mukai (Pilot 29)
Tadashi Kaneko	LCDR	60	*Hiyō* group leader	14 Nov 1942	Guadalcanal	*Ryūjō,* 15th Air Group, 12th Air Group, *Shōkaku,* 6th Air Group
Masaji Suganami	LT	61	Air Group 252 group leader	14 Nov 1942	Guadalcanal	13th Air Group, *Sōryū*
Tsumoru Ōkura	CPO	Pilot 36	Air Group 253	14 Nov 1942	Guadalcanal	Kanoya Air Group, also PO1c Meiji Hikuma (Kō 5) and PO1c Minoru Tanaka (Pilot 54)
Sanae Matsumoto	PO1c	Pilot 42	Air Group 204	14 Nov 1942	Guadalcanal	Also PO2c Kōichi Hoshino (Kō 6) and PO2c Toshio Nagata (Otsu 11)
Masahiro Ueno	LdgSea	Hei 3	*Hiyō*	15 Nov 1942	Guadalcanal	
Yoshikazu Ōhara	PO1c	Otsu 9	Air Group 582	18 Nov 1942	Solomons	3rd Air Group
Iwao Gōno	PO2c	Hei 3	Air Group 252	20 Nov 1942	Lae	Also LdgSea Yasutaka Kanoya (Hei 3)
Tōru Oda	PO3c	Pilot 56	Air Group 252	22 Nov 1942	Lae	Also LdgSea Tomio Maeda (Hei 3)
Tomoyuku Sakai	LTJG	66	Air Group 582	30 Nov 1942	Buna	Attacked vessels, *Hiryū;* also PO1c Takashi Yokoyama (Otsu 9)
Shigeru Yoshihashi	CPO	Kō 1	Air Group 252	3 Dec 1942	Rabaul	Emergency landing
Nao Uematsu	PO2c	Otsu 10	Air Group 582	7 Dec 1942	Buna	
Nobumichi Takebe	LdgSea	Hei 3	Air Group 204	10 Dec 1942	Solomons	
Jirō Tanaka	CPO	Pilot 41	*Hiyō*	10 Dec 1942	Munda	*Sōryū;* also PO2c Shigeo Motegi (Otsu 10)
Toshimi Satō	LdgSea	Hei 3	Air Group 582	14 Dec 1942	Buna	
Yaichirō Fukunishi	Res. ENS	Res. 8	Air Group 252	24 Dec 1942	Munda	Also LdgSea Kazufusa Harano
Chuichirō Hata	LdgSea	Hei 2	Air Group 252	27 Dec 1942	Munda	
Susumu Ōtsuki	PO2c	Hei 2	Air Group 582	7 Jan 1943	Lae	
Hikoji Kawata	PO2c	Hei 2	Air Group 204	9 Jan 1943	Buin	
Sueji Itsukaichi	CPO	Pilot 32	Air Group 204	11 Jan 1943	Munda	12th Air Group
Tatenoshin Tanoue	LTJG	68	Air Group 204	15 Jan 1943	Munda	Also LdgSea Shō-ichi Fujisada (Hei 3) and LdgSea Yutaka Kimoto (Hei 4)
Mitsuoki Asano	Res. ENS	Res. 8	Air Group 582	17 Jan 1942	Rabi	
Saburō Kitahata	WO	Pilot 21	*Junyō*	23 Jan 1943	Wewak	Intercepted B-29s [B-24s], 12th Air Group
Taka-aki Satō	CPO	Pilot 43	*Junyō*	23 Jan 1943	Wewak	Ramming, *Hiryū*
Kiyoharu Shibuya	LTJG	67	Air Group 204	23 Jan 1943	Guadalcanal	Also PO2c Yoshio Imamura (Otsu 11)
Mitsunori Nakajima	WO	Pilot 29	Air Group 253	24 Jan 1943	Guadalcanal	POW, returned, 13th Air Group, 12th Air Group

(*continued*)

KEY FIGHTER PILOTS KILLED IN ACTION (by Date) (*continued*)

Name	Rank	Class		Unit	Date of Death	Place	Major Unit History and Other Data
Shin Iwamoto	PO1c	Kō	5	Air Group 253	25 Jan 1943	Guadalcanal	
Mitsuyoshi Inoue	PO1c	Hei	2	Air Group 202	28 Jan 1943	Ambon	
Korenobu Nishide	CPO	Kō	1	Air Group 252	1 Feb 1943	Guadalcanal	*Shōkaku*
Saburō Horida	PO2c	Hei	2	Air Group 582	1 Feb 1943	Guadalcanal	Also PO2c Tatsuo Morioka (Otsu 10)
Katsuma Shigemi	WO	Pilot 20		*Zuikaku*	4 Feb 1943	Guadalcanal	*Kaga*, 14th Air Group, *Ryūjō*; also CPO Sōji Chiba (Pilot 40)
Masami Takemoto	CPO	Pilot 37		Air Group 582	7 Feb 1943	Guadalcanal	12th Air Group, 3rd Air Group
Sahei Yamashita	WO	Otsu	5	Air Group 201	9 Feb 1943	Nauru	Intercepted B-17s, Chitose Air Group, Tainan Air Group
Hifumi Yamamoto	LdgSea	Hei	6	Air Group 204	13 Feb 1943	Buin	
Kōtaro Takano	PO2c	Otsu 11		Air Group 252	13 Feb 1943	Buin	
Yoshio Yoshida	PO2c	Otsu 11		Air Group 252	14 Feb 1943	Ballale	
Yō-ichi Kenmochi	LTJG		68	Air Group 253	19 Feb 1943	Surumi [New Britain Island]	
*Masanao Maki	LdgSea	Hei	3	*Zuihō*	3 Mar 1943	Off Lae	Ramming
Takio Dannoue	CPO	Kō	1	*Zuihō*	3 Mar 1943	Off Lae	12th Air Group
Shizuki Nishiyama	PO2c	Pilot 54		Air Group 204	3 Mar 1943	Off Lae	Tainan Air Group
Kan-ichi Kashimura	WO	Pilot 24		Air Group 582	6 Mar 1943	Russell	13th Air Group, 12th Air Group
Sei-ichi Kitaoka	PO1c	Pilot 45		*Zuihō*	11 Mar 1943	Buna	Also LdgSea Hiroshi Koyama (Hei 3)
Seiji Tajiri	PO2c	Pilot 50		Air Group 202	15 Mar 1943	Darwin	
Kō-ichi Yoshida	LT	Res.	4	Air Group 252 division officer	26 Mar 1943	Nauru	Killed by bombing, 14th Air Group
Asao Inoue	WO	Otsu	5	Air Group 253	28 Mar 1943	Oro Bay	Also PO2c Kaneyuki Kamikata-hira (Kō 6)
Shigeto Kawahara	LTJG		68	Air Group 204	1 Apr 1943	Russell	Also PO2c Ei-ichi Sugiyama (Kō 6)
Kiyoshi Ono	PO2c	Hei	2	Air Group 253	1 Apr 1943	Russell	
Hideo Shimizu	PO1c	Otsu	9	Air Group 253	1 Apr 1943	Russell	Re the above two pilots: also PO2c Ichirō Kawahata and PO2c Izumi Tanaka (both Kō 6), LdgSea Yoshiharu Izumi (Hei 4), and SupSea Sueo Mizuno (Hei 6)
Makoto Murata	LdgSea	Hei	3	Air Group 204	7 Apr 1943	Guadalcanal	
Tsuguo Matsuyama	WO	Otsu	3	*Hiyō*	7 Apr 1943	Guadalcanal	13th Air Group, *Hiryū*
Shōzō Katayama	WO	Pilot 21		*Junyō*	7 Apr 1943	Guadalcanal	12th Air Group
Chiune Yotsumoto	PO1c	Kō	5	*Junyō*	7 Apr 1943		*Ryūjō*. Re the above two pilots: also LTJG Shirō Itesono (69), CPO Matsutarō Kobayashi (Kō 3), PO2c Yūji Andō (Pilot 48), and LdgSea Ippei Ninomiya
Yasuo Kanemitsu	LdgSea	Hei	3	Air Group 253	7 Apr 1943	Guadalcanal	
Taizō Okamoto	LTJG	Pilot 16		*Zuikaku*	11 Apr 1943	Oro Bay	12th Air Group, also PO1c Shūryū Uenuma (Otsu 9)
Sadakazu Iwaki	PO2c	Hei	3	Air Group 253	11 Apr 1943	Oro Bay	
Jirō Mitsumoto	WO	Otsu	6	*Zuikaku*	14 Apr 1943	Milne Bay	*Zuihō*
Tadashi Torakuma	WO	Pilot 20		Omura Air Group	16 Apr 1943	Kyūshū	Accident, 13th Air Group, 12th Air Group, Air Group 253
Tomekichi Hinako	LT	Pilot 1		Sasebo Air Group	2 May 1943	Kyūshū	Accident

KEY FIGHTER PILOTS KILLED IN ACTION (by Date) (*continued*)

NAME	RANK	CLASS	UNIT	DATE OF DEATH	PLACE	MAJOR UNIT HISTORY AND OTHER DATA
Hayato Noda	WO	Otsu 4	Air Group 204	13 May 1943	Russell	Also PO2c Yūhi Kariya (Hei 2)
Ryū Tanigaki	PO2c	Otsu 11	Air Group 253	13 May 1943	Buin	
Shōgo Sasaki	PO2c	Hei 4	Air Group 582	13 May 1943	Russell	
Akira Kimura	LT	65	Air Group 251 division officer	15 May 1943	New Britain	Also PO2c Gi-ichi Nakayama (Hei 2)
Kuratoshi Yasuda	PO1c	Hei 2	Air Group 202	15 May 1943	Dutch East Indies	
Jun-ichi Takahashi	PO1c	Otsu 10	Air Group 253	17 May 1943	Kavieng	Accident; also PO1c Katsutoshi Maetsuji (Kō 2)
Satoru Ogawa	PO1c	Hei 2	Air Group 582	5 Jun 1943	Buin	3rd Air Group; also PO2c Shigehiko Itō (Hei 3)
Yoshimi Hidaka	CPO	Pilot 48	Air Group 204	7 Jun 1943	Russell	Also PO1c Yasushi Okazaki (Kō 6) and PO2c Kameji Yamane (Hei 3)
Masuaki Endō	PO1c	Otsu 9	Air Group 251	7 Jun 1943	Russell	
Toshitaro Sekiguchi	PO2c	Kō 7	Air Group 251	7 Jun 1943	Russell	Re two pilots above: also PO2c Kan-ichi Masuda (Otsu 11), PO2c Setsu Matsuyoshi (Hei 3), and PO2c Yutaka Fukano (Hei 7)
Gi-ichi Noguchi	LTJG	68	Air Group 582	12 Jun 1943	Russell	Also PO2c Muneichi Fujioka (Hei 6)
Shigenobu Kōzuki	PO2c	Hei 7	Air Group 251	12 Jun 1943	Russell	Also PO2c Katsujirō Matsumoto (Kō 7)
★Zenjirō Miyano	LT	65	Air Group 204	16 Jun 1943	Lunga Point	12th Air Group, 3rd Air Group; also PO2c Yamato Tamura (Hei 3)
Takeshi Morizaki	Res. LTJG	Res. 7	Air Group 204	16 Jun 1943	Lunga Point	Also PO2c Saji Kanda (Hei 2)
Daizō Fukumori	PO1c	Otsu 10	Air Group 582	16 Jun 1943	Lunga Point	Also PO1c Katsumi Furumoto (Otsu 10) and PO2c Mototami Ishibashi (Hei 4)
Ken-ichi Shinozuba	PO2c	Hei 2	Air Group 582	16 Jun 1943	Lunga Point	
Shūhei Ōya	LTJG	Pilot 14	Air Group 251	16 Jun 1943	Lunga Point	12th Air Group
Yoshio Ōki	WO	Pilot 37	Air Group 251	16 Jun 1943	Lunga Point	12th Air Group Re the three pilots above: also PO2c Suehiro Yamamoto (Hei 1), PO2c Hiroshi Kanda (Hei 7), and PO2c Ikuzō Shimizu (Kō 7)
Takashi Kōshita	LTJG	69	Air Group 251	16 Jun 1943	Lunga Point	
Takumi Hoashi	LT	63	Testing Department	16 Jun 1943	Yokosuka	14th Air Group, *Shōkaku*, accident during test of the Raiden
Ichirō Mukai	LT	63	Air Group 251 group leader	30 Jun 1943	Rendova	12th Air Group
Takeyoshi Ōno	LTJG	68	Air Group 251	30 June 1943	Rendova	
Mitsuteru Hashimoto	LTJG	69	Air Group 251	30 Jun 1943	Rendova	Re the above three pilots: also PO2c Hiroshi Iwano (Kō 7), PO2c Nobuo Konishi (Kō 7), PO2c Uichirō Andō (Hei 3), PO2c Kazuo Fukui (Hei 7), and PO2c Shun-ichi Hiromori
Nobutaka Yatsunami	PO1c	Hei 5	Air Group 582	30 Jun 1943	Rendova	Also PO2c Takamichi Sasamoto (Hei 3)
Toyomitsu Tsujinoue	CPO	Kō 5	Air Group 204	1 Jul 1943	Rendova	

(*continued*)

KEY FIGHTER PILOTS KILLED IN ACTION (by Date) (*continued*)

NAME	RANK	CLASS		UNIT	DATE OF DEATH	PLACE	MAJOR UNIT HISTORY AND OTHER DATA
Yosaburō Shinomiya	PO1c	Otsu	9	Air Group 251	1 Jul 1943	Rendova	Also PO2c Hideo Tsukamoto (Hei 4)
Ichirōbei Yamazaki	PO1c	Pilot 54		Air Group 251	4 Jul 1943	Rendova	4th Air Group
Mitsugu Ōtani	CPO	Pilot 41		*Ryūhō*	7 Jul 1943	Rendova	*Hiyō*
Takeo Ōtsu	PO2c	Otsu 12		Air Group 253	7 Jul 1943	Rendova	
Saburō Nozawa	CPO	Pilot 45		Air Group 253	9 Jul 1943	Rendova	12th Air Group
Jisuke Iwase	PO2c	Hei	3	*Ryūhō*	11 Jul 1943	Rendova	
Yoshio Ōsawa	PO2c	Hei	3	Air Group 582	11 Jul 1943	Rendova	POW, returned
Tsukijirō Fujii	PO2c	Otsu 11		Air Group 253	11 Jul 1943	Rendova	
Fusayoshi Murasaki	CPO	Pilot 41		Air Group 582	12 Jul 1943	Rendova	Also PO2c Rokei Ōmiya (Otsu 11)
Tamotsu Tsujioka	PO2c	Hei	7	Air Group 251	12 Jul 1943	Rendova	POW, returned; also PO1c Hakuji Ishizaki (Kō 6)
Saburō Saitō	LTJG	68		Air Group 253	15 Jul 1943	Rendova	Also PO2c Shichirō Nagai and PO2c Fukumitsu Shimada, (both Hei 3)
Taiji Suzuki	PO2c	Hei	3	*Ryūhō*	15 Jul 1943	Rendova	*Shōkaku*
Sei-ichi Nakasawa	PO2c	Hei	4	Air Group 204	16 Jul 1943	Buin	
Kenji Moriyama	CPO	Pilot 35		*Junyō*	17 Jul 1943	Buin	
Hisa-aki Fujimaki	LTJG	68		*Junyō*	17 Jul 1943	Buin	Re the two pilots above: also PO1c Kiyoshi Kojima (Kō 6) and PO1c Hidenari Takesawa (Otsu 10)
Masaharu Hiramoto	CPO	Pilot 38		*Ryūhō*	17 Jul 1943	Buin	Also PO2c Yoshio Nakasono (Hei 3)
Kisaku Koshida	LTJG	69		Air Group 204	17 Jul 1943	Buin	
Minoru Kuranaga	PO2c	Hei	2	Air Group 201	25 Jul 1943	Buin	Also LdgSea Takeshi Ōura (Hei 7)
Tetsurō Nihei	PO1c	Kō	6	Air Group 204	25 Jul 1943	Rendova	Also PO2c Kenkichi Nemoto (Hei 4)
Sachio Hayama	PO2c	Hei	2	Air Group 252	25 Jul 1943	Wake	Also PO2c Kenji Wada (Hei 3)
Kiyoshi Ōsuga	PO2c	Hei	2	Air Group 252	27 Jul 1943	Wake	
Chūji Sakagami	CPO	Pilot 45		Air Group 251	4 Aug 1943	Rendova	
Matsuhimaru Kashibō	PO2c	Pilot 54		Air Group 201	4 Aug 1943	Buin	Also PO2c Fukuyoshi Morino (Hei 3)
Sei-ichi Kurosawa	PO2c	Hei	4	Air Group 204	6 Aug 1943	Buin	
Yasuhiro Nakamura	PO2c	Hei	3	*Junyō*	13 Aug 1943	Buin	
Keigo Fujiwara	LTJG	68		*Junyō*	15 Aug 1943	Ballale	Also PO2c Munenori Shimizu (Kō 7)
Masao Shimada	LTJG	69		Air Group 204	15 Aug 1943	Ballale	
Seizaburō Watanabe	PO2c	Hei	3	Air Group 204	15 Aug 1943	Ballale	Re the two pilots above: also PO1c Norimasa Narahara, PO2c Motoharu Imazeki (Otsu 11), and PO2c Tetsuo Hidaka (Hei 3)
Takeshi Takahashi	CPO	Pilot 42		Air Group 202	16 Aug 1943	Balikpapan	14th Air Group
Jisaku Kaneko	PO2c	Hei	1	Air Group 201	30 Aug 1943	Ballale	
Iki Arita	CPO	Pilot 41		Air Group 251	30 Aug 1943	Buin	12th Air Group, also PO2c Shigeo Hayashi (Otsu 12)
Michitaka Kashihara	PO1c	Otsu 10		Air Group 251	4 Sep 1943	Buin	
Yoshikazu Nagahama	CPO	Kō	2	Tsuiki Air Group	6 Sep 1943	Homeland	Accident, *Kaga, Zuikaku*
Yoshio Terai	PO1c	Kō	6	Air Group 202	7 Sep 1943	Darwin	
Tsukasa Kondō	WO	Otsu	6	Air Group 201	9 Sep 1943	Buin	12th Air Group
Morio Miyaguchi	ENS	Otsu	1	Air Group 202	9 Sep 1943	Merauke	*Ryūjō*, 12th Air Group, attached to 22nd Air Flotilla Command
Kuraichi Gotō	PO1c	Kō	6	Air Group 202	9 Sep 1943	Merauke	Also PO2c Kōshirō Agawa (Kō 7)

KEY FIGHTER PILOTS KILLED IN ACTION (by Date) (*continued*)

NAME	RANK	CLASS	UNIT	DATE OF DEATH	PLACE	MAJOR UNIT HISTORY AND OTHER DATA
Wataru Kubota	WO	Pilot 36	Yokosuka Air Group	12 Sep 1943	Homeland	Accident, *Sōryū*
En-ichi Yokota	CPO	Pilot 43	Yokosuka Air Group	12 Sep 1943	Homeland	12th Air Group, *Zuikaku*
Sato-o Yoshizawa	CPO	Otsu 6	Yokosuka Air Group	12 Sep 1943	Homeland	Accident
Makoto Terao	PO2c	Otsu 11	Air Group 204	14 Sep 1943	Buin	Also PO2c Tokuji Yoshizaki (Hei 4)
Eiji Nishida	PO2c	Hei 3	Air Group 201	14 Sep 1943	Buin	Also PO2c Hiroshi Mure (Hei 3)
Tetsuji Ueno	LTJG	69	Air Group 204	16 Sep 1943	Buin	Also LTJG Sueichi Ōshima (69)
Ryōitsu Ōkubo	WO	Pilot 29	Air Group 204	18 Sep 1943	Buin	
Yukuo Nanao	PO2c	Hei 6	Air Group 331	22 Sep 1943	Car Nicobar	
Takeo Okumura	CPO	Pilot 42	Air Group 201	22 Sep 1943	Cape Cretin	14th Air Group, *Ryūjō*, Tainan Air Group
Shunzō Hongō	WO	Pilot 30	Air Group 201	22 Sep 1943	Cape Cretin	13th Air Group, 12th Air Group; also Res. ENS Minoru Tanaka (Res. 10)
Toshihisa Shirakawa	PO1c	Kō 6	Air Group 204	22 Sep 1943	Cape Cretin	
Shigeru Tanaka	SupSea	Hei 11	Air Group 204	23 Sep 1943	Viroa	
Sei-ichi Enomoto	CPO	Hei 1	Air Group 204	25 Sep 1943	Viroa	3rd Air Group, Air Group 582
Hachirō Tsuboya	PO1c	Kō 6	Air Group 204	3 Oct 1943	Munda	Also LdgSea Yutaka Shimizu (Hei 10)
Toshiyuki Sueda	WO	Pilot 32	Air Group 252	6 Oct 1943	Wake	13th Air Group, 12th Air Group
Bunkichi Nakajima	CPO	Pilot 33	Air Group 252	6 Oct 1943	Wake	13th Air Group, 15th Air Group, 3rd Air Group
Yukuo Miyauchi	CPO	Kō 3	Air Group 252	6 Oct 1943	Wake	
Hisashi Hide	CPO	Otsu 7	Air Group 252	6 Oct 1943	Wake	
Yoshio Shiode	PO2c	Otsu 11	Air Group 252	6 Oct 1943	Wake	Re the three pilots above: also CPO Kazuo Tobita (Hei 3), PO1c Tamotsu Okabayashi (Hei 3), PO1c Soyō Shibata (Kō 6), Saburō Fujiuma (Hei 4), PO2c Katsunobu Shiba, PO2c Kazuyoshi Tokuhara (Hei 6), and PO2c Kiyoshi Takei (Otsu 12)
Takao Banno	PO2c	Pilot 53	Air Group 204	7 Oct 1943	Vella Lavella	*Kaga, Shōhō, Junyō*
Kōshio Enomoto	SupSea	Hei 10	Air Group 201	10 Oct 1943	Buin	Also SupSea Hisa Akahori (Hei 10)
Makoto Endō	WO	Pilot 25	Air Group 253	12 Oct 1943	Rabaul	12th Air Group, *Ryūjō*
Tomokichi Arai	LTJG	Pilot 15	Air Group 201 division officer	15 Oct 1943	Buin	13th Air Group
Shigenobu Adachi	PO1c	Otsu 9	Air Group 204	15 Oct 1943	Buin	Also PO2c Kisaku Tanaka (Hei 3)
Tsunehiro Yamagami	CPO	Kō 3	Air Group 253	15 Oct 1943	Buna	12th Air Group, also PO2c Eiji Sekiguchi (Otsu 12)
Hisayoshi Mōri	PO2c	Hei 3	Air Group 253	15 Oct 1943	Buna	
Haruo Sagara	LTJG	69	Air Group 253	17 Oct 1943	Buna	SupSea Ittoku Mishima (Hei 10)
Yoshiharu Matsumoto	WO	Pilot 28	Air Group 253	17 Oct 1943	Buna	15th Air Group
Yoshimi Yamauchi	PO2c	Hei 3	Air Group 204	17 Oct 1943	Buin	Also PO2c Shunji Itō (Hei 4)
Yūji Yokoyama	CPO	Pilot 38	Air Group 204	18 Oct 1943	Rabaul	

(*continued*)

KEY FIGHTER PILOTS KILLED IN ACTION (by Date) (*continued*)

NAME	RANK	CLASS	UNIT	DATE OF DEATH	PLACE	MAJOR UNIT HISTORY AND OTHER DATA
Yoshio Aizawa	Res. ENS	Res. 9	Air Group 201	18 Oct 1943	Buin	Also PO1c Yoshio Mogi (Otsu 9)
Hidemichi Moriyama	Res. ENS	Res. 10	Air Group 204	23 Oct 1943	Rabaul	
Shizu-o Ishi-i	CPO	Pilot 50	Air Group 204	24 Oct 1943	Rabaul	12th Air Group, Tainan Air Group, *Junyō*
Tsuyoshi Tanaka	PO1c	Hei 6	Air Group 204	24 Oct 1943	Rabaul	12th Air Group, Tainan Air Group, *Junyō* Re two pilots above: also PO2c Masaru Kubo (Otsu 13) and PO2c Masakazu Kobayashi (Hei 2)
Yoshinori Noguchi	PO1c	Otsu 9	Air Group 201	29 Oct 1943	Rabaul	
Shigetsune Ōgane	CPO	Pilot 45	Air Group 201	1 Nov 1943	Bougainville	
Gen-ichi Seki	CPO	Kō 5	Air Group 201	1 Nov 1943	Bougainville	Re two pilots above: also PO1c Ichirō Yamashita, PO1c Manabu Yoshi-i, and PO1c Yonehachirō Ishikura, (all Kō 7)
Yutaka Ōtani	WO	Kō 3	Air Group 204	1 Nov 1943	Bougainville	Attached to 22nd Air Flotilla Command, Kanoya Air Group
Masatsugu Kawamura	CPO	Kō 6	*Shōkaku*	2 Nov 1943	Rabaul	Also PO1c Genshichi Satō (Hei 3) and PO1c Take-o Yamamoto (Hei 6)
Shigeru Ōkura	CPO	Pilot 41	*Zuikaku*	2 Nov 1943	Rabaul	
Kazu-o Komaba	PO1c	Hei 3	*Zuikaku*	2 Nov 1943	Rabaul	Re two pilots above: also PO1c Saburō Yoshida (Kō 7) and PO2c Masayoshi Miyakawa (Hei 7)
Fusa-ichi Kaneko	PO1c	Hei 3	Air Group 204	2 Nov 1943	Rabaul	Also CPO Katsumi Shima-moto (Kō 6)
Kazunori Miyabe	LTJG	Otsu 2	*Shōkaku*	3 Nov 1943	Rabaul	12th Air Group, injured the previous day
Kosaku Minato	CPO	Pilot 44	*Zuihō*	5 Nov 1943	Rabaul	Tainan Air Group
Hiroshi Nishimura	PO1c	Otsu 11	*Zuikaku*	5 Nov 1943	Rabaul	
*Kenjirō Nōtomi	LT	62	*Zuikaku* group leader	8 Nov 1943	Bougainville	*Shōhō, Ryūjō*
Nobutaka Muraoka	PO1c	Hei 3	*Zuihō*	8 Nov 1943	Bougainville	
Shigeru Araki	LT	67	*Zuikaku* division officer	11 Nov 1943	Rabaul	
Masao Satō	LT	63	*Zuihō* group leader	11 Nov 1943	Bougainville	12th Air Group, *Zuikaku, Kaga;* also Res. ENS Shōichirō Yamada (Res. 9)
Hitoshi Satō	WO	Pilot 6	*Shōkaku*	11 Nov 1943	Bougainville	15th Air Group; also PO1c Kazuo Tachizumi (Otsu 11) and PO1c Ryūzō Isobe (Hei 7)
Yukio Aisō	ENS	Otsu 3	Air Group 201	17 Nov 1943	Torokina	Also PO1c Jisuke Yoshino (Kō 8)
Masateru Tomoishi	WO	Pilot 44	Air Group 253	21 Nov 1943	Torokina	14th Air Group, *Ryūjō;* also PO1c Hidemichi Matsu-mura and PO1c Isao Fu-kuda (Hei 3)
Shōtoku Yamaguchi	PO1c	Hei 3	Air Group 204	22 Nov 1943	Cape Torokina	Also PO1c Yorihisa Kobay-ashi (Otsu 11)
Masahiro Chikanami	Res. LTJG	Res. 7	Air Group 252	24 Nov 1943	Makin	

KEY FIGHTER PILOTS KILLED IN ACTION (by Date) (*continued*)

NAME	RANK	CLASS	UNIT	DATE OF DEATH	PLACE	MAJOR UNIT HISTORY AND OTHER DATA
Tsutomu Kawai	LTJG	69	Air Group 252	24 Nov 1943	Makin	
Masao Kuramoto	LTJG	Res. 8 (Seinan Gakuin)	Air Group 252	24 Nov 1943	Makin	Re the three pilots above: also WO Kumaji Tsugane (Otsu 4), PO1c Hiroshi Ueda (Otsu 11), and PO1c Kiyoshi Tokunaga (Hei 3)
Shin-ichi Yamawaki	PO1c	Hei 4	Air Group 252	24 Nov 1943	Makin	Also PO1c Morimasa Hirai (Hei 6)
Shizuo Kojima	WO	Pilot 32	Air Group 252	25 Nov 1943	Makin	
Kumaichi Katō	PO1c	Otsu 11	Air Group 252	25 Nov 1943	Makin	Re the two pilots above: 13th Air Group; also PO1c Shigeichi Suzuki (Hei 4), PO1c Kōichi Ishikawa (Otsu 12), and PO2c Seiji Sakamaki (Hei 11)
Genshichirō Ōyama	Res. ENS	Res. 9	*Zuikaku*	5 Dec 1943	Roi	
Hisashi Aoyama	WO	Pilot 39	*Zuikaku*	5 Dec 1943	Roi	Re the two pilots above: also PO1c Yasukichi Yamakawa (Hei 6) and PO1c Osamu Ichikawa (Kō 7)
Yoshio Yoshida	WO	Pilot 46	*Zuikaku*	5 Dec 1943	Roi	
Ichirō Imamura	LTJG	69	Air Group 281	5 Dec 1943	Roi	
Shigeru Tagami	PO1c	Hei 3	Air Group 281	5 Dec 1943	Roi	Re the two pilots above: also PO1c Sadamu Imazono and PO1c Itsurō Kubo (both Kō 8)
Ten-ichi Tagami	PO1c	Hei 3	Air Group 201	16 Dec 1943	Cape Marcus	
Kazuo Umeki	CPO	Kō 5	Air Group 201	19 Dec 1943	Rabaul	
Kanemori Shimizu	Res. ENS	Res. 10	Air Group 253	19 Dec 1943	Rabaul	Also PO1c Tokio Yokoi (Otsu 12)
Kōichirō Takinoshita	LdgSea	Hei 10	Air Group 281	19 Dec 1943	Mili	
Nihei Iwano	PO1c	Kō 8	Air Group 281	20 Dec 1943	Mili	
*Yoshio Ōba	LTJG	69	Air Group 201	23 Dec 1943	Rabaul	Also PO1c Shōyō Kijiya (Otsu 12)
Kagemitsu Matsuo	Res. ENS	Res. 10	Air Group 253	23 Dec 1943	Rabaul	
Takeshi Fujii	CPO	Kō 6	Air Group 204	23 Dec 1943	Rabaul	Also PO1c Jirō Uchida (Otsu 12)
Jinkichirō Kudō	WO	Pilot 31	Air Group 281	24 Dec 1943	Mili	14th Air Group
Tadashi Hirai	PO1c	Otsu 11	Air Group 253	26 Dec 1943	Tsurubu, Cape Gloucester, New Britain	Also PO1c Chikara Kitaguchi (Hei 6)
Yasujirō Ōno	CPO	Pilot 43	Air Group 253	27 Dec 1943	Rabaul	12th Air Group, *Zuihō;* also PO1c Matsukichi Matsui (Hei 3)
Manzō Iwaki	LTJG	Pilot 13	*Hiyo*	1 Jan 1944	Kavieng	Also PO1c Hitoshi Nagano (Kō 7)
Michio Takeshita	PO1c	Kō 7	Air Group 201	1 Jan 1944	Rabaul	Also PO1c Tsuneo Suzuki (Otsu 13)
Den Katayama	Res. ENS	Res. 9	Air Group 204	2 Jan 1944	Rabaul	Also PO1c Tokio Iishi (Hei 6)

(*continued*)

KEY FIGHTER PILOTS KILLED IN ACTION (by Date) *(continued)*

Name	Rank	Class	Unit	Date of Death	Place	Major Unit History and Other Data
Itsugi Yamazaki	PO1c	Otsu 11	Air Group 251 (night fighters)	2 Jan 1944	Rabaul	
Toshio Fujita	PO2c	Otsu 15	Air Group 204	7 Jan 1944	Rabaul	
Hiroshi Shibagaki	SupSea	Hei 12	Air Group 204	22 Jan 1944	Rabaul	
Hiroshi Ōiwa	CPO	Pilot 40	Air Group 204	23 Jan 1944	Rabaul	Also PO1c Susumu Kanenobu (Kō 8) and PO1c Namio Hashimasa (Otsu 11)
Takeshige Senuma	PO1c	Otsu 11	Air Group 202	23 Jan 1944	Rangour (near Ambon, Ambon Island, Indonesia)	
Hei-ichi Kubota	PO1c	Otsu 13	Air Group 253	23 Jan 1944	Rabaul	Also PO1c Takeshi Katayama (Otsu 12), Air Group 204
Kiyoshi Shimizu	PO1c	Hei 7	Air Group 253	26 Jan 1944	Rabaul	Air Group 204
Sanemori Yoshioka	PO1c	Otsu 14	*Ryūhō*	26 Jan 1944	Rabaul	
Fujikazu Koizumi	LTJG	Otsu 2	*Hiyō*	27 Jan 1944	Rabaul	12th Air Group, 3rd Air Group
Nobu Mae	LTJG	69	*Junyō*	27 Jan 1944	Rabaul	Also CPO Sukeo Kawasaki (Otsu 9)
Yoshiaki Hatakeyama	WO	Kō 1	Air Group 252	27 Jan 1944	Maloelap	3rd Air Group; also PO1c Shirō Tsukahara (Hei 3)
Toshio Komiya	PO1c	Hei 3	Air Group 252	27 Jan 1944	Maloelap	
Masashi Ishida	PO1c	Pilot 56	Air Group 253	28 Jan 1944	Rabaul	*Akagi, Shōkaku*
Shigeru Tsuda	PO1c	Otsu 14	*Junyō*	28 Jan 1944		
Yoshihide Ishizawa	CPO	Otsu 10	*Ryūhō*	28 Jan 1944	Rabaul	*Shōkaku*
Minoru Kitasaki	PO1c	Otsu 12	Air Group 253	29 Jan 1944	Rabaul	Also PO2c Shōzo Hara (Otsu 15)
Hiroshi Arai	PO1c	Otsu 14	*Ryūhō*	30 Jan 1944	Rabaul	
Keizaburō Yamazaki	CPO	Kō 6	Air Group 252	30 Jan 1944	Roi	
Teruo Sugiyama	WO	Otsu 7	Air Group 253	4 Feb 1944	Rabaul	*Ryūjō*, Air Group 201, Air Group 204
Takaichi Hasuo	LT	65	Air Group 281 group leader	6 Feb 1944	Roi	Banzai attack death, 12th Air Group, 3rd Air Group; also LTJG Masayuki Gotō (Res. 10)
Isamu Mochizuki	LTJG	Pilot 9	Air Group 281 division officer	6 Feb 1944	Roi	Banzai attack death, 13th Air Group
Yoshijirō Minegishi	ENS	Otsu 2	Air Group 281	6 Feb 1944	Roi	Banzai attack death, 15th Air Group, *Hiryū;* also CPO Shunji Nakasawa and CPO Shigeichi Sasa (both Otsu 10)
Akira Kikuchi	WO	Pilot 31	Air Group 281	6 Feb 1944	Roi	Banzai attack death, 12th Air Group; also PO1c Toshikazu Yahiro (Hei 7) and PO1c Sakae Okamura (Otsu 12)
Taketoshi Iio	PO1c	Otsu 11	Air Group 281	6 Feb 1944	Roi	Also PO1c Fumio Katō (Hei 3)
Ginji Kiyosue	WO	Kō 2	*Ryūhō*	7 Feb 1944	Rabaul	*Shōkaku, Zuikaku*
Toshio Itō	Res. LTJG	Res. 10	Air Group 253	9 Feb 1944	Rabaul	
Kaoru Takaiwa	PO1c	Otsu 13	Air Group 253	10 Feb 1944	Rabaul	Air Group 201
Shichijirō Mae	PO1c	Pilot 54	*Junyō*	11 Feb 1944	Rabaul	*Zuikaku*
Sanenori Kuroki	CPO	Pilot 42	*Hiyō*	12 Feb 1944	Rabaul	
Nobuo Ogiya	WO	Pilot 48	Air Group 253	13 Feb 1944	Rabaul	Chitose Air Group, Air Group 281, Air Group 204
Takeru Kobayashi	PO1c	Hei 2	Air Group 254	14 Feb 1944	Nanning	

KEY FIGHTER PILOTS KILLED IN ACTION (by Date) (*continued*)

Name	Rank	Class	Unit	Date of Death	Place	Major Unit History and Other Data
Sukeichi Yamashita	Res. LTJG	Res. 10	Air Group 252	16 Feb 1944	Micronesia	On transport aircraft, also CPO Jūji Kido (Kō 6)
*Hideo Maeda	WO	Kō 1	Air Group 204	17 Feb 1944	Truk	12th Air Group
Hisao Harada	WO	Otsu 7	Air Group 204	17 Feb 1944	Truk	Re the two pilots above: also LTJG Tadao Satō (70), PO1c Iwao Taneda (Hei 6), and PO1c Yasumasa Tsutsumi
Haruo Tomita	CPO	Kō 6	Air Group 201	17 Feb 1944	Truk	
Hiroshi Sonokawa	LT	62	Air Group 251 (night fighters)	17 Feb 1944	Truk	
Yoshihiro Yoshikawa	LTJG	70	Air Group 263	23 Feb 1944	Marianas	Also PO1c Tomimasa Ōkubo and PO1c Ryōzō Okada (both Kō 7)
Yoshio Wajima	LTJG	Pilot 18	Air Group 263	23 Feb 1944	Marianas	12th Air Group, 14th Air Group, Chitose Air Group, Air Group 582
Kazuo Ikumi	CPO	Otsu 10	Air Group 203	15 Mar 1944	Atsugi	Accident, Air Group 582
Masaru Tsukiji	PO1c	Otsu 13	Air Group 253	24 Mar 1944	Cape Torokina	
Yasuto Abe	CPO	Kō 6	Air Group 202	27 Mar 1944	Ponape	
Kaoru Miyazaki	PO1c	Hei 3	Yokosuka Air Group	27 Mar 1944	Homeland	
Mitsutami Noda	WO	Kō 6	Air Group 202	29 Mar 1944	Truk	Also PO1c Furuo Yoshimitsu (Hei 4)
Koshirō Yamashita	ENS	Pilot 17	Air Group 201	30 Mar 1944	Peleliu	*Ryūjō*, 12th Air Group
Kazuo Hattori	LdgSea	Hei 10	Air Group 201	30 Mar 1944	Peleliu	
Shin-ichi Suzuki	CPO	Pilot 45	Air Group 201	30 Mar 1944	Peleliu	Re the two pilots above: also LTJG Shigeo Hayashi (70), CPO Haruo Kunihiro (Kō 6), and PO1c Masao Wada (Kō 9)
Tomojirō Yamaguchi	LT	69	Fighter Hikōtai 351	30 Mar 1944	Peleliu	
Masato Okasako	LTJG	70	Air Group 261	31 Mar 1944	Peleliu	
Masao Shibuya	Res. ENS	Res. 11	Air Group 261	31 Mar 1944	Peleliu	Re the two pilots above: also PO2c Kenji Nihonmori (Pilot 45), PO1c Shigeru Hayashi (Pilot 55), PO1c Tashirō Koga (Otsu 11), and PO2c Ken-ichi Iryū (Otsu 15)
Nobuhiko Mutō	LT	70	Air Group 263	31 Mar 1944	Peleliu	
Takeichi Kikuchi	WO	Kō 1	Air Group 263	31 Mar 1944	Peleliu	Re the two pilots above: also Res. ENS Yoshito Shimoda (Res. 11), WO Masarō Nagase (Kō 1), CPO Shōji Kurita (Kō 6), and CPO Shōkichi Nishimoto (Otsu 10)
Ken Okui	CPO	Kō 5	Air Group 253	5 Apr 1944	Truk	
Tsuneo Nakahara	LTJG	Pilot 12	Sanya Air Group	5 Apr 1944	Nanning	Tainan Air Group
Takeo Kume	CPO	Otsu 9	Sanya Air Group	5 Apr 1944	Nanning	Tainan Air Group Re the two pilots above: also PO1c Tasuke Okabe, PO1c Tomio Kitaoka (both Otsu 13), and PO1c Asagorō Ishioka (Otsu 12)

(*continued*)

KEY FIGHTER PILOTS KILLED IN ACTION (by Date) (*continued*)

NAME	RANK	CLASS	UNIT	DATE OF DEATH	PLACE	MAJOR UNIT HISTORY AND OTHER DATA
Kaname Yoshimatsu	CPO	Pilot 41	Kaiko Air Group	5 Apr 1944	Nanning	*Sōryū, Hiryū*, also CPO Sakae Mori (Pilot 50)
Hiroshi Maeda	LT	69	Air Group 254	8 Apr 1944	Hainan Island	
Takumi Tahara	CPO	Pilot 45	Sanya Air Group	9 Apr 1944	Hainan Island	*Hiryū*
Kishiro Ayukawa	LTJG	70	Air Group 261	16 Apr 1944	Mariaon [Woleai]	
Matao Ichioka	PO2c	Hei 12	Air Group 253	19 Apr 1944	Solomons	
Shirō Kawakubo	LT	69	Air Group 202	30 Apr 1944	Truk	
Hiroshi Suzuki	Res. LTJG	Res. 9	Air Group 202	30 Apr 1944	Truk	Re foregoing two pilots: also PO1c Noboru Nakaoka (Kō 9), PO1c Hiroshi Nishida (Otsu 12), and PO1c Kikuo Ikeda (Kō 7)
Usao Nishimura	PO1c	Kō 9	Air Group 253	30 Apr 1944	Truk	Also PO2c Masaru Moriyama (Hei 6)
Shunji Horiguchi	CPO	Pilot 51	Air Group 265	5 May 1944	Saipan	*Shōkaku, Junyō*, accident; also PO1c Norio Nakajima (Kō 10)
Ken-ichi Honda	LT	69	Air Group 263	7 May 1944	Guam	Also Res. ENS Shōzō Kajikawa (Res. 11)
San-ichirō Tanaka	WO	Pilot 43	Air Group 263	7 May 1944	Guam	12th Air Group, Tainan Air Group
Sukemasa Katō	WO	Otsu 7	Fighter Hikōtai 311	7 May 1944	Biak	Also CPO Tsutomu Shibata (Otsu 9)
Sanenobu Maehara	WO		Air Group 203 (night fighters)	13 May 1944	Northern Kuriles	
Shinji Ishida	WO	Kō 1	Fighter Hikōtai 311	29 May 1944	Biak	Also CPO Tadashi Gotō (Kō 8)
Yūji Satō	WO	Kō 2	Air Group 202	2 Jun 1944	Biak	Air Group 331; also CPO Kenji Yamashita (Kō 9)
Hiroo Takao	LT	69	Fighter Hikōtai 603 division officer	3 Jun 1944	Babo	Also CPO Michiaki Ichikawa (Kō 9)
Toshio Ushikubo	Res. LTJG	Res. 10 (Kiryu Higher Technical School)	Fighter Hikōtai 301	3 Jun 1944	Babo	Also CPO Kōshichi Izumida (Otsu 12)
Otojirō Sakaguchi	WO	Kō 1	Fighter Hikōtai 301	3 Jun 1944	Biak	POW, returned
Ryutarō Masuda	LT	70	Air Group 253	9 Jun 1944	Truk	Intercepted B-24s
Kunishige Hasegawa	WO	Otsu 6	Fighter Hikōtai 901 (night fighters)	10 Jun 1944	Truk	
Jūji Torimoto	LT	69	Fighter Hikōtai 316 division officer	11 Jun 1944	Saipan	
Tetsuji Koga	WO	Otsu 7	Fighter Hikōtai 316	11 Jun 1944	Saipan	Re the two pilots above: also Ryōji Saitō, CPO Tsuneaki Shimada (Kō 9), and PO1c Yūki Kasuda (Kō 10)
Nobuyuku Ikura	LT	70	Air Group 265	11 Jun 1944	Saipan	

KEY FIGHTER PILOTS KILLED IN ACTION (by Date) (*continued*)

Name	Rank	Class	Unit	Date of Death	Place	Major Unit History and Other Data
Katsushi Tanaka	WO	Kō 1	Air Group 265	11 Jun 1944	Saipan	Re the two pilots above: *Akagi;* also ENS Seiji Yoshifuku (Res. 11), CPO Ryō-ichi Sugiura (Kō 5), PO1c Nobuya Sugita (Kō 10), and PO2c Gunji Kawauchi (Hei 10)
Ryūzo Yamamoto	CPO	Kō 8	Air Group 261	11 Jun 1944	Saipan	
Zenji Saitō	CPO	Kō 8	Air Group 261	11 Jun 1944	Saipan	Re the two pilots above: also CPO Kiyoshi Fushimi (Otsu 14) and CPO Yōtarō Ishikawa (Kō 9)
Ryuichi Jirōmaru	PO1c	Kō 10	Air Group 263	11 Jun 1944	Marianas	
Kōji Shimizu	CPO	Otsu 11	Air Group 343	12 Jun 1944	Marianas	Also CPO Kiyohira Kane-yama (Otsu 13)
Motoi Kaneko	LT	69	Fighter Hikōtai 401 division officer	15 Jun 1944	Iwo Jima	Also PO1c Toshirō Kanazawa and PO1c Rinzō Toya (both Kō 10)
Yoshio Torishima	CPO	Hei 2	Fighter Hikōtai 401	15 Jun 1944	Iwo Jima	3rd Air Group
Mamoru Shimura	LTJG	Pilot 18	Air Group 265	15 Jun 1944	Iwo Jima	
Shigeo Jūni	LT	67	Fighter Hikōtai 316 group leader	15 Jun 1944	Iwo Jima	
Suminori Kawahata	CPO	Pilot 43	Fighter Hikōtai 316	15 Jun 1944	Iwo Jima	Also Res. LTJG Chōbei Morita (Res. 9) and CPO Kazuo Ōishi (Otsu 14)
Shirō Sakamoto	Res. ENS	Res. 11	Fighter Hikōtai 301	15 Jun 1944	Saipan	
Aiji Satō	PO1c	Kō 10	Air Group 265	15 Jun 1944	Saipan	Also PO1c Kei Tomioka (Kō 10)
Zentoku Satō	CPO	Otsu 12	Air Group 201	15 Jun 1944	Naha	Also CPO Shinkichi Ōshima (Hei 3)
Tetsuo Kadomatsu	PO1c	Kō 10	Air Group 343	17 Jun 1944	Marianas	
Hiroshi Kurihara	WO	Kō 1	Air Group 201	18 Jun 1944	Marianas	12th Air Group, *Ryūjō*
Zenji Kaburagi	CPO	Hei 3	Air Group 263	18 Jun 1944	Marianas	
Ikurō Sakami	LT	69	Air Group 601 division officer	19 Jun 1944	Battle of Philippine Sea	Also LT Kiyoshi Fukagawa (70)
Toshitada Kawazoe	LT	67	Air Group 601 division officer	19 Jun 1944	Battle of Philippine Sea	3rd Air Group; also CPO Mamoru Morita (Otsu 9)
Akira Maruyama	ENS	Otsu 4	Air Group 601	19 Jun 1944	Battle of Philippine Sea	12th Air Group, 14th Air Group, *Ryūjō, Shōkaku*
Ichirō Yamamoto	WO	Pilot 50	Air Group 601	19 Jun 1944	Battle of Philippine Sea	*Shōkaku;* also CPO Masayuki Hanamura (Kō 7)
Saburō Sugai	WO	Pilot 26	Air Group 601	19 Jun 1944	Battle of Philippine Sea	*Ryūhō;* also CPO Shun-ichi Koyanagi (Hei 3)

(*continued*)

KEY FIGHTER PILOTS KILLED IN ACTION (by Date) *(continued)*

Name	Rank	Class		Unit	Date of Death	Place	Major Unit History and Other Data
Hiroshi Yoshimura	LT		68	Air Group 652 division officer	19 Jun 1944	Battle of Philippine Sea	*Ryūhō,* also LT Kenkichi Takasawa (69)
Yoshihiko Takenaka	WO	Kō	1	Air Group 652	19 Jun 1944	Battle of Philippine Sea	3rd Air Group
Kenta Komiyama	WO	Otsu	7	Air Group 652	19 Jun 1944	Battle of Philippine Sea	*Zuikaku*
Kō-ichi Imamura	CPO	Pilot	56	Air Group 652	19 Jun 1944	Battle of Philippine Sea	
Hiroshi Shiozaka	LT		70	Air Group 653	19 Jun 1944	Battle of Philippine Sea	Also PO1c Kiyotaka Sawazaki (Hei 3)
Isao Kondō	CPO	Kō	6	Air Group 653	19 Jun 1944	Battle of Philippine Sea	
Kōzaburō Yasui	WO	Pilot	40	Air Group 652	19 Jun 1944	Battle of Philippine Sea	14th Air Group, attached to 22nd Air Flotilla Command, Tainan Air Group; also CPO Masami Komaru (Hei 7)
Tetsuo Kikuchi	CPO	Pilot	39	Air Group 652	19 Jun 1944	Battle of Philippine Sea	14th Air Group, *Akagi, Shōkaku, Ryūhō*
Fumio Yamagata	LT		70	Air Group 601	19 Jun 1944	Battle of Philippine Sea	Also LT Yutaka Yagi (70)
Toshio Fukushima	LT		70	Air Group 601	19 Jun 1944	Battle of Philippine Sea	Also CPO Fumio Itō (Otsu 12)
Mitsunobu Kaga	LTJG	Otsu	2	Air Group 601	19 Jun 1944	Battle of Philippine Sea	Also CPO Iwao Yamamoto (Otsu 11)
Susumu Horio	LT		70	Air Group 601	19 Jun 1944	Battle of Philippine Sea	Also CPO Takeo Nagai (Pilot 44)
Shinya Ozaki	LT		68	Air Group 343 group leader	19 Jun 1944	Guam	
Isao Doikawa	CPO	Pilot	47	Air Group 343	19 Jun 1944	Guam	*Sōryū;* also PO1c Kiyoshi Yoshioka (Kō 10)
Tatsuo Hirano	LT	Engineering 47		Fighter Hikōtai 309 group leader	19 Jun 1944	Guam	
Yoshinao Tokuji	WO	Otsu	6	Air Group 253	19 Jun 1944	Guam	12th Air Group, 3rd Air Group; also CPO Noboru Kayahara (Kō 9)
Kō-ichi Yamauchi	CPO	Otsu	12	Air Group 201	19 Jun 1944	Off Saipan	
Naoto Satō	CPO	Kō	8	Air Group 261	19 Jun 1944	Guam	Also CPO Shigenori Hayashi (Otsu 14)
Takumi Kai	WO	Otsu	8	Air Group 652	20 Jun 1944	Battle of Philippine Sea	*Kaga, Zuikaku*
Jirō Imura	WO	Otsu	7	Air Group 652	20 Jun 1944	Battle of Philippine Sea	*Hōshō;* also CPO Masahiro Motoki (Kō 8)

KEY FIGHTER PILOTS KILLED IN ACTION (by Date) (*continued*)

NAME	RANK	CLASS	UNIT	DATE OF DEATH	PLACE	MAJOR UNIT HISTORY AND OTHER DATA
Masamichi Minogata	LT	69	Air Group 253	23 Jun 1944	Guam	
Toshiharu Ikeda	LT	67	Fighter Hikōtai 603 group leader	23 Jun 1944	Off Saipan	
Saneo Imamura	WO	Pilot 23	Fighter Hikōtai 603	23 Jun 1944	Off Saipan	Air Group 331
Tadashi Nakamoto	CPO	Kō 5	Air Group 201	23 Jun 1944	Off Saipan	Tainan Air Group; also CPO Toshio Tanaka (Kō 9)
Kakurō Kawamura	LT	69	Air Group 343 division officer	24 Jun 1944	Iwo Jima	Also LTJG Naoyoshi Yonemasu (71)
Katsumi Kōda	LT	69	Fighter Hikōtai 601 division officer	24 Jun 1944	Iwo Jima	
Nobuo Awa	LT	69	Air Group 252 group leader	24 Jun 1944	Iwo Jima	
Sadayoshi Masumoto	LT	70	Air Group 252	24 Jun 1944	Iwo Jima	Re the two pilots above: also WO Mitsuzō Hashimoto (Kō 2), CPO Makoto Nagura (Kō 9), and Res. ENS Masao Katsuta (Res. 11)
Tadao Shiratori	WO	Kō 3	Yokosuka Air Group	24 Jun 1944	Iwo Jima	Also CPO Takao Banno (Hei 3)
Kiyoshi Sekiya	CPO	Hei 3	Yokosuka Air Group	24 Jun 1944	Iwo Jima	3rd Air Group, Air Group 582, Air Group 204
Kazuo Ōhata	LT	70	Yokosuka Air Group	24 Jun 1944	Iwo Jima	Attack task forces
Toshitsugu Nisugi	CPO	Pilot 54	Yokosuka Air Group	24 Jun 1944	Iwo Jima	PO1c Kinji Koike (Otsu 16)
Tomezō Yamamoto	CPO	Hei 2	Air Group 203	24 Jun 1944	Shumshu Islands	Accident, Air Group 582
Masateru Kurokawa	Res. ENS	Res. 11	Air Group 261	24 Jun 1944	Marianas	
Mitsuho Tanaka	LT	70	Air Group 253	26 Jun 1944	Truk	Intercepted B-24s
Susumu Ishida	CPO	Otsu 8	Air Group 252	3 Jul 1944	Iwo Jima	Chitose Air Group; also CPO Akio Maeda (Hei 4)
Junzō Okutani	WO	Kō 41	Fighter Hikōtai 601	3 Jul 1944	Iwo Jima	
Korekiyo Kawakita	LT	70	Fighter Hikōtai 601	3 Jul 1944	Iwo Jima	
Mibuichi Shimada	CPO	Pilot 54	Fighter Hikōtai 601	3 Jul 1944	Iwo Jima	Re the three pilots above: also CPO Yoshio Gotō (Otsu 11), CPO Kikuichi Ishikawa (Otsu 14), and PO1c Teruo Doi (Otsu 16)
Sadao Yamaguchi	LT	67	Yokosuka Air Group division officer	4 Jul 1944	Iwo Jima	3rd Air Group
Bangorō Myōkei	CPO	Hei 3	Yokosuka Air Group	4 Jul 1944	Iwo Jima	Air Group 582; also CPO Sadao Kubo (Hei 3)
Masami Iwatsubo	CPO	Hei 3	Air Group 301	4 Jul 1944	Iwo Jima	
Iwao Mita	WO	Kō 2	Air Group 301	4 Jul 1944	Iwo Jima	*Sōryū*, *Hiyō*; also PO2c Takayoshi Morita (Hei 10)

(*continued*)

KEY FIGHTER PILOTS KILLED IN ACTION (by Date) *(continued)*

NAME	RANK	CLASS	UNIT	DATE OF DEATH	PLACE	MAJOR UNIT HISTORY AND OTHER DATA
Tomotoshi Ishikawa	WO	Kō 1	Omura Air Group	6 Jul 1944	Homeland	Accident
Ryōgo Nakabachi	PO1c	Kō 10	Air Group 265	7 Jul 1944	Saipan	Banzai attack death; also Sakurō Takahashi and PO1c Keima Miwa (Kō 10)
Hitoshi Ishibashi	PO1c	Kō 10	Air Group 261	7 Jul 1944	Saipan	Banzai attack death; also Setsu Suzuki, PO1c Tamotsu Harada (Kō 10)
*Yasuhiro Shigematsu	LT	66	Air Group 263 group leader	8 Jul 1944	Marianas	*Hiryū, Junyō;* also LTJG Hōshi Dokushima (Res. 11)
Jizō Nishiyama	CPO	Kō 5	Air Group 201	8 Jul 1944	Marianas	Also CPO Shigehisa Aoki (Otsu 13)
Ichirō Higashiyama	LTJG	Otsu 2	Air Group 261 division officer	8 Jul 1944	Saipan	Banzai attack death, 15th Air Group, 12th Air Group
Tetsutarō Kumagaya	WO	Pilot 28	Air Group 253	8 Jul 1944	Saipan	Banzai attack death, 13th Air Group, 14th Air Group, Air Group 253, Air Group 204
Kenzō Asatsu	CPO	Otsu 11	Air Group 301	8 Jul 1944	Saipan	Banzai attack death
Teiji Kagami	Res. LT	Res. 7 (Nagoya Pharmaceutical College)	Fighter Hikōtai 603 division officer	11 Jul 1944	Micronesia	
Tetsuo Matsuo	PO1c	Kō 10	Air Group 201	21 Jul 1944	Yap	Rammed into a B-29; also PO1c Ryūji Tomita (Kō 10)
Shigeru Itaya	LCDR	57	51st Air Flotilla staff	24 Jul 1944	Kuriles	Accident, *Ryūjō,* 15th Air Group, 12th Air Group, *Akagi*
Yasuhiko Ukimura	LT	70	Fighter Hikōtai 301 division officer	25 Jul 1944	Micronesia	Air Group 265
Jirō Iwai	CPO	Otsu 10	Air Group 331	25 Jul 1944	Sabang	*Hiyō;* also PO1c Hiroshi Kataoka (Kō 10)
Rikio Aizawa	CPO	Kō 8	Air Group 254	29 Jul 1944	Sanya	
Ichirō Shimoda	LT	66	Air Group 321 group leader	2 Aug 1944	Tinian	Banzai attack death; also LT Hideo Kume and LT Tametsugu Yonishi (both 70)
Ken-ichi Ban	LT	69	Fighter Hikōtai 306 group leader	10 Aug 1944	Guam	Banzai attack death
Yoshio Iwabuchi	CPO	Pilot 56	Air Group 601	10 Aug 1944	Guam	*Sōryū,* banzai attack death
Mizuho Tanaka	LT	70	Fighter Hikōtai 301 division officer	17 Aug 1944	Truk	Intercepted B-24s
Shin Yamauchi	LT	69	Fighter Hikōtai 311 division officer	20 Aug 1944	Borneo	Accident
Rikio Tomioka	LT	70	Fighter Hikōtai 315	31 Aug 1944	Iwo Jima	

KEY FIGHTER PILOTS KILLED IN ACTION (by Date) (*continued*)

Name	Rank	Class	Unit	Date of Death	Place	Major Unit History and Other Data
Kunio Mori	LT	69	Fighter Hikōtai 902 division officer	10 Sep 1944	Off Leyte	Also LTJG Nobuichi Takahata (14th Reconnaissance)
Hiroshi Mori-i	LT	69	Fighter Hikōtai 306 group leader	12 Sep 1944	Cebu	Res. LTJG Hayao Ishihashi (Res. 11)
Hideo Ōishi	WO	Pilot 26	Air Group 201	12 Sep 1944	Cebu	*Hōshō, Sōryū*, 12th Air Group
Tadahiro Sakai	WO	Kō 4	Air Group 201	12 Sep 1944	Cebu	3rd Air Group
Hyakurō Makiyama	CPO	Hei 3	Air Group 201	12 Sep 1944	Cebu	Air Group 582
Shinsaku Tanaka	CPO	Otsu 12	Air Group 201	12 Sep 1944	Cebu	Re the three pilots above: also CPO Masami Futatsugi (Otsu 10), CPO Tokuharu Noda (Otsu 11), CPO Tsuneji Mitani (Kō 9), and CPO Hiroshi Yasumatsu (Hei 4)
Kishio Kadota	CPO	Otsu 10	Air Group 201	12 Sep 1944	Legaspi	
Shitau Satō	Res. ENS	Res. 13	Air Group 201	13 Sep 1944	Bacolod	Also PO1c Sumio Sasamoto (Kō 10)
Shigenobu Takahara	WO	Otsu 8	Fighter Hikōtai 311	21 Sep 1944	Manila	*Akagi*
Nobuo Takano	LT	70	Fighter Hikōtai 311	21 Sep 1944	Manila	Re the two pilots above: also CPO Kikuo Nishimori (Otsu 10) and PO1c Tadashi Ikeda (Otsu 16)
Hisateru Tabuchi	LTJG	Pilot 14	Fighter Hikōtai 901 division officer (night fighters)	21 Sep 1944	East of Philippines	
Tetsuya Yanogawa	PO1c	Kō 10	Air Group 201	22 Sep 1944	East of Philippines	
Yukio Maki	LT	65	Tsukuba Air Group group leader	28 Sep 1944	Homeland	Accident, 14th Air Group, Tainan Air Group, 6th Air Group
Keisaburō Uchiyama	Res. LTJG		Fighter Hikōtai 602	3 Oct 1944	Balikpapan	Also CPO Kitami Kikuchi (Otsu 14)
Eizō Ōta	CPO	Otsu 12	Fighter Hikōtai 602	10 Oct 1944	Balikpapan	
Sadao Ozaki	LT	Res. 7 (Kansai Univ.)	Fighter Hikōtai 902 division officer (night fighters)	10 Oct 1944	Balikpapan	
Akira Tanaka	LT	Res. 8 (Kantō Gakuin College)	Fighter Hikōtai 309 group leader	10 Oct 1944	Balikpapan	Also CPO Tsumirō Tanaka (Otsu 13) and PO1c Akio Fukui (Kō 10)
Yoshio Murata	Res. LT	Res. 4 (Nippon Univ.)	Takao Air Group group leader	12 Oct 1944	Taiwan	Also LT Toshikazu Taguchi (Engineer 50) and CPO Toshihiro Matsunaga (Otsu 13)
Ryō-ichi Iwakawa	CPO	Pilot 56	Takao Air Group	12 Oct 1944	Taiwan	3rd Air Group, Air Group 253
Noboru Okugawa	CPO	Pilot 29	Tainan Air Group	12 Oct 1944	Taiwan	*Zuikaku;* also LTJG Ken Kihara (72)

(*continued*)

KEY FIGHTER PILOTS KILLED IN ACTION (by Date) (*continued*)

Name	Rank	Class	Unit	Date of Death	Place	Major Unit History and Other Data
Junjirō Itō	WO	Kō 1	Air Group 221	12 Oct 1944	Taiwan	12th Air Group, *Zuikaku*
Katsuhiko Kawasaki	CPO	Hei 2	Air Group 221	12 Oct 1944	Taiwan	Air Group 253
						Re the two pilots above: also LTJG Yosaburō Ōtsuki (71), CPO Kiyoshi Yamazaki (Otsu 11), and Res. LTJG Takeo Kawaguchi (Res. 11)
Fumio Shigeta	LT	69	Fighter Hikōtai 304 division officer	12 Oct 1944	Taiwan	
Shigemi Wakabayashi	LTJG	71	Fighter Hikōtai 401	12 Oct 1944	Taiwan	Also LTJG Katsumi Yamaguchi (72)
Usaburō Suzuki	LT	68	Fighter Hikōtai 301 group leader	13 Oct 1944	Off Taiwan	Air Group 202, Air Group 582, Air Group 204
Tadashi Sakai	CPO	Hei 2	Air Group 341	13 Oct 1944	Taiwan	
Hiroshi Suzuki	CPO	Kō 5	Air Group 201	13 Oct 1944	Off Philippines	
Kunio Kimura	LT	70	Fighter Hikōtai 302	14 Oct 1944	Taiwan	
Masao Iizuka	LT	66	Fighter Hikōtai 302 group leader	15 Oct 1944	Off Taiwan	*Kaga;* also LTJG Mitsuo Tanabe (72)
Osamu Takahashi	LT	70	Fighter Hikōtai 308	15 Oct 1944	Off Taiwan	Also PO1c Jinpei Isozaki (Otsu 15)
Hiromichi Hōjō	CPO	Pilot 43	Fighter Hikōtai 315	15 Oct 1944	Off Taiwan	3rd Air Group, *Hiyō*
Hiroshi Nagakura	CPO	Kō 7	Air Group 653	15 Oct 1944	Off Taiwan	
Satoshi Kanō	WO	Otsu 6	Air Group 254	16 Oct 1944	Off Taiwan	*Zuikaku*
★Hidehiro Nakama	LT	70	Fighter Hikōtai 317 division officer	21 Oct 1944	Iwo Jima	Rammed into B-24
Yoshiyasu Kunō	Res. LTJG	Res. 11 (Hōsei Univ.)	Fighter Hikōtai 301	21 Oct 1944	Off Leyte	Special attack forces
★Naohisa Uemura	Res. ENS	Res. 13 (Rikkyō Univ.)	Air Group 201	21 Oct 1944	Off Leyte	Special attack forces
Minoru Tsukahara	CPO	Kō 9	Air Group 221	21 Oct 1944	Morotai	
★Kaoru Satō	CPO	Hei 4	Air Group 201	23 Oct 1944	Off Leyte	Special attack forces, Air Group 253
Minoru Kobayashi	LCDR	64	Fighter Hikōtai 312 group leader	24 Oct 1944	East of Philippines	*Ryūjō*, 3rd Air Group
Iwao Akiyama	LT	Engineering 51	Fighter Hikōtai 316 division officer	24 Oct 1944	East of Philippines	Re the two pilots above: also CPO Bun-ichi Fujise (Otsu 11) and CPO Takeru Wada (Kō 7)
Sumio Fukuda	LT	69	Fighter Hikōtai 163 group leader	24 Oct 1944	East of Philippines	*Junyō*, Air Group 204; also WO Mamoru Ishii (Pilot 44)
Yukiharu Ozeki	WO	Pilot 32	Air Group 203	24 Oct 1944	East of Philippines	13th Air Group, 12th Air Group, 3rd Air Group, 6th Air Group
Minoru Shibamura	WO	Pilot 48	Fighter Hikōtai 402	24 Oct 1944	East of Philippines	Also CPO Rokusaburō Shinohara (Otsu 11)

KEY FIGHTER PILOTS KILLED IN ACTION (by Date) (*continued*)

Name	Rank	Class	Unit	Date of Death	Place	Major Unit History and Other Data
Hiroshi Tanaka	LT	70	Fighter Hikōtai 407	24 Oct 1944	East of Philippines	
Saneo Miyauchi	LT	70	Fighter Hikōtai 313	24 Oct 1944	East of Philippines	Also CPO Yoshito Azukihata (Otsu 12)
Hisaya Hirusawa	LT	Engineering 50	Fighter Hikōtai 313 group leader	24 Oct 1944	East of Philippines	Also LT Hisao Kawanishi (70)
Kazunari Koyama	CPO	Kō 9	Air Group 653	24 Oct 1944	East of Philippines	Also PO1c Mitsuo Senda (Otsu 16)
Hōhei Kobayashi	LT	67	Fighter Hikōtai 161 group leader	25 Oct 1944	East of Philippines	
Yoshiteru Mine	LT	70	Fighter Hikōtai 161 division leader	25 Oct 1944	East of Philippines	Re the two pilots above: *Shōkaku;* also PO1c Takeo Ohkawa (Kō 10), CPO Takeo Yamashiro (Otsu 10), and CPO Denshin Kataoka (Otsu 10)
Momoto Matsumura	WO	Pilot 29	Air Group 161	25 Oct 1944	East of Philippines	12th Air Group, 13th Air Group, Air Group 204; also CPO Yasuo Iguchi (Kō 7)
Mitsuo Ōfuji	LT	70	Fighter Hikōtai 165 division officer	25 Oct 1944	East of Philippines	
Seikichi Kubota	WO	Otsu 7	Fighter Hikōtai 165	25 Oct 1944	East of Philippines	*Shōkaku;* Air Group 601, also CPO Oto Kataoka (Kō 8)
Yoshirō Hashiguchi	CPO	Pilot 42	Fighter Hikōtai 164	25 Oct 1944	East of Philippines	12th Air Group, 3rd Air Group, Air Group 601; also CPO Masakazu Suzuki (Kō 6)
Eiji Sanada	CPO	Pilot 56	Air Group 634	25 Oct 1944	East of Philippines	*Junyō*
Yasuhide Aoki	Res. LTJG	Res. 11	Fighter Hikōtai 304	25 Oct 1944	East of Philippines	Also PO1c Hisao Fujii (Otsu 15)
*Yukio Seki	LT	70	Fighter Hikōtai 301 division officer	25 Oct 1944	Off Leyte	Special attack forces, PO1c Nobuo Tani and PO1c Iwao Nakano (Kō 10)
Misao Sugawa	LdgSea	Hei 15	Air Group 201	25 Oct 1944	Off Leyte	Special attack forces escort
Masaru Sometani	LTJG	71	Fighter Hikōtai 401	25 Oct 1944	Philippines	
Dai Nakajima	LT	69	Fighter Hikōtai 161 division officer	26 Oct 1944	Sibuyan Sea	
*Tomisaku Katsumata	PO1c	Kō 10	Fighter Hikōtai 301	26 Oct 1944	Off Leyte	Special attack forces
*Hiroyoshi Nishizawa	WO	Otsu 7	Fighter Hikōtai 303	26 Oct 1944	Mindoro	On board transport aircraft, Chitose Air Group, Air Group 251, Air Group 203, Air Group 253
Shingo Honda	CPO	Hei 4	Fighter Hikōtai 303	26 Oct 1944	Mindoro	
Katsumasa Matsumoto	CPO	Otsu 9	Air Group 762	26 Oct 1944	Cebu	
Tomokazu Ema	WO	Pilot 22	Air Group 354	29 Oct 1944	Manila	14th Air Group, 6th Air Group; also LTJG Gi-ichi Minami (Otsu 2)
Kyōji Handa	CPO	Hei 3	Air Group 341	29 Oct 1944	Manila	
Tsuneishi Nakamura	CPO	Kō 6	Air Group 653	29 Oct 1944	Bamban	
Tsunesaku Sakai	CPO	Hei 4	Air Group 203	1 Nov 1944	Cebu	

(*continued*)

KEY FIGHTER PILOTS KILLED IN ACTION (by Date) *(continued)*

NAME	RANK	CLASS	UNIT	DATE OF DEATH	PLACE	MAJOR UNIT HISTORY AND OTHER DATA
Shōji Katō	CPO	Kō 9	Air Group 203	2 Nov 1944	Leyte	
Chōzō Nakaya	CPO	Otsu 15	Air Group 653	2 Nov 1944	Leyte	
Kenji Nakagawa	LT	67	Fighter Hikōtai 165 group leader	3 Nov 1944	Leyte	*Zuihō, Zuikaku,* Air Group 653; also LTJG Satōru Iguchi (72)
Tei-ichi Katō	Res. LTJG	Res. 10 (Tokyo Univ.)	Fighter Hikōtai 303	4 Nov 1944	Cebu	
Torajirō Haruta	LT	69	Fighter Hikōtai 316 group leader	5 Nov 1944	Mabalacat	Air Group 253; also CPO Sōji Wakatsu (Otsu 16)
Makoto Inoue	WO	Pilot 46	Air Group 203	5 Nov 1944	Bamban	12th Air Group, 3rd Air Group, Air Group 253
Yoshinori Nakada	LdgSea	Special Otsu 2	Fighter Hikōtai 407	5 Nov 1944	Bamban	
Ki-ichi Nagano	CPO	Pilot 56	Air Group 203	6 Nov 1944	Bamban	Air Group 582
Shoku Kimura	LTJG	72	Air Group 254	11 Nov 1944	Leyte	
*Korekiyo Otsuji	LTJG	71	Fighter Hikōtai 163 division officer	12 Nov 1944	Leyte	Special attack forces; also CPO Yaozō Wada (Otsu 13)
Munesaburō Takahashi	ENS	Pilot 30	Air Group 341	18 Nov 1944	Tacloban	13th Air Group, 12th Air Group, *Sōryū, Hiyō*
*Yoshita Toda	LTJG	72	Air Group 221	19 Nov 1944	Leyte	Special attack forces
*Mikihiko Sakamoto	LTJG	71	Air Group 352	21 Nov 1944	Omura	Rammed into B-29
Masa-aki Kawahara	ENS	Pilot 26	Omura Air Group	21 Nov 1944	Omura	Intercepted B-29s
Aya-o Shirane	LCDR	64	Fighter Hikōtai 701 group leader	24 Nov 1944	Ormoc Bay	12th Air Group, *Akagi, Zuikaku;* also CPO Sadao Koike (Otsu 10)
Akira Yamamoto	ENS	Pilot 24	Yokosuka Air Group	24 Nov 1944	Over Yachimata	Intercepted B-29s, *Hōshō, Ryūjō,* 12th Air Group, *Kaga, Zuihō*
*Yoshimi Minami	ENS	Pilot 30	Fighter Hikōtai 302	25 Nov 1944	Philippines	Special attack forces, 12th Air Group, *Shōkaku*
Tatsu Nagato	LTJG	Res. 11 (Hikone Higher Commercial School)	Fighter Hikōtai 305	26 Nov 1944	Philippines	Special attack forces
Masa-ichi Ōshōdani	CPO	Otsu 9	Yokosuka Air Group	26 Nov 1944	Atsugi	Accident, Air Group 204
Susumu Takeda	LTJG	71	Fighter Hikōtai 303 division officer	27 Nov 1944		Also, CPO Kyōichi Inuzuka (Otsu 8)
*Yasunori Ono	WO	Kō 2	Air Group 252	27 Nov 1944	Saipan	Special attack forces; also LTJG Kenji Ōmura (72)
Keiji Kataki	LT	70	Fighter Hikōtai 312 division officer	29 Nov 1944	Philippines	Also PO1c Tsunehiro Yoshii (Otsu 16)
Masuzō Setō	LCDR	64	Fighter Hikōtai 315 group leader	4 Dec 1944	Off Taiwan	Tainan Air Group, *Shōkaku,* ditched
*Tetsurō Yano	Res. LTJG	Res. 11	Fighter Hikōtai 316	7 Dec 1944	Philippines	Special attack forces
Ushi-o Nishimura	CPO	Kō 9	Fighter Hikōtai 302	8 Dec 1944	Iwo Jima	

KEY FIGHTER PILOTS KILLED IN ACTION (by Date) (*continued*)

NAME	RANK	CLASS	UNIT	DATE OF DEATH	PLACE	MAJOR UNIT HISTORY AND OTHER DATA
Ki-ichi Oda	WO	Pilot 18	Fighter Hikōtai 306	10 Dec 1944	Off Ogasa-wara	Died in action on board submarine; *Kaga,* 15th Air Group, *Sōryū*
Yoshiharu Kagami	CPO	Otsu 12	Fighter Hikōtai 701	14 Dec 1944	Philippines	Also LT Sumio Arikawa (71)
Seiya Nakajima	LT	71	Fighter Hikōtai 402 division leader	15 Dec 1944	Philippines	
Takumi Chōsokabe	CPO	Otsu 13	Fighter Hikōtai 602	20 Dec 1944	Balikpapan	
Shirō Kawai	LCDR	64	Fighter Hikōtai 308 group leader	24 Dec 1944	Clark	12th Air Group, Tainan Air Group, Air Group 201, missing after parachuting
Tadashi Yoneda	CPO	Pilot 56	Fighter Hikōtai 315	25 Dec 1944	Clark	Air Group 251; also CPO Masakazu Kuwabara (Hei 3)
Yoshio Kinoshita	LT	71	Fighter Hikōtai 308 division officer	3 Jan 1945	Taiwan	Also ENS Shigemasa Nishio (Otsu 6)
Saburō Mitsuoka	CPO	Otsu 11	Air Group 341	4 Jan 1945	Malcott	Died in action as result of gun shots
*Shin-ichi Kanaya	LT	71	Air Group 201	5 Jan 1945	Philippines	Special attack forces
Akira Sugiura	LT	Res. 8 (Aoyama)	Air Group 901 division officer	5 Jan 1945	Hainan Islands	Also LT Tsunekata Maki (71), LTJG Takeshi Inoue (Res. 11)
Masami Iwatsubo	CPO	Hei 3	Air Group 352	6 Jan 1945	Northern Kyūshū	Also LTJG Kō-ichi Sawada (72)
*Shigenobu Manabe	CPO	Hei 7	Air Group 252	7 Jan 1945	Philippines	Special attack forces
Yoshio Yamazaki	WO	Kō 4	Fighter Hikōtai 902 (night fighters)	8 Jan 1945	Balikpapan	
Tokushige Yoshizawa	CPO	Hei 7	Air Group 105 base unit	9 Jan 1945	New Britain	Air Group 201, Air Group 204
*Yukio Endō	LT	Otsu 1	Air Group 302 (night fighters)	14 Jan 1945	Atsumi Peninsula	Intercepted B-29s, Air Group 251, Air Group 352
Yoshio Orihara	CPO	Kō 1	Fighter Hikōtai 314	15 Jan 1945		*Hiyō,* Air Group 601
Tetsuo Endō	LT	67	Fighter Hikōtai 314 group leader	16 Jan 1945	Luzon	
Hajime Toji	CPO	Otsu 9	Hikōtai 901 (Air Group 254)	16 Jan 1945	Sanya	*Junyō;* also CPO Hisashi Kamata (Otsu 10)
*Minoru Kawazoe	LT	69	Fighter Hikōtai 317 group leader	21 Jan 1945	Off Taiwan	Special attack forces; also LT Sei-ichi Saitō (71)
*Hidenobu Sumino	Res. LTJG	Res. 13	Air Group 201	25 Jan 1945	Lingayen Gulf	Special attack forces
Toshio Imada	CPO	Otsu 10	Fighter Hikōtai 602	6 Feb 1945	Balikpapan	Intercepted B-24s
Toshio Araki	LT	67	Air Group 302 group leader	16 Feb 1945	Kantō Plains	
Jirō Ishikawa	CPO	Kō 6	Air Group 252	16 Feb 1945	Kantō Plains	*Hiyō;* also CPO Shigemi Izumi (Kō 6)
Kōzō Kobayashi	LT	71	Tsukuba Air Group	16 Feb 1944	Kantō Plains	Air Group 202
Rokuya Yoneyama	CPO	Hei 6	Tsukuba Air Group	16 Feb 1945	Kantō Plains	Re the two pilots above: also LT Itaru Yamashita (71) and CPO Shūji Furuuchi (Kō 6)

(*continued*)

KEY FIGHTER PILOTS KILLED IN ACTION (by Date) (*continued*)

Name	Rank	Class	Unit	Date of Death	Place	Major Unit History and Other Data
Noboru Matsu-ura	Res. LTJG	Res. 11	Yatabe Air Group	16 Feb 1945	Kantō Plains	
Hachirō Sakai	CPO	Otsu 16	Air Group 601	16 Feb 1945	Kantō Plains	
Kenkō Akai	LTJG	72	Air Group 302	17 Feb 1945	Kantō Plains	Also PO1c Tadashi Saka (Hei 10)
Shinkai Fujimori	LT	69	Tsukuba Air Group	17 Feb 1945	Kantō Plains	
Takashi Yamazaki	CPO	Hei 3	Yokosuka Air Group	17 Feb 1945	Kantō Plains	*Zuikaku*
Sanemasa Nanjō	CPO	Kō 7	Fighter Hikōtai 304	17 Feb 1945	Kantō Plains	
Ryōkei Shinohara	WO	Otsu 8	Yatabe Air Group	25 Feb 1945	Kantō Plains	12th Air Group, Tainan Air Group
Toshihide Kihara	LT	71	Tsukuba Air Group	25 Feb 1945	Kantō Plains	
Katsumi Sugie	LTJG	72	Air Group 601	25 Feb 1945	Kantō Plains	
Morito Yamaguchi	LT	71	Air Group 901 division officer	25 Feb 1945	Hainan Island	
Masajirō Kawato	PO1c	Hei 12	Air Group 105 base unit	9 Mar 1945	New Britain	POW, returned
Mitsuru Ōnuma	LT	Res. 9 (Waseda Univ.)	Air Group 203	18 Mar 1945	Southern Kyūshū	Also PO1c Mitsunori Kojima (Otsu 16)
Mankichi Satō	CPO	Otsu 11	Air Group 221	18 Mar 1945	Southern Kyūshū	
Kunio Matsuzaki	LT	71	Air Group 343 division officer	19 Mar 1945	Matsuyama	
Kōzō Shima	LT	71	Air Group 343 division officer	19 Mar 1945	Matsuyama	
Shirō Endō	CPO	Kō 7	Air Group 343	19 Mar 1945	Matsuyama	Re the three pilots above: also CPO Yasuharu Nikkō (Kō 10), CPO Kiku-ichi Ishikawa (Otsu 14), PO1c Mitsuo Nakajima (Otsu 16), Res. LTJG Isaburō Inoue (Res. 11), PO1c Haruhiko Takeshima (Kō 11), and LdgSea Yō-ichi Saiki (Special Hei 1)
★Mutsuo Urushiyama	LT	70	Fighter Hikōtai 307 division officer	21 Mar 1945	Off Tosa	Jinrai special attack force escort
★Yū-ichi Izawa	LT	71	Fighter Hikōtai 306 division officer	21 Mar 1945	Off Tosa	
★Kōjirō Murakami	CPO	Otsu 11	Fighter Hikōtai 306	21 Mar 1945	Off Tosa	
★Gorō Tsuda	CPO	Hei 2	Fighter Hikōtai 306	21 Mar 1945	Off Tosa	Re the three pilots above: *Jinrai* special attack force escort; also CPO Ichizen Kobayashi (Kō 7) and CPO Toshikazu Nakano (Hei 3)

KEY FIGHTER PILOTS KILLED IN ACTION (by Date) (*continued*)

Name	Rank	Class	Unit	Date of Death	Place	Major Unit History and Other Data
Nao Sugisaki	LT	69	Air Group 352 group leader	31 Mar 1945	Kyūshū	
*Iwao Fumoto	PO1c	Otsu 17	Air Group 721	1 Apr 1945	Okinawa	Ōka [Baka bomb] special attack forces
Yōzō Tsuboi	LT	Yo 9 (Doshisha Univ.)	Air Group 302 division officer	1 Apr 1945	Kantō Plains	
Hiroyuki Fujishima	CPO	Kō 8	Air Group 601	3 Apr 1945	Okinawa	Also CPO Tatsu Nakatani (Kō 10)
Yū-ichi Kobayashi	CPO	Hei 4	Air Group 205	5 Apr 1945	Okinawa	
Kunio Kanzaki	LT	68	Fighter Hikōtai 312 group leader	6 Apr 1945	Okinawa	Air Group 381
Hiroshi Matano	LT	71	Fighter Hikōtai 312	6 Apr 1945	Okinawa	Re the two pilots above: also, ENS Akira Ozeki (Pilot 25), Res. LTJG Chisato Akiyama, and Res. LTJG Shōgo Kobayashi (both Res. 11)
Noboru Yamakawa	LT	Otsu 1	Ōmura Air Group	6 Apr 1945	Okinawa	13th Air Group, *Kaga*, 15th Air Group, Tainan Air Group
Shinzō Tabata	CPO	Otsu 14	Ōmura Air Group	6 Apr 1945	Okinawa	Also CPO Kazuo Tanio (Otsu 16)
Nobutaka Kurata	CPO	Pilot 54	Air Group 252	6 Apr 1945	Okinawa	*Zuikaku*, Air Group 203, Air Group 352; also PO2c Masakazu Koyanagi
*Yūhei Watanabe	PO1c	Hei 11	Fighter Hikōtai 313	7 Apr 1945	Chiba	Rammed into B-29
Kōji Chikama	LT	Otsu 11	Fighter Hikōtai 306	12 Apr 1945	Okinawa	Also LT Manabu Ishimori (71)
Ei-ichi Kawabata	LT	69	Fighter Hikōtai 804 group leader	12 Apr 1945	Okinawa	
Shō-ichi Takahashi	LT	70	Tsukuba Air Group	12 Apr 1945	Okinawa	
Ichigo Katayama	LTJG	72	Air Group 302	12 Apr 1945	Okinawa	
Tatsutoshi Hashimoto	LTJG	72	Air Group 343	12 Apr 1945	Okinawa	Also CPO Yoshio Aoyama (Kō 10)
*Tenshin Suzuki	LTJG	73	Yatabe Air Group	14 Apr 1945	Okinawa	
*Tadashi Ōmoto	LTJG	Res. 13	Yatabe Air Group	14 Apr 1945	Okinawa	Re the two pilots above: special attack forces; also ENS Hachirō Sasaki (Res. 14) and PO2c Hideo Sumihiro (Otsu 18)
*Shō-ichi Sugita	PO1c	Hei 3	Fighter Hikōtai 301	15 Apr 1945	Kanoya	6th Air Group, Air Group 343, Air Group 201
Megumi Yoshioka	CPO	Otsu 16	Air Group 302	15 Apr 1945	Kanoya	Also CPO Masao Oikawa (Otsu 15)
Masa-aki Asakawa	LT	69	Air Group 332 group leader	16 Apr 1945	Naruo	Accident, Air Group 341
Makoto Oku-umi	LTJG	72	Air Group 601	16 Apr 1945	Kikaiga-shima	
Teigo Ishida	CPO	Hei 6	Fighter Hikōtai 407	16 Apr 1945	Okinawa	Air Group 202, Air Group 204; also LdgSea Hitoshi Kotake (Special Otsu 2)

(*continued*)

KEY FIGHTER PILOTS KILLED IN ACTION (by Date) (*continued*)

NAME	RANK	CLASS	UNIT	DATE OF DEATH	PLACE	MAJOR UNIT HISTORY AND OTHER DATA
Yasuo Isobe	CPO	Pilot 53	Genzan Air Group	16 Apr 1945	Okinawa	
Hiroshi Tajiri	LTJG	72	Air Group 352	16 Apr 1945	Okinawa	Also LTJG Kazuyoshi Mori (72)
Kyōji Takahashi	LT	71	Air Group 252 division officer	16 Apr 1945	Okinawa	Also CPOP Yūzō Komatsu (I Iei 6)
Katsuyoshi Tanaka	CPO	Hei 3	Air Group 343	16 Apr 1945	Okinawa	Also CPO Katsue Katō (Kō 9)
Takao Ōtani	CPO	Kō 8	Air Group 302	16 Apr 1945	Okinawa	
Hachirō Yanagisawa	LCDR	64	Fighter Hikōtai 304 group leader	17 Apr 1945	Okinawa	
Mutsuo Uemura	CPO	Hei 2	Fighter Hikōtai 311	17 Apr 1945	Okinawa	
*Nobuo Saitō	WO	Pilot 42	Air Group 205	17 Apr 1945	Okinawa	Special attack forces
Ei Fukuda	LTJG	72	Air Group 302	19 Apr 1945	Kantō Plains	Also CPO Shirō Toriyama (Hei 3)
Yoshishige Hayashi	LT	69	Fighter Hikōtai 407 group leader	21 Apr 1945	Southern Kyūshū	Intercepted B-29s, Air Group 251; also PO1c Toshinobu Shimizu (Otsu 14)
Sō-ichirō Yamada	CPO	Otsu 15	Yokosuka Air Group	21 Apr 1945	Southern Kyūshū	Intercepted B-29s
Takehiko Kobayashi	LT	Engineering 52	Ōmura Air Group division officer	22 Apr 1945	Southern Kyūshū	
Shigenobu Nakada	CPO	Pilot 40	Air Group 201	24 Apr 1945	Luzon	Air Group 204, Air Group 201, died in action on the ground; also CPO Seiji Katō (Kō 8)
Saburō Yoneda	ENS	Kō 2	Fighter Hikōtai 901 (night fighters)	28 Apr 1945	Okinawa	
Shirō Hamada	CPO	Kō 10	Air Group 343	28 Apr 1945	Okinawa	
Seiji Jōnoshita	LT	70	Fighter Hikōtai 312 group leader	29 Apr 1945	Homeland	Died from diseases contracted at the front, Air Group 253
Seikichi Izawa	CPO	Hei 7	Air Group 302	3 May 1945	Atsugi	
Katsujirō Nakano	ENS	Pilot 37	Fighter Hikōtai 311	4 May 1945	Okinawa	3rd Air Group, Air Group 202, Air Group 221
Tatsumi Soga	CPO	Otsu 11	Air Group 203	4 May 1945	Okinawa	
*Yoshio Ōishi	WO	Otsu 9	Air Group 205	4 May 1945	Okinawa	Special attack forces, *Zuikaku*
Tei-ichirō Hayashida	WO	Kō 4	Ōmura Air Group	4 May 1945	Okinawa	Special attack forces, *Shōhō*
Hideaki Maeda	CPO	Otsu 11	Air Group 205	9 May 1945	Off Taiwan	
Masayoshi Urano	WO	Kō 5	Fighter Hikōtai 312	11 Apr 1945	Okinawa	Air Group 201; also CPO Isamu Ishii (Hei 10)
Hamashige Yamaguchi	WO	Otsu 9	Fighter Hikōtai 312	11 Apr 1945	Okinawa	Tainan Air Group, Air Group 201
Shigeo Kimura	ENS	Pilot 41	Fighter Hikōtai 313	11 Apr 1945	Okinawa	14th Air Group, attached to the 22nd Air Flotilla Command, Air Group 331; also CPO Akira Saitō (Hei 2)
Yōji Amari	ENS	Kō 2 observation planes	Fighter Hikōtai 812	13 May 1945	Okinawa	

KEY FIGHTER PILOTS KILLED IN ACTION (by Date) (*continued*)

Name	Rank	Class	Unit	Date of Death	Place	Major Unit History and Other Data
Hiroshi Nemoto	Res. ENS	Res. 13	Yatabe Air Group	13 May 1945	Okinawa	Special attack forces; also PO2c Gi-ichi Hoshino (Otsu 18)
Nobuyoshi Osada	WO	Pilot 35	Fighter Hikōtai 303	14 May 1945	Okinawa	Also PO1c Tōbei Rikitake (Otsu 11)
Naosuke Yoshida	LCDR	Res. 4 (Yokohama Higher Technical College)	Fighter Hikōtai 312 group leader	28 May 1945	Okinawa	Also ENS Atsuki Mezaki (Kō 1) and CPO Sakuji Hayashi (Hei 2)
Nobuyuki Tanabe	CPO	Kō 11	Air Group 601	29 May 1945	Yokohama	Also CPO Jun-ichi Hoshino (Hei 10)
Takao Katō	CPO	Otsu 11	Air Group 252	29 May 1945	Yokohama	
Seijō Bōji	Res. LTJG	Res. 11 (Ryūkoku Univ.)	Air Group 302	29 May 1945	Yokohama	
Jirō Funakoshi	CPO	Otsu 14	Air Group 343	2 Jun 1945	Kyūshū	Also CPO Eiji Mikami (Kō 11)
Susumu Kawasaki	LTJG	Otsu 3	Air Group 252	3 Jun 1945	Okinawa	Air Group 352
Sunao Nishikane	WO	Otsu 10	Fighter Hikōtai 303	7 Jun 1945	Southern Kyūshū	Air Group 253
Naraichi Murai	CPO	Hei 6	Air Group 601	10 Jun 1945	Kantō Plains	Air Group 252
Takio Yoshida	WO	Pilot 39	Fighter Hikōtai 402	10 Jun 1945	Kantō Plains	Air Group 253
Hideo Andō	WO	Otsu 10	Fighter Hikōtai 901	13 Jun 1945	Okinawa	
Keijirō Hayashi	LT	70	Fighter Hikōtai 407 group leader	22 Jun 1945	Kyūshū	Air Group 381; also CPO Takashi Yanagisawa (Kō 9)
Junji Yamazaki	CPO	Kō 9	Fighter Hikōtai 311	22 Jun 1945	Okinawa	
Katsuji Kobayashi	CPO	Kō 8	Air Group 302	23 Jun 1945	Yokohama	Air Group 204; also LT Norio Ueno (71)
Shūzō Enomoto	LTJG	73	Fighter Hikōtai 308	23 Jun 1945	Kantō Plains	Also CPO Katsumi Niimoto (Kō 8)
Hitoshi Hikosaka	CPO	Kō 11	Air Group 332	26 Jun 1945	Kinki	
Shōjirō Ishii	PO1c	Hei 10	Air Group 343	2 Jul 1945	Kyūshū	Also CPO Takashi Sakuma (Kō 10)
Isshū Kinoshita	Res. LT	Res. 10 (Tokyo Univ.)	Fighter Hikōtai 701 division officer	5 Jul 1945	Northern Kyūshū	Also CPO Seishi To-yohara (Hei 12)
Mitsuo Asakura	CPO	Kō 10	Tsukuba Air Group	8 Jul 1945	Kantō Plains	
Takashi Shimada	LTJG	73	Air Group 332	10 Jul 1945	Akashi	
Akira Sugawara	LT	69	Yokosuka Air Group division officer (night fighters)	11 Jul 1945	Homeland	
Takashi Oshibuchi	LT	68	Fighter Hikōtai 701 group leader	24 Jul 1945	Bungo Strait	Air Group 251, Air Group 253, Air Group 203; also CPO Jirō Hat-sushima (Kō 9)
Kaneyoshi Mutō	ENS	Pilot 32	Fighter Hikōtai 301	24 Jul 1945	Bungo Strait	13th Air Group, 12th Air Group, 3rd Air Group, Yokosuka Air Group
Eiji Okuda	CPO	Otsu 17	Fighter Hikōtai 303	25 Jul 1945	Southern Kyūshū	

(*continued*)

KEY FIGHTER PILOTS KILLED IN ACTION (by Date) (*continued*)

Name	Rank	Class	Unit	Date of Death	Place	Major Unit History and Other Data
*Naoshi Kanno	LT	70	Fighter Hikōtai 301 group leader	1 Aug 1945	Over Yakushima	Air Group 343, Air Group 201; also CPO Yasuo Yoshioka (Kō 10)
Seiji Noma	CPO	Otsu 12	Fighter Hikōtai 407	2 Aug 1945	Southern Kyūshū	
Yoshio Saitō	LT	71	Fighter Hikōtai 304 division officer	5 Aug 1945	Bōsō Peninsula	Air Group 332
Sei-ichirō Sako	CPO	Kō 7	Air Group 203	7 Aug 1945	Southern Kyūshū	Also CPO Bu-ichi Kamo (Otsu 13)
Gorō Kitano	LTJG	73	Fighter Hikōtai 303	7 Aug 1945	Southern Kyūshū	
*Takeaki Shimizu	ENS	Kō 1	Fighter Hikōtai 901 (night fighters)	8 Aug 1945	Okinawa	
Mitsuo Ishizuka	ENS	Pilot 22	Fighter Hikōtai 407	8 Aug 1945	Southern Kyūshū	
Masayuki Tadami		Kō 9	Fighter Hikōtai 407	8 Aug 1945	Southern Kyūshū	Also CPO Sakae Masumoto (Kō 10)
Keishichirō Hattori	LT	Engineering 52	Fighter Hikōtai 701	8 Aug 1945	Southern Kyūshū	Also CPO Kan-emon Yokobori (Kō 10)
Hiroshi Ōhara	WO	Pilot 50	Fighter Hikōtai 401	9 Aug 1945		Died from injuries received in action, *Akagi, Shōkaku*
*Shirō Okajima	LTJG	Res. 13	Air Group 721	11 Aug 1945	Okinawa	Special attack forces; also PO1c Minoru Hoshino (Kō 12)
Sadao Ōshio	LT	72	Air Group 343	12 Aug 1945	Kyūshū	
Kazumasa Sagara	CPO	Kō 10	Air Group 302	13 Aug 1945	Off Honshū	
Eiji Matsuyama	ENS	Kō 3	Air Group 601	14 Aug 1945	Over Lake Biwa	Also LTJG Kan-ichi Hyōdō (Res. 13)
Mitsuo Taguchi	LT	Pilot 18	Air Group 302 division officer	15 Aug 1945	Kantō Plains	Also LTJG Yoshikane Kuramoto (73) and CPO Ikki Takeda (Hei 6)
Kaoru Tamura	CPO	Otsu 16	Air Group 252	15 Aug 1945	Chiba Prefecture	Also CPO Kōhei Sugiyama (Otsu 15)

APPENDIX C

NAVAL FIGHTER PILOTS (BY CLASS)

1. This table shows all naval pilots who have specialized in fighters from the day that naval aviation was born through the Pacific War, arranged by class. Because of the fact that official records are not complete, we enlisted the help of many other people. It was not possible to prepare a complete list as such; in addition, because of page limitations, the following have been omitted: 40th class [also 41st and 42nd], Aviation Student Course; Hei 7th class; Kō 8th class; Otsu 14th class; and classes after the 12th class, Flight Reserve Student Course.
2. Marks following names have the following meaning: (H) Honors recipient, (K) Killed in action, and (A) Accidental death.
3. Parentheses around a name indicate pilots who changed from specializing in one type of aircraft to another. In 1936, with the separation of the land attack forces, a large number of personnel changed to a different branch.
4. Pilots who converted from other specialities to that of fighter pilot are grouped together, at the end of each class listing. From the middle point of the Pacific War on, there were a large number of personnel who converted from seaplane fighters and from two-seater reconnaissance floatplanes.
5. Pilots of night fighters (such as the Gekkō and others) and float fighter units were not included.
6. Designations of type of aircraft are in accordance with the practices of the period: carrier-based planes, seaplanes, carrier fighters, and so on.

Aviation Students

1. The systematic training of pilots began in July 1912 with the 1st Class, Aviation Technical Research Committee Members (Kōkū Gijutsu Kenkyū-iin), and ended with its 6th Class. With the establishment of the Yokosuka Air Group in April 1916, the name was changed to "Aviation Technical Student" (Kōkū Gijutsu Gakusei). When the Kasumigaura Air Group was established in November 1922, student training was shifted to Kasumigaura; starting with the 12th Class, students were referred to as "Aviation Students" (Hikō Gakusei), and this name lasted until the 42nd Class graduated in February 1945.
2. Before the 18th Class, Aviation Student Course, the specialization by type of aircraft was not too clear because of the early developmental stage of training at the time. The names of all personnel have been listed in such cases. From the 19th Class on, only those who specialized in fighter aircraft have been listed.
3. Parentheses following a name indicate the Naval Academy (Naval Engineering College) class.
4. For a complete list of aviation students, please refer to the "Naval Aviation Duty (Officer) Listing" (Kaigun Kūchū Kimmusha (Shikan) Meibo), compiled by the Kaikū Kai (Naval Air Society).

Before the 1st Class
(*Five persons*)
Shirō Aihara (29)
Kanehiko Umekita (29)
Yōzō Kaneko (30)
Sankichi Kawano (31)
Chūji Yamada (33)

1st Class, Aviation Technical Research Committee Members
(*October 1912–May 1913; four persons*)
Tōzaburō Adachi (36) (A)
Fumio Inoue (33) (A)

Shōkei Hirose (36)
Masatsune Fujise (36)

2nd Class, Aviation Technical Research Committee Members
(*June 1913–; three [sic] persons*)
Teruo Nanba (37)
Hideho Wada (34)

3rd Class, Aviation Technical Research Committee Members
(*February–August 1944; five persons*)

Teizō Iigura (37)
Yukinobu Ōsaki (36)
Takao Takebe (37) (A)
Kishichi Magoshi (37)
Junpei Yamamoto (38)

4th Class, Aviation Technical Research Committee Members
(*February–June 1915; six persons*)

Shinji Abe (37) (A)
Masaru Kaiya (38)
Torao Kuwabara (37)
Kōsaku Tsuda (39)

Senji Tsuyuki (36)
Nakajirō Mikami (38)

**5th Class, Aviation
Technical Research
Committee Members**
(*May 1915–March 1916; five
persons*)
Misato Asada (39)
Naota Gotō (39)
Akitomo Beppu (38)
Toshikazu Yashima (39)
Misao Wada (39)

**6th Class, Aviation
Technical Research
Committee Members**
(*December 1915–March 1916;
six persons*)
Tamotsu Araki (40)
Takijiro Ōnishi (40)
Munetaka Sakamoto (40)
Torasaburō Shōji (40)
Tomeo Muroi (39)
Saburō Yamaguchi (39)

**First Class, Aviation
Technical Students**
(*June 1916–June 1917; five
persons*)
Osamu Imamura (40)
Masuo Kani (40)
Shin-ichi Sakamoto (40)   (A)
Morihiko Miki (40)
Toyoo Yamamura (40)   (A)

**2nd Class, Aviation
Technical Students**
(*December 1916–December
1917; six persons*)
Seiki Katō (40)
Shun-ichi Kira (40)
Tomo Shirase (38)
Sadatoshi Senda   (K)
Masanao Tanba (40)
Saburō Yamanouchi (40)   (A)

**3rd Class, Aviation
Technical Students**
(*December 1917–December
1918; twelve persons*)
Rinosuke Ichimaru (41)   (A)
Keizō Ueno (41)
Yoshio Katō (41)
Seigo Kadowaki (41)
Tokichi Kokura (41)   (K)
Takeo Komaki (40)   (A)
Masaki Sakakibara (41)   (A)
Munetaka Sakamaki (41)   (H)
Kōji Shirai (41)
Tsutomu Tomeoka (41)   (A)
Jirō Miyake (41)   (A)
Ichitarō Yonezawa (41)

**4th Class, Aviation
Technical Students**
(*December 1918–December
1919; twelve persons*)
Hisakichi Akaishi (42)   (A)
Kanjō Akashiba (42)
Makoto Awaya (41)
Tomeo Kaku (42)   (K)
Akio Kawazoe (42)
Taksane Furuse (42)
Kiyosaku Shimura (41)   (A)
Jirō Shimoyama (41)
Shigeho Tameda (42)   (A)
Torao Nara (42)   (A)
Sadayoshi Yamada (42)   (H)
Michiyuki Yamada (42)   (K)

**5th Class, Aviation
Technical Students**
(*December 1919–December
1920; seven persons*)
Yoshiaki Itō (43)
Yoshio Ueda (44)   (A)
Komatarō Kawaguchi (44) (A)
Ushie Sugimoto (44)   (K)
Michio Sumikawa (45)   (H)
Tomiyoshi Maehara (44)
Keikichi Mori (Araki) (45)

**6th Class, Aviation
Technical Students**
(*December 1920–July 1921;
eleven persons*)
Sanji Iwabuchi (43)   (K)
Kaoru Umetani (46)
Tadao Katō (45)
Yoshio Kamei (46)   (K)
Masaharu Kondō (46)
Tadamasa Suganuma (44)   (A)
Ō Takehiko (46)
Aizō Nakamura (44)   (H)
Atsuma Baba (46)   (A)
Tatsuji Fujimatsu (46)
Hidemi Machida (44)

**7th Class, Aviation
Technical Students**
(*March–November 1922; eight
persons*)
Fujirō Ōhashi (46)
Asazō Kikuchi (45)
Kazuo Hoshi (46)
Shigetoshi Miyazaki (46)   (K)
Shinnosuke Muneyuki (45)(A)
Chikao Yamamoto (46)   (H)
Toshiyuki Yokoi (46)
Saburō Wada (46)

**8th Class, Aviation
Technical Students**
(*December 1922–November
1923; nine persons*)

Masahisa Saitō (47)
Kōsuke Sasaki (47)   (A)
Senjun Takahashi (47)
Nobukichi Takahashi (47) (K)
Tarō Taguchi (47)   (H)
Takanari Maeda (47)
Kenji Matsumura (47)   (A)
Kenzō Yamazaki (47)   (A)
Sakae Yamamoto (46)

**9th Class, Aviation
Technical Students**
(*June 1923–May 1924; ten
persons*)
Hideo Kōda (48)   (A)
Ei-ichirō Jō (47)   (K)
Hideo Tsukada (48)
Daizō Nakajima (48)
Den Nakajima (48)
Ayao Nishijima (48)   (A)
Katsumi Hayami (47)   (A)
Masashi Maruyama (48)   (A)
Kanzō Miura (47)   (H)
Yoshitoshi Miwa (48)   (K)

**10th Class, Aviation
Technical Students**
(*December 1923–November
1924; ten persons*)
Toshihiko Odawara (48)
    (H, K)
Shigetoyo Shirahama (49) (A)
Shinzō Susumu (48)   (A)
Yoshiharu Soga (49)
Shigeru Tanno (49)   (A)
Tsukasa Noguchi (48)   (A)
Saneyasu Hidaka (49)   (A)
Yoshitarō Horikoshi (49) (A)
Iwao Minematsu (48)
Shigeshi Wakamatsu (49)

**11th Class, Aviation
Technical Students**
(*May 1924–March 1925; ten
persons*)
Ryō-ichi Asaka (49)
Teruyuki Kakita (48)
Sakae Kamura (Yamashita)
    (49)
Tokujirō Kikuoka (49)
Yoshito Kobayashi (49)
Eikichi Nakajima (49)   (A)
Kiyoma Maeda (49)   (A)
Toshio Mizunaga (49)   (A)
Ryutarō Yamanaka (49)
Masahiro Watanabe (49)   (A)

**12th Class, Aviation
Students [all subsequent
classes]**
(*February 1925–November
1925; eight persons*)

Kenji Kimura (49)
Toshiki Kurimoto (48)   (K)
Shizuo Tateishi (50)   (A)
Takashi Tsue (50)   (A)
Misao Terada (50)
Chisato Morita (49)
Yoshitane Yanagimura
  (49)   (H, K)
Shigeo Watanabe (50)

13th Class, Aviation Students
(September 1925–May 1926; nine [sic] persons)
Sadagorō Uchida (50)
Motoharu Okamura (50)
Naota Sata (50)
Haruo Satō (50)
Shō-ichi Sawabe (50)   (H, A)
Kunizō Terai (50)
Jirō Tokui (50)   (K)
Tarō Fukuda (50)

14th Class
(March–November 1926; nine persons)
Tatsuo Aizawa (51)   (K)
Sakaye Ichikawa (50)   (A)
Yasuna Kozono (51)
Akira Kuroi (51)   (A)
Masami Kojima (51)
Chujirō Nakano (51)   (H)
Nenosuke Nakamura (51)   (K)
Takeo Yasunobu (51)   (A)
Tetsujirō Wada (51)   (A)

15th Class
(September 1926–May 1927; ten persons)
Tsugio Ikegami (51)
Masatsugu Iwao (51)   (K)
Yoneji Utsu (51)
Kiyoshi Katsuhata (51)
Chū-ichi Kawashima (51)   (A)
Shigeo Kurioka (51)   (A)
Hidetoshi Tamura (51)   (A)
Masae Handa (51)   (A)
Kurio Okehata (51)   (H, K)
Gorō Hirayama (51)   (A)

16th Class
(March–November 1927; fourteen persons)
Takeshi Aoki (51)
Sukemitsu Itō (51)
Ichirō Imamura (51)
Saburō Katsuta (51)   (K)
Yoshinari Kojima (51)   (A)
Toshikazu Sugiyama (51)   (H)
Yoshijirō Suzuki (51)
Toshimasa Taira (51)   (A)
Yoshiteru Take (51)

Hisatsugu Tate (51)
Kōrokurō Tatemi (51)
Shigehachirō Tokoro (51)   (K)
Shigeki Negoro (51)
Yoshio Fukumori (51)   (A)

17th Class
(September 1927–May 1928; eleven persons)
Takahisa Amagai (51)
Yasuo Iwai (51)   (K)
Shō-ichi Ogasawara (51)
Yūsuke Kakinuma (51)   (A)
Shunji Kamide (51)
Tokutarō Kubo (51)   (K)
Sadao Koike (51)   (H)
Keizō Suda (51)
Shin-ichi Nitta (51)   (K)
Tatsukichi Miyo (51)
Minoru Mori (51)   (K)

18th Class
(March–December 1928; sixteen persons)
Shin-ichi Akumi (52)   (A)
Taisuke Itō (52)   (H)
Tsutomu Inoue (52)   (A)
Iroku Ōuchi (52)   (A)
Ikuto Kusumoto (52)   (K)
Hiroshi Kogure (52)
Masayoshi Saitō (52)   (A)
Takeo Shibata (52)
Hiroshi Shimizu (52)   (K)
Masakazu Suzuki (52)
Nakazaemon Tokunaga (52)
Yorimi Tsuchihashi (52)   (A)
Shinroku Nishizawa (52)
Shūsaku Fukuoka (52)   (A)
Masami Matsumoto (52)
Hideo Muramatsu (52)   (A)

19th Class
(December 1928–November 1929; eighteen persons)
Nokiji Ikuta (52)
Nobuo Itō (52)
Minoru Genda (52)   (H)
Asa-ichi Tamai (52)
Shirō Watanabe (52)   (A)

20th Class
(December 1929–November 1930; fourteen persons)
Takeo Ide (54)   (A)
Shigeharu Nagano (54)   (A)
Tadao Funaki (54)   (K)
Katsutoshi Yagi (54)

21st Class
(December 1930–November 1931; twenty-six persons)
Norito Ōbayashi (55)   (K)
Kiyoji Sakakibara (55)

Mikuma Minowa (55)
Saburō Momosaki (55)   (A)
Shigema Yoshitomi (55)

22nd Class
(December 1931–November 1932; twenty-three persons)
Chikamasa Igarashi (56)
Juroku Shimizu (56)   (A)
Ryōsuke Nomura (56)   (H)
Mochifumi Nangō (55)   (K)

23rd Class
(December 1932–July 1933; twenty-eight persons)
Shigeru Itaya (57)   (K)
Ryōhei Ushioda (57)   (K)
Kiyoto Hanamoto (57)   (A)
Shichirō Yamashita (57)   (K)

24th Class
(April–November 1933; thirty-two persons)
Naoichi Ishikawa (58)   (A)
Mambei Shimokawa (58)   (A)
Shigeo Taguma (58)   (K)
Hideo Teshima (58)   (K)
Tadashi Nakajima (58)
Sei-ichi Maki (58)

25th Class
(November 1933–July 1934; thirty-three persons)
Takahide Aioi (59)
Yoshimitsu Oku (58)   (H, A)
Takashi Kaneko (59)   (K)
Mitsugu Kofukuda (59)
Yoshitami Komatsu (59)
Hideki Shingō (59)

26th Class
(November 1934–July 1935; thirty-four persons)
Kiyokazu Ikenouchi (60)   (A)
Mitsuo Ishikawa (60)   (A)
Toshitaka Itō (60)
Harutoshi Okamoto (60)
Tadashi Kaneko (60)   (K)
Saburō Shindō (60)
Minoru Suzuki (60)
Masao Yamashita (60)
Tamotsu Yokoyama (59)

27th Class
(November 1935–November 1936; thirty-five persons)
Kai Ikeda (61)   (K)
Masaji Suganami (61)   (K)
Kenzō Tanaka (61)   (A)
Sumio Nōno (61)   (K)

28th Class
(December 1936–September 1937; thirty-seven persons)

Fusata Iida (62)   (H, K)
Bunji Gotō (62)   (A)
Yoshio Shiga (Yotsumoto) (62)
Naohisa Shinjō (62)   (K)
Motonari Suhō (62)
Shō-ichi Takahashi (62)   (A)

29th Class
(*October 1937–May 1938; twenty-one persons*)
Kanetake Okazaki (62)   (K)
Kiyokuma Okajima (63)
Takeo Kurosawa (63)
Kenjirō Nōtomi (62)   (H, K)
Takumi Hoashi (63)   (A)

30th Class
(*December 1937–July 1938; twenty-seven persons*)
Masao Asai (63)   (K)
Muneyoshi Aratake (63)   (A)
Yoshio Kurakane (63)
Masao Satō (63)   (K)
Ichirō Mukai (63)   (K)

31st Class
(*August 1938–March 1939; fifty-nine persons*)
Isamu Ikeda (64)   (H, A)
Kiku-ichi Inano (Takabayashi) (64)
Shirō Kawai (63)   (K)
Minoru Kobayashi (64)   (K)
Aya-o Shirane (64)   (K)
Masuzō Setō (64)   (K)
Tadatsune Tokaji (64)   (K)
Yasushi Nikaidō (64)   (A)
Masayoshi Murakami (64)   (A)
Shigeru Mori (64)   (K)
[*Converted*]
Hachirō Yanagisawa (64)   (K)
Kushichirō Yamada (64)

32nd Class
(*September 1939–April 1940; sixty-four persons*)
Masanobu Ibusuki (65)
Yuzuru Nakano (65)   (A)
Takaichi Hasuo (65)   (K)
Yukio Maki (65)   (A)
Masatoshi Makino (65)   (K)
Akira Wakao (65)   (K)

33rd Class
(*November 1939–June 1940; twenty-nine persons*)
Tomoyuki Sakai (66)   (H, K)
Tadashi Hara (66)   (A)
Moriyasu Hidaka (66)
Iyozō Fujita (66)
Jōji Yamashita (66)   (K)

34th Class
(*April 1940–April 1941; forty-eight persons*)
Masao Iizuka (66)   (K)
Yasuhiro Shigematsu (66)   (K)
Yūzō Tsukamoto (66)
Hisayoshi Miyajima (66)
Shigehisa Yamamoto (66)

35th Class
(*November 1940–November 1941; 158 persons*)
Shigeru Araki (67)   (K)
Nobuhiro Iwasaki (67)   (K)
Toshitada Kawazoe (67)   (K)
Katsutoshi Kawamata (67)   (K)
Katsumi Kurihara (67)   (K)
Jun-ichi Sasai (67)   (K)
Kiyoharu Shibuya (67)   (K)
Masayoshi Baba (67)   (K)
Tadashi Hayashiya (67)   (K)
Kaoru Yamaguchi (67)   (K)
Sadao Yamaguchi (67)   (K)
[*Converted*]
Toshio Araki (67)   (K)
Toshiharu Ikeda (67)   (K)
Tetsuo Endō (67)   (K)
Shigeo Jūni (67)   (K)
Takeo Yokoyama (67)

36th Class
(*May 1941–June 1942; 125 persons*)
Shū-ichi Utsumi (68)   (K)
Takeyoshi Ōno (68)   (K)
Takashi Oshibuchi (68)   (K)
Toshio Katō (68)   (A)
Mukumi Kanemitsu (68)   (K)
Shigeto Kawahara (68)   (K)
Masakazu Kusakari (68)
Yōichi Kenmochi (68)   (K)
Hōhei Kobayashi (68)   (K)
Saburō Saitō (68)   (K)
Tadashi Satō (68)   (K)
Toshio Shiozuru (68)
Usaburō Suzuki (68)   (K)
Kennosuke Tanouchi (68)   (K)
Shunkichi Tashiro (68)   (K)
Kenji Nakagawa (68)   (H, K)
Daihachi Nakajima (68)
Yoshikazu Noguchi (68)   (K)
Kazuto Kuba (68)   (K)
Hisanori Fujimaki (68)   (K)
Keigo Fujiwara (68)   (K)
Hidetane Futagami (68)   (K)
Kazumasa Mitsumori (68)
Isao Murata (68)   (K)
Kunisuke Yūki (68)   (K)
Hiroshi Yoshimura (68)   (K)
Torio Watanabe (67)   (K)

[*Converted*]
Shinya Ozaki (68)   (K)
Keizō Yamazaki (68)

37th Class
(*November 1941–February 1943; 139 persons*)
Nobuo Awa (69)   (K)
Shirō Itezono (69)   (K)
Ichirō Imamura (69)   (K)
Kunio Iwashita (69)   (H)
Tetsushi Ueno (69)   (K)
Takeshi Uemura (69)
Sue-ichi Ōshima (69)   (K)
Yoshio Ōba (69)   (K)
Takashi Kōnoshita (69)   (K)
Motoi Kaneko (69)   (K)
Tsutomu Kawai (69)   (K)
Kakurō Kawamura (69)   (K)
Kunio Kanzaki (69)   (K)
Kisaku Koshida (69)   (K)
Ikurō Sakami (69)   (K)
Haruo Sagara (69)   (K)
Masao Shimada (69)   (K)
Naoshi Sugisaki (69)   (K)
Takeo Sekiya (69)
Hiroo Takao (69)   (K)
Kenkichi Takasawa (69)   (K)
Dai Nakajima (69)   (K)
Mitsuteru Hashimoto (69)   (K)
Yoshishige Hayashi (69)   (K)
Torajirō Haruta (69)   (K)
Ken-ichi Ban (69)   (K)
Sumio Fukuda (69)   (K)
Shoku Mae (69)   (K)
Hiroshi Maeda (69)   (K)
Yasuo Masuyama (69)
Shigeo Mizorogi (69)   (K)
Nobuhiko Mutō (69)   (K)
Hiroshi Morii (69)   (K)
Tatsuo Hirano (Engineering 47)   (K)
[*Converted*]
Shirō Kawakubo (69)   (K)
Minoru Kawazoe (69)   (K)
Katsumi Kōda (69)   (K)
Jūji Torimoto (69)   (K)
Masamichi Minogata (69)   (K)

38th Class
(*June 1942–September 1943; 130 persons*)
Masa-aki Asakawa (69)   (K)
Jun Abe (70)   (A)
Kishichirō Ayukawa (70)   (K)
Nobuyuki Ikura (70)   (K)
Mutsuo Urushiyama (70)   (K)
Kazuo Ōhata (70)   (K)
Mitsuo Ōfuji (70)   (K)
Masato Okasako (70)   (K)

Keiji Kataki (70) (K)
Hideo Katori (70)
Korekiyo Kawakita (70) (K)
Naoshi Kanno (70) (K)
Seiji Kinoshita (70) (K)
Kunio Kimura (70) (K)
Tadao Satō (70) (K)
Hiroshi Shiosaka (70) (K)
Nobuo Takano (70) (K)
Masao Takahashi (70) (K)
Jirō Takamure (70) (K)
Mizuho Tanaka (70) (K)
Kōji Chikama (70) (K)
Takeo Tsutsumi (70) (K)
Keijirō Hayashi (70) (K)
Shigeo Hayashi (70) (K)
Yoshihiro Hayashi (70)
Kakichi Hirata (70)
Kiyoshi Fukagawa (70) (K)
Toshio Fukushima (70) (K)
Susumu Horio (70) (K)
Ken-ichi Honda (70) (K)
Ryutarō Masuda (70) (K)
Masayoshi Masumoto (70) (K)
Takuo Mitsumoto (70)
Yoshiteru Mine (70) (K)
Yutaka Yagi (70) (K)
Fumio Yamagata (70) (K)
Yoshihiro Yoshikawa (70) (K)

[Converted]
Toyohiko Inuzuka (70) (A)
Akira Satomura (70) (K)
Shinkai Fujimori (70) (K)
Takeshi Murakami (70)
Hiroshi Morioka (70)

39th Class
(*January 1943–January 1944;*
165 persons)
Yukio Ayukawa (71) (K)
Manabu Ishimori (71) (K)
Katsuo Imawaka (71) (K)
Tadashi Iwano (71) (K)
Yasuhiko Ukimura (70) (K)
Tsuguo Ōtsubo (71) (K)
Takashi Ōhira (71) (K)
Hiroshi Ōbuchi (71) (K)
Korekiyo Otsuji (71) (K)
Tamon Kawaguchi (71) (A)
Hisao Kawanishi (70) (K)
Tsutomu Kariya (70) (A)
Ei-ichi Kawashima (70) (K)
Takatoshi Kikuchi (71)
Osamu Kurata (70)
Hiroshi Kotajima (70) (A)
Jun Saitō (70)
Osamu Takahashi (70) (K)
Iwao Takeishi (70) (K)
Akira Takeda (70)
Kōsuke Tabuchi (70)
Hiroshi Tanaka (70) (K)
Rikio Tomioka (70) (K)
Hidehiro Nakama (70) (K)
Yasusuke Nakamura (71) (K)
Tomoyoshi Nagatomo
(71) (K)
Kisuke Hasegawa (70)
Fujio Hayashi (71)
Susumu Fukuoka (71) (K)
Ei-ichi Furusawa (71) (K)
Hiroshi Matano (71) (K)
Yasushi Matsui (71) (K)

Kunio Matsusaki (71) (K)
Chikashi Matsuyama (71) (A)
Tomiya Miyazaki (70)
Saneo Miyawaki (70) (K)
Sumihiro Meguro (71)
Isao Yagi (70)
Shin Yamauchi (69) (K)
Naomi Yonemitsu (71) (K)
Taisuke Yonemura (71)
Keizō Wada (71) (K)
Ichirō Watanabe (K)
Iwao Akiyama (Engineering
51) (K)
Toshikazu Taguchi
(Engineering 50) (K)
Hisaya Hirusawa
(Engineering 50) (K)
Taka-aki Yokote
(Engineering 50) (K)
[Converted]
Yukio Seki (70) (K)
Shizuhiko Chikuma (70)
Yoshita Tada (71) (K)

40th Class
(*June 1943–June 1944; 185*
persons)

41st Class
(*September 1943–July 1944;*
323 persons)

42nd Class
(*March 1944–February 1945;*
466 persons)

Pilot Trainee Students and Hei Flight Reserve Enlisted Trainee Class Students

PILOT TRAINEE STUDENTS

1. Initially only officers were considered for use as pilots; however, in March 1914 noncommissioned officers were used experimentally in a test program of training. As a result, in May 1928 a Flight Trainee (Hikōjutsu Renshū-sei) system was started. In June 1930 the system's name was changed to "Pilot Trainee" (Sōju Renshū-sei, Sōren). Basic pilot training was conducted at Kasumigaura and later at Yatabe, Tsukuba, and elsewhere. The period of training varied depending on the class or year when it was being conducted; it ranged from five months to one year in length.

   Immediately upon graduation from the course, students were converted into aviation seaman (Kōkū-hei). (In June 1941, the name was changed to flight seaman, "Hikō-hei.") Courses for instruction in the actual use of aircraft were conducted after graduation (granting of pilot insignia) at the various air groups (courses are referred to as advanced training, Enchō Kyōiku). Training in the use of fighter aircraft was for the most part conducted at the Ōita Air Group. The 54th through 56th classes were granted their pilot insignia upon completion of their training at Ōita.

2. The names of all personnel that attended the 1st through 12th classes during the earliest period of training are listed in their entirety because it was not always possible to ascertain their aircraft specialities. Starting with the 13th Class, the names listed are those that specialized in fighters. Also, during the period of the 13th through 50th class, the training course for carrier-based planes was not yet independent so the number of such trainees has not been listed.

Hei Flight Reserve Enlisted Trainee Class Students

1. Ever since the establishment of the Flight Reserve Enlisted Trainee Class system (Yoka Renshū-sei Seido) in June 1930, the training of noncommissioned officer flight personnel was conducted in parallel; in other words, for graduates of the flight reserve class system itself and for those personnel recruited from noncommissioned officer ranks in general (Sōren, the Pilot Trainee Course). Starting in October 1940, the latter group of trainees was used as Hei type Flight Reserve Enlisted Trainees; following general training, which lasted around two months, the trainees were then sent on to the Flight Trainee Course (Hikō Renshu-sei Kyōtei). The Flight Trainee Course was common for both Kō and Otsu category trainees. Carrier fighter training for flight trainees was conducted at the Ōmura and Tokushima air groups and elsewhere, in addition to that being conducted at the Ōita Air Group. Because of training capacity limitations, flight trainee classes were sometimes held in two or more different locations.

Before Regular Training Courses Started
Shinzaburō Yokochi
Saburō Fujii
Kyōjirō Ueno (A)
Genji Terada
Kōgorō Kisaki (A)
Shikazō Koshimizu
Teruki Sakao
Togō Takahashi
Tadashi Hayakawa
Kaneyoshi Yokoyama

1st Class
(May 1920–May 1921; eight persons)
Daijirō Aoki (A)
Tsutomu Abe
Torao Ishikawa (A)
Genzō Ōkubo
Goichi Kawabe
Fukuzō Takahashi
Sei-ichirō Takahashi (A)
Tomekichi Hinako (A)

3rd Class
(December 1922–August 1923; nineteen persons)
Yoshihisa Itō
Hideyoshi Iwamoto
Hiko-o Egusa (A)
Kenzaburō Ōwatari
Yoshitaka Kajima
Jōkichi Kawakami
Kōzō Kokumai
Ryōnosuke Suzuki
Eiji Sorabayashi
Masami Takahashi
Torakichi Tanaka
Yoshizō Hanawa
Kinji Haryū
Taiki Furuyama
Mamoru Miyoshi
Sakumatsu Meguro
Yotsuo Yashima
Tsunetarō Yamamoto (A)
Yaichi Watanabe (A)

4th Class
(June 1923–May 1924; twenty-one persons)
Mikio Aoki (A)
Shirō Akisawa
Akio Aso
Tomokazu Ejima
Ichirō Ōura
Takao Kaji
Yoshinobu Kawano
Masayuki Shimokawa
Isamu Takahashi
Ichiji Takekawa
Tōjirō Takeshita
Iwaji Chikada
Seikō Chikano (A)
Takuma Chiku
Tadashi Nakamura (H, A)
Eisaku Nagashima
Hisamatsu Nori (A)
Chōjirō Hayashi (K)
Ryōgo Fujii (A)
Mitsuo Fujita (A)
Sōshirō Matsuno (A)

5th Class
(December 1923–November 1924; seventeen persons)
Takashi Abe
Ryōsaku Iyama
Masayuki Iwai (A)
Shunji Ōmura
Saburō Kameda (A)
Kiyoshi Kitayama (A)
Gunji Saitō
Haruo Suematsu
Heisuke Suzuki
Kaneo Tanaka (A)
Tamizō Tengu
Shin-ichi Nakanishi
Tsuruo Hashiguchi
Genhachi Fukami
Yoshito Fujisada (H)
Shichinosuke Maeda
Isao Matsumoto

6th Class
(June 1924–March 1925; seventeen persons)
Tadao Iwabe
Sakae Ueno
Shizunori Uchimura
Yoshio Oikawa (K)
Shin-ichi Ōishi
Keijirō Kaneko (A)
Shinzō Takamura
Yoshinosuke Dōchi
Sei-ichi Nakano
Senjirō Nishiyama
Tsuneo Fujimaki
Tomeji Fuse
Kiyoshi Maruyama
Takeji Miura (H, K)
Rokuzō Moriyama (K)
Shō-ichi Yamada
Takashi Yokoyama (A)

7th Class
(February 1925–November 1925; eleven persons)
Jutsuhei Ashizawa
Kesaju Ishikawa (A)
Taneo Inuzuka (K)
Tasamatsu Kobayashi
Hitokazu Sakurasawa
Tsuneshichi Shibata
Yoshitarō Suga (A)
Saijirō Teramoto (H)
Toshio Nakamura
(Yasumoto) (A)
Man-ichi Hama (A)
Norikazu Fujisaki

8th Class
(September 1925–May 1926; fifteen persons)
Kiyoe Aoki
Yūkichi Andō
Shōjiro Iwahori
Isao Kubota (A)
Ryōji Komatsu (A)
Teruo Komine (A)
Shōsuke Sasa-ō (K)

Tadashi Satō (A)
Kōzō Susa
Hei-ichiro Mase (H, K)
Yoshio Matsuo (A)
Toyotsugu Miyata
Yasumi Murayama
Isao Morikawa
Shigeru Yamada (K)

9th Class
*(February–November 1926;
carrier and floatplanes, nineteen
persons)*
Atau Aoki
Isamu Itō
Yōsuke Ōta
Shinji Ōhara (A)
Nobuyuki Ogawa (A)
Tadashi Ono (Tsuda)
Asakichi Kurokawa (Yoshida)
Shin-ichi Kawano
Miyoji Kobayashi (Tanaka)
Isamu Koine (Mochizuki)
Jin Sasaki
Tomezō Shiraishi
Kumezō Suzuki
Takeo Tozawa
Kunkichi Moto
Toshio Mori
Yoshimi Mori
Makoto Yanai (H)
Motoyuki Yokota

10th Class
*(July 1926–May 1927; carrier
and seaplanes, seventeen persons)*
Michiyoshi Ichimaru
Gi-ichi Ogura
Nao Kai (A)
Shigeo Katayama
Keijirō Katō
Tsurukichi Kawasaki
Shōji Kikuchi
Sakae Kimura
Mamoru Kubota (A)
Takeo Saitō
Bukichi Takano
Tokuji Tatemichi
Kōji Tariki
Hiroshi Nakanome
Yutaka Haraguchi
Heitarō Hiragawara
Heiji Yamamoto

11th Class
*(January–November 1927;
carrier and seaplanes, nineteen
persons)*
Bungo Abe
Shinsuke Ishii

Chikashi Itō (A)
Shinpei Ōsuga
Tomoshiro Ōmori
Hajime Oshikawa
Tadato Katagiri
Sakae Katō (K)
Takeo Koba
Sanshirō Kudō (A)
Shinkichi Gotō
Ryōji Satō
Shigejirō Takahashi
Takeyoshi Taguchi (A)
Michimori Higo (A, H)
Takeji Matsumoto
Yoshio Masuda (A)
Yoshio Marugame
Tei-ichi Watanabe

12th Class
*(July 1927–May 1928; carrier
and seaplanes, sixteen persons)*
Sumio Anami (A)
Akio Arai
Masao Andō
Yūzo Ishii
Kōshirō Ebina (A)
Nagao Ōmomo
Munetsugu Satō
Tadayoshi Suzuki
Mitsuo Toyoda
Tsuneo Nakahara (K)
Takao Hirama
Rikimatsu Hirayama
Shigezō Fujii (K)
Heitarō Morita
Norimasa Yamaguchi
Yatarō Yamamoto

13th Class
*(March–December 1928; carrier
and seaplanes, twenty-two
persons)*
Yoshio Inoue (A)
Manzō Iwaki (K)
Masao Ono
Ichio Kaneko (A)
Toshio Kuroiwa (K)
Fumiaki Takimoto
Kazuo Takeo
Hideo Funatsu

14th Class
*(July 1928–May 1929; carrier
and seaplanes, thirty persons)*
Akira Eitoku (K)
Shūhei Ōya (K)
Wasuke Otokuni
(Seizaburō Kurosaki)
Hajime Koga
Mineichi Shibata

Mitsugu Mori
Yasukichi Yamagawa
(Egawa) (A)

15th Class
*(June 1929–April 1930; carrier
and seaplanes, thirty persons)*
Tomokichi Arai (H, K)
Noboru Ōzeki
Katsumi Shima
Jirō Chōno (K)
Katsuji Matsushima (K)

16th Class
*(May 1930–May 1931; carrier
and seaplanes, twenty-five
persons)*
Masahiro Ishii
(Hiratsuchi Ujiki) (K)
Taizō Okamoto (K)
Sadao Kawano
Kiyoto Koga (A)
Eisaku Shibayama
Sakeo Nishiyama

17th Class
*(June 1931–March 1932;
carrier and seaplanes, thirty-two
persons)*
Sadaaki Akamatsu
Kikkō Ishikawa (A)
Shōjiro Itō
Keiji Kubo
Bunji Shimizu (A)
Kiyoteru Terashita
Sakae Fukuchi (H, A)
Koshirō Yamashita (K)

18th Class
*(May–November 1932; carrier
and seaplanes, forty persons)*
Ki-ichi Oda (Nakamura) (K)
Kyūshichi Kobayashi (K)
Chiyoyuki Shibata
Sukeichi Tanaka (A)
Matsukatsu Matsuoka (H, A)
Kazumasa Yokoyama (A)
Yoshio Wajima (K)
[Converted]
Mamoru Shimura (K)
Mitsuo Taguchi (K)

19th Class
*(October 1932–Mar 1938;
carrier and seaplanes, forty-one
persons)*
(Yasuyoshi Akaike) (H, K)
Takeo Inaba (K)
Chitoshi Isozaki
Matsuya Katō (Tsukamoto)
Ippei Gotō (K)

Taira Tanaka
Ken-ichi Takahashi (K)
Watari Handa

20th Class
*(February–July 1933; carrier
and seaplanes, thirty-seven
persons)*
(Tomiji Kawaguchi) (K)
Katsuma Shigemi (K)
Tadashi Torakuma
  (Kimoto) (A)
(Masao Naitō)
Kōji Hanagaki
Fusaji Miyata
[*Converted*]
Shinki Satō (H)

21st Class
*(April–September 1933; carrier
and seaplanes, thirty persons)*
Hachirō Aizawa
Masumi Okuyama (A)
Shōzō Katayama (K)
Tsutomu Kawakami (A)
Saburō Kitahata (K)
Katsuo Nakamura (A)
Kōsaburō Yamanaka

22nd Class
*(June–December 1933; carrier
and seaplanes, twenty-eight
persons)*
Mitsuo Ishizuka (K)
Tomokazu Ema (K)
Takanobu Kobata
(Tadashi Koike)
Katsumi Shirakami
Toraichi Takatsuka (K)
(Rikichi Hiwatari) (A)

23rd Class
*(October 1933–April 1934;
carrier and seaplanes, thirty-four
persons)*
Saneo Imamura (K)
Takenori Kusumoto (A)
Tetsutarō Kumagaya (K)
Nobuo Kuro-iwa (Itō)
Tsukasa Taguchi (A)
Torajirō Nakatsuchi
(Takeshi Furukawa)
[*Converted*]
Namio Nishikawa

24th Class
*(February–September 1934;
carrier planes, thirty-seven
persons)*
Kazuo Kagawa (A)
Kan-ichi Kashimura (K)

Noboru Kawase
Taketeru Sentō (A)
Masumi Tsutsumi
  (Yamaguchi) (K)
Haruo Nakagawa (A)
Kijirō Noguchi
Hatsuo Hidaka
Akira Yamamoto (A)

25th Class
*(June–November 1934; carrier
planes, thirty persons)*
Kyōsaku Aoki
Torakichi Inaha (A)
(Ma-ari Uehara)
Makoto Endō (K)
Jihei Kaneko
Hideyoshi Kume (A)
Toshiyuki Sakai (K)
Saburō Sugai (K)
Torata Takiguchi (K)
(Masaichi Tōhata) (A)
Chiharu Naitō
(Masao Nakajima) (K)
Katsuhiro Hashimoto
(Kunitada Matsushita) (A)
[*Converted*]
Akira Ozeki (K)

26th Class
*(September 1934–March 1935;
carrier planes, thirty-nine
persons)*
Terumi Aihara (A)
Hideo Ōishi (K)
Takejirō Onozuka (A)
Masa-aki Kawahara (K)
Kunimori Saeki (A)
Hitoshi Satō (K)
Takeo Sugiyama
Tsuyoshi Sumita (K)
(Toyozō Takehara) (A)
Takeo Tanaka (A)
Hachitarō Hayashi
Yoshio Fukui
Akio Matsuba

27th Class
*(January–July 1935; carrier
planes, thirty-eight persons)*
Tetsuo Imabayashi (A)
Ryō-itsu Ōkubo (Saka) (K)
Kikue Otokuni
Masaichi Kondō
Yoshimichi Saeki
(Nobuyoshi Sumi)
Yūsaburō Toguchi
Masato Hino (K)
Isao Hiraishi (H, K)
Yoshiharu Fujimoto (A)

Toyoshige Fukunaga (A)
Hitoshi Fukazawa (K)
Shigeru Makino (K)

28th Class
*(February–August 1935; carrier
planes, thirty-two persons)*
Shirō Ayukawa (A)
(Shizuo Okunishi) (K)
Katsuyoshi Ogasawara (K)
Morinori Kurachi (A)
Einosuke Shitama (A)
Kiyonobu Suzuki (K)
Kamezō Tarui
Matsuo Hagiri
(Kinta Hatakeyama)
Kihei Fujiwara
Kōichi Magara (K)
Yoshiharu Matsumoto (K)
Toshio Mori
Tadashi Yokote (K)

29th Class
*(May–November 1935; land
planes, thirty-three persons)*
Shigeshi Imamura (K)
(Keitarō Iwase) (K)
Noboru Okugawa (K)
(Harunobu Oda) (K)
Takashi Kikuchi (A)
Tomihiko Tanaka (K)
Mitsunori Nakajima
Kōji Hayakawa (K)
Suezō Harada (K)
Kinji Fujiwara (K)
Momoto Matsumura (K)
Kōji Miyazaki (K)
Tasuke Mukai (K)
Shōtarō Yamashita

30th Class
*(May–November 1935; carrier
planes, forty-one persons)*
Masazumi Ino (K)
Yoshihiro Inoue
Shinya Kashikura (H)
(Tatsugorō Katō) (K)
Toshio Kaneko (K)
(Eikichi Koga) (A)
Maresuke Gokan (A)
Hatsutarō Koshimizu (A)
Munesaburō Takahashi (K)
Kōsaku Toyoda
Susumu Nakagaki (A)
Tsugio Ogiwara (K)
Shunzō Hongō (K)
Namitarō Matsushima
Hideyori Matsumoto
Yoshimi Minami (K)

31st Class
(September 1935–March 1936; carrier planes, thirty-two persons)
(Norio Ōtake)
Jūzō Okamoto (K)
Hisao Ochi (K)
(Harumi Kawano)
Akira Kikuchi (K)
Jinkichirō Kudō (K)
(Yoshitatsu Kurahara) (K)
Sadao Konno (H)
Kuniyoshi Tanaka
Tadashi Teramatsu (K)
Tadashi Nakamoto (K)
(Tsukasa Muramatsu) (K)

32nd Class
(January–July 1936; carrier planes, thirty-three persons)
Fujio Ayabe (K)
(Tsune Ino)
Sueji Itsukaichi (K)
Nagaharu Umeda (K)
Yukiharu Ozeki (K)
Shizuo Kojima (K)
(Bunpei Kondō) (A)
Kizō Shizu (K)
Toshiyuki Sueda (K)
(Isshō Numata) (K)
Kaneyoshi Mutō (K)
Isao Murata (K)

33rd Class
(February–September 1936; carrier planes, thirty persons)
Shigetaka Ōmori (K)
Hiromori Shimomura (K)
(Minoru Tasaki (Ishii))
Bunkichi Nakajima (K)
Hideo Fukawa
(Mitsugu Maeda) (K)
[Converted]
Masao Suizu

34th Class
(April–December 1936; carrier planes, twenty-seven persons)
Ki-ichi Iwase (K)
Tetsuzō Iwamoto
Kiyomi Kuwabara
Morinosuke Hatanaka
Ineo Hamada (K)
Sadao Yamashita (K)
Kyōichi Yoshii

35th Class
(June 1936–February 1937; carrier planes, twenty-seven persons)
Tsuneyoshi Iono

Shime Inoue (A)
(Masayuki Tanimoto)
Tōru Haneda (K)
Kaname Harada (A)
Gonji Moriyama (K)

36th Class
(October 1936–June 1937; carrier planes, twenty-six persons)
Tsumugu Ōkura (K)
(Osamu Kamikawa)
(Takeo Kawashima) (K)
Wataru Kubota (Tsukada) (A)
Mankichi Sawada
Hiromitsu Takahara (K)

37th Class
(December 1936–July 1937; carrier planes, twenty-one persons)
Yoshio Ōki (K)
Yū-ichi Tanaka (A)
Katsujirō Nakano (K)
Kazuki Mikami
Masami Takemoto (K)

38th Class
(March–November 1937; carrier planes, twenty-five persons)
Masayoshi Okazaki
Kenji Okabe
Hiroshi Kawanishi (K)
Saburō Sakai (H)
Masaharu Hiramoto (K)
Iwao Hirayama (K)
(Minoru Maeda) (A)
Yanosuke Nagashima
Inuki Hirose
Yūji Yokoyama (K)

39th Class
(May 1937–January 1938; carrier planes, thirty persons)
Hisashi Aoyama (K)
Tetsuo Kikuchi (K)
Jūzō Saitō
Masanosuke Suzuki (K)
Jirō Tanaka (H, K)
Yoshisuke Hoshiya (K)
Takio Yoshida (K)

40th Class
(July 1937–February 1938; carrier planes, thirty-six persons)
Saburō Ishii (K)
Toshikazu Iwata (K)
Hiroshi Ōiwa (K)
Genkichi Ogawa (K)
Sōji Chiba (K)
Michisuke Tokuda (K)
Takashi Nakajima (K)

Shigenobu Nakata (K)
Masaharu Hika (K)
Kōzaburō Yasui (K)
Tōru Yamamoto (K)
Hatsumasa Yamaya (K)
Kazuo Yokogawa

41st Class
(November 1937–June 1938; carrier planes, thirty-six persons)
Iki Arita (K)
Isamu Ochi (A)
Shigeru Ōkura (K)
Mitsugu Ōtani (K)
Shigeo Kimura (K)
Tetsuo Satō (K)
Seinoshin Sano (K)
Jirō Shōji (K)
Jūsaku Tanabe (A)
Toshiaki Harada
Fusayoshi Murasaki (K)
Hideo Morinio (H)
(Tsumo-o Yamazaki) (K)
Kaname Yoshimatsu (K)

42nd Class
(February–September 1938; carrier planes, sixty-two persons)
Rokuzō Iwamoto (H,K)
Ken-ichirō Ueda (A)
Takeo Okumura (K)
Masakatsu Obata (A)
Ganji Kuragami
Saneatsu Kuroki
Tamotsu Kojima (K)
Nobuo Saitō (K)
Naokichi Suzuki (K)
Norio Tokushige (K)
Jinsaku Nojima (K)
Yoshirō Hashiguchi (K)
Teisaburō Hida (K)
Hiroshi Fujita (K)
Sanae Matsumoto (K)
Takeshi Yamamoto
(Takahashi) (K)

43rd Class
(April–November 1938; carrier planes, fifty-six persons)
(Gorō Abe) (K)
Yasujirō Ōno (K)
Takashi Okamoto
Suminori Kawabata (K)
Yoshinao Kodaira (K)
Gorō Sakaida (K)
Taka-aki Satō (K)
San-ichiro Tanaka (K)
(Kuraichi Nishida) (K)
(Kōsaku Hisamatsu) (K)
Hiromichi Hōjō (K)
Teizō Hosomura (A)

Takashi Honda
Sukeji Majima (K)
En-ichi Yokoda (H, A)

44th Class
(*June 1938–January 1939;*
carrier planes, fifty-five persons)
Chin Ishii (K)
(Kōsaku Itō) (A)
Kyō-ichirō Ogino (K)
Torakichi Okazaki (K)
Takeo Kanamaru
Hiroshi Kuratomi (K)
Saburō Saitō
Ryōseki Sakuraba (K)
Takeo Takashima (K)
Toshio Tomiya (A)
Masateru Tomoishi (K)
(Teru Nakai) (K)
Yasunobu Nahara
Ryō-ichi Hanabusa
(Masayoshi Higashima) (A)
Kosaku Minato (K)
Shigeru Yano (K)
Isaburō Yawata (K)
Tadao Yamanaka (H)
Mototsuna Yoshida (K)

45th Class
(*October 1938–May 1939;*
carrier planes, forty-eight
persons)
Fumio Itō (K)
Shigetsune Ōkane (K)
Sei-ichi Kitaoka (K)
Takashi Kurauchi
Hisao Komori (K)
Chūji Sakaue (K)
Shin-ichi Suzuki (K)
Isao Tahara (K)
Saburō Nozawa (K)
Nobutoshi Furukawa (K)
Kenzō Futamotomori (K)
Saburō Yoshi-i (K)

46th Class
(*January–September 1939;*
carrier planes, forty-nine persons)
Makoto Inoue (K)
Toshio Ōta (K)
Shigeto Sawano (K)
Kaneo Suzuki (K)
Tetsujirō Suzuki (A)
Yoshizō Tanaka (K)
Tomeyoshi Nagata (A)
Yoshio Hirose (K)
Yoshio Yoshida (K)

47th Class
(*March–October 1939; carrier*
planes, forty-nine persons)

Hiroyoshi Itō (K)
Zenji Ōkubo (A)
Enji Kakimoto (K)
Keiji Kikuchi (K)
Masakichi Sonoyama (K)
Isao Doikawa (K)
Tomita Hara (Atake)

48th Class
(*June 1939–January 1940;*
carrier planes, eighty-two
persons)
Yūji Andō (K)
Gen Ishikami (A)
Seiji Ishikawa
Nobuo Ogiya (K)
Kishirō Kobayashi (K)
Minoru Shibamura (K)
Shō-ichi Shōji (K)
Sakae Nakazawa (A)
Haruo Nitta (K)
Yasuji Notani (K)
Makoto Bandō
Yoshimi Hidaka (K)
Zenpei Matsumoto (K)

49th Class
(*November 1939–June 1940;*
carrier planes, seventy persons)
Takeichi Kokubun (K)
Katsutarō Kobayashi
Sadamu Komachi
Shinpei Sano (K)
Tetsuo Sentō (A)
Katsuaki Nagatomo (K)
Toshiaki Honda (K)
Masao Masuyama
Tomikichi Maruta (A)
Nobuo Yamamoto (A)

50th Class
(*December 1939–June 1940;*
carrier fighters, eleven persons)
Seiji Iishi (K)
Shizuo Ishii (K)
Hiroshi Ōhara (K)
Masami Shiga
Seiji Tajiri (K)
Yutaka Chiyoshima (K)
Genzō Nagasawa (K)
Shin-ichi Nagata (K)
Sakae Mori (K)
Ichirō Yamamoto (K)
Tatsu Matsumoto (K)

51st Class
(*December 1939–July 1940;*
carrier fighters, six persons)
Shigeru Kawano
Mitsuyoshi Takasuga (K)
Masao Taniguchi (50
advanced)

Tōichirō Hanyu (K)
Shunji Horiguchi (A)
Haruo Miyata (A)
[*Converted*]
Keiji Sunami (H)
Gōzō Teruyama

52nd Class
(*February–July 1940; no carrier*
fighter pilots)

53rd Class
(*February–August 1940; carrier*
fighters, eleven persons)
Yasuo Isobe (K)
Shinkō Itō (K)
Yoshio Egawa
Michiyuki Kitaoki
Yukio Kitasato (K)
Masa-aki Shimakawa
Ei-ichi Takahashi (K)
Takashi Nakaue (K)
Takao Banno (H, K)
Haruo Fujibayashi
Yoshio Motokichi (K)
[*Converted*]
Katsuaki Nagamawari

54th Class
(*May 1941; Ōita Air Group*
graduates, carrier fighters,
twenty-one persons)
Genkichi Ōishi (A)
Hiroshi Okano
Matsuhimaru Kashibō
Teruo Kawamata (K)
Nobutaka Kurata (K)
Kenji Kotaka (A)
Mibuichi Shimada (K)
Hiroshi Suyama (K)
Mitsuo Suizu (K)
Minoru Tanaka (K)
Matsutarō Takaoka (K)
Toshitsugu Nisugi (K)
Shizuki Nishiyama (K)
Osamu Hatanaka (A)
Kō-ichi Fujii (A)
Shichijirō Mae (K)
Shirō Murakami (K)
Ichirōbei Yamazaki (K)
Ken-ichirō Yamamoto (K)
Ippei Yoshida
Sueyoshi Yūmoto (K)
[*Converted*]
Kōkichi Ōtsuki (A)

55th Class
(*July 1941; Ōita Air Group*
graduates; carrier fighters, nine
persons)
Minoru Ishii (K)

Masashi Ishida (K)
Shōji Ishihara (K)
Mitsumasa Ujihara (A)
Kyōji Kobayashi (K)
Eiji Sanada (K)
Kihachi Ninomiya (K)
Shigeru Hayashi (K)
Yasuo Matsumoto

56th Class
(*July 1941; Ōita Air Group graduate; carrier fighters, nineteen persons*)
Yoshio Aoki (K)
Sachio Azuma (K)
Kōichi Imamura (K)
Ryōichi Iwakawa (K)
Yoshio Iwabuchi (K)
Tomekichi Ōtsuki (K)
Tōru Oda (K)
Haruo Kawanishi (K)
Heikichi Kitao (K)
Takeshi Sakamoto
Shin Suematsu (K)
Mikio Tanikawa (K)
Mitsuru Tsuruoka (A)
Hajime Toyoshima (K)
Ki-ichi Nagano (K)
Takeo Matsuda (K)
Masayoshi Yonekawa (A)
Tadashi Yoneda (K)
Keisaku Yoshimura (K)

[*Converted*]
Heisaku Satō (K)
Yoshijirō Shirahama

57th Class
(*October 1941; Hakata Air Group graduates; seaplanes, thirty-three persons*)
[*Converted*]
Hideo Uemura (Saitō)
Masakazu Enomoto (K)
Kaneo Oita (K)
Jisaku Kaneko (K)
Tomematsu Matsunaga (K)
Kazuo Yamazaki (A)
Suehiro Yamamoto (K)

Hei 2nd Class (Flight Trainee Course 12th Class)
(*November 1941; Ōita Air Group graduates, thirty-seven persons*)
Toshiyuki Ichiki
Kiyoshi Itō
Manri Itō (K)
Ken-ichi Inagaki
Naoshi Ubukata (K)
Kiyoshi Ōsuga (K)

Shigeru Kawazu (K)
Saji Kanda (K)
Magoichi Kosaka (K)
Tamio Kobayashi
Takeshi Kobayashi (K)
Yū-ichi Kobayashi (K)
Akira Saitō (K)
Ken-ichi Jōzuka (K)
Yoshiyuki Shimozuru
Yōzō Sugawara (K)
Chinta Takagi (K)
Wataru Takeda (K)
Sadamu Tamai (K)
Jūfuku Tanji (K)
Gorō Tsuda (K)
Yoshio Torishima (K)
Tsuneyoshi Nakazawa (K)
Yoshi-ichi Nakatani
Gi-ichi Nakayama (K)
Chuichirō Hata (K)
Ayunosuke Hattori (A)
Sakuji Hayashi (K)
Takeichirō Hidaka (K)
Yoshimitsu Maeda (K)
Toshimi Matsugeta
Shigejirō Murakami (K)
Danji Yatsukura (K)
Kuratoshi Yasuda (K)
Tomezō Yamamoto (A)
Kōki Yoneda (K)
Masao Watanabe (K)

[*Converted*]
Tadashi Sakai (K)

(*November 1941; Usa Air Group graduates: converted from dive-bombers, eighteen persons*)
Kunishige Iizuka
Mitsuyoshi Inoue (K)
Satoru Ogawa (K)
Tetsuo Kamata
Yūki Kariya (K)
Shigetsugu Kawai
Katsuhiko Kawasaki (K)
Hikoji Kawada (K)
Minoru Kuranaga (K)
Shigehiro Sugihara (K)
Katsuji Hijiya (A)
Hiroyuki Hihara (K)
Tsunesaku Hayashi
Sachio Hayama (K)
Tadashi Fujimoto (K)
Hidetaro Hosoya (K)
Isamu Miyazaki
Hideo Watanabe

(*November 1941; Usa Air Group graduates: converted from carrier attack planes, ten persons*)
Mutsu-o Uemura (K)

Kiyoshi Ono (K)
Susumu Ōtsuki (K)
Tsugio Kawagishi (A)
Masayoshi Kojima (A)
Kiyoshi Sekiya (K)
Ten-ichi Tanoue (K)
Yoshihira Hashiguchi (A)
Saburō Hotta (K)
Shigeru Mukumoto (K)

Hei 3rd Class (Flight Trainee Course 17th Class)
(*March 1942; Ōita Air Group graduates, eighty persons; Ōmura Air Group graduates, unknown number of persons*)
Hisashi Aoki (K)
Yūichirō Andō (K)
Takesaburō Ikeda (K)
Izumi Ishihara (Sanada)
Tomitaro Itō (K)
Shigehiko Itō (K)
Yoshifusa Iwasaka (K)
Jisuke Iwase (K)
Jinzō Ueno (A)
Masahiro Ueno (K)
Noboru Uehara (K)
Yoshio Ōsawa
Tōru Ōbayashi (A)
Tamotsu Okabayashi (K)
Kunio Okishige (K)
Mitsuyasu Ozaki (K)
Hiroshi Ochi (K)
Jūkichi Ono (K)
Yoshi-ichiro Katō (K)
Masao Katō (K)
Yasutaka Kaya (K)
Fusakazu Kaneko (K)
Shigeto Kawakami (K)
Sōroku Kawakami (K)
Yukio Kitano (K)
Hide-aki Kiyosawa (A)
Shō-ichi Kuwahara (K)
Ichihei Kobayashi (K)
Toshio Komiya (K)
Hiroshi Koyama (K)
Kazuo Gotō (K)
Mitsuo Gotō (K)
Gen Gōno (K)
Takao Banno (K)
Takamichi Sasamoto (K)
Genshichi Satō (K)
Toshimi Satō (K)
Kiyotaka Sawasaki (K)
Ichizō Shigematsu (A)
Yoshio Shōji (A)
Katsuo Sugano (K)
Shō-ichi Sugita (K)
Kazuo Sugino

Taiji Suzuki (K)
Takashi Sekiya (K)
Masanobu Shiba (K)
Takashi Takayama (K)
Toji Tatebe (K)
Takeo Tanimizu
Kazu Tamura (K)
Hideo Tsukamoto (K)
Shizuo Doi (K)
Kiyoshi Tokunaga (K)
Tatsuo Tokunaga (K)
Kazuo Tobita (K)
Sachio Nakatsukasa (K)
Masa-aki Nakane (K)
Toshikazu Nakano (K)
Tomokazu Nakano (K)
Yasuhiro Nakamura (K)
Kiyoshi Nakamoto (K)
Nobuto Nagao (K)
Shin-ichi Nishisaka (K)
Eiji Nishida (K)
Yoshio Nishida (K)
Ippei Ninomiya (K)
Hisahide Hashimoto (K)
Haruo Hamanaka
Kōkichi Hamano (K)
Tokutarō Harami-ishi
  (Suzuki) (K)
Kazufusa Harano (K)
Shinjirō Hinoda (K)
Tetsuo Hidaka (K)
Sadao Hirai
Shigeo Hirano (K)
Shin-ichi Hirabayashi
Imio Fukuda
Tsugio Fukutome (K)
Masakazu Fujisada (K)
Aihiko Fujita (A)
Seiji Hosono (K)
Hidemasa Honda (K)
Tomio Maeda (K)
Masanao Maki (K)
Bangorō Myōkei (K)
Hachirō Mitsunaga (K)
Shinkō Muraoka (K)
Hiroshi Mure (K)
Fukuyoshi Morino (K)
Motosuke Yato (K)
Ryō-ichi Yasuda (A)
Nobutaka Yanami (K)
Kenji Yanagiya
Yoshimi Yamauchi (K)
Shōtoku Yamaguchi (K)
Taku Yamazaki (K)
Kameji Yamane (K)
Shin-ichi Yamawaki
Ryōzō Wakabayashi (K)
Seizaburō Watanabe (K)
Kenji Wada (K)

Hei 3rd Class (Flight Trainee Course 18th Class)
(May 1942; Ōmura Air Group graduates; carrier fighters, thirty persons)

Shigemasa Asami (K)
Yoshimizu Arata (K)
Takematsu Imabayashi (A)
Masami Iwatsubo (K)
Sumio Uehara (A)
Sachio Egawa (K)
Yoneji Kanazawa (K)
Ikuji Kaburagi (K)
Motoyasu Kitamura (K)
Sadao Kubo (K)
Kazuo Komaba (K)
Toshikazu Koyanagi (K)
Hachirō Satō (K)
Itaru Shikano
Katsuyoshi Tanaka (K)
Kisaku Tanaka (K)
Sakuji Tanaka (K)
Shirō Tsukahara (K)
Shirō Toriyama (K)
Ryōji Handa (K)
Sakuichi Fukuda (K)
Kichirō Maekawa
Momo-o Makiyama (K)
Matsukichi Matsui (K)
Setsu Matsukichi (K)
Kaoru Miyazaki (A)
Toshio Miyanishi (K)
Takashi Yamashita (A)
Makio Yamato (K)
Takamori Yamanaka (K)

(July 1942; Ōmura Air Group graduates; carrier fighters, twenty-seven persons)

Shunji Itō (K)
Sadakazu Iwaki (K)
Seijirō Uemura (K)
Kiyoshi Ogawa
Fumio Katō (K)
Yasuo Kanemitsu (K)
Bunji Kamihira (K)
Atsushi Kubo (A)
Susumu Kubota (K)
Masakichi Kurihara
Sei-ichi Kurosawa (K)
Hikoji Gotō (K)
Toshikatsu Satō (K)
Fukumitsu Shimada (K)
Shigeru Tanoue (K)
Isamu Tanaka (K)
Toshio Nakazono (H, K)
Yoshio Nakamura
Shichirō Nagai (K)
Hisao Nishimoto

Shin-ichi Hasegawa
Kijū Hitomi (K)
Fukuda
Hidemichi Matsumura (K)
Makoto Murata (K)
Hisayoshi Mori (K)
Hiroshi Yasumatsu (K)

Hei 4th Class (Flight Trainee Course 21st Class)
(July 1942; Ōita Air Group graduates; carrier fighters, twenty-nine persons)

Tsurumi Ichiki (K)
Moto-omi Ishibashi (K)
Yoshiharu Izumi (K)
Sanjirō Imai (K)
Ichijō Umezu
Ryōji Ōhara
Masanori Oka (K)
Yutaka Kimoto (K)
Tomokazu Kobayashi (K)
Ichijirō Saitō
Seikichi Sakae (K)
Shōgo Sasaki (K)
Kaoru Satō (K)
Shigekazu Suzuki (K)
Masakazu Nakazawa (K)
Mitsuo Nakahara (A)
Masaichi Nakamura (K)
Wataru Nakamichi
Kanekichi Nemoto (K)
Takeshi Hayashi (K)
Noboru Hayashi (K)
Hirano
Saburō Fujiuma (K)
Toshiaki Maeda (K)
Takayuki Murakami (K)
Shin-ichi Yamawaki (K)
Tokuji Yoshizaki (K)
Furuo Yoshimitsu (K)

[Converted]
Shinkichi Ōshima (K)
Sachio Kamihara
Shingo Honda (K)
Tsunesaku Sakai (K)
Eikichi Nakazaki (K)

Hei 6th Class (Flight Trainee Course 23rd Class)
(September 1942; Ōmura Air Group graduates, twenty-seven persons; Tokushima Air Group graduates, thirty persons; Ōita Air Group graduates, unknown number)

Hideo Iijima (K)
Tokio I-ishi (K)
Kane-ichi Ishi-i (A)
Teigo Ishida (K)

Bunji Ishida	(K)	Tsuyoshi Tanaka	(K)	Sueo Mizuno	(K)
Ryūzō Isobe	(K)	Hiroshi Takebe	(K)	Mitsuzō Miyagaki	
Sue-o Inoue	(K)	Iwao Taneda	(K)	Hisakazu Miyamoto	(K)
Yoshiyuki Ueki	(K)	Yoshitaka Tamura	(K)	Minoru Miwa	(K)
Kazuo Endō	(K)	Kiyoshi Tamaki	(K)	Naraichi Murai	(K)
Michizō Egashira	(K)	Kazuyoshi Tokuhara	(K)	Kaname Mori	(K)
Matsukichi Ōtomo	(K)	Minoru Tomisono	(K)	Katsu Moriyama	(K)
Chikara Kitakuchi	(K)	Akira Nakazawa	(K)	Kei-ichi Kadoma	(K)
Kunio Kidokoro	(K)	Hayao Nakabeppu	(K)	Ryūji Yagi	
Kensuke Kurosawa	(K)	Yukuo Nanao	(K)	Yasukichi Yamakawa	(K)
Masakazu Kobayashi	(K)	Dō Nishi	(K)	Takeo Yamamoto	(K)
Shōjirō Kobayashi	(K)	Noboru Nishio	(K)	Hifumi Yamamoto	(K)
Yūzō Komatsu	(K)	Takeo Hashimoto	(K)	Hiroshi Yamamoto	(K)
Eigorō Saitō		Shujirō Hasegawa	(A)	Ken-ichiro Yoshioka	(K)
Sōji Saitō	(K)	Denjirō Baba	(K)	Rokuya Yoneyama	(K)
Tomoharu Shi-ina	(K)	Takayuki Hamasaki	(A)	[Converted]	
Kenzō Shiokawa		Morimasa Hirai	(K)	Takeji Ōmori	(K)
Katsunobu Shiba	(K)	Tarō Fukuhara	(K)	Tadanobu Okamoto	(A)
Shigeru Shibukawa		Muneichi Fujioka	(K)	Yōichi Katsumata	
Ikki Takeda	(K)	Kinpei Hoshino	(K)	Takeshi Katō	(K)
Tadami Takemoto	(K)	Toshimitsu Matsuzaki	(A)	Toshikazu Hyōdō	
Tai-ichi Tashiro	(K)	Gen-ichi Matsuda	(A)		
Hideo Takanabe	(K)	Masanari Mizusawa	(K)		

Kō, Otsu Flight Reserve Enlisted Trainee Class Students

1. The Flight Reserve Enlisted Trainee (Yoka Renshū-sei) system was inaugurated by order of the Ministry of the Navy in December 1929. In June 1930, students for the 1st class were assigned. Paralleling the army's Youth Flight Enlisted Trainee (Shōnen Hikō-hei) program, the navy program focused on youths aged fifteen through seventeen who had knowledge approximately equivalent to graduates of the higher elementary schools (Kōtō Shogakkō). Flight Reserve Enlisted Trainees were trained for a period of two and a half to three years, primarily centered around general education subjects; at a later date, the program was shortened to two years. After graduation, trainees were assigned to Flight Trainee Courses (Hikō Renshū-sei Katei) for basic pilot training. After completing the latter, trainees moved on to a course where they were trained in the actual use of aircraft. From the Flight Trainee Course level on, training was common with that given under the Hei Flight Reserve Enlisted Trainee Course.
2. In order to satisfy the need for an increase in flight personnel in May 1937, it was decided to use personnel with a higher educational background than that required for the Flight Reserve Enlisted Trainee Class system; such personnel were placed in the Kō Flight Reserve Enlisted Trainee Class system. Students for the 1st class entered the program in September. Qualification requirements were the equivalent of high school (chūgakkō) graduation. The period of training for the program ranged from one year two months to one year six months (later reduced to one year). Further, with the establishment of the Kō Flight Trainee Course system, it was decided to change the name of the previous Flight Reserve Enlisted Trainee Class to Otsu Flight Trainee Course.
3. Initially, Flight Reserve Enlisted Trainee Class training was conducted within the Yokosuka Air Group; in March 1939, training was moved to Tsuchiura. In November 1940, the program was made independent as the Tsuchiura Air Group. Later, because of the increase in the number of personnel being trained, the Mie Air Group was organized in August 1942. Such groups continued to be established successively; in the spring of 1945, there were eighteen training air groups that specialized in the Flight Reserve Enlisted Trainee Class program.
4. For the relationship between the Kō, Otsu, Hei Flight Reserve Enlisted Trainee Class system and the Flight Trainee Course system, please refer to the table on page 424.

Otsu 1st Class
(Entered June 1930; May 1933 graduates of Flight Trainee Course; carrier planes, twenty persons)
Yasujirō Abe
Shōzō Okabe
Jirōkichi Kusunoki
Yoshimitsu Harada (K)
Morio Miyaguchi (K)
Shigeo Miyamoto (K)
Noboru Yamakawa (K)
Hiroyuki Yamaguchi (K)
Hitoshi Watanabe (A)

[*Converted*]
Susumu Itō

Otsu 2nd Class
(Entered June 1931; April 1935 graduates of Flight Trainee Course; carrier planes, forty-eight persons)
Sei-ichi Okabe
Masanori Ōhashi (A)
Suekichi Osanai (K)
Zenji Ono (K)
Yasuji Kanemitsu (A)
Osamu Kudō (K)
Fujikazu Koizumi (K)
Yoshimi Kodama (K)
Sukesada Senda (A)
Jirō Nasu (A)
Hiro-o Natori (A)
Ichirō Higashiyama (H, K)
Mi-uma Hirai (K)
Yoshijirō Minegishi (K)
Masatsugu Miyauchi (A)
Kazunori Miyabe (K)
Sakutsuchi Yamada (A)
Gi-ichi Yamanouchi (K)
Nao Watanabe (K)

[*Converted*]
Minobu Kaga (K)
Gi-ichi Minami (K)

Otsu 3rd Class
(Entered June 1932; April 1936 graduates of Flight Trainee Course; carrier planes, forty-six persons)
Sachi-o Aiso (K)
Kazumi Aramaki (A)
Mitsuo Kaneko (A)
Seizaburō Sugino
Yoshio Suzuki (A)
Torakichi Tanaka (Ozawa)
Ryō-ichi Nakamizo (K)
(Takuo Noda)
(Keigo Noborimoto)
Tsugio Matsuyama (K)

Sachi-o Miyasato (K)
Yūji Mōri (K)
Akitsugu Yamazaki

[*Converted*]
Susumu Kawasaki

Otsu 4th Class
(Entered May 1933; May 1937 graduates of Flight Trainee Course; carrier planes, forty-one persons)
(Satarō Abe) (K)
Yoshiharu Kusakabe (A)
(Tatsu Kotani) (K)
Rokuo Sagara
Hayato Noda (K)
Yutaka Matsuzaki (A)
Akira Maruyama (K)
Gitarō Miyazaki (K)
Yoshio Yoshie

[*Converted*]
Kumaji Tsugane (K)

Otsu 5th Class
(Entered June 1934; March 1938 graduates of Flight Trainee Course; carrier planes, forty-three persons)
Tomo-o Inoue (K)
(Takeru Ōhara) (H, K)
Shigeru Okamoto (K)
Ei-ichi Kimura (K)
Yoshihiro Kobayashi (K)
Tsutomu Kobayashi (A)
Yū-ichi Sagara (K)
Shigeo Sugio
Kazuo Tsunoda
Masayuki Nakase (K)
Yukuo Hanzawa (K)
Masayuki Mitsumasu (A)
Sahei Yamashita (K)
Satoshi Yoshino (K)

[*Converted*]
Kunio Shintani (K)
Masahiko Nakamine
Tsutomu Hamada

Otsu 6th Class
(Entered June 1935; August 1938 graduates of Flight Trainee Course; carrier planes, fifty-one persons)
Sueji Ide (K)
Tsutomu Iwai
Tatsuo Uchimura (A)
Ichizō Ōmori
Satoshi Kanō (K)
Masao Kawasaki (K)
Susumu Gotō (K)
Tsukasa Kondō (H, K)

Toyo-o Sakai (K)
Yasuhisa Satō (K)
Toshirō San-ō
Kō-ichi Takafuji (A)
Yukuo Tanaka (K)
Yoshinao Tokuji (K)
Tatsuo Higashinaka
Masami Fukazawa
(Otokichi Funakawa) (K)
Jirō Mitsumoto (K)
Kazuo Muranaka
Tomio Yoshizawa (H, A)

[*Converted*]
Shigemasa Nishio (K)

Otsu 7th Class
(Entered June 1936; March 1939 graduates of Flight Trainee Course; carrier planes, seventy-one persons)
Tomio Inenaga (K)
Jirō Imura (K)
Fumio Ōzumi (K)
Yūsuke Katō (K)
Toshio Kikuchi (K)
Haruyoshi Kubota (K)
Yasujirō Kawano (K)
Kenta Komiyama (K)
Teruo Sugiyama (K)
Gunji Suzuki (K)
Kazuo Suzuri (K)
Ryō Takahashi
Akira Takamori (A)
Tokiharu Tezuka (K)
Hiroyoshi Nishizawa (K)
Fujio Hayashi (K)
Eijirō Higaki (K)
Hisashi Hide (K)
Shigeo Fukumoto

[*Converted*]
Fukuju Kawakami
Tetsuji Koga (K)
Taiji Takayama
Kazutoshi Nagano (A)
Hisao Harada (K)
Toshiaki Maeda (A)

Otsu 8th Class
(Entered June 1937; March 1940 graduates of Flight Trainee Course; carrier fighters, eleven persons)
Shigeo Okazaki
Nobuo Osanai (A)
Takumi Kai (K)
Ichirō Kaneko (A)
Ichirō Sakai (K)
Ryōkei Shinohara (K)
Shigenobu Takahara (K)
Noboru Todaka (K)

Kunimori Nakakariya
Tatsuzō Hasegawa (K)
Akira Hongō (A)
Hisashi Matsumoto (K)
[Converted]
Susumu Ishida (K)
Kyō-ichi Inuzuka (K)
Fujiki Azuma

Otsu 9th Class
(Entered June 1938; October
1941 graduates of Flight Trainee
Course, 10th class; Ōita Air
Group graduates, twenty-three
persons)
Shigenobu Adachi (K)
Masami Arai (K)
Makoto Ueda (K)
Chikatatsu Uenuma (K)
Sadao Uehara
Kazushi Utō (K)
So-ichi Ōshōdani (A)
Sukeo Kawasaki (K)
Yutaka Kimura (K)
Ken-ichi Kumagaya (K)
Takeo Kume (K)
Tatsusuke Gotō (K)
Noboru Satō (K)
Tsutomu Shibata (K)
Matsumi Suzuki (K)
Akimizu Seki (K)
Shigeru Nomura (H)
Kiyotake Fukuyama (K)
Yoshio Mogi (K)
Masaru Morita (K)
Toyo-o Moriura (K)
Takashi Yokoyama (K)
Kametsugu Watamura

(October 1941 graduates of Usa
Air Group: converted from
carrier bombers, ten persons)
Ken-ichi Abe
Daizō Ihara (K)
Masuaki Endō (K)
Yoshio Ōishi (K)
Yoshizō Ōnishi (K)
Shin Nakano (K)
Noboru Nishiyama (K)
Sa-ichi Matsumoto
Mamoru Morita (K)
Shigematsu Yamashita

(October 1941 graduates of
Kisarazu Air Group: converted
from medium attack planes)
Gi-ichi Ōhara (K)
Takashi Konno (K)
Hideo Shimizu (K)
Yosaburō Shinomiya (K)

Hajime Tochi (K)
Yoshinori Noguchi (K)
Katsumasa Matsumoto (K)
Toyo-o Mori-ura (K)
Hamashige Yamaguchi (K)

Persons who converted from
other branches to the Otsu 9th
Class to receive training
November 1941–February
1942 were to be trained in
fighters by the Sasebo Air
Group unit dispatched to
Izumi.

Otsu 10th Class
(Entered November 1938,
graduated March 1942 from
Flight Trainee Course; Ōita Air
Group graduates, thirty-five
persons)
Minoru Awao (K)
Kazuo Ikumi (A)
Mitsuji Ikeda (K)
Yoshihide Ishizawa (K)
Isao Itō (K)
Jirō Iwai (K)
Nao Uematsu (K)
Noboru Ōta
Michitaka Kashiwara (K)
Kishio Kadota (K)
Toyonobu Kuzuhara
Sadao Koike (K)
Shigekazu Sasa (K)
Zensaburō Suzuki (A)
Jun-ichi Takahashi (K)
Tōru Takeuchi
Hideya Takesawa (K)
Kisaku Takeda (A)
Shunji Nakasawa (K)
Atsuo Nishikane (K)
Shōkichi Nishimoto (K)
Kikuo Nishimori (K)
Yoshiyuki Hirata (K)
Daizō Fukumori (K)
Tamotsu Fujita
Masami Futaki (K)
Katsuki Furumoto (K)
Mitsuo Hori (Mikami)
Shigeo Motegi (K)
Tatsuo Morioka (K)
Toshio Morita (K)
Sakae Yamashita
Takeo Yamashiro (K)
Mitsuo Yamada
Isamu Yoshiwara (K)

[Converted]
Toshio Imada (K)
Hisashi Kamata (K)
Shūgo Takahashi

Otsu 11th Class
(Entered June 1939; 21st Class
of Flight Trainee Course; July
1942 graduates of Ōita Air
Group, fourteen persons)
Masanori Arimura (K)
Gen-ichi Uchida (K)
Kumaichi Katō (K)
Shigeru Kimata (K)
Matagorō Kimura (K)
Yorihisa Kobayashi (K)
Kōji Shimizu (K)
Takeshige Senuma (K)
Kōtarō Takano (K)
Akira Takita (K)
Tamaru Tanigaki (K)
Toshio Nagata (K)
Hiroshi Hirai (K)
Tadao Wakimoto (A)

[Converted]
Kenzō Asatsu (K)
Katsuyoshi Itō (K)
Ryōzō Soejima
Teruyuki Naoi
Satoyuki Hayase
Saburō Mitsuoka (K)

(23rd Class of Flight Trainee
Course; September 1942
graduates of Ōita Air Group;
forty-eight persons)
Shin-ichi Ando
Taketoshi Iio (K)
Masao Ishii (K)
Eikichi Ichimura (A)
Hisashi Ichiyanagi
Motoharu Imazeki (K)
Yoshio Imamura (K)
Hiroshi Ueda (K)
Rizō Ōkubo
Minoru Ōta (A)
Rokei Ōmiya (K)
Takemi Okada (K)
Takao Katō (K)
Mitsuo Kusano
Tashirō Koga (K)
Yoshio Gotō (K)
Toshiyuki Koba
Shigeru Sasako (A)
Mankichi Satō (K)
Yoshio Shiode (K)
Rokusaburō Shinohara (K)
Masa Shimada (K)
Hideo Suzuki (K)
Hideo Seki
Tatsumi Soga (K)
Kazuo Tachizumi (K)
Minpo Tanaka
Toshio Tanaka

Makoto Terao (K)
Hiroshi Nishimura (K)
Tokuharu Noda (K)
Namio Hashimasa (K)
Hisashi Hayakawa (K)
Tadashi Hirai (K)
Tsukijirō Fujii (K)
Bun-ichi Fujise (K)
Hideaki Maeda (K)
Ryōhei Masajima (A)
Kan-ichi Masuda (K)
Kōjirō Murakami (K, H)
Kiyoshi Yamazaki (K)
Tadao Yamashita (K)
Rikusuke Yamashita (K)
Iwao Yamamoto (K)
Yoshio Yoshida (K)
Masuo Yoneyama (K)

Otsu 12th Class
(*Entered November 1939;*
January 1943 graduates of 25th
Class Flight Trainee Course;
carrier fighters, fifty-eight
persons)
Eisaburō Asakage (K)
Yoshito Azukihata (K)
Fusao Ariga (K)
Kō-ichi Ishikawa (K)
Asagorō Ishida (K)
Kōshichi Izumida (K)
Noboru Itō (K)
Fumio Itō (K)
Jirō Uchida (K)
Eizō Ōta (K)
Takeo Ōtsu (A)
Mamoru Ōtsuka (K)
Sakae Okamura (K)
Shizumu Ono (K)
Tsunemichi Kōnoue
Yoshiharu Kagami (K)
Tomonobu Kameyama (K)
Shōyō Kijiya (K)
Kei Kishi (K)
Minoru Kitasaki (K)
Kinya Kunihiro (K)
Yoshinari Kumada (K)
Kusuo Kuriyama (K)
Noboru Koizumi (K)
Kaname Koide (K)
Masao Kotaki (K)
Yukuhiro Kodama (K)
Kaoru Gotō (K)
Bun-ichi Gotō (K)
Zentoku Satō (A)
Kazuo Shibayama (K)
Eiji Sekiguchi (K)
Kiyoshi Takei (K)
Tadamori Tajima (K)

Shinsaku Tanaka (K)
Tsugio Terada (K)
Setsuo Tominaga (K)
Katsumi Nakamura (K)
Hideo Ni-imichi
Satoshi Nishioka
Yō-ichi Nishikura (K)
Hiroshi Nishida (K)
Yoshikazu Nishimoto
Seiji Noma (K)
Shigeo Hayashi
Noriyuki Haraguchi (K)
Shun-ichi Hiromori (K)
Yoshio Mazaki (K)
Fukukichi Masago
Tadayoshi Matsui (A)
Seisuke Matsuda (K)
Kimiyoshi Miyamoto (K)
Shirō Miwa (S)
Toshi-aki Murata (K)
Kiyota Yanagi (K)
Kō-ichi Yamauchi (K)
Tokio Yokoi (K)
Sadatoshi Yoshino (K)
[*Converted*]
Yu Inoue
Takeshi Tsuji
Yoshiharu Dōmoto
Kōshi Nosue (K)
Keisuke Yamamura
Takafumi Yokobayashi (K)

Otsu 13th Class
(*Entered June 1940; March*
1943 graduates of 26th Class
Flight Trainee Course; carrier
fighters, forty-one persons)
Shigehisa Aoki (K)
Moritsugu Akiba (K)
Genbō Adachi (A)
Yoshiaki Ikenaga (A)
Yukuo Ikoma (K)
Seiroku Inoue
Kōji Ueda (K)
Shigeru Ueno (K)
Kiyomizu Ō-e (A)
Tasuke Okabe (K)
Teruo Ogawa (K)
Etsuo Okimura (K)
Kiyohira Kaneyama (K)
Mineo Kanzaki (K)
Tomio Kitaoka (K)
Masaru Kubo (K)
Taira Kubota (K)
Chōsatsu Koga (K)
Shigeo Saitō (K)
Tadashi Sakai (K)
Sekizen Shibayama
Yoshi-ichi Shima (K)

Iso-o Sugiura
Tsuneo Suzuki (K)
Hideo Suzuki (K)
Mitsugu Suzuki
Kazuo Sudō (K)
Kaoru Takaiwa (K)
Ken-ichi Takahashi
Harukuni Tanaka (K)
Tsumio Tanaka (K)
Isao Chōsokabe
Masaru Tsukiji (K)
Nobuyoshi Nakamura
Shigeru Nishiyama (K)
Yoshimoto Hattori (K)
Kōji Fujishiro
Toshihiro Matsunaga (K)
Ichitarō Muramoto (K)
Keizō Yamaguchi
Yaozō Wada (K)
[*Converted*]
Suehiro Ikeda (K)
Isao Itō
Take-ichi Kamo (K)
Soto-o Saitō (K)
Hideshi Tanimoto (K)
Shinjirō Nakajima (K)
Takeshi Nishio

Kō 1st Class
(*Entered September 1937; June*
1939 graduates of Flight Trainee
Course; carrier planes,
seventy-six persons)
Junjirō Itō (K)
Tomotoshi Ishikawa (A)
Takeru Imahashi (K)
Tōru Ōshima (K)
Keishū Kamihira
Koreo Kimura
Hiroshi Kurihara (K)
Yoshio Koike
Otojirō Sakaguchi
Yoshikane Sasaki (K)
Yoshihiko Takenaka (K)
Katsumi Tanaka (K)
Takio Dannoue (K)
Terusada Chūman (K)
Kazuyoshi Toyoda
Korenobu Nishide (K)
Yoshiaki Hatakeyama (K)
Naoyuki Hayashi (A)
Takashi Hirano (K)
Hideo Maeda (K)
Toshio Makinota
  (Minamoto) (K)
Jirō Matsuda
Hisao Murabyashi
Kōroku Yūsaki (A)
Shigeru Yoshihashi (K)

[*Converted*]
Shinji Ishida (K)
Take-ichi Kikuchi (K)
Masarō Nagase (K)
Atsuki Mesaki (K)

Kō 2nd Class
(*Entered April 1938; December
1939 graduates of Flight Trainee
Course; carrier planes,
eighty-one persons*)
Akira Atsumi (K)
Yoshio Iwashiro (K)
Shinji Iwama (K)
Tomio Kamei (K)
Ginji Kiyomatsu (K)
Yūji Satō (K)
Sei-ichi Tsukuda
Yoshikazu Nagahama (A)
Shigenori Nishikaichi (K)
Mitsuomi Noda (K)
Iwao Mita (K)
[*Converted*]
Masanobu Ibusuki
Mitsuzō Hashimoto (K)

Kō 3rd Class
(*Entered October 1938; April
1941 graduates of 1st Class,
Flight Trainee Course; carrier
fighters, twenty-one persons*)
Yoshisuke Arita (K)
Susumu Ishihara
Hideo Izumi (K)
Yutaka Ōtani (K)
Jin-ichirō Kawanishi (K)
Sakyō Kikuchi (K)
Tadayoshi Koga (K)
Tokusuke Konishi (A)
Ichirō Kobayashi (K)
Kazuo Kobayashi
Katsumi Kobayashi (K)
Matsutarō Kobayashi (K)
Hitoshi Sasaki
Tsugio Shikada
Taka-aki Shimotaba (A)
Tamotsu Nakamura (A)
Yoshio Matsuura (A)
Takeo Miyasawa (K)
Yukuo Miyauchi (K)
Tsunehiro Yamakami (K)
Takurō Yoshie (K)
[*Converted*]
Yasunori Ono (K)
Masashi Shibata
Tadao Shiratori (K)
Eiji Matsuyama (K)

Kō 4th Class
(*Entered April 1939; September
1941 graduates of 9th Class,*

*Flight Trainee Course; carrier
fighters, twenty-one persons*)
Chikao Aoki (K)
Hisashi Ichinose (K)
Tsutomu Itō (K)
Takeo Inoue (K)
Junzō Okutani (K)
Yozō Kawada (K)
Yasuzō Kimura (A)
Eikichi Onigashira (A)
Tadahiro Sakai (K)
Yoshimi Sakai (K)
Masao Sasakibara
Tomotsugu Sawada (K)
Toshikazu Tamura (K)
Yukihisa Tan (K)
Kunimatsu Nishiura (K)
Tamotsu Nishioka (A)
Hideyoshi Nomura (A)
Tei-ichirō Hayashida (K)
Susumu Matsuki (K)
Tatsuo Maruyama (K)
Un-ichi Miya (K)

Kō 5th Class
(*Entered October 1939; 15th
Class, Flight Trainee Course;
January 1942 Ōita Air Group
graduates, twenty-eight persons*)
Shirō Ishikawa
Makoto Iwamoto (K)
Kazuo Umeki (K)
Masanori Eguchi (K)
Toshiharu Ōkubo (K)
Takeshi Okui (K)
Bungorō Kawamata (K)
Masa-aki Kanda (Kō 4th
  Advanced Training) (A)
Hachirō Kuwabara (K)
Itsumi Shimizu (K)
Yutaka Shimizu (A)
Akira Imoto
Shinpei Sugiura (K)
Hiroshi Suzuki (K)
Mikiya Takada (K)
Shigeru Takahashi
Harumi Tomita (K)
Masashi Tomita (K)
Tadashi Nakamoto (K)
Mitsuo Nakayama
Fumi Nishiyama (K)
Yoshirō Nozu (K)
Yukio Hayasaka (K)
Tasuku Fukuyama (K)
Tadao Fujiwara (K)
Minoru Honda
Ya-ichi Yazawa (A)
Iwao Yamada (K)
Chi-une Yotsumoto (K)

(*February 1942 graduates of Usa
Air Group, twelve persons*)
Masayoshi Urano (K)
Chūji Sakurai (K)
Katsumi Shimura (K)
Ryō-ichi Sugiura (K)
Gen-ichi Seki (K)
Jōji Taniguchi (K)
Toyomitsu Tsujinoue (K)
Norimasa Narahara (K)
Takehiko Baba
Meiji Hikuma (K)
Nao-ichi Maeda (K)
Katsutoshi Maetsuji (K)

Kō 6th Class
(*Entered April 1940; July 1942
graduates of 21st Class, Flight
Trainee Course; carrier fighters,
forty-one persons*)
Yasuto Abe (K)
Jirō Ishikawa (K)
Hirotsugu Ishizaki (K)
Shigeyoshi Izumi (K)
Kōji Inamura (A)
Kesaji Iriki (K)
Yasushi Okazaki (K)
Yoneki Ochi (K)
Kaneyuki Kamikatahira (K)
Motomu Kawakami (K)
Ichirō Kawabata (K)
Masatsugu Kawamura (K)
Shigeharu Kido (K)
Haruo Kunihiro (K)
Kiyoshi Kojima (K)
Kurakazu Gotō (K)
Isao Kondō (K)
Kunio Sakai (K)
Moriji Sako (H)
Soyō Shibata (K)
Katsumi Shimamoto (K)
Toshihisa Shirakawa (K)
Tomio Shiraki (K)
Ei-ichi Sugiyama (K)
Shinpei Takagaki (K)
Izumi Tanaka (K)
Hachirō Tsuboya (K)
Yoshio Terai (K)
Tokihiro Tokuoka (K)
Haruo Tomita (K)
Takashi Nakamichi (A)
Tsuneishi Nakamura (K)
Tetsurō Nihei (K)
Rokurō Fukuda (K)
Takeshi Fujii (K)
Kō-ichi Hoshino (K)
Takeo Matsubayashi (K)
Takeo Maruyama (K)
Toshitsune Misawa (K)
Keizaburō Yamasaki (K)

[*Converted*]
Kiyoshi Akizuki
Mamoru Irio
Katsushi Kurita (K)
Masakazu Suzuki (K)
Misao Chō (K)
Hideji Furuuchi (K)

Kō 7th Class
(*Entered October 1940;*
November 1942 graduates of
24th Class, Flight Trainee
Course; carrier fighters, forty-one
persons)
Shizuo Aoki (A)
Kōshirō Agawa (K)
Yonehachirō Ishihara (K)
Shigeru Ishizuka (K)
Yasuo Iguchi (K)
Ichiji Ikeda (K)
Kikuo Ikeda (K)
Osamu Ichikawa (K)

Hiroshi Iwano (K)
Tomimasa Ōkubo (K)
Fumi-o Ōsumi (K)
Ryōzō Okada (K)
Tadashi Okamitsu (K)
Masakazu Kai (K)
Fusao Kinoshita (K)
Nobuo Konishi (K)
Shigemitsu Kōzuma (K)
Misao Sakanoue (A)
Sanpei Shiono
Munenori Shimizu (K)
Ikuzō Shimizu (K)
Toshitarō Sekiguchi (K)
Miyoshi Tanaka (K)
Michio Takeshita (K)
Gihachirō Taniguchi (A)
Yoshinobu Tsurusaki (K)
Yoshio Nakajima (K)
Hiroshi Nagakura (K)
Hitoshi Nagano (K)
Mitsuru Hama (A)

Katsujirō Matsumoto (K)
Yoshiyuki Miura
Jirō Murata
Isshun Morimoto (K)
Shigeaki Morita (A)
Ichirō Yamashita (K)
Ken-ichi Yamamoto (A)
Shigetarō Yamamoto (K)
Takashi Yoshii (K)
Saburō Yoshida (K)
Kenzō Yonemoto (A)
Takeru Wada (K)

[*Converted*]
Shirō Endō (K)
Yū-ichi Okada (K)
Ichizen Kobayashi (K)
Masuo Doi
Sanemasa Nanjō (K)
Masayuki Hanamura (K)
Kenjirō Honma (K)
Hidenori Matsunaga

Aviation Reserve Students

1. The Aviation Reserve Students (Kōkū Yobi Gakusei) program started in November 1934, structured around the Oceanic Division, Japanese Student Aviation League (Nihon Gakusei Kōkū Remmei Kaiyō-bu), which itself was later renamed the Student Oceanic Aviation Group (Gakusei Kaiyō Hikō-dan) and then the Naval Reserve Aviation Group (Kaigun Yobi Kōkū-dan). Trainees were generally selected from among graduates of universities and colleges; until 1942, the majority of them were from the oceanographic discipline. After their selection, Aviation Reserve Students were given about two months of general education, followed by ten months of pilot training. Following graduation, they were commissioned as ensigns (after 1942, a portion of these reserve students were integrated into regular active duty service).
2. Up through the 3rd Class, students specializing in land aircraft were provided specialized training in carrier attack aircraft; those specializing in seaplanes, received training in the piloting of observation seaplanes. Starting with the 4th Class, training was conducted for each type of aircraft by the speciality involved.

Yo (Reserve) 1st Class
(*November 1934–November*
1935; all types of aircraft, five
persons)

[*Converted*]
Isamu Matsubara

Yo 2nd Class
(*May 1935–April 1936; total of*
all aircraft types, fourteen
persons; no fighters)

Yo 3rd Class
(*April 1936–March 1937; total*
of all aircraft types, seventeen
persons; no fighters)

Yo 4th Class
(*April 1937–January 1938; total*
of all aircraft types, twelve

persons; fighters, two persons)
Yoshio Murata (K)
Kō-ichi Yoshida (K)

[*Converted*]
Naonori Yoshida (K)

Yo 5th Class
(*April 1938–March 1939; total*
of all types of aircraft, nineteen
persons; no fighters)

Yo 6th Class
(*April 1939–April 1940; total*
of all types of aircraft, twenty-
six persons; no fighters)

Yo 7th Class
(*April 1940–April 1941; total*
of all types of aircraft, thirty-two
persons; fighters, two persons)

Masahiro Chikanami (K)
Takeshi Morisaki (K)

[*Converted*]
Teiji Kagami (K)

Yo 8th Class
(*April 1941–April 1942; total*
of all types of aircraft, forty-three
persons)
Mitsuoki Asano (K)
Masao Kuramoto (K)
Akira Sugiura (K)
Akira Tanaka (K)
Ya-ichirō Fukunishi (K)
Shigeo Morimoto (A)

[*Converted*]
Takeo Hirose

Yo 9th Class
(*January 1942–January 1943;
total of all types of aircraft,
thirty-four persons*)
Yoshio Aizawa (K)
Mitsuru Ōnuma (K)
Genshichirō Ōyama (K)
Den Katayama (K)
Kenjō Kusaka (A)
Hiroshi Suzuki (K)
Shō-ichirō Yamada (K)

[*Converted*]
Yōzō Tsuboi (K)
Chōbei Morita (K)

Yo 10th Class
(*January 1942–January 1943;
total of all types of aircraft,
forty-eight persons; carrier
fighters, thirteen persons*)
Izumi Ashida
Suzuo Itō (K)
Toshio Ushikubo (K)
Akira Kasahara (A)
Kazuo Kayaki
Isshū Kinoshita (K)
Masayuki Gotō (K)

Kinshi Shimizu (K)
Sanenori Takamatsu (A)
Minoru Tanaka (K)
Kagemitsu Matsuo (K)
Hidezō Moriyama (K)
Suke-ichi Yamashita (K)

[*Converted*]
Tei-ichi Katō (K)

Yo 11th Class
(*September 1942–November
1943; total of all types of
aircraft, eighty-five persons;
carrier fighters, thirty-seven
persons*)
Yasuhide Aoki (K)
Yoshihiro Aoki
Chisato Akiyama (K)
Hayao Ishibashi (K)
Isaburō Inoue (K)
Takeshi Inoue (K)
Kazuo Uji-ie (A)
Takao Okakura (K)
Katsuzō Kajikawa (K)
Seijō Bōji (K)
Masao Katsuta (K)
Takeo Kawaguchi (K)

Hikomori Kimiyama (A)
Kōfu Kunō (K)
Masateru Kurokawa (K)
Hiroshi Kojima (A)
Yatarō Koizumi (K)
Shōgo Kobayashi (K)
Mitsurō Sakamoto (K)
Noriyasu Satō
Masao Shibuya (K)
Yoshito Shimada (K)
Tatsu Nagato (K)
Teruhisa Hatai
Kikumasa Fujita (K)
Yoshishi Busujima (K)
Yoshio Hotta (K)
Noboru Matsu-ura (K)
Takashi Matsumoto (K)
Naoyasu Matsudaira
Mitsuo Yatomi (A)
Tetsurō Yano (K)
Keizō Yamakawa (K)
Takashi Yamazaki (A)
Tatsuo Yui (A)
Sadakatsu Yuchi (K)
Masatsugu Yoshitomi (K)

Relationship Between the Flight Reserve Enlisted Trainee Class System (Yokaren) and Flight Trainee Course (Hiren)

Note: Figures in parentheses under the Graduates column indicate the number who went on active duty.

FLIGHT RESERVE ENLISTED TRAINEE PROGRAM CLASSES			FLIGHT TRAINEE COURSE		REMARKS
Class	Graduates	Period	Class	Period	
Kō 3 Pilot Kō 3 Recon.	253	Oct 1938–Apr 1940	1	Apr 1940–Apr 1941	
———			2		Only reconnaissance studied
Pilot 54	83	———	3	Mar 1940–May 1941	
———			4		Only reconnaissance studied
			5	Aug 1940–Jun 1941	Only communications studied
Pilot 55		———	6	Jun 1940–Jul 1941	
Pilot 56		———	7	Jun 1940–Jul 1941	
———			8	Aug 1940–Jul 1941	Only communications studied
Kō 4 Pilot Kō 4 Recon.	258	Apr 1939–Sep 1940	9	Sep 1940–Sep 1941	
Otsu 9 Pilot Otsu 9 Recon.	(200)	Jun 1938–Nov 1940	10	Nov 1940–Oct 1941	
Hei 1 Pilot	31	Aug 1940–Nov 1940	11	Nov 1940–Oct 1941	Pilot 57 class; seaplanes only
Hei 2 Pilot	225	Nov 1940–Jan 1941	12	Jan 1941–Nov 1941	
———	117		13	Mar 1941–Jan 1942	Only reconnaissance studied
	73		14	Jan 1941–Dec 1941	Only communications studied

(*continued*)

Flight Reserve Enlisted Trainee Program Classes			Flight Trainee Course		Remarks
Class	Graduates	Period	Class	Period	
Kō 5 Pilot ⎱ Kō 5 Recon. ⎰	252	Oct 1939–Mar 1941	15	Mar 1941–Feb 1942	
Otsu 10 Pilot ⎱ Otsu 10 Recon. ⎰	(233)	Nov 1938–May 1941	16	May 1941–Mar 1942	
Hei 3 Pilot	317	Feb 1941–Apr 1941	⎧ 17 ⎱ 18	Apr 1941–Mar 1942 ⎰ Jul 1941–May 1942 ⎰ Jul 1941–Jul 1942	
Hei 3 Recon.	157	Feb 1941–Apr 1941	17	Apr 1941–Aug 1941	
———	131		19	Jul 1941–Apr 1942	Only communications studied
———	127		20	Aug 1941–May 1942	Only communications studied
Hei 4 Pilot	217	May 1941–Jul 1941	⎧ 18 ⎱ 21 ⎱ 22	Jul 1941–May 1942 Sep 1941–Jul 1942 Mar 1942–Jul 1942	Larger aircraft only
Hei 4 Recon.	198	May 1941–Jul 1941	18	Jul 1941–Oct 1941	
Kō 6 Pilot ⎱ Kō 6 Recon. ⎰	262	Apr 1940–Sep 1941	21 ⎱ 21	Sep 1941–Jul 1942 Sep 1941–Aug 1942	
Otsu 11 Pilot ⎱ ⎱ ⎱ Otsu 11 Recon. ⎰	386	Jun 1939–Sep 1941	⎧ 21 ⎱ 23	Sep 1941–Jul 1942 Nov 1941–Sep 1942	
Hei 5 Recon.	201	Jun 1941–Aug 1941	21	Sep 1941–Dec 1941	Only reconnaissance studied
Hei 6 Pilot	262	Aug 1941–Oct 1941	23	Nov 1941–Sep 1942	
Hei 6 Recon.	170		23	Nov 1941–Jul 1942	
Kō 7 Pilot ⎱ Kō 7 Recon. ⎰	312	Oct 1940–Jan 1942	24	Jan 1942–Nov 1942	
Hei 7 Pilot	259	Oct 1941–Jan 1942	24	Jan 1942–Nov 1942	
Hei 7 Recon.	170		24	Jan 1942–Sep 1942	
Hei 8 Pilot	117	Dec 1941–Jan 1942 Dec 1941–Mar 1942	24 ⎱ 25	Jan 1942–Nov 1942 ⎰ Mar 1942–Jan 1943 ⎰	Only seaplanes
Hei 8 Recon.	140	Dec 1941–Mar 1942	25	Apr 1942–Sep 1942	Only reconnaissance studied
Hei 9 Recon.	209	Dec 1941–Mar 1942	25	Mar 1942–Sept 1942	Only reconnaissance studied
Otsu 12 Pilot ⎱ Otsu 12 Recon. ⎰	(365)	Nov 1939–Mar 1942	25	Mar 1942–Jan 1943	
Hei 10 Pilot	188	Feb 1942–Mar 1942	⎧ 25 ⎱ 26	Mar 1942–Jan 1943 May 1942–Mar 1943	
Hei 10 Recon.			26	May 1942–Nov 1942	
Otsu 13 Pilot ⎱ Otsu 13 Recon. ⎰	(294)	Jun 1940–May 1942	26	May 1942–Mar 1943	
Otsu 14 Pilot ⎱ Otsu 14 Recon. ⎰	(325)	Aug 1940–Jul 1942	27	Jul 1942–May 1943	
Hei 11 Pilot	385	May 1942–Jul 1942	27	Jul 1942–May 1943	
Hei 11 Recon.	183		27	Jul 1942–Jan 1943	
Special Hei 11 Pilot	186	Aug 1942–Sep 1942	28	Sep 1942–Sep 1943	Larger aircraft only
Kō 8 Pilot ⎱ Kō 8 Recon. ⎰	(455)	Apr 1941–Sep 1942	28	Sep 1942–Jul 1943	
Hei 12 Pilot	291	Aug 1942–Sep 1942	28	Sep 1942–Jul 1943	
Hei 12 Recon.	177		28	Sep 1942–Mar 1943	
Hei 13 Pilot	158	Sep 1942–Nov 1942	29	Nov 1942–Sep 1943	
Hei 13 Recon.	165		29	Nov 1942–May 1943	
Otsu 15 Pilot ⎱ Otsu 15 Recon. ⎰	(630)	Dec 1940–Nov 1942	29 29	Nov 1942–Sep 1943 Nov 1942–May 1943	
Kō 9 Pilot ⎱ Kō 9 Recon. ⎰	790	Oct 1941–Jan 1943	30 30	Jan 1943–Nov 1943 Jan 1943–Sep 1943	
Hei 14 Pilot	238	Nov 1942–Jan 1943	30	Jan 1943–Nov 1943	
Hei 14 Recon.	159		30	Jan 1943–Jul 1943	

FLIGHT RESERVE ENLISTED TRAINEE PROGRAM CLASSES			FLIGHT TRAINEE COURSE		REMARKS
Class	Graduates	Period	Class	Period	
Special Hei 14 Pilot	144	Dec 1942–Mar 1943	31	Mar 1943–Oct 1943	
Hei 15 Pilot	142	Nov 1942–Mar 1943	31	Mar 1943–Jan 1944	
Hei 15 Recon.	140		31	Mar 1943–Sep 1943	
Kō 10 Pilot	(1,097)	Apr 1942–May 1943	32	May 1943–Nov 1943	
Kō 10 Recon.			32	May 1943–Dec 1943	
			33	Jul 1943–Feb 1944	
Otsu 16 Pilot	(1,237)	May 1941–May 1943	32	May 1943–Mar 1944	
Otsu 16 Recon.			33	Jul 1943–Mar 1944	
Hei 16 Pilot	141	Jan 1943–May 1943	32	May 1943–Mar 1944	
	118	Feb 1943–May 1943	32	May 1943–Mar 1944	
Hei 16 Recon.	133	Jan 1943–May 1943	32	May 1943–Nov 1943	
Hei 17 Pilot	438	Mar 1943–Jul 1943	33	Jul 1943–Mar 1944	Final Hei flight training course
Special Otsu 1 Pilot	(1,585)	Apr 1943–Sep 1943	34	Sep 1943–Jul 1944	
Special Otsu 1 Recon.			34	Sep 1943–Feb 1944	
Special Otsu 2 Pilot	(625)	Jun 1943–Nov 1943	35	Nov 1943 –Apr 1944 –Aug 1944	
Special Otsu 2 Recon.			35	Nov 1943–Mar 1944	
Kō 11 Pilot	(1,185)	Oct 1942–Nov 1943	36	Nov 1943–Jul 1944	
Kō 11 Recon.		Oct 1942–Jan 1944			
Kō 12 Pilot	(3,242)	Apr 1943–Mar 1944 Jun 1943–Mar 1944	37	Mar 1944–Sep 1944	
Kō 12 Recon.		Aug 1943	37	Mar 1944–Sep 1944	
Otsu 17	(1,209)	Dec 1941–Feb 1944	37	Feb 1944–Sep 1944	
Special Otsu 3 Pilot	(526)	Aug 1943–Mar 1944	37	Mar 1943–Sep 1944	
Special Otsu 3 Recon.			37	Mar 1944–Sep 1944 May 1944–Dec 1944	
Otsu 18	(1,480)	May 1942–Mar 1944	38		
		Oct 1943–Jul 1944		June 1944– May 1944–Dec 1944	
Kō 13	(28,111)	Dec 1943–Sep 1944	38–42	Feb 1945–	
Special Otsu 4 Pilot	(787)	Oct 1943–May 1944	38	May 1944–Dec 1944	
Special Otsu 4 Recon.			38	May 1944–Feb 1945	
Special Otsu 5 Pilot	(938)	Dec 1943–Dec 1944	——	——	
Special Otsu 5 Recon.			41	Nov 1944–Feb 1945 (Mar 1945)	
Otsu 19	1,500	Dec 1942–Jan 1945	42	Jan 1945 Feb 1945 –Mar 1945	Flight training course closed down
Kō 14	(52,115)	Apr 1944 Jun 1944 –Mar 1945	——	——	

APPENDIX D

MAJOR AIR BATTLES (By Date)

This table summarizes data about the major air battles that naval fighter units participated in during the China Incident and World War II. Data were taken from the official records of each battle. In order to show differences between the battle results recorded on each side, we have tried to contrast our data with official and unofficial data of the other side [United States, England, and China]. Note: the word "own" refers to the country of the origin of the data.

U.S. Navy Aircraft Abbreviations Used:

VT	Carrier attack plane (kankō)	VB	Carrier bomber (kanbaku)
VFB	Fighter bomber (bakusen, senbaku)	VF	Fighter (sentō-ki)
VA	Land attack plane (riku-kō)	VA	Land-based bomber (rikubaku)
VOS	Reconnaissance seaplane (suitei)		

Parentheses indicate probables.
Destroyed means destroyed and/or set on fire on ground.

Air Battle	Date	Participating Forces	Victories	Japanese Losses	Other Records (China, U.S., England)
Attack on Nanking (*First raid*)	19 Sep 1937	16 VOS, 17 VB, 12 VF	Shot down 33 (6)	3 VB, 1 VOS	11 own [Chinese] shot down, 1 enemy shot down
Attack on Canton	21 Sep 1937	24 VF, 6 VT, 24 VB	Shot down 16 (1)	5 VF ditched	11 own shot down
Attack on Nanking	12 Oct 1937	11 VF, 9 VA	Shot down 5, destroyed 2	3 VF	
Attack on Nanking	2 Dec 1937	6 VF, 8 VT	Shot down 13 (3)	None	10 own lost
Attack on Nanking	12 Oct 1937	11 VF, 9 VA	Shot down 5, destroyed 2	3 VF	
Attack on Nanchang	9 Dec 1937	8 VF, 15 VA	Shot down 12, destroyed 12	1 VF	
Attack on Nanchang	22 Dec 1937	12 VF, 11 VA	Shot down 17 (4), destroyed 13	1 VF	
Attack on Hankow	18 Feb 1938	11 VF, 15 VA	Shot down 18 (1), destroyed 5	4 VF	5 own lost, 14 enemy shot down
Attack on Nanchang	25 Feb 1938	18 VF, 35 VA	Shot down 42 (13)	2 VF	6 own lost, 3 enemy shot down
Attack on Canton	13 Apr 1938	6 VF, 18 VB	Shot down 15 (3)	3 VF	
Attack on Hankow	29 Apr 1938	28 VF, 18 VA	Shot down 51 (11)	2 VF and 2 VA	Own 13 shot down, 24 enemy shot down
Attack on Hankow	31 May 1938	35 VF, 18 VA	Shot down 20 (2)	1 VF	
Attack on Nanchang	26 Jun 1938	28 VF, 18 VA	Shot down 19 (4), destroyed 2	None	
Attack on Nanchang	4 Jul 1938	23 VF, 26 VA	Shot down 45 (5), destroyed 9	2 VF	
Attack on Nanchang	16 Jul 1938	15 VF, 18 VA	Shot down 10, destroyed 3	None	

Air Battle	Date	Participating Forces	Victories	Japanese Losses	Other Records (China, U.S., England)
Attack on Nanchang	18 Jul 1938	6 VF, 14 VB, 5 VT	Shot down 9 (2), destroyed 19	1 VF	
Attack on Hankow	3 Aug 1938	29 VF, 18 VA	Shot down 32 (5), destroyed 7	3 VF	
Attack on Nan-yung	30 Aug 1938	6 VF, 5 VB, 4 VT	Shot down 17	2 VF	
Attack on Liuchow	30 Dec 1939	13 VF	Shot down 14	1 VF	
Attack on Kweilin	10 Jan 1940	26 VF, 27 VA	Shot down 16, destroyed 9	None	
Attack on Chungking	13 Sep 1940	13 VF, 27 VA	Shot down 27	None	13 own lost
Attack on Chengtu	4 Oct 1940	8 VF, 27 VA	Shot down 6, destroyed 19	None	
Attack on Kunming	7 Oct 1940	7 VF, 27 VA	Shot down 14, destroyed 4	None	
Attack on Chengtu	26 Oct 1940	8 VF	Shot down 10	None	
Attack on Chengtu	14 Mar 1941	12 VF, 10 VT	Shot down 27 (3), destroyed 7	None	16 own lost, 6 enemy shot down
Attack on Hawaii	7 Dec 1941	78 VF, 129 VB, 143 VT	Shot down 14, destroyed 450	9 VF, 15 VB, 5 VT	Total of 347 own lost
Attack on Luzon	8 Dec 1941	89 VF, 108 VA	Shot down 25 (2), destroyed 80	7 VF	15–23 own shot down, 72–85 own destroyed
Attack on Luzon	10 Dec 1941	56 VF, 81 VA	Shot down 43, destroyed 61	2 VF	13 own shot down
Attack on Singapore	18 Jan 1942	11 VF, 26 VA	Shot down 15 (5)	2 VF	
Attack on Singapore	22 Jan 1942	9 VF, 52 VA	Shot down 12	2 VF	
Attack on Darwin	29 Jan 1942	36 VF, 71 VB, 81 VT, 54 VA	Shot down 8, destroyed 21	1 VF, 1 VB	4 own shot down, 14 own destroyed
Marshall intercept operations	1 Feb 1942	34 VF (cumulative)	Shot down 17 (3 probables)	None [1 VF]	5 enemy shot down, 10 own shot down
Attack on Surabaya	3 Feb 1942	58 VF, 37 VA	Shot down 48, 36 destroyed	3 VF	20 own lost
Attack on Batavia	9 Feb 1942	15 VF, 17 VA	Shot down 12		
Attack on Surabaya	18 Feb 1942	8 VF, 23 VA	Shot down 9 (3)		
Attack on Surabaya	19 Feb 1942	23 VF, 18 VA	Shot down 17 (3)		
Attack on Colombo	5 Apr 1942	36 VF, 38 VB, 53 VT	Shot down 55 (10)	1 VF, 6 VB	21 enemy shot down, 25 own shot down
Attack on Trincomalee	9 Apr 1942	38 VT, 91 VT	Shot down 42 (3), destroyed 4	3 VF, 1 VT	15 enemy shot down, 14 own shot down
Attack on Darwin	27 Apr 1942	21 VF	Shot down 19 (6)		4 own lost, 7 enemy shot down
Battle of the Coral Sea (attack on task force)	8 May 1942	18 VF, 33 VB, 18 VT	Shot down 64 (5)	2 VF, 9 VB, 8 VT	33 own shot down, 36 shot down over water and sunk
Battle of the Coral Sea (combat air patrol)	8 May 1942	19 VF	Shot down 40 (7)		
Attack on Moresby	28 May 1942	26 VF	Shot down 13 (4)	None	
Attack on Midway	4 Jun 1942	36 VF, 36 VB, 36 VT	Shot down 45	2 VF, 1 VB, 1 VT	17 own shot down
Battle of Midway	4 Jun 1942	120 VF (cumulative)	Shot down 90	13 VF	76 own missing
Attack on Guadalcanal	7 Aug 1942	17 VF, 9 VB, 27 VA	Shot down 48 (8)	2 VF, 9 VB, 5 VA	12 own shot down

(continued)

Air Battle	Date	Participating Forces	Victories	Japanese Losses	Other Records (China, U.S., England)
Attack on Guadalcanal	24 Aug 1942	15 VF, 6 VT	Shot down 15	2 VF, 3 VT	16 enemy shot down, 3 own shot down
Second Battle of the Solomons (attack on task force)	24 Aug 1942	19 VF, 54 VB, 12 VT	Shot down 10 (1)	3 VF, 21 VB	90 enemy shot down
Attack on Guadalcanal	30 Aug 1942	18 VF	Shot down 10 (4)	7 VF	14 enemy shot down, 4 own shot down
Attack on Guadalcanal	13 Sep 1942	21 VF, 26 VA	Shot down 17 (2)	4 VF	11 enemy shot down, 5 own shot down
Combat air patrol over ship convoy off Guadalcanal	15 Oct 1942	52 VF (cumulative)	Shot down 32 (9)	2 VF	8 enemy shot down, 7 own shot down
Attack on Guadalcanal	25 Oct 1942	40 VF (cumulative)	Shot down 10	6 VF	22 enemy shot down
Battle of Santa Cruz (attack on American fleet)	26 Oct 1942	47 VF, 59 VB, 49 VT (cumulative) }	} Shot down 55	6 VF, 31 VB, 21 VT }	} 74 own lost
Battle of Santa Cruz (combat air patrol)	26 Oct 1942	51 VF (cumulative)		5 VF	
Attack on Guadalcanal	11 Nov 1942	44 VF, 9 VB, 25 VA	Shot down 25 (5)	2 VF, 5 VB and 4 VA	11 enemy shot down, 7 own shot down
Attack on Guadalcanal	12 Nov 1942	30 VF, 19 VA	Shot down 20 (7)	12 VA	5 enemy shot down, 4 own shot down
Combat air patrol over Solomons ship convoy	14 Nov 1942	20 VF	Shot down 15 (7)	7 VF	8 own shot down
Attack on vessels off Isabel Island	1 Feb 1943	81 VF, 15 VB	Shot down 28	4 VF, 5 VB	21 enemy shot down, 8 own shot down
Combat air patrol over fleet off Guadalcanal	4 Feb 1943	22 VF (+ Army)	Shot down 17	3 VF	17 enemy shot down, 10 own shot down
Attack on Buin	14 Feb 1942	27 VF	Shot down 19	1 VF	5 enemy shot down, 10 own shot down
Drive on Russell Islands	1 Apr 1943	57 VF	Shot down 47 (7)	9 VF	18 enemy shot down, 6 own down
Attack off Guadalcanal	7 Apr 1943	157 VF, 67 VB	Shot down 41 (13)	12 VF, 9 VB	39 enemy shot down, 7 own shot down
Attack on Oro Bay	11 Apr 1943	71 VF, 21 VB	Shot down 21 (9)	2 VF, 4 VB	17 enemy shot down
Attack on Moresby	12 Apr 1943	124 VF, 43 VA	Shot down 28 (7)	2 VF, 6 VA	22 enemy shot down, 2 own shot down, 15 own destroyed
Attack on Milne Bay	14 Apr 1943	129 VF, 75 VB, 44 VA	Shot down 45 (9)	1 VF, 3 VB and 3 VA	5 enemy shot down, 3 own shot down
Escort of Yamamoto Aircraft	18 Apr 1943	6 VF, 2 VA	Shot down 6 (3)	2 VA	5 enemy shot down, 1 own shot down
Attack on Darwin	2 May 1943	27 VF, 18 VA	Shot down 21 (4)	None	6 enemy shot down, 13 own shot down

Air Battle	Date	Participating Forces	Victories	Japanese Losses	Other Records (China, U.S., England)
Drive on Russell Islands	13 May 1943	54 VF	Shot down 38 (10)	4 VF	16 enemy shot down, 3 own shot down
Attack on Oro Bay	14 May 1943	33 VF, 18 VA	Shot down 15	4 VA	16 enemy shot down, 2 own shot down
Attack on Russell Islands	7 Jun 1943	81 VF	Shot down 41 (8)	9 VF	23 enemy shot down, 9 own shot down
Attack on Russell Islands	12 Jun 1943	74 VF	Shot down 33 (8)	6 VF	31 enemy shot down; 6 own shot down
Attack off Guadalcanal	16 Jun 1943	70 VF, 24 VB	Shot down 32 (5)	15 VF, 13 VB	66 enemy shot down, 6 own shot down
Attack on Rendova	30 Jun 1943	72 VF, 8 VB, 26 VA	Shot down 49 (8)	13 VF, 17 VA	58 enemy shot down, 17 own shot down
Attack on Brocks Creek	30 Jun 1943	27 VF, 22 VA	Shot down 16 (3)	None	8 enemy shot down, 6 own shot down
Attack on Brocks Creek	6 Jul 1943	27 VF, 22 VA	Shot down 17 (3)	2 VA	7 enemy shot down, 8 own shot down
Attack on Rubiana	15 Jul 1943	44 VF, 8 VA	Shot down 19 (12)	5 VF, 5 VA	44 enemy shot down, 3 own shot down
Interception over Buin	17 Jul 1943	46 VF	Shot down 58 (13)	9 VF	48 enemy shot down, 6 own shot down
Interception over Buin	12 Aug 1943	45 VF	Shot down 33	1 VF, 24 destroyed on ground	
Attack on Vella Lavella	15 Aug 1943	149 VF, 25 VB, 11 VT, 24 VA (cumulative)	Shot down 29 (9)	9 VF, 8 VB	44 enemy shot down
Attack on Brocks Creek	7 Sep 1943	36 VF	Shot down 18 (3)	1 VF	7 enemy shot down, 3 own shot down
Attack on Buin	14 Sep 1943	258 VF (cumulative)	Shot down 60 (6)	5 VF, 9 destroyed on ground	
Attack on Cape Cretin	22 Sep 1943	35 VF, 8 VA	Shot down 14	8 VF, 6 VA	39 enemy shot down, 3 own shot down
Interceptions over Wake Island	6 Oct 1943	23 VF	Shot down 10	14 VF	6 own shot down, 22 enemy shot down
Interceptions over Rabaul	12 Oct 1943	34 VF	Shot down 9	2 VF, 12 destroyed on ground	26 enemy shot down, 100 enemy destroyed, 5 own shot down
Attack on Buna	15 Oct 1943	39 VF, 15 VB	Shot down 14	5 VF, 14 VB	47 enemy shot down, 1 own shot down
Attack on Cape Torokina	1 Nov 1943	79 VF, 16 VB, 9 VT	Shot down 3	23 VF, 5 VB, 3 VT	22 enemy shot down, 4 own shot down

(continued)

Air Battle	Date	Participating Forces	Victories	Japanese Losses	Other Records (China, U.S., England)
Interceptions over Rabaul	2 Nov 1943	115 VF	Shot down 119 (22)	18 VF	68 enemy shot down, 19 own shot down
Interceptions over Rabaul	5 Nov 1943	59 VF	Shot down 49 (20)	2 VF	25 enemy shot down, 13 own shot down
Interceptions over Rabaul	7 Nov 1943	58 VF	Shot down 16	?	23 enemy shot down, 16 enemy destroyed, 5 own shot down
Interceptions over Rabaul	11 Nov 1943	68 VF	Shot down 71	11 VF	135 enemy shot down, 7 own shot down
Attack on Calcutta	5 Dec 1943	27 VF, 9 VA	Shot down 6 (2)	None	
Interceptions over Roi	5 Dec 1943	53 VF	Shot down 24 (6)	16 VF, 15 destroyed on ground	28 enemy shot down, 4 own shot down
Interceptions over Rabaul	23 Dec 1943	99 VF (cumulative)	Shot down 24	6 VF	30 enemy shot down, 3 own destroyed
Attack on Cape Marcus	26 Dec 1943	63 VF, 25 VB	Shot down 20 (5)	4 VF, 13 VB	75 enemy shot down, 7 own shot down
Interceptions over Rabaul	9 Jan 1944	72 VF	Shot down 33	2 VF	21 enemy shot down, 5 own shot down
Interceptions over Rabaul	17 Jan 1944	79 VF	Shot down 87	?	17 enemy shot down, 12 own shot down
Interceptions over Rabaul	13 Feb 1944	40 VF	Shot down 23 (7)	2 VF	
Interceptions over Truk	17 Feb 1944	64 VF (cumulative)	Shot down 31	31 VF, 81 destroyed on ground	56 enemy shot down, 19 own shot down
Interceptions over Rabaul	19 Feb 1944	36 VF	Shot down 37 (6)	5 VF	23 enemy shot down
Interceptions over Marianas	23 Feb 1944	20 VF		11 VF, 30 destroyed on ground	60 enemy shot down, 6 own shot down
Interceptions over Palau	30 Mar 1944	22 VF	Shot down 19 (3)	14 VF	70 enemy shot down, 25 own shot down
Interceptions over Palau	31 Mar 1944	66 VF	Shot down 40 (3)	35 VF	
Attack on Nanning	5 Apr 1944	32 VF	Shot down 9 (2)	9 VF	9 enemy shot down, 1 own shot down
Interceptions over Truk	30 Apr 1944	54 VF	Shot down 32 (2)	28 VF	59 enemy shot down, 34 enemy destroyed; 35 own shot down
Interceptions over Marianas	11 Jun 1944	139 VF (cumulative)	Shot down 9	22 VF	11 own shot down, 70 enemy shot down

Air Battle	Date	Participating Forces	Victories	Japanese Losses	Other Records (China, U.S., England)
Interceptions over Iwo Jima	15 Jun 1944	37 VF	Shot down 4	16 VF	20 enemy shot down, 7 enemy destroyed, 2 own shot down
Attack on vessels off Saipan	15 Jun 1944	11 VF, 3 VB, 10 VA	Shot down 2	1 VF, 1 VB, 8 VA	
Attack on vessels off Saipan	18 Jun 1944	36 VF, 24 VFB, 2 VB, 8 VA	Shot down 5	13 VF, 1 VFB, 7 VA	
Battle of Philippine Sea (attack on enemy fleet)	19 Jun 1944	107 VF, 80 VFB, 89 VB, 50 VT	Shot down 24 (8)	60 VF, 45 VFB, 56 VB, 31 VT	} 269 enemy shot down, 29 own shot down, 73 own sunk
Battle of Philippines (combat air patrol)	20 Jun 1944	34 VF	Shot down 26 (3)	12 VF	
Interceptions over Guam	19 Jun 1944	56 VF	Shot down 26 (1)	12 VF	
Interceptions over Iwo Jima	24 Jun 1944	59 VF	Shot down 37 (10)	23 VF	29 enemy shot down, 6 own shot down
Interceptions over Iwo Jima	3 Jul 1944	110 VF (cumulative)	Shot down 39 (3)	31 VF	
Interceptions over Iwo Jima	4 Jul 1944	45 VF (cumulative)	Shot down 26 (1)	12 VF	70 enemy shot down
Interceptions over Central Philippines	12 Sep 1944	41 VF +	Shot down 23 (3)	27 VF, 30 destroyed on ground	45 enemy shot down, 36 enemy destroyed, 9 own shot down
Interceptions over Central Philippines	13 Sep 1944	24 VF	Shot down 7	9 VF	
Interceptions over Manila	21 Sep 1944	42 VF	Shot down 27	20 VF, 10 destroyed on ground	38 enemy shot down, 10 destroyed, 15 own missing
Interceptions over Taiwan	12–13 Oct 1944			} Total of 312	500 enemy shot down and/or destroyed, as well as 71 own missing
Air battles off Taiwan	12–16 Oct 1944	Cumulative about 650 aircraft of all types	Shot down 112		
Interceptions over Balikpapan	14 Oct 1944		Shot down 38		43 enemy shot down, 7 own shot down
Attack on enemy fleet east of the Philippines	24 Oct 1944	Total of 199 (126 VF)	Shot down 32	Total of 67	
Air battle off Philippines (off Cape Engano)	24 Oct 1944	30 VF, 19 VFB, 2 VB, 5 VT	Shot down 8 (1)		
Attack on enemy fleet east of the Philippines	25 Oct 1944	18 VF, 28 VB	Shot down 7	Total of 10	
Interceptions over Luzon	29 Oct 1944	142 VF (cumulative)	Shot down 40	21 VF, 8 destroyed on ground	71 enemy shot down, 11 own shot down
Interceptions over Luzon	5 Nov 1944	82 VF (cumulative)	Shot down 45	32 VF, 33 destroyed on ground	25 own shot down

(continued)

Air Battle	Date	Participating Forces	Victories	Japanese Losses	Other Records (China, U.S., England)
Interceptions over eastern Japan (American carrier aircraft)	16–17 Feb 1945		Shot down 98	30 missing	332 enemy shot down, 177 enemy destroyed, 49 own missing
Interceptions over eastern Japan (American carrier aircraft)	25 Feb 1945		Shot down 10		25 enemy shot down, 30 enemy destroyed, 9 own shot down
Interceptions over Matsuyama	19 Mar 1945	70 VF	Shot down 52	16 VF	
Attack on American fleet off Shikoku	21 Mar 1945	30 VF, 18 VA	Shot down 7 (3)	10 VF, 18 VA	
Okinawa special attack force escort operations	3 Apr 1945	40 VF	Shot down 17 (6)	8 VF	
Okinawa special attack force escort operations	12 Apr 1945	75 VF	Shot down 25	20 VF	
Okinawa special attack force escort operations	16 Apr 1945	93 VF	Shot down 23 (1)	17 VF	
Interceptions over Bungo Suidō	24 Jul 1945	31 VF	Shot down 19	6 VF	

NAME INDEX

1. The rank listed is the highest attained by the individual.
2. Page numbers of the main biographical entry for an ace are in **boldface** type.
3. Page numbers where aces appear in photographs or are mentioned in illustration captions are in *italics*.

UNIT INDEX

1. Page numbers where the battle record of the unit is discussed in detail appear in **boldface** type.
2. Page numbers where a unit is featured in illustrations or mentioned in captions are in *italics*.

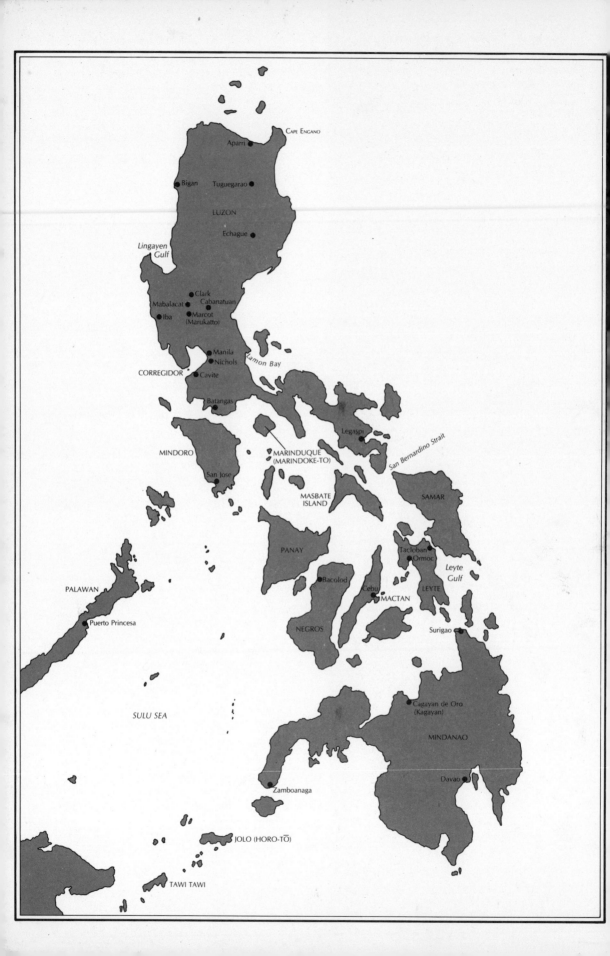